MANAGING PERFORMANCE THROUGH TRAINING AND DEVELOPMENT

EIGHTH EDITION

ALAN M. SAKS
University of Toronto

ROBERT R. HACCOUN
Université de Montréal

SERIES EDITOR:
MONICA BELCOURT
School of Human Resource Management,
Faculty of Liberal Arts and Professional Studies,
York University

NELSON

NELSON

Managing Performance through Training and Development, Eighth Edition

by Alan M. Saks and Robert R. Haccoun

VP, Product and Partnership Solutions:
Claudine O'Donnell

Publisher, Digital and Print Content:
Alexis Hood

Executive Marketing Manager:
Amanda Henry

Content Development Manager:
Elke Price

Photo and Permissions Researcher:
Julie Pratt

Production Project Manager:
Shannon Martin

Production Service:
SPi-Global

Copy Editor:
Linda Jenkins

Proofreader:
SPi-Global

Indexer:
SPi-Global

Design Director:
Ken Phipps

Post-secondary Design Project Manager:
Pamela Johnston

Interior Design:
Jen Spinner

Cover Design:
Jen Spinner

Compositor:
SPi-Global

COPYRIGHT © 2019, 2016, 2013, 2010 by Nelson Education Ltd.

Printed and bound in Canada
8 9 10 23 22

For more information contact Nelson Education Ltd., 1120 Birchmount Road, Toronto, Ontario, M1K 5G4. Or you can visit our Internet site at nelson.com

Cognero and Full-Circle Assessment are registered trademarks of Madeira Station LLC.

Library and Archives Canada Cataloguing in Publication

Saks, Alan M. (Alan Michael), author
Managing performance through training and development / Alan M. Saks, University of Toronto, Robert R. Haccoun, University of Montreal.—Eighth edition.

Issued in print and electronic formats. ISBN 978-0-17-679807-9 (softcover).—ISBN 978-0-17-684842-2 (PDF)

1. Employees—Training of—Textbooks.
2. Textbooks. I. Haccoun, Robert R., author II. Title.

HF5549.5.T7S23 2018
658.3'124
C2018-903528-5
C2018-903529-3

ISBN-13: 978-0-17-679807-9
ISBN-10: 0-17-679807-2

In memory of my father, Simon Saks
Alan M. Saks

To the little ones: Orli, Amit, Erez, and Micah
Robert R. Haccoun

BRIEF CONTENTS

CONTENTS

ABOUT THE SERIES

The management of human resources has become the most important source of innovation, competitive advantage, and productivity. More than ever, human resources management (HRM) professionals need the knowledge and skills to design HRM policies and practices that not only meet legal requirements but also are effective in supporting organizational strategy. Increasingly, these professionals turn to published research and books on best practices for assistance in the development of effective HR strategies. The books in the *Nelson Series in Human Resources Management* are the best source in Canada for reliable, valid, and current knowledge about practices in HRM.

The texts in this series include the following:

- Managing Performance through Training and Development
- Management of Occupational Health and Safety
- Recruitment and Selection in Canada
- Strategic Compensation in Canada
- Strategic Human Resources Planning
- Industrial Relations in Canada

The *Nelson Series in Human Resources Management* represents a significant development in the field of HRM for many reasons. Each book in the series is the first and now best-selling text in the functional area. Furthermore, HR professionals in Canada must work with Canadian laws, statistics, policies, and values. This series serves their needs. It is the only opportunity that students and practitioners have to access a complete set of HRM books, standardized in presentation, which enables them to access information quickly across many HRM disciplines. Students who are pursuing the HR professional designation through their provincial HR associations will find the books in this series invaluable in preparing for the knowledge exams. This one-stop resource will prove useful to anyone looking for solutions for the effective management of people.

The publication of this series signals that the HRM field has advanced to the stage where theory and applied research guide practice. The books in the series present the best and most current research in the functional areas of HRM. Research is supplemented with examples of the best practices used by Canadian companies that are leaders in HRM. Each text begins with a general model of the discipline, and then describes the implementation of effective strategies. The books serve as an introduction to the functional area for the new student of HR and as a validation source for the more experienced HRM practitioner. Cases, exercises, and endnotes provide opportunities for further discussion and analysis.

As you read and consult the books in this series, I hope you share my excitement in being involved and knowledgeable about a profession that has such a significant impact on the achievement of organizational goals, and on employees' lives.

Monica Belcourt, PhD, FCHRL
Series Editor
March 2018

ABOUT THE AUTHORS

Alan M. Saks

Alan M. Saks, PhD, is a Professor of Human Resources Management at the University of Toronto in the Department of Management–UTSC and the Centre for Industrial Relations and Human Resources. Prior to joining the University of Toronto, Professor Saks was a member of the Department of Management in the Faculty of Commerce and Administration at Concordia University and in the School of Administrative Studies at York University.

Professor Saks earned his HBA in Psychology from the University of Western Ontario, an MASc in Industrial/Organizational Psychology from the University of Waterloo, and a PhD in Organizational Behaviour and Human Resources from the University of Toronto. He conducts research in a number of areas in human resources management including recruitment, job search, training, employee engagement, and the socialization and on-boarding of new employees. His research has been published in refereed journals such as the *Journal of Applied Psychology, Personnel Psychology, Academy of Management Journal, Journal of Organizational Behavior, Journal of Vocational Behavior, Human Resource Management, Human Resource Management Review, Journal of Business and Psychology, Journal of Organizational Effectiveness: People and Performance*, and the *International Journal of Training and Development*, as well as in professional journals such as *HR Professional* Magazine, the *Canadian Learning Journal*, and *Canadian HR Reporter*. In addition to this text, he is also the author of *Research, Measurement and Evaluation of Human Resources*, and co-author of *Organizational Behaviour: Understanding and Managing Life at Work*.

Robert R. Haccoun

Educated at McGill University (BA 1969) and the Ohio State University (MA 1970, PhD 1973), Robert R. Haccoun is Full Professor of Psychology and Director of the Industrial and Organizational Psychology program at the Université de Montréal. Prior to returning to academia in 1978, Professor Haccoun was a research scientist for Bell Canada in Montreal. He is a founding member and past president of the Industrial-Organizational Psychology section of the Canadian Psychological Association.

Professor Haccoun has led a number of research studies, mainly focused on training, absenteeism, and research methodology, and delivered papers at scientific conferences. His research articles are published in Canada in journals that include *Canadian Psychologist, Canadian Journal of Behavioural Science*, and the *Canadian Journal of Administrative Studies*. Internationally, his research is published in *Personnel Psychology*, the *Journal of Applied Psychology, Organizational Behavior and Human Decision Processes*, the *Journal of Organizational Behavior*, and *Applied Psychology: An International Review*. He has contributed chapters to several books, and his co-authored research book, *Comprendre l'organisation: Approches de recherches*, has been translated into Spanish. His statistics text-book, published in 2007, is in its second edition (2010). He is a reviewer for many scientific journals and has served on scientific advisory boards for provincial, national, and international research funding agencies.

He has received a number of awards, including the Prize of Professional Excellence from Quebec's Society of Work Psychology and the Teaching Excellence prize from his university.

Active in the transfer of knowledge from academia to applied settings, he has also published non-technical articles and delivered conferences aimed at professional audiences. His consulting services have been called upon by organizations in Canada, the United States, and Europe.

PREFACE

Increasing global competition and economic challenges along with new and changing technology, an increasingly knowledge-based economy, skilled labour shortages and skills mismatches, and demographic changes in the workforce have made learning more important than ever for employees, organizations, governments, and society. These challenges require organizations to provide training and development programs for employees so that they have the knowledge, skills, abilities, and attitudes that are necessary to be productive and innovative, and so that organizations have the human capital they need to be competitive and survive.

Continuous learning and skill development is a fundamental requirement for organizations today. The ability to compete, adapt, innovate, and achieve an organization's goals and objectives in today's increasingly competitive and uncertain environment depends in large part on the provision and effectiveness of training and development—the focus of this textbook.

Since the last edition of this text was published, the science and practice of training and development has continued to advance. The increasing use of technology, learning on demand, blended approaches to training delivery, social media, mobile (m-) learning, microlearning, MOOCs, and synthetic learning environments are just some examples of the exciting developments in training and development. The eighth edition of *Managing Performance through Training and Development* reflects the many advances in both the science and practice of training and development.

As with the five previous editions, the eighth edition is co-authored by Alan Saks and Robert Haccoun. The two authors have been involved in training research for over 20 years and have collaborated on numerous research projects. With the eighth edition, they have continued to develop and improve this textbook in many ways.

// WHAT'S NEW IN THE EIGHTH EDITION

The eighth edition represents one of the most revised and restructured. In response to the excellent comments we have received from reviewers over the years, we have decided to remove the chapter on Organizational Learning (Chapter 2 in previous editions). As a result, there are now 14 rather than 15 chapters in the text.

Although the chapter on organizational learning has been removed, many of the key topics from that chapter can still be found in the eighth edition. For example, human capital is now discussed in Chapter 1 (The Training and Development Process); workplace learning and informal learning can now be found in Chapter 2 (Learning and Motivation); learning culture is now defined in Chapter 3 (The Needs Analysis Process); communities of practice can now be found in Chapter 7 (Technology-Based Training Methods); and organizational learning, the learning organization, and the multilevel systems model of organizational learning are now in Chapter 14 (The Evolution and Future of Training and Development).

Another major change to the eighth edition is the removal of the material on motivation theories from the chapter on learning and motivation (now Chapter 2). Many reviewers have told us that the motivation theories are covered in other courses and do not need to be covered in the text. Therefore, we have removed the material on intrinsic and extrinsic motivation, need theories, and expectancy theory. We have, however, retained the material on goal setting theory, proximal and distal goals, and goal orientation because it continues to be important in training research and practice.

We have also made a number of changes to Chapter 14 (The Evolution and Future of Training and Development). The section on ethics has been moved to Chapter 8 (Training Delivery) and, as already indicated, the multilevel systems model of organizational learning, organizational learning, and the learning organization are now in Chapter 14. We have also added a new section in Chapter 14 on how to make training and development programs effective, along with a new Trainer's Notebook that summarizes the main factors that contribute to the effectiveness of training and development programs.

In addition to these major changes, you will also find new content (e.g., synthetic learning environments, Chapter 7); new definitions (e.g., learner engagement, Chapter 4); expanded coverage of existing topics (e.g., adult learning theory and learning styles, Chapter 2); updated material (e.g., training and development in Canada, Chapter 1); new tables and figures (Table 4.3: Bloom's taxonomy of learning objectives, Chapter 4); new chapter-opening vignettes (e.g., Calfrac Well Services, Chapter 7); new Training Today features (Training Today 7.1, Virtual Reality Training at BNSF Railway, Chapter 7); and new The Trainer's Notebook features (The Trainer's Notebook 8.2, Getting Trainees Engaged) throughout the eighth edition of *Managing Performance through Training and Development*.

// FEATURES

As with the last several editions, our goal has been to make this textbook integrative by including features such as Make the Connection, Flashback and Flash Forward Case Questions, a Running Case Study, and an Integrative Case.

Make the Connection alerts the reader to material in a chapter that has a connection to material that was presented in a previous chapter. For example, when reading about a self-management transfer of training intervention in Chapter 9 (Transfer of Training), the reader is reminded about material on self-regulation and social cognitive theory in Chapter 2 (Learning and Motivation). The purpose of this feature is to help students integrate material across chapters and understand how material in one chapter is related to material that was presented in a previous chapter.

The Make the Connection feature appears in two ways. A puzzle icon in the margin alerts the reader to a Make the Connection feature and indicates the chapter and page number where the material was first presented. The connection is also explained to the reader in the text. This feature is meant to help readers understand how the material throughout the text is linked and interconnected.

The **Flashback case questions** ask students to consider the case study in each chapter in terms of several of the chapters and topics discussed in previous chapters. For example, the flashback questions for the case study in Chapter 9 (Transfer of Training) ask students to consider the use of different instructional methods from Chapter 5, learning theories from Chapter 2, and training design activities from Chapter 4. These questions require students to integrate material from various chapters so they learn how material covered in previous chapters is relevant for each case study.

The **Flash Forward case questions,** which follow the Flashback case questions, ask students to consider the case in each chapter in terms of a topic covered in the next chapter. This is meant to get students thinking about the next chapter before they actually study it. It is also another way to integrate material from different chapters when solving a particular case. For example, the Flash Forward question in Chapter 9 (Transfer of Training) asks about how the training program in the case was evaluated and how it should be evaluated, thereby getting students to begin thinking about the next chapter in the text, which is on training evaluation. These questions can be used by an instructor to encourage students to think about the next chapter after they have discussed a case in the context of the current chapter.

The Flashback and Flash Forward questions allow instructors to use a case study from any chapter to teach material in other chapters. In other words, every case study in the text is a *flexible* case because instructors have the ability to decide how and when they will use it in terms of topics, content, and chapters.

Another integrative feature is the **Running Case Study.** The Running Case Study (Dirty Pools) appears at the end of Chapter 1 and is followed by questions that pertain to the content of the chapter. Each subsequent chapter (with the exception of Chapter 13, Management and Leadership Development) has a series of chapter-relevant questions about the Running Case Study. Thus, instructors can relate the case to the material in every chapter as they cover it. This provides students with the continuity of returning to the same case throughout the course, and it allows them to apply the material from each chapter to the case, thereby building on each chapter in the process.

Like the previous edition, this edition includes two **Integrative Cases,** both of which are in the Appendix. The purpose of this feature is to provide students with an oppor-tunity to work on a case that requires them to use and apply material from most of the chapters. The relevant chapters for the integrative case questions are indicated so that instructors can use the integrative cases throughout the course as each chapter is covered. Alternatively, the integrative cases can be used at the end of a course as a review of all the chapters. This feature is meant to help students integrate and apply their learning throughout the text to one particular training situation.

In addition to these integrative features, the eighth edition continues to provide students and instructors with a wide range of pedagogical features. For example, every chapter has a **Case Study** with questions on the main topics, principles, concepts, and theories covered in the chapter as well as flashback and flash forward questions.

The eighth edition includes two new case studies that can be found in Chapters 3 (The Needs Analysis Process) and Chapter 7 (Technology-Based Training Methods). The new case study in Chapter 7 (The Korea Ginseng Corporation) is in addition to the case study that has been in previous editions of the text (E-Learning at Flotation Ltd.), and unlike other case studies in the text, it consists of several parts that are followed by a series of questions. This case study provides an example of how an actual organization used technology in the design of a new training program.

The eighth edition also includes a new kind of case study question called ***Rewrite the Case***. Every case study has one Rewrite the Case question. These questions require students to write a paragraph or two for the case study in order to rectify something important that is either absent or poorly performed. For example, the rewrite the case question in Chapter 8 (Training Delivery) asks students to add a section in which they describe the trainer making use of Gagné's nine events of instruction.

The Rewrite the Case questions serve a number of purposes. First, they require students to think carefully about how to make the training program described in the case more effective using material from the chapter. Second, students have to write their answer so that it fits into the case rather than just stating an answer to a question. And third, we think this type of question might be more fun and engaging for students. Instructors can use the Rewrite the Case questions for class discussion, assignments, or for class presentations. Whatever their use, the Rewrite the Case questions provide instructors with another way to teach the cases in addition to the main discussion questions and the flashback and flash forward questions.

In addition to the Case Study, every chapter has a **Case Incident** that consists of a short description of a training problem followed by several questions. They can be used to begin a discussion at the start of class or later in class when students are ready to apply the chapter material.

As with the previous edition, the eighth edition has two types of exercises in every chapter. **In-Class Exercises** can be completed during class time without any pre-class preparation. **In-the-Field Exercises** require students to gather information in the field by talking to HR and training professionals and by searching the Web to answer chapter-relevant questions. These exercises can also be used as projects and assignments.

Each chapter has Discussion Questions and The Great Training Debate. The **Discussion Questions** focus on the main issues, principles, and theories described in a chapter. **The Great Training Debate** presents an issue for students to debate either early in a class to get them thinking about a topic or later in a class so they can begin to apply the chapter material to an important training issue. For example, The Great Training Debate in Chapter 1 asks students to debate whether all provinces should enact training legislation similar to the training law in Quebec.

As in the previous edition of the text, every chapter begins with a **chapter-opening vignette**. Each vignette tells the story of an actual training program in an organization that is relevant to the material covered in the chapter. Many of the vignettes feature Canadian organizations, and the eighth edition includes several new ones that feature a variety of types of organizations (e.g., financial, health, service, law enforcement, manufacturing, educational, broadcasting, public transit) from across the country.

As with previous editions, you will also find in each chapter The Trainer's Notebook and Training Today features. **The Trainer's Notebook** presents practical, hands-on information for trainers and practitioners (e.g., Chapter 8, The Trainer's Notebook 8.2: Getting Trainees Engaged). The **Training Today** feature describes the latest in training research and practice (e.g., Chapter 9, Training Today 9.1: The Effects of Follow-Up Sessions on the Transfer of Training).

We have also retained other features that appeared in previous editions, including **Chapter Learning Outcomes** at the beginning of every chapter; **Key Terms**, which appear in the text in bold and in the margins and are also listed at the end of each chapter; and a chapter-ending **Summary** that reviews the main content of each chapter.

In summary, the eighth edition of *Managing Performance through Training and Development* offers a wide variety of pedagogical material in every chapter. Our intent is to provide instructors and students with many options for pedagogical material to choose from to best suit their learning needs, styles, and preferences.

// STRUCTURE OF THE BOOK

Managing Performance through Training and Development is structured in a manner that follows the sequence of the instructional systems design (ISD) model of training and development: needs analysis, training design and delivery, and training evaluation.

The text begins with an overview of the training and development process. **Chapter 1** describes the importance and benefits of training and development for employees, organizations, and society. "Training and development" is defined and presented in the larger context of the performance management process as well as the organization's external environment, the organizational context, and the HR management system. Chapter 1 also describes the ISD model of the training and development process, which sets the stage for the subsequent chapters.

The focus of **Chapter 2** is learning, which is first and foremost what training and development is all about. We believe it is important for students to first understand learning before they begin to learn about training and development. Therefore, Chapter 2 describes how individuals learn and their motivation to learn. Formal and informal learning, learning outcomes, stages of learning, learning styles, learning theories, adult learning theory, goal-setting theory, and training motivation are described, along with their implications for training and development. The chapter concludes with a model of training effectiveness that shows the variables that influence learning and retention, and how learning and retention are related to individual behaviour, individual performance, and organizational effectiveness. The training effectiveness model is further developed in Chapters 4 and 9.

The training and development process begins with a needs analysis, the focus of **Chapter 3**. This chapter describes the needs analysis process with particular emphasis on the three levels of needs analysis (organizational, task, and person) and how to determine solutions to performance problems. The chapter also describes the methods and sources of needs analysis and some of the obstacles to conducting a needs analysis.

Chapter 4 describes how to design training and development programs. The chapter begins with an overview of the importance of training objectives and how to write them. The chapter then proceeds to cover the main steps involved in the design of training programs, including whether to purchase or design a training program; requests for proposals; training content; training methods; active practice and conditions of practice; active learning and adaptive expertise; and error-management training.

One of the most important steps in the design of a training program is the choice of training methods. Given the vast array of training methods and instructional techniques available, Chapters 5, 6, and 7 are devoted to this topic.

Chapter 5 describes the most frequently used off-the-job instructional methods, including lectures, discussions, case studies, case incidents, behaviour modelling training, role plays, simulations, games, and action learning. Each training method is defined and described, along with tips for trainers. The chapter also describes instructional media and concludes with a discussion of the factors to consider when choosing training methods and the importance of a blended approach.

In **Chapter 6,** we turn to on-the-job training methods, including job instruction training, performance aids, job rotation, apprenticeship programs, coaching, and mentoring. As in Chapter 5, we define and describe each method and provide tips for trainers. The chapter concludes with a discussion of the advantages and disadvantages of off-the-job and on-the-job training methods.

Chapter 7 is devoted to technology-based training methods. The chapter begins with a definition of technology-based training, followed by a description of computer-based training and e-learning. Distinctions are made between instructor-led training and self-directed learning, and between asynchronous and synchronous training. This is followed by a discussion of online and distance education, electronic performance support systems, the virtual classroom, social media and Web 2.0 technology, mobile (m-) learning, and synthetic learning environments. The chapter then discusses how to design technology-based training programs, their advantages and disadvantages, and the effectiveness of technology-based training methods.

The focus of **Chapter 8** is training delivery. The chapter begins with a description of a lesson plan and then describes the main components of a lesson plan, including the trainer, trainees, training materials and equipment, the training site, and scheduling training programs. The chapter also describes the role of ethics in training and development, how to create a climate for learning, Gagné's nine events of instruction, and common training delivery problems and solutions.

One of the biggest problems facing trainers and organizations is the transfer of training, the focus of **Chapter 9**. The chapter begins with a review of the transfer problem and barriers to transfer, followed by a description of Baldwin and Ford's (1988) model of the transfer process. The chapter then describes strategies that can be undertaken by managers, trainers, and trainees to improve the transfer of training before, during, and after training. The chapter also describes transfer of training interventions, post-training supplements, and the transfer system.

Once a training program has been designed and delivered, it needs to be evaluated. Chapters 10 and 11 are devoted to training evaluation. In **Chapter 10,** we describe the purpose and barriers of training evaluation and three training evaluation models. The chapter also describes how to measure key variables for training evaluation and the different types of training evaluation designs.

In **Chapter 11,** the focus shifts to the costs and benefits of training. Chapter 11 describes how to calculate the costs of training programs as well as the benefits (e.g., net benefit, benefit–cost ratio, return on investment, and utility). The importance of the credibility of estimates is also discussed.

Chapters 12 and 13 describe the types of training programs that are provided in organizations. **Chapter 12** describes the most common types of training that employees receive, including orientation training, essential skills training, technical and non-technical skills training, information technology training, computer software training, health and safety training, total quality management training, team training, sales training, customer-service training, sexual and racial harassment training, ethics training, diversity training, cross-cultural training, health and wellness training, and mental health training.

Chapter 13 is devoted entirely to management and leadership development. This reflects both its importance to organizations and the large investments made by organizations in the development of management and leadership talent. The chapter begins with definitions of "management" and "management development." It then describes the core managerial roles and functions, management skills, emotional intelligence, and transactional, transformational, charismatic, and authentic leadership. Models of management skill development are also described, as well as error training for management development and the content and methods of management development programs. The chapter concludes with a discussion of research on the effectiveness of management development.

Finally, **Chapter 14** concludes the text with a discussion of the evolution and future of training and development. The chapter begins with a discussion of the evolution of learning in organizations. This is followed by a description of a multilevel systems model of organizational learning that highlights the importance of learning at the individual, group, and organization levels. The changing role of learning professionals is then discussed along with the skills and competencies required by learning professionals today and in the future. The chapter concludes with a review of the main factors that make training and development programs effective.

Throughout this textbook we have tried to maintain a balance between theory and research on the one hand, and practice and application on the other. We have also tried to provide examples of the concepts and principles presented in the text by showcasing effective training programs. Overall, we have tried to provide a thorough and comprehensive text on training and development that reflects both the science and practice of the field as well as our excitement and genuine love of the topic. We hope that the combination of text material and the many pedagogical features will motivate students to learn about the science and practice of training and development.

// INSTRUCTOR RESOURCES

The **Nelson Education Teaching Advantage (NETA)** program delivers research-based instructor resources that promote student engagement and higher-order thinking to enable the success of Canadian students and educators. Visit Nelson Education's **Inspired Instruction** website at nelson.com/inspired to find out more about NETA.

The following instructor resources have been created for *Managing Performance through Training and Development*, Eighth Edition. Access these ultimate tools for customizing lectures and presentations at nelson.com/instructor.

NETA TEST BANK

This resource was written by one of the book's co-authors, Alan Saks. It includes over 480 multiple-choice questions written according to NETA guidelines for effective construction and development of higher-order questions. Also included are over 350 true/false questions and over 120 short-answer questions.

The NETA Test Bank is available in a new, cloud-based platform. **Nelson Testing Powered by Cognero®** is a secure online testing system that allows instructors to author, edit, and manage test bank content from anywhere Internet access is available. No special installations or downloads are needed, and the desktop-inspired interface, with its drop-down menus and familiar, intuitive tools, allows instructors to create and manage tests with ease. Multiple test versions can be created in an instant, and content can be imported or exported into other systems. Tests can be delivered from a learning management system, the classroom, or wherever an instructor chooses. Nelson Testing Powered by Cognero for *Managing Performance through Training and Development* can also be accessed through nelson.com/instructor.

NETA POWERPOINT

Microsoft® PowerPoint® lecture slides for every chapter have been adapted by one of the book's co-authors, Alan Saks. There is an average of 45 slides per chapter. The slides provide a basic outline of the chapter and many feature key figures, tables, and photographs from *Managing Performance through Training and Development*, Eighth Edition. NETA principles of clear design and engaging content have been incorporated throughout, making it simple for instructors to customize the deck for their courses.

IMAGE LIBRARY

This resource consists of digital copies of figures, short tables, and photographs used in the book. Instructors may use these JPEGs to customize the NETA PowerPoint or create their own PowerPoint presentations. An Image Library Key describes the images and lists the codes under which the JPEGs are saved. Codes normally reflect the Chapter number (e.g., C01 for Chapter 1), the Figure or Photo number (e.g., F15 for Figure 15), and the page in the textbook. C01-F15-pg26 corresponds to Figure 1-15 on page 26.

NETA INSTRUCTOR GUIDE

This resource was written by Steven G. Robinson at Georgian College. It is organized according to the textbook chapters and addresses key educational concerns, such as typical stumbling blocks students face and how to address them, as well as suggested classroom activities to give you the support you need to engage your students in the classroom. Other features include chapter summaries, sample lecture outlines, and suggested answers to end-of-chapter exercises, case incidents, and case studies.

// STUDENT ANCILLARIES

MINDTAP

Stay organized and efficient with **MindTap**—a single destination with all the course material and study aids you need to succeed.

Built-in apps leverage social media and the latest learning technology. For example,

- ReadSpeaker will read the text to you.
- Flashcards are pre-populated to provide you with a jump start for review—or you can create your own.
- You can highlight text and make notes in your MindTap Reader. Your notes will flow into Evernote, the electronic notebook app that you can access anywhere when it's time to study for the exam.
- Self-quizzing allows you to assess your understanding.
- Videos provide additional insights into topics discussed in the textbook.

Visit nelson.com/student to start using MindTap. Enter the Online Access Code from the card included with your text. If a code card is not provided, you can purchase instant access at NELSONbrain.com.

ACKNOWLEDGMENTS

Writing a textbook requires the support and assistance of many people who directly or indirectly make important contributions to the process and outcome. We wish to thank all those who have played important roles in our lives and in writing this edition as well as previous editions of this text.

First, we thank all the reviewers who provided us with insightful and constructive feedback over the past few editions that led to many changes and improvements:

Lynne Bard, *Conestoga College*
Gordon Barnard, *Durham College*
Lisa Bering, *Humber College*
Anna Bortolon, *Conestoga College*
Holly Catalfamo, *Niagara College*
Alfonsina Chang, *Seneca College*
Genevieve Farrell, *Ryerson University*
Susan Fitzrandolph, *Ryerson University*
Morai Forer, *Saskatchewan Polytechnic*
Bernadette Gatien, *Saint Mary's University*
Stefan Gröschl, *University of Guelph*
Jamie Gruman, *University of Guelph*
John Hardisty, *Sheridan College*
Jill Leedham, *Mohawk College*
Donna Leibham, *University of Calgary*
Barbara Lipton, *Seneca College*
Edward Marinos, *Sheridan College*
Kenneth McBey, *York University*
Thomas Medcof, *University of Guelph*
Jody Merritt, *St. Clair College*
Grace O'Farrell, *University of Winnipeg*
Louis Pike, *Ryerson University*
Steve Robinson, *Georgian College*
Carol Ann Samhaber, *Algonquin College*
Enda Sooster, *Georgian College*
Jennifer Souch, *Durham College*
Tracey Starrett, *The Starrett Group*
Wiktor J. Tutlewski, *Kwantlen Polytechnic University*
Michelle White, *Fanshawe College*
Valerie Whyte, *University of New Brunswick*
Jeff Young, *Saint Mary's University*

Each one contributed to this text by lending us their expertise and by taking the time to share their teaching experiences. Their comments and feedback have helped us to improve each edition of this text.

Second, we wish to express our gratitude to the team at Nelson Education that helped us develop and produce this text: Publisher, Jackie Wood; Content Manager,

Elke Price; Production Project Manager, Shannon Martin; Executive Marketing Manager, Amanda Henry; and Permissions Manager, Lynn McLeod. We are grateful for their support and all their hard work and feel very lucky to be working with a team of dedicated professionals who care so much about what they do and their authors.

Finally, we also wish to thank our families, who have had to endure the burden of living with busy, tired, and overworked authors who sometimes don't have time to play or sleep! Alan Saks is grateful to Kelly, Justin, and Brooke for making it all worthwhile. Robert Haccoun is grateful to his family, especially the little ones: Orli, Amit, Erez, and Micah. Our love for them grows as they do.

Alan M. Saks
Robert R. Haccoun

THE TRAINING AND DEVELOPMENT PROCESS

CHAPTER LEARNING OUTCOMES

AFTER READING THIS CHAPTER, YOU SHOULD BE ABLE TO:

- explain the differences between performance management, training, and development, and how they are related
- discuss the role of training and development in the performance management process
- explain how training and development benefits organizations, employees, and society
- explain why some organizations invest more than others in training and development
- discuss the context of training and development and the relationships between the different factors
- explain the instructional systems design (ISD) model of training and development and its implications for the training and development process

Several years ago police officers at the Edmonton Police Service (EPS) participated in a one-day mental health training program on how to effectively recognize and deal with individuals suffering from mental illness and in crisis situations. Officers participated in role-playing exercises involving highly trained actors who represented various mental illnesses. According to Sgt. David DeMarco, the officer in charge of the tactics training team, the program filled a void in officer training, since new recruits at the EPS receive training on mental health issues but there is very little related training after that.

The goal of the training was to improve interactions between police officers and mentally ill individuals by improving officers' empathy, communication skills, and ability to de-escalate potentially difficult situations. The program encouraged police behaviours such as verbally expressing empathy, maintaining eye contact, using non-threatening body language, "mirroring" the actor's movements, and sharing non-threatening information.

More than 650 officers from the police service participated in the training program. Each officer went through six realistic scenarios:

- a depressed individual who was belligerent and potentially violent with a weapon nearby
- a psychotic individual who was experiencing hallucinations
- an excited individual behaving strangely on a public street
- an individual with presumed alcohol dependence collapsed on the street
- a couple arguing about the man's gambling addiction
- a depressed individual who may have overdosed

According to Peter Silverstone of the University of Alberta, who helped develop the program, "We were trying to reflect the common interactions the police have and trying to get them to see things in a different light than they may have originally. For example, the manic presentation was very similar to an individual who may be taking a stimulant or other drugs, so we tried to get the police to not take the situation for granted and start to think about what actually may be presented to them."

The actors who portrayed the individuals with mental illnesses really enhanced the officers' training, said

Courtesy of the Edmonton Police Service

Police officers at Edmonton Police Services participated in a mental health training program to recognize and deal with individuals suffering from mental illness.

Sgt. DeMarco, especially since other types of in-service training usually have police officers acting the part rather than professionally trained actors. The actors also offered feedback to the officers after the role playing, describing how the officers' actions made them feel. For example: "I was frightened when you came that close to me." Supervisors and psychologists also provided feedback to the officers after they dealt with each scenario. They offered tips for how to improve their interaction, such as changing their body language to mirror that of the individual, looking her in the eye, and sharing their names with her.

Six months after the program, the participating officers were able to deal with persons with mental illness more effectively and better recognize mental health issues. There was a 40 percent increase in officers' ability to recognize mental health issues as the reason for a call. There was also an improvement in police officers' ability to communicate with the public and to verbally de-escalate a situation, and in their level of empathy in dealing with the public. Participating officers also used less physical force or fewer weapons when interacting with persons who had a mental illness.

Officers who participated in the training program also improved their efficiency in dealing with mental health issues. They were able to spend less time on calls, which translated into a cost savings of more than $80,000 in the six months after the program.

The EPS mental health training program is now part of regular training. In a report to the Canadian Association of Chiefs of Police, the Mental Health Commission of Canada

(MHCC) commended the Edmonton Police Service for how its officers deal with people in crisis.[1]

Sources: Silliker, A. (2013, May 20). Mental illness training for cops effective: Study. Canadian HR Reporter, 26(10), 1, 6. Reprinted by permission of Canadian HR Reporter. © Copyright Thomson Reuters Canada Ltd. (2013), Toronto, Ontario, 1-800-387-5164. Web: www. hrreporter.com; Krameddine, Y. I., DeMarco, D., Hassel, R., & Silverstone, P. H. (2013, March 18). A novel training program for police officers that improves interactions with mentally ill individuals and is cost-effective. Frontiers in Psychiatry, doi:10.3389/fpsyt.2013.00009; Maurier, R. (2013, March 18). Helping police protect and serve people with mental illness. University of Alberta, http://uofa.ualberta. ca/news-and-events/newsarticles/2013/. . . (2014, September 5); Edmonton cops commended by Mental Health Commission. Edmonton Sun, http://www.edmontonsun.com/2014/09/05/edmonton-cops-commended-by-mental-health-commission (2014, September 5); Specialized training helps officers safely deal with people in crisis, Edmonton Police Media Release, http://www.edmontonpolice.ca/News/MediaReleases/Specializedtraininghelpsofficerssafel. . . .

// INTRODUCTION

The EPS's mental health training program is a great example of the role and importance of training and development in organizations. The program ensures that police officers are prepared to answer calls that involve persons who have a mental illness and are in a crisis situation. It is also an excellent example of how to design, deliver, and evaluate training and development programs, just what this book is all about.

It is not hard to understand how investments in the training and development of employees can improve an organization's success and competitiveness. In fact, later in this chapter you will learn how training and development benefits employees, organizations, and society. But have you ever wondered how employee training benefits you and can affect *your* life?

Consider the police shooting deaths of several mentally ill people in Toronto over the last 15 years. Five emotionally disturbed people were shot by police in Toronto between 2002 and 2012, and 18-year-old Sammy Yatim was shot on a streetcar in 2013.

An inquest into the deaths of three of the fatal shootings made 74 recommendations. One of those recommendations calls for police officers to consider mental state and whether a person is in crisis when advancing with a sharp weapon. However, police officers are trained to react to behaviour when facing a threatening situation regardless of a person's mental health. As a result, many of the recommendations call for changes to police training, such as emphasizing verbal de-escalation techniques. The report recommends that officers be trained to stop shouting commands such as "Stop, police!" or "Drop the weapon!" and try different defusing strategies if an emotionally disturbed person has failed to respond to the standard police commands. The report also recommends that training emphasize that there is no fixed distance at which shooting is necessary.[2]

In 2014, a landmark report by former Supreme Court Justice Frank Iacobucci into the use of lethal force by the Toronto Police Service made 84 recommendations to improve police officers' interactions with emotionally disturbed or mentally ill persons in crisis situations. Several of the recommendations call for training that emphasizes containment of crisis situations, de-escalation techniques, and communication instead of force, making all officers complete a mental health first aid course, and additional mental health training for sergeants. According to the report, "Police must be trained not only in techniques for calming a situation or negotiating with someone in crisis, but also in areas of recognizing crisis symptoms, assessing the physical and mental capabilities of the subject, anticipating unexpected responses to routine commands or actions, exercising discretion in decisions to apprehend, arrest or divert an individual, and combatting the effects of stigma on their decisions making" (p. 144).[3]

CHAPTER 1 The Training and Development Process

In 2017, an inquest into the police shooting death of Michael MacIsaac emphasized the need for better de-escalation techniques for police officers and the need for mental health training. In particular, it recommended extending police training at the Ontario Police College by one week to focus exclusively on de-escalation training and training on the use of different communication techniques when an individual does not respond to shouting of commands. Thus, like the Iacobucci report, a major recommendation is for better police training in dealing with individuals in crisis situations and in the use of more effective methods of de-escalation.[4]

The EPS mental health training program described in the chapter-opening vignette is consistent with many of the recommendations of both these inquires and the Iacobucci report. Recall that six months after the EPS mental health training program began, participating officers were able to deal with persons with mental illness more effectively and better recognize mental health issues, and there was a 40 percent increase in officers' ability to recognize mental health issues as the reason for a call. There was an improvement in police officers' ability to verbally de-escalate a situation, and officers used less physical force or fewer weapons when interacting with persons who had a mental illness. Thus, mental health training for police officers can make a big difference in police officers' attitudes and behaviour, and save lives.

As you can see, employees who are not properly trained can make mistakes that result in accidents that threaten public safety and well-being. While these examples are among the most extreme, it is important to recognize that poorly trained employees produce defective products and provide poor service. Thus, training is of vital importance not only to employees and organizations, but to all of us who use public transportation and purchase goods and services every day of our lives. To learn more about the potential consequences of failing to provide adequate training, see Training Today 1.1, "The Risks and Consequences of Failing to Provide Training."

TRAINING TODAY 1.1

THE RISKS AND CONSEQUENCES OF FAILING TO PROVIDE TRAINING

Although much is known about the benefits of training, much less is known about the risks and consequences of failing to provide training, especially when it comes to occupational health and safety and harassment.

There are many negative outcomes that are possible when an organization does not provide proper training. It can be as simple as an employee or department failing to perform their job adequately because they did not receive the necessary skills training and development. However, it can be much more serious, such as when there are lapses in safety training or training on workplace policies that can have legal consequences. Failure to provide training on proper procedures, safety training, or ergonomics can result in disability claims, which can be very costly for organizations.

There are also legal consequences for organizations that do not provide proper safety training and Workplace Hazardous Materials Information System (WHMIS) training in compliance with the *Occupational Health and Safety Act*. In addition, directors and owners of organizations are susceptible to personal liability if they are aware of unsafe working conditions and allow them to continue.

In 2015 two corporate directors with NewMex Canada, a furniture retailer based in Brampton, Ontario, received jail time and a $250,000 fine for failing to provide health and safety training which, along with other safety violations, was found to be the cause behind the death of a forklift operator. The two directors were charged with failing to take reasonable care and NewMex pleaded guilty to failing to provide information, instruction, and supervision to a worker regarding fall protection and working from a height.

There can also be consequences for failing to provide proper training on psychological safety and workplace

(continued)

harassment. For example, in 2015 the Canadian Olympic Committee came under fire after receiving media attention for a so-called "culture of harassment" within the organization. Former president Marcel Aubut stepped down after being accused by multiple women of unwanted touching and sexual comments.

Investigators found that there was insufficient training on workplace harassment at the organization and recommended education, including a mandatory training session for staff and board members on harassment policies and procedures. The organization received a significant amount of negative media attention and reputational damage as a result of the incident.

Failing to provide training on workplace harassment can also lead to employees taking stress leave, and employees who are injured as a result of an organization's failure to provide adequate training must be accommodated as required under the human rights code.

Thus, failure to provide necessary and adequate training can result in considerable risks to employees and negative consequences for management and organizations.

Source: Based on Bernier, L. (2016, February 8). More than just a good idea or nice-to-have: A look at the potential consequences for failing to provide adequate training. *Canadian HR Reporter*, 29(2), 14–15.

For organizations, success and competitiveness are highly dependent on training and development. In fact, continuous learning and skill development has become a key factor for the success of individuals and organizations. Whether an organization is adopting new technology, improving quality, or simply trying to remain competitive, training and development is a critical and necessary part of the process.

A report by the Conference Board of Canada on learning and development in Canadian organizations concluded that continuous learning and the transfer of knowledge are key factors in fostering creativity and promoting organizational excellence.[5] Not surprisingly, training and development is one of the distinguishing characteristics of the best companies to work for in Canada.[6]

Therefore, it should not surprise you that organizations invest millions of dollars each year on training and development. This textbook will teach you about the training and development process and how to design, deliver, and evaluate effective training and development programs.

In this chapter, we introduce you to the topic of training and development and describe the training and development process. We begin with a discussion of performance management, since training and development is first and foremost about managing performance in organizations.

// PERFORMANCE MANAGEMENT

As the title of the textbook indicates, training and development is about managing performance. This is especially important in light of a recent study that found that half of Canadian workers believe they are less productive at work than they could be. One of the causes for this is a lack of training and development. A lack of productivity also highlights the need for performance management.[7]

Performance management is the process of establishing performance goals and designing interventions and programs to motivate and develop employees to improve their performance and, ultimately, organization performance. This process signals to employees what is really important in the organization, ensures accountability for behaviour and results, and helps improve performance.[8]

> **Performance management**
> The process of establishing performance goals and designing interventions and programs to motivate and develop employees to improve their performance

FIGURE 1.1

THE PERFORMANCE MANAGEMENT PROCESS

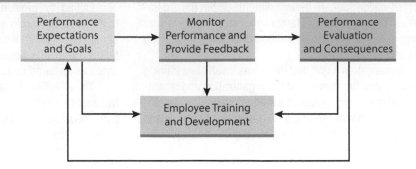

Performance management is not a single event, like a performance appraisal or a training program; rather, it is a comprehensive, ongoing, and continuous process that involves various activities and programs designed to develop employees and improve their performance.[9]

As shown in Figure 1.1, the performance management process involves several components that are closely related to one another. The starting point of the process is defining performance, setting performance expectations, and setting performance goals. Managers meet with employees to discuss performance expectations and agree on performance goals. These goals should stem from organizational or department-level goals and objectives. This ensures that employee goals are aligned with department and organizational goals.[10]

The goal-setting process should make the organization or superordinate goal clear and concrete to employees. Managers can do this by setting **SMART goals**—goals that are specific, measureable, attainable, relevant, and have a time frame.[11] To learn more about SMART goals, see the Trainer's Notebook 1.1.

SMART goals
Goals that are specific, measurable, attainable, relevant, and have a time frame

THE TRAINER'S NOTEBOOK   1.1

SMART GOALS

SMART goals are specific, measurable, attainable, relevant, and have a time frame.

Specific: Goals must be specific regarding the behaviour to be performed or the level of performance. Specific goals are more effective than general or do-your-best goals.

Measurable: It must be possible to determine whether goals have been achieved. Therefore, when setting goals the criteria of success must be indicated.

Attainable: Goals should be challenging but attainable. Goals should not be too difficult or too easy.

Relevant: Goals should be relevant and meaningful to the individual. They should be clearly linked to unit and organization objectives.

Time frame: A time frame within which the goal will be achieved must be indicated.

Source: Latham, G. P. (2003). Goal setting: A five-step approach to behavior change. *Organizational Dynamics*, 32, 309–318.

Once the manager and employee have set SMART goals, it is important for managers to monitor employee performance and provide ongoing feedback so that employees know whether they are accomplishing their goals. For example, at First West Credit

Union, employees identify their performance goals and then discuss them with their manager, who ensures that the goals tie back to the company's core strategic objectives. Employees obtain feedback from colleagues during the year, which is then used as part of the review and assessment with their manager.[12]

In addition to informal feedback, a key part of the performance management process is a formal performance evaluation. This usually involves the use of a standard rating form on which the manager and employee (self-appraisal) evaluate the employee's performance on a number of behavioural/performance dimensions and review the extent to which the employee has accomplished his/her goals. The performance evaluation also involves performance consequences to reward employees for accomplishing their goals and serves to reinforce employee behaviour and performance. The process then repeats itself with the setting of new or revised performance expectations and goals.[13]

A critical component of the performance management process is employee training and development and the creation of a development plan for employees. This involves programs and activities that are designed to help employees achieve their goals and improve their performance. This, of course, is where training and development fits into the performance management process. Employee training and development can include formal training and development programs in the classroom as well as on-the-job training such as coaching and mentoring. At First West Credit Union, learning and development are a key part of the performance management process.[14]

Employee training and development is shown in the middle of Figure 1.1 because it connects to all of the other components of the performance management process. In other words, each of the components of the performance management process provides information on the developmental needs of employees.[15] For example, when setting goals it might be determined that attending a training program will help an employee achieve his/her goals. Thus, part of the goal-setting process might include a development plan that will enable employees to achieve their goals. Feedback might suggest the need for additional training to address an employee problem or weakness. The formal performance evaluation identifies employee strengths and weaknesses as well as areas that need improvement. This has further implications for employee development and the creation of an employee development plan that will set the stage for the next round of the performance management process.[16] Thus, each component of the performance management process can identify an employee's training needs and lead to action plans for employee training and development.

In summary, performance management is a key factor for the improvement and management of employee performance, and training and development is a central and necessary component of the performance management process. But what exactly is training and development?

// TRAINING AND DEVELOPMENT

Training and development is one of the most important ways that performance can be improved in organizations. **Training** refers to formal and planned efforts to help employees acquire knowledge, skills, and abilities to improve performance in their current job.[17] Training usually consists of a short-term focus on acquiring skills to perform one's job. You have probably experienced this type of training, such as when your company sends you to a workshop to learn a software package or to learn how to better serve customers. The goal is to help you learn to do your current job better.

As indicated at the beginning of the chapter, the objective of the Edmonton Police Service mental health training program is to improve interactions between police officers

> **Training**
> Formal and planned efforts to help employees acquire knowledge, skills, and abilities to improve performance in their current job

and mentally ill individuals by improving officers' empathy, communication skills, and ability to de-escalate potentially difficult situations.

Development refers to formal and planned efforts to help employees acquire the knowledge, skills, and abilities required to perform future job responsibilities and for the long-term achievement of individual career goals and organizational objectives. The goal is to prepare individuals for promotions and future jobs as well as additional job responsibilities. This process might consist of extensive programs, such as leadership development, and might include seminars and workshops, job rotation, coaching, and other assignments. The goal is to prepare employees for future responsibilities and often for managerial careers. You can read more about management development in Chapter 13.

Thus, the primary objective of training and development is to develop and maximize an organization's human capital. **Human capital** refers to the knowledge, skills, and abilities of an organization's employees. It has been found to be a key determinant of an organization's performance and one of the most important resources for competitive advantage.[18] Human capital development is one of the top areas of concern for organizations, and increased training and development for employees is one of the top strategies for developing human capital.[19]

Training and development can also facilitate the development of **social capital**, which refers to the social resources that an individual obtains from participation in a social structure. It has to do with relationships within an organization and between members of the organization and external stakeholders. Like human capital, social capital can also be used by employees to achieve their goals, and it contributes to employee and organization performance.[20]

In summary, through training and development, organizations strive to develop human capital and social capital to improve individual and group performance, and ultimately the organization's performance. As described in the next section, training and development benefits organizations, employees, and society at large.

// BENEFITS OF TRAINING AND DEVELOPMENT

Organizations that invest in the training and development of their employees reap many benefits. But so do employees and the society in which they live. In this section, we describe the benefits of training and development to organizations, employees, and society. As you will see, training and development plays a critical role in the success and well-being of organizations, employees, and society.

BENEFITS TO ORGANIZATIONS

Organizations that invest in training and development benefit in many ways that help them obtain a sustained competitive advantage. Training and development can facilitate an organization's strategy, increase effectiveness, and improve employee recruitment, engagement, and retention.

STRATEGY

The goal of all organizations is to survive and prosper. Training and development can help organizations achieve these goals. Organizations can be successful by training employees so they have the knowledge and skills necessary to help achieve organization

---

Development
Formal and planned efforts to help employees acquire knowledge, skills, and abilities required to perform future job responsibilities

Human capital
The knowledge, skills, and abilities of an organization's employees

Social capital
The social resources that an individual obtains from participation in a social structure

goals and objectives. By linking training to an organization's strategy, training becomes a strategic activity that operates in concert with other organization programs and activities to achieve an organization's strategic business objectives. We will have more to say about what makes training strategic later in the chapter.

EFFECTIVENESS

There is a calculable benefit to training employees. Trained employees can do more and better work, make fewer errors, require less supervision, have more positive attitudes, and have lower rates of turnover. Trained employees also produce higher-quality products and services.[21] These benefits have a positive effect on an organization's competitiveness and performance.

The link between training and organization performance is strongly supported by research. For example, a survey conducted by the American Management Association found that companies that expanded their training programs showed gains in productivity and larger operating profits.[22] In another study, a 10 percent increase in training produced a 3 percent increase in productivity over two years.[23] A review of research on training and organizational effectiveness found that training is positively related to human resource outcomes (e.g., employee attitudes, motivation, and behaviours), organizational performance outcomes (e.g., performance and productivity), and financial outcomes (e.g., profit and financial indicators).[24]

In addition, research has found that companies that invest more in training have higher revenues, profits, and productivity growth than firms that invest less in training.[25] Research by the Conference Board of Canada found that organizations that spend the most on training and development outperform those that spend the least on training and development on a number of performance indicators, such as employee satisfaction, customer satisfaction, profitability, and productivity.[26] A study of companies in South Korea found that those that invest more in workplace learning achieve higher levels of learning outcomes (i.e., employee competence, labour productivity, and employee enthusiasm) and financial performance. In other words, investment in workplace training influences organizational performance through learning outcomes.[27]

Training has also been found to be more effective than other interventions. For example, a study that compared the impact of human resource practices to practices that place greater emphasis on operational initiatives, such as advanced manufacturing technology, found that the human resource practices were directly related to the productivity of 308 companies over 22 years, while none of the operational manufacturing practices related to productivity. Both empowerment and extensive training were related to productivity, and together they accounted for a 9 percent increase in value added per employee.[28]

Training is so important for organizations that it can even make the difference between the success or failure of a business. For example, research has found that a key factor associated with the success of a franchisee is the length of training (the number of weeks that franchisees underwent initial training). The more robust and lengthy the training program for the franchisee, the more likely the franchisee is to succeed. Franchises with the shortest franchisee training programs are the most likely to fail.[29]

To learn more about the effects of training on productivity and firm profits, see Training Today 1.2, "The Effects of Training on Firm Productivity and Profits."

THE EFFECTS OF TRAINING ON FIRM PRODUCTIVITY AND PROFITS

Is training related to firm profits? If so, how? To find out, Youngsang Kim and Robert Ployhart conducted a study of 359 firms over a period of 12 years before (2000–2007) and after (2008–2011) the recent recession. They argue that training develops firm-specific human capital resources that will result in higher productivity. Furthermore, greater productivity will provide greater financial resources that can be used for profit-generating opportunities, which in turn will lead to greater profit growth in a strong and growing economy (the period before the recession). In a weak economy or during economic downturns (the period during and after the recession), firms that provide more extensive training should be more prepared and able to quickly recover from an economic downturn. This is because the slack financial resources that result from higher productivity can be used to counter the effects of a recession.

Training was measured in terms of the overall percentage of full-time employees trained internally on the job. Organizations with a higher percentage of employees who are trained on the job should have greater firm-specific knowledge and skills, which will increase productivity. As predicted, firms with more internal training had greater productivity and profit growth, and the relationship between training and profit growth was due in part to greater productivity. The authors also found that firms with more extensive training generated resources that help them to buffer and more quickly recover from the recession.

The results of this study demonstrate that training influences firm profit growth through its effect on productivity. In other words, the effects of training on profit growth are due to its direct effect on productivity. The most important practical implication of this study is that firms that use more extensive internal training produce and perform better than competitors and recover more quickly from a recession.

Source: Kim, Y., & Ployhart, R. E. (2014). The effects of staffing and training on firm productivity and profit growth before, during, and after the great recession. *Journal of Applied Psychology*, 99(3), 361–389.

EMPLOYEE RECRUITMENT, ENGAGEMENT, AND RETENTION

Training and development is considered an effective tool for attracting and retaining top talent, especially for employees under the age of 30 who consider their career growth and professional development more important than salary.[30]

Training is often used by organizations to increase their attractiveness to prospective employees and to retain their current employees. For many organizations today, training is the number-one attraction and retention strategy.[31] For example, construction company EllisDon offers employees a range of courses and programs through its EllisDon University (EDU), which is part of the company's attraction and retention strategy.[32] At CIBC, continuing education and training is an important business and retention tool.[33] Keller Williams Realty Inc. invites competitors and prospects to their training programs, since training plays a major role in the recruitment of agents.[34]

An organization that fails to provide training opportunities to its employees will be at a disadvantage in attracting new employees and retaining current ones. In one study, 99 percent of the respondents said that there are job areas in which training would be useful to them, and in which training decreases their willingness to move to another company.[35] Research conducted by the Conference Board of Canada found that organizations that spend more per employee on training and development have significantly lower voluntary and involuntary turnover rates.[36]

Training and opportunities for learning and development also have implications for employees' work engagement. **Work engagement** is a positive, fulfilling, work-related

> **Work engagement**
> A positive, fulfilling, work-related state of mind that is characterized by vigour, dedication, and absorption

state of mind that is characterized by vigour, dedication, and absorption. *Vigour* involves high levels of energy and mental resilience while working; *dedication* refers to being strongly involved in one's work and experiencing a sense of significance, enthusiasm, and challenge; and *absorption* refers to being fully concentrated and engrossed in one's work.[37]

Employees who receive formal workplace training report that it makes them feel more engaged in their job. Opportunities for learning and development and a positive learning climate have also been found to be positively related to employees' work engagement, and work engagement is positively related to employee attitudes, behaviours, job performance, and well-being as well as organizational performance. Thus, when employees have opportunities for learning, training, and development they are more likely to be engaged.[38]

BENEFITS TO EMPLOYEES

Training and development also has benefits for employees. These can be categorized as internal or intrinsic to an individual, such as knowledge and attitudes, and those that are external to an individual, such as salary.

INTRINSIC BENEFITS

Trained employees benefit by acquiring new knowledge and skills that enable them to perform their jobs better. Research has shown that training has a positive effect on employees' job behaviour and job performance.[39] In addition to improving knowledge and skills, trained employees also develop greater confidence or self-efficacy (see Chapter 2 for a discussion of self-efficacy) in their ability to perform their job. They describe feelings of increased usefulness and belonging in the organization, and they seek out opportunities to fully exploit their new skills and abilities.[40] Trained employees also have more positive attitudes toward their job and organization.[41]

EXTRINSIC BENEFITS

Extrinsic benefits include things such as higher earnings as a result of increased knowledge and skills, improved marketability, greater security of employment, and enhanced opportunities for advancement and promotion. A number of studies have found that company-sponsored training programs increase workers' wages by 4 to 11 percent.[42] According to one study, immigrants to Canada who have completed apprenticeship training are more likely to be employed and to earn more money than immigrants who have only a high school diploma.[43] Many workers who have been laid off attend training programs to acquire new skills to obtain employment.[44]

BENEFITS TO SOCIETY

Training and development also has benefits for society that extend beyond the workplace. The training and development that organizations provide for their employees has implications for public health and safety, and it helps to create an educated and skilled population that benefits the economy and a country's standard of living.

CHAPTER 1 The Training and Development Process

EDUCATED AND EMPLOYED POPULATION

Education and training are fundamental for reducing unemployment, especially among youth, where it has been rising.[45] The knowledge and skills that employees acquire through training help to create an employable, educated, and skilled workforce. For example, some organizations offer literacy and numeracy training for employees who did not obtain it through regular educational channels but who require it to perform their jobs. This training also enables employees to function more effectively in their daily lives and therefore has a number of societal benefits.

Employees who have participated in organization-sponsored training programs report using their new skills to better manage their personal lives. They are more likely to be able to read instructions for assembling products and to be able to calculate bills and expenses. They are also more likely to be able to find employment if they are laid off or their employer closes a plant.

HEALTH AND SAFETY

As is evident from the examples provided at the beginning of the chapter, training and development has important implications for public health and safety. Effective training programs not only improve employee performance, but they can also reduce errors, improve safety, and even save people's lives. Training can reduce life-threatening errors in high-risk environments and improve the safety of employees and the public.

A good example of the effect of training on public health and safety is the Edmonton Police Service's mental health training program, which was described in the chapter-opening vignette. Another good example is the new mandatory entry-level training for commercial truck drivers in Ontario. Mandatory training was implemented in 2017 to ensure that commercial truck drivers are properly trained before they are allowed to take a road test, to improve road safety, and to eliminate inadequate and unregulated training provided by unregistered truck training schools. Previously, drivers could obtain a licence without any formal training. The mandatory training will include at least 103.5 hours of instruction and will cover the entry-level knowledge and skills required to safely operate a large truck.[46] Thus, training not only ensures the health, safety, and well-being of employees and the public, it can also save lives.

ECONOMY AND STANDARD OF LIVING

Key to a country's standard of living, incomes, and overall prosperity are its productivity and productivity growth. Unfortunately, Canada's economic performance and competitiveness in the global marketplace has been declining. Canada lags behind its major competitors in its productivity growth and innovation. Canada ranks 9th among 16 peer countries in productivity and 14th on the Global Competitiveness Index.[47] Among the G7 countries, Canada is the second-least productive country and 27 percent below the productivity of the United States.[48] A strong Canadian economy and a high standard of living require an improvement in the productivity, innovation, and performance competitiveness of Canadian organizations.[49]

There are a number of ways to improve productivity, and one of them is by improving and investing in the knowledge and skills of the workforce.[50] Investing in training and development is one of the key ways to improve Canada's productivity, economy, and standard of living.

Investing in the development of the workforce through training and development is considered to be a primary means for the economic development of nations.[51] Countries with higher education levels have more and better employment opportunities and lower unemployment rates.[52] Training investments and a skilled workforce also attract employers and lead to job creation, more job opportunities, and higher paying jobs. The most skilled workers earn 60 percent more than the lowest skilled.[53]

The federal government spends billions of dollars annually on education and training because it sees a strong link between an educated workforce and a high-wage economy. In 2013 the Canadian government made skills training a centrepiece of the federal budget and introduced the Canada Job Grant.[54] The Canada Job Grant is a program to help employers train new or existing employees so that employees have the skills needed to fill vacant jobs and to address Canada's skills mismatch.[55]

The Canada Job Grant is a program to help employers train new or existing employees to address Canada's skills mismatch.

A **skills mismatch** (or shortage) means that an insufficient number of workers with the needed skills are available to satisfy the number of available jobs. In other words, there is a mismatch between the skilled labour available and the market demand. The shortage of skilled trades is considered to be one of the barriers to Canada's economic prosperity.[56] According to the Conference Board of Canada, there will be a shortage of a million workers by 2020.[57]

Skills mismatch
An insufficient number of workers with the skills needed are available to satisfy the number of available jobs

Under the Canada Job Grant, employers can receive up to $10,000 to train each worker and workers can receive up to $15,000 to upgrade their skills and help them find a new or better job. Having skilled workers is critical to the growth and competitiveness of organizations as well as economic growth and prosperity. The skills gap and skills mismatch are a major concern of organizations today, and training and development is an important part of the solution to reduce the gap and ensure that employees have the knowledge and skills required by organizations today.[58]

Another solution is to provide students with **work-integrated learning** in which they acquire work experience as part of their education through internships, apprenticeships, and cooperative placements. In 2017, the federal government introduced the Student Work-Integrated Learning Program, which provides employers in the STEM (science, technology, engineering, mathematics) and business sectors with payroll subsidies for hiring students. The goal is to ensure that post-secondary students have the skills required by organizations when they graduate which will help to close the skills gap.[59]

Work-integrated learning
Providing students with work experience through internships, apprenticeships, and cooperative placements

Of course, for organizations, employees, and society to reap the benefits of training, organizations must invest in training and development. In the next section, we discuss investments in training and development by Canadian organizations.

// TRAINING AND DEVELOPMENT IN CANADA

In order to benefit from training and development, organizations must invest in training their workforce and provide employees with training opportunities. However, not all workers have access to employer-sponsored training. It has frequently been reported that just over half (56 percent) of the workers in Canada have access to employer-sponsored training, while some 44 percent do not. What's more, some workers are less likely to receive training than others. In particular, part-time and temporary workers as well as those who are less educated and older are less likely to receive training, compared to those who are employed in small- and medium-sized organizations.[60]

Furthermore, Canadian organizations have not been leaders when it comes to investing in training and development. For example, a recent survey found that less than half (47 percent) of Canadian organizations provide training to their employees.[61] According to the Conference Board of Canada, Canadian organizations have for many years underinvested in training and development.[62]

However, the results of the most recent survey indicate a positive and progressive trend in learning and development investments by Canadian organizations. According to the Conference Board of Canada, Canadian organizations have turned a corner when it comes to investments in learning and development.[63]

Although Canadian organizations have lagged in the amount spent on training per employee, there has been a steady and gradual increase in learning over the past several years. In 2017, the average direct investment in training and development per employee was $889, which is up from $800 in 2015.[64] By comparison, organizations in the United States spent on average $1,075 per employee in 2017.[65] Canadian organizations spend on average 81 cents for every dollar spent by organizations in the United States on learning and development. Thus, although Canadian organizations continue to lag behind those in the United States when it comes to investments in training and development, the gap has narrowed as Canadian organizations have gained substantial ground.[66]

In addition, the average number of hours of training received by employees at Canadian organizations increased slightly to 32 hours in 2017 from 31 hours in 2015. As shown in Table 1.1, senior management and executives receive the most hours of training (35) while non-technical (17) and trades (18) employees receive the least. Employees in services (32 hours) and not-for-profit organizations (30 hours) receive the most training,

TABLE 1.1

TRAINING AND DEVELOPMENT IN CANADA

- Total average training investment per employee in 2017: $889.
- Total average training investment per employee by organization type in 2013: private sector $773; federal/provincial/Crown $947; municipal/university/hospital/school board $190; not-for-profit sector $381.
- Total average training investment per employee by organization size in 2013: fewer than 250 employees $997; 250–499 employees $1,127; 500–1499 employees $666; 1500 or more employees $349.
- Total average training investment per employee by level of unionization in 2013: non-union $779; low unionized $560; high unionized $683.
- Annual training expenditure per employee by region 2004–2008: Quebec $1,158; Alberta $979; Manitoba/Saskatchewan $829; British Columbia $811; Ontario $802; Atlantic provinces $611.
- Percentage of payroll spent on training and development in 2017: 1.39.
- Percentage of annual revenues spent on training and development in 2017: 1.12.
- Average number of training hours received annually per employee in 2017: 32.
- Average number of training hours received annually by employee category in 2017: senior management and executive 35; middle management 29; supervisory 23; professional, technical, and scientific 26; trades 18; non-technical 17.

Sources: Hughes, P. D., & Campbell, A. (2009). Learning & development outlook 2009: Learning in tough times. Ottawa: The Conference Board of Canada; Lavis, C. (2011). Learning & development outlook 2011: Are organizations ready for learning 2.0? Ottawa: The Conference Board of Canada; Hall, C. (2014). Learning & development outlook—12th edition: Strong learning organizations, strong leadership. Ottawa: The Conference Board of Canada; Cotsman, S., & Hall, C. (2018). Learning cultures lead the way: Learning & development outlook—14th edition. Ottawa: The Conference Board of Canada.

while those in wholesale/retail (22 hours) receive the least. By comparison, employees in the United States received an average of 47.61 hours of training per employee in 2017.[67] Canada ranked second-last on annual training days per employee in a study that included 12 comparator countries.[68]

The average investment in training and development as a percentage of payroll in Canada dropped in 2017 to 1.39 percent, down from 1.41 in 2015.[69]

What type of training should organizations provide their employees? A survey of 800 Canadian employers found that the most strategically relevant skills for a business are thinking/problem solving, customer service, essential skills, and oral/communication. However, less than 50 percent of the employers indicated that they are willing to provide training in these areas. The results shown in Table 1.2 indicated a large gap between the skills that employers value and their willingness to provide training to improve these valued skills.[70]

Information about training and development in Canada is summarized in Table 1.1. This information will allow you to compare your organization and training experience against that of others. This information also highlights some differences in training across job categories and types of organizations. In the next section, we consider how beliefs that training is an investment or an expense can influence spending on training and development.

TABLE 1.2

VALUE OF SKILLS VERSUS WILLINGNESS TO PROVIDE TRAINING

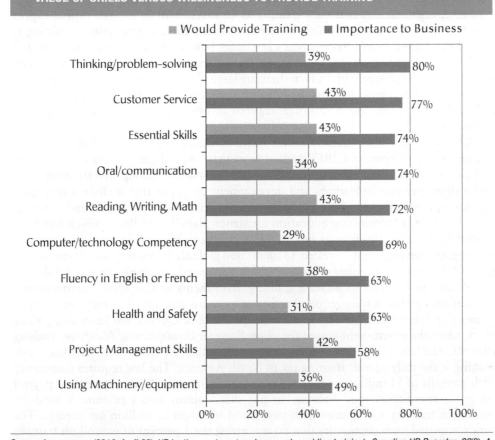

Source: Anonymous. (2013, April 22). HR by the numbers (employers not providing training). *Canadian HR Reporter, 26*(8), 4.

// IS TRAINING AN INVESTMENT OR AN EXPENSE?

Given the many benefits of training and development, it is surprising that Canadian organizations do not invest more, and it raises the question "Why don't organizations invest more in training and development?"

One reason is that learning and training are not considered a high priority in Canadian organizations. In a survey of Canadian organizations, only 50 percent of respondents agreed or strongly agreed that learning is a top priority in their organization. Furthermore, Canada ranked 20th out of 63 countries on the importance organizations placed on workforce training in 2017. This ranking places Canada behind top-ranking countries such as Japan, Switzerland, and Denmark.[71] In another study, Canadian executives were found to be less likely than those in comparator countries to believe that training is a high priority; Canada ranked 30th out of the 55 countries that were surveyed.[72]

Another reason for the underinvestment in training and development is the perception that training, learning, and development expenditures represent a cost rather than an investment. Organizations that view training and development as an expense believe that training budgets can be cut in difficult times. According to the Conference Board of Canada, many organizations in Canada view training and development as a necessary operating expense or cost that should be minimized.[73]

Organizations that view training as a cost tend to limit their training investments to only what is required by law or necessary to survive. As a result, training is often one of the first things to go when times are tough and there are cuts to discretionary spending.[74] However, organizations that view training as an investment in human capital expect direct benefits and a return on their investment. For these organizations, training is part of the organization's strategy and a key factor in its competitiveness and success.[75]

This is not to suggest that there are no Canadian organizations that invest heavily in training and development. In fact, there are large differences in the amount spent on training and development across organizations and industries. The Conference Board of Canada found that one in five organizations invests more than 3 percent of payroll in training.[76]

Organizations in the financial sector spend hundreds of millions of dollars a year in training and development. CIBC invested more than $61 million globally on corporate-wide learning and development in 2017.[77] BMO Financial Group invests more than $90 million per year in learning and development programs that include a corporate university, orientation programs, leadership, sales and service programs, and a tuition refund policy or "continuing education assistance plan."[78] TD Bank, which has been ranked by *Training Magazine* as one of 125 top organizations that excel in employee training and development, invested $81.8 million globally in training and development in 2017. The average number of days of training invested per employee was 4.8 days.[79]

What can be done to increase training investments in Canadian organizations? What if organizations were required to invest a certain amount of money each year in training and development? That is what the province of Quebec has been doing since 1995, when the government passed the *Act to Foster the Development of Manpower Training* (Bill 90, which is often referred to by employers as the "1 percent" or "training" law), making it the only payroll training tax in North America. The law requires companies with payrolls of $1 million or more to invest a minimum of 1 percent of their payroll on government-sanctioned training, or pay that amount into a provincial fund for workforce training. Companies with payrolls of less than $1 million are exempt. The funds acquired from companies that do not invest the 1 percent of payroll on training are placed in a government fund that supports training initiatives in the province.[80]

Organizations in the financial sector invest hundreds of millions of dollars a year in training and development.

A report analyzed the landmark law, concluding that it has had a significant effect on the way Quebec firms organize and deliver training, and has resulted in substantial growth in adult learning and training over the last decade. In fact, the participation rate in workplace training in Quebec increased from 21 percent to 33 percent between 1997 and 2002, making it the fastest growth rate in Canada and closing the gap between Quebec and other provinces.[81]

According to the Conference Board of Canada, organizations in Quebec spend on average more per employee on training and development than those in other provinces, providing additional evidence that the Quebec law has had a positive effect on training investments.[82]

Some organizations try to ensure that they benefit from their training programs by having employees sign a training bond. A **training bond** is a contract between the employer and employee that states that the employer will pay for the employee's training as long as the employee remains with the organization for a minimum period of time upon completion of a training program. If the employee fails to remain for the agreed-upon period of time, then he/she must reimburse the organization for the cost of the training.[83]

So far in this chapter we have focused on the role, importance, and impact of training and development. However, training and development takes place within a larger context that can influence the extent to which organizations provide training and the type of training they provide. Let's now take a closer look at the context of training and development.

> **Training bond**
> A contract between the employer and employee that states that the employer will pay for the employee's training as long as the employee remains with the organization for a minimum period of time following completion of the training program

// THE CONTEXT OF TRAINING AND DEVELOPMENT

Training and development are embedded in a larger context that can influence the extent to which training and development is provided in an organization as well as the type of training provided. As shown in Figure 1.2, training and development is just one part of a system of human resource practices that is influenced by internal and external factors.

The human resources system is influenced by environmental and organizational factors. Environmental factors such as legislation, the economic climate, competition, demographics, and social values have an impact on organizations. For example, if a

FIGURE 1.2

THE CONTEXT OF TRAINING AND DEVELOPMENT

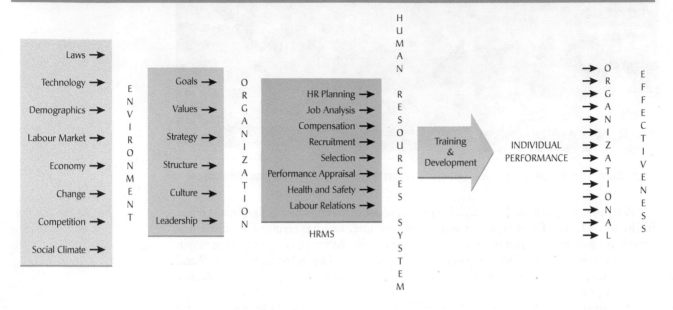

competitor introduces a lower-priced product, the organization will have to decide whether to match the competitor's actions or compete in other ways, such as by providing superior service. This strategic decision can in turn affect costs, the ability to pay employees, and/or the need to train and reward employees for effective performance. Events and concerns inside and outside an organization can lead to the need for new knowledge, skills, abilities, and training programs.

Sometimes sudden and unexpected changes in the environment can lead to changes in organizations themselves and in human resources policies and practices. For example, consider how concerns over terrorism have affected airport and flight security training. The Transportation Security Administration in the United States developed new guidelines for the training of baggage screeners and flight crews and made airport security fully federalized. The training of baggage screeners now includes technical training on metal detectors, X-ray scanners, and bag searching, and how to deal with difficult passengers and manage stress. Training was increased to 40 hours of classroom training and 60 hours of on-the-job training. Pilots and flight attendants receive training on how to assess and react to dangerous situations.[84] Other changes in training as a result of the threat of terrorism include a shift to distance technologies and e-learning and an increase in training programs on diversity, security, stress management, and change management.[85]

Let's now consider how changes in specific environmental and organizational factors can affect the human resources system and training and development.

THE ENVIRONMENTAL CONTEXT OF TRAINING AND DEVELOPMENT

Some of the key environmental factors that drive human resources and training and development are global competition, technology, the labour market, and environmental change.

GLOBAL COMPETITION

Increasing global competition has forced organizations to improve their productivity and the quality of their goods and services. Improvements in the production process and quality initiatives almost always require employees to learn new skills. When Canadian organizations send workers on assignments in foreign countries, they need to provide them with cross-cultural training so they will be able to adapt and function in a different culture (see Chapter 12 to learn about cross-cultural training). Thus, global competition can require numerous changes to human resource practices and the need for training and development.

TECHNOLOGY

Technology has had a profound effect on the way organizations operate and compete. New technologies can provide organizations with improvements in productivity and a competitive advantage. However, such improvements depend on the training that employees receive. Technology will lead to productivity gains only when employees receive the necessary training to exploit the technology.[86] Thus, the adoption of new technologies will have a direct impact on the training needs of employees who will be required to use the technology. A good example of this is when Yellow Pages Group (YPG) had to transform itself from print publishing to digital media.[87]

THE LABOUR MARKET

Changes in the labour market can have a major effect on training and development. For example, consider the implications of a shortage of skilled labour in Canada. It has been estimated that a critical shortage of skilled workers in Canada could reach 1 million by the year 2020. It has also been reported that there is a significant skills mismatch in Canada, since some occupations have a labour surplus while others have a shortage.[88] To deal with this looming crisis, the country will have to change its approach to education and training.[89] If organizations cannot hire people with the necessary knowledge and skills, they will have to provide more training if they are to compete and survive. Changes in the labour market and the supply of talent require changes in the amount and type of training.

Changes in immigration patterns also have implications for training and development. For example, the successful integration of Syrian refugees into the Canadian workforce requires organizations to provide cultural competency training so that the refugees will feel welcome and comfortable in the workplace. This also means that current employees require diversity training (see Chapter 12) so that they learn to understand and accept cultural differences.[90]

ENVIRONMENTAL CHANGE

The technological revolution, increasing globalization, and competition have resulted in a highly uncertain and constantly changing environment. In order to survive and remain competitive, organizations must adapt and change. As a result, managing change has become a normal part of organizational life, and training and development is almost always a key part of the process. This often involves training programs on the change process as well as training that is part of the change program. For example, if an organization implements a change program that involves a team-based work system, then employees will require team training (see Chapter 12 for a description of team training).

THE ORGANIZATIONAL CONTEXT OF TRAINING AND DEVELOPMENT

Training and development is also affected by internal events in the organization. Among the most important internal factors are an organization's strategy, structure, and culture.

STRATEGY

Strategy refers to an organization's objectives and action plans for realizing its objectives and gaining a competitive advantage. It is one of the most important factors influencing training and development. As indicated earlier, training and development can help an organization achieve its strategic objectives and gain a competitive advantage when it is aligned with an organization's strategy.

The alignment of human resources practices with an organization's business strategy is known as **strategic human resource management (SHRM)**. Organizations that have greater alignment between their HR practices and their strategies have been found to have superior performance.[91]

HR practices like training and development can also be strategic rather than independent or isolated activities when they are aligned with the organization's business strategy and therefore enable an organization to achieve its strategic goals and objectives. Thus, **strategic training and development (ST&D)** refers to the alignment of an organization's training needs and programs with an organization's strategy and objectives. Whether an organization has a strategy for quality, innovation, or customer service, training as well as other human resources practices must be designed to reinforce and support the strategy.

For example, if an organization decides to improve customer service or product quality, then employees will require training to learn how to provide better service or improve product quality. If an organization's strategy is to grow as rapidly as possible, then employees need to be trained in the management of mergers, acquisitions, joint ventures, and international ventures. All these growth components necessitate the building of new skills, and training and development is required to do this.

Strategy is often a key factor driving the need for and type of training and development in organizations. For example, several years ago, Bayshore Home Health, the largest provider of home and community healthcare services in Canada, launched a workforce diversity strategy. A key part of the strategy involved employee education about diversity that consisted of workshops on cultural competence and specific diversity workshops to address local needs.[93] At Hallmark Tubular Solutions Ltd. of Calgary, safety is a key part of its strategy. This is reflected in various training programs, such as an emergency response program to train staff on medical emergency evacuations and severe weather events, a journey–risk management program, a driver training program, and a mentorship program that ends with new hires being evaluated for safety competence. The company has been recognized as one of Canada's Safest Employers.[93]

By linking training to business strategy, training becomes strategic rather than an isolated and independent activity; thus, it is more likely to be effective. In fact, training can lower an organization's market value when it is not strategically focused.[94] There is

Strategy
An organization's objectives and action plans for realizing its objectives and gaining a competitive advantage

Strategic human resource management (SHRM)
The alignment of human resources practices with an organization's business strategy

Strategic training and development (ST&D)
The alignment of an organization's training needs and programs with an organization's strategy and objectives

FIGURE 1.3

A STRATEGIC MODEL OF TRAINING AND DEVELOPMENT

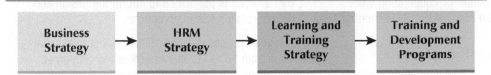

also some evidence that employees are more likely to participate in training when they perceive a strong alignment between a training program and the strategic direction of the organization.[95]

Figure 1.3 depicts the role that strategy plays in the training and development process. The model shows how an organization's business strategy will have implications for its human resource management (HRM) strategy. The HRM strategy will then influence the organization's strategy for learning and training, which will in turn determine the type of training and development activities and programs required.

However, in order for training and development to be strategic, the training and development function must be strategically aligned with strategic organization objectives. This requires that members of the training and development function have business knowledge, business skills, business abilities, and a cooperative relationship with line managers. To assess the strategic alignment of the training and development function in your organization, refer to the Trainer's Notebook 1.2, "The Strategic Alignment of Training and Development."

THE TRAINER'S NOTEBOOK   1.2

THE STRATEGIC ALIGNMENT OF TRAINING AND DEVELOPMENT

Strategic alignment between the learning and development function and an organization's strategy is a critical requirement for an organization to provide strategic training and development programs and to contribute to an organization's performance. The following scale was designed to assess the perceived strategic alignment of the learning and talent development (LTD) function in organizations.

The learning and talent development strategic alignment (LDSA) scale consists of 15 items that measure two dimensions of strategic alignment: LTD business knowledge, skills, and abilities (items 1 to 8), and cooperation (the cooperative relationship between LTD practitioners and line managers).

To find out about the strategic alignment of the LTD function in your organization, answer the 15 questions below using the following scale:

1 = Strongly disagree

2 = Disagree

3 = Neither agree nor disagree

4 = Agree

5 = Strongly agree

1. LTD understands the emerging needs of the business.

2. LTD knows the business value chain.

3. LTD has confidence to speak in business terms to line executives.

4. LTD strategic plans are communicated in business language.

5. LTD understands the context in which the business operates.

6. LTD is deeply aware of what is necessary to execute a firm's strategies.

7. LTD understands how its efforts are linked to the organization's mission.

8. LTD provides ongoing communication of the business case for learning decisions.

(continued)

9. The learning function works proactively with line managers to develop trust.

10. There is an internal climate of cooperation where the learning function can exercise its role in creating strategic alignment.

11. LTD receives support from line managers.

12. The learning function plans how interventions will be integrated throughout the organization.

13. Just-in-time learning solutions are offered to address current business needs.

14. The learning function has ongoing dialogue with line managers.

15. Gap analysis is performed to inform the design and delivery of strategic interventions.

Add your responses for all 15 items. Your total score can range from 15 to 75. Higher scores indicate greater strategic alignment. To determine scores for each dimension, add responses for items 1 to 8 for LTD business knowledge, skills, and abilities (scores can range from 8 to 40), and add responses for items 9 to 15 for cooperation (scores can range from 7 to 35).

Source: Republished with permission of Learning Systems Institute, from Hicks, K. (2016). Construct validation of strategic alignment in learning and talent development. *Performance Improvement Quarterly, 28*(4), 71–89; permission conveyed through Copyright Clearance Center, Inc.

STRUCTURE

The structure of an organization also affects training and development. Organizations are increasingly becoming flatter, with fewer levels of management. Employees are expected to perform tasks that were once considered managerial tasks, so they must be trained in traditional managerial activities such as problem solving, decision making, and teamwork. Many organizations have experienced dramatic structural changes such as downsizing and re-engineering in an effort to survive. These changes to an organization's structure often lead to changes in employees' tasks and responsibilities and necessitate the need for training.

CULTURE

Organizational culture refers to the shared beliefs, values, and assumptions that exist in an organization. An organization's culture is important because it determines the norms that exist in an organization and the expected behaviours. The culture of an organization and its norms and expected behaviours are often communicated to employees through training programs.

For example, ethical practices are deeply ingrained in the culture of Molson Coors Brewing Company and are communicated to employees through the company's ethics training programs. The company's training programs reflect a culture of integrity and the importance of acting in an honest and trustworthy manner based on business ethics and moral conviction.[96] Thus, the training programs are consistent with the company's core values and are a catalyst for achieving its business goals.

krivenko/Shutterstock.com

At Hallmark Tubular Solutions Ltd. safety is a key part of its strategy and is reflected in its training programs.

THE HUMAN RESOURCES SYSTEM

The human resources system and other human resource functions also influence training and development. In fact, in addition to being linked to business strategy, human resources practices should also be aligned and linked to each other. Thus, strategic human resource management involves two kinds of linkages. First, human resource practices should be linked to business strategy. Second, human resource practices should also be linked to one another so they work together to achieve an organization's strategy. Thus, what is most important is not individual human resource practices but rather the entire system of practices and the extent to which they are aligned with an organization's strategy and with one another. In combination, the practices form an integrated and tightly linked human resources system that is known as a high-performance work system.

A **high-performance work system (HPWS)** consists of an integrated system of human resource practices and policies that includes rigorous recruitment and selection procedures, performance-contingent incentive compensation, performance management, a commitment to employee involvement, and extensive training and development programs. High-performance work practices develop employees' knowledge, skills, abilities, and increase their motivation. This leads to more positive attitudes, lower turnover, and higher productivity, which results in higher organizational performance. Many studies have found that organizations with HPWSs have superior productivity and financial performance.[97]

In summary, external factors influence an organization's strategy, structure, and the way human resources are managed, and these factors in turn influence the design and delivery of training and development programs. Training and development should be tightly aligned with an organization's business strategy and other human resources practices in the human resources system. In other words, there should be a good fit or match between strategy and training and development, and between training and development and other human resources practices. In this way, training and development is strategic and an important part of a HPWS that can improve individual performance and, ultimately, organizational effectiveness.

// THE INSTRUCTIONAL SYSTEMS DESIGN (ISD) MODEL OF TRAINING AND DEVELOPMENT

In this section, we describe a systematic approach to the training and development process called the instructional systems design (ISD) model of training and development. The **instructional systems design (ISD) model** depicts training and development as a rational and scientific process that consists of three major steps: needs analysis, design and delivery, and evaluation.[98] The ISD model is a streamlined version of an earlier model of instructional design known as **ADDIE**, in which each letter represents a different action: analysis, design, development, implementation, and evaluation.[99]

According to the ISD model, the training process begins with a performance gap. A performance gap is something in the organization that is not quite right or is of concern to management. Perhaps customer complaints are up, quality is low, market share is being lost, or employees are frustrated by management or technology. Or perhaps there is a performance problem that is making it difficult for employees or departments to achieve goals or meet standards. If some part of the organization has a problem, or if there are concerns about the performance of individual employees or departments, then the problem needs to be analyzed. Recall in the chapter-opening vignette that the

Organizational culture
The shared beliefs, values, and assumptions that exist in an organization

High-performance work system (HPWS)
An integrated system of human resource practices and policies that usually includes rigorous recruitment and selection procedures, performance-contingent incentive compensation, performance management, a commitment to employee involvement, and extensive training and development programs

Instructional systems design (ISD) model
A rational and scientific model of the training and development process that consists of a needs analysis, training design and delivery, and training evaluation

ADDIE
Analysis, design, development, implementation, and evaluation

Edmonton Police Services training program was implemented to fill a void in officer training related to mental health issues.

A critical first step in the ISD model is a needs analysis to determine the nature of the problem and whether training is the best solution. A needs analysis is performed to determine the difference or gap between the way things are and the way things should be.

Needs analysis consists of three levels known as an organizational analysis, a task analysis, and a person analysis. Each level of a needs analysis is conducted to gather important information about problems and the need for training. An organizational analysis gathers information on where training is needed in an organization, a task analysis indicates what training is required, and a person analysis identifies who in the organization needs to be trained.

Based on the data collected from managers, employees, customers, and/or corporate documents, strategies for closing the gap are considered. Before training is determined to be the best solution to the problem, alternatives must be assessed. The solution to the performance gap might be feedback, incentives, or other human resource interventions. If training is determined to be the best solution, then objectives—or measurable goals—are written to improve the situation and reduce the gap. The needs analysis, the consideration of alternative strategies, and the setting of objectives force trainers to focus on performance improvement, not the delivery of a training program. Training is only one solution, and not necessarily the best one, to performance problems.

If training is the solution to a performance problem, a number of factors must be considered in the design and delivery of a training program. The needs analysis information is used to write training objectives and to determine the content of a training program. Then the best training methods for achieving the objectives and for learning the training content must be identified.

After a training program has been designed and delivered, the next stage is training evaluation. The needs analysis and training objectives provide important information about what should be evaluated to determine whether a training program has been effective. In this stage, the trainer has to decide what to measure as part of the evaluation of a training program as well as how to design an evaluation study. On the basis of a training evaluation, decisions can be made about what aspects of a training program should be retained, modified, or discarded.

The purpose of all training and development efforts is ultimately to improve employee performance and organizational effectiveness. Thus, it is important to know whether employee job performance has changed and whether the organization has improved following a training program. As indicated in the chapter-opening vignette, the Edmonton Police Service mental health training program resulted in a 40 percent increase in officers' ability to recognize mental health issues as the reason for a call, an improvement in police officers' ability to communicate with the public and to verbally de-escalate a situation, and an increase in their level of empathy in dealing with the public. And because less time was being spent on calls, there was a cost savings of more than $80,000 in the six months after the program.

Figure 1.4 shows the ISD model of training and development. As we have described, each stage leads into the subsequent stage, with needs analysis being the first critical step—it sets the stage for the design and delivery and the evaluation stages. Also notice that there are feedback loops from evaluation to needs analysis and training design and delivery. This indicates the process is a closed-loop system in which evaluation feeds back into needs analysis and into training design and delivery. In this way, it is possible to know whether performance gaps identified in the needs analysis stage have been closed, and whether changes are required in the design and delivery of a training

FIGURE 1.4

THE INSTRUCTIONAL SYSTEMS DESIGN MODEL OF TRAINING AND DEVELOPMENT

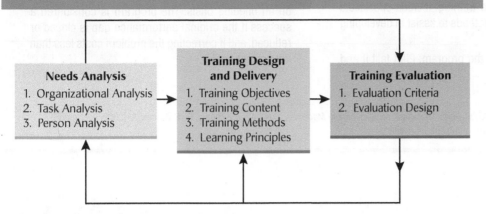

program to make it more effective. Thus, training programs are continuously modified and improved on the basis of training evaluation.

Although the ISD model is considered to be the best approach for managing the training and development process, in reality many organizations do not follow all of the steps of the ISD model. In other words, many organizations do not conduct a needs analysis, they implement training programs that are poorly designed, and they do not evaluate their training programs. As a result, many organizations implement training programs that are not effective. One recent survey reported that the effectiveness of employee training programs across several industries ranged from 24 percent to 49 percent.[100] Making training programs more effective begins with the ISD model, which remains the best approach for managing the training and development process.[101]

We will have more to say about each stage of the training and development process as they are covered in the remainder of the textbook. For now, you should understand the ISD model and the sequence of activities that are involved in the training and development process. To learn more about how to apply the ISD model, see The Trainer's Notebook 1.3, "The Application of the ISD Model."

THE TRAINER'S NOTEBOOK   1.3

THE APPLICATION OF THE ISD MODEL

The instructional systems design model begins when somebody identifies a performance gap in the organization. According to the ISD model, the recognition of a performance gap should lead to the following sequence of activities:

1. Conduct an organizational analysis to investigate the performance gap and determine whether training is a possible solution (i.e., when the cause of the problem is a lack of knowledge or skills).

2. If training is a possible solution, conduct a task analysis to determine how the job or jobs in question should be performed and the things that a skilled employee must know and be able to do.

3. Conduct a person analysis to determine how employees currently perform the job compared to how they should perform and how best to train them (i.e., training methods).

(continued)

4. Design a training program using those methods and approaches that will be most effective to train employees who require training. Include specialists in various media and methods to assist in developing training material.

5. Develop and fine-tune the program. Pilot test it and revise as needed.

6. Deliver the program to its intended audience.

7. Monitor and evaluate the program and its results on an ongoing basis. The program is considered a success if the original performance gap is closed or reduced, and if correcting the problem costs less than not correcting it.

Sources: Gordon, J., & Zemke, R. (2000, April). The attack on ISD. *Training Magazine*, 37(4), 42–53; Zemke, R., & Rossett, A. (2002, February). A hard look at ISD. *Training Magazine*, 39(2), 26–34. Trainingmag.com

// SUMMARY AND ROAD MAP

This chapter introduced you to the training and development process and emphasized the important role that training and development plays in organizations and in performance management. The benefits of training and development for organizations, employees, and society were described, as was the state of training and development in Canadian organizations. We also described how training and development is embedded in the environmental and organizational context and is part of the human resources system. It was also noted that for training to be effective, it should be aligned with the organization's business strategy and with other human resource practices, and part of a high-performance work system (HPWS). Finally, we described the instructional systems design (ISD) model of training and development that sets the stage for the remainder of the textbook.

In Chapter 2, we focus on learning—which is, after all, what training and development is all about. You will learn about learning theories and the learning process as well as training motivation. Chapter 2 is the foundation for the remainder of the textbook and sets the stage for the chapters that follow.

Chapters 3 through 11 focus on the steps of the ISD model. Chapter 3 deals with the needs analysis process. Chapters 4 through 9 focus on the design and delivery of training and development programs. This includes chapters on how to design training programs (Chapter 4), off-the-job training methods (Chapter 5), on-the-job training methods (Chapter 6), and technology-based training methods (Chapter 7). Chapter 8 focuses on how to deliver training programs, and in Chapter 9 you will learn how to design training programs so that employees apply what they learn in training on the job, or what is known as the transfer of training. Chapters 10 and 11 focus on the final stage of the ISD model, training evaluation. The focus of Chapter 10 is evaluation criteria and evaluation design; the focus of Chapter 11 is how to determine the costs and benefits of training programs.

In Chapter 12 you will learn about different types of training programs, and in Chapter 13 you will learn about management and leadership development. The textbook concludes with Chapter 14, which provides an overview of the evolution and future of training and development and how to make training and development programs effective.

KEY TERMS

ADDIE p. 23
development p. 8
high-performance work system (HPWS) p. 23
human capital p. 8
instructional systems design (ISD) model p. 23
organizational culture p. 23
performance management p. 5
skills mismatch p. 13
SMART goals p. 6
social capital p. 8
strategic human resource management (SHRM) p. 20
strategic training and development (ST&D) p. 20
strategy p. 20
training p. 7
training bond p. 17
work engagement p. 10
work-integrated learning p. 13

DISCUSSION QUESTIONS

1. According to the Conference Board of Canada, the investments made by Canadian organizations in training and development have remained relatively constant over the last decade. Comment on the implications of this for organizations, employees, and the Canadian economy. Should governments get involved and enact laws that require organizations to invest a certain percentage of their payroll in training and development, as they have in Quebec? Why or why not?

2. Studies comparing the competitive performance of Canadian corporations indicate that among the countries in the G7 (Canada, United States, Japan, Germany, France, Italy, and United Kingdom) and compared with the European Union, Canada ranks very low. Do you think that training and development in Canada has anything to do with this? If so, what should governments and businesses do?

3. Discuss some of the reasons why organizations often fail to implement the instructional systems design (ISD) model of training and development. The ISD model has been challenged and at times criticized. Why do you think this is the case, and do you think it is warranted?

4. Refer to the chapter-opening vignette on the Edmonton Police Service mental health training program and discuss the extent to which the instructional systems design (ISD) model was used. In other words, describe the training program in terms of each stage of the ISD model (i.e., what the needs were, how the program was designed and delivered, and how it was evaluated).

5. Research on training and organizational effectiveness has found that training is positively related to human resource and performance outcomes as well as financial outcomes. Explain why and how training is related to these outcomes. What are the implications of these findings for organizations?

6. Why do some organizations view learning, training, and development as an expense rather than an investment? What are the implications of this? What can be done

CHAPTER 1 The Training and Development Process

to change this perception so that organizations view training and development as an investment? What are the implications of changing perceptions for employees, organizations, and society?

7. Discuss some of the reasons why Canadian organizations have been slow to increase their investments in training and development over the last few decades and continue to lag behind organizations in the United States. Do you think they should increase their investments in training and development? What would be the implications for employees, organizations, and society? Explain your answer.

8. Should organizations require employees to sign a training bond in which they agree to pay back the organization the cost of the training they received if they leave the organization? Explain your answer. What would be your response if your organization or an organization that you wanted to work for required you to sign a training bond?

THE GREAT TRAINING DEBATE

1. Debate the following: Training and development is the single most important factor for the competitiveness and success of organizations.

2. Debate the following: All provinces should enact training legislation similar to the training law in Quebec.

3. Debate the following: Training is an operating cost and should be limited to only what is required by law and absolutely necessary.

4. Debate the following: Employees who receive training from their organization should be required to sign a training bond that requires them to pay the cost of their training if they leave the organization before a specified period of time.

EXERCISES

IN-CLASS

1. Review the training and development facts in Table 1.1. Benchmark your experiences in a current or previous organization against the statistics in the table. Based on the statistics in the table, you might consider things such as the following: How does your organization compare to the Canadian averages in areas such as the number of training hours employees receive a year and the amount spent per employee on training? Does your organization fare better or worse than the average Canadian organization? What do the results tell you about your organization? What are the implications of your findings for your learning and job performance? What are the implications for your organization?

2. Consider how training and development is influenced by, and in turn can influence, other human resources functions. In particular, give an example of how training and development can influence and be influenced by each of the following human resources functions: recruitment, selection, HR planning, performance appraisal, compensation, and health and safety.

3. Use the ISD model of training and development to examine one of your university or college courses. That is, what did your instructor have to do in terms of a needs analysis? How did he or she design and deliver the course? How was the course evaluated, or how should it be evaluated?

4. Assume you are a director of training and development in a small organization. In order to reduce expenses, the company president has decided to cut the training budget in half and reduce the amount of training provided to employees. The president has asked to meet with you to discuss these plans. Your job is to prepare a short presentation to persuade the president to change his or her mind. What will you say and what can you do to convince the president of the importance of and need for more, not less, training and development?

5. Recall the last time you attended an organization-sponsored training program. Describe the objectives and content of the training program and whether you think the program was strategic. In other words, was it an example of strategic training and development? Be specific about why you think it was or was not a good example of strategic training and development. What would have made it more strategic?

6. Recall the last time you attended an organization-sponsored training program. Describe the objectives and content of the training program and whether you think the ISD model was used to develop the program. Be specific about the extent to which each stage of the model was used in the development of the program. How effective was the training program in terms of your learning and in achieving the program's objectives? Based on your analysis, what else could have been done to use the ISD model more fully, and what effect might this have had on the effectiveness of the program?

IN-THE-FIELD

1. Contact the human resource department of your own or another organization to discuss the organization's training programs. Try to learn about the extent to which the human resource department follows the ISD model of training and development. Find out about each stage of the model and the extent to which it is used. Which aspects of the model are adequately carried out and which ones are not? If some of the stages are not adequately conducted, find out why this is the case and why the HR department does or does not rigorously adhere to the ISD model. Based on the responses, what advice would you give the HR department about its training and development programs?

2. A number of associations and government departments provide useful information and services related to learning, training, and development. To learn more about some of these associations, visit the following websites:

   www.performanceandlearning.ca (The Institute for Performance and Learning)

   www.td.org (Association for Talent Development)

   www.esdc.gc.ca/eng/home.shtml (Employment and Social Development Canada)

   Write a brief report in which you describe the association and the information that can be obtained from each website about learning, education, and training and development.

CASE INCIDENT

BEER AMBASSADORS

Several years ago, the Beer Store invested $30 million as part of a plan to update its store branding. This involved building new stores and renovating existing ones. The plan was to open 13 new stores across Ontario and to renovate 61 existing stores. The new stores and those renovated were designed to fit a new Beer Store brand.

Part of the new Beer Store brand was to make the stores more efficient and customer-friendly and to improve the customer shopping experience. To improve the shopping experience the new and renovated stores would have better lighting and music and employees who will be more helpful. According to Beer Store president Ted Moroz, Beer Store customers want to walk around the stores so that they can see and touch the products.

Large stores will have an open layout that will allow customers to walk around the store and see the products as well as signs that indicate what foods go best with different beers. In small stores, customers will be able to use touch screens to find out details about different beers and to place their orders.

The investment also includes new training for employees or what the Beer Store refers to as "beer college" so that employees will learn how to provide a great shopping experience for customers. Employees will receive training on different products as well as customer relations. The plan is to make Beer Store employees beer "ambassadors" who will be able to discuss different types of beer with customers and what food goes best with different beers. Employees will receive new uniforms with the new Beer Store logo and various slogans such as "Beer Champion" and "Beer Enthusiast."

QUESTIONS

1. Explain the context of training and development (Figure 1.2) in relation to the changes at the Beer Store. What factors have changed and why? What are the implications of the changes for individual performance and organizational effectiveness?

2. What makes training strategic? Is the training that employees receive at the Beer Store strategic? Explain your answer.

3. Discuss the instructional systems design (ISD) model of training and development in relation to the training being provided to employees at the Beer Store. Be sure to indicate the need for training, training content and objectives, and how the training should be evaluated.

Sources: Karstens-Smith, G. (2013, December 17). Beer Store pouring over $30-million store renovations. *Toronto Star*, pp. B1, B4; Lewis, M. (2013, May 7). Beer store: A high-tech makeover. *Toronto Star*, www.thestar.com; Anonymous. (2014, July 13). Beer Store invests $30 million in redesign. *Brampton Guardian*, www.mississauga.com; Adams, M. I. (2014, January 7). Local Beer Store undergoing makeover. *Enterprise-Bulletin*, www.theenterprisebulletin.com.

CASE STUDY	FLOTATION LTD.

"Great course, Sam!" said the trainees as they walked out the door and headed for the parking lot. Just like all the others. Sam Harris, a veteran trainer with Flotation Ltd., a manufacturer of life jackets and other flotation devices, smiled as he gathered his notes together.

He had just finished two hours of wisecracking and slightly off-colour storytelling as he worked his way through the third session of a human relations course for supervisors. "Keep 'em happy" was Sam's motto. Give the troops what they want, keep your enrolments up, and no one will complain.

Sam was good at it, too! For 25 years, he had earned an easy living, working the politics, producing good numbers of trainees for the top brass to brag about ("We give each employee up to 30 hours of training every year!"), and generally promoting his small training group as a beehive of activity.

Everybody knew Sam and everybody liked him. His courses were fun. He had no trouble convincing managers to send their people. He put out a catalogue with his course list every year in January. He hadn't had a cancellation in more than 10 years. Some managers said that training was the best reward they had. Now, only two years from retirement, Sam intended to coast comfortably into pension-land. All his favourite courses had long been prepared. All he had to do was make adjustments here and there and create some trendy new titles.

But times were changing. The company president was thinking differently. "I need somebody to take a close look at our training function," he said. Sitting in the president's office, Jenny Stoppard, the newly hired vice-president of human resources, wondered what he meant. Flotation Ltd. had a reputation as a company with a well-trained workforce.

"We need to increase our productivity per person by 50 percent over the next three years," the president continued. "And you are going to spearhead that effort. We spend a lot on training and we cycle people through a lot of courses. But I'm not satisfied with the bottom line. I know that while Dad was president he swore by Sam and said he was the greatest. I don't know anymore. Maybe a whole new approach is needed. Anyway, I want you to take a close look at Sam's operation."

Later in the day, the president called Sam into his office. "Sam, I want you to meet Jenny Stoppard. I've just hired her as vice-president of human resources. She's your new boss. I think the next three years are going to be very exciting around here, and Jenny is going to be a key player in the drive to increase our competitiveness. I want you to do everything in your power to cooperate with her."

QUESTIONS

1. Comment on Sam's approach to training. Would you want him working for your organization? What are the benefits of his training programs to employees and the organization?

2. To what extent is training and development at Flotation Ltd. strategic? What would make it more strategic?

3. To what extent does Sam use the instructional systems design (ISD) model of training and development? If he were to use the ISD model more fully, what would he do? Comment on each step of the ISD model.

4. How does Sam evaluate his training programs? Compare Sam's evaluation to the president's objectives. If Sam were to evaluate training based on the president's objectives, what would he have to do? What do you think the results might be?

5. The president has asked Jenny to "take a close look at Sam's operation." What should she do, and what should she report back to the president?

FLASH FORWARD QUESTION

What do you think employees are learning in Sam's training programs? What are some possible learning outcomes? If the president wants to increase productivity per person by 50 percent over the next three years, what learning outcomes should result from Flotation Ltd.'s training and development programs?

RUNNING CASE STUDY DIRTY POOLS

In August 2011, the *Toronto Star* conducted an investigation of pools and hot tubs at condominiums, health clubs, and swimming pools across the city of Toronto. They discovered that many pools and hot tubs in Toronto have repeatedly violated public health and safety rules. This means that bathers are potentially being exposed to injury and disease.

Public health inspectors conduct inspections of the approximately 1600 recreational water facilities in the City of Toronto. Every recreational water facility in the city is inspected at least two times a year and no less than once every three months while operating. Those facilities that operate year-round might receive up to four inspections per year. These inspections are unannounced and based on mandated inspection frequencies. Owners receive an inspection report and written instructions that outline the corrective actions they must take to correct any identified deficiencies. When an imminent health and safety hazard is identified a facility can be closed. A closed facility is allowed to reopen once it has met certain conditions as determined by a re-inspection. There are no set fines, and public health inspectors cannot issue tickets.

The data obtained by the *Toronto Star* indicates more than 10 000 violations by pools and spas over the past two years at luxury condominiums, private schools, spas, hotels, and fitness clubs. Many have repeatedly failed to meet health and safety standards set by the city with little penalty or public knowledge, thereby putting unwitting swimmers at risk of disease and injury.

Health infractions include things such as failure to maintain safe and sanitary conditions and equipment in sanitary and working order, poor water clarity, unsafe storage of chemicals, failing to keep proper records, improper chemical balance such as pH levels, and a hot tub's vacuum release system not working properly (a safety device that prevents the pool's suction mechanism from trapping bathers to the whirlpool floor). Inspectors reported 635 incidents of improper pH levels in two years.

Health inspectors can close a pool for a variety of violations, such as cloudy water, missing emergency equipment such as a spine board or two buoyant safety rings, or loose or missing pool outlet covers. Since 2009, more than 300 pools have been closed for various violations, including faulty mechanics, missing emergency equipment, and dirty water.

Poorly maintained pools can be breeding grounds for bacteria that can cause serious gastrointestinal illnesses. Recreational water illnesses are caused by germs spread by swallowing or having contact with contaminated water. Swallowing a small amount of pool water with cryptosporidium can make a person sick and has become a leading cause of swimming pool–related outbreaks of diarrheal illness. Illnesses include gastrointestinal, skin, ear, respiratory, eye, and neurologic infections. The most common symptom is diarrhea, which is caused by germs such as cryptosporidium, giardia, shigella, norovirus, and *E. coli*. Other symptoms include rashes and burning eyes.

The root of pool problems and infractions is poor training. In Ontario, however, there are no standardized training requirements. In 2009 and 2010, inspectors reported 114 cases of staff who were not adequately trained to run a hot tub or pool safely. City officials cited 23 facilities multiple times for this infraction, suggesting that they failed to get the necessary training despite the inspector's warning. Although health officials can order an operator be retrained as part of their inspections, there is no standardized training. As a result, a re-training order just means that when the inspector returns the operator must show that he/she can perform the procedure in question.

In response to the *Toronto Star* investigation, safety experts called for the province of Ontario to enforce standardized training for swimming pool operators. Toronto's Board of Health has also asked the province to require standardized training for operators. Ontario's health minister said the province may consider introducing a certification program for pool operators.

At a meeting on September 13, 2011, the Board of Health requested that the medical officer amend the current regulations and require standardized training for public pool and public spa operators with respect to water chemistry analysis and promoting health and safety and injury prevention. Ontario health regulations require training for pool and hot tub operators but it does not indicate to what extent. As a result, some operators receive rigorous two-day courses while others receive brief instructions on how to check chemical levels. Furthermore, while regular training is mandatory for operators at municipal pools in Toronto, this is not the case for operators of facilities at condos or hotels.

Government-sanctioned training for pool operators is enforced in the province of Alberta, where two-day training programs are offered by public and private government-approved agencies across the province. Operators are certified if they receive 70 percent or higher on a final exam.

On April 28, 2014, the Toronto Board of Health adopted a proposal from the medical officer of health that the city should draft a bylaw that requires all recreational water facilities including public swimming pools, public spas (hot tubs), and wading pools to post a sign or document on site showing notices disclosing inspection results to inform the public of whether any health and safety violations have taken place. The final decision must still be made by Toronto City Council.

Toronto City Councillor John Filion, who has been a strong advocate for facilities to display evidence that they have met city standards, said he expects the recommended bylaw will ensure that standards are being adhered to, boost public confidence, and improve conditions at pools and spas. He also believes that inspectors should have the power to issue fines, something that requires provincial approval.

Sources: E. Mathieu, "Pool operators could be forced to post their inspection results," *Toronto Star*, pp. A1, A4, April 18, 2014; D. Zlomislic & J. McLean, "Board of health vows crackdown on bad pools," *Toronto Star*, Aug. 20, 2011, www.thestar.com/news/gta/2011/08/20/board_of_health_vows_crackdown_on_bad . . .; J. McLean & D. Zlomislic, "Toronto pools' dirty secrets," *Toronto Star*, pp. A1, A20, Aug. 20, 2011; J. McLean & D. Zlomislic, "Training standards urged to clean up dirty pools," *Toronto Star*, pp. A1, A20, Aug. 27, 2011; J. McLean, "Toronto cracks down on bad pools," *Toronto Star*, p. A3, Sept. 14, 2011; Onsite posting of inspection results for recreational water facilities, City of Toronto, *Staff Report*.

QUESTIONS

1. Discuss the implications of a lack of mandatory standardized training for pool operators for the operators, their employees, and the public. What does this say about the role of training in organizations?

2. Do you think pool operators should receive mandatory, standardized training? If so, what will be some of the benefits for operators and the public?

3. Discuss the context of training and development with respect to the current training situation for pool operators. Use Figure 1.2 to explain your answer. Now explain the situation if training becomes mandatory. What factors in the model will change, and what are the implications? What if a bylaw requires operators to post inspection results? What if operators can be fined for infractions?

4. Describe how the ISD model can be used in the development of a standardized training program for pool operators. Be sure to explain each step of the ISD model as it pertains to a training program for pool operators.

// REFERENCES

1. Silliker, A. (2013, May 20). Mental illness training for cops effective: Study. *Canadian HR Reporter, 26*(10), 1, 6; Krameddine, Y. I., DeMarco, D., Hassel, R., & Silverstone, P. H. (2013). A novel training program for police officers that improves interactions with mentally ill individuals and is cost-effective. *Frontiers in Psychiatry, 4*, 9. doi:10.3389/fpsyt.2013.00009; Maurier, R. (2013, March 18). Helping police protect and serve people with mental illness. Retrieved from http://uofa.ualberta.ca/news-and-events/newsarticles/2013/march/helping-police-protect-and-serve-people-with-mental-illness; Edmonton cops commended by Mental Health Commission. (2014, September 5). *Edmonton Sun*. Retrieved from http://www.edmontonsun.com/2014/09/05/edmonton-cops-commended-by-mental-health-commission; Edmonton Police. (2014, September 5). *Specialized training helps officers safely deal with people in crisis* [Media release]. Retrieved from http://releases3017.rssing.com/chan-9611048/all_p32.html

2. Kane, L. (2014, February 12). Toronto police shootings inquest rules deaths as homicides; recommends training changes. *Toronto Star*. Retrieved from http://www.thestar.com/news/crime/2014/02/12/police_shootings_inquest_rules_deaths_as_homicides.html

3. Iacobucci, F. (2014). *Police encounters with people in crisis*. Toronto: Toronto Police Service.

4. Gallant, J. (2017, August 3). Inquest jury zeroes in on police training. *Toronto Star*, pp. A1, A10.

5. Parker, R. O., & Cooney, J. (2005). *Learning & development outlook 2005*. Ottawa: The Conference Board of Canada.

6. Gordon, A. (2000, February). 35 best companies to work for. *Report on Business Magazine*, 24–33.

7. Vander Wier, M. (2017, January 23). Half of workers suffer from "productivity deficit": Survey. *Canadian HR Reporter, 30*(1), 1, 2.

8. Gosselin, A., Werner, J., & Hall, N. (1997). Ratee preferences concerning performance management and appraisal. *Human Resource Development Quarterly, 8*(4), 315–333.

9. Aguinis, H. (2009). *Performance management* (2nd ed.). Upper Saddle River, NJ: Pearson Prentice Hall.

10. Kinicki, A. J., Jacobson, K. J. L., Peterson, S. J., & Prussia, G. E. (2013). Development and validation of the performance management behavior questionnaire. *Personnel Psychology, 66,* 1–45.

11. Latham, G. P. (2003). Goal setting: A five-step approach to behavior change. *Organizational Dynamics, 32,* 309–318.

12. Dobson, S. (2013, January 28). Upgrading talent management processes leads to fully integrated approach, efficiencies. *Canadian HR Reporter, 26*(2), 20.

13. Kinicki et al. (2013).

14. Dobson (2013).

15. Aguinis (2009).

16. Smither, J. W., & London, M. (2009). Best practices in performance management. In J. W. Smither & M. London (Eds.), *Performance management: Putting research into action* (pp. 585–625). San Francisco, CA: Jossey-Bass; Squires, P. (2009). The role of on-the-job and informal development in performance management. In J. W. Smither & M. London (Eds.), *Performance management: Putting research into action* (pp. 157–195). San Francisco, CA: Jossey-Bass.

17. Brown, K. G., & Sitzmann, T. (2011). Training and employee development for improved performance. In S. Zedeck (Ed.), *Handbook of industrial and organizational psychology* (Vol. 2, pp. 469–503). Washington, DC: American Psychological Association.

18. Crook, T. R., Todd, S. Y., Combs, J. G., Woehr, D. J., & Ketchen, D. J., Jr. (2011). Does human capital matter? A meta-analysis of the relationship between human capital and firm performance. *Journal of Applied Psychology, 96,* 443–456; McFarland, L A.., & Ployhart, R. E. (2018). Strategic training and development and their role in shaping competitive advantage. In K. G. Brown (Ed.), *The Cambridge handbook of workplace training and employee development* (pp. 545–565). New York, NY: Cambridge University.

19. Cotsman, S., & Hall, C. (2018). *Learning cultures lead the way: Learning & development outlook–14th edition.* Ottawa: The Conference Board of Canada.

20. Brown, K. G., & Van Buren, M. E. (2007). Applying a social capital perspective to the evaluation of distance training. In S. M. Fiore & E. Salas (Eds.), *Where is the learning in distance learning? Toward a science of distributed learning and training* (pp.41–63). Washington, DC: American Psychological Association.

21. Bowsher, J. (1990). Making the call on the CEO. *Training and Development Journal, 44*(5), 65–66.

22. Adams, M. (1999). Training employees as partners. *HR Magazine, 44*(2), 64–70.

23. Bernstein, A., & Magnusson, P. (1993, February 22). How much good will training do? *Business Week*, pp. 76–77.

24. Tharenou, P., Saks, A. M., & Moore, C. (2007). A review and critique of research on training and organizational-level outcomes. *Human Resource Management Review, 17*, 251–273.

25. Betcherman, G., Leckie, N., & McMullen, K. (1997). *Developing skills in the Canadian workplace*. Ottawa: Canadian Policy Research Networks; Arthur, W., Jr., Bennett, W., Jr., Edens, P. S., & Bell, S. T. (2003). Effectiveness of training in organizations: A meta-analysis of design and evaluation features. *Journal of Applied Psychology, 88*, 234–245.

26. Hughes, P. D., & Campbell, A. (2009). *Learning & development outlook 2009: Learning in tough times*. Ottawa: The Conference Board of Canada.

27. Park, Y., & Jacobs, R. (2011). The influence of investment in workplace learning on learning outcomes and organizational performance. *Human Resource Development Quarterly, 22*, 437–458.

28. Birdi, K., Clegg, C., Patterson, M., Robinson, A., Stride, C. B., Wall, T. D., & Wood, S. J. (2008). The impact of human resource and operational management practices on company productivity: A longitudinal study. *Personnel Psychology, 61*, 467–501.

29. Michael, S. C., & Combs, J. G. (2008). Entrepreneurial failure: The case of franchisees. *Journal of Small Business Management, 46*(1), 73–90; Webb, W. (2008). Training = franchise success, *Training, 45*(8), 54.

30. Hirsh, L. (2008, November 3). Non-monetary rewards gaining traction. *Canadian HR Reporter, 21*(19), 24; Harder, D. (2007). More than money. *Canadian HR Reporter, 20*(19), 21.

31. HR by the numbers (Top retention strategies). (2014, September 22). *Canadian HR Reporter, 27*(16), 4.

32. Dobson, S. (2010, February 8). Constructive education. *Canadian HR Reporter, 23*(3), 14, 15.

33. Israelson, D. (2014, March 20). Why companies need a smart training culture. *The Globe and Mail*. Retrieved from www.theglobeandmail.com

34. Freifeld, L. (2017, January–February). Keller Williams Realty's view from the top. *Training, 54*(1), 26–32.

35. Schaaf, D. (1998). What workers really think about training. *Training, 35*(9), 59–66.

36. Hughes & Campbell (2009).

37. Bakker, A. B., & Demerouti, E. (2008). Towards a model of work engagement. *Career Development International, 13*, 209–223.

38. Bakker & Demerouti (2008); Noe, R. A., Clarke, A. D. M., & Klein, H. J. (2014). Learning in the twenty-first century workplace. *Annual Review of Organizational Psychology and Organizational Behavior, 1*, 245–275; Eldor, L., & Harpaz, I. (2016). A process model of employee engagement: The learning climate and its relationship with extra-role performance behaviors. *Journal of Organizational Behavior, 37*, 213–235; Anonymous (2017, March). Effectiveness of formal workplace training uncovered. *TD: Talent Development, 71*(3), 19;

Christian, M. S., Garza, A. S., & Slaughter, J. E. (2011). Work engagement: A quantitative review and test of its relations with task and contextual performance. *Personnel Psychology, 64*, 89–136; Saks, A. M. (2006). Antecedents and consequences of employee engagement. *Journal of Managerial Psychology, 21*, 600–619.

39. Arthur et al. (2003).

40. Garavan, T. N., Costine, P., & Heraty, N. (1995). *Training and development in Ireland: Context policy and practice.* Dublin: Oak Tree Press.

41. Schaaf (1998).

42. Bernstein & Magnusson (1993).

43. Silliker, A. (2011, April 11). Apprenticeships close immigrant wage gap. *Canadian HR Reporter, 24*(7), 8.

44. Howlett, K., & Church, E. (2009, January 13). Training for the new economy. *The Globe and Mail*, p. A4.

45. Flavelle, D. (2013, January 30). Jobless youth costs $10,7 billion in lost wages, TD report says. *Toronto Star*, pp. B1, B4.

46. Wallace, K., & Ormsby, M. (2016, February 23). Province will make training mandatory for big-rig drivers. *Toronto Star*, pp. A1, A10.

47. *Innovation provincial rankings – How Canada Performs.* The Conference Board of Canada. Retrieved from The Conference Board of Canada website: www.conferenceboard.ca/hcp/provincial/innovation.aspx; *Canada ranks 14th on the world economic forum's 2017 global competitiveness.* The Conference Board of Canada. Retrieved from The Conference Board of Canada website: www.conferenceboard.ca/press/blog-item/trending-insights/2017/09/27/canada-ranks...

48. Wong, R. (2017, July 10). Combining HR and finance to improve productivity metrics. *The Globe and Mail*, p. B8.

49. Hughes & Campbell (2009).

50. Crane, D. (2002, October 27). Innovation means productivity gains. *Toronto Star*, p. C2.

51. Salas, E., Tannenbaum, S. I., Kraiger, K., & Smith-Jentsch, K. A. (2012). The science of training and development in organizations: What matters in practice. *Psychological Science in the Public Interest, 13*, 74–101.

52. Klie, S. (2007, December 3). Higher education leads to higher productivity. *Canadian HR Reporter, 20*(21), 7.

53. Bernstein & Magnusson (1993).

54. Campion-Smith, B., & Consiglio, A. (2013, March 22). Split over skills training grant. *Toronto Star*, p. A19.

55. Flavelle, D. (2013, October 8). Digital skills give Canada an edge. *Toronto Star*, pp. B1, B5.

56. Flavelle, D. (2013, March 15). Invest in skilled trades, Stronach urges. *Toronto Star*, p. B3.

57. Wright, L. (2014, March 26). Watchdog dismisses skills shortage. *Toronto Star*, pp. B1, B6.

58. Bernier, L. (2013, November 4). Skills mismatch bad—and it will get worse. *Canadian HR Reporter*, *26*(19), 1–10; Mas, S. (2014, June 29). Canada job grant won't be in place July 1 in most provinces. *CBC News*, www.cbc.ca/news/politics/canada

59. Vander Wier, M. (2017, October 2). Feds move to close skills gap. *Canadian HR Reporter*, *30*(16), 1, 10.

60. Cooke, G. B., Chowhan, J., & Brown, T. (2011). Declining versus participating in employer-supported training in Canada. *International Journal of Training and Development*, *15*, 271–289; Silliker, A. (2012, February 27). Many workers not offered training: Study. *Canadian HR Reporter*, *25*(4), 3, 12.

61. Vander Wier, M. (2017, February 6). New grads face tough road when transitioning to workplace: Surveys. *Canadian HR Reporter*, *30*(2), 3, 8.

62. Harris-Lalonde, S. (2001). *Training and development outlook.* Ottawa: The Conference Board of Canada.

63. Cotsman & Hall (2018).

64. Cotsman & Hall (2018).

65. Anonymous (2017, November/December). 2017 Training industry report. *Training*, *54*(6), 20–33.

66. Cotsman & Hall (2018).

67. Hughes & Campbell (2009).

68. Cotsman & Hall (2018).

69. Cotsman & Hall (2018).

70. HR by the numbers (Employers not providing training). (2013, April 22). *Canadian HR Reporter*, *26*(8), 4.

71. Cotsman & Hall (2018).

72. Hughes & Campbell (2009).

73. Hughes & Campbell (2009).

74. Fair, B. (2010, October 18). How to stop C-suite yawn over training. *Canadian HR Reporter*, *23*(18), 21, 25.

75. Hughes, P. D., & Grant, M. (2007). *Learning & development outlook 2007.* Ottawa: The Conference Board of Canada.

76. Parker & Cooney (2005).

77. http://corporateresponsibilityreport.cibc.com/engaging-employees.html

78. Dobson, S. (2010, March 22). Reimbursing tuition reinforces development. *Canadian HR Reporter*, *23*(6), 14, 18. Retrieved from www.bmo.com

79. Anonymous (2017, January/February). Top 125. *Training*, *54*(1), 60–95; Anonymous (2017). Opening doors for an inclusive tomorrow: 2017 Corporate Responsibility Report (TD). https://www.td.com/document/PDF/corporateresponsibility/2017-Final-CRR_EN.pdf

80. Bélanger, P., & Robitaille, M. (2008). A portrait of work-related learning in Quebec. Ottawa: Work and Learning Knowledge Centre.

81. Bélanger & Robitaille (2008).

82. Hughes & Campbell (2009).

83. Mitchell, T. (2011, January 17). When the employer is the victim. *Canadian HR Reporter, 24*(1), 13–14.

84. Anonymous (2002). Airport training ready to take off. *Training and Development, 56*(4), 17–18.

85. Caudron, S. (2002, February). Training in the post-terrorism era. *Training and Development, 56*(2), 25–30.

86. Crane, D. (1998, March 28). Time to take worker training seriously. *Toronto Star*, p. B2.

87. Lavoie, L. (2013, July 15). Dialing up a new workforce. *Canadian HR Reporter, 26*(13), 11–12.

88. Silliker, A. (2013, January 28). Canada facing significant labour mismatch: CIBC. *Canadian HR Reporter, 26*(2), 1, 27.

89. McCarthy, S. (2001, February 27). Skilled-worker shortage could reach one million. *The Globe and Mail*, p. A1.

90. Foster, L. (2016, February 22). Syrian refugees welcomed by employers. *Canadian HR Reporter, 29*(3), 1–3.

91. Becker, B. E., & Huselid, M. A. (1998). High performance work systems and firm performance: A synthesis of research and managerial implications. *Research in Personnel and Human Resources Management*, 16, 53–101.

92. Klie, S. (2009, December 14). Cultural competence affects patient health. *Canadian HR Reporter, 22*(22), 12.

93. Dobson, S. (2013, November 18). A 'Hallmark' of safety. *Canadian HR Reporter, 26*(20), 17.

94. Gibb-Clark, M. (2000, February 11). Employee training can backfire on firms: Survey. *The Globe and Mail*, p. B10.

95. Montesino, M. U. (2002). Strategic alignment of training, transfer-enhancing behaviors, and training usage: A posttraining study. *Human Resource Development Quarterly, 13*(1), 89–108.

96. Greengard, S. (2005). Golden values. *Workforce Management, 84*(3), 52–53.

97. Becker & Huselid (1998); Combs, J., Liu, Y., Hall, A., & Ketchen, D. (2006). How much do high-performance work practices matter? A metaanalysis of their effects on organizational performance. *Personnel Psychology*, 59, 501–528.

98. Dipboye, R. L. (1997). Organizational barriers to implementing a rational model of training. In M. A. Quinones & A. Ehrenstein (Eds.), *Training for a rapidly changing workplace*. Washington, DC: American Psychological Association.

99. Gordon, J., & Zemke, R. (2000). The attack on ISD. *Training, 37*(4), 42–53; Zemke, R., & Rossett, A. (2002). A hard look at ISD. *Training, 39*(2), 26–34; Weinstein, M. G., & Shuck, B. (2011). Social ecology and worksite training and development: Introducing the social in instructional system design. *Human Resource Development Review*, 10, 286–303.

100. Silliker, A. (2013, February 25). HR by the numbers (American workers unhappy with training). *Canadian HR Reporter, 26*(4), 4.

101. Gordon & Zemke (2000); Zemke & Rossett (2002).

CHAPTER

2

LEARNING AND MOTIVATION

CHAPTER LEARNING OUTCOMES

AFTER READING THIS CHAPTER, YOU SHOULD BE ABLE TO:

- define learning and workplace learning and describe how individuals learn through formal and informal learning methods
- describe how to classify learning outcomes
- explain how people learn using the three stages of learning and resource allocation theory
- use Kolb's learning model and the VARK model to distinguish and describe the different ways people learn and the implications for training
- compare the different theories of learning and discuss their implications for training
- describe the six core principles of andragogy and their implications for training programs
- explain goal-setting theory and why training motivation is important for learning and training effectiveness
- describe the model of training effectiveness

Abbott Point of Care in Ottawa is a state-of-the-art manufacturing facility that develops, manufactures, and markets hand-held medical diagnostic and data management products for rapid blood analysis at a patient's bedside.

Abbott has made significant investments to help support its growth by purchasing automated equipment. Given the advanced technical properties of the new equipment, the company needed a highly skilled workforce to successfully and efficiently manage it, and to meet Abbott's rigorous safety and quality standards.

To help employees adapt and develop the specific technical skills to successfully operate the equipment, Abbott launched a microelectronics manufacturer apprenticeship program to train its employees in-house to become instrumentation and control technicians. The program was created in partnership with Algonquin College and with support from the Ontario Ministry of Training, Colleges, and Universities.

The microelectronics manufacturer apprenticeship program was mandatory for employees in certain positions (such as operators) and was taught in-house during working hours at the manufacturing facility over a period of three years. With a total of 304 hours of classes involving 19 college credit courses, apprentices learned to better operate and monitor high-technology automated equipment while learning the necessary skills to improve processes and automation. Beyond formal academic training, the program included essential soft-skills training such as teamwork and adapting to change.

Participating employees also gained enhanced skills in communication, science and mathematics, quality regulations, critical thinking, and problem solving. The apprenticeship program has been a special chance to upgrade education for apprentices and increase their opportunity for mobility within the company.

Courtesy of Abbott Point of Care

Abbott Point of Care launched a microelectronics manufacturer apprenticeship program to train its employees to become instrumentation and control technicians.

Following the program's success, Abbott introduced an instrumentation and control technician apprenticeship program to train employees to become instrumentation and control technicians. This program features a customized curriculum that includes 15 college courses over three years, which are offered free of charge to employees.

The program was awarded the Minister's Apprenticeship Recognition Award, which recognizes employers for their contribution and commitment to improving the skills and training of apprentices in Ontario.[1]

Sources: C. Lewis, "Keeping your employees up with the times—free of charge," *Canadian HR Reporter*, Mar. 24, 2014, Vol. 27 (6), p. 22. Reprinted by permission of *Canadian HR Reporter*. © Thomson Reuters Canada Ltd., 2014, Toronto, Ontario, 1-800-387-5164. Web: www.hrreporter.com; "Abbott launches a new apprenticeship program for its Ottawa-based manufacturing sector," Abbott Point of Care, *News*, http://www.abbott.ca/docs/2013_Abbott_Point_of_Care_Apprenticeship_Release-Aug28-2013.pdf.

// INTRODUCTION

Abbott Point of Care's apprenticeship programs are a good example of the importance of learning for employees and organizations. Abbott employees not only acquired new skills that were necessary to perform their jobs, but were also motivated to participate in the apprenticeship programs and to learn new skills. But just what is learning and how do employees learn?

In this chapter, we focus on how people learn and their motivation to learn. First, we define what we mean by learning and workplace learning, distinguish formal from informal learning, and describe learning outcomes. Then we discuss the stages of learning and learning styles, followed by a review of learning theories and their implications for training. We then discuss training motivation and conclude the chapter with a model that links training and individual factors to learning, behaviour, and organizational effectiveness.

// WHAT IS LEARNING?

Although training and development is the focus of this textbook, it is important to keep in mind that what we are trying to accomplish through training and development is learning. In other words, training and development is the means for accomplishing the goal, and the goal is learning.

Learning is the process of acquiring knowledge and skills. It involves a change of state that makes possible a corresponding change in one's behaviour. Learning is the result of experiences that enable one to exhibit newly acquired behaviours.[2] Learning occurs "when one experiences a new way of acting, thinking, or feeling, finds the new pattern gratifying or useful, and incorporates it into the repertoire of behaviours."[3] When a behaviour has been learned, it can be thought of as a skill. Apprentices who participated in Abbott's microelectronics manufacturer apprenticeship program learned to operate and monitor high-technology automated equipment, acquired skills to improve processes and automation, and enhanced their skills in communication, science and mathematics, quality regulations, critical thinking, and problem solving.

Let's now consider how employees learn in the workplace.

// WORKPLACE LEARNING

Workplace learning is the process of acquiring job-related knowledge and skills through formal training programs and informal social interactions among employees.[4] Although the focus of this book is formal training and development programs, it is important to recognize that employees also acquire information and learn through informal interactions with others and from their experiences on the job. In fact, it is generally recognized that when it comes to workplace learning, about 70 percent comes from on-the-job experiences and assignments, 20 percent from relationships and interactions with others, and 10 percent from formal learning activities and events. This breakdown is known as the **70–20–10 model**.[5]

In effect, what the 70–20–10 model highlights is that a great deal of what employees learn at work is through informal learning. **Informal learning** is learning that occurs naturally as part of work and is not planned or designed by the organization. Informal learning is spontaneous, immediate, and task-specific. By comparison, **formal learning** has an expressed goal set by the organization and a defined process that is structured and sponsored by the organization.[6]

Table 2.1 provides a more detailed definition of formal and informal learning, and Table 2.2 describes some of the differences between formal and informal learning.

Learning
The process of acquiring knowledge and skills, and a change in individual behaviour as a result of some experience

Workplace learning
The process of acquiring job-related knowledge and skills through formal training programs and informal social interactions among employees

70–20–10 model
Seventy percent of workplace learning comes from on-the-job experiences, 20 percent from interactions with others, and 10 percent from formal learning activities and events

Informal learning
Learning that occurs naturally as part of work and is not planned or designed by the organization

Formal learning
Learning that is structured and planned by the organization

TABLE 2.1

FORMAL AND INFORMAL LEARNING

Formal Learning

Learning that involves formal, planned, and structured activities or the organized transfer of work-related skills, knowledge, and information. It includes activities such as classroom instruction, structured on-the-job programs, workshops, seminars, e-learning, and courses offered at external institutions.

Informal Learning

Learning that occurs primarily spontaneously and outside of formal, designed activities; the unstructured transfer of work-related skills, knowledge, and information, usually during work. It is usually initiated by learners and it can involve asking co-workers for help, ad hoc problem solving, incidental conversations, seeking out expert knowledge on the Internet, some types of coaching and mentoring, group problem-solving, and lunch-and-learn sessions.

Sources: Cotsman, S., & Hall, C. (2018). Learning cultures lead the way: Learning and development outlook—14th Edition. Ottawa: The Conference Board of Canada; Hughes, P. D., & Grant, M. (2007). *Learning and development outlook 2007.* Ottawa: The Conference Board of Canada.

It has been reported that 70 to 90 percent of what employees learn and know about their jobs is learned through informal processes rather than through formal programs. According to the Conference Board of Canada, informal learning is on the rise in Canadian organizations. Some of the reasons for the increase in informal learning are an increase in the need for knowledge transfer, an increased strategic emphasis on informal learning, informal activities being initiated by employees, and increased leadership support.[7]

Between 70 and 90 percent of what employees learn and know about their jobs is learned informally.

TABLE 2.2

DIFFERENCES BETWEEN FORMAL AND INFORMAL LEARNING

FACTOR	FORMAL LEARNING	INFORMAL LEARNING
Control	The control of learning rests primarily in the hands of the organization	The control of learning rests primarily in the hands of the learner
Relevance	Variable relevance to participants because it is not tailored to the individual	Highly relevant and need-specific to the individual
Timing	There is usually a delay; what is learned is not immediately used on the job	What is learned tends to be used immediately on the job
Structure	Highly structured and scheduled	Usually unstructured and occurs spontaneously
Outcomes	Tends to have specific outcomes	May not have specific outcomes

Sources: Day, N. (1998, June). Informal learning gets results. *Workforce management, 77*(6), 31–35; Parker, R. O., & Cooney, J. (2005). *Learning and development outlook 2005.* Ottawa: The Conference Board of Canada, Ottawa.

Employees have always learned through informal means. For example, an employee might show co-workers a way to save time by combining two steps in handling customer complaints. Sometimes learning occurs when an employee returns from a formal training session and teaches others what he or she has learned. In fact, when a research team studied informal training at Motorola, they discovered that every hour of formal training yielded four hours of informal training. Thus, there is a strong connection between informal learning and formal training, and there is evidence that informal learning has a significant effect on performance.[8]

An essential part of informal learning is informal learning behaviours. To find out more, see Training Today 2.1, "Informal Learning Behaviours."

Organizations are beginning to discover the importance and benefits of informal learning. For example, at Boeing Commercial Airplanes, researchers found that teams, personal documentation, supervisor–employee relationships, and shift changes provided rich examples of informal learning. At Motorola, during shift changes that overlap by half an hour or more, assembly-line shift workers and their supervisors update the next shift on any problems that had occurred as well as the probable causes and possible solutions.

Given the increasing pace of work and the constant changes in technology, organizations are finding that informal learning is more important than ever, as there often is not enough time for formal training.[9]

Employees learn about many things through informal means, such as new general knowledge, teamwork, problem solving, communication skills, new job tasks, computers, health and safety, new equipment, and even politics in the workplace.[10] One study found that email was the most-used method for informal learning followed by accessing information from the organization's intranet. Other forms of informal

INFORMAL LEARNING BEHAVIOURS

It is generally believed that 70 to 90 percent of learning in organizations takes place informally rather than through formal means. It is therefore important to better understand the antecedents and outcomes of informal learning.

First, it is necessary to make an important distinction between informal learning and informal learning behaviours (ILBs). Informal learning refers to knowledge and skills that are acquired through ILBs. In contrast, formal learning refers to knowledge and skills that are acquired through formal learning behaviours such as attending a training program.

Informal learning behaviours (ILBs) are noncurricular behaviours and activities pursued for the purpose of knowledge and skill acquisition that take place outside formally designated learning contexts. Such activities are predominantly self-directed, intentional, and field based. Informal learning behaviours are not syllabus based, discrete, or linear. ILBs occur in the workplace outside of formal learning and can involve various activities such as observing a co-worker, asking questions, discussing a problem with a supervisor, and practice. Engaging in ILBs is essential for informal learning.

In contrast, formal learning behaviours are curricular behaviours and activities pursued for the purpose of knowledge and skill acquisition that take place within formally designated learning contexts. Thus, they are organizationally sanctioned, externally directed, and are classroom and/or course based. Such activities are prescribed or scheduled by a syllabus or instructor and often have well-established learning objectives. They tend to proceed in a linear fashion and have a discrete beginning and end.

A recent study examined research on the antecedents and outcomes of ILBs. With respect to the antecedents, they found that personal and situational antecedents are positively related to ILBs. Individual predispositions such as personality variables (e.g., openness to experience), learning-related motives (e.g., self-efficacy), and demographics (e.g., education) were positively related to ILBs. Situational antecedents such as job/task characteristics (e.g., control and autonomy), support (e.g., support from supervisors and co-workers), and opportunities for learning (e.g., potential exists for new learning) were also positively related to ILBs.

With respect to outcomes, they found that ILBs are related to various work outcomes. As expected, engagement in ILBs is positively related to positive work attitudes, knowledge and skill acquisition, and performance.

These results indicate that engagement in ILBs is a function of personal factors (e.g., personality) as well as situational factors (e.g., support), and engaging in ILBs results in more positive work attitudes, greater knowledge and skill acquisition, and higher performance. Thus, it is clearly beneficial for organizations to encourage and support informal learning behaviours.

Source: Based on Cerasoli, C. P., Alliger, G. M., Donsbach, J. S., Mathieu, J. E., Tannenbaum, S. I., & Orvis, K. A. (2018, April). Antecedents and outcomes of informal learning behaviors: A meta-analysis. *Journal of Business and Psychology*, *33*(2), 203–230.

learning include Internet searches, communities of practice, voluntary mentoring, and coaching. Most of the best practices identified involved the use of technology for information exchange (e.g., a social networking site for the company) and creating time for face-to-face interactions (e.g., team lunches and rearranging office layout to facilitate conversations).[11]

To learn how organizations can facilitate informal learning, see The Trainer's Notebook 2.1, "Facilitating Informal Learning in Organizations."

Regardless of whether learning is formal or informal, a fundamental issue is whether employees have learned what they need to learn to be able to perform their jobs effectively.[12] Let's now consider the outcomes of workplace learning.

FACILITATING INFORMAL LEARNING IN ORGANIZATIONS

Here are some strategies for facilitating informal learning in organizations:

- Encourage employees to actively foster informal learning opportunities on their own.
- Form casual discussion groups among employees with similar projects and tasks.
- Create meeting areas and spaces where employees can congregate and communicate with each other (e.g., water cooler, cafeteria).
- Remove physical barriers (e.g., office walls) that prevent employees from interacting and communicating.
- Create overlaps between shifts so workers on different shifts or from different departments can get to know each other and discuss work-related issues.
- Create small teams with a specialized focus on a product or problem.
- Allow groups to break from their routines for team discussions.
- Provide work teams with some autonomy to modify work processes when they find a better way of doing things.
- Eliminate barriers to communication and give employees the authority to take training on themselves.
- Condense office spaces and make room for an open gathering area for coffee breaks and socializing.
- Match new hires with seasoned employees so they can learn from casual interaction and explicit teaching and mentoring.

Sources: Lavis, C. (2011). *Learning and development outlook 2011: Are organizations ready for learning 2.0?* Ottawa: The Conference Board of Canada; www.vancity.com.

// LEARNING OUTCOMES

Learning can be described in terms of domains or outcomes of learning. Table 2.3 shows the learning outcomes of two categorization schemes. The first one is by Robert Gagné, who developed the best-known classification of learning outcomes. According to Gagné, learning outcomes can be classified according to five general categories[13]:

1. *Verbal information.* Facts, knowledge, principles, and packages of information, or what is known as "declarative knowledge."
2. *Intellectual skills.* Concepts, rules, and procedures that are known as "procedural knowledge." Procedural rules govern many activities in our daily lives, such as driving an automobile or shopping in a supermarket.
3. *Cognitive strategies.* The application of information and techniques, and understanding how and when to use knowledge and information.
4. *Motor skills.* The coordination and execution of physical movements that involve the use of muscles, such as learning to swim.
5. *Attitudes.* Preferences and internal states associated with one's beliefs and feelings. Attitudes are learned and can be changed. However, they are considered to be the most difficult domain to influence through training.[14]

TABLE 2.3		
LEARNING OUTCOMES CLASSIFICATION SCHEMES		
Gagné's Classification Scheme		
Verbal information (declarative knowledge)		
Intellectual skills (procedural knowledge)		
Cognitive strategies (how and when to use information and knowledge)		
Motor skills (physical movements)		
Attitudes (internal states)		
Kraiger, Ford, & Salas Classification Scheme		
COGNITIVE (QUANTITY AND TYPE OF KNOWLEDGE)		
• Verbal knowledge		
• Knowledge organization		
• Cognitive strategies		
SKILL-BASED (TECHNICAL AND MOTOR SKILLS)		
• Compilation (proceduralization and composition)		
• Automaticity		
AFFECTIVE (ATTITUDINAL AND MOTIVATIONAL)		
• Attitudinal		
• Motivational (goal orientation, self-efficacy, goals)		

Sources: Gagné, R. M. (1984). Learning outcomes and their effects: Useful categories of human performance. *American Psychologist*, *39*, 377–385; Kraiger, K., Ford, J. K., & Salas, E. (1993). Application of cognitive, skill-based, and affective theories of learning outcomes to new methods of training evaluation. *Journal of Applied Psychology*, 78, 311–328.

Drawing on Gagné's classification scheme, Kurt Kraiger and colleagues developed a multidimensional classification scheme of learning outcomes that includes some additional indicators of learning. Their classification scheme consists of three broad categories of learning outcomes. Each category has several more specific indicators of learning[15]:

1. *Cognitive outcomes.* The quantity and type of knowledge and the relationships among knowledge elements. This includes *verbal knowledge* (declarative knowledge), *knowledge organization* (procedural knowledge and structures for organizing knowledge or mental models), and *cognitive strategies* (mental activities that facilitate knowledge acquisition and application, or what is known as metacognition).

2. *Skill-based outcomes.* This involves the development of technical or motor skills and includes *compilation* (fast and fluid performance of a task as a result of proceduralization and composition) and *automaticity* (ability to perform a task without conscious monitoring).

3. *Affective outcomes.* These are outcomes that are neither cognitively based nor skills based; they include *attitudinal* (affective internal state that affects behaviour) and *motivational* outcomes (goal orientation, self-efficacy, goals).

A training program can focus on one or more of the learning outcomes and, as you will see in the next section, some of the outcomes are associated with certain stages of the learning process. It is also important to realize that the extent to which a training program has an effect on any of these outcomes depends in large part on the objectives of a training program. In addition, different training methods are more or less effective depending on the learning outcome a training program was designed to influence. In other words, the best training method for a training program depends in part on the desired learning outcome. According to Gagné, different instructional events and conditions of learning are required for each of the learning outcomes. Furthermore, the learning outcomes are interrelated, which means that changes in one might result in changes in another.[16]

Regardless of the learning outcome, learning generally occurs over a period of time and progresses through a series of stages, as described in the next section.

// STAGES OF LEARNING AND RESOURCE ALLOCATION THEORY

Learning and the acquisition of new knowledge and skills occur over a period of time and in a meaningful sequence across several stages. A theory developed by John Anderson called the adaptive character of thought theory, or ACT theory, describes the learning process as it unfolds across three stages.[17]

According to **ACT theory**, learning takes place in three stages that are known as declarative knowledge, knowledge compilation, and procedural knowledge or proceduralization. A related theory called Resource Allocation theory explains how people learn during each of the stages as a function of the resources required to learn a new task.

Resource allocation theory explains what happens during each stage and recognizes that individuals possess limited cognitive resources that can be used to learn a new task. Performance of a new task is determined by individual differences in attentional and cognitive resources, the requirements of the task (task complexity), and self-regulatory activities (e.g., self-monitoring and self-evaluation) used to allocate attention across tasks.[18]

As you will see, the amount of cognitive resources an individual can allocate to learning a new task varies across the three stages. Table 2.4 provides a summary of learning and performance at the three stages of learning.

The first stage of learning is called **declarative knowledge**. It involves the learning of knowledge, facts, and information. For example, think of what it was like when you learned how to drive a car. At first, you acquired a great deal of information, such as what to do when you get into the car, how to start the car and put it in gear, how to change gears if it is a standard shift, and so on. These pieces or units of information are called chunks.

During this first stage of learning one must devote all of one's attention and cognitive resources to the task of learning. In other words, it is not likely that you would be able to make a phone call, listen to

Learning takes place in three stages: declarative knowledge, knowledge compilation, and procedural knowledge.

TABLE 2.4

THE STAGES OF LEARNING

STAGE 1

DECLARATIVE KNOWLEDGE

Learning: Knowledge, facts, and information
Performance: Resource dependent

STAGE 2

KNOWLEDGE COMPILATION

Learning: Integrating tasks into sequences
Performance: Fragmented and piecemeal

STAGE 3

PROCEDURAL KNOWLEDGE

Learning: Task mastery
Performance: Automatic and habitual; resource insensitive

music, or carry on a conversation during this period of learning to drive a car. This is because all of your attention and cognitive resources are required to learn the task of driving. Furthermore, your driving performance at this stage is slow and prone to errors.

In the declarative stage of learning, performance is resource dependent because all of one's attention and cognitive resources are required to learn the task. Any diversion of attention is likely to affect your learning and lower your performance. Just think of what it is like when you are in class and somebody starts talking to you. Your learning is seriously affected because you need all of your attention and cognitive resources for the task of learning. Listening or talking to somebody during class will require your attention, and your learning will suffer.

The second stage of learning is called **knowledge compilation**. Knowledge compilation involves integrating tasks into sequences to simplify and streamline the task. The learner acquires the ability to translate the declarative knowledge acquired in the first stage into action. During this stage, performance becomes faster and more accurate. For example, when learning how to drive a car, you are able to get into the car and begin to drive without having to think about every single thing you must do. In other words, what was once many single and independent tasks during the declarative stage (e.g., put on your seatbelt, lock the car, adjust the seat, adjust the mirror, start the car, etc.) is now one smooth sequence of tasks. You get into the car and do all of the tasks as part of an integrated sequence.

Although the attention requirements during the knowledge compilation stage are lower than in the declarative stage, performance is still somewhat fragmented and piecemeal. So when you are learning to drive a car, this might mean popping the clutch from time to time and occasionally rolling backwards when on an incline, stalling the car, and so on.

The final stage of learning is called **procedural knowledge** or proceduralization. During this stage, the learner has mastered the task and performance is automatic and habitual. In other words, the task can now be performed without much thought.

> **Knowledge compilation**
> Integrating tasks into sequences to simplify and streamline the task

> **Procedural knowledge**
> The learner has mastered the task and performance is automatic and habitual

CHAPTER 2 Learning and Motivation

The transition from knowledge acquisition to application is complete. This is what most of us experience when we drive. We get into a car and drive without giving much thought about what we are doing. The task of driving becomes habitual and automatic.

Because tasks at this stage can be performed with relatively little attention, it is possible to divert one's attention and cognitive resources to other tasks, such as talking with passengers or listening to music. Performance at this stage is fast and accurate, and the task can be performed with little impairment even when attention is devoted to another task (as long as we keep our eyes on the road and hands on the wheel!). At this stage, performance is said to be resource insensitive because changes in attention will not have much of an impact on performance.

IMPLICATIONS FOR TRAINING What are the implications of ACT theory for learning and training? First, ACT theory recognizes that learning is a sequential and stage-like process that involves three important stages. Second, it indicates that different types of learning take place at different stages. And third, motivational interventions might be more or less effective depending on the stage of learning. As you will learn later in the chapter, research has shown that goal setting can be harmful to learning during the early stages of learning, when all of one's attention and cognitive resources are devoted to learning. This follows from resource allocation theory, which states that during the early stages of learning, cognitive ability is more important than motivational strategies.

However, when goals are set during the later stages of learning (e.g., procedural knowledge) they can have a positive effect on performance. Cognitive ability becomes less important than it was during the declarative stage of learning. Thus, the effects of both cognitive ability and motivational interventions on learning and performance depend on the stage of learning.[19]

// LEARNING STYLES

An important aspect of learning is the way in which people learn. Individuals differ in how they prefer to learn and how they learn best. These differences in learning preferences are known as **learning styles**. However, the exact meaning of a learning style depends on the model of learning style. In this section, we discuss two of the best-known models of learning style: David Kolb's experiential learning theory model and Neil Fleming's VARK model.

David **Kolb's learning style** has to do with the way people gather information and process and evaluate it during the learning process.[20] Table 2.5 shows Kolb's four learning modes and how they combine to form the four learning styles.

Learning modes involve the way people gather information (concrete experience, or CE, and abstract conceptualization, or AC) and the way people process or evaluate information (active experimentation, or AE, and reflective observation, or RO). It is the combination of these "learning modes" (the way a person gathers information and the way a person processes information) that results in a learning style.

People who prefer to gather information through direct experience and involvement are CE types (feeling). Those who prefer to gather information by thinking about issues, ideas, and concepts are AC types (thinking). If you prefer to process information by observing and reflecting on information and different points of view, you are an RO type (watching). If you prefer to process information by acting on it and actually doing something to see its practical value, you are an AE type (doing).[21]

TABLE 2.5

LEARNING STYLES

LEARNING STYLE	LEARNING MODES	MEANING
CONVERGING	Abstract conceptualization (AC) and active experimentation (AE)	Thinking and doing
DIVERGING	Concrete experience (CE) and reflective observation (RO)	Feeling and watching
ASSIMILATING	Abstract conceptualization (AC) and reflective observation (RO)	Thinking and watching
ACCOMMODATING	Concrete experience (CE) and active experimentation (AE)	Feeling and doing

Thus, according to Kolb, an individual's learning style is a function of how they gather information and how they process information. For example, a *converging* learning style combines abstract conceptualization and active experimentation (thinking and doing). People with this learning style focus on problem solving and the practical application of ideas and theories. A *diverging* learning style combines concrete experience and reflective observation (feeling and watching). People with this orientation view concrete situations from different points of view and generate alternative courses of action. An *assimilating* style combines abstract conceptualization and reflective observation (thinking and watching). These people like to process and integrate information and ideas into logical forms and theoretical models. Finally, an *accommodating* learning style combines concrete experience and active experimentation (feeling and doing). People with this learning style prefer hands-on experience and like to learn by being involved in new and challenging experiences.[22]

Although people might prefer a particular learning style, ideally people can learn best by using all four styles. In fact, Kolb notes the importance of a **learning cycle** in which people use each of the four modes of learning in a sequence. The learning cycle begins with concrete experience (learning by experience), followed by reflective observation (learning by reflecting), then abstract conceptualization (learning by thinking), and finally active experimentation (learning by doing). This kind of learning cycle has been shown to improve learning and retention as well as the development of behavioural skills. Learning is most effective when all four steps in the learning cycle are part of the learning experience.[23]

The second model of learning styles is the VARK model developed by Fleming. **Fleming's learning style** is an individual's preferred ways of gathering, organizing, and thinking about information. It has to do with the different ways that individuals take in and give out information. There are four different perceptual preferences for how people prefer to learn. **VARK** is an acronym for the four different perceptual preferences or learning styles[24]:

V = visual
A = aural/auditory
R = read/write
K = kinesthetic

Learning cycle
People use each of the four modes of learning in a sequence that begins with concrete experience followed by reflective observation, abstract conceptualization, and active experimentation

Fleming's learning style
An individual's preferred ways of gathering, organizing, and thinking about information

VARK
Visual, aural/auditory, read/write, and kinesthetic

Thus, the VARK model is based on how individuals prefer to receive information through four sensory modalities. Individuals who prefer to learn through the *visual* modality like to learn from charts, maps, graphs, diagrams, and other visual symbolic devices. Those who prefer to learn through the *aural/auditory* modality like to learn from talking, explaining, and discussing things such as in lectures and group discussions. Individuals who prefer the *read/write* modality like to learn from printed material and readings such as books, reports, manuals, and note taking. Those who prefer the *kinesthetic* modality like to learn from direct practice, demonstrations, and experience such as simulations, role plays, and case studies. These people prefer to learn by actually doing something.[25]

Fleming has developed a questionnaire to measure the learning styles (the VARK questionnaire). An individual's score indicates their learning style preference as well as the strength of their learning style. This is because in addition to a single learning style preference, it is possible to have a combination of two, three, or four learning style preferences. The VARK questionnaire provides a profile of a person's scores on the four modalities. While some people might have one primary learning style, others might have multiple learning styles (two, three, or four) or what is known as a multimodal learning style.[26]

The VARK questionnaire can be used for learners to determine their learning style which can help them choose learning activities that will be best suited to their learning preferences. In addition, instructors can adjust their learning activities and strategies to match that of their learners. There is some evidence that students perform better in courses in which the learning activities match their learning style.[27]

IMPLICATIONS FOR TRAINING Learning styles have several implications for training. First, they recognize that people differ in how they prefer to learn. This means that a person's comfort, motivation, and success in training will depend on how well the training (e.g., its design, content, methods, and delivery) matches their learning style. Thus, trainers should be aware of these differences and design training programs to appeal to different learning styles. At AmeriCredit, an auto finance company in Fort Worth, Texas, course facilitators receive a report prior to a training session that allows them to adjust course delivery, content, and design based on the learning styles of the trainees.[28] The use of technology in training makes it much easier to tailor learning and training to a trainee's learning style.

Second, trainees can also benefit from an awareness of their VARK learning style so that they can focus on their primary style(s) when learning, and make informed choices regarding training programs and opportunities to attend. Trainees might also make adjustments to their learning behaviours when attending a training program to maximize their learning. This might involve readings prior to training, taking additional notes during training, asking questions and participating in discussions, and/or practicing what has been learned in training.[29]

Third, training programs should be designed with each learning mode and style included and as part of a sequence of learning experiences in accordance with Kolb's learning cycle (CE-RO-AC-AE). At Capital One Financial Corp., after employees are taught a new set of skills they are given work projects to implement the skills, and then they must report on the experience. The approach closely mirrors the learning cycle.[30]

Using Fleming's VARK model, trainers should use a multimodal approach that includes activities and methods that will appeal to the visual (e.g., diagrams, charts), aural/auditory (e.g., lectures, discussions), read/write (e.g., readings, handouts), and the kinesthetic (e.g., demonstrations, practice) learning styles.[31]

Now let's consider the learning process and how people learn according to several learning theories.

// LEARNING THEORIES

The learning process and how people learn is explained by several theories of learning. Learning theories are important because they help us understand how people learn and how to design training programs to maximize learning and retention. In this section, we describe two learning theories that have important implications for training: conditioning theory and social cognitive theory.

CONDITIONING THEORY

The famous psychologist B. F. Skinner defined learning as a relatively permanent change in behaviour in response to a particular stimulus or set of stimuli.[32] Skinner and the behaviourist school of psychology believe that learning is a result of reward and punishment contingencies that follow a response to a stimulus.

The basic idea is that a stimulus or cue is followed by a response, which is then followed by a positive or negative consequence (which is known as positive or negative reinforcement). If the response is positively reinforced, it strengthens the likelihood that the response will occur again and that learning will result.

Behaviourists argue that similar principles are at work when an adult submits an innovative proposal and is praised, and when a pigeon pecks a red dot and is given a pellet of food. When a response is reinforced through food, money, attention, or anything pleasurable, then the response is more likely to be repeated. If there is no reinforcement, then over time the response will cease, which is known as extinction. If the response is punished, then it will not be repeated. Conditioning theory is illustrated in Figure 2.1.

While positive reinforcement involves the application of something positive following a desired response so that the behaviour will continue, negative reinforcement involves the removal of a stimulus after an action. For example, when an instructor praises students for participating in class discussions and answering questions he/she is using positive reinforcement which results in continued participation. Now think of an instructor chewing out a class for not participating in class discussions and threatening to pick students at random to answer questions. When students participate, the instructor stops chewing them out and threatening to choose students at random. Thus, the response is increased class participation which is due to the removal of a negative stimulus. Both positive and negative reinforcement are used to increase the likelihood of a desired behaviour.

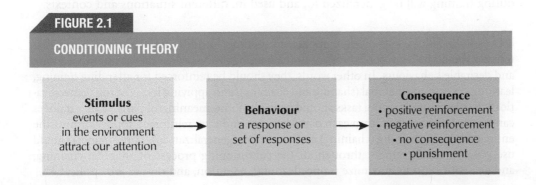

FIGURE 2.1

CONDITIONING THEORY

Stimulus
events or cues
in the environment
attract our attention

Behaviour
a response or
set of responses

Consequence
• positive reinforcement
• negative reinforcement
• no consequence
• punishment

CHAPTER 2 Learning and Motivation

It is important to realize that negative reinforcement is not the same as punishment, which involves the application of a negative consequence in response to an undesirable behaviour to decrease or eliminate the occurrence of the behaviour. In the example above, a desirable behaviour is being learned and increased (i.e., class participation) by a negative reinforcer that is removed when the desirable behaviour occurs.

Managers and trainers use conditioning theory principles when they attempt to influence employee behaviour. For example, at the financial services company Capital One, new hires attend monthly reinforcement sessions in which they discuss what they did on the job that directly relates to the skills they are developing. Once the skills are mastered they are taught new skills, and the reinforcement cycle continues.[33] Let's now take a closer look at the conditioning process.

THE CONDITIONING PROCESS

The conditioning process involves linking desired behaviour to pleasurable consequences. This is accomplished through three connected concepts: *shaping, chaining,* and *generalization*. **Shaping** refers to the reinforcement of each step in the process until it is mastered, and then withdrawing the reinforcer until the next step is mastered. Shaping is extremely important for learning complex behaviour. Behaviour modelling training is a training method (see Chapter 5) that makes extensive use of this concept by rewarding trainees for the acquisition of separate skills performed sequentially.

Chaining is the second concept and involves the reinforcement of entire sequences of a task. During shaping, an individual learns each separate step of a task and is reinforced for each successive step. The goal is to learn to combine each step and perform the entire response. This combination is what chaining involves, and it is accomplished by reinforcing entire sequences of the task and eventually reinforcing only the complete task after each of the steps have been learned.

The third concept is **generalization**, which means that the conditioned response occurs in circumstances different from those during learning.[34] Thus, while a trainee might have learned a task through shaping and chaining, he or she might not be able to perform the task in a different situation or outside of the classroom. To achieve generalization, the trainer must provide trainees with opportunities to perform the task in a variety of situations.

For example, the trainer can change a role-play script from negotiating with one's supervisor the deadline of a project to negotiating the starting salary with a new employer. As a result, the trainee learns to generalize the skill from a simple, controlled environment to a different, more difficult one. This is a goal of training—that learning acquired during training will be generalized to, and used in, different situations and contexts.

IMPLICATIONS FOR TRAINING When applied to training, conditioning theory suggests that trainees should be reinforced throughout the training process when they engage in learning and desirable behaviours. In other words, they should be reinforced for attending training, learning the training material (shaping and chaining), and applying it on the job (generalization). Furthermore, training tasks should be broken into meaningful parts so that trainees can be reinforced as they learn each part (shaping), and then reinforced for performing the entire task during training (chaining) and on the job (generalization). Thus, trainers should use positive reinforcement throughout the conditioning process of shaping, chaining, and generalization to maximize trainee learning, retention, and on-the-job application.

Shaping
The reinforcement of each step in a process until it is mastered

Chaining
The reinforcement of entire sequences of a task

Generalization
The conditioned response occurs in circumstances different from those during learning

SOCIAL COGNITIVE THEORY

If you think about how you learn, you will realize that learning does not just occur as a result of reward and punishment contingencies. Learning also occurs through cognitive processes such as observation and modelling, and this is best explained by social cognitive theory.

The central premise of social cognitive theory is **social learning**, which involves learning through interactions with others. Social learning can be either formal (e.g., mentoring programs) or informal (e.g., collaborative work).[35] According to social cognitive theory, people learn by observing the behaviour of others, making choices about different courses of action to pursue, and managing their own behaviour in the process of learning.[36] We observe the actions of others and make note of the reinforcing or punishing outcomes of their behaviour. We then imitate what we have observed and expect certain consequences to follow. Considerable research has shown that people observe and reproduce the actions and attitudes of others.[37]

Social cognitive theory involves three key components: observation, self-efficacy, and self-regulation.

> **Social learning**
> Learning through inter-actions with others

OBSERVATION

As you have probably experienced in yourself and others, people learn by **observation**. They observe the actions of others and the consequences of those actions. If the person being observed (the role model) is credible and knowledgeable, their behaviour is more likely to be imitated. The imitation will occur particularly if the role model is reinforced for the behaviour. New recruits watch the intense work hours of the senior staff. They then work the same long hours, in the expectation that they, too, will be rewarded with promotions and pay raises.

Four key elements are critical for observational learning to take place: attention, retention, reproduction, and reinforcement. Learners must first attend to the behaviour (i.e., be aware of the skills that are observable). Second, they must remember what they observed and encode it in their own repertoire so that they can recall the skills. Third, they must then try out the skill (i.e., try to reproduce it) through practice and rehearsal. Fourth, if the reproduction results in positive outcomes (i.e., it is reinforced), then the learner is likely to continue to reproduce the behaviour and retain the new skills.

Many training programs use social cognitive theory concepts in which a model is used to exhibit desired behaviour that is then followed by opportunities for practice and positive reinforcement. Some organizations assign new recruits to mentors or senior co-workers so that they can learn by observing them. The financial services firm Edward Jones has a mentoring program in which new investment representatives are paired with more established ones. New employees shadow their mentor for three weeks to learn about the company and how things are done.[38]

> **Observation**
> Learning by observing the actions of others and the consequences

SELF-EFFICACY

While observation may provide the observer with information necessary to imitate the observed behaviour, we know that people do not always attempt to do things they observe other people doing. For example, a novice skier might observe his friends make their way down a steep hill but refuse to imitate their behaviour and follow them down the hill. This is because he might not have the confidence or the belief that he will be able to do it. Such beliefs are known as self-efficacy beliefs.

Self-efficacy refers to beliefs that people have about their ability to successfully perform a specific task. Self-efficacy is a cognitive belief that is task specific, as in the example of the skier's confidence that he can ski down a steep hill. The novice skier might have low self-efficacy to ski down the hill but very high self-efficacy that he can get an "A" in a training course!

Self-efficacy is influenced by four sources of information. In order of importance, they are task mastery, observation, verbal persuasion and social influence, and one's physiological or emotional state.[39] So how would you strengthen the self-efficacy of the novice skier who is afraid to follow his friends down the hill? The self-efficacy of the novice skier can be strengthened not only by having him observe his friends' behaviour, but also by encouraging him and providing assurance that he can do it; making him feel comfortable and relaxed rather than fearsome and anxious; and, most importantly, by ensuring that he first experiences some success—perhaps by trying some less threatening ski hills.

Self-efficacy has been shown to have a strong effect on people's attitudes, emotions, and behaviour in many areas of human functioning. Self-efficacy influences the activities people choose to perform, the amount of effort and persistence they devote to a task, their affective and stress reactions, and performance outcomes.[40]

Self-efficacy has also been found to be very important for training. Research has shown that training effectiveness involves strengthening trainees' self-efficacy to perform the training task. In other words, training increases trainees' self-efficacy to perform a task, and self-efficacy leads to improved task performance.[41]

Self-efficacy
Beliefs that people have about their ability to successfully perform a specific task

Christophe Testi/Shutterstock.com

Self-efficacy influences the activities people choose to perform and the amount of effort and persistence they devote to a task.

SELF-REGULATION

According to conditioning theory, an individual's behaviour is regulated by external agents who administer rewards and punishments. However, the third component of social cognitive theory suggests that people can regulate their own behaviour and do not require external rewards and punishment to learn and change their behaviour. This is known as **self-regulation** and it involves managing one's own behaviour. Self-regulation not only enables people to function effectively in their personal lives, but it also helps people acquire the knowledge and skills they need to succeed in education and in the workplace.[42]

Self-regulated learning involves the use of affective, cognitive, and behavioural processes during a learning experience to reach a desired level of achievement.[43] Self-regulation is a goal-oriented cyclical process in which trainees set goals and establish a plan for learning, develop learning strategies, focus their attention on learning, monitor their learning outcomes, and modify their behaviours over time.[44] Thus, self-regulation enables people to structure and motivate their own learning and behaviour through the use of various internal processes. These internal processes involve observing and monitoring one's own behaviour (self-monitoring) as well as the behaviour of others, setting performance goals (goal setting), practising and rehearsing new and desired behaviours,

Self-regulation
Managing one's own behaviour through a series of internal processes

Self-regulated learning
The use of affective, cognitive, and behavioural processes during a learning experience to reach a desired level of achievement

keeping track of one's progress and performance, comparing performance with one's goals (self-evaluation), and rewarding oneself for goal achievement (self-reinforcement).[45]

Self-regulation has been found to be related to cognitive, affective, and behavioural outcomes. It has also been shown to be an effective method of training. For example, one study found that self-regulation training increased the job attendance of employees with above-average absenteeism. Compared to a group that did not receive self-regulation training, employees who received self-regulation training had higher self-efficacy for attending work and increased their job attendance. These results were shown to continue for up to nine months following training.[46] An increasing number of studies have also found that self-regulation training leads to improvements in skill acquisition, maintenance, and performance. Thus, trainees who engage in self-regulated learning learn more than those who do not self-regulate their learning.[47]

IMPLICATIONS FOR TRAINING Social cognitive theory has several important implications for the design of training programs. In particular, learning can be improved by providing trainees with models who demonstrate how to perform a training task; by strengthening trainee self-efficacy for successfully learning and performing the task; and by teaching trainees how to regulate their behaviour and performance while learning and on the job. These principles have been incorporated into a training method called behaviour modelling training, which is described in Chapter 5.

In addition, there is some evidence that trainees can be encouraged to self-regulate their learning during training by having them set learning goals and asking them questions about their self-regulatory activities. **Self-regulation prompts** ask trainees questions about their learning, goals, and their goal progress to encourage self-regulation during training. Several studies have shown that trainees who were prompted with questions about their self-regulation during training (e.g., whether they are concentrating on learning the training material, evaluating their knowledge, and monitoring the effectiveness of their learning strategies) showed a significant improvement in their declarative and procedural knowledge over time as well as their performance. Trainees also spent more time reviewing the course material and were less likely to withdraw from an online training course before completion.[48]

Thus, trainers might incorporate self-regulation prompts into training programs to remind trainees to self-regulate their learning. To be most effective, self-regulation prompts should be provided periodically throughout a training program. To find out how to prompt trainee self-regulation during training, see The Trainer's Notebook 2.2, "Prompting Self-Regulation."

> **Self-regulation prompts**
> Asking trainees questions about their learning, goals, and goal progress to encourage self-regulation during training

THE TRAINER'S NOTEBOOK   2.2

PROMPTING SELF-REGULATION

The following questions can be used during training to prompt self-regulation. Trainees should be asked these questions periodically throughout a training program. They can respond using a 5-point scale with anchors 1 = not at all to 5 = definitely. Trainees should be given the following message before they begin the training:

Research has shown that asking yourself questions about whether you are concentrating on learning the training material will increase how much you learn during training. The training program will periodically ask you questions about where you are directing your mental resources and whether you are making progress toward learning the

(continued)

training material. Respond honestly to these questions and use your responses to direct your learning during training.

- Am I concentrating on learning the training material?
- Do I understand all of the key points of the training material?
- Are the study strategies I'm using helping me learn the training material?
- Have I spent enough time reviewing to remember the information after I finish the course?
- Am I setting goals to help me remember the material after I finish the course?
- Would I do better on the next quiz if I studied more?

- Am I focusing my mental effort on the training material?
- Do I need to continue to review to ensure I will remember the material after I finish the course?
- Are the study tactics I have been using effective for learning the training material?
- Do I know enough about the training material to remember the material after I finish the course?
- Am I setting goals to ensure I have a thorough understanding of the training material?
- Do I know enough about the training material to answer all of the questions correctly on the quiz for this module?

Sources: Sitzmann, T., & Ely, K. (2010). Sometimes you need a reminder: The effects of prompting self-regulation on regulatory process, learning, and attrition. *Journal of Applied Psychology*, 95, 132–144.

// ADULT LEARNING THEORY

A final theory of learning that is important for training and development is adult learning theory which is based on the differences between adults and children and the implications of these differences for learning. Consider the learning environment that children experience for much of their education. They are told what, when, and how to learn. Learning is supposed to pay off in some unknown way in the distant future. But is this an appropriate way to educate adults? To answer this question, we first have to consider how adults are different from children.

First, adults have acquired a great deal of knowledge and work-related experience that they bring with them to a training program. Adults like to know why they are learning something, the practical implications of what they are learning, and its relevance to their problems and needs. Adults are problem centred in their approach to learning and prefer to be self-directed. They like to learn independently and they are motivated to learn by both extrinsic and intrinsic factors. (See Table 2.6 for some other differences between adults and children.)

These differences have led to the development of an adult learning theory known as andragogy. **Andragogy** refers to an adult-oriented approach to learning that takes into account the differences between adult and child learners. By contrast, the term **pedagogy** refers to the more traditional approach of learning used to educate children and youth. Pedagogy assigns full responsibility to the instructor for making decisions about what, how, and when something will be learned and if it has been learned. As a result, the learner has a submissive role of simply following the instructions of the instructor.[49]

Andragogy makes six core assumptions about the adult learner (need to know, learner self-concept, learner's experience, readiness to learn, orientation to learning, and motivation to learn). These six adult learning principles form the basis of andragogy.

Andragogy
An adult-oriented approach to learning that takes into account the differences between adult and child learners

Pedagogy
The traditional approach to learning used to educate children and youth

TABLE 2.6

TEACHING CHILDREN VERSUS ADULTS

FACTOR	CHILDREN	ADULTS
PERSONALITY	Dependent	Independent
MOTIVATION	Extrinsic	Intrinsic
ROLES	Student	Employee
	Child	Parent, volunteer, spouse, citizen
OPENNESS TO CHANGE	Open	Ingrained habits and attitudes
BARRIERS TO CHANGE	Few	Negative self-concept
	Limited opportunities	
	Time	
	Inappropriate teaching methods	
EXPERIENCE	Limited	Vast
ORIENTATION TO LEARNING	Subject-centred	Problem-centred

First, adults need to know why they must learn something before they learn it. They need to know how the learning will be conducted, what learning will occur, and why it is important. They also need to know how the learning will benefit them and what the consequences will be. Second, adults have a self-concept of themselves that they are responsible for their own life decisions. As a result, they prefer to be treated in a way that acknowledges their self-concept for self-direction and self-directed learning.

Third, adults have acquired a great deal of experience in their lives and they differ from children and youth in terms of both the quantity and quality of experiences. These experiences can have both positive and negative implications for learning. That is, while they can be a rich source for learning they can also result in habits and biases that can hinder one's willingness to learn new things.

Fourth, adults are ready to learn when there are things they need to know to improve and manage aspects of their life or to perform a task. Fifth, while children and youth's orientation to learning is subject-oriented, adults' orientation to learning is life-centred and focused on task performance and solving problems. Adults are motivated to learn things that will help them do things better and solve problems in their life. They will learn better when they see real-life applications of the learning material and experience. Sixth, while adults respond positively to external motivators such as promotions and pay raises, they are primarily motivated by internal motivators such as self-esteem and opportunities for growth and development.

Thus, andragogy includes the learner in the learning process by providing the learner with procedures and resources to acquire knowledge and skills. It makes the learning experience of adults more consistent with their needs, self-concept, life experiences, orientation to learning, and motivation to learn. This means that adult learning should be self-directed and problem-centred, and should take into account the learner's existing knowledge and experiences.[50]

IMPLICATIONS FOR TRAINING Adult learning theory has important implications for learning throughout the training and development process. First, adult learners should be involved in the planning of training and development which should be a collaborative process. This means that they should have input into the training they need and will receive (e.g., training objectives and content) as well as how it will be designed (e.g., training methods), delivered, and evaluated.

Second, the design and instruction of training programs should be the joint responsibility of the trainer and trainees and based on trainees' self-assessment of their needs. Third, the training climate should be conducive for learning which means that it should be collaborative and supportive, and include self-directed learning as well as experiential learning techniques.[51]

The Trainer's Notebook 2.3, "Implications of Adult Learning Theory for Training and Development Programs," summarizes the implications of adult learning theory for training and development. Now let's consider the role of motivation in the training and development process.

THE TRAINER'S NOTEBOOK   2.3

IMPLICATIONS OF ADULT LEARNING THEORY FOR TRAINING AND DEVELOPMENT

- Adult trainees should be informed about the importance, relevance, and benefits of training.
- Adult trainees should be involved and have input into the planning and design of training programs.
- Adult trainees should be involved in the needs analysis and have input into training objectives, training content, and training methods.
- The designers of training programs should consider the needs and interests of adult trainees.
- The training content should be meaningful and relevant to adult trainees' work-related needs, concerns, and problems.

- Trainers should be aware of adult trainees' experiences and use them as examples.
- Adult trainees can learn independently and may prefer to do so.
- Adult trainees are motivated by both intrinsic and extrinsic rewards.
- Adult trainees should be given safe practice opportunities.
- Adult trainees should be involved in the evaluation of training and re-diagnosis of training needs

---

// MOTIVATION

You might be familiar with the topic of motivation with respect to employee motivation and job performance. But did you know that learning and the effectiveness of training programs are also a function of people's motivation? In fact, motivation is an important predictor of task performance, job performance, learning, and the effectiveness of training programs.

Motivation refers to the degree of persistent effort that one directs toward a goal. Motivation has to do with *effort*, or how hard one works; *persistence*, or the extent to which one keeps at a task; and *direction*, or the extent to which one applies effort and persistence toward a meaningful goal.

In organizations, motivation has to do with the extent to which employees direct their effort and persistence toward organization goals or in a manner that will benefit the organization, such as high productivity or excellent customer service. One of the best known and most studied theories of motivation that is important for training and development is goal setting theory.

GOAL-SETTING THEORY

In Chapter 1, it was noted that an important part of the performance management process is goal setting. You were also informed that managers and employees should set SMART goals—goals that are specific, measureable, attainable, relevant, and have a time frame. The basis for SMART goals is goal-setting theory.

Goal-setting theory is based on the idea that people's intentions are a good predictor of their behaviour. A **goal** is the object or aim of an action.[52] According to goal-setting theory, goals are motivational because they direct people's efforts and energies and lead to the development of strategies to help them reach their goals. For goals to be motivational, however, they must have a number of characteristics.

First, goals must be *specific* in terms of their level and time frame. General goals that lack specificity tend not to be motivational. Second, goals must be *challenging* to be motivational. Goals should not be so easy that they require little effort to achieve, and they should not be so difficult that they are impossible to reach. Third, goals must be accompanied by *feedback* so that it is possible to know how well one is doing and how close one is to goal accomplishment. Finally, for goals to be motivational, people must accept them and be *committed* to them.[53]

Research on goal-setting theory has provided strong support for the motivational effects of goals. Studies across a wide variety of settings have consistently shown that challenging and specific goals that are accompanied with performance feedback result in higher levels of individual and group performance.[54]

However, although specific and challenging goals have been found to be motivational, the effects of goals on learning and performance depend on the type of goal that is set. Two important distinctions are whether a goal is proximal or distal and whether the goal is a performance goal or a learning goal.

PROXIMAL AND DISTAL GOALS

An important distinction with respect to a goal is whether it is a distal goal or proximal goal. A **distal goal** is a long-term or end goal, such as achieving a certain level of sales performance. A **proximal goal** is a short-term goal or sub-goal that is instrumental for achieving a distal goal. Proximal goals involve breaking down a distal goal into smaller, more attainable sub-goals. Proximal goals provide clear markers of progress toward a distal goal because they result in more frequent feedback. As a result, individuals can evaluate their ongoing performance and identify appropriate strategies for the attainment of a distal goal. Distal goals are too far removed to provide markers of one's progress, making it difficult for individuals to know how they are doing and to adjust their strategies.[55]

Motivation
The degree of persistent effort that one directs toward a goal

For more information see Chapter 1, pp. 6–7

Goal
The object or aim of an action

Distal goal
A long-term or end goal

Proximal goal
A short-term goal or sub-goal

Proximal goals are especially important for complex tasks. Research has found that distal goals can have a negative effect on the performance of a complex task. However, when distal goals are accompanied with proximal goals, they have a significant positive effect on the discovery and use of task-relevant strategies, self-efficacy, and performance.[56]

A study of provincial and federal government managers who attended a self-awareness training program found that trainees who set distal and proximal outcome goals at the end of the training program were more likely to apply what they learned in training on the job six weeks after training than those who set only a distal outcome goal. Thus, distal goals are effective for learning a new task only when they are accompanied by proximal goals.[57]

GOAL ORIENTATION

Another important characteristic of goals is goal orientation. **Goal orientation** is a dispositional or situational goal preference in achievement situations.[58] Goal orientation has been found to be a stable individual difference. Individuals differ with respect to their goal orientation and the goals they will pursue in learning situations.

For example, some individuals have a **learning goal orientation (LGO)**, which means that they are most concerned about developing competence by acquiring new skills and mastering new tasks. Individuals with a performance goal orientation are more concerned about their task performance and focus on either demonstrating their competence by seeking favourable judgments from others or avoiding negative judgments. Individuals who are most concerned about favourable judgments about their performance and demonstrating their capabilities to others have a **prove performance goal orientation (PPGO)**. Individuals who are most concerned about avoiding negative judgments from others about their performance have an **avoid performance goal orientation (APGO)**.[59]

Goal orientation is important because it can influence cognitive, affective, and motivational processes as well as skill acquisition, learning, and task performance. Trainees who have learning goals have been found to have higher intrinsic motivation, self-efficacy, self-set goals, and metacognitive activity, and these factors are all related to learning and performance.[60]

Although individuals differ in their goal orientations, goal setting can involve learning goals as well as performance goals. **Learning goals** are process-oriented and focus on the learning process. They enhance understanding of the task and the use of task strategies. **Performance goals** are outcome-oriented goals that focus on the achievement of specific performance outcomes.

As indicated earlier, challenging and specific goals that are accompanied by performance feedback have been shown to result in higher performance. However, high-performance goals are not always the most effective. For example, recall from the discussion on the stages of learning and resource allocation theory that goal setting can be harmful for learning during the declarative stage, when trainees' attention and cognitive resources are required to learn the task. Setting high-performance goals can interfere with learning because they force trainees to focus on the outcomes of their effort rather than on learning. This is especially a concern for learning complex tasks in situations in which trainees lack the knowledge and skill to perform the task and require all of their cognitive resources for learning. Setting a high-performance goal is more effective for tasks that are less complex and more routine and straightforward.

Learning goals, however, are especially important for learning new tasks because individuals must first acquire knowledge and learn strategies needed to perform a task. When learning to perform a new task, setting a difficult performance outcome goal has

Goal orientation
A dispositional or situational goal preference in achievement situations

Learning goal orientation (LGO)
A focus on developing competence by acquiring new skills and mastering new tasks

Prove performance goal orientation (PPGO)
A focus on favourable judgments from others for one's performance outcomes

Avoid performance goal orientation (APGO)
A focus on avoiding negative judgments from others for one's performance outcomes

Learning goals
Process-oriented goals that focus on the learning process

Performance goals
Outcome-oriented goals that focus on the achievement of specific performance outcomes

been found to be detrimental for performance. This is because performance goals can detract attention from learning. Thus, during the learning process a specific, difficult learning goal should be set, as this has been shown to result in higher self-efficacy and performance. Once an individual has acquired the knowledge and skills necessary to perform a new task, he/she can focus on performance goals.[61]

IMPLICATIONS FOR TRAINING Goal-setting theory has a number of implications for training. For example, prior to a training program trainees should have specific and challenging goals for learning, and they should be given feedback during and after the training program so that they know whether they have achieved their goals. Setting specific and challenging goals should improve trainees' motivation to learn as well as their performance on the training task. Thus, as described in Chapter 1, in practice it is important to set SMART goals.

However, it should be kept in mind that setting high-performance goals during the declarative stage of learning can be detrimental for learning, especially for complex tasks. Therefore, special attention needs to be given to the stage at which goals are set and the complexity of the task. In addition, attention must also be given to the type of goal. For tasks that are novel and complex, a distal goal should be accompanied with proximal goals. Proximal goals should be set for knowledge and skill acquisition during training.

Research on goal orientation suggests that trainers should consider the goal orientation of trainees and the type of goals that are set for training. Learning goals that focus on skill development are particularly important for learning, especially for individuals who have a performance goal orientation and need to be assigned learning goals. Thus, trainers should emphasize the importance of learning and the need to focus on learning goals during training. High learning goals appear to be especially important for challenging tasks and when new skills must be learned. Setting high-performance goals for a task that is still being learned can be detrimental for learning and performance. Therefore, learning goals should be set for learning new tasks and performance goals for motivating performance once learning and task mastery have been achieved.

// TRAINING MOTIVATION

As indicated earlier, learning and the effectiveness of training programs is influenced by motivation. In this section, we focus on the role of motivation in training. In particular, we introduce the concept of *training motivation* and describe the predictors and consequences of trainees' motivation to learn.

Training motivation (also known as motivation to learn) refers to the direction, intensity, and persistence of learning-directed behaviour in training contexts. Research has found that training motivation predicts learning and training outcomes, and it is influenced by individual and situational factors.[62]

Among the individual factors that predict training motivation, personality variables and factors associated with one's job and career are important. Personality variables that predict training motivation include locus of control, achievement motivation, anxiety, and conscientiousness.

Locus of control refers to people's beliefs about whether their behaviour is controlled mainly by internal or external forces. Persons with an internal locus of control

Training motivation
The direction, intensity, and persistence of learning-directed behaviour in training contexts

Locus of control
People's beliefs about whether their behaviour is controlled mainly by internal or external forces

believe that the opportunity to control their own behaviour resides within themselves. Persons with an external locus of control believe that external forces determine their behaviour. Thus, internals perceive stronger links between the effort they put into something and the outcome or performance level they achieve. Persons with an internal locus of control tend to have higher levels of training motivation.

In addition, persons who are high in **achievement motivation** or the desire to perform challenging tasks and high on **conscientiousness** (responsible and achievement-oriented) also tend to have high training motivation. Persons with higher anxiety, however, tend to have lower training motivation. Self-efficacy is also positively related to training motivation.

Several job and career variables are also related to training motivation. For example, employees with higher **job involvement**—or the degree to which an individual identifies psychologically with work and the importance of work to their self-image—have higher training motivation. Organizational commitment and career planning and exploration are also associated with higher training motivation. Organizational factors such as supervisor support, peer support, and a positive climate also predict training motivation.

Training motivation has been found to be related to many training outcomes. For example, training motivation is positively related to declarative knowledge, skill acquisition, trainees' reactions to training, and the likelihood that trainees apply on the job what they learn in training (i.e., transfer of training). What's more, training motivation predicts training outcomes beyond the effects of cognitive ability.[63]

In summary, training motivation is an important factor in the training process that is related to many training outcomes. Training is more likely to be effective and result in learning, skill acquisition, and improved job performance when trainees have high levels of training motivation.

IMPLICATIONS FOR TRAINING There are several things that trainers and managers can do to ensure that trainees' training motivation is high. First, they can assess trainee personality to determine whether trainees are high on the personality factors that are related to training motivation (e.g., locus of control). Second, they can assess trainee motivation prior to a training program to ensure that trainees are motivated to learn, and select those trainees with high training motivation to attend a training program. In fact, this is what the auto finance company AmeriCredit does. Employees complete a motivation questionnaire that is used to predict their likelihood of success in learning from a training program.[64]

Trainers should also consider influencing some of the factors that predict training motivation in an effort to increase trainees' motivation to learn. For example, they might lower trainees' anxiety, increase self-efficacy, and improve trainee attitudes. Finally, trainers should consider situational factors that influence training motivation and ensure that supervisors and peers provide trainees with support and that there is a positive climate for learning and training.

// A MODEL OF TRAINING EFFECTIVENESS

In this final section of the chapter, we present a model of training effectiveness that highlights the linkages between training and learning and between learning and individual performance and organizational effectiveness.

Achievement motivation The desire to perform challenging tasks

Conscientiousness The degree to which a person is responsible and achievement-oriented

Job involvement The degree to which an individual identifies psychologically with work, and the importance of work to their self-image

Figure 2.2 presents a model of training effectiveness. Recall from Chapter 1 that *training* involves the acquisition of knowledge, skills, and abilities to improve performance on one's current job, and *development* involves the acquisition of knowledge, skills, and abilities required to perform future job responsibilities. Thus, the first important link in the model is from training and development to learning and retention. In other words, training and development leads to declarative knowledge, the acquisition of skills and abilities, and retention of learned material.

In addition to training and development, we also know that there are personal and individual factors that influence learning. Among the most important is cognitive ability. **Cognitive ability** is similar to intelligence. It reflects an individual's basic information-processing capacities and cognitive resources. It refers to the knowledge and skills an individual possesses and may include cognitive skills and psychomotor skills. Examples of cognitive skills include basic numeracy and literacy, the intelligence to learn complex rules and procedures, and so on. Cognitive ability (verbal comprehension, quantitative ability, and reasoning ability) determines how much and how quickly people learn; it is related to the ability to learn and to succeed on the job.[65]

Recall the earlier discussion of ACT theory and resource allocation theory, in which it was noted that cognitive ability is particularly important during the early stages of learning. In fact, research has consistently shown that general cognitive ability is a

For more information see Chapter 1, p. 7

Cognitive ability
An individual's basic information-processing capacities and cognitive resources

FIGURE 2.2

MODEL OF TRAINING EFFECTIVENESS

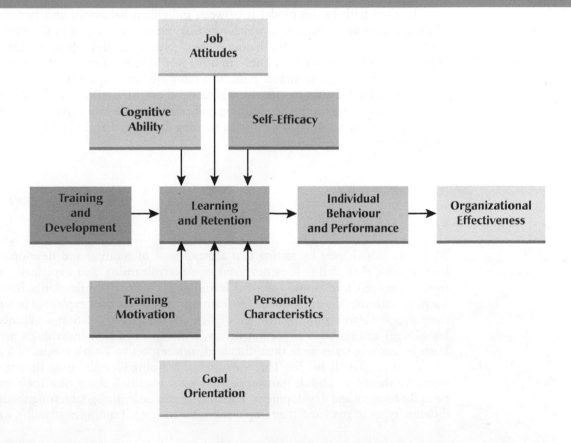

CHAPTER 2 Learning and Motivation

strong predictor of learning, training success, and job performance. It is an especially good predictor of job performance on complex jobs. In training research, cognitive ability has been found to predict declarative knowledge, skill acquisition, and the application of trained skills on the job.[66]

Training motivation is also a strong predictor of learning and training outcomes. Like cognitive ability, training motivation predicts declarative knowledge, skill acquisition, and the application of trained skills on the job. Self-efficacy, goal orientation, and personality characteristics also influence learning. Trainees with higher self-efficacy and a learning goal orientation are more likely to learn during training. In addition, trainees with an internal locus of control and a high need for achievement learn more during training.[67]

Another important personality variable is **core self-evaluations (CSE)** which represents an individual's self-appraisal of their worthiness, competence, and capability as a person. It is a broad personality variable that consists of four specific traits (general self-efficacy, self-esteem, locus of control, and emotional stability). CSE has been found to have direct and indirect effects on affective (e.g., self-efficacy), cognitive (e.g., declarative knowledge), and skill-based (e.g., proficiency) learning outcomes.[68]

An additional factor that can influence learning is trainees' attitudes. Three attitudinal variables that are important for learning are job involvement, job satisfaction, and organizational commitment. Employees with higher job attitudes are more likely to learn and apply what they learn in training on the job.[69]

The model also shows a path from learning to individual behaviour and performance. This is called transfer of training (see Chapter 9) and refers to the application of learning on the job. Employees must first learn and retain training content in order to change their behaviour and improve their job performance.

The final path in the model is between individual behaviour and performance and organizational effectiveness which was first introduced to you in Chapter 1 (see Figure 1.2). This path indicates that employees' behaviour and job performance will influence organizational effectiveness. In other words, more effective employee behaviours and higher job performance result in a more effective organization.

In summary, the training effectiveness model shows how training and development and individual factors influence learning and retention. We will expand and develop the model in Chapter 4 when we discuss training design and again in Chapter 9 when we discuss the transfer of training.

Core self-evaluations (CSE)
An individual's self-appraisal of their worthiness, competence, and capability as a person that consists of four specific traits (general self-efficacy, self-esteem, locus of control, and emotional stability)

// SUMMARY

We began this chapter by stating that a major goal of training and development is learning. We then defined learning and workplace learning and explained the difference between formal and informal learning. Then two classification schemes for learning outcomes were described. The learning process was then explained in terms of three stages of learning (declarative knowledge, knowledge compilation, and procedural knowledge) and resource allocation theory. Differences in how individuals prefer to learn or learning styles were then discussed with respect to Kolb's model of learning styles and the VARK model. Three theories of learning (conditioning theory, social cognitive theory, and adult learning theory) were described along with their implications for training and development. The chapter also described goal setting theory and different types of goals and their implications for training. Training motivation was also discussed, along with its predictors and consequences. The chapter concluded with a model of training effectiveness that shows the linkages between training and development, individual factors, trainee attitudes, learning and retention, individual behaviour and performance, and organizational effectiveness.

KEY TERMS

achievement motivation p. 64
ACT theory p. 48
andragogy p. 58
avoid performance goal orientation (APGO) p. 62
chaining p. 54
cognitive ability p. 65
conscientiousness p. 64
core self-evaluations (CSE) p. 66
declarative knowledge p. 48
distal goal p. 61
Fleming's learning style p. 51
formal learning p. 42
generalization p. 54
goal p. 61
goal orientation p. 62
Informal learning p. 42
job involvement p. 64
knowledge compilation p. 49
Kolb's learning style p. 50
learning p. 42
learning cycle p. 51
learning goal orientation (LGO) p. 62
learning goals p. 62
learning style p. 50
locus of control p. 63
motivation p. 61
observation p. 55
pedagogy p. 58
performance goals p. 62
procedural knowledge p. 49
prove performance goal orientation (PPGO) p. 62
proximal goal p. 61
resource allocation theory p. 48
self-efficacy p. 56
self-regulated learning p. 56
self-regulation p. 56
self-regulation prompts p. 57
shaping p. 54
social learning, p. 55
training motivation p. 63
VARK p. 51
Workplace learning p. 42
70–20–10 model p. 42

DISCUSSION QUESTIONS

1. Given the importance of motivation for learning and training outcomes, what should trainers do to ensure that trainees are motivated to learn? What should managers do? Discuss the pros and cons of different approaches.

2. What are the differences between pedagogy and andragogy, and what are the implications of each model for the design of training programs?

3. Discuss Kolb's and Fleming's models of learning styles and their implications for the design of training programs. What are the similarities and differences between the two models? Using each model, describe how training programs should be designed for learners with different learning styles?

4. What are the sources of information that influence self-efficacy? How can trainers improve trainees' self-efficacy? How can supervisors improve trainees' self-efficacy? What can trainees do to improve their own self-efficacy?

5. What are the three stages of learning according to ACT theory? Give an example of how a training program might be designed according to ACT theory.

6. If an instructor of one of your courses wanted to maximize student learning, what should he/she do according to conditioning theory, social cognitive theory, and adult learning theory? If he/she wanted to motivate students to attend class and learn, what should he/she do according to goal-setting theory?

7. Discuss how goal-setting theory can be used to improve trainee learning in a training program. What kind of goal should be set for trainees? Discuss the relevance of task complexity, goal orientation, and type of goal (proximal and distal).

8. Compare and contrast the two learning outcomes classification schemes in Table 2.1. How are they similar and how do they differ?

9. Based on the description at the beginning of the chapter of Abbott Point of Care's apprenticeship training program, what are some of the learning outcomes that the program is designed to achieve? What activities are being used to achieve each learning outcome? Use both classification schemes in Table 2.1 to answer this question.

10. Describe what self-regulation is and how it can help trainees learn during training. How can self-regulated learning be encouraged during training, and what effect might this have on trainees?

11. What are the six core principles of adult learning theory and what are the implications of each of them for the design of training and development programs?

12. What is the difference between formal and informal learning, and what can organizations do to facilitate informal learning? What are the advantages and disadvantages of formal and informal learning?

THE GREAT TRAINING DEBATE

1. Debate the following: Given that cognitive ability (or training motivation) is a strong predictor of learning, only trainees with high cognitive ability (or high training motivation) should be allowed to attend training programs, since those with low cognitive ability (or low training motivation) are not likely to learn or benefit from training.

2. Debate the following: When it comes to learning, the only thing that really matters is a person's cognitive ability.

3. Debate the following: Given that so much learning in the workplace is informal, formal learning programs are no longer necessary. Organizations should emphasize informal learning and reduce their spending on formal training programs.

EXERCISES

IN-CLASS

1. You have a friend whose grandmother is about to attend a training program on how to use computers, and she has very low self-efficacy about her ability to learn and to use a computer. Describe some of the things your friend should do prior to the training program to increase her grandmother's self-efficacy.

2. Consider Kolb's four learning modes and styles and how they might apply to your course on training and development or another course you are taking. How should the course be designed so it follows Kolb's learning cycle (concrete experience, reflective observation, abstract conceptualization, and active experimentation)? Be specific about what the instructor will have students do at each stage of the learning cycle. Now consider Fleming's VARK model. How should the course be designed so that it is multimodal?

3. Using the material on goal-setting theory, set a goal for your training and development course. That is, set a specific and challenging goal that you will be committed to. In addition, determine how and when you will be able to obtain feedback. Be sure to also set a learning goal, a performance goal, a proximal goal, and distal goal. Once you have set your goals, meet with another member of the class to review and evaluate each other's goals for the course.

4. Consider a course you are currently taking and examine it in terms of adult learning theory. To what extent does your course incorporate the principles of adult learning theory? Which aspects of the course incorporate adult learning theory and which aspects do not? If you were to redesign the course to make it more consistent with the principles of adult learning theory, what are some of the things you would change?

5. Training motivation is an important predictor of training outcomes, so it is important that trainers ensure trainees' training motivation is high. You might have noticed how your own training motivation influences your learning and performance in a course or training program. What are some of the things that a trainer or course instructor should do so that trainees' training motivation is high? Be sure to consider individual and situational factors.

6. Review the model of training effectiveness in Figure 2.2. Assess your potential learning and retention of a course you are currently taking by evaluating yourself as best you can on each of the predictors in the model (i.e., cognitive ability, attitudes, self-efficacy, goal orientation, personality characteristics, and training motivation). Based on your assessment, how successful will your learning and retention of the course material be? What predictors can you try to change to enhance your learning and retention of the course material?

7. Review the material on self-regulation in the chapter and then design a self-regulation training program to help you learn and improve a skill or behaviour that you want to improve (i.e., making presentations, time management, exercising, quitting smoking, etc.). Once you have chosen a skill or behaviour, prepare a self-regulation program. Be specific about what exactly you are going to do at each step in the process (i.e., how and when you will observe and keep track of your behaviour and observe the behaviour of others; set specific goals; when you will practise and rehearse the desired behaviours; how you will keep track of your progress; and how you will reward yourself for goal achievement). Once you have prepared your program, meet with another member of the class to review and evaluate each other's self-regulation program.

8. Technocell Canada (TCC) is a subsidiary of the German group Felix Schoeller Holding, the world's largest producer of photographic and décor paper. After implementing a training program, the benefits listed below were realized. Use Gagné's learning outcomes classification scheme as well as Kraiger, Ford, and Salas' to classify each of the benefits:

   • improved literacy and numeracy skills
   • enhanced understanding by machine operators, managers, and supervisors of the importance of basic skills in the workplace
   • improved attitudes and behaviour, and a stronger sense of community in the workplace
   • enhanced teamwork
   • improved employee motivation to do better and take pride in their work
   • improved ability of employees to troubleshoot
   • improved workplace safety record
   • increased self-confidence, self-esteem, and activity in the workplace and community

9. Make a list of three to five of the most important things you learned on a current or previous job. Once you have made your learning list, indicate how you learned each item on your list. Was it through formal or informal learning? Be specific about the formal or informal activities that contributed to your learning. What does your list tell you about learning in organizations? What should you do if you want to improve your learning in the future? What should organizations do?

10. As a student, you spend a great deal of time learning. But how exactly do you learn? Make a list of the formal and informal ways you learn. Do you learn more from formal or informal methods? If you want to improve your learning, what are some of the things you might do? Be specific in terms of both formal and informal ways to improve your learning.

IN-THE-FIELD

1. Contact the human resource department of your own or another organization to discuss the organization's training programs. Find out the extent to which the principles and components of the following learning theories are used to improve trainees' learning: conditioning theory, social cognitive theory, and adult learning theory. What principles and components of each theory are being used for training and what can the HR area do to improve trainee learning?

2. What is your VARK learning style? To find out, go to http://vark-learn.com/the-vark-questionnaire/ and complete the VARK questionnaire.

Answer the following questions:

a. What are your VARK results?

b. What is your learning style? What does this tell you about how you prefer to learn?

c. What are the implications of the results for how you learn? Identify learning strategies that match your VARK preference by going to http://vark-learn.com/strategies/ and clicking on the links for your learning style(s). What strategies can you use to improve your learning?

d. How can the information from VARK questionnaire be used by trainers to improve learning and the effectiveness of training programs?

e. How can this information help you to learn better and improve your learning outcomes in your courses and in training programs?

3. Conduct an interview with several people you know who are currently employed. Interview them about how they learn in their organization. Ask questions about how and what they have learned through formal and informal learning opportunities. Based on their responses, answer the following questions:

a. Did they learn more from formal or informal learning?

b. Did they have more formal or informal opportunities for learning?

c. Which type of learning was most effective for them, formal or informal learning?

d. What did they learn from formal and informal learning? Did they learn similar or different things from each?

e. What kinds of practices were used in their organization for formal and informal learning?

f. What can you conclude about how people learn in organizations and the use and effectiveness of informal and formal learning in organizations?

CASE INCIDENT

MANAGEMENT TRAINING AT IKEA

IKEA is a Sweden-based home furnishings chain with stores in Canada and the United States. A single store can have 40 managers, making the task of training enough new managers quickly and well a challenge. To get managers trained for new store openings, IKEA has established certain stores as centres of excellence. These centres of excellence become learning sites for one or more management competencies that managers must master.

Manager trainees have a carefully developed, objectives-based curriculum and access to a 17-module online learning program that covers the basics of each of nine management competencies. Once a trainee has mastered the learning material and a series of practicum assignments, he or she is eligible to be certified as successful by the competence centre store manager. Trainees can be at a competence centre for two to six weeks depending on the competency to be mastered and number of competencies to be mastered at each centre.

Part of the process involves shadowing successful managers. This is followed by two weeks of classroom training at IKEA Business College, where managers are introduced to the philosophies and theories behind IKEA store operations. They get exposed to the "big picture," the theory of how the company operates, and what the IKEA vision is all about. Six months after a location opens, managers begin rotating back to Business College for advanced store operations training.

QUESTIONS

1. What are the learning outcomes of the IKEA manager training program? What do managers learn and how do they learn?

2. To what extent does the manager training program follow the learning process and stages of learning according to ACT theory? What changes, if any, would you suggest and why?

3. Discuss Kolb's learning styles, modes, and cycle with respect to the manager training program. To what extent does the program incorporate Kolb's four learning modes and follow the learning cycle? What changes, if any, would you make to the program so that it includes all four learning modes and adheres to Kolb's learning cycle?

Source: Zemke, R. (2004). Training top 100: Editor's choice: IKEA U.S.A. *Training Magazine*, *41*(3), 70. Trainingmag.com

| CASE STUDY | THE PERFORMANCE APPRAISAL TRAINING PROGRAM |

Nurse supervisors at a large hospital seldom conducted performance appraisal interviews and some refused to do them. They complained that there was no time to meet with every nurse, and that it was a difficult, time-consuming, and unpleasant process that was a big waste of time. Some were uncomfortable with the process and found it to be stressful for everybody involved. They said it caused a lot of anxiety for them and the nurses.

However, the administration was in the process of introducing a new model of nursing that required all nurses to perform certain critical behaviours when interacting with and counselling patients and their families. It was therefore imperative that performance appraisals be conducted to ensure that nurses were implementing the new model of nursing and performing these critical behaviours.

The nurse supervisors would be required to evaluate their nurses' performance every six months and then conduct a performance appraisal interview with each nurse in which the previous six months' performance would be discussed. An action plan would then be developed with specific goals for improvement.

The administration decided to hire a performance management consultant to provide a one-day workshop on how to conduct performance appraisals for all nurse supervisors. The training program was mandatory and all nurse supervisors had to attend. Many of them did so reluctantly, complaining that it would be a waste of time and that it would not make any difference in how things were done in the hospital.

The training program began with a lecture on performance management and how to conduct performance appraisal interviews. The consultant first explained that the purpose of a performance appraisal interview is to give feedback to employees on how well they are performing their jobs and then plan for future growth and development. He then discussed different types of performance appraisal interviews such as the "tell-and-sell interview," the "tell-and-listen interview," and the "problem-solving interview." This was followed by a list of guidelines on how to conduct effective interviews, such as asking the employee to do a self-assessment, focusing on behaviour not the person, minimizing criticism, focusing on problem solving, and being supportive. The trainees were then instructed on how to set goals and develop an action plan for improvement.

After the lecture, the trainees were asked to participate in a role play in which they would take turns playing the part of a supervisor and an employee. They were provided with information about a nurse's job performance to discuss in the role play and then develop an action plan. However, some of the trainees left the session, refusing to participate. Others did not take it seriously and made a joke out of it. There was a lot of laughing and joking throughout this part of the program After the role play there was a group discussion about the role play followed by a review of the key points to remember when conducting performance appraisal interviews.

Although the supervisors were supposed to begin conducting performance reviews and interviews shortly after the training program, very few actually did. Some said they tried to do them but could not find time to interview all of their nurses. Others said that they followed the consultant's guidelines but they did not see any improvement in how they conducted interviews or in how nurses reacted to them. Some said it continued to be a stressful experience that was uncomfortable for them and the nurses, so they decided to stop doing them.

One year later, performance appraisals were still a rare occurrence at the hospital. Furthermore, many of the nurses were not practising the new nursing model and, as a result, nursing care and performance were inconsistent throughout the hospital and often unsatisfactory.

QUESTIONS

1. Consider Gagné's learning outcomes for the performance appraisal training program. What were the expected learning outcomes of the training program and what did trainees learn? What learning outcomes were not learned? What learning outcomes should have been the focus of the training program?

2. Explain the success of the training program using conditioning theory and social cognitive theory. How do these theories explain why the training program was not more effective? How could the program be improved by using some of the concepts, principles, and components of each theory?

3. Discuss the extent to which adult learning theory principles were incorporated into the training program. Which principles were included and which ones were absent? What could the consultant have done differently to make better use of adult learning theory?

4. Describe the training program in terms of Kolb's learning styles and the VARK model learning styles. What aspects of the program relate to each of the modes and styles of learning from Kolb's model and the VARK model? What trainee learning style or styles are most likely to benefit from the program, and which ones are not likely to benefit? How could the program be changed to make better use of Kolb's learning cycle? How could the program be changed to make it multimodal?

5. Describe the supervisors' training motivation. What effect did their training motivation have on the success of the training program? What factors that influence training motivation should be considered to improve supervisors' training motivation? What are some things the consultant might have done to make sure that the trainees' were motivated to learn?

FLASHBACK QUESTIONS

1. Explain how the performance appraisal training program can benefit the hospital, employees, patients, and society. What are the potential consequences of an ineffective training program for the hospital, patients, employees, and society?

2. To what extent has the performance appraisal training program followed the instructional systems design (ISD) model of training and development? If you were to redesign the program, what changes would you make based on the ISD model?

FLASH FORWARD QUESTION

1. If a needs analysis is a process to identify gaps or deficiencies in employee and organizational performance, what is the gap at the hospital and what additional information would be helpful to learn about the nature of the gap and possible solutions for closing it? Do you think there might be other solutions for closing the gap besides training? If so, what are they? Is training a good solution for closing the gap?

REWRITE THE CASE QUESTION: KOLB'S LEARNING CYCLE

Rewrite the case to describe the consultant providing the training using Kolb's learning cycle. In other words, write a paragraph in which you illustrate the consultant's use of each of Kolb's modes of learning in the proper sequence. Be sure to indicate exactly what the consultant is doing when using each mode of learning.

QUESTIONS

Refer to the case at the end of Chapter 1 to answer the following questions.

1. What learning outcomes will be most important for a training program for pool operators and employees? Discuss the extent to which each of Gagné's learning outcomes will be relevant. Refer to the Kraiger, Ford, and Salas' learning outcomes and describe the relevance of each of their learning outcomes for the training of pool operators and employees. What learning outcomes should be the focus of a standardized training program for pool operators and employees? Explain your answer.

2. What principles from conditioning theory and social cognitive theory will be important for training pool operators and employees? Explain your answer.

3. Explain how the principles from adult learning theory can be used to train pool operators and employees. What aspects of adult learning theory would you want to include in the training program?

4. Describe how research on training motivation can be used to motivate pool operators and employees to attend training and learn and apply the training material on the job. What do you think will be most important to increase training motivation? Explain your answer.

5. To what extent can formal and informal learning improve the health and safety of pools and hot tubs? What type of learning would you recommend and why? Can formal learning be effective without informal learning? Can informal learning be effective without formal learning?

// REFERENCES

1. Lewis, C. (2014, March 24). Keeping your employees up with the times—Free of charge. *Canadian HR Reporter*, *27*(6), 22; Abbott. (2013, August 28). Abbott launches a new apprenticeship program for its Ottawa-based manufacturing sector [Media release]. Retrieved from http://www.abbott.ca/docs/2013_Abbott_Point_of_Care_Apprenticeship_Release-Aug28-2013.pdf.

2. Hinrichs, J. R. (1976). Personnel training. In M. D. Dunnette (Ed.), *Handbook of industrial and organizational psychology* (pp. 829–860). Skokie, IL: Rand McNally; Gagné, R. M. (1984). Learning outcomes and their effects: Useful categories of human performance. *American Psychologist*, *39*, 377–385.

3. Hinrichs (1976), p. 833.

4. Park, Y., & Jacobs, R. (2011). The influence of investment in workplace learning on learning outcomes and organizational performance. *Human Resource Development Quarterly*, *22*, 437–458.

5. Biech, E. (2016, December). The 90% solution. *TD: Talent Development*, *70*(12), 58–63.

6. Stamps, D. (1998). Learning ecologies. *Training, 35*(1), 32–38; Roseman, E. (2001, August 29). Delta Hotels knows how to keep workers. *Toronto Star*, p. E2.

7. Day, N. (1998). Informal learning gets results. *Workforce Management, 77*(6), 31–35; Dobbs, K. (2000). Simple moments of learning. *Training, 37*(1), 52–58; Lavis, C. (2011). *Learning and development outlook 2011: Are organizations ready for learning 2.0?* Ottawa: The Conference Board of Canada; Hall, C. (2014). *Learning and development outlook–12th edition: Strong learning organizations, strong leadership.* Ottawa: The Conference Board of Canada.

8. Day (1998).

9. Stamps (1998); Dobbs (2000).

10. Livingstone, D. W., & Scholtz, A. (2006). *Work and lifelong learning in Canada: Basic findings of the 2004 WALL survey.* Toronto: Ontario Institute for Studies in Education.

11. Paradise, A. (2008). Informal learning: Overlooked or overhyped? *T+D, 62*(7), 52–53.

12. Kraiger, K., Ford, J. K., & Salas, E. (1993). Application of cognitive, skill-based, and affective theories of learning outcomes to new methods of training evaluation. *Journal of Applied Psychology, 78*, 311–328.

13. Gagné (1984).

14. Zemke, R. (1999). Toward a science of training. *Training, 36*(7), 32–36.

15. Kraiger et al. (1993).

16. Kraiger et al. (1993).

17. Kanfer, R., & Ackerman, P. L. (1989). Motivation and cognitive abilities: An integrative/aptitude-treatment interaction approach to skill acquisition. *Journal of Applied Psychology, 74*, 657–690.

18. Carter, M., & Beier, M. E. (2010). The effectiveness of error management training with working-aged adults. *Personnel Psychology, 63*, 641–675.

19. Kanfer & Ackerman (1989).

20. Kolb, D. A. (1984). *Experiential learning.* Englewood Cliffs, NJ: Prentice-Hall.

21. Kolb (1984).

22. Kolb (1984).

23. Whetten, D. A., & Cameron, K. S. (2002). *Developing management skills* (5th ed.). Upper Saddle River, NJ: Prentice Hall.

24. Hawk, T. F., & Shah, A. J. (2007). Using learning style instruments to enhance student learning. *Decision Sciences Journal of Innovative Education, 5*, 1–19; Leite, W. L., Svinicki, M., & Shi, Y. (2010). Attempted validation of the scores of the VARK: Learning styles inventory with multitrait-multimethod confirmatory factor analysis models. *Educational and Psychological Measurement, 70*, 32–339.

25. Hawk & Shah (2007); Leite, Svinicki, & Shi (2010).

26. Hawk & Shah (2007); Leite, Svinicki, & Shi (2010).

27. Hawk & Shah (2007).

28. Barbian, J. (2002). Training top 100: AmeriCredit. *Training, 39*(3), 46–47.

29. Hawk & Shah (2007).

30. Delahoussaye, M. (2001). Training top 50: Capital One. *Training, 38*(3), 70–71.

31. Fleming, N. D., & Mills, C. (1992). Not another inventory, rather a catalyst for reflection. *To Improve the Academy, 11*, 137–155.

32. Skinner, B. F. (1953). *Science and human behavior.* New York: McMillan.

33. Delahoussaye (2001).

34. Pearce, J. M. (1987). A model of stimulus generalization in Pavlovian conditioning. *Psychological Review, 94*, 61–73.

35. Lavis, C. (2011). *Learning and development outlook 2011: Are organizations ready for learning 2.0?* Ottawa: The Conference Board of Canada.

36. Bandura, A. (1986). *Social foundations of thought and action: A social cognitive theory.* Englewood Cliffs, NJ: Prentice-Hall.

37. Luthans, F., & Davis, T. (1983). Beyond modelling: Managing social learning processes in human resource training and development. In C. Baird, E. Schneier, & D. Laird (Eds.), *The training and development sourcebook.* Amherst, MA: Human Resource Development Press.

38. McLaughlin, K. (2001). Training top 50: Edward Jones. *Training, 38*(3), 78–79.

39. Bandura, A. (1997). *Self-efficacy: The exercise of control.* New York: W. H. Freeman.

40. Bandura (1997).

41. Haccoun, R. R., & Saks, A. M. (1998). Training in the twenty-first century: Some lessons from the last one. *Canadian Psychology, 39*, 33–51.

42. Sitzmann, T., & Ely, K. (2011). A meta-analysis of self-regulated learning in work-related training and educational attainment: What we know and where we need to go. *Psychological Bulletin, 137*, 421–442.

43. Sitzmann & Ely (2011).

44. Sitzmann, T., & Johnson, S. K. (2012). The best laid plans: Examining the conditions under which a planning intervention improves learning and reduces attrition. *Journal of Applied Psychology, 97*, 967–981.

45. Bandura (1986).

46. Frayne, C. A., & Latham, G. P. (1987). Application of social learning theory to employee self-management of attendance. *Journal of Applied Psychology, 72*, 387–392; Latham, G. P., & Frayne, C. A. (1989). Self-management training for increasing job attendance: A follow-up and a replication. *Journal of Applied Psychology, 74*, 411–416.

47. Gist, M. E., Stevens, C. K., & Bavetta, A. G. (1991). Effects of self-efficacy and post-training intervention on the acquisition and maintenance of complex interpersonal skills. *Personnel Psychology, 44*, 837–861; Sitzmann & Ely (2011).

48. Sitzmann, T., Bell, B. S., Kraiger, K., & Kanar, A. M. (2009). A multilevel analysis of the effect of prompting self-regulation in technology-delivered

instruction. *Personnel Psychology, 62,* 697–734; Sitzmann, T., & Ely, K. (2010). Sometimes you need a reminder: The effects of prompting self-regulation on regulatory processes, learning, and attrition. *Journal of Applied Psychology, 95,* 132–144.

49. Knowles, M. (1990). *The adult learner.* Houston, TX: Gulf.

50. Knowles, M. S., Holton, E. F. III, & Swanson, R. A. (2015). *The adult learner* (8th ed.). New York: Routledge.

51. Holton, E. F. III, Swanson Wilson, L., & Bates, R. A. (2009). Toward development of a generalized instrument to measure andragogy. *Human Resource Development Quarterly, 20,* 169–193.

52. Locke, E. A., & Latham, G. P. (2002). Building a practically useful theory of goal setting and task motivation. *American Psychologist, 57,* 705–717.

53. Locke, E. A., & Latham, G. P. (1990). *A theory of goal setting and task performance.* Englewood Cliffs, NJ: Prentice-Hall.

54. Locke & Latham (1990).

55. Seijts, G. H., & Latham, G. P. (2001). The effect of distal learning, outcome, and proximal goals on a moderately complex task. *Journal of Organizational Behavior, 22,* 291–307; Latham, G. P., & Seijts, G. H. (1999). The effects of proximal and distal goals on performance on a moderately complex task. *Journal of Organizational Behavior, 20,* 421–429.

56. Seijts & Latham (2001).

57. Brown, T. C. (2005). Effectiveness of distal and proximal goals as transfer-of-training interventions: A field experiment. *Human Resource Development Quarterly, 16,* 369–387.

58. Payne, S. C., Youngcourt, S. S., & Beaubien, J. M. (2007). A meta-analytic examination of the goal orientation nomological net. *Journal of Applied Psychology, 92,* 128–150.

59. Watson, A. M., Thompson, L. F., Rudolph, J. V., Whelan, T. J., Behrend, T. S., & Gissel, A. L. (2013). When big brother is watching: Goal orientation shapes reactions to electronic monitoring during online training. *Journal of Applied Psychology, 98,* 642–657.

60. Bell, B. S., & Kozlowski, S. W. J. (2008). Active learning: Effects of core training design elements on self-regulatory processes, learning, and adaptability. *Journal of Applied Psychology, 93,* 296–316; Cannon-Bowers, J. A., Rhodenizer, L., Salas, E., & Bowers, C. A. (1998). A framework for understanding pre-practice conditions and their impact on learning. *Personnel Psychology, 51,* 291–320; Payne et al. (2007).

61. Seijts & Latham (2001); VandeWalle, D., Cron, W. L., & Slocum, J. W., Jr. (2001). The role of goal orientation following performance feedback. *Journal of Applied Psychology, 86,* 629–640; VandeWalle, D., Brown, S. P., Cron, W. L., & Slocum, J. W., Jr. (1999). The influence of goal orientation and self-regulation tactics on sales performance: A longitudinal field test. *Journal of Applied Psychology, 84,* 249–259.

62. Colquitt, J. A., Lepine, A., & Noe, R. A. (2000). Toward an integrative theory of training motivation: A meta-analytic path analysis of 20 years of research. *Journal of Applied Psychology, 85,* 678–707.

63. Colquitt et al. (2000).

64. Barbian, J. (2002). Training top 100: AmeriCredit. *Training, 39*(3), 46–47.

65. Brown, K. G., & Sitzmann, T. (2011). Training and employee development for improved performance. In S. Zedeck (Ed.), *Handbook of industrial and organizational psychology* (Vol. 2, pp. 469–503). Washington, DC: American Psychological Association.

66. Colquitt et al. (2000).

67. Colquitt et al. (2000).

68. Stanhope, D. S., Pond, S. B. III, & Surface, E. A. (2013). Core self-evaluations and training effectiveness: Prediction through motivational intervening mechanisms. *Journal of Applied Psychology, 98*, 820–831.

69. Burke, L. A. (2001). Training transfer: Ensuring training gets used on the job. In L. A. Burke (Ed.), *High-impact training solutions: Top issues troubling trainers*. Westport, CT: Quorum Books; Colquitt et al. (2000).

3

THE NEEDS ANALYSIS PROCESS

CHAPTER LEARNING OUTCOMES

AFTER READING THIS CHAPTER, YOU SHOULD BE ABLE TO:

- define "needs analysis" and describe the needs analysis process
- explain how to conduct an organizational, a task, and a person analysis as well as a cognitive task analysis and a team task analysis
- describe how to determine solutions to performance problems and when training is the best solution for a performance problem
- compare and contrast different methods and sources for conducting a needs analysis
- describe the obstacles to conducting a needs analysis and how to conduct a rapid needs analysis

Several years ago, TD Bank became concerned about the growing number of robberies at its branches. It was clear that something had to be done to protect employees and customers. The first thing they did was conduct a needs analysis that included focus groups, interviews, and surveys.

The needs analysis revealed the need to design a training program that would focus not just on robbery prevention but also on what happens afterward. An outline was developed for a training program that centred on three areas: the most common types of robberies, what happens during robbery attempts, and what processes and behaviours are considered best practices in the financial sector.

The objectives of the training program were to reduce the number of robberies, enhance risk-management practices, improve robbery prevention, and reduce financial losses. The instructional designers worked with external subject-matter experts and networks to determine learning objectives. They also partnered with the RCMP and an armed robbery association in the United States to ensure there was a good North America–wide perspective.

The various components were designed, reviewed, deployed, and tested, and the program was piloted with trainers; a train-the-trainer leader's guide was developed, followed by train-the-trainer sessions.

The course content includes strategy tools; tactics for robbery prevention; procedures and actions to follow during a robbery; employee and customer safety standards procedures; documentation and communication strategies; and tips, tactics, and tools for dealing with trauma.

The training program uses a blended learning approach that includes e-learning, in-branch training sessions, and ongoing coaching. The e-learning course focuses on what to do before, during, and after a robbery, and it includes video clips. The e-learning takes about 30 minutes and has to be completed before the in-branch training. Employees also take a test that requires them to achieve a score of 80 percent to receive credit for the course.

TD Bank's Robbery Prevention and Awareness training program won a silver award for training excellence from the Institute for Performance and Learning.

The in-branch training program reviews the key learning points from the e-learning training, and includes role plays and debriefing sessions. A second in-branch session is provided six months later. In addition, each year employees are required to review the e-learning course, including a "What's New" section. Once the training is completed, participants and stakeholders give quantitative and qualitative formal evaluations.

More than 21 000 employees have completed the Robbery Prevention and Awareness training program and are now better prepared to face a robbery situation. TD has seen a reduction in the number of robberies, enhanced risk management practices and procedures, improved prevention through ongoing vigilance, and improved the safety of customers and employees. In addition, there was a 41 percent reduction in cash losses and an 11 percent decrease in the number of robberies. In addition, TD's Robbery Prevention and Awareness training program won a silver award for training excellence from the Institute for Performance and Learning.[1]

Source: Dobson, S. (2010, November 29). Learning to avoid the bad guys. *Canadian HR Reporter, 23*(21), p. 24. Reprinted by permission of *Canadian HR Reporter*. © Copyright Thomson Reuters Canada Ltd., 2010, Toronto, Ontario, 1-800-387-5164. Web: www.hrreporter.com.

// INTRODUCTION

TD's Robbery Prevention and Awareness training program highlights an important aspect of the training and development process. It shows how organization concerns often lead to the need for training, and how a needs analysis is first required to determine who needs training and what type of training they need. In addition, it shows that a needs analysis has implications for training objectives, training content, training methods, and training evaluation. As you can tell from this example, needs analysis is a critical first step in the training and development process.

In Chapter 1 you were introduced to the instructional systems design (ISD) model of training and development, which depicts training and development as a rational and scientific process that consists of three major steps: needs analysis, design and delivery, and evaluation. The process involves an analysis of current performance and ends with improved performance. The critical first step in the ISD model is a needs analysis to determine the nature of the problem and whether training is the best solution. A needs analysis is performed to determine the difference or gap between the way things are and the way things should be. In this chapter, you will learn about the needs analysis process and how to determine if training is the best solution to performance problems.

For more information see
Chapter 1, pp. 23–26

// WHAT IS A NEEDS ANALYSIS?

Needs analysis (also known as needs assessment) is the cornerstone and foundation of training and development. In fact, it is often referred to as the most important step in the training and development process.[2]

Needs analysis is a process designed to identify gaps or deficiencies in employee and organizational performance. Needs analysis is concerned with the gaps between actual performance and desired performance. It is a "formal process of identifying needs as gaps between current and desired results, placing those needs in priority order based on the cost to meet each need versus the cost of ignoring it, and selecting the most important needs (problems or opportunities) for reduction or elimination."[3]

While a **need** is a gap between the way things are (current results) versus the way they should be (desired results), needs analysis is the process to identify gaps or deficiencies in individual, group, or organizational performance. The way to identify performance gaps is to solicit information from those who are affected by the performance problem. A needs analyst gathers information from key people in an organization about the organization, jobs, and employees to determine the nature of performance problems. This information identifies the problem, which is the difference between the way the work is being done and the most cost-effective way of doing it. In the simplest terms, needs = required results – current results.[4]

The goal of needs analysis is to identify the difference between what is and what is desired or required in terms of results, and to compare the magnitude of gaps against the cost of reducing them or ignoring them. Obviously, performance gaps could be the result of many factors, and the solutions might include training as well as other interventions. A thorough needs analysis can help an organization prioritize its needs and make informed decisions about what problems need to be resolved. Thus, needs analysis identifies, prioritizes, and selects needs that will affect internal and external stakeholders.[5] Needs analysis helps to identify the causes of and solutions to performance problems.

Needs analysis
A process to identify gaps or deficiencies in employee and organizational performance

Need
A gap between current and desired results

// THE NEEDS ANALYSIS PROCESS

Figure 3.1 shows that needs analysis is a process that consists of a series of interrelated steps. As described in Chapter 1, the process starts with an "itch" or a problem. If the performance problem is important, stakeholders are consulted and a needs analysis is conducted. There are three levels of needs analysis: an organizational analysis, a task analysis, and a person analysis. The collection of information and the needs analysis process conclude with a number of important outcomes.

For more information see Chapter 1, p. 25

FIGURE 3.1

THE NEEDS ANALYSIS PROCESS

Concern

↓

Important?

Yes   No → Terminate

↓

Consult Stakeholders

↓

Collect Information

Organizational Analysis	**Task Analysis**	**Person Analysis**
1. Strategic alignment 2. Environment 3. Resource analysis 4. Organizational context	1. Identify target jobs 2. Obtain description 3. Develop rating scales 4. Survey incumbents 5. Analyze and interpret information 6. Provide feedback	1. Define desired performance 2. Determine gap 3. Identify obstacles

Outcomes

1. Performance gaps
2. Solutions to performance gaps
3. Where training is needed
4. The type of training needed
5. Who needs to be trained
6. Specification of learning objectives
7. How training should be designed and delivered
8. The development of criteria for evaluation

STEP ONE: A CONCERN

The process of identifying training needs originates slowly and informally with a concern. This concern is sometimes referred to as an itch or a pressure point—something that causes managers to notice it. This concern might be as subtle as noticing that employees are treating customers in an abrupt manner, or observing that employees are spending a lot of time asking one another for help with a new system. Other concerns might be recognizing a shift in regular activities, such as an increase in defective parts, accidents, or complaints.[6] TD Bank was concerned about the growing number of robberies and the safety of employees and customers.

In other cases, the concern might come from dangers on the job or perhaps an awareness of a skills gap. For example, a labour ministry inspector in Ontario ordered self-defence training and protective equipment for guards at the Roy McMurtry youth jail in Brampton following a series of violent attacks in which several guards were injured.[7] At Boston Pizza, the top casual dining chain in Canada, a growing skills gap among the company's store managers was noticed. Although managers were familiar with the Boston Pizza concept and had the necessary hard skills, they were lacking in soft skills because most of them came up through the ranks and had not had any formal management education. In order to remedy the soft-skills concern, the company launched Boston Pizza College, a classroom-based management training program.[8]

Sometimes the pressure comes from the external environment, such as when legislation regarding employee relations is changed, when the competition introduces a highly competitive service feature, or when problems that threaten public health and safety are recognized.

STEP TWO: IMPORTANCE

After a concern has been raised, the next step is to determine whether the concern is central to the effectiveness of the organization. The training manager must be aware of the strategic orientation of the organization. The goals; plans; introduction of products and services; and changes in technology, practices, and regulations should be clear. Human resource policies must be linked with the strategic directions of the company (as discussed in Chapter 1), and the training strategy should support the organization's efforts to achieve its goals.[9]

Another important concern is the cost implications of a problem. Does current performance cost the company in lost productivity or dissatisfied customers? If the performance problem is important, then there must be some way to demonstrate that correcting the problem will result in increased productivity or client satisfaction. A concern is important (i.e., worthy of further exploration and analysis) if it has an impact on outcomes that are important to the organization and its effectiveness. Clearly, bank robberies are a major concern to TD Bank and all financial institutions.

STEP THREE: CONSULT STAKEHOLDERS

The next step in the needs analysis process is to involve the stakeholders who have a vested interest in the process and outcomes. Support from key players in the organization is necessary from the beginning of the needs analysis process.

At a minimum, top management should understand the rationale for the needs analysis. Training analysts must obtain agreement on why the needs analysis is being done and who will be involved. Managerial expectations must be clarified.[10] Likewise, other stakeholders, such as employees or their collective representatives, should be consulted and included in the needs analysis process. All stakeholders must have input and buy into the needs analysis process to ensure that the data collection will result in accurate information and that they have a vested interest in the success of the program.

STEP FOUR: DATA COLLECTION

The next stage in the needs analysis process is the most extensive and involves the documentation of the concern through the collection of information from three levels of analysis. Recall from the chapter-opening vignette that before TD Bank's robbery prevention training program was designed and delivered, a needs analysis was conducted.

The three levels of needs analysis are the *organizational*, the *task*, and the *person* or *employee*. Although overlaps among the three areas of analysis occur, each plays a distinctive role. The analysis of the organization provides information about its strategies and context and answers the question *Where is training needed in the organization?* The task analysis provides information about the tasks and the relevant knowledge, skills, and abilities needed to perform selected jobs and answers the question *What knowledge, skills, and abilities are required to perform the job effectively?* A person analysis provides information about an employee's level of performance and answers the question *Who needs to be trained?*

NEEDS ANALYSIS OUTCOMES

At the beginning of this chapter we referred to needs analysis as the cornerstone of the training and development process. This is due in large part to the many outcomes of needs analysis, as shown in Figure 3.1.

The needs analysis results in a number of outcomes that set the stage for the rest of the training and development process. Besides clarifying the nature of performance gaps, a needs analysis helps to determine whether training and development is a good solution to performance problems or whether some other intervention might be more effective. If training and development is part of the solution, needs analysis information is used to determine where training is needed in the organization, what type of training is required, and who in the organization should receive training.

Needs analysis information is also used to write training objectives and to design training programs (e.g., what training content should be included in the training program, what training methods would be most effective, etc.). TD Bank's needs analysis indicated the need for a training program to focus on robbery prevention as well as on what happens after a robbery. Finally, the information from a needs analysis is used in the development of measures for training evaluation.

In summary, the needs analysis process helps to determine the best solution to performance problems and how to proceed if training is part of the solution. Later in the chapter we discuss a process for determining solutions to performance problems. In the following sections, we describe how to conduct an organizational, a task, and a person needs analysis.

// ORGANIZATIONAL ANALYSIS

Organizational analysis involves the study of the entire organization: its strategy, environment, resources, and context. An understanding of each of these components provides information not only for the identification of training needs, but also on the probability of the success of a training program. Key to an organizational analysis is finding out if a training program is aligned with an organization's strategy, the existence of any constraints, and the extent of support for the delivery and success of a training program. An organizational analysis can help identify potential constraints and problems that can derail a training program so that they can be dealt with prior to or during the design and delivery of a costly program. Let's take a closer look at each of the components of an organizational analysis.

STRATEGIC ALIGNMENT

Most organizations have a strategy that consists of the organization's mission, goals, and objectives, such as a dedication to quality or innovation. These broad statements trickle down to specific goals and objectives for each department or unit, and reflect an organization's plan for growth, adaptation, profitability, and survival.

In the past, an organization's strategy was set and implemented independently of the training and development function and human resources. However, it has become increasingly apparent that human resource functions such as training and development are essential to an organization's strategy and the accomplishment of its objectives. As a result, vice presidents and directors of human resources are now often involved in the setting of an organization's strategy, and the human resource function has become more strategic.

For more information see
Chapter 1, p. 20

In Chapter 1, we defined strategic human resource management (SHRM) as the alignment of human resource practices with an organization's business strategy. Although SHRM refers in general to the human resource system, it involves aligning specific HRM functions and activities with an organization's business strategy. In this regard, we can describe HR functions such as training and development as being strategic.

Strategic training and development (ST&D) involves the alignment of an organization's training needs and programs with an organization's strategy and objectives. You might recall from Chapter 1 that one of the organization benefits of training and development is facilitating and supporting an organization's strategy.

It is important to consider an organization's strategy during the needs analysis process so that training and development programs are consistent with an organization's strategy and are designed to help an organization achieve its goals and objectives. Thus, an organization's strategy should indicate the type and amount of training and development required. For example, at construction company EllisDon, the organization's strategic priorities are the basis for determining the competencies that employees will need to move the company forward. They make sure that training is aligned with business needs and the organization's strategic goals.[11]

Training is more likely to be effective and contribute to an organization's success and provide a competitive advantage when it is congruent or aligned with its business strategy. When training and development programs are designed and implemented in isolation of an organization's strategy, they are not likely to be effective in helping an organization achieve its goals.

As indicated in Chapter 1, there is some evidence that training can detract from an organization's bottom line and negatively impact shareholder value if it is not aligned with an organization's strategy. Training that is not linked to an organization's strategy can lower a company's market value.[12] To find out how one company aligns their training and development programs with their strategy, see Training Today 3.1, "Strategic Alignment at MillerCoors."

ENVIRONMENT

In Chapter 1, we described how training and development is embedded in the external environment and how factors in the environment can affect the organization, human resource practices, and training and development. The environment is dynamic and uncertain. New technologies, competitors, recessions, and trade agreements can profoundly affect not only the need for and content of training, but also employees' receptivity to being trained.

Training programs are often mandated and a direct result of government legislation and regulations (such as safety regulations, bullying, harassment) as well as industry (e.g., trucking, financial) and organization policies (e.g., privacy, security) or what is generally known as **compliance training**. For example, occupational health and safety policies in British Columbia require employers to take steps to prevent or minimize workplace bullying and harassment. As a result, employees and supervisors must be trained on how to recognize the potential for bullying and harassment, how to respond to bullying and harassment, and procedures for reporting incidents of bullying and harassment.[13]

In Ontario, all workers and supervisors who are subject to the *Occupational Health and Safety Act* (OHSA) must complete a mandatory health and safety awareness training program introduced by the Ministry of Labour in 2014. The training program is designed to inform workers of their rights and responsibilities when it comes to workplace health and safety.[14] Organizations in Ontario must also provide all of their employees accessibility training on how to interact with people with different disabilities in accordance with the *Accessibility for Ontarians with Disabilities Act* (AODA).[15]

Sometimes training is mandated in response to public pressure over particular issues and concerns. For example, all new judges in Ontario are now required to undergo mandatory training on sexual assault issues. The mandatory training is a result of a number of cases from across the country in which judges made questionable comments and rulings in sexual assault cases.[16]

Besides legal and regulatory factors, organizations are also conscious of the strategies of their competitors and social concerns. For example, the nature of a training program can be a direct result of an organization's attempt to establish a new market niche, manufacture a new product, or offer new services. In the social realm, many organizations are concerned about privacy and protecting the personal information of customers and clients. As a result, many organizations now provide privacy training to employees and managers who handle personal information. In fact, some privacy laws in Canada require organizations to provide privacy training to front-line employees and management.[17] In addition, organizations have also become concerned about how they are perceived by the public and the use of social media, and this has led to the need for media training for organizational leaders and senior staff.[18]

Another example that was described in Chapter 1 is the increasing concern of police forces about how best to deal with people who have mental health issues. As a result, many police forces across the country now train their officers on how to identify different mental illnesses and to use that knowledge to de-escalate situations. This is the number one issue for the Ontario Provincial Police (OPP), whose goal is to ensure that at least one officer on every shift has taken 40 hours of Crisis Intervention Training.[19]

In summary, an organizational analysis is important for determining changes in an organization's external environment whether they are legal, social, political, or competitive that might require some form of training and development.

In Ontario, all workers and supervisors who are subject to the *Occupational Health and Safety Act* (OHSA) must complete a mandatory health and safety awareness training program.

Zorandim/Shutterstock.com

RESOURCE ANALYSIS

An important component of an organizational analysis is determining the organization's ability to design and deliver a training program. Does the organization have the resources (money, time, and expertise) to design and deliver a training program if one is needed?

A **resource analysis** involves identifying the resources available in the organization that might be required to design and implement training and development programs. Training programs are costly and require considerable resources. In addition to the financial costs, the design and implementation of a training program requires considerable time and expertise. Not all organizations have the expertise required to design and deliver training programs. In addition, the human resource staff might not have the time required to design new training programs. Training programs also require materials, equipment, and facilities, which can also be expensive.

A resource analysis enables an organization to determine whether it has the resources required for a training and development solution or whether another, less costly solution would be better. Ultimately, one must answer the question of whether the organization has the resources required for training and development if it is needed.

ORGANIZATIONAL CONTEXT

Organizations consist of more than buildings, equipment, and paper. They are social entities made up of people. The people in the buildings have feelings, attitudes, and values that make up the climate of an organization. **Organizational climate** refers to the collective attitudes of employees toward work, supervision, and company goals, policies, and procedures. One aspect of climate that is particularly important for training is the training transfer climate.

Training transfer climate refers to characteristics in the work environment that can either facilitate or inhibit the application of training on the job. A strong training transfer climate is one in which there are cues that remind employees to apply training material on the job, positive consequences such as feedback and rewards for applying training on the job, and supervisor and peer support for the use of newly acquired skills and abilities. The training transfer climate has been found to be a strong predictor of training effectiveness and of whether trainees apply newly trained skills on the job.[20]

Another important component of an organization's context is its culture for learning. A **learning culture** refers to the attitudes and practices within the organization regarding the importance placed on organizational learning and employee development. In a similar vein, a **continuous learning culture** is a culture in which members of an organization believe that knowledge and skill acquisition are part of their job responsibilities and that learning is an important part of work life in the organization.[21]

Information about an organization's training transfer climate and continuous learning culture is important because it indicates whether the work environment will support a training program and whether a training program is likely to be effective. It can also identify potential obstacles to the success of a training program and whether a pre-training intervention will be required to improve the climate and/or culture prior to the design and delivery of a training program. It might also indicate that an alternative solution to a performance problem would be more effective than a training program. This is an important part of an organizational analysis because training is not likely to be effective in organizations in which the climate for training transfer and/or the culture for learning are not strong.

The influence of the training transfer climate and a continuous learning culture on training effectiveness demonstrates the importance of the organizational context for a training program's success and the need to conduct an organizational analysis. Whether employees apply what they learn in training on the job has a lot to do with an organization's transfer climate and a continuous learning culture, because they can either facilitate or hinder the implementation and success of a training program.

Resource analysis
The identification of the resources available in an organization that might be required to design and implement training and development programs

Organizational climate
The collective attitudes of employees toward work, supervision, and company goals, policies, and procedures

Training transfer climate
Characteristics in the work environment that can either facilitate or inhibit the application of training on the job

Learning culture
The attitudes and practices within the organization regarding the importance placed on organizational learning and employee development

Continuous learning culture
A culture in which members of an organization believe that knowledge and skill acquisition are part of their job responsibilities and that learning is an important part of work life in the organization

CHAPTER 3 The Needs Analysis Process

The Trainer's Notebook 3.1, "Continuous Learning Culture Diagnosis," describes how to determine whether an organization has a continuous learning culture. We discuss the role of the training transfer climate and a continuous learning culture in more detail in Chapter 9.

Once the strategy, environment, resources, and context of an organization have been assessed, the information gathered can be used to determine whether a training program is required to help the organization achieve its goals and objectives and whether it will be successful. However, even if training is needed, it is still not clear what kind of training is needed and who needs to be trained. To answer these questions, additional information is required about the tasks that employees perform and how well employees perform them. This information can be obtained by conducting a task analysis and a person analysis.

// TASK ANALYSIS

A **task analysis** consists of a description of the activities or work operations performed on a job and the conditions under which these activities are performed. A task analysis reveals the tasks required for a person to perform a job and the knowledge, skills, and abilities (KSAs) that are required to perform the tasks successfully.

Task analysis
The process of obtaining information about a job by determining the duties, tasks, and activities involved and the knowledge, skills, and abilities (KSAs) required to perform the tasks

There are six steps involved in a task analysis:

1. Identify the target jobs.
2. Obtain a job description.
3. Develop rating scales to rate the importance and difficulty of each task and the frequency with which it is performed.
4. Survey a sample of job incumbents.
5. Analyze and interpret the information.
6. Provide feedback on the results.

IDENTIFY THE TARGET JOBS After a problem or performance discrepancy has been identified in an organization, the focus shifts to the job level to determine which jobs are contributing to the performance problem and have a performance gap.

OBTAIN A JOB DESCRIPTION A **job description** lists the specific duties carried out through the completion of several tasks. In large organizations, most positions have a description of the tasks and minimum qualifications required to do the job. If this description has not been updated within the last year, consult with both the manager and several employees in the position to obtain a current listing of tasks and qualifications. The job description should contain a summary of the major duties of the job, a list of these duties, the KSAs required to perform the tasks, and the conditions under which the tasks are performed. All tools and specialized knowledge should be listed.

After preparing a job description, the list of duties should be reviewed with subject-matter experts, managers, and job incumbents in interviews or focus groups. The analyst then develops a list of tasks to be performed, the KSAs needed to perform the tasks, and the necessary tools, software, or equipment, along with an understanding of the conditions under which the tasks are performed. The result looks very much like a job description with job specifications (a job specification is a statement of the KSAs required to perform a job).

Creating job descriptions and making lists of tasks and duties does have its downside. Critics argue that jobs change so rapidly that these lists are quickly out of date. Therefore, some job analysts have begun to develop a list of job competencies. A **competency** is a cluster of related KSAs that forms a major part of a job and that enables the job holder to perform effectively.[22] Competencies are behaviours that distinguish effective performers from ineffective performers. Competencies can be knowledge, skills, behaviour, or personality traits.

Examples of competencies for managers include setting goals and standards, coaching, making decisions, and organizing. As you can see, competencies are very similar to skills. Skills, however, can be very specific, such as "negotiate a collective agreement," whereas competencies are generic and universal, such as "win agreement on goals, standards, expectations, and time frames."

The goal is to develop competencies that are teachable (i.e., we can observe them and describe them). If these competencies are then associated with effective performance, we can use them as a base to increase the effectiveness of an employee's on-the-job behaviour. Competencies can then be used instead of job descriptions.

DEVELOP RATING SCALES TO RATE THE IMPORTANCE AND DIFFICULTY OF EACH TASK AND THE FREQUENCY WITH WHICH IT IS PERFORMED Rating scales are developed to rate the importance of each task, its difficulty, and how often it is performed. Tasks that are more important for the effective performance of a job and those that are difficult and frequently

Job description
A statement of the tasks, duties, and responsibilities of a job

Competency
A cluster of related knowledge, skills, and abilities that enables the job holder to perform effectively

performed need to be identified. These ratings are important for determining the content of a training program and for identifying what employees must do in order to perform a job effectively.

SURVEY A SAMPLE OF JOB INCUMBENTS Job incumbents, supervisors, and subject-matter experts who are familiar with the job must then provide ratings of task importance, difficulty, and frequency. A questionnaire and a structured interview as well as observation of employees performing their jobs can be used to rate the importance and difficulty of tasks and the frequency with which they are performed. An example of a survey is shown in Table 3.1.

ANALYZE AND INTERPRET THE INFORMATION Once the tasks have been identified and the importance, difficulty, and frequency ratings have been made, the information must be analyzed and interpreted. This usually involves some elementary statistical analyses to identify those tasks that are the most important and difficult, and most frequently performed. Statistical software packages can assist in this task and can be used for more complex analyses. Comparisons between groups may reveal additional important information such as differences between senior employees and newcomers.

PROVIDE FEEDBACK ON THE RESULTS Because employees and managers might not be aware of the need for training, it is important to provide small groups of managers and employees with feedback about the responses to the task analysis. This feedback encourages employees to talk about areas of strengths and weaknesses and to propose solutions to problems. By owning the problem and generating the solution, employees may be more willing to change their behaviours and managers will be more likely to support a training program.

TABLE 3.1

SAMPLE TASK ANALYSIS SURVEY

For each of the following tasks, please make three ratings. Looking at your own job, assess the importance of the task by circling a number from 1 (not important) to 5 (very important) and the difficulty of the task by circling a number from 1 (not very difficult) to 5 (very difficult). Then, consider how frequently you perform the task and rate it from 1 (very infrequently) to 5 (very frequently).

Task	Importance	Difficulty	Frequency
Knowledge: Explain technical information to co-workers	1 2 3 4 5	1 2 3 4 5	1 2 3 4 5
Control: Develop procedures to monitor and evaluate activities	1 2 3 4 5	1 2 3 4 5	1 2 3 4 5
Planning: Schedule time, tasks, and activities efficiently	1 2 3 4 5	1 2 3 4 5	1 2 3 4 5
Coaching: Provide verbal feedback to assist in the development of more effective ways of handling situations	1 2 3 4 5	1 2 3 4 5	1 2 3 4 5

The result of a task analysis should be information on the key task requirements for certain job categories and the associated job specifications (knowledge, skills, and abilities). This sets the stage for the design of training programs because it specifies the tasks that employees must be trained to perform as well as the knowledge and skills that they need to learn.

Limitations of a task analysis, however, are that it emphasizes observable behaviours rather than mental processes, and it assumes that the tasks are performed by individuals rather than groups. Many jobs today, however, involve mental processes and teamwork. In the following sections, we describe two approaches to task analysis that focus on mental processes and teamwork: cognitive task analysis and team task analysis.

// COGNITIVE TASK ANALYSIS

The traditional approach to a task analysis focuses on behaviours rather than mental processes such as decision making. However, many jobs today are knowledge based and involve complex mental tasks. How then does one conduct a task analysis for jobs that involve mental tasks that are not easy to observe? The answer is a cognitive task analysis.

A **cognitive task analysis (CTA)** is a set of procedures that focuses on understanding the mental and cognitive processes and skills required for performing a job.[23] It differs from the more conventional task analysis in that the focus is on the mental and cognitive aspects of a job rather than observable behaviours, such as typing or driving, that are the focus of a traditional task analysis.

CTA describes mental and cognitive activities that are not directly observable, such as decision making, problem solving, pattern recognition, and situational assessment. A traditional task analysis focuses on what gets done, while a cognitive task analysis focuses more on the details of how tasks get done.

Although CTA is useful for any job that has cognitive elements, it is especially useful in jobs that require an extensive knowledge base, involve complex judgments in dynamic and uncertain environments, and have high-stakes outcomes.[24] It can identify elements of job performance such as decisions, cues, judgments, and perceptions that are important for effective job performance and are not identified by a traditional task analysis. As a result, important cognitive elements can be incorporated into training and development programs. The most common approaches used to conduct a CTA are interviews and observation.[25]

// TEAM TASK ANALYSIS

As indicated earlier, the traditional task analysis is not suited to the analysis of jobs that involve group work. However, many jobs today involve groups of individuals working together on team-related tasks. Thus, a task analysis must be able to identify the knowledge and team-related skills required to work in a group.

A **team task analysis** is similar to a task analysis in that the tasks of the job must be identified. However, an assessment of team-based competencies (knowledge, skills, and attitudes) associated with the tasks is also required.

A team task analysis identifies the knowledge and team-related skills required to work in a group.

Cognitive task analysis (CTA)
A set of procedures that focuses on understanding the mental processes and skills required for performing a job

Team task analysis
An analysis of tasks as well as the team-based competencies (knowledge, skills, and attitudes) associated with the tasks

Teamwork competencies include things such as how to communicate, interact, and coordinate tasks effectively with team members. The main objective is to identify the key team competencies required for the tasks of the job, which will be used to write training objectives and to design a training program.[26]

There are a number of important differences between a traditional task analysis and a team task analysis. The main difference is that a team task analysis must identify the interdependencies of the job as well as the skills required for task coordination. Another difference is that a team task analysis must also identify the cognitive skills that are required for interacting in a team.

In general, a team task analysis should focus on the knowledge of task-specific goals; knowledge of task procedures, strategies, and timing; knowledge of team members' roles and responsibilities; and knowledge of teamwork. A team task analysis can be conducted using individual and group interviews, a review of existing documents, observation, and questionnaires, and by examining past important events.[27]

// PERSON ANALYSIS

Task analysis, cognitive task analysis, and team task analysis identify the tasks an employee must be able to perform and the KSAs required. However, they do not indicate how well employees are able to perform the tasks or whether they have the necessary knowledge, skills, and abilities. This information must be obtained from a person analysis, which is the third level of a needs analysis. A person analysis focuses on the person performing a job and helps to determine who needs training and whether they are ready for training.

Person analysis is the process of studying employee behaviour and performance to determine whether performance meets the work standards. A standard is the desired level of performance—ideally, the quantifiable output of a specific job. A person analysis examines how well an employee performs the critical tasks and their knowledge, skills, and abilities. The objective is to provide answers to these kinds of questions: *How well does the employee perform the tasks? Who, within the organization, needs training? What kind of training do they need?*

A three-step process can answer these questions:

1. Define the desired performance.
2. Determine the gap between desired and actual performance.
3. Identify the obstacles to effective performance.

> Person analysis
> The process of studying employee behaviour and performance to determine whether performance meets standards

DEFINE THE DESIRED PERFORMANCE The first step is to establish standards for performance. These standards will be important in the needs analysis, during training, and in evaluating the effectiveness of training. The idea is to determine the standard or the acceptable level of task performance. This enables a comparison of each employee's performance level against the standard in order to identify discrepancies and the need for training.

DETERMINE THE GAP BETWEEN DESIRED AND ACTUAL PERFORMANCE In this step, a comparison is made between the standard level of performance and each employee's performance. Employee performance data can be obtained from performance appraisals, work samples, observations, self-assessments of competencies, and formal tests.

IDENTIFY THE OBSTACLES TO EFFECTIVE PERFORMANCE When a gap exists between the standard and an employee's performance, it is necessary to determine the cause of or reason for the gap. Performance problems can be the result of deficiencies in execution as well as deficiencies in KSAs. Sometimes, the gap is the result of the worker not knowing the standard, not receiving adequate feedback about performance relative to the standard, and/or not being rewarded for meeting the standard. A lack of goals and feedback is often the reason for substandard performance.

In addition to determining how well an employee performs the critical tasks, a person analysis can also examine the personal and individual factors described in Chapter 2, such as self-efficacy, goal orientation, training motivation, and personality, that can influence learning and training success. Since these factors can indicate who will benefit from training, it is important to measure them before training and take any actions necessary to improve them (e.g., increase trainee motivation to learn) before trainees attend a training program. In addition, some characteristics of trainees might also have implications for the content and methods of a training program.[28]

Once the needs analysis has been completed, the next step is to determine solutions to performance problems and whether training is part of the solution to a performance problem. In the next section, we describe the process of determining solutions to performance problems.

For more information see Chapter 2, pp. 65–66

// DETERMINING SOLUTIONS TO PERFORMANCE PROBLEMS

Table 3.2 lists a variety of potential barriers to effective performance. If you consider all the barriers to performance listed in Table 3.2, only the first two (lack of knowledge and skills) suggest a training solution. Other barriers have to do with motivation and the work environment. Clearly, the solution to performance problems is not always

TABLE 3.2

BARRIERS TO EFFECTIVE PERFORMANCE

HUMAN	TECHNICAL	INFORMATION	STRUCTURAL
Lack of knowledge	Poor job design	Ill-defined goals/objectives	Overlapping roles and responsibilities
Lack of skills	Lack of tools/equipment	Lack of performance measurements	Lack of flexibility
Lack of motivation	Lack of standardized procedures	Raw data, not normative or comparative data	Lack of control systems
Counterproductive reward systems	Rapid change in technology	Resources sub-optimized	Organizational political climate
Group norms	Ineffective feedback	Informal leaders	

Source: Republished with permission of International Society for Performance Improvement, from R. Chevalier, "Analyzing performance discrepancies with Line Managers," *Performance Improvement*, Vol. 29, No. 10, p. 23; permission conveyed through Copyright Clearance Center, Inc.

training. Saying "I've got a training problem" is like going to the doctor and saying you have an Aspirin problem.[29] Training, like Aspirin, is a solution, not a problem. How, then, do we determine whether training is the best solution to performance problems?

Figure 3.2 presents a flowchart developed by Mager and Pipe to assist in analyzing performance problems and determining solutions to performance problems. Let's review the steps in the flowchart.

When there is a performance problem, the manager must describe the problem and decide whether it is worth spending time and money to correct. For example, a manager might be irritated by employees who wear their hair shoulder-length, but having short hair will make absolutely no difference to productivity or other measures of performance. The exception might be in a manufacturing environment, where long hair would pose a safety hazard (solved easily by wearing a head covering). When a performance problem is important and worth pursuing, the true analysis begins.

First, we consider some basic solutions or quick fixes. For example, are the work expectations, standards, and goals clear? Does the employee have adequate resources? Is the outcome of the employee's performance visible and known to the employee? If the answer to any of these questions is *No*, then the solution might involve clarifying expectations and standards, setting goals, providing necessary resources, and/or providing performance feedback.

If the problem cannot be solved by these quick fixes, the analyst must then attempt to determine the cause of poor performance by asking a number of additional questions about the environment and reward and punishment contingencies.

For example, is the person punished for desired performance? While this question seems odd, organizational life is full of examples of punishment for good performance. The assistant who works twice as hard as co-workers is punished by being given more work. The manager who stays within his/her budget is punished by having it slashed the following year. In these and other cases, behaviour that should be rewarded is actually punished. Such penalties and punishments for what is good performance should be eliminated.

Sometimes undesirable performance is rewarded, such as when employees get paid for each unit produced. Under these circumstances, you might find that employees are very good at producing lots of defective units. Of course, if they get paid for each unit produced they will continue to produce as many as they can regardless of quality. Thus, it is also important to ensure that undesirable behaviour is not rewarded. High volume should not be rewarded if quality is desired.

The next issue is whether rewards are linked to effective performance. Are there positive consequences for performing as desired? Sometimes when an employee does something good, the manager says nothing, on the assumption that the employee is being paid to do the work. Good performance that is not rewarded will eventually disappear. Sometimes, employees assume that their performance does not matter to anyone. When managers sit in their offices and fume over sloppy work but give no feedback to employees, or arrange no consequences for poor performance, the sloppy work will continue.

Working with the human resource staff, managers need to develop contingency management programs that reward employees for good performance. **Contingency management** is grounded in the belief that every act has a consequence and if the consequence is a reward, then the act will be repeated. If there is no consequence or the consequence is something negative or punishing, the action will not be repeated. If this sounds familiar to you, it is because it has its basis in conditioning theory, which was described in Chapter 2.

Recall that according to conditioning theory, learning is the result of reward and punishment contingencies that follow a response to a stimulus. Thus, contingency management is an application of conditioning theory.

Contingency management
Practices based on the belief that every act has a consequence and if the consequence is a reward, then the act will be repeated

FIGURE 3.2

MAGER AND PIPE'S PERFORMANCE ANALYSIS FLOWCHART FOR DETERMINING SOLUTIONS TO PERFORMANCE PROBLEMS

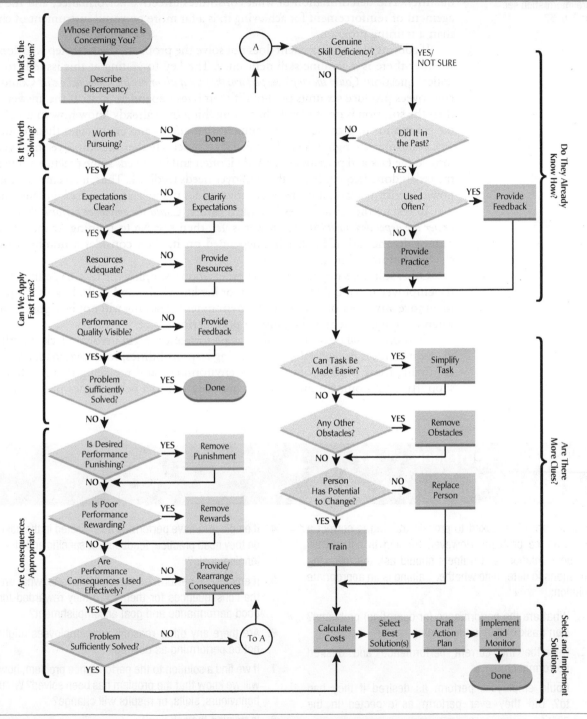

Source: © 2012 Mager Associates, Inc. Adapted from Mager, R. F., & Pipe, P. (1997). *Analyzing performance problems* (3rd ed.).

For more information see
Chapter 2, p. 53

By analyzing rewards and punishments, managers might realize that they are asking for safe procedures but punishing those who slow down production. Quality might be the all-important word on the sign in the factory, but employees might be praised for quantity. The determination of what constitutes effective performance, and the management of reinforcement for achieving it, is a far more powerful instrument of change than a training program.

If contingency management does not solve the problem, the next step is to consider whether there is a genuine skill deficiency. The key to getting at this issue is to ask a critical question: *Could the employee perform the task if his or her life depended on it?* Could your employees produce six units per hour if their lives depended on it? If the answer is *Yes*, then the solution is not to teach them something they already know how to do. Rather, the solution is to provide an environment that allows and encourages them to do it.

Following the right side of Figure 3.2, consider whether the employee has ever performed the task and perhaps does not do it often and just needs some practice. Or perhaps the task is done frequently and the employee needs feedback. Thus, if an employee knows how to perform a task, it is important to consider practice and feedback before training.

To restate the critical question asked earlier, *Could the employee perform the task if his or her life depended on it?* If the answer is *Yes*, then say *No* to training. If the employee cannot do the task if his/her life depended on it, then consider a number of other changes before training.

Other solutions might be to lower expectations, simplify the task, or perhaps transfer the employee to a job that better fits his or her knowledge and skills. It is also important to remove any other obstacles in the environment. Training will not be a good solution when the environment is the cause of poor performance.

Environmental obstacles to effective performance might involve a lack of authority, inadequate tools or technology, conflicting responsibilities, work overload, and so on. Removing these obstacles in the work environment and replacing them with a more supportive environment might be the best solution to a performance problem.

THE TRAINER'S NOTEBOOK   3.2

THE TRAINING SOLUTION CHECKLIST

Trainers are often asked to provide training to correct a performance problem. However, training is not always the best solution, and trainers should ask the following questions to determine whether training is an appropriate solution:

1. What are the performance (or operating) problems? Don't ask, "What is the training need?"

2. Describe the current performance and desired performance.

3. Could employees perform as desired if they had to? Did they ever perform as expected in the past?

4. If employees have performed as expected in the past, do they need practice, feedback, or specific and challenging goals?

5. If employees perform as you want them to, what are the consequences for them? Are they rewarded for good performance and goal accomplishment?

6. Are there any other reasons why employees might not be performing as desired?

7. If we find a solution to the performance problem, how will we know that the problem has been solved? What behaviours, skills, or results will change?

8. Is training the solution?

TABLE 3.3

PERFORMANCE PROBLEMS AND TRAINING

Training is often the best solution to performance problems under the following conditions:

- The task is performed frequently.
- The task is difficult.
- Correct performance is critical.
- The employee does not know how to perform as required (cannot do it).
- Performance expectations and goals are clear, and employees receive feedback on their performance.
- There are (or will be) positive consequences for correct work behaviour; there are not negative consequences for performing as required.
- Other solutions (such as coaching) are ineffective or too expensive (e.g., terminating employees and rehiring those with required skills).

Finally, if there exists a genuine skill deficiency and the person does not have the potential to change, then replacing the person might be the only solution. If, however, the person does have the potential to change, then consider training as a potential solution.

In summary, the best way to determine whether training is an appropriate solution to performance problems is to first conduct a thorough needs analysis, identify performance obstacles, and then consider various solutions to a performance problem, as shown in Figure 3.2. A checklist of the questions to ask to determine whether training is the best solution to performance problems is provided in The Trainer's Notebook 3.2, "The Training Solution Checklist." Table 3.3 provides a list of the conditions under which training is most likely to be the best solution to performance problems.

// NEEDS ANALYSIS METHODS

In the chapter-opening vignette, it states that focus groups, interviews, and surveys were used to conduct the needs analysis at TD Bank. These are examples of needs analysis methods. There are many methods and techniques for conducting a needs analysis. The methods differ in terms of the quality and type of information obtained, as well as the time and cost of collecting it. This section describes some of the most common methods of needs analysis.

Table 3.4 describes nine basic needs analysis methods, along with their advantages and disadvantages. The nine methods are: observation, questionnaires, key consultation, print media, interviews, group discussion, tests, records and reports, and work samples.

Some methods of needs analysis are better than others in terms of response rate, quality, usefulness of the data, and cost. One study tested three techniques: closed-ended survey, open-ended survey, and focus groups. A combination of the closed-ended survey and focus-group interviews provided the most practical, useful, and cost-effective information.[30] The best method, however, depends on the time and money available, the experience of the analyst, and the nature of the responses.

Surveys are one of the most often used methods of needs analysis due to their low cost and the ability to collect information from large numbers of respondents. Some

TABLE 3.4

ADVANTAGES AND DISADVANTAGES OF NINE BASIC NEEDS ANALYSIS METHODS

METHODS	ADVANTAGES	DISADVANTAGES
OBSERVATION		
• can be as technical as time–motion studies or as functionally or behaviourally specific as observing a new board or staff member interacting during a meeting	• minimizes interruption of routine work flow or group activity	• requires a highly skilled observer with both process and content knowledge (unlike an interviewer, who needs, for the most part, only process skills)
• may be as unstructured as walking through an agency's offices on the lookout for evidence of communication barriers	• generates *in situ* data, highly relevant to the situation affected by response to identified training needs/interests will impact	• carries limitations that derive from being able to collect data only within the work setting (the other side of the first advantage listed in the preceding column)
• can be used normatively to distinguish between effective and ineffective behaviours, organizational structures, and/or process	• (when combined with a feedback step) provides for important comparison checks between inferences of the observer and the respondent	• holds potential for respondents to perceive the observation activity as "spying"
QUESTIONNAIRES		
• may be in the form of surveys or polls of a random or stratified sample of respondents, or an enumeration of an entire "population"	• can reach a large number of people in a short time	• make little provision for free expression of unanticipated responses
• can use a variety of question formats: open ended, projective, forced choice, priority ranking	• are relatively inexpensive	• require substantial time (and technical skills, especially in survey mode) for development of effective instruments
• can take alternative forms such as Q-sorts, or slip-sorts, rating scales, either predesigned or self-generated by respondent(s)	• give opportunity for expression without fear of embarrassment	• are of limited utility in getting at causes of problems or possible solutions
• may be self-administered (by mail) under controlled or uncontrolled conditions, or may require the presence of an interpreter or assistant	• yield data easily summarized and reported	• suffer low return rates (mailed), grudging responses, or unintended and/or inappropriate respondents
KEY CONSULTATION		
• secures information from those persons who, by virtue of their formal or informal standing, are in a good position to know what the training needs of a particular group are:	• is relatively simple and inexpensive to conduct	• carries a built-in bias, since it is based on views of those who tend to see training needs from their own individual or organizational perspective

TABLE 3.4 (*Continued*)

ADVANTAGES AND DISADVANTAGES OF NINE BASIC NEEDS ANALYSIS METHODS

a. board chairman b. related service providers c. members of professional associations d. individuals from the service population	• permits input and interaction of a number of individuals, each with his or her own perspectives of the needs of the area, discipline, group, etc.	• may result in only a partial picture of training needs due to the typically nonrepresentative nature (in a statistical sense) of a key informant group
	• establishes and strengthens lines of communication between participants in the process	

PRINT MEDIA

• can include professional journals, legislative news/notes, industry "rags," trade magazines, in-house publications	• is an excellent source of information for uncovering and clarifying normative needs	• can be a problem when it comes to the data analysis and synthesis into a usable form (use of clipping service or key consultants can make this type of data more usable)
	• provides information that is current, if not forward-looking	
	• is readily available and is apt to have already been reviewed by the client group	

INTERVIEWS

• can be formal or casual, structured or unstructured, or somewhere in between • may be used with a sample of a particular group (board, staff, committee) or conducted with everyone concerned • can be done in person, by phone, at the work site, or away from it	• are adept at revealing feelings, causes of, and possible solutions to problems that the client is facing (or anticipates); provide maximum opportunity for the client to represent himself spontaneously on his own terms (especially when conducted in an open-ended, non-directive manner)	• are usually time-consuming • can be difficult to analyze and quantify results (especially from unstructured formats) • unless the interviewer is skilled, the client(s) can easily be made to feel self-conscious • relies for success on a skillful interviewer who can generate data without making client(s) feel self-conscious, suspicious, etc.

GROUP DISCUSSION

• resembles face-to-face interview technique, e.g., structured or unstructured, formal or informal, or somewhere in between	• permits on-the-spot synthesis of different viewpoints	• is time-consuming (therefore initially expensive) both for the consultant and the agency

CHAPTER 3 The Needs Analysis Process

TABLE 3.4 (*Continued*)

ADVANTAGES AND DISADVANTAGES OF NINE BASIC NEEDS ANALYSIS METHODS

• can be focused on job (role) analysis, group problem analysis, group goal setting, or any number of group tasks or themes, e.g., "leadership training needs of the board"	• builds support for the particular service response that is ultimately decided on	• can produce data that are difficult to synthesize and quantify (more of a problem with the less structured techniques)
• uses one or several of the familiar group facilitating techniques: brainstorming, nominal group process, force fields, consensus rankings, organizational mirroring, simulation, and sculpting	• decreases client's "dependence response" toward the service provided, since data analysis is (or can be) a shared function	
	• helps participants become better problem analysts, better listeners, etc.	

TESTS

• are a hybridized form of questionnaire	• can be especially helpful in determining whether the cause of a recognized problem is a deficiency in knowledge, skill, or—by elimination—attitude	• the availability of a relatively small number of tests that are validated for a specific situation
• can be very functionally oriented (like observations) to test a board, staff, or committee member's proficiency	• results are easily quantifiable and comparable	• do not indicate whether measured knowledge and skills are actually being used in the on-the-job or "back home group" situation
• may be used to sample learned ideas and facts		
• can be administered with or without the presence of an assistant		

RECORDS AND REPORTS

• can consist of organizational charts, planning documents, policy manuals, audits, and budget reports	• provide excellent clues to trouble spots	• causes of problems or possible solutions often do not show up
• employee records (grievances, turnover, accidents, etc.)	• provide objective evidence of the results of problems within the agency or group	• carry perspectives that generally reflect the past situation rather than the current one (or recent changes)
• includes minutes of meetings, weekly/monthly program reports, memoranda, agency service records, program evaluation studies	• can be collected with minimum effort and interruption of work flow, since they already exist at the work site	• need a skilled data analyst if clear patterns and trends are to emerge from such technical and diffuse raw data

TABLE 3.4 *(Continued)*

ADVANTAGES AND DISADVANTAGES OF NINE BASIC NEEDS ANALYSIS METHODS

WORK SAMPLES

• are similar to observation but in written form	• carry most of the advantage of records and reports data	• case study method will take time away from actual work of the organization
• can be products generated in the course of the organization's work, e.g., ad layouts, program proposals, market analyses, letters, training designs, or	• are the organization's data (its own output)	• need specialized content analysts
• written responses to a hypothetical but relevant case study provided by the consultant		• analyst's assessment of strengths/ weaknesses disclosed by samples can be challenged as "too subjective"

Source: Adapted with permission of the Association for Talent Development (ATD), from Steadham, S. V. (1980, January). Learning to select a needs assessment strategy. *Training and Development Journal, 34*(1), 58. Permission conveyed through Copyright Clearance Center, Inc.

software firms have developed surveys that can be customized to include questions from broad-climate issues to specific job standards. Many firms have designed needs analysis software, some of which can be tailored to clients' needs. This technology allows HR staff to develop customized surveys quickly, and to analyze results by region, unit, and so on.

// NEEDS ANALYSIS SOURCES

There are many sources of needs analysis information. Among the most important and often used are employees, managers, human resource staff, and subject-matter experts who are familiar with a job. Some retail stores assess the competence of their sales staff through the use of professional shoppers who rate sales performance against established standards.

In many cases, data on employees' performance and training needs are obtained from employees who rate their own performance and indicate their training needs. This is usually referred to as self-assessment. For example, Source Atlantic, an industrial distribution and services company in Saint John, had sales employees do self-assessments to identify areas where they could benefit from training. Employees then had access to a number of training programs that helped them improve their skills and better meet customer needs.[31]

Self-assessment has both benefits and limitations. Employees might be more motivated to be trained if they have some input in deciding on their needs. However, expressions of needs include feelings or desires and may have no relation to performance.[32]

Several studies have found weak relationships between employees' self-assessments of performance and managerial assessments.[33] A review of 55 studies failed to find a strong relationship between self-evaluation of ability and other measures of performance.[34]

However, a study at IBM demonstrated that employees can be trained in self-assessment by learning to break down a job into its component parts and to analyze skills.[35] This method has the added benefit of the employees accepting ownership of their development plans.

In summary, there are many methods and sources for conducting a needs analysis. Because of the differences in information provided by the various methods and sources, the best approach is one that includes multiple methods and sources. Surveying only job incumbents about their perceptions of their own abilities might not result in the most objective information about performance gaps. Employees may have wish lists for training that do not meet the needs of their units or that do not address their own weaknesses. Managers, too, should be asked for their performance evaluations. Those who have frequent interaction with job incumbents, such as customers and employees in other departments, should also be surveyed. These different perspectives result in more accurate and complete information. They also enable analysts to distinguish between perceived needs (what training employees feel they need), demand needs (what managers request), and normative needs (training needed to meet industry, unit, or job comparative standards).

// OBSTACLES TO NEEDS ANALYSIS

Now that you are familiar with the needs analysis process, you might be surprised to learn that many organizations do not conduct a thorough or complete needs analysis, at least not to the extent that they should.[36] Given the importance of needs analysis in the training process, you might wonder why this is the case.

As it turns out, there are a number of obstacles to conducting a formal needs analysis. Understanding these obstacles is important because if you are aware of them you can learn how to overcome them.

To begin with, trainers often claim that they are not rewarded for taking the time (and money) to conduct a needs analysis. Managers prefer action over analysis and they want to see training resources used to train employees. They may also believe that they can identify training needs accurately and that more analysis is a waste of time and money. Managers may even have their own agendas, such as rewarding employees by sending them to exotic locations for training, and therefore resist any attempt to identify training needs.

Time can also be a constraint. For example, new equipment might be arriving and it is easier to train all employees on all procedures instead of determining who needs training on which aspects of the new equipment. In fact, time is increasingly a concern. Needs analysis can take months to complete, and yet employees need to be trained and back on the job in a matter of weeks or even days.

Ultimately, what everyone is most concerned about is getting people trained as soon as possible. Because needs analysis is costly and time consuming, it is often seen as an unnecessary constraint on resources, staff, and time. The cost, time, and effort necessary to perform a needs analysis means that many organizations do not conduct a needs analysis at all or not to the extent that they should.

However, conducting some data collection and analysis, rather than having no information, will almost always result in a better training program. It is therefore important for trainers to persuade management of the importance of conducting a needs analysis, and to ensure that it is included in the training budget. Another solution is to conduct a quick and inexpensive needs analysis or what is known as a rapid needs analysis.

A **rapid needs analysis** involves gathering available information and using data that already exist.[37] Thus, trainers need to be creative in finding ways to conduct a needs analysis within the time and resource constraints that exist in their organizations. To learn about some creative techniques for conducting a rapid needs analysis, see The Trainer's Notebook 3.3, "How to Conduct a Rapid Needs Analysis."

> **Rapid needs analysis**
> A quick and inexpensive needs analysis that involves gathering available information and using data that already exist

---

THE TRAINER'S NOTEBOOK 3.3

HOW TO CONDUCT A RAPID NEEDS ANALYSIS

- *Ask a series of questions.* When a manager demands a training course for employees, the trainer should start by asking questions related to the nature of the problem and its impact on the business. Some trainers even agree to conduct a training course, as per the manager's demand, and then renegotiate the assignment as information emerges from interviews with employees before the course. Managers may be receptive to the emerging data, recognizing the need to design solutions that solve the problem.

- *Use existing information.* Surveys, interviews, and observations are expensive data-collection methods. But most organizations keep customer complaint letters, grievance files, exit interviews, and sales data, which can be re-assessed for needs analysis purposes.

- *Speed up data collection.* Use the company intranet to survey employees. Start discussion groups about issues, concerns, and problems.

- *Link assessment and delivery.* Rather than conduct a lengthy needs analysis and then design a training program, some trainers attempt to join the two together, in small steps. For example, if there are star performers, bring them together in a forum with poorer performers to discuss effective techniques. The poorer performers can compare performance and learn how to improve at the same time.

Source: Adapted from Zemke, R. (1998). How to do a needs assessment when you think you don't have time. *Training Magazine, 35*(3), 38–44. Trainingmag.com

---

// SUMMARY

This chapter described the needs analysis process. Three levels of needs analysis were described—organizational, task, and person analysis—as well as cognitive task analysis and team task analysis. We also described the process of how to determine solutions to performance problems. Needs analysis methods and sources were also described, as well as the obstacles to needs analysis. It should now be clear to you that a needs analysis is critical for determining the nature of performance problems and whether training and development is the solution to a performance problem. The importance of a needs analysis, however, does not end here. As you will see in Chapter 4, a needs analysis is necessary for writing training objectives and designing a training program.

CHAPTER 3 The Needs Analysis Process

KEY TERMS

cognitive task analysis (CTA) p. 93
competency p. 91
compliance training p. 88
contingency management p. 96
continuous learning culture p. 89
job description p. 91
learning culture p. 89
need p. 82
needs analysis p. 82
organizational analysis p. 86
organizational climate p. 89
person analysis p. 94
rapid needs analysis p. 105
resource analysis p. 89
strategic training and development (ST&D) p. 86
task analysis p. 90
team task analysis p. 93
training transfer climate p. 89

DISCUSSION QUESTIONS

1. Organizations often have data on file that can be used for a needs analysis. Discuss the kinds of information that might exist in an organization and how it might be useful for an organizational, a task, and/or a person analysis.

2. If needs analysis information has not been used as the basis for the design and delivery of a training program, what are some of the reasons that organizations provide training? Are these good reasons for investing in training and development programs?

3. Discuss the reasons why organizations do not always conduct a needs analysis and what a trainer might do to overcome needs analysis obstacles. What are the implications of designing and implementing a training program without conducting a needs analysis?

4. Discuss the advantages and disadvantages of the different sources of needs analysis information. What sources are best for a person, a task, and an organizational needs analysis?

5. Discuss the process involved in determining solutions to performance problems. When is training likely to be a good solution? When is training not likely to be a good solution?

6. What is the difference between a training transfer climate and a continuous learning culture? Why should an organization obtain information about the transfer climate and continuous learning culture before designing and implementing a training program?

7. What is the difference between a task analysis, a cognitive task analysis, and a team task analysis? Discuss when and how each type of needs analysis should be conducted.

8. In recent years, the Toronto Transit Commission (TTC) has been criticized for its poor customer service and complaints about discourteous employees. Explain how you could use the needs analysis process (Figure 3.1) to address these problems. In other words, discuss the concern, its importance, consulting stakeholders, and collecting information. What can we learn about the TTC and its problems from the needs analysis process?

THE GREAT TRAINING DEBATE

1. Debate the following: Needs analysis is a waste of time. What is most important is getting employees trained as soon as possible rather than wasting time and resources to find out if training is needed.

2. Debate the following: Training is costly and time consuming for organizations and should only be considered after other, less costly interventions have failed.

EXERCISES

IN-CLASS

1. Think of a problem you had or were aware of at an organization that you worked for. Describe the problem and then use Mager and Pipe's flowchart for determining solutions to performance problems (Figure 3.2) to determine the best solution. Consider each solution in the figure and explain why it would or would not be a good solution to the problem. Finally, if you know what the organization did about the problem, describe what it did and whether it was an effective solution.

2. Consider your job and performance as a student and conduct each of the following types of needs analysis: (a) task analysis, (b) cognitive task analysis, (c) team task analysis, and (d) person analysis. Based on your results, indicate the critical tasks of a student, how well you perform each task, and on which tasks you need to improve your performance. What do you need to do to become a better student?

3. Find a partner in the class and take turns conducting a task analysis interview. Before beginning your interview, prepare a task analysis interview guide with questions that will help you identify tasks; rate their importance, difficulty, and frequency; and determine the task specifications (knowledge, skills, and abilities). The interviewee can refer to a current or previous job when answering the interviewer's questions. Also consider the relevance of a cognitive task analysis and a team task analysis.

4. Table 3.4 describes nine methods of needs analysis. Review each method and then explain which method you think would be most appropriate for each of the following kinds of needs analysis: (a) organizational analysis, (b) task analysis, (c) cognitive task analysis, (d) team task analysis, and (e) person analysis. Be sure to explain your reasoning as to why a particular method would be best for each type of needs analysis.

5. Recall a training program that you have attended as part of a current or previous job. To what extent do you think the program was based on organizational, task, and person analysis? Try to relate specific aspects of the training program to each level of needs analysis. What performance problem was the training designed to address, and how effective was the program as a solution to the performance problem?

6. Imagine that you are a trainer in an organization that prides itself on providing employees with frequent opportunities for training. The president of the company has asked you to design and deliver a training program on team skills so that employees will be able to work in groups. He or she wants you to start training employees as soon as possible and does not want you to spend time and money conducting a needs analysis. He or she wants you to develop an action plan for the design and delivery of the program and present it in one week. How will you handle the needs analysis issue and what will you recommend? Prepare your presentation and present it to the class.

7. Review the chapter-opening vignette on TD Bank's Robbery Prevention and Awareness training program and answer the following questions:

a. What was the concern?

b. Why was a needs analysis conducted?

c. How was the needs analysis conducted?

d. What were the objectives of the training program?

e. What was the content of the training program?

f. What training methods were used?

g. How was the training program evaluated?

h. Was the training program effective?

What does this case tell you about the role of needs analysis in the training and development process?

IN-THE-FIELD

1. To find out about the extent to which organizations conduct needs analyses, contact the human resources staff of an organization and request an interview about needs analysis. In particular, find out whether the staff conduct organizational, task, and person analysis; the kinds of information they gather when they conduct each level of needs analysis; what methods and sources they use to gather the information; and what they do with the information and how it is used in the training and development process. If they do not conduct needs analyses, find out why and how they determine training needs. You should come to class prepared to present the results of your interview.

2. To find out how organizations determine whether training is the solution to performance problems, contact the human resources staff of an organization and request an interview about their training programs. In particular, find out what the problem was that a particular training program was designed for and how they determined that training was the best solution. In addition, find out whether they considered the other solutions in Mager and Pipe's flowchart for determining solutions to performance problems (Figure 3.2). Be sure to find out how they reached the decision that training was the best solution to the problem and whether the training program did, in fact, solve the problem. You should come to class prepared to present the results of your interview.

CASE INCIDENT

THE ASTHMA ATTACK

In March of 2013, a teenage boy visiting a Tim Hortons franchise in London, Ontario, suffered an asthma attack. The 17-year-old boy was having difficulty breathing and was gasping for air as he tried to get the attention of employees.

According to a customer who witnessed the incident, an employee asked "What do you want?" kind of rudely and all the boy could say was "Help" and "Phone." Employees told him the phone wasn't for customers and directed him to a payphone across the street at a variety store.

According to the witness, "The teen boy was going between the two tills, there were five or six employees . . . he was visibly in distress. They didn't ask if he needed help. The whole time, not one of them came out from behind the counter to see if he was OK."

The customer who witnessed the incident called 911 and stayed with the boy until paramedics arrived. However, when they arrived they found themselves at an exit-only door. The employees did not open the door to let them in, so the paramedics had to pry the door open to get to the boy and take him to the hospital.

QUESTIONS

1. Run the asthma attack incident through the needs analysis process (Figure 3.1). What is the performance problem and is it important? Who are the stakeholders? What information would you collect by doing organizational, task, and person analysis? What are some of the outcomes that would result from the needs analysis process?

2. If Tim Hortons was to conduct a needs analysis following the asthma attack, what methods and sources should they use? Explain the advantages and disadvantages of each method and source.

3. Do you think training is needed to solve the performance problem? Consider some other solutions to performance problems and whether they would be appropriate. How would you know if training was the best solution to the performance problem?

Sources: Silliker, A. (2013, April 8). Will your staff help if customer falls ill? *Canadian HR Reporter*, *26*(7),1, 12; Dubinski, K. (2013, March 5). Tim Horton's denies phone to teen having asthma attack. *The London Free Press*, http://www.lfpress.com/2013/03/04/tim-hortons-denies-phone-to-teen-having-asthma-attack; Canadian Press (2013, March 5). Tim Horton's staff looked on as boy had asthma attack in London, Ont. store, customer says. *National Post*, http://news.nationalpost.com/2013/03/05/tim-hortons-staff-looked-on-as-boy-had-asthma-attack-in-london-ont-store-customer-says/

CASE STUDY	THE INCIDENT AND APOLOGY

On a Saturday night in the fall of 2015, a woman was attending a charity event at a golf and country club in Toronto along with her baby and partner. During the dinner her two-and-a-half-month old baby became hungry so she went into a secluded hallway in a discreet corner outside of the dining area where she sat in a chair to feed him.

While seated in the chair feeding her baby, a male service manager approached her with a large tablecloth to shield her from view because of complaints from people who did not want to see her breastfeeding while they were eating. She was told that she was visible to patrons in a members-only dining area. Although she was seated in a chair in the corner of the hallway, she was told that she was still visible to patrons.

The woman was then escorted to the basement to continue feeding her baby and told that she would be "more comfortable there," a move that she felt was an attempt to accommodate people who are intolerant of something natural. "I thought, why are people disgusted or upset by the sight of a child eating while they are eating? It didn't make any sense to me," said the mother. "I took Jacob (her baby) off the breast and covered up and he led me downstairs to the basement," she said.

"The way it was handled, I was slightly embarrassed because he made me feel like it was a shameful thing by sort of covering me up and saying people didn't want to see it." She did not say anything to the manager at the time because she was so surprised. "I kind of went along with it," she said. "And then I felt like, wait a minute, what just happened here? And why didn't I kind of stand up for myself at the time?" She left shortly after and the charity's organizers said they would speak with the golf club.

The woman's partner took a photo of her breastfeeding and posted it and a description of the incident on Facebook. People from all around the world sent messages of support and outrage over the incident. The post also prompted a backlash from parents and patrons of the club. By Sunday afternoon, the page was full of comments from people condemning the club's actions. The club's Facebook page also received dozens of one-star reviews.

"After getting a flood of support, I suddenly realized that a lot of women don't really know the law, don't really know that it's not OK for people to ask you to move and make you feel like you're doing something wrong breastfeeding," she said. "Personally, I feel why should I have to cover up when I'm breastfeeding? The baby's head covers the breast anyway, this is a perfectly natural thing to do. It's necessary to sustain life, so why are we made to feel shameful of it?"

The Ontario Human Rights Commission says that women have the right to breastfeed in a public area and not to be disturbed or asked to move to a more discreet location. The commission also states that such services including those offered by restaurants, cafes, stores, and at parks must be provided to breastfeeding women without discrimination.

The following Monday, the president of the club's board of governors and the chief operating officer sent an apology to the woman and posted it publicly. The letter stated, "Our staff member should have acted differently and not have asked you to move to another location at the club to continue feeding your baby. We deeply regret that this caused you to feel embarrassed." The letter also stated, "We recognize that you and other mothers who come to the [club] as members or guests are entitled to breastfeed their children without covering up and should not be asked to move from a location that is comfortable and convenient for them," and "We unreservedly apologize for the discomfort this caused you."

The apology also indicated that the club plans to make sure its staff are aware of the province's human rights code as it applies to women breastfeeding and will provide sensitivity training to its staff to make them aware "of the needs and rights of breastfeeding mothers."

The women accepted the apology and said, "Well I'm very pleased. First of all because the apology was public and second of all it was going to come with sensitivity training for the staff." She said the club took the corrective measures she wanted, but she has a message for those who discriminate against breastfeeding mothers. "I say that this is a beautiful act. It's an act that sustains life. It's very important as a way of bonding between mother and child, and it's a human right."

Sources: Dolski, M. (2016, October 18). Nursing mom gets an apology from golf club. Toronto Star, GT1, GT3; D'Amore, R. (2016, October 16). West-end golf club facing online backlash after breastfeeding mom says she was sent to basement. CTV Toronto, http://toronto.ctvnews.ca/west-end-golf-club-facing-online-backlash-after-breastfeeding . . .; Westoll, N. (2016, October 17). Toronto golf club apologizes after mom was asked to breastfeed son in basement. Courtesy of Global News, https://globalnews.ca/news/3008151/toronto-golf-club-apologizes-after-mom-was-asked-to-breastfeed-son-in-basement/; Ghebreslassie, M. (2016, October 17). Breastfeeding mom banished to basement of Toronto country club "very pleased" with apology. CBC News, http://www.cbc.ca/news/canada/toronto/breastfeeding-country-club-1.3808294; Howells, L. (2016, October 17). Breastfeeding Toronto woman says she was escorted to country club basement. CBC News, www.cbc.ca/news/canada/toronto/breastfeeding-country-club-1.3807819. Reproduced by permission of CBC Licensing.

QUESTIONS

1. What do you think of the incident and the way the club handled it?

2. Do you think the club should have conducted a needs analysis before deciding on what they will do? What information would they have obtained if they had conducted a needs analysis?

3. Use the needs analysis process model (Figure 3.1) to better understand what happened at the club. Be sure to consider each step in the process. Describe what you would learn from organizational, task, and person analysis and what the outcomes would be.

4. What methods and sources would you use to conduct a needs analysis at the club? What methods and sources would you use for organizational, task, and person analysis and why?

5. Use the Mager and Pipe's flowchart in Figure 3.2 to determine some possible solutions to the problem. Do you think training is part of the solution? If so, who should be trained and what kind of training should they receive? Do you think that the club should provide all of its employees with sensitivity training? What other solutions might be necessary?

6. What do you think the club should do to prevent similar incidents from happening again? Explain your answer.

FLASHBACK QUESTIONS

1. Refer to Figure 1.2 in Chapter 1 (The Context of Training and Development) and use it to explain if training is needed at the golf and country club and what kind of training might be needed. What factors might affect the extent to which the club provides training to its employees and the type of training they provide?

2. Refer to the ISD model in Figure 1.4 in Chapter 1 (The Instructional Systems Design Model of Training and Development) and describe how it can be used to design and deliver a training program for employees at the golf and country club. Be specific about the training objectives, training content, and how you would evaluate the training program.

FLASH FORWARD QUESTION

1. If a training objective is a statement of what trainees are expected to be able to do after a training program, what would be the training objective of a training program for employees at the golf and country club? What content would you include in a training program for the employees at the club?

REWRITE THE CASE QUESTION: THE NEEDS ANALYSIS PROCESS

Rewrite the case so that it includes the needs analysis process (see Figure 3.1) and a description of each of the steps. In other words, write a description for the case in which you describe what the club has done at each step of the needs analysis process. Be sure to indicate a response at each step (e.g., what is the concern, is it important, what stakeholders were consulted, needs analysis, etc.).

RUNNING CASE STUDY DIRTY POOLS

QUESTIONS

Refer to the case at the end of Chapter 1 to answer the following questions.

1. Explain what a need and a needs analysis are and relate both to the information provided in the case. Be sure to explain any gaps or deficiencies, the current situation, and the desired situation.

2. Explain the needs analysis process using Figure 3.1 in relation to the information and situation described in the case. In other words, describe the concern, its importance, the stakeholders, and the information that can be obtained from a needs analysis. What are some of the outcomes that might result from this process? Be sure to refer to the case in describing each step and the outcomes.

3. If each facility were to conduct a needs analysis, what would they find out from conducting organizational, task, and person analysis?

4. What methods and sources of information should be used to conduct a needs analysis and why? How would this information be helpful in the design of a training program for pool operators and employees?

5. Do you think pool operators and employees should be required to attend a standardized training program? To answer this question, run the situation through Mager and Pipe's performance analysis flowchart (Figure 3.2). Do you think training is the best solution to the problems identified in the case? Are there other possible solutions? Explain your answer.

// REFERENCES

1. Dobson, S. (2010, November 29). Learning to avoid the bad guys. *Canadian HR Reporter*, *23*(21), 24. Reprinted by permission of *Canadian HR Reporter*. © Copyright Thomson Reuters Canada Ltd., 2010, Toronto, Ontario, 1-800-387-5164. Web: www.hrreporter.com.

2. Salas, E., & Cannon-Bowers, J. A. (2001). The science of training: A decade of progress. *Annual Review of Psychology*, *52*, 471–499.

3. Leigh, D., Watkins, R., Platt, W. A., & Kaufman, R. (2000). Alternate models of needs assessment: Selecting the right one for your organization. *Human Resource Development Quarterly, 11*, 87–93.

4. Kaufman, R. (1991). *Strategic planning plus: An organizational guide.* Glenview, IL: Scott Foreman Professional Books.

5. Leigh et al. (2000).

6. Mills, G. R., Pace, W., & Peterson, B. (1989). *Analysis in human resource training and organization development.* Reading, MA: Addison-Wesley.

7. Winsa, P. (2014, June 26). Guards seek self-defence training. *Toronto Star,* pp. GT1, GT4.

8. Hall, B. (2003). The top training priorities for 2003. *Training, 40*(2), 38–42.

9. Carr, C. (1992). The three Rs of training. *Training, 29*(6), 60–61.

10. Goldstein, I. L. (1993). *Training in organizations* (3rd ed.). Pacific Grove, CA: Brooks/Cole.

11. Dobson, S. (2010, February 8). Constructive education. *Canadian HR Reporter, 23*(3), 14, 15.

12. Gibb-Clark, M. (2000, February 11). Employee training can backfire on firms: Survey. *The Globe and Mail,* p. B10.

13. Dobson, S. (2013, November 4). B.C. confronting bullies. *Canadian HR Reporter, 26*(19), 1, 6.

14. Bernier, L. (2013, December 16). Safety training to be mandatory in Ontario. *Canadian HR Reporter, 26*(22), 1, 6.

15. Bernier, L. (2016, July 11). All Ontario employees need accessibility training. *Canadian HR Reporter, 29*(12), 1, 6.

16. Rushowy, K. (2017, May 18). New judges to undergo mandatory training. *Toronto Star,* pp. A1, A18; Hasham, A. (2017, July 2). As courts adapt to societal change, judges go back to school. *Toronto Star,* pp. A1, A4.

17. Shields, R. (2014, May 5). Training around privacy. *Canadian HR Reporter, 27*(9), 12.

18. Bernier, L. (2015, October 19). Wanted: Execs with media expertise. *Canadian HR Reporter, 28*(17), 1, 14.

19. Brennan, R. J. (2014, July 13). Making mental health issues a priority. *Toronto Star,* pp. A3.

20. Rouiller, J. Z., & Goldstein, I. L. (1993). The relationship between organizational transfer climate and positive transfer of training. *Human Resource Development Quarterly, 4*, 377–390.

21. Tracey, J. B., Tannenbaum, S. I., & Kavanagh, M. J. (1995). Applying trained skills on the job: The importance of the work environment. *Journal of Applied Psychology, 80*, 239–252.

22. Parry, S. B. (1998). Just what is a competency? *Training, 35*(6), 58–64.

23. Salas & Cannon-Bowers (2001).

24. Brown, K. G., & Sitzmann, T. (2011). Training and employee development for improved performance. In S. Zedeck (Ed.), *Handbook of industrial and organizational psychology* (Vol. 2, pp. 469–503). Washington, DC: American Psychological Association.

25. DuBois, D. A. (2002). Leveraging hidden expertise: Why, when, and how to use cognitive task analysis. In K. Kraiger (Ed.), *Creating, implementing, and managing effective training and development: State-of-the-art lessons for practice* (pp. 80–114). San Francisco, CA: Jossey-Bass; Brown & Sitzmann (2011).

26. Salas, E., Burke, C. S., & Cannon-Bowers, J. A. (2002). What we know about designing and delivering team training: Tips and guidelines. In K. Kraiger (Ed.), *Creating, implementing, and managing effective training and development: State-of-the-art lessons for practice* (pp. 234–259). San Francisco, CA: Jossey-Bass.

27. Salas et al. (2002).

28. Salas, E., Tannenbaum, S. I., Kraiger, K., & Smith-Jentsch, K. A. (2012). The science of training and development in organizations: What matters in practice. *Psychological Science in the Public Interest*, *13*, 74–101.

29. Mager, R. F., & Pipe, P. (1970). *Analyzing performance problems: Or, you really oughta wanna*. Belmont, CA: Lear Siegler/Fearon.

30. Preskill, H. (1991). A comparison of data collection methods for assessing training needs. *Human Resource Development Quarterly*, *2*(2), 143–156.

31. Silliker, A. (2013, January 14). Recognizing HR excellence in N.B. *Canadian HR Reporter*, *26*(1), 2.

32. Latham, G. P. (1988). Human resource training and development. *Annual Review of Psychology*, *39*, 545–582.

33. McEnery, J., & McEnery, J. M. (1987). Self-rating in management training needs assessment: A neglected opportunity. *Journal of Occupational Psychology*, *60*, 49–60; Staley, C. C., & Shockley-Zalaback, P. (1986). Communication proficiency and future training needs of the female professional: Self-assessment versus supervisors' evaluations. *Human Relations*, *39*, 891–902.

34. Mabe, P. A., & West, S. G. (1982). Validity of self-evaluation of ability: A review and a meta-analysis. *Journal of Applied Psychology*, *67*, 280–296.

35. Bardsely, C. A. (1987). Improving employee awareness of opportunity at IBM. *Personnel*, *64*(4), 58–63.

36. Saari, L. M., Johnson, T. R., McLaughlin, S. D., & Zimmerle, D. M. (1988). A survey of management training and education practices in U.S. companies. *Personnel Psychology*, *41*(4), 731–744.

37. Dachner, A. M., Saxton, B. M., Noe, R. A., & Keeton, K. E. (2013). To infinity and beyond: Using a narrative approach to identify training needs for unknown and dynamic situations. *Human Resource Development Quarterly*, *24*, 239–267.

TRAINING DESIGN

CHAPTER LEARNING OUTCOMES

AFTER READING THIS CHAPTER, YOU SHOULD BE ABLE TO:

- write a training objective that includes the four elements and three components of an objective
- explain how to decide to purchase or design a training program and how to write a request for proposal (RFP)
- describe how to determine the content of a training program and the different types of training methods
- explain how to use the conditions of practice to maximize the benefits of active practice
- compare and contrast routine expertise and adaptive expertise
- explain how to design a training program for active learning
- explain how, when, and why you would design an error-management training program

Mindfulness training is all the rage these days. With many employees stressed out, overworked or overwhelmed, more employers are offering the training as a way for people to learn how to relax, rewind, and rejuvenate.

"It's about employee engagement; it's about employee wellness and employee productivity—there's so many different angles to it," says Geoff Soloway, training director at MindWell Canada.

"It's a training that supports the person and the profession, so the person is more focused, less stressed. That's going to benefit the employee personally – they're going to be happier . . . and they're going to do their work better.

It's cultivating awareness in our lives at a very basic level."

But one of the challenges with the training is traditionally it's offered over six to eight weeks, with two hours per week. For that reason, MindWell Canada launched a pilot program that is 30 days long and available online.

"One of the biggest barriers to mindfulness training thus far is that it's typically run in a multi-week structure . . . and that's logistically and financially difficult for organizations, for busy people," says Soloway.

Moving the program online will make it more accessible, as will shifts in the language and type of practices taught, he says.

"We're trying to broaden that stroke so more people are interested in taking the training."

The online training will also ask participants to invite a buddy to accompany them in the training because people are more likely to follow through if they have a workout buddy in physical exercise, and this is a mental exercise, says Soloway.

The pilot program, which will look at impacts on areas such as productivity, retention, stress reduction, and conflict management—will ideally start with in-person workshops to familiarize people with the program.

"The 30-Day Challenge was designed using similar principles to the eight-week course so that participants learn new skills and are able to integrate them into daily life with daily support and guidance, yet the content is available anytime, anywhere, and on any device, making it more relevant and accessible to a wider population, many of whom can't sign up for a weekly course because of their work schedules," he says.

University of British Columbia

The University of British Columbia participated in a 30-day online mindfulness training program.

The University of British Columbia signed on for the 30-day pilot program after going through a research study on mindfulness at work back in 2014. That six-week program involved 84 participants led by Soloway for two hours each week, as well as a four-hour mini-retreat between weeks four and five.

The mindfulness-based stress reduction program consisted of practices such as yoga, body scans, focused awareness and open awareness, mindful eating and walking, and meditation. Participants could access the mindfulness practices using smartphone applications or the Internet. They were asked to complete a 10- to 20-minute daily practice outside of work, as well as a three- to five-minute daily practice at work.

They were also to complete weekly readings, reflective exercises and weekly logs, participate as a learning partner with another participant on a weekly basis, and received a weekly email from the instructor reviewing homework for the week.

In the end, the researchers found the Mindfulness@ Work program increased participants' overall levels of mindfulness; creativity increased in the training groups; participants were less likely to report feeling powerless and withdraw from conflict situations; and there were significant improvements in emotional regulation, according to Soloway.

The self-reported increases after the program were in people's ability to handle stress, personal resiliency when faced with challenges, and workplace productivity, says Miranda Massie, health promotions co-ordinator, health, well-being and benefits, human resources at UBC in Vancouver.

The 30-day on-line Mindfulness Challenge program as well as in-person mindfulness training is now available on an annual basis for the UBC community.[1]

Source: Dobson, S. (2015, July 13). Taking mindfulness online. *Canadian HR Reporter, 28*(12), 15. Reprinted by permission of *Canadian HR Reporter.* © Copyright Thomson Reuters Canada Ltd., (2015), Toronto, Ontario, 1-800-387-5164. Web: www.hrreporter.com

// INTRODUCTION

The University of British Columbia (UBC) is a good example of an organization that invests a great deal of resources in the design of training and development programs. In order to stay competitive and ensure that employees have the knowledge and skills to perform their jobs, companies regularly design new training programs. In the case of UBC, it participated in a newly designed online mindfulness training program.

In Chapter 3, we described the process of identifying training needs and determining solutions to performance problems. Once it has been determined that training is part of the solution to performance problems, a training program must be designed.

Training design involves preparing and planning events to facilitate learning.[2] How a training program is designed not only affects learning, it also influences learner engagement. **Learner engagement** is the extent to which trainees are cognitively, physically, and emotionally immersed in the training content and the learning process. Trainees who are more engaged in a training program will be more likely to learn and retain the training material.[3]

As shown in Table 4.1, the training design involves many important decisions, such as whether to purchase a training program from a vendor or design it in-house, what content to include, what training methods to use, how to provide trainees with opportunities for practice, and what strategies to include to maximize the potential effects of practice on learning and retention. The starting point that connects the needs analysis to training design is writing training objectives.

Training design
The process of preparing and planning events to facilitate learning

Learner engagement
The extent to which learners are cognitively, physically, and emotionally immersed in the training content and the learning process

TABLE 4.1
TRAINING DESIGN ACTIVITIES

1. Write training objectives.
2. Decide to purchase or design a training program.
3. Create a request for proposal (RFP) to purchase training services and programs.
4. Determine the training content.
5. Decide on the training methods.
6. Incorporate active practice and conditions of practice into the training program.
7. Consider design elements for active learning if adaptive expertise is required.

// TRAINING OBJECTIVES

A **training objective** is a statement that answers the question, *What should trainees be able to do at the end of a training program?* Put another way, an objective is the expected or intended outcome of training. Training objectives also describe the knowledge and skills to be acquired.

The emphasis of training is usually on learning, on-the-job behaviour, and job performance. Learning involves the process of acquiring new knowledge, skills, and attitudes, while performance involves the use of these new skills, knowledge, and attitudes on the job. Training objectives usually refer to the acquisition of knowledge and/ or skills as well as behaviour and performance on the job.

Training objectives are an important link between the needs analysis stage and the other stages of the training and development process. In addition to stating what employees will learn and be able to do following a training program, training objectives serve a number of purposes for trainees, trainers, and managers; these are described in Table 4.2. Thus, it is important to write training objectives prior to designing a training program.

TABLE 4.2

PURPOSES OF TRAINING OBJECTIVES

Training objectives serve a number of purposes for trainers, trainees, and managers.

TRAINERS

1. Trainees can be assessed prior to training to determine if they have mastered any of the objectives. Depending on the results, trainees can either omit certain sections of a training program or undertake additional training to master the prerequisites.

2. The selection of training content and methods is simplified by objectives. The choice of content and methods is guided by the need to achieve certain objectives.

3. Learning objectives enable trainers to develop measures for evaluation, to determine how to evaluate a training program, and how to calculate the benefits of a program.

TRAINEES

4. Objectives inform trainees of the goals of a training program and what they will be expected to learn and do at the end of a training program.

5. Objectives allow trainees to focus their energies on achieving specific goals, rather than waste energy on irrelevant tasks or on trying to figure out what is required of them.

6. Objectives communicate to employees that training is important and that they will be accountable for what they learn in training.

MANAGERS

7. Objectives communicate to managers, professional groups, and others what the trainee is expected to have learned by the end of a training program and what the trainee should be able to do.

8. Management and supervisors know exactly what is expected of trainees and can reinforce and support newly trained knowledge and skills on the job.

WRITING TRAINING OBJECTIVES

Writing training objectives involves more than making lists of behaviour verbs such as *recognize* and *evaluate*. The real skill is the ability to rework needs analysis information into performance outcomes. A training objective should contain four key elements of the desired outcome, as follows:

1. *Who is to perform the desired behaviour?* Employees and managers are the easiest to identify. In a training situation more accurate descriptors might be "all first-level supervisors," "anyone conducting selection interviews," or "all employees with more than one month of experience." The trainer is not the "who," although it is tempting for some trainees to write, for example, that the trainer will present five hours of information on communication. The goal of the instructor is to maximize the efficiency with which all trainees achieve the specified objectives, not just present the information.[4]

2. *What is the actual behaviour to be used to demonstrate mastery of the training content or objective?* Actions described by verbs like *type*, *run*, and *calculate* can be measured easily. Other mental activities, such as *comprehend* and *analyze* can also be described in measurable ways. This represents the essence of what it is that the trainee must be able to do as a result of the training. Therefore, it is important to clearly indicate what that behaviour will be. One way to do this is to use Bloom's taxonomy of learning objectives, which includes six main categories (remember, understand, apply, analyze, evaluate, and create) that are ordered from simple to complex and concrete to abstract.[5] Table 4.3 lists the six main categories and subcategories.

3. *Where and when is the behaviour to be demonstrated and evaluated (i.e., under what conditions)?* These could include "during a 60-second typing test," "on a ski hill with icy conditions," "when presented with a diagram," or "when asked to design a training session." The tools, equipment, information, and other source materials for training should be specified. Included in this list may be things the trainee may not use, such as calculators.

4. *What is the standard by which the behaviour will be judged?* Is the trainee expected to type 60 words per minute with fewer than three errors? Can the trainee list five out of six purposes for training objectives?

An example of a training objective that includes the four elements is as follows:

The sales representative (who) *will be able to make 10 calls a day to new customers* (what) *in the territory assigned* (where *and* when) *and will be able to generate three (30 percent) sales worth at least $500 from these calls* (how *or* the criterion).

Training objectives should closely resemble the task analysis. For example, one task of the job of a receptionist could be: *The receptionist* (who) *sorts 100 pieces of incoming mail by categories of complaints, requests for information, and invoices* (what) *within 60 minutes, with less than one percent processing errors* (how). This could easily become a training objective. A training objective that reads like a job behaviour is more likely to be approved, learned, and used on the job.

When the four elements are included in a training objective, the final written objective should contain three key components:

1. *Performance:* What the trainee will be able to do after the training. In other words, what work behaviour the trainee will be able to display.

TABLE 4.3	

BLOOM'S TAXONOMY OF LEARNING OBJECTIVES	
1.0	*Remember*: Retrieving relevant knowledge from long-term memory. 1.1 Recognizing 1.2 Recalling
2.0	*Understand*: Determining the meaning of instructional messages, including oral, written, and graphic communication. 2.1 Interpreting 2.2 Exemplifying 2.3 Classifying 2.4 Summarizing 2.5 Inferring 2.6 Comparing 2.7 Explaining
3.0	*Apply*: Carrying out or using a procedure in a given situation. 3.1 Executing 3.2 Implementing
4.0	*Analyze*: Breaking material into its constituent parts and detecting how the parts relate to one another and to an overall structure or purpose. 4.1 Differentiating 4.2 Organizing 4.3 Attributing
5.0	*Evaluate*: Making judgments based on criteria and standards. 5.1 Checking 5.2 Critiquing
6.0	*Create*: Putting elements together to form a novel, coherent whole or make an original product. 6.1 Generating 6.2 Planning 6.3 Producing

Source: Krathwohl, D. R. (2002). A revision of Bloom's taxonomy: An overview. *Theory into Practice, 41*(4), 212–218. Reprinted by permission of the publisher Taylor & Francis Ltd, http://www.tandfonline.com

2. *Condition:* The tools, time, and situation under which the trainee is expected to perform the behaviour. In other words, where and when the behaviour will occur.

3. *Criterion:* The level of acceptable performance, standard, or criteria against which performance will be judged.

Representative workers should be involved in the development of the training objectives. A team consisting of the trainer, trainees, and their supervisors would be ideal.[6] At some point, the objectives should be reviewed with, and approved by, the managers and the supervisors of the trainees.

In summary, a training objective contains an observable action with a measurable criterion outlining the conditions of performance. Once training objectives have been developed, the next step is to design a training program. However, at this point the organization has to decide whether a training program should be designed in-house by the HR or training staff or by an external consultant or vendor. This is known as the purchase-or-design decision and is described in the next section.

// THE PURCHASE-OR-DESIGN DECISION

Once the training objectives have been developed, the organization faces a make-or-purchase decision. Many private training companies and consultants in Canada offer an extensive array of courses on general topics such as health and safety and customer service. The use of external sources to provide training and development programs and services is known as **outsourcing**. In Canada, organizations allocate 39 percent of direct learning and development expenditures to external sources, which is similar to learning and development salaries.[7] The main reasons for outsourcing are cost savings, time savings, and improvements in compliance and accuracy.[8]

In many cases, it is more economical for an organization to purchase training materials, packaged in a professional format, than to develop the materials themselves, which in many cases will be used only once or twice.

For example, most organizations do not design training courses in basic skills; rather, they form alliances with educational institutions, community colleges, or private organizations that specialize in developing and delivering basic skills training programs.[9] Recall from the chapter-opening vignette that the online mindfulness training program at UBC was designed by MindWell Canada.

Organizations are particularly likely to purchase training programs that do not require organization-specific content and are of a more generic nature. For example, organizations prefer to use outside consultants for sexual harassment training.[10]

The advantages of packaged programs are high quality, immediate delivery, ancillary services (tests, videos), the potential to customize the package to the organization, benefits from others' implementation experience, extensive testing, and often a lower price than internally developed programs.[11]

Training programs developed internally by an organization also have some advantages, including security and confidentiality, use of the organization's language, incorporation of the organization's values, use of internal content expertise, understanding of the specific target audience and organization, and the pride and credibility of having a customized program.[12]

Let's now consider how an organization decides whether they should design a training program in-house or purchase one from a training vendor or consultant.

> **Outsourcing**
> The use of an external supplier to provide training and development programs and services

PURCHASE DECISION FACTORS

Given the pros and cons of purchasing and designing a training program, what factors should be considered when making such a decision? One of the most important factors is the cost of each alternative. A cost–benefit analysis is necessary to determine the best option. As indicated in the chapter-opening vignette, the online mindfulness training program takes less time to complete and is less costly than the more traditional program. Some organizations, such as Enbridge and Shoppers Drug Mart, have purchased training programs and deliver them in-house to save on residential costs.[13]

In addition to the cost of training, other factors should also be considered. For example, the human resource staff must have the time and expertise to design a training program. Designing a training program requires expertise in many areas, such as training methods and the principles and theories of learning. If the human resource department does not have this expertise in-house, it will need to purchase all or part of a training program. As well, developing a training program is time consuming. Unless a human resource department has a training function and training staff or is otherwise well staffed, it may not have the time to design training programs.

Time is also a factor in terms of how soon an organization wants to begin training. Given the amount of time required to design a new training program, if there is a need or desire to begin training as soon as possible, then the organization will need to purchase a training program. In effect, the sooner the organization wants to begin training, the less likely there will be sufficient time to design a new training program.

Another important factor is the number of employees who need to be trained and the extent to which future employees will require training. If a relatively small number of employees require training, then it is probably not worthwhile to design a new training program. However, if a large number of employees need to receive training now and in the future, designing a new training program in-house makes more sense. Thus, to the extent that the training program will be used for many employees in both the short and the long term, a decision to design the program in-house is more likely.

When purchasing training products and services, organizations have several options. For example, they can purchase an off-the-shelf training program that is already designed and contains all the materials required to deliver a training program such as the online mindfulness training program. Alternatively, a consultant can be hired to design and/or deliver a training program, or a purchased training program can be delivered by training staff or subject-matter experts within an organization.

When an organization decides to purchase a training program, it must choose a vendor or consultant who will design and/or deliver the program. This requires a request for proposal and is described in the next section.

// REQUEST FOR PROPOSAL (RFP)

Request for proposal (RFP)
A document that outlines to potential vendors and consultants an organization's training and project needs

The process of identifying and hiring a vendor or consultant begins with a **request for proposal (RFP)**, which is a document that outlines to potential vendors and consultants the organization's training and project needs. Vendors and consultants can review the RFP and determine whether they are able to provide the products and services required by the organization and whether they should prepare a proposal and bid on the job. The organization must then evaluate the proposals it receives and choose a vendor that can provide the best solution and is also a good match for the organization.

An RFP should provide detailed information about the organization's training needs and the nature of the project. It also often includes a detailed statement of the work, instructions on how to respond, and a schedule for the RFP and the selection process.[14]

Creating an RFP is an important step in searching for a vendor because it requires the organization to describe its most critical training needs and the nature of the training solution required. This will help to ensure that the organization purchases what it really needs and communicates the training needs and required project to stakeholders and potential vendors.

Failure to prepare a detailed RFP can result in an organization purchasing a program that it really does not need and at a much higher cost than necessary. There are many stories of companies that failed to create a good RFP and then purchased programs and systems that went well beyond what they really needed.[15] Thus, it is important that an organization determine the extent to which a vendor's products and services match its needs for training services and products. To learn more about how to write an effective RFP, see The Trainer's Notebook 4.1, "An Effective Request for Proposal (RFP)."

// TRAINING CONTENT

If a decision is made to design a training program, the next step is to determine the training content. The training content should be relevant for task performance and it should also be meaningful to trainees. Training content has greater **meaningfulness** to trainees when it is rich in associations and it is easily understood.[16] Recall that the content of the mindfulness training program includes yoga, body scans, focused awareness and open awareness, mindful eating and walking, and meditation. This content is both relevant and meaningful to trainees, and thus it will facilitate learning and retention.

This is a crucial stage in training design because the training content must be based on the training needs and objectives. As noted by Campbell, "By far the highest-priority question for designers, users, and investigators of training is, 'What is to be learned?'

> **Meaningfulness**
> Training content that is rich in associations and is easily understood by trainees

That is, what (specifically) should a training program try to accomplish, and what should the training content be?"[17]

To understand the importance of this, consider an organization that sells dental equipment and supplies. Although the company regularly offers new products, they do not sell very well. The reason is that the sales force concentrates on repeat sales of more common supplies and materials. There are a number of reasons why this might be the case. For example, the sales force might not be sufficiently informed about the new products, or they might not have the skills required to sell them. Other reasons could be a lack of motivation or an attitude problem. Obviously, designing a training program to inform the sales force about the new products will not be very effective if what they are actually lacking are sales skills. Getting the content right is one of the most important stages in training design.

A trainer will have a good idea about the required training content from the needs analysis and training objectives. This is another reason why it is important to conduct a thorough needs analysis prior to designing a training program. In fact, a review of research on managerial training found that managerial training programs were more effective when the training content was based on an analysis of the tasks or skill requirements of the job.[18] Training content can also be determined by comparing employees' current levels of knowledge and skills to the organization's desired levels as indicated by the performance goals or objectives. The gap between the two represents the organization's training needs and the required content of a training program.

At the Canadian National Exhibition, each department is asked about situations summer staff can expect to encounter in each job. The departments then provide real-life scenarios and the best ways to handle them. As a result, the training content is tailored to department needs and specific jobs. The training content for supervisors includes handling conflict between staff members, escalating and de-escalating complaints, taking corrective action, recognizing staff for initiative and great service, and evaluating performance.[19]

According to Donald Kirkpatrick, trainers should ask themselves "What topics should be presented to meet the needs and accomplish the objectives?"[20] In some cases, the required training is legislated, such as the Workplace Hazardous Materials Information System (WHMIS), which requires that workers in certain occupations receive training on the potential hazards of chemicals in the workplace and emergency procedures for the clean-up and disposal of a spill (see Chapter 12). In such cases, the content of training is specified in the legislation and in the requirements for employee certification.

Subject-matter expert (SME) A person who is familiar with the knowledge, skills, and abilities required to perform a task or a job

In other cases, it might be necessary to consult a **subject-matter expert (SME)** who is familiar with the knowledge, skills, and abilities required to perform a task or a job and who can specify the training content.[21] For example, to determine the content of a training program on sales techniques, one might consult with experienced salespersons, consultants, or managers. At BMO, they survey the highest-ranking commercial account managers in order to identify their best work habits and key drivers of success. Their responses are then incorporated into a guide that is given to all employees in the account management sales force.[22]

In Chapter 3, it was noted that a priority for police forces today is how best to deal with people who have mental health issues. As a result, many police forces, like the Ontario Provincial Police (OPP), train their forces in mental health. But what content should be included in these training programs? The OPP provides a three-day Crisis Intervention training program that includes content on the *Mental Health Act*, different mental health issues people might have and the signs and symptoms, how to de-escalate

The Ontario Provincial Police provides its forces with a three-day Crisis Intervention training program.

and diffuse high-risk situations, proper procedures to help persons with mental illness, and the community resources that are available.[23]

We also noted in Chapter 3 the increasing concerns about privacy and protection of customer and client personal information, and that many organizations must now provide their employees and managers with privacy training. But what content would you include in a privacy training program? To learn more, see The Trainer's Notebook 4.2, "Training Content for Privacy Training."

THE TRAINER'S NOTEBOOK 4.2

TRAINING CONTENT FOR PRIVACY TRAINING

Although the content of a privacy training program depends on an organization's activities, policies, and procedures, as well [as] the privacy laws that it must abide by, the following are some common areas that should be part of the content of a privacy training program:

- some privacy-related background information that provides context for the training
- a discussion of key terms
- a brief review of applicable privacy laws
- an examination of key privacy concepts

- a description of the organization's ongoing dealings with, and holdings of, personal information or personal health information
- a review of the organization's policies and procedures that relate to privacy and data security
- an introduction to the organization's privacy officer or team, and a description of her roles and responsibilities
- a reminder of each staff member's personal responsibilities relating to privacy/data security

Source: Shields, R. (2014, May 5). Training around privacy. *Canadian HR Reporter*, p. 12. Reprinted by permission of *Canadian HR Reporter*.
© Copyright Thomson Reuters Canada Ltd., (2014), Toronto, Ontario, 1-800-387-5164. Web: www.hrreporter.com

// TRAINING METHODS

Once the training content has been determined, the next step is to decide what training methods will be used.[24] The topic of training methods is extensive, and the next three chapters are devoted to it. For now we will present a brief introduction to this important part of training design.

Training methods can be classified into a number of different categories, such as active versus passive methods, one-way versus two-way communication, or informational versus experiential. For our purposes, we distinguish training methods in terms of where they take place, since this is a fairly tangible distinction. That is, some training methods take place on the job, such as coaching and performance aids, while others take place off the job in a classroom with an instructor. A third category includes methods that use technology to deliver training, such as the online mindfulness training program described at the beginning of the chapter.

A variety of off-the-job and on-the-job training methods are described in Chapters 5 and 6, and technology-based training methods are described in Chapter 7. The effectiveness of these methods differs depending on the type of training content and the learning outcomes. There are many training methods from which to choose, and the choice will be influenced by many factors, such as the training objectives, time, money, and tradition.

Research shows that learning and retention are best achieved through the use of training methods that promote productive responses from trainees and actively engage trainees in learning the training material, which is a key part of the mindfulness training program.[25] **Productive responses** are those in which the trainee actively uses the training content rather than passively watching, listening to, or imitating the trainer. In addition, training methods that encourage active participation during training also enhance learner engagement and learning.[26]

Ultimately, the objectives of a training program and the training content should determine the most appropriate training methods. For many organizations, however, the best approach is a **blended training** approach that consists of a combination of classroom training, on-the-job training, and computer technology. According to the Conference Board of Canada, many Canadian organizations use a blend of training methods as opposed to a single training method.[27]

For example, at construction company EllisDon, employees receive classroom training, self-guided e-learning and webinars, lunch and learn programs, and on-the-job training.[28] Training for new hires at Best Buy includes role plays, on-the-job training, and online training.[29]

Andrey Popov/Shutterstock.com

Trainees learn and acquire new knowledge and skills through active practice.

> **Productive responses**
> The trainee actively uses the training content rather than passively watching, listening to, or imitating the trainer
>
> **Blended training**
> The use of a combination of approaches to training, such as classroom training, on-the-job training, and computer technology

> **Practice**
> Physical or mental rehearsal of a task, skill, or knowledge in order to achieve some level of proficiency in performing the task or skill or demonstrating the knowledge

// ACTIVE PRACTICE

One of the most important ways that people learn and acquire new skills is through practice.[30] It is therefore important to incorporate practice into the design of a training program. But what exactly is practice?

Practice is physical or mental rehearsal of a task, skill, or knowledge in order to achieve some level of proficiency in performing the task or skill or demonstrating the knowledge.[31] There is a certain degree of truth to the adage "practice makes perfect." A student who practises answering exam questions will learn more than a student who just reads the textbook. A manager will probably learn more about interviewing by actually conducting a mock interview than by listening to a lecture on interviewing. In general, both adults and children learn through practice.

In training, we refer to **active practice**, which means that trainees are given opportunities to practise the task or use the knowledge being learned during training. Recall from the chapter-opening vignette that the online mindfulness training program required participants to complete a 10- to 20-minute daily practice outside of work and a three- to five-minute daily practice at work. Another example of a training program that includes active practice is IBM's Global Sales School, which prepares new sellers with the skills they need to differentiate IBM and win in the marketplace. The program focuses on learning by doing and includes practising sales skills, writing proposals, developing solutions, prospecting and identifying opportunities, negotiating and closing deals, and contributing to account and territory planning. Trainees also practise sales meetings that involve mock client meetings with experienced IBM sellers who play the role of a client.[32]

Training programs that include opportunities for active practice not only maximize learning but also facilitate learner engagement and a change in behaviour. The active engagement of trainees in learning training content has been shown to enhance and maximize learning.[33] However, the effectiveness of active practice depends on conditions of practice that occur before and during training.

In the following sections, we describe **conditions of practice** that can be implemented before (pre-training) and during training to enhance the effectiveness of active practice and maximize trainee learning and retention.

Table 4.4 summarizes the conditions of practice before and during training. Some of these conditions are especially important when designing training programs for older workers. To learn more, see Training Today 4.1, "Designing Training Programs for Older Workers."

> **Active practice**
> Providing trainees with opportunities to practise performing a training task or using knowledge during training

> **Conditions of practice**
> Practice conditions that are implemented before and during training to enhance the effectiveness of active practice and maximize learning and retention

TRAINING TODAY 4.1

DESIGNING TRAINING PROGRAMS FOR OLDER WORKERS

One of the most important demographic changes occurring in North America and Europe is the aging of the workforce. Besides the fact that the workforce is getting older, workers are staying longer in the workforce, returning to work after retirement, and working past the typical retirement age. In addition, the nature and types of jobs available for older workers is also changing, which means that many older workers will need to learn new skills to remain employed. Thus, there are and there will continue to be a greater percentage of older workers (those over 50) than ever before. As a result, the need to effectively train older workers has never been greater. The question, however, is *How do you design training programs to be most effective for older workers?*

The starting point for answering this question is an awareness of some of the differences between older and younger workers. It is well known that there are many physical and cognitive changes that occur over the adult lifespan. For example, aging impacts cognitive processing, which can result in slower reaction time and longer times required to process information. Slower processing speeds can make it difficult to acknowledge, encode, and act upon novel information. Age can also influence the maintenance and manipulation of information that is necessary for comprehension and learning. In addition, attentional resources can diminish with age, and this can affect one's ability to coordinate and integrate information. There are also

(continued)

motivational changes associated with aging. For example, there is some evidence that motivation to learn and self-efficacy decline with age.

So how should training programs be designed for older workers? There are two approaches that address this question. First, age-specific training is designed specifically for older trainees and aims to minimize or limit cognitive (or physical or motivational) limitations. This might involve presenting the training material at a slower rate or in smaller chunks of information. However, age-specific training in which older workers receive their own special training program runs the risk of stigmatizing them and reinforcing negative stereotypes of older workers that can result in negative consequences.

In contrast, age-general training involves designing training programs that will be effective for and benefit trainees of all ages. Indeed the research indicates that sound instructional principles have positive effects on young and older trainees. Furthermore, well-designed training programs based on sound instructional principles should be particularly beneficial for older trainees. For example, advance organizers have been found to be more beneficial for older trainees, although they are also beneficial for younger trainees.

So what approach is better – age-specific training or age-general training? According to Kurt Kraiger, the answer is both. Age-general training because best practices should be incorporated into the design of all training programs and sound instructional principles will be effective for trainees of all ages. At the same time, there is no reason why small or reasonable changes to accommodate older trainees should not also be incorporated into the design of training programs. Thus, the best solution is to combine elements of age-specific and age-general training in the design of training programs that include older trainees.

With respect to training design principles that might be especially effective for older employees, Kraiger suggests several practices. For example, training should be framed as an intrinsic benefit and training assignments should appeal to motives such as greater autonomy, greater self-determination, and positive relationships with co-workers and supervisors. It is also important to be clear about the purpose and relevance of the training. Pre-training practices might also include some instruction on cognitive strategies to enhance learning and training performance.

In addition, the training content should be organized into well-defined units in which each successive lesson builds on prior ones. The use of behaviour modelling, a training method that involves the observation of models performing training tasks, is also recommended as it has been found to be especially effective for older trainees. Several studies have also found that increasing the total training time and allowing self-pacing during training are also beneficial for older trainees' learning. There should also be some accommodations to the training environment such as providing comfortable furniture, proper lighting, loud enough audio, and avoiding extraneous outside distractions.

Thus, when it comes to training design for older workers, the best approach incorporates best practices in instructional design that maximize the learning of trainees of all ages, combined with several specific training practices that are particularly effective for the learning of older trainees.

Source: Based on Kraiger, K. (2017). Designing effective training for older workers. In E. Parry & J. McCarthy (Eds.). *The Palgrave Handbook of Age Diversity and Work* (Chapter 26, pp. 639–667). London: Palgrave Macmillan.

PRE-TRAINING INTERVENTIONS

Pre-training interventions
Activities or material provided before a training program or practice session to improve the potential for learning as well as the efficiency and effectiveness of practice during training

Conditions of practice that are implemented prior to a training program to prepare trainees for active practice are known as pre-training interventions. **Pre-training interventions** are activities or material provided before a training program or practice session to improve the potential for learning as well as the efficiency and effectiveness of practice during training.[34]

Pre-practice interventions prepare trainees for receiving and using information.[35] In this section, we discuss six pre-training interventions: (1) attentional advice, (2) metacognitive strategies, (3) advance organizers, (4) goal orientation, (5) preparatory information, and (6) pre-practice briefs.

TABLE 4.4

THE CONDITIONS OF PRACTICE

The following conditions of practice can be implemented before and during training to enhance the effectiveness of practice and maximize trainee learning and retention.

PRE-TRAINING INTERVENTIONS

1. *Attentional advice.* Providing trainees with information about the task process and general task strategies that can help them learn and perform a task.

2. *Metacognitive strategies.* Ways in which trainees can be instructed to self-regulate their learning of a task.

3. *Advance organizers.* Activities that provide trainees with a structure or framework to help them assimilate and integrate information acquired during practice.

4. *Goal orientation.* The type of goal that is set during training (learning or performance).

5. *Preparatory information.* Providing trainees with information about what they can expect to occur during practice sessions.

6. *Pre-practice briefs.* Sessions in which team members establish their roles and responsibilities and establish performance expectations prior to a team practice session.

CONDITIONS OF PRACTICE DURING TRAINING

1. *Massed or distributed practice.* How the segments of a training program are divided and whether the training is conducted in a single session or divided into several sessions with breaks or rest periods between them.

2. *Whole or part learning.* Whether the training material is learned and practised at one time or one part at a time.

3. *Overlearning.* Continued practice even after trainees have mastered a task so that the behaviour becomes automatic.

4. *Task sequencing.* Dividing training material into an organized and logical sequence of sub-tasks.

5. *Feedback and knowledge of results.* Providing trainees with information and knowledge about their performance on a training task.

ATTENTIONAL ADVICE

Attentional advice involves providing trainees with information about the task process and general task strategies that can help them learn to perform a task. Attentional advice helps to focus or direct trainees' attention on specific aspects of the training or practice session and task strategies and to assimilate the training material with existing knowledge. This can aid in learning a task, performing the task, and generalizing what is learned in practice to other situations in which the strategies can be applied. Attentional advice has been found to have positive effects on cognitive learning, skill-based learning, and affective learning.[36]

METACOGNITIVE STRATEGIES

Trainees can also benefit more from practice if they know how to regulate their learning through a process known as metacognition. **Metacognition** has been described as

Attentional advice
Providing trainees with information about the task process and general task strategies that can help them learn and perform a task

Metacognition
A self-regulatory process that helps people guide their learning and performance

For more information see Chapter 2, p. 47

"thinking about one's thinking" and refers to a self-regulatory process that helps people guide their learning and performance. Metacognition allows people to assess and adjust their progress and strategies while learning to perform a task. You might recall the discussion of learning outcomes in Chapter 2, in which metacognition was described as a cognitive learning outcome.

Metacognition consists of two primary functions: monitoring and control. *Monitoring* involves identifying the task, checking and evaluating one's progress, and predicting the outcomes of that progress. *Control* involves decisions about where to allocate one's resources, the specific steps to complete a task, the speed and intensity required to work on a task, and the prioritization of activities.[37]

Metacognitive strategies
Strategies trainees can use to self-regulate their learning of a task

Metacognition involves the use of metacognitive activities or strategies to monitor one's progress during training. **Metacognitive strategies** (e.g., thinking out loud, self-diagnosing weaknesses, posing questions to yourself during practice, answering the question, "Do I understand this?") are strategies trainees can use to self-regulate their learning of a task. Metacognitive strategies can be taught to trainees prior to training so they can self-regulate and guide their own learning and performance during practice sessions. This enables trainees to identify any problems they are having and the need to modify their learning strategies. The use of metacognitive strategies prior to training has been found to enhance cognitive, skill, and affective learning (especially self-efficacy).[38]

ADVANCE ORGANIZERS

Advance organizers
Structures or frameworks to help trainees assimilate and integrate training content

Advance organizers are structures or frameworks to help trainees assimilate and integrate training content. In other words, they provide trainees with a structure or framework for organizing the training material and for integrating it with their existing knowledge. Advance organizers can include outlines, text, diagrams, and graphic organizers. Research on advance organizers has found that they improve cognitive and skill-based learning, and that they are particularly useful for learning highly complex and factual material and for low-ability trainees.[39]

GOAL ORIENTATION

For more information see Chapter 2, pp. 62–63

Goal orientation
The type of goal (learning goal or performance goal) that is set during training

Goal orientation refers to the type of goal that is set during training. You might recall the discussion in Chapter 2 about the two types of goal orientations: a learning goal orientation and a performance goal orientation. *Learning goals* focus trainees' attention on the learning process, while *performance goals* focus attention on the achievement of specific performance outcomes.

When used as a pre-training intervention, goal orientation involves having trainees set a goal at the start of the training or prior to a practice session. Since learning goals focus trainees' attention on the process of learning and skill acquisition, they tend to be more effective for learning. In fact, learning goals have been found to be related to more metacognitive activity and to result in faster skill acquisition. Thus, learning goals appear to be most effective for practice because they focus trainees' attention on learning the task rather than on their performance. However, research has found that both learning and performance pre-training goals result in higher cognitive, skill-based, and affective learning. In other words, any pre-training goal is more effective than no goal at all. Nonetheless, learning goals have been found to result in higher levels of skill-based and affective learning when compared to performance goals. Thus, it is recommended that learning goals be encouraged as a pre-training intervention.[40]

PREPARATORY INFORMATION

Preparatory information involves providing trainees with information about what to expect during training and practice sessions (e.g., events and consequences). This enables trainees to prepare for events that will take place during practice and to develop strategies to overcome performance obstacles. This also helps to minimize the effects of stress. Thus, trainees provided with preparatory information are better prepared to learn and perform a task. They know what to expect and how to deal with performance obstacles.

Preparatory information is particularly useful for learning to perform stressful tasks in which the ability to cope and overcome obstacles is critical for task performance. Research on the effects of preparatory information has found that it has positive effects on skill-based learning and affective learning outcomes (self-efficacy, attitudes toward training, and intention to use training material on the job).[41]

> **Preparatory information**
> Information about what trainees can expect to occur during practice sessions so that they can develop strategies to overcome performance obstacles

PRE-PRACTICE BRIEFS

The final example of a pre-training intervention is called pre-practice briefs and is specific to team training. **Pre-practice briefs** involve sessions in which team members establish their roles, responsibilities, and performance expectations prior to a team practice session. Pre-practice briefs can improve team practice sessions, especially for tasks that are fast-paced and stressful. Teams that have engaged in pre-practice briefs have been found to perform better than those that did not. This is partly due to better coordination and communication strategies.[42]

> **Pre-practice briefs**
> Sessions in which team members establish their roles, responsibilities, and performance expectations prior to a team practice session

> **Massed versus distributed practice**
> How the segments of a training program are divided and whether the training is conducted in a single session (massed) or is divided into several sessions with breaks or rest periods between them (distributed)

CONDITIONS OF PRACTICE DURING TRAINING

Practice conditions that can be implemented during training include: (1) massed or distributed practice, (2) whole or part learning, (3) overlearning, (4) task sequencing, and (5) feedback and knowledge of results.

MASSED VERSUS DISTRIBUTED PRACTICE

Massed versus distributed practice has to do with how segments of a training program are divided. Massed practice, or cramming, is practice with virtually no rest periods, such as when the training is conducted in a single session instead of being divided into several sessions with breaks or rest periods between them. Distributed or spaced practice conditions include rest intervals during the practice session.

Students might argue that they can succeed on an exam for which they have crammed, but research shows that memory loss after cramming is greater than if a student had studied over several weeks. Furthermore, organizations would prefer that trainees retain material over many months, rather than just knowing it for the course, test, or simulation.

Research has shown that material that was learned under distributed practice is retained longer.[43] Furthermore, a review

Massed practice or practice with no rest periods is not very effective for retention and performance.

of research on practice conditions found that distributed practice sessions resulted in higher performance than massed practice conditions.[44] Thus, practice is more effective when practice periods are spread over time, rather than massed together. Trainers teaching a new skill, such as negotiation, could increase learning by spacing the training and practices over a week of two-hour sessions, rather than cramming it into an eight-hour day. Distributed practice is most effective for trainees with little or no experience, when the rest periods are shorter early on but longer later in training, and for learning motor skills.[45]

WHOLE VERSUS PART LEARNING

Whole versus part learning has to do with whether all of the training material is learned and practised at one time or one part at a time.[46] For example, piano students often learn complex pieces one hand at a time. Research has found that the best strategy depends on the trainee and the nature of the task. Whole learning is more effective when the trainee has high intelligence, practice is distributed, the task organization of the training material is high, and task complexity is low. Generally speaking, when the task itself is composed of relatively clear and different parts or sub-tasks, it is best for trainees to learn and practise each part at a time and then perform all parts in one whole sequence. However, if the task itself is relatively simple and consists of a number of closely related tasks, then a strategy of whole learning makes more sense.[47]

OVERLEARNING

Overlearning refers to learning something until the behaviour becomes automatic. In other words, trainees are provided with continued opportunities for practice even after they have mastered the task.[48] It is an effective way to train people for emergency responses or for complex skills when there is little time to think in a job situation. It is also important for skills that employees might not need to use very often on the job.

Overlearning helps ensure that task performance will become habitual or automatic. **Automaticity** refers to the performance of a skill to the point at which little attention from the brain is required to respond correctly.[49] You might recall the discussion of learning outcomes in Chapter 2, where automaticity was described as a skill-based learning outcome.

Overlearning has been found to be an effective method for improving retention for both cognitive and physical tasks. The greater the overlearning, the longer the resulting retention of the training material. However, the benefits of overlearning for retention are reduced by half after 19 days and to zero after five to six weeks. Thus, additional training is required after about three weeks to maintain the benefits of overlearning.[50]

For more information see Chapter 2, p. 48

TASK SEQUENCING

Task sequencing has to do with the manner in which the learning tasks are organized and arranged. The basic idea is that learning can be improved by dividing the training material into an organized sequence of sub-tasks. The idea behind task sequencing was proposed by Robert Gagné, who argued that practice is not enough for learning to occur.[51] Rather, what is most important is that the distinct sub-tasks are identified and arranged in a logical sequence. In this manner, a trainee will learn each successive sub-task before the total task is performed. The trainee learns to perform each step or task in the proper order or sequence.

According to Gagné, what is most important for learning when designing a training program is identifying the component tasks or sub-tasks and arranging them into a meaningful, logical, and suitable sequence.[52]

FEEDBACK AND KNOWLEDGE OF RESULTS

Feedback and knowledge of results involves providing trainees with feedback and information about their performance on a training task so they know how they are performing. Research indicates that feedback is critical for learning for at least five reasons.[53]

First, feedback lets trainees know whether they are performing the training task effectively. This enables them to correct mistakes and improve their performance. Second, positive feedback can help build confidence and strengthen trainees' self-efficacy. Third, positive feedback can be reinforcing and stimulate continued efforts and learning. Fourth, feedback is necessary for trainees to know whether they have attained their goals and whether they need to revise them or set new ones. And fifth, clear, detailed, and timely feedback throughout training will maximize learner engagement.[54]

During training, **corrective feedback** can be provided when trainees' performance is below the standard to guide them to learn and improve new behaviours. This feedback should be designed to correct behaviour and performance. When incorrect responses are given, the feedback should include the correct response. Negative feedback ("You failed to acknowledge the client's problem") will not be perceived as punishing if the source is knowledgeable, friendly, trustworthy, and powerful enough to affect outcomes like promotions and it is accompanied by the correct response.[55]

To be most effective, feedback should be accurate, specific, credible, timely, and positive.[56] In a study of the effect of feedback on the performance of hourly workers, Miller concluded that the relevance, specificity, timing, and accuracy of the feedback are the critical factors in mastery of learning.[57] Trainees receiving this type of feedback are more likely to adjust their responses toward the correct behaviour, more likely to be motivated to change, and more likely to set goals for improving or maintaining performance.[58]

In some training methods, such as computer-assisted instruction and behaviour modelling, feedback is an integral component. For guidelines on how to provide feedback, see The Trainer's Notebook 4.3, "How to Give Training Feedback."

Feedback and knowledge of results Providing trainees with feedback and information about their performance on a training task

Corrective feedback Feedback that is meant to correct behaviour and performance

---

THE TRAINER'S NOTEBOOK   4.3

HOW TO GIVE TRAINING FEEDBACK

Feedback during training can be very effective for learning and changing behaviour if the feedback is perceived as being constructive rather than critical. Here are some tips on how to give effective training feedback.

- *Timing.* Try to provide the feedback immediately after the behaviour or performance is observed.

- *Be specific.* Feedback works best when it is specific. Don't say "You moved the arm wrong"; say "You have the arm tilted at 30 degrees."

- *Correct performance.* After discussing what was incorrectly done, provide guidance and demonstrate the correct performance. ("You had the arm tilted at a 30-degree angle; you will find it easier or quicker to tilt it 90 degrees.")

- *Reinforce correct performance.* Provide positive feedback and reinforcement following correct performance: "Good, you have the correct 90-degree angle."

// ACTIVE LEARNING

The traditional approach to training is to teach trainees to reproduce specific behaviours in similar settings and situations. This is known as **routine expertise**, and many training programs are designed for this purpose. However, routine expertise is not as effective for complex jobs that involve novel, unstructured, ill-defined, or changing task demands and work environments.

For complex jobs and tasks, employees must be able to adapt their knowledge and skills to different problems and situations. This requires **adaptive expertise**, which is the ability to use knowledge and skills across a range of tasks, settings, and situations. Adaptive expertise requires a much deeper understanding of a task because the learner has to understand how to use his/her knowledge and skills in new and novel situations. This has important implications for the design of training programs.[59]

A key factor in training design for adaptive expertise is active learning. **Active learning** is an approach to training that gives trainees control over their learning so that they become active participants in their own learning experience. For example, the learner has responsibility for choosing learning activities and monitoring and judging progress. In contrast, traditional approaches to training give the trainer primary responsibility for learning decisions and limits trainees' control. Active learning promotes an *inductive* learning process in which the learner is provided with unstructured opportunities to discover rules, principles, and strategies for performing a task on their own through exploration and experimentation. Trainees make decisions about what to explore and when to seek guidance, and this is what gives them control of and responsibility for their own learning. Traditional approaches to learning are *deductive* because they transmit knowledge to the learner and provide more guidance and structure on how and what to learn.[60]

But how do you design a training program for active learning? Several design elements have been identified, including exploratory or discovery learning, error framing, and emotion control. **Exploratory/discovery learning** provides trainees with the opportunity to explore and experiment with training tasks to infer and learn the rules, principles, and strategies for effective task performance. By contrast, **proceduralized instruction** provides trainees with step-by-step instructions on how to perform a task and the rules, principles, and strategies for effective performance.[61]

Error framing involves encouraging trainees to make errors and to view errors as instrumental for learning. In other words, trainees are encouraged to make and learn from errors during practice. We discuss this in more detail in the next section, on error-management training.

Emotion control is a strategy to help trainees control their emotions during training, which is important given that active learning can provoke stress and anxiety that can hinder learning and performance. For example, trainees might be instructed to manage negative emotions by increasing positive thoughts and self-statements and avoiding negative ones.[62]

Research on active learning has found that it is effective for developing adaptive expertise. A key reason for the effectiveness of active learning is the development and use of metacognitive strategies. Recall that metacognitive strategies are ways in which trainees self-regulate their learning. Research has found that active learning stimulates metacognitive activities to a greater extent than proceduralized instruction and helps to explain the effects of active learning strategies on adaptive learning and performance.[63] Let's now take a closer look at error-management training.

// ERROR-MANAGEMENT TRAINING (EMT)

In the previous section, we described training design elements that can be used to promote active learning. One of the design elements encourages trainees to make errors and to view them as instrumental for learning. At first, this might seem like an unusual idea. After all, people usually try to avoid making errors because they can be frustrating and lead to anxiety, anger, and despair. But think again. Isn't it the case that errors and mistakes happen quite frequently during the learning process and when people make mistakes they want to learn how to correct them? If so, why not design training programs so that trainees make errors and learn from them?

First, it is helpful to understand why errors might be important for learning. According to Michael Frese and his colleagues, errors are a source of negative feedback that can have a positive and informative function in training. In fact, they argue that negative feedback is a necessary prerequisite for learning. Thus, rather than being avoided, errors should be incorporated into the training process, a method known as error-management training.[64]

Error-management training (EMT) involves explicitly encouraging trainees to make errors during training and to learn from them. This can be done by providing trainees with only basic information or minimal instructions about how to perform a task. As a result, trainees try out different approaches when practising a task, which means that they will inevitably make errors. In contrast, when the training is **error-avoidant**, it is highly structured and trainees are given detailed step-by-step instructions on how to perform a task so they are less likely to make errors. If they do make an error, the trainer intervenes and corrects them.[65]

There are two key characteristics of EMT. First, trainees are provided with only basic training-relevant information and introduced to various problems that they are told to explore and solve on their own (active exploration). Thus, trainees are provided with little guidance and active exploration is encouraged. Because they have insufficient information they are very likely to make errors.

Second, because making errors can be frustrating, trainees are told to expect errors and to frame them positively. Thus, making errors is encouraged during training. This is known as **error-management instructions** and involves instructions that errors are a necessary and natural part of learning. Trainees are told that they should make errors and learn from them. Error-management instructions reduce the negative effects of errors and enable trainees to be open to learning from error feedback.[66] For example, when learning a new task, instructors might repeat statements such as "The more errors you make, the more you learn" and "You have made an error? Great! Because now you can learn something new!"[67]

Error training can improve learning and performance for a number of reasons. First, errors inform trainees of knowledge and skills that need improvement and what they should focus on. Second, errors force trainees to develop thoughtful strategies and a deeper processing of information, which leads to mental models of how to perform a task. Third, errors can lead to greater practice because trainees tend to practise those things they have not yet mastered. Fourth, errors force trainees to learn "error-recovery strategies," which means they are better able to respond to and correct errors, which can lead to improved performance. And fifth, errors lead to greater exploration because people often want to find out why an error has occurred. Thus, errors are likely to result in greater learning and therefore better performance of the learned task.[68]

Error-management training (EMT)
Training that explicitly encourages trainees to make errors during training and to learn from them

Error-avoidant
Training that is highly structured and provides trainees with detailed step-by-step instructions on how to perform a task so they are less likely to make errors

Error-management instructions
Statements that errors are a necessary and natural part of learning and emphasize the positive function of errors

Several studies have found that EMT is more effective than error-avoidant training for learning and performance. However, some studies have found that EMT is not more effective than error-avoidant training and is, in some cases, less effective. To better understand this discrepancy in results, Nina Keith and Michael Frese reviewed all of the studies that have compared EMT to error-avoidant training. They found that overall, EMT results in more positive training outcomes than training that does not encourage errors. However, they also found that EMT is especially effective in certain circumstances.[69]

First, EMT is effective for post-training performance but not performance during training. This should not be surprising because it is only after training that the benefits of EMT are realized. During training, trainees are involved in active exploration and are making errors that will lower their performance. Second, EMT was found to be more effective for the performance of tasks that require adaptive expertise or what are known as **adaptive tasks** (tasks that differ from those worked on during training and require different solutions) than for tasks that require routine expertise or **analogical tasks** (tasks that are similar to those worked on during training). This follows from the previous discussion of active learning. Recall that EMT is an element of active learning, and so it follows that it is more effective for tasks that require adaptive expertise.[70]

Finally, EMT was most effective when it was accompanied by error-management instructions. In other words, it is the combination of active exploration and error-management instructions that results in more positive training outcomes.[71] Interestingly, error-management instructions have also been found to benefit trainees even when the training is error avoidant. In particular, error-management instructions improve the performance of older trainees as well as younger trainees with lower cognitive ability when the training was highly structured and error avoidant. Thus, error-management instructions can be beneficial with or without error-management training.[72]

// MODEL OF TRAINING EFFECTIVENESS—TRAINING DESIGN

Before concluding this chapter, let's return to the model of training effectiveness that was introduced in Chapter 2. Recall that the model shows that in addition to training and development, trainees' cognitive ability, training motivation, self-efficacy, goal orientation, personality, and attitudes influence trainee learning and retention; learning and retention lead to individual behaviour and performance; and individual behaviour and performance influence organizational effectiveness.

Based on what you have learned in this chapter, we can add training design to the model. Recall that training methods, active practice, and practice conditions before training and during training influence learning and retention. As well, design elements that promote active learning (exploratory/discovery learning, emotion control, and EMT) are necessary to develop adaptive expertise.

Figure 4.1 above shows a revised model of training effectiveness in which training and development, trainee characteristics, and training design influence learning and retention. Thus, learning and retention are also influenced by how a training program is designed.

Adaptive tasks
Tasks that differ from those worked on during training and require different solutions

Analogical tasks
Tasks that are similar to those worked on during training

FIGURE 4.1

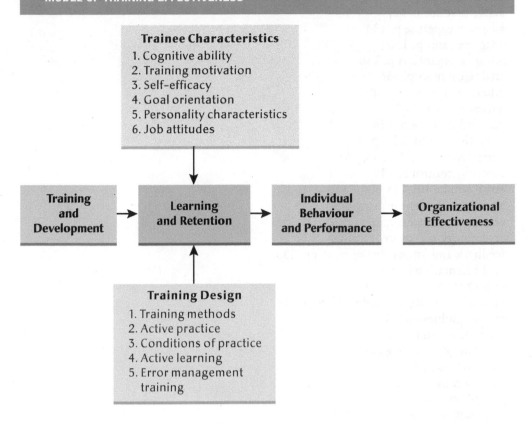

// SUMMARY

This chapter described the main activities involved in training design. First, we described how to write training objectives in terms of the key elements and components. Next, we discussed the decision to purchase or design a training program and the factors to consider when making a purchase-or-design decision. The importance of a request for proposal (RFP) was also discussed. We then described the factors involved in the design of a training program, including training content, methods, active practice, and the conditions of practice. This was followed by a discussion of active learning and design elements that promote adaptive expertise. The chapter concluded with a discussion of error-management training and the model of training effectiveness.

One of the most important design factors discussed in this chapter was training methods. As you will see in the next three chapters, there are many types of off-the-job (Chapter 5) and on-the-job training methods (Chapter 6) as well as many forms of technology-based training (Chapter 7).

KEY TERMS

active learning p. 134
active practice p. 127
adaptive expertise p. 134
adaptive tasks p. 136
advance organizers p. 130
analogical tasks p. 136
attentional advice p. 129
automaticity p. 132
blended training p. 126
conditions of practice p. 127
corrective feedback p. 133
emotion control p. 134
error-avoidant p. 135
error-management instructions p. 135
error-management training (EMT) p. 135
exploratory/discovery learning p. 134
feedback and knowledge of results p. 133
goal orientation p. 130
learner engagement p. 117
massed versus distributed practice p. 131
meaningfulness p. 123
metacognition p. 129
metacognitive strategies p. 130
outsourcing p. 121
overlearning p. 132
practice p. 126
preparatory information p. 131
pre-practice briefs p. 131
pre-training interventions p. 128
proceduralized instruction p. 134
productive responses p. 126
request for proposal (RFP) p. 122
routine expertise p. 134
subject-matter expert (SME) p. 124
task sequencing p.132
training design p. 117
training objective p. 117
whole versus part learning p. 132

DISCUSSION QUESTIONS

1. Discuss the purpose of training objectives for trainees, trainers, and managers. How would trainees, trainers, and managers be affected if a training program did not have training objectives?

2. What factors should an organization consider when deciding to purchase or design a training program?

3. What are the advantages and disadvantages of purchasing a training program and designing a training program in-house?

4. Why is it important to include active practice in a training program? Give an example of how active practice was used in a training program you have attended.

5. Discuss the conditions of practice before (pre-training interventions) and during training, and how they can improve learning and retention.

6. Explain how error-management training (EMT) works and the circumstances in which it is most likely to be effective. When should EMT be used?

7. Explain what a request for proposal (RFP) is and why an organization should write one before purchasing a training program.

8. What should be included in a request for proposal (RFP), and what are the eight things to consider when creating one?

9. What is the difference between active practice and active learning, and what are the implications of each for the design of training programs?

10. Explain how you would design (a) an error-avoidant training program, and (b) an EMT (error-management training) program. Describe each training program and how it would proceed. Be sure to describe the task that trainees are learning to perform.

11. Why do you think error-management instructions have been found to be beneficial even for structured training that is error avoidant? Why is this especially the case for older trainees as well as younger trainees who have lower cognitive ability?

12. What are some of the differences between older and younger workers and what are the implications of these differences for the design of training programs? Explain the difference between age-specific training and age-general training and how you would design a training program based on each approach.

13. Describe the six categories of Bloom's taxonomy of learning objectives and then write six training objectives for your training and development course using the six categories (refer to Table 4.3).

THE GREAT TRAINING DEBATE

1. Debate the following: Practice makes perfect and enough practice will always lead to learning and retention.

2. Debate the following: Errors are frustrating and upsetting to trainees and should be avoided in training.

EXERCISES

IN-CLASS

1. Think of the best and worst training experience you have ever had. For each one, indicate the purpose of the training, the objectives, content, and methods. Then, using the material presented in this chapter, make a list of all the reasons why you think it was your best or worst training experience. Based on your lists, what are some of the things that make a training program effective?

2. If you have a driver's licence, you probably remember what it was like to learn to drive. Chances are you stepped into a car with a friend or family member who told you what to do. And if you have ever taught someone how to drive, you probably did the same thing. Did you remember to tell them everything they needed to know? What did you tell them to do first? Could you have done a better job teaching them to drive? Refer to the section of this chapter on task sequencing. Recall that task sequencing involves dividing a task into its component parts or sub-tasks, and then ordering them into a meaningful and logical sequence. Now try to design a driver training program based on task sequencing. In other words, make a list of all of the sub-tasks involved in driving a car and then organize them into a logical sequence for the purpose of teaching somebody how to drive.

3. Have you ever wondered what your instructor does to prepare for a class? To find out, choose one of your classes and try to describe each of the following:
   - the objectives of the class
   - the content of the class
   - the training methods used
   - opportunities for active practice
   - conditions of practice
   - active learning

   Based on your description, how well was the class designed? How effective was it for your learning? How could it be improved?

4. Recall a training program that you attended in a previous or current job. Describe the objectives and content of the program and any opportunities for active practice. What did you practise and how helpful was it for your learning and retention? Describe the extent to which any of the conditions of practice were used either before or during the training program, and how they affected your learning and retention. What changes would you recommend to improve learning and retention?

5. Identify a skill that you would like to acquire. Some examples might be to use a particular software package or perhaps to improve your written or oral presentation skills. Now develop training objectives for a training program on the skill that you have chosen, using the four elements and three components of training objectives described in the chapter. Exchange your objectives with another student and evaluate each other's objectives in terms of the criteria outlined in the chapter for writing training objectives.

6. Read the following training objectives and identify what is wrong with them. Then rewrite them so that they conform to the elements and components of training objectives described in the chapter.
   - The trainer will spend 30 minutes discussing time-management tips.
   - The trainees will be able to manage their time more effectively.
   - The purpose of the seminar is to teach time-management techniques.
   - After attending the course, employees will be able to make lists and put letters beside the items on the list, enabling them to manage time more effectively.

7. Recall a training program that you attended in a previous or current job. Describe the objectives and content of the program and the extent to which errors were part of the program. Did you make any errors while learning? If so, what effect did this have on your learning and the training experience? If you were to redesign this training program, how would you change it so that it included error-management training?

IN-THE-FIELD

1. Contact the human resources department of an organization and request a meeting with a department member whom you can interview about the organization's training programs. Prepare some questions so you can learn about each of the following design factors of a particular training program that the organization has implemented:

   - Was the training program designed by the organization or purchased? What were the reasons for designing or purchasing the program?
   - If the training program was purchased, was a request for proposal (RFP) used and what was included in it?
   - What is the content of the training program and how was it developed?
   - What training methods were used and why?
   - Was active practice designed into the training program? If so, what kind of practice opportunities did trainees have?
   - To what extent were the conditions of practice listed in Table 4.4 incorporated into the training program?

   Using the information you have obtained, evaluate the training program in terms of how well it was designed and list some recommendations for improvement.

2. Contact the human resources department of an organization and request a meeting with a department member whom you can interview about the use of requests for proposals for training. Prepare some questions so you can learn about the creation and use of RFPs. For example,

   - Why do they use an RFP for training?
   - What information do they include and request in RFPs?
   - Who is involved in creating RFPs?
   - How do they use RFPs to choose a vendor?
   - How effective are RFPs for purchasing training products and services?

   Using the information you have obtained, prepare a short report and/or presentation on the organization's use of RFPs for training. What have you learned about RFPs, and what recommendations can you suggest to organizations about using and preparing them?

CASE INCIDENT

WE ID 25

The Beer Store in Ontario has a strict policy to keep alcohol from being sold to people who are underage or intoxicated. One of the ways in which this policy is enforced is through a program called We ID 25. The program requires Beer Store staff to ask for proper identification of age from anyone who appears to be 25 years of age or younger, even though the legal drinking age in Ontario is 19. In addition, customers who appear to be intoxicated can be refused service.

According to the Beer Store, preventing sales to minors is a matter of strict protocols, training, and experience. Extensive training and retraining is provided to all employees who deal with the public. An Employee Orientation package is provided to new staff that includes the We ID 25 program as well as Beer Store policies, practices, and procedures relating to the customer service standard. There are also 16 online courses for new hires.

The Beer Store tests the We ID 25 program regularly to ensure that employees are maintaining the standard. They send mystery shoppers to all of its stores at least three times a year to make sure the program is working. In 2015, almost 3.7 million customers were asked for age identification or challenged for intoxication, and about 50 000 individuals were refused service.

QUESTIONS

1. Describe what a training objective for the We ID 25 training program might focus on. In other words, what should trainees be able to do after training? Now write a training objective for the We ID 25 program. Be sure to include the four key elements and the three key components.

2. What content should be included in the We ID 25 training program? Be sure to indicate how the content you believe should be included will enable employees to enforce the policy to not sell alcohol to people who are underage or intoxicated.

Sources: Gordon, A. (2014, February 13). Rising to a minor challenge. *Toronto Star*, pp. L1, L4, www. thebeerstore.ca/about-us/social-responsibility; The Beer Store. *The Canadian Business Journal*, http://www. cbj.ca/the_beer_store/; Backgrounder: Responsible alcohol retailing. (2014, April 15). CNW, www.newswire.ca

CASE STUDY	TRAINING THE SALES FORCE

Sales at a large telecommunications company were down for the third quarter. Management reviewed several strategies to improve sales and concluded that one solution would be to improve training for the large, dispersed sales force.

For the sake of expediency, the training department began using a needs analysis it had conducted several years before as a basis to develop enhanced training. Their plan was first to update the original needs analysis, and then to develop new training strategies on the basis of what they found. They also began investigating new training technologies as a possible way to reduce training delivery costs. However, management was so intent on doing something quickly that the training department was ultimately pressured into purchasing a generic, off-the-shelf training package from a local vendor.

One of the features of the package that appealed to management was that the course could be delivered over the Web, saving the time and expense of having the sales force travel to the main office to receive the training. Hence, even though the package was costly to purchase, the company believed that it was a bargain compared to the expense of developing a new package in-house and delivering it in person to the sales force.

Six months after the training had been delivered, sales were still declining. Management turned to the training department for answers. Because no measures of training performance had been collected, the training department had little information upon which to base its diagnosis. For lack of a better idea, members of the training department began questioning the sales force to see if they could determine why the training was not working.

Among other things, the sales people reported that the training was slow and boring, and that it did not teach them any new sales techniques. They also complained that without an instructor, it was impossible to get clarification on things they did not understand. Moreover, they reported that they believed that sales were off not because they needed training in basic sales techniques, but because so many new products were being introduced that they could not keep up. In fact, several of the sales people requested meetings with design engineers just so they could get updated product information.

The training department took these findings back to management and requested that they be allowed to design a new training package, beginning with an updated needs analysis to determine the real training deficiencies.

Source: Republished with permission of Blackwell Publishing Inc. from Salas, E., & Cannon-Bowers, J. A. (2000). Design training systematically. In E. A. Locke (Ed.), *Handbook of principles of organizational behavior* (pp. 56–57). Oxford, UK. Blackwell Publishers Ltd. Permission conveyed through Copyright Clearance Center, Inc. Case questions prepared by Alan Saks.

QUESTIONS

1. What were the objectives of the training program? Write a training objective for the program described in the case that contains the key elements and components of a training objective. How would your training objective have helped in the choice/design of a training program? How would it have helped trainees and managers?

2. Comment on the company's decision to purchase a generic, off-the-shelf training package by a local vendor. What were the advantages and disadvantages? Do you think it was a good idea for the company to purchase the training rather than to have it designed in-house? Explain your answer.

3. Explain how using a request for proposal (RFP) might have changed the company's decision to purchase the training program. Do you think the company would have purchased the same training program from the same vendor if they had created a detailed RFP? Explain your answer.

4. What effect did the use of the original needs analysis have on the content of the training program and the decision to have it delivered over the Web? Do you think a new needs analysis should have been conducted? If so, what effect might it have had on the design of the training program?

5. Comment on the use of the Web as the main method of training. What are the advantages and disadvantages of this method of training? What other methods might have been more effective?

6. If you were to design the training program, describe what you would do differently in terms of (a) training objectives, (b) training content, (c) training methods, (d) active practice and conditions of practice, and (e) active learning. How would your training program be different from the one described in the case? Would your program be more effective?

FLASHBACK QUESTIONS

1. To what extent was the instructional systems design (ISD) model of training and development used at the telecommunications company? If it had been used to a greater extent, what would have been done differently? Comment on each step of the ISD model.

2. Comment on how company management concluded that one solution to the sales problem was to improve training. Do you think that improving training is the best solution to the sales problem? Explain your answer using Mager and Pipe's performance analysis flowchart for determining solutions to performance problems (see Chapter 3, Figure 3.2). What are some other possible solutions for improving sales?

3. The training department has requested that they be allowed to design a new training program for the sales force, beginning with an updated needs analysis. Explain how they should conduct a new needs analysis. Refer to Figure 3.1 when answering this question.

4. If a new needs analysis is conducted, what will be learned from an organizational, a task, and a person analysis? How will this information help in the design of a new training program?

FLASH FORWARD QUESTION

1. Do you think the sales training program would have been more effective if off-the-job training methods were used instead of the Web as the main method of training? What off-the-job training methods do you think should have been used? Explain your answer. (To answer this question, refer to Table 5.1 in Chapter 5.)

REWRITE THE CASE QUESTION: PURCHASE DECISION AND REQUEST FOR PROPOSAL

Rewrite the case by describing the factors that should be considered in the decision to purchase a generic, off-the-shelf training package from a local vendor and the use of an RFP. In other words, rewrite the case to indicate how the company decided to purchase rather than design a training program and how they used an RFP to select a vendor.

QUESTIONS

Refer to the case at the end of Chapter 1 to answer the following questions.

1. Consider what trainees might be expected to do after attending a standardized training program for pool operators and employees. Write a training objective and be sure to include the four key elements and the three components of a training objective. Also, consider the six categories in Bloom's taxonomy of learning objectives (see Table 4.3).

2. Given the concerns raised in the case regarding the various infractions, what do pool operators and employees need to learn? What content should be included in a standardized training program for pool operators and their employees?

3. Should a standardized training program for pool operators and employees include active practice? Explain your answer. Describe how active practice might be used in a training program for pool operators and their employees.

4. Consider the conditions of practice during training for a training program for pool operators and employees. What conditions of practice during training would you recommend, and why?

5. Would a training program for pool operators and their employees involve routine expertise or adaptive expertise? What are the implications of your answer for the design of a training program?

// REFERENCES

1. Dobson, S. (2015, July 13). Taking mindfulness online. *Canadian HR Reporter, 28*(12), 15.

2. Brown, K. G., & Sitzmann, T. (2011). Training and employee development for improved performance. In S. Zedeck (Ed.), *Handbook of industrial and organizational psychology* (Vol. 2, pp. 469–503). Washington, DC: American Psychological Association.

3. Kraiger, K., & Mattingly, V. P. (2018). Cognitive and neural foundations of learning. In K. G. Brown (Ed.), *The Cambridge handbook of workplace training and employee development* (pp. 11–37). New York: Cambridge University.

4. Kibler, R. J., Barker, L. L., & Miles, D. T. (1970). *Behavioral objectives and instruction.* Boston: Allyn and Bacon.

5. Krathwohl, D. R. (2002). A revision of Bloom's taxonomy: An overview. *Theory into Practice, 41*(4), 212–218.

6. Laird, D. (1985). *Approaches to training and development* (2nd ed.). Reading, MA: Addison-Wesley.

7. Cotsman, S., & Hall, C. (2018). *Learning cultures lead the way: Learning & development outlook—14th edition.* Ottawa: The Conference Board of Canada.

8. Johnson, G. (2004). To outsource or not to outsource . . . that is the question. *Training Magazine, 41*(8), 26–29.

9. Hays, S. (1999). Basic skills training 101. *Workforce Management, 78*(4), 76–78.

10. Ganzel, R. (1998). What sexual harassment training really prevents. *Training Magazine, 35*(10), 86–94.

11. Nadler, L., & Nadler, Z. (1990). *The handbook of human resource development* (2nd ed.). New York: John Wiley and Sons.

12. Nadler & Nadler (1990).

13. Klie (2009).

14. Chapman, B. (2004). How to create the ideal RFP. *Training Magazine, 41*(1), 40–43.

15. Chapman (2004).

16. Wexley, K. N., & Latham, G. P. (1991). Developing and training human resources in organizations (2nd ed.). New York: HarperCollins.

17. Campbell, J. P. (1988). Training design for performance improvement. In J. P. Campbell & R. J. Campbell, R. J. (Eds.), *Productivity in organizations: Frontiers of industrial and organizational psychology* (pp. 177–216). San Francisco, CA: Jossey-Bass.

18. Taylor, P. J., Russ-Eft, D. F., & Taylor, H. (2009). Transfer of management training from alternative perspectives. *Journal of Applied Psychology, 94*, 104–121.

19. Akkerman, E. (2014, September 8). "Let's go to the Ex," *Canadian HR Reporter, 27*(15), 14.

20. Kirkpatrick, D. L. (1994). *Evaluating training programs: The four levels* (p. 11). San Francisco, CA: Berrett-Koehler Publishers.

21. Campbell, J. P. (1988).

22. Waxer, C. (2005). Bank of Montreal opens its checkbook in the name of employee development. *Workforce Management, 84*(11), 46–49.

23. South, W. (2014, December 1). Local police take the time to learn about mental health. *Goderich Signal Star,* www.goderichsignalstar.com; Tapley, J. (2014, March 19). Crisis intervention training gives police better understanding of mental health issues. *Ingersoll Times,* www.ingersolltimes.com.

24. Campbell, J. P. (1988).

25. Campbell, J. P. (1988).

26. Thoms, P., & Klein, H. J. (1994). Participation and evaluative outcomes in management training. *Human Resource Development Quarterly, 5*, 27–39.

27. Hughes, P. D., & Campbell, A. (2009). *Learning & development outlook 2009: Learning in tough times.* Ottawa: The Conference Board of Canada.

28. Dobson, S. (2010, February 8). Constructive education. *Canadian HR Reporter, 23*(3), 14, 15.

29. Klie, S. (2010, November 1). Social media, training help with holiday hires. *Canadian HR Reporter, 23*(19), 1, 9.

30. Hinrichs, J. R. (1976). Personnel training. In M. D. Dunnette (Ed.), *Handbook of industrial and organizational psychology* (pp. 829–860). Skokie, IL: Rand McNally.

31. Cannon-Bowers, J. A., Rhodenizer, L., Salas, E., & Bowers, C. A. (1998). A framework for understanding pre-practice conditions and their impact on learning. *Personnel Psychology, 51*, 291–320.

32. Anonymous (2016, January/February). Outstanding training initiatives (IBM: Global sales school redesign and business impact study). *Training Magazine, 53*(1), 58–59.

33. Sitzmann, T. (2011). A meta-analytic examination of the instructional effectiveness of computer-based simulation games. *Personnel Psychology, 64*, 489–528.

34. Mesmer-Magnus, J., & Viswesvaran, C. (2010). The role of pre-training interventions in learning: A meta-analysis and integrative review. *Human Resource Management Review, 20*, 261–282.

35. Cannon-Bowers et al. (1998).

36. Mesmer-Magnus & Viswesvaran (2010).

37. Schmidt, A. M., & Ford, J. K. (2003). Learning within a learner control training environment: The interactive effects of goal orientation and metacognitive instruction on learning outcomes. *Personnel Psychology, 56*, 405–429.

38. Mesmer-Magnus & Viswesvaran (2010).

39. Mesmer-Magnus & Viswesvaran (2010).

40. Mesmer-Magnus & Viswesvaran (2010).

41. Mesmer-Magnus & Viswesvaran (2010).

42. Cannon-Bowers et al. (1998).

43. Baldwin, T. T., & Ford, J. K. (1988). Transfer of training: A review and directions for future research. *Personnel Psychology, 41*, 63–105.

44. Donovan, J. J., & Radosevich, D. J. (1999). A meta-analytic review of the distribution of practice effect: Now you see it, now you don't. *Journal of Applied Psychology, 84*, 795–805.

45. Bass, B. M., & Vaughn, J. A. (1969). *Training in industry: The management of learning.* Belmont, CA: Wadsworth; Donovan & Radosevich (1999).

46. Baldwin & Ford (1988).

47. Baldwin & Ford (1988).

48. Baldwin & Ford (1988).

49. Yelon, S., & Berge, Z. (1992). Practice-centered training. *Performance & Instruction, 31*(8), 8–12.

50. Driskell, J. E., Willis, R. P., & Copper, C. (1992). Effects of overlearning on retention. *Journal of Applied Psychology, 77*, 615–622.

51. Gagné, R. M. (1962). Military training and principles of learning. *American Psychologist, 17*, 83–91.

52. Gagné (1962).

53. Baldwin & Ford (1988).

54. Kraiger & Mattingly (2018).

55. Waldersee, R., & Luthans, F. (1994). The impact of positive and corrective feedback on customer service performance. *Journal of Organizational Behavior, 15*, 83–95; Ilgen, D. R., Fisher, C. D., & Taylor, M. S. (1979). Consequences of individual feedback on behaviour in organizations. *Journal of Applied Psychology, 64*, 349–371.

56. Campbell, J. P. (1988).

57. Miller, L. (1965). *The use of knowledge of results in improving the performance of hourly operators*. Detroit, MI: General Electric Company, Behavioral Research Service.

58. Locke, E. A., & Latham, G. P. (1990). *A theory of goal setting and task performance*. Englewood Cliffs, NJ: Prentice-Hall.

59. Machin, M. A. (2002). Planning, managing, and optimizing transfer of training. In K. Kraiger (Ed.), *Creating, implementing, and managing effective training and development* (pp. 263–301). San Francisco, CA: Jossey-Bass; Smith, E. M., Ford, J. K., & Kozlowski, S. W. J. (1997). Building adaptive expertise: Implications for training design strategies. In M. A. Quinones and A. Ehrenstein (Eds.), *Training for a rapidly changing workplace*. Washington, DC: American Psychological Association.

60. Bell, B. S., & Kozlowski, S. W. J. (2008). Active learning: Effects of core training design elements on self-regulatory processes, learning, and adaptability. *Journal of Applied Psychology*, *93*, 296–316; Katz-Navon, T., Naveh, E., & Stern, Z. (2009). Active learning: When is more better? The case of resident physicians' medical errors. *Journal of Applied Psychology*, *94*, 1200–1209.

61. Bell & Kozlowski (2008).

62. Bell & Kozlowski (2008).

63. Bell & Kozlowski (2008).

64. Heimbeck, D., Frese, M., Sonnentag, S., & Keith, N. (2003). Integrating errors into the training process: The function of error management instructions and the role of goal orientation. *Personnel Psychology*, *56*, 333–361.

65. Heimbeck et al. (2003).

66. Keith, N., & Frese, M. (2008). Effectiveness of error management training: A meta-analysis. *Journal of Applied Psychology*, *93*, 59–69.

67. Keith & Frese (2008).

68. Heimbeck et al. (2003).

69. Keith & Frese (2008).

70. Keith & Frese (2008).

71. Keith & Frese (2008).

72. Carter, M., & Beier, M. E. (2010). The effectiveness of error management training with working-aged adults. *Personnel Psychology*, *63*, 641–675.

CHAPTER 5

OFF-THE-JOB TRAINING METHODS

CHAPTER LEARNING OUTCOMES

AFTER READING THIS CHAPTER, YOU SHOULD BE ABLE TO:

- explain the difference between instructional methods and instructional media
- compare and contrast the use and effectiveness of different instructional methods
- explain how to design a simulation with high physical and psychological fidelity
- choose an appropriate instructional method for a training program
- discuss the implications of an aptitude–treatment interaction for training

At Queen's University, the Faculty of Health Sciences includes the schools of medicine, nursing, and rehabilitative therapy. To improve the training of its residents in surgery and resuscitation, a New Medical Building includes an 8000 square feet [approximately 750 square metres] clinical simulation centre that was built to provide state-of-the art mannequins and manipulative computer programs.

In the past, much of the learning was done at the bedside with real patients says Bob McGraw, director of the clinical simulation centre. However, this is not always the best approach for the resident or patient and it does not provide enough opportunities for learning. "You really need to have a focused, repetitive practice of skills to get good at something, and trying to do this in a hospital or clinic-based setting really isn't efficient and you really can't take your learner as far as you want to take them," he says. "The educational philosophy of a centre like this, the bottom line is that practice makes perfect and the more you practice any skill, the better you get at it—particularly if it's under a supervised setting."

New technologies allow the faculty to closely mimic real situations. For instance, a piece of plastic skin can be draped over a board and used for suturing practice. More complex simulators allow a resident to practice removing a gall bladder by seemingly cutting specific vessels, doing cautery and controlling the bleeding. Working off a video screen, they have instruments connected to a computer that can track where the instruments are moving relative to the patient and push back and resist—known as haptic feedback—to make it feel as if the instruments are touching a real person.

Residents are able to practise their technique many times, such as several times on a weekend instead of once per week or month, says McGraw. Computers track the performance of each resident and generate reports that tell the faculty how long it took a resident to do a procedure, if there were any complications, and how the instruments were moving during the procedure. "What we're focused on is a level of competency that we want to get all residents up to, so they do it as many times as they need to demonstrate that they're where we need them to be, and this is all before we let them into the operating room."

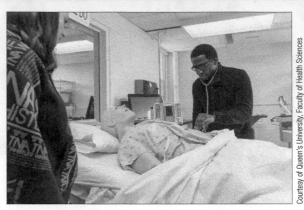

Students in the Faculty of Health Sciences at Queen's University learn to perform medical procedures in a new state-of-the art clinical simulation centre.

And because certain events like a cardiac arrest do not happen very often in a hospital, it is difficult for residents to get experience working together as a team in an emergency situation. However, thanks to the clinical simulation centre, on any given Friday morning the residents can participate in 10 or 20 emergency simulations. According to McGraw, "We can make sure that they are exposed to certain important rescue cases."

The school also provides training on resuscitation and the managing of critically ill patients, such as defibrillation. The training uses very sophisticated mannequins that produce vital signals such as a heart rate, blood pressure, and dilated pupils.

Although the mannequins and computer programs are not exactly the same as real patients, students are able to suspend reality and buy into the situation, says McGraw. "It's not precise but it does accomplish what we want it to accomplish—we can create complex scenarios, we can engage our students so that they're completely focused on the problem. And we have no problem having them suspend reality—this is the real thing."[1]

// INTRODUCTION

As you learned in Chapter 4, training methods are an important component in the design of training programs. This chapter is the first of three chapters on training methods. In this chapter, we focus on instructional methods that take place off the job.

Instructional methods are the techniques used to stimulate learning.[2] Instructional methods are usually used in a classroom or formal setting for the purpose of learning. Queen's University's clinical simulation centre is a good example of the use of simulations, which is an instructional training method discussed in this chapter.

Although the instructional methods described in this chapter usually take place in a classroom, some instructional methods, such as games and simulations, can also take place outside of a classroom and can be incorporated into computer-based training programs, as you will learn in Chapter 7.

In Canada and the United States, instructor-led classroom training remains the primary and most popular method of providing training, although it has been on the decline. In 2000, 80 percent of all training was delivered in the classroom in Canadian organizations. Today, it represents just 48 percent of all training. However, according to the Conference Board of Canada, instructor-led classroom training is still the most widely used training method in Canadian organizations and is used by 94 percent of organizations. In the United States, 42 percent of training hours are delivered by an instructor in a classroom, and 13 percent of organizations use instructor-led classroom training exclusively or mostly.[3] A survey of Canadian workers found that over one-third of them consider in-house, instructor-led workshops as the most valued type of training.[4]

This chapter describes the most common instructional training methods. The instructional methods are presented in order of degree of trainee involvement, from passive to active. We start with lectures, because there is relatively little trainee input, and end with action learning, where trainees manage the learning process.

Table 5.1 lists and defines the nine instructional methods described in this chapter.

> **Instructional methods**
> The techniques used to stimulate learning

TABLE 5.1

INSTRUCTIONAL METHODS

1. *Lecture.* The trainer presents to trainees the content to be learned.
2. *Discussion.* Two-way communication between the trainer and the trainees as well as among trainees.
3. *Case study.* Trainees discuss, analyze, and solve problems based on a real situation.
4. *Case incident.* A problem, concept, or issue is presented for analysis.
5. *Behaviour modelling training.* Trainees observe a model performing a task and then attempt to imitate the observed behaviour.
6. *Role play.* Trainees practise new behaviours in a safe environment.
7. *Simulations.* The use of operating models of physical or social events designed to represent reality.
8. *Games.* Structured competition that allows employees to learn specific skills.
9. *Action learning.* Trainees study and solve real-world problems and accept responsibility for the solution.

// LECTURE METHOD

Most people have experienced a lecture, given its widespread use in education and training. A **lecture** is a training method in which the trainer presents to trainees the training content to be learned. It involves a unidirectional flow of information from the trainer to the trainee. Although lectures have a reputation as a boring training method, the research evidence indicates that lectures are effective for training several types of skills and tasks.[5]

Lectures offer a number of advantages. Large amounts of information can be provided to large groups of trainees in a relatively short period of time at a minimal expense, which makes the lecture method very efficient. Key points can be emphasized and repeated. Trainers can be assured that trainees are all hearing the same message, which is useful when the message is extremely important, such as instructions or changes in procedures. A lecture is also useful as a method to explain to trainees what is to follow in the rest of a training session. For example, a lecture could be used to highlight the key learning points of a video or role play. Many employees are comfortable with the lecture method because they are familiar with it and it requires little participation.

However, as some of us have experienced, lectures also have some drawbacks as a training method. While useful for the acquisition of declarative knowledge and immediate recall, they are not as effective for the development of skills or for changing attitudes. The lecture does not accommodate differences in trainee ability, and all trainees are forced to absorb information at the same rate. Trainees are also forced to be passive learners with little opportunity to connect the content to their own work environment, or to receive feedback on their understanding of the material.

To overcome the disadvantages of lectures, trainers often include time for discussion, questions and answers, and other opportunities for trainee involvement. Trainers can also supplement a lecture with instructional media (e.g., video) as well as other instructional methods (e.g., case study).

A recent instructional strategy for making lectures more interesting and engaging is a **flipped classroom** (also known as an inverted classroom), in which participants view a video lecture outside of the classroom and then spend class time working on engaging and collaborative activities that are facilitated by the instructor. Thus, the training content is delivered outside of the classroom, and activities that usually take place outside of the classroom (e.g., projects, assignments) are worked on in the classroom. The flipped classroom might be especially effective for teaching procedural knowledge.[6]

Lectures are most effective for learning declarative knowledge.

Matej Kastelic/Shutterstock.com

TIPS FOR TRAINERS

Trainers can use the lecture method effectively by following a number of guidelines. For example, "Where do I begin?" is a question asked by most first-time trainers. The answer is "First you have to know what you want to do (the objective) and how much information you need to impart." The trainer should begin a lecture with an introduction to the topic and inform trainees about what they will learn and/or be able to do or accomplish by the end of the lecture.

The trainer must then present the content or body of the lecture. Either through previously gained knowledge or the ability to research a topic, the trainer will gather and arrange information in a logical manner. Logic could dictate a progression from the general to the specific or from the specific to the general, depending on the subject matter. This information can be transcribed onto cards or sheets of paper. An effective technique is to rule off a wide (5 cm to 8 cm) margin down the right-hand side of each page. Detailed information can then be placed in the body of the page, while headings are written in the margins.

It has been suggested that no more than six major points be presented during each half hour of a lecture.[7] It takes practice to get the timing of a lecture right. Only through experience can one judge the amount of material needed for any given amount of time. It is helpful to break the lecture into 10- to 15-minute segments with a short stretch of time in between, and to summarize the material at both the beginning and the end, stopping occasionally to allow trainees to catch up and to write their own summaries.

A trainer who drones on for an entire hour is rarely effective. The delivery should be punctuated with a variety of supplementary material or exercises. Stories, case incidents, graphics, humour, trainee presentations, videos, and question-and-answer sessions are some of the techniques a trainer can use to maintain interest and, perhaps even more important, impart in the trainee the love of—or at least respect for—the subject matter. The trainer should conclude the lecture with a summary of the key learning points followed by some time for questions and answers.

// DISCUSSION METHOD

The **discussion method** is a method of training that allows for two-way communication between the trainer and the trainees as well as among trainees. It is one of the primary ways to increase trainee involvement in the learning process. Group discussion serves at least five purposes:

> **Discussion method**
> Two-way communication between the trainer and trainees as well as among trainees

1. It helps trainees recognize what they do not know but should know.
2. It is an opportunity for trainees to get answers to questions.
3. It allows trainees to get advice on matters that are of concern to them.
4. It allows trainees to share ideas and derive a common wisdom.
5. It is a way for trainees to learn about one another as people.[8]

Group discussions facilitate the exchange of ideas and are good ways to develop critical thinking skills. Social and interpersonal skills are also enhanced. However, group discussions are not effective with large numbers of participants because many remain silent or are unable to participate. Some group members will dominate while the contributions of others will not be useful. Still others may become dogmatic in their positions on issues. Group discussions take a lot of training time and must be carefully facilitated to manage the outcomes.

TIPS FOR TRAINERS

The discussion method is most effective when the trainer can convince group members that a collective approach has some advantage over individual approaches to a problem.[9] Thus, the trainer should create a participative culture at the beginning of a training program. The trainer's task is to get trainees to buy into the process as an activity that is both interesting and useful.

The major difficulty with the discussion method is that comments tend to be addressed to the trainer. When faced with this situation, it is best to reflect the questions or comments back to the trainees. Positive reinforcement is critical. Reluctant participants are drawn out, while the trainer uses the energy of more assertive individuals. When the group strays off topic, the trainer gently refocuses the discussion, supporting the participation while changing the substance.[10]

The key to successful discussions is to ensure that one trainee does not dominate the discussion. The trainer does not have to be obvious (e.g., by putting all the dominant personalities together). More subtle techniques can be used. For example, trainees can be given roles that change with each discussion—scribe, presenter, and discussion leader. If groups are kept small—four to six seems to work best—then most trainees have something to do, increasing participation and decreasing chances for some individuals to dominate the process. It is harder to be aggressive when taking notes or trying to summarize the thoughts of others.

Trainers dealing with groups of mixed educational backgrounds must also be aware of reading speed and literacy problems. Often group discussions require trainees to read a passage, a case incident, or a problem. Hostility or reluctance to do so might point to literacy difficulties. Be gentle; work the informal group process by finding a place in a hallway for someone to quietly read the material. Or, if this process is too obvious, summarize the main points before you assign the work. People who don't read well often have excellent memories; with care, they'll get by.[11]

// CASE STUDY METHOD

A **case study** is a training method in which trainees discuss, analyze, and solve problems that are usually based on a real situation. The primary use of the case study method is to encourage open discussion and analysis of problems and events. Trainees apply business-management concepts to relevant real-life situations. Most cases present situations in which the problems are correctable.

The objectives of a case study are to

1. introduce realism into trainees' learning;
2. deal with a variety of problems, goals, facts, conditions, and conflicts that often occur in the real world;
3. teach trainees how to make decisions; and
4. teach trainees to be creative and think independently.[12]

The case study method teaches trainees to think for themselves and develop analytical and problem-solving skills while the trainer functions as a catalyst for learning. Case studies develop analytical ability, sharpen problem-solving skills, encourage creativity, and improve the organization of thoughts and ideas.[13]

The case study method is often used in business schools to teach students how to analyze and solve realistic organizational problems. Several studies have found that using cases improves communication skills and problem solving, and enables students to better understand management situations.[14]

Cases vary depending on the intended purpose of the writer and according to the issue being examined. Some case studies disclose what management decisions were made when attempting to solve an organization's problems, while others require the trainee(s) to develop solutions and recommend courses of action.

For the case method to be effective, certain requirements must be met. For example, the qualifications of both the trainees and the trainer affect the ability to analyze cases and draw conclusions. As well, space and time dimensions are important. Trainees need time to analyze cases properly. Finally, case studies and discussions work best in an open and informal atmosphere.[15]

Cases may be written in various styles, presenting either single problems or a number of complex, interdependent situations. They may be concerned with corporate strategy, organizational change, management, or any problem relating to a company's financial situation, marketing, human resources, or a combination of these activities. Some case reports describe the organization's difficulties in vague terms, while others may state the major problems explicitly.

In addition to the various styles of case writing, methods of presentation also differ. Cases do not always have to be in written form. Sometimes it is more effective to present cases using audio-visual techniques. This approach has advantages for both the trainees and the trainers. For example, trainers do not have to do as much research and writing, and trainees are able to identify better with the characters.[16]

TIPS FOR TRAINERS

Certain requirements should be met when writing a case study. The case should be a product of a real organizational situation. A fictitious case could be regarded with boredom and distrust, since the setting might seem too unrealistic.[17] Ideally, cases should be written by more than one person. Collaboration on the presentation of facts ensures a more realistic situation and helps to reduce biases. Although it is difficult, the case writer must not make assumptions and should include only facts. The author of a case must relate core issues to the reader, not personal bias.

Because a case study is a description of a typical management situation, it is often difficult to know what to include and what to omit. Most cases give an overall description of the company and the industry situation, although the length of a case report varies. A typical case, however, will be up to 20 typewritten pages. The key issues and the relevant details should be included to give the reader enough information to make a qualified decision.

A teaching note provides communication between the case writer and those who teach the case. In its strictest sense, a teaching note would include information on approaches to teaching a specific case. Some teaching notes, however, are more detailed, containing samples of analyses and computations. In addition, teaching notes may state the objectives of the case and contain additional company information not available to trainees.[18]

// CASE INCIDENT METHOD

Unlike the typical case study, a **case incident** is usually no more than one page in length and is designed to illustrate or probe one specific problem, concept, or issue. Most management textbooks include a case incident at the end of each chapter. The case incident has become one of the most accessible ways of adding an experiential or real-world component into a lecture.

Case incidents are useful when the trainer wants to focus on one topic or concept. Because they are short, trainees can read them during a training session and valuable time will not be taken up by differences in trainees' reading speeds. When larger, more

> **Case incident**
> A training method in which one problem, concept, or issue is presented for analysis

traditional cases are used, advance preparation is necessary to read and review the case material. The brevity of a case incident reduces the need for preparation and reading skills, so all trainees can participate without a lot of advance reading and preparation.

Another advantage of a case incident is that trainees are able to use their own experiences. If the material is written well, the problem presented in each incident will encourage the application of current knowledge, leading to increased confidence and trainee input and participation.

The main disadvantage of case incidents is that some trainees are bothered by the lack of background material. Indeed, at times it is necessary for trainees to make assumptions, and trainers may be asked by some trainees to sketch in the background. They can be especially problematic for trainees who have limited knowledge and work experience. A lack of work or life experiences tends to elicit shallow answers based on speculation and ill-informed opinion.

Case incidents have been used successfully in higher education and organizations. Supervisors like the hands-on aspects of solving a specific management problem. Similarly, students have found the case incident method to be a welcome relief from the traditional lecture method.

TIPS FOR TRAINERS

Case incidents can be used in several ways. Trainees can be divided into groups with one member assigned the task of making notes while another can be designated the group spokesperson. The groups discuss the case incident and answer case questions. The trainer then has each group spokesperson present his or her answers. This process can then lead into a general group discussion.

Another approach is to have trainees read the case incident, answer the case questions, and then have a class discussion. This method is especially useful when an example is needed to illustrate a specific point. The trainer asks the trainees to read the incident and think about a question, and then leads the group in a short discussion. As soon as the point has been made, the trainer should continue quickly, so as not to lose the trainees' interest. Alternatively, a case incident can be used to illustrate a point at the start of a training program, or used as an exercise at the end of a training program.

For more information see Chapter 2, pp. 55–56

Behaviour modelling training (BMT)
A training method in which trainees observe a model performing a task and then attempt to imitate the observed behaviour

// BEHAVIOUR MODELLING TRAINING

As you know from Chapter 2, people learn by observing the behaviour of others. So it should not surprise you that observational learning is a popular and effective method of training.

Behaviour modelling training (BMT) is a training method in which trainees observe a model performing a task and then attempt to imitate the observed behaviour. It is based on social cognitive theory and observational learning.

You might recall from Chapter 2 that four key elements are critical for observational learning to take place: attention, retention, reproduction, and reinforcement. These are also important for BMT, which is a very effective method for learning skills and behaviours.

BMT is one of the most widely used and researched training methods.[19] It has been used to teach interpersonal skills such as supervision, negotiation, communication, and sales, as well as motor skills. It is the most popular method for teaching interpersonal and supervisory skills. In recent years it has been extended to other areas such as cross-cultural skills and technical skills.[20]

BMT is based on four general principles of learning:[21]

1. observation (modelling)
2. rehearsal (practice)
3. reinforcement (reward)
4. transfer

The process is fairly straightforward. Trainees observe a model performing a specific task, such as handling a customer complaint or operating a machine, and then practise performing the task. The performance of a task can be observed on video or performed live.

The training task should be broken down into key learning points or behaviours to be learned as a series of critical steps that can be modelled independently. After viewing the model, the participants practise the behaviour, one step at a time. When one step is mastered and reinforced, the trainer moves to the next critical skill (recall the discussion of shaping and chaining in Chapter 2). Specific feedback must follow the performance of each step. This step-by-step process results in the development of skills and the self-efficacy needed to use them. The final step involves specific actions to maximize the transfer of learning on the job.

A review of research on BMT found that it has a particularly strong effect on learning, but it also has a positive effect on skills development and job behaviour. The effect on skills development was greatest when learning points were used and presented as rules to be followed and when training time was longest. Transfer of learning on the job was greatest when models displaying both positive and negative behaviours were used, when trainees were instructed to set goals, when trainees' superiors were trained, and when rewards and sanctions were provided for using or failing to use newly learned skills on the job.[22]

For more information see Chapter 2, p. 54

TIPS FOR TRAINERS

The model used in BMT should be someone with whom the trainee can identify and who is perceived as credible. Under these conditions, the trainee is more likely to want to imitate the model's behaviour. In addition, trainers must carefully plan BMT and ensure that trainees are provided with opportunities to practise the observed behaviour, that they receive feedback on their performance of the task, and that they are motivated to use the new behaviour on the job. Trainees will resist behaviour modelling if the behaviours are incongruent with common work practices.

Sometimes, an ineffective model is demonstrated first to increase motivation to try the new positive behaviour. This approach is known as a **mixed modelling strategy** because it shows trainees what should be done (a positive model) as well as what should not be done (a negative model).[23]

There is some evidence that exposing trainees to a mixed model is more effective for behavioural generalization (using the trained skills on a task that was different from the training task) than exposing trainees to a positive-only model that only shows what should be done. However, exposure to a positive-only model has been shown to be effective for behavioural reproduction of the training task.[24] There is also some evidence that a mixed model is most likely to result in behavioural reproduction for trainees with a learning goal orientation.[25]

> **Mixed modelling strategy**
> BMT that shows trainees what should be done (a positive model) and what should not be done (a negative model)

For more information see
Chapter 4, pp. 132–133

Transfer of the new skill and behaviours to the workplace is the weakest link in the process. Old patterns are comfortable and familiar, especially when there is some resistance in the work environment to new ways of doing things. However, by over-learning the skill as discussed in Chapter 4, its use can become automatic. In addition, the reinforcement of newly acquired skills on the job ensures their repetition and continued application. When reinforcers are in place, BMT can have long-lasting and positive outcomes.[26]

For guidelines to implement BMT, see The Trainer's Notebook 5.1, "Implementing Behaviour Modelling Training."

THE TRAINER'S NOTEBOOK   5.1

IMPLEMENTING BEHAVIOUR MODELLING TRAINING

1. Describe to trainees a set of well-defined behaviours (skills) to be learned.

2. Provide a model or models displaying the effective use of those behaviours.

3. Provide opportunities for trainees to practise using those behaviours.

4. Provide feedback and social reinforcement to trainees following practice.

5. Take steps to maximize the transfer of those behaviours to the job.

Source: Taylor, P. J., Russ-Eft, D. F., & Chan, D. W. L. (2005). A meta-analytic review of behavior modeling training. *Journal of Applied Psychology, 90,* 692–709.

// ROLE PLAY

Role play
A training method in which trainees are given the opportunity to practise new behaviours in a safe environment

A **role play** is a method of training in which trainees are given the opportunity to practise new behaviours in a safe environment. In effect, they allow trainees the opportunity to experience a role and what the role entails. Thus, the emphasis is on doing and experiencing. Role plays are most useful for acquiring interpersonal and human relations skills and for changing attitudes. They are often used in training programs that involve interpersonal skills such as communication, sales, performance appraisal, counselling, mentoring, team building, and leadership, and in certain settings (e.g., social services) where participants can take on the roles of workers and clients.[27] For example, at L'Oréal Canada junior sales representatives participate in role plays in which the vice president of sales and sales directors play the role of customers.[28]

A role play consists of three phases: (1) development, (2) enactment, and (3) debriefing. First, a role play must be carefully *developed* to achieve its objectives. A role play usually consists of a scenario in which there are two actors. For example, if sales clerks are learning how to interact with customers, a role play might involve a customer returning an item and asking for a refund. The scenario provides information on the time, place, roles, encounter, and instructions on what each role player should do.

During the *enactment* phase, trainees are provided with the role-play information and scenarios and are assigned roles. There are usually two role players and sometimes a third trainee who is an observer. Trainees are given some time to become familiar with the scenario and their roles, and then act out the role play. Trainees will then switch roles so that each one spends some time in each role.

Although in many cases a trainee will play his/her own role in a role play, it is also possible for the trainee to play another role, which is called a reverse role play. In a **reverse role play**, trainees are required to put themselves in another person's position.[29] By playing the role of another person, trainees can develop empathy for others and learn what it feels like to be in a particular role. For example, when a customer service representative is given instructions to play the part of a disgruntled customer with a major problem, he or she can experience the frustrations of responses like "That's not my department" and "Just fill in that form over there, no, not that one." As a result, the trainee develops an awareness of the other person's feelings and attitudes, which can lead to a change in trainee attitudes and behaviour.

> **Reverse role play**
> Role plays in which trainees put themselves in another person's position

After the enactment phase is the *debriefing* phase, which is considered to be the most important phase of a role play. It should last two to three times longer than the enactment phase. In this phase, participants discuss their experiences and the outcomes of their role play. Correct behaviours are reinforced and connections with key learning points and trainees' jobs are made. This is done by establishing the facts (what happened, what was experienced), analyzing the causes and effects of behaviours, and planning for skill or attitude changes on the job.

> **Multiple role play**
> Groups of trainees acting out various roles

Role playing can take on various forms and does not always have to involve just two actors. A role play can involve groups of trainees acting out various roles in what is known as a **multiple role play**. Another variation is to have a role play performed and observed by trainees. In other cases, it might be preferable to have all of the trainees participate in a role play. The type of role play will depend on the training content and objectives.

Role plays can also vary in how much detail and structure the actors are given. In some role plays the actors are given a great deal of detail about what they are supposed to do and how they should feel, while less structured role plays might just indicate the actors' roles without any detail about them.

Role plays provide the opportunity to practise new behaviours in a safe environment.

TIPS FOR TRAINERS

While role playing allows trainees to practise and learn new skills, trainees sometimes resist it. As a result, the role of the trainer is crucial. Trust has to be established and an open and participative climate is necessary. Trainees should be warmed up by involving them in minor role situations. The trainer can reinforce risk taking and use mistakes as learning opportunities. Trainers can ask trainees to show all the incorrect ways to handle an angry customer. When a critical mistake is made, the trainer can point it out and then start again. In one role play, a police officer was testing methods of talking to a potential suicide victim on a bridge. The officer made the fatal mistake of saying "Go ahead, I dare you," and the role-play partner jumped. The trainer immediately stated, "Well, that approach didn't work, would you like to try another?" This demonstrates the true value of role playing—the opportunity to practise behaviours in a safe environment.

One of the limitations of a role play is that, unlike behaviour modelling, trainees are not shown exactly what to do and how to behave prior to participating in a role play. As a result, some trainees might not be successful in a role play and might even display incorrect behaviours. Furthermore, much of what happens during a role play is left in the hands of the role players. This means that it is extremely important for the trainer to draw out the incorrect and correct behaviours during the debriefing phase. Otherwise, trainees might not learn the appropriate behaviours. Role plays are most successful when they mirror the reality and setting of the organization and participants relate to it on an emotional level.[30]

To learn how to implement roles plays, see The Trainer's Notebook 5.2, "Steps for Effective Role Plays."

THE TRAINER'S NOTEBOOK   5.2

STEPS FOR EFFECTIVE ROLE PLAYS

1. Consider role plays when the training involves communication or interpersonal skills.
2. Define the learning outcomes of the session.
3. Study the relevant organizational roles.
4. Create the role-play scripts—one with a general context, and the other that's specific to the role.
5. Prepare the observation sheets with pertinent points to be observed.

6. See that the setting is right for the role play—stage, A/V tools, light, and so on.
7. Call for volunteers.
8. Facilitate and debrief after the role play.
9. Do not leave any issue unresolved.

Source: Republished with permission of the Association for Talent Development (ATD), from Karve, S. (2011). Setting the stage for effective role plays. *T+D*, *65*(11), 76–77. Permission conveyed through Copyright Clearance Center, Inc.

// SIMULATIONS

Simulations are a form of training that involves the use of operating models of physical or social events that are designed to represent reality. Thus, a simulation is a working representation of reality.[31]

Simulations
The use of operating models of physical or social events designed to represent reality

Simulations attempt to recreate situations by simplifying them to a manageable size and structure. They are models or active representations of work situations that are designed to increase trainee motivation, involvement, and learning. They are also used when training in the real world might involve danger or extreme costs. Simulations can involve individuals working alone or groups of individuals working together.

Simulations are a popular method of training and are widely used in business, education, healthcare, and the military. For example, simulations are typically used in medicine, maintenance, law enforcement, and emergency management settings. As described in the chapter-opening vignette, Queen's University's clinical simulation centre is used to train medical residents. The military and the commercial aviation industry are purported to be the biggest users of simulation-based training.[32]

A good example of an equipment simulator is a flight simulator used to train pilots.

pcruciatti/Shutterstock.com

There are a number of different types of simulations. **Equipment simulators** are mechanical devices that are similar to those that employees use on the job. They are designed to simulate the kinds of procedures, movements, and/or decisions required in the work environment. A good example of an equipment simulator is a flight simulator used to train pilots. Flight simulators mimic flights exactly but pose no risk to humans or equipment. Equipment simulators are also used to train astronauts, air traffic controllers, and maintenance workers. Trucking companies have also begun to use simulations to train new drivers.

Simulations can also be used to develop managerial and interpersonal skills. For example, organizational simulations require participants to solve problems, make decisions, and interact with various stakeholders. Trainees learn how organizations operate and acquire important managerial and business skills.

Simulations are also used to train employees involved in emergency response work, such as firefighters and police officers. For example, several years ago Ontario hospital workers and emergency crews responded to an explosion as a result of a chemical accident while also dealing with a respiratory outbreak. Fortunately, it was a mock crisis and the explosion was fictitious. The two-and-a-half-hour simulation involved 350 participants and was designed to prepare medical first responders and healthcare workers for a major urban disaster that could send hundreds of people to hospital.[33]

A major disadvantage of simulations is that they are expensive to develop and, in the case of emergency response simulations, very expensive to stage. On the positive side, simulations are an excellent way to add some realism to a training program. They are especially useful in situations where it would be too costly or dangerous to train employees on the actual equipment used on the job.

Equipment simulators Mechanical devices that are similar to those that employees use on the job

CHAPTER 5 Off-the-Job Training Methods

TIPS FOR TRAINERS

A successful simulation involves four steps: preparing for the simulation (consider the participants and learning objectives when choosing a simulation), delivering the simulation (let participants know why they are being asked to participate in the simulation and the expected outcomes), debriefing the simulation (discuss the simulation and make connections to the workplace), and following up on the simulation (post-simulation activities to maintain learning). Like role plays, the debriefing is the most important step because it allows the participants to step back and reflect on the experience and understand how it relates to their work.[34]

To be most effective, simulations should have physical and psychological fidelity. **Physical fidelity** has to do with the similarity of the physical aspects of a simulation (e.g., equipment, tasks, and surroundings) to the actual job. Simulators should be designed to physically replicate and resemble the work environment. That is, the simulation should have the appearance of the actual work site. For example, a flight simulator should look like the cockpit of an actual airplane with respect to the various controls, lights, and instruments.

Psychological fidelity has to do with the similarity of the psychological conditions of the simulation to the actual work environment. Simulations should be designed so that the experience is as similar as possible to what trainees experience on the job. In other words, the simulation should include on-the-job psychological conditions such as time pressures, problems, conflicts, and so on. The simulations described in the chapter-opening vignette in which medical students practise removing a gall bladder and practise on sophisticated mannequins are good examples of physical and psychological fidelity.

Simulations allow a great deal of flexibility, since complicating factors or unexpected events can be built into the program. For example, in a pilot-training simulation, a blizzard can be introduced. For a good example of a simulation, see Training Today 5.1, "Simulations for Sales Success."

Physical fidelity
The similarity of the physical aspects of a simulation (e.g., equipment, tasks, and surroundings) to the actual job

Psychological fidelity
The similarity of the psychological conditions of the simulation to the actual work environment

---

TRAINING TODAY 5.1

SIMULATIONS FOR SALES SUCCESS

B. Braun Medical Inc. is a manufacturer of infusion therapy and pain management products. In 2007, the sales of one of B. Braun's flagship products, the Introcan Safety IV catheter, had slowed to 1.5 percent despite a concerted investment of staff and company resources. In addition, customer trial-to-conversions came in at 25 percent, with retention rates measured at only 40 percent six months post-conversion.

The sales representatives didn't believe they had the clinical expertise necessary to establish credibility with their customers or correctly set expectations for use of the IV catheter. A learning-style survey showed that the sales force collectively held a variety of learning styles, which led B. Braun to create a new blended training program.

B. Braun designed the program to include product training via learning modules, peer coaching, and a teach-back component, followed by hands-on didactic training during live classroom sessions. Then, in September 2010, they launched a two-day simulation training program. The goal was for reps to repetitively practise placing the IV catheter through scenario-based simulation training so they could understand what clinicians experienced when they used the product.

On the first day of the simulation, participants take a pre-test to determine their current knowledge of venipuncture. Part of this assessment includes the reps' immersion in a real-life scenario. They are asked to place an IV catheter using a "demo arm" with blood pressure and fake blood.

(continued)

Participants receive grades based on a 30-point checklist. Following the pre-test, a nurse teaches a venipuncture certification course.

On the second day of the simulation, participants are placed on a computer simulator with a haptics device (which allows them to "feel" the virtual IV catheter insertion) to practise the process of placing the IV catheter. The reps coach one another and engage in clinical discussions while completing the scenarios.

The training concludes with a real-life scenario in which participants work on a patient who is wearing a demo arm. The reps are assigned a scenario and tasked with selecting the correct supplies and placing the IV catheter. An observer uses the 30-point checklist to grade the reps' performance improvement. Participants also complete a written post-training test to measure their knowledge gain.

B. Braun has documented a 22 to 25 percent increase in participants' knowledge and skills. Since the company re-launched the Introcan Safety IV catheter with the new training program, customer trial-to-conversion rates have increased to 95 percent and customer retention rates have increased to better than 85 percent six months post-conversion.

Source: Adapted with permission of the Association for Talent Development (ATD), from Anonymous, "Simulations for selling success," T+D, January 2012, 66(1), p. 80; permission conveyed through Copyright Clearance Center, Inc.

// GAMES

Games are training methods that involve structured competition that allows trainees to learn specific skills. Games tend to have rules, principles, and a system for scoring. However, unlike simulations, games do not have to represent reality, and they are often designed to be entertaining. For example, an employment law game called Winning through Prevention teaches human resource managers about lawful termination, discrimination, and workplace safety. Players who answer correctly get promoted and those who answer incorrectly are faced with a lawsuit.[35]

> Games
> Training methods that involve structured competition that allows trainees to learn specific skills

Business games often require teams of players to compete against each other to gain a strategic advantage, to gain market share, or to maximize profits. They can involve all areas of management practice and often require the players to gather and analyze information and to make business management decisions. As a result, business games tend to focus on the development of problem-solving, interpersonal, and decision-making skills.

Some business games are relatively simple and focus on a particular functional area, such as marketing, human resources, or finance. Other games are much more complex and try to model an entire organization. Participants might have to operate a company and make all kinds of decisions and solve business problems. They then receive feedback and have the opportunity to practise particular skills.

Games incorporate many principles of learning, such as learning from experience, active practice, and direct application to real problems. They are used to enhance the learning process by injecting fun and competition, generating energy, and providing opportunities for people to work together.

A disadvantage of games is the possibility of learning the wrong things, a weak relation to training objectives, and an emphasis on winning.[36] In addition, trainees sometimes get so caught up in the game that they lose sight of the importance of learning. Although trainees seem to enjoy games and respond enthusiastically to them, there is not very much evidence on how effective they are for improving skills and on-the-job performance.

TIPS FOR TRAINERS

The design of a game begins with a critical question: "What is the key task to be learned?" At the beginning of the game, the trainer should state the learning objective so that trainees don't just focus on winning the game but understand what they will learn. In addition, the roles of the players must be clearly defined.

Games should be as realistic as possible and be a meaningful representation of the kind of work that participants do. If they are not realistic, participants might not take them seriously. This will undermine learning and the application of new skills on the job. To be most effective, games should be well planned and prepared, linked to training objectives, and include a debriefing session so that trainees understand the purpose of the game and the critical skills and behaviours to be learned.[37] As well, because many kinds of games are available, trainers need to be familiar with them and carefully choose one that best meets an organization's needs and objectives.

// ACTION LEARNING

Some training methods that are known as **problem-based learning** require trainees to solve real or simulated open-ended problems.[38] A good example of this is action learning. **Action learning** requires trainees to identify problems; develop possible solutions; test these solutions in a real-world, real-time situation; and evaluate the consequences. The aims are to solve an actual business problem and to test theories in the real world.

Reginald Revans, the originator of action learning principles, emphasizes that the learner develops skills through responsible involvement in some real, complex, and stressful problem.[39] The goals of action learning are to involve and challenge the trainee, and to move employees from passive observation to identification with the people and the vision of the organization. This method moves trainees from information receivers to problem solvers.

Action learning incorporates more of the adult learning principles than any other method of training. Recall from Chapter 2 that adults are problem centred in their approach to learning and prefer to be self-directed and to learn independently.

The majority of the time spent in action learning is dedicated to diagnosing problems in the field. The problems and the inherent value systems supporting the problems are assessed and challenged. This work is always done in groups, and learning outcomes include group and interpersonal skills, risk taking, responsibility, and accountability.[40]

Many professions use action learning to train and socialize their students. For example, students in social work are often sent to work with the homeless or welfare recipients. These students are encouraged to apply their theoretical knowledge in the field. Organizations are using the precepts of action learning when employees take responsibility for quality-improvement projects.

Action learning requires a commitment of energy and time from participants and their managers. Solving real organizational problems can be stressful for trainees. The difficulties of working in teams on real problems can lead to conflict and increased anxiety and stress.

Although action learning is more popular in Europe than in North America, a number of companies in Canada and the United States have developed action learning programs. For example, TD Bank Financial Group has a leadership development program in which action learning plays an integral part. The bank's senior managers attend

Problem-based learning
Training methods that require trainees to solve real or simulated open-ended problems

Action learning
A training method in which trainees solve real-world problems and accept responsibility for the solution

For more information see Chapter 2, pp. 58–60

a three-day course to learn about the competencies that comprise a new leadership profile. Then they must use the learning to solve an action learning opportunity that they identified before attending the program.

TELUS has an action learning program for its director-level managers. The company partnered with several universities to deliver courses in several key areas. After taking the courses, participants are expected to use the learning to solve work-related problems, and they are held accountable for applying the learning and making changes.[41]

Automatic Data Processing, Inc. (ADP), one of the world's largest providers of business outsourcing solutions, has teams of 10 participants address real business opportunities or challenges and then present recommendations to their executive sponsor(s) and senior leaders.[42]

TIPS FOR TRAINERS

Action learning projects must be challenging and deal with real organizational concerns. Trainees should buy into the importance of the project and the organizational problem and receive some release time to work on the project. In addition, some training in group skills to enable collaboration might also be necessary. The group working on the project should be small enough (four to seven members) to develop trust but contain a diverse set of skills to enable creative solutions. The learning process should be monitored and the trainees held accountable for their proposed solutions.

// INSTRUCTIONAL MEDIA

In addition to instructional methods, the design of training and development programs involves choosing instructional media, which should be distinguished from the training content and instructional methods.

Instructional media refers to the medium or media used to deliver the training content and methods to trainees. For example, a lecture can be delivered face-to-face in a classroom or through the use of various media such as online video or DVD.[43] Instructional media can also be used with most of the instructional methods. A good example of this is audio-visual methods.

Audio-visual methods refer to various forms of media that trainers can use in the classroom to illustrate key points or demonstrate certain actions or behaviours. Trainers often use slides, videos, and DVDs to supplement lectures and discussions.

Slides are often used to highlight important parts of a lecture or a discussion, allowing trainees to remember key points. A video is often used to illustrate how to behave in a certain situation or to demonstrate effective and ineffective behaviours.

For example, at pharmaceutical company Nycomed Canada, a performance management training program for managers uses videos of performance management scenarios to guide managers through the process and show them how to handle different issues.[44] Many managers have learned correct interviewing techniques through videos.

One advantage of audio-visual methods is the ability to control the pace of training. A slide or a video clip can be used to clarify a concept. Trainees receive consistent information from these methods no matter where or how often the training is given. Most important, a video can show a situation that is difficult for a trainer to describe, such as a hostile customer or a dangerous malfunction in equipment.

Instructional media
The medium or media used to deliver the training content and methods to trainees

Audio-visual methods
Various forms of media that are used to illustrate key points or demonstrate certain actions or behaviours

Video allows a trainer to show complex and dynamic situations in a realistic manner. The use of videos has been made easier with the Internet, since trainers can now find relevant video clips online that can be shown during training. Not surprisingly, videos remain one of the most popular forms of instructional media.

TIPS FOR TRAINERS

When using instructional media, such as a video, to supplement an instructional method, the trainer should discuss the learning objectives and the key points, and instruct trainees to pay particular attention to certain key parts. Trainees should understand how the video fits into the rest of the training program and be given sufficient guidance so that they know what to look for and what they should focus on.

Slides should not overwhelm trainees with information, and they should be easy to read and follow. Too much information or print that is too small and difficult to read can undermine their usefulness. Finally, it is important to keep in mind that the use of instructional media should be guided by the training content and the instructional methods being used.

// CHOOSING AN INSTRUCTIONAL METHOD

In this chapter, we have described some of the most common instructional methods of training. In Chapter 6, you will learn about on-the-job training methods, and in Chapter 7 you will find out about technology-based training methods. With so many instructional methods available, it is natural to ask, "What method is best?" and "How does a trainer choose an instructional method?" There is no easy or straightforward answer to this question. However, we will try to provide some guidelines for making this important decision.

Two large surveys of training directors found that nine training methods were effective in achieving different types of training goals.[45] For example, the case study method was rated most effective for problem-solving skills, and computer-based instruction was rated best for knowledge retention. The role-play method was evaluated best for changing attitudes and developing interpersonal skills. However, these are only individual perceptions, and they do not provide information on actual training outcomes.

It is important to realize that the effectiveness of an instructional method depends on the training objectives and learning outcomes. Thus, the choice of which method to use for a particular training program should start with the program's objectives. For example, if the objective is for trainees to learn declarative knowledge, you might choose the lecture method. However, if the objective is the acquisition of interpersonal skills, you might want to use the role-play method.

In general, the lecture method is most effective when you want to impart large amounts of information quickly and at low cost to large groups of trainees. To teach interpersonal skills such as interviewing or negotiations, the most effective methods are behaviour modelling training and role playing.

In addition to training objectives, other factors that should be considered when choosing an instructional method include cost and resource availability, on-the-job application, trainer skill and preferences, and trainee preferences and characteristics. We will now briefly discuss each of these factors.

COST AND RESOURCE AVAILABILITY

An instructional method might be extremely effective for achieving a program's objectives, but it might be too costly to design and deliver. For example, a simulation might be appropriate for a training objective but very expensive. Thus, trainers must consider the cost and resources available for designing and delivering instructional methods.

ON-THE-JOB APPLICATION

Another important factor to consider is on-the-job applications. Trainers will choose some methods over others if trainees are expected to apply the newly acquired knowledge and skills on the job. For example, a lecture is not a good choice if the objective is on-the-job application. If trainees are expected to apply new knowledge and skills on the job, then a role play, simulation, or behaviour modelling training will be more effective.

TRAINER SKILL AND PREFERENCES

A trainer might be more skilled at using some methods and might have a personal preference for using certain methods. For example, if a trainer is not experienced or comfortable conducting role plays or using a case study, then these methods might not be considered. Thus, the choice of an instructional method also depends on the skills and preferences of trainers.

TRAINEE PREFERENCES AND CHARACTERISTICS

When choosing an instructional method, the trainer should consider what is best for trainees with respect to their preferences and characteristics. For starters, you might recall the discussion of learning styles in Chapter 2. Learning style refers to the way individuals prefer to learn. Trainees with different learning styles are likely to prefer different instructional methods (e.g., lecture versus role playing), and different methods will maximize their learning.

For more information see Chapter 2, pp. 50–52

Also important is a trainee's ability to benefit from a particular method of instruction. There is some evidence that training methods have differential effects on trainees as a result of differences in trainee characteristics and aptitudes (e.g., abilities, skills, and knowledge). This is known as an aptitude–treatment interaction.

An **aptitude–treatment interaction (ATI)** refers to situations in which the effect of a training method on trainees depends on trainee characteristics (e.g., aptitude, self-efficacy, and demographics). For example, some methods of training might be more or less effective depending on a trainee's aptitude.

An **aptitude** is broadly defined as any characteristic of trainees that affects their ability to learn from the training method. For example, there is some evidence that high-ability trainees benefit more from programs with less structure and greater complexity, while low-ability trainees benefit more from explicit and structured programs.[46] There is also evidence that self-pacing methods are especially effective for older trainees.[47]

Another example of an aptitude–treatment interaction was described earlier in the chapter in the section on behaviour modelling training, when it was noted that a mixed model strategy is most effective for trainees with a learning goal orientation. Thus, it is

Aptitude–treatment interaction (ATI)
Situations in which the effect of a training method depends on trainee characteristics

Aptitude
Any characteristic of trainees that affects their ability to learn from a training method

important that the training methods chosen are suitable for and matched to trainees' aptitudes and characteristics.

BLENDED TRAINING

Although we have been discussing instructional methods as if only one can be used in a training program, in reality trainers mix and combine them (e.g., case studies with lecturing). In fact, you might recall that in Chapter 4 we defined **blended training** as an approach that combines classroom training, on-the-job training, and computer technology. This usually involves the use of face-to-face instruction—be it on the job or in the classroom—as well as some aspect of online instruction.[48]

Blended training programs are becoming more common and, increasingly, the norm. A blended delivery approach has a number of benefits. It allows participants to learn in ways that are most suitable to their needs, styles, and preferences, allows multiple learning outcomes to be achieved, and increases the possibility that the training will be applied on the job. Therefore, trainers must be skilled in a variety of instructional methods.

In conclusion, when it comes to choosing an instructional method, each method has its place and there are many factors to consider. Ultimately, mixing, combining, and blending instructional methods is the best approach for maximizing trainee engagement, learning, retention, and on-the-job application.

> **Blended training**
> The use of a combination of methods to training, such as classroom training, on-the-job training, and computer technology

// SUMMARY

This chapter described nine of the most common instructional training methods. The advantages and disadvantages of each method were described, as well as suggestions for their use to maximize trainee learning and retention. We also discussed instructional media and how it can be used with instructional methods. The chapter concluded with a discussion of the factors to consider when choosing instructional methods. Particular emphasis was given to aptitude–treatment interactions and the need to consider trainee aptitudes and characteristics when choosing an instructional method. The importance of combining instructional methods and using a blended delivery approach was also discussed.

KEY TERMS

action learning p. 164
aptitude p. 167
aptitude–treatment interaction (ATI) p. 167
audio-visual methods p. 165
behaviour modelling training (BMT) p. 156
blended training p. 168
case incident p. 155
case study p. 154
discussion method p. 153
equipment simulators p. 161
flipped classroom p. 152

DISCUSSION QUESTIONS

1. What is the difference between a role play and behaviour modelling training, and what are the advantages and disadvantages of each method? When would it be preferable to use one or the other? What method do you prefer, and why?

2. Review the instructional methods listed in Table 5.1 and discuss the advantages and disadvantages of using each method to train airport passenger and baggage screeners. What methods do you think would be most effective, and why?

3. What are the advantages and disadvantages of each of the instructional methods listed in Table 5.1, and when would it be best to use each method? What method do you prefer, and why?

4. What are the main factors a trainer should consider when choosing an instructional method? Explain how each factor will suggest some methods over others.

5. What is the difference between physical fidelity and psychological fidelity, and how would you design a simulation to have both?

6. What is an aptitude–treatment interaction, and how is it relevant for choosing an instructional methods?

7. What is a blended training program and what are the implications of blended training for trainers and trainees?

8. What is the difference between games and simulations, and what are the advantages and disadvantages of each method? When would it be best to use a game versus a simulation?

9. Explain how the four key elements of observational learning (attention, retention, reproduction, and reinforcement) are relevant to behaviour modelling training.

10. What are the advantages and disadvantages of the lecture method? What can a trainer do to make a lecture more interesting and engaging?

THE GREAT TRAINING DEBATE

1. Debate the following: Lectures are not a very effective method of training and they should never or seldom be used for training.

2. Debate the following: No single instructional training method is best, and all training programs should use a blended approach.

3. Debate the following: Games might make a training program fun for trainees but they are a waste of time and money when it comes to learning, on-the-job behaviour, and job performance.

EXERCISES

IN-CLASS

1. Prepare a five-minute lecture on a topic of your choice using the information on lectures described in the text. Find a partner in your class and review each other's lecture. If time permits, give your lecture to the class or a small group and discuss its effectiveness. What would make your lecture more effective?

2. Choose a training program you have taken that you really liked and one that you did not like. For each one, indicate the instructional methods that were used (see Table 5.1) and how they were used. What effect did the methods have on your satisfaction with the program and your learning? What methods might have improved your satisfaction and learning?

3. Think of a work situation you have either experienced or observed that would lend itself to a role play (e.g., a customer complaining to an employee). Design a role play in which you describe a scenario and the role of two role players. Be clear about the purpose of the role play—its objectives and what the role players are expected to learn. Be sure to include instructions to participants about the scenario and the relationship between the characters. The instructor can have you describe your role play to the class and/or have class members enact it. If role plays are enacted, be sure to also include a debriefing session afterward.

4. Describe the major tasks involved in performing a previous or current job and how employees are trained. Then review each of the instructional methods in Table 5.1 and describe how they might be used to train employees for the job. What instructional methods do you think would be most effective? What methods would you recommend, and why?

5. For this exercise, your task is to design a short game that can be played in class to learn an interpersonal skill such as communication, team skills, leadership, or negotiation. In groups of two or three, choose a skill to focus on, and then design a game to learn the skill. Your game must be designed so that other members of the class can play it during class time. Write a brief description of your game indicating the objectives, the players, the rules, and what team members have to do to get points or win. The instructor can either have you describe your game to the class and/or have class members actually play it. After playing the game, be sure to discuss how effective it was for learning the skill and the participants' reaction to it.

6. Consider your course on training and development. Do you think action learning would be an effective instructional method? Design an action learning project for your training and development course. Be specific about the objectives, the skills to be developed, and the problems to be worked on and solved.

7. For this exercise you are to design a training program for a task you currently perform or have performed on a job. Once you have decided on a task, prepare an outline of a lecture that you could use to train other employees to perform the task. Be sure to indicate the main content and points you will include in your lecture.

When your outline is complete, review the instructional methods in Table 5.1 and consider adding some of them to your training program. What other instructional methods will you include, and why? At what point in your lecture will you include them? Be specific when describing how the other instructional methods will be incorporated into your training program and what they will involve.

8. Many organizations use structured employment interviews as part of the selection process. However, not all interviewers or managers know how to conduct a structured employment interview. If your task was to design a training program on how to conduct a structured employment interview, what instructional training method(s) would you use, and why? For each of the methods in Table 5.1, indicate whether you would use it for your training program. Be sure to explain your reasoning. Once you have decided which method(s) you will use, briefly describe how and why you will use them, and for what purpose.

IN-THE-FIELD

1. Contact the human resources department of an organization to learn about the instructional methods they use to train employees. In particular, you should inquire about the following:

   - What instructional methods do they use, what do they use them for, and why do they use them? (Refer to Table 5.1.)
   - Do they use a blended approach to training? If so, what methods are used?
   - Do they use certain methods for particular training programs?
   - Do they prefer to use certain methods more than others?
   - What methods do they believe are the most effective for training employees in their organization?
   - What factors do they consider when choosing instructional methods?

2. To learn more about action learning, visit the World Institute for Action Learning at **www.wial.org** and answer the following questions:

   a. What is action learning?
   b. What is action learning particularly effective for?
   c. What are the WIAL solution spheres?
   d. How can you benefit from WIAL action learning?
   e. What are the components of action learning?

CASE INCIDENT

THE ALTERCATION

In March 2014, a video showing an altercation between an angry customer and a Sears Canada employee at a store in Winnipeg was posted online. The video was made after the salesperson asked the customer to remove his children from lawn tractors that were on display. In the video, the salesperson says to the customer, "Let me guess, you just came off the boat?" The customer then calls the employee racist and follows him around the store swearing at him and demanding that he be fired.

Sears reacted quickly to the incident and initially suspended the employee but then fired him. Vincent Power, vice-president of corporate affairs and communications at Sears Canada, said: "We have a code of conduct, a code of ethics and we also have a respect in the workplace policy, and those were broken, basically."

When it comes to training, Sears' code of conduct deals with major areas such as the proper use of company assets, conflicts of interest and protection of physical and intellectual property, said Power. There's also a workshop about respect in the workplace dealing with mutual respect, harassment, workplace violence, inappropriate behaviour and bullying, along with tips on what managers can do to create respectful workplaces. Every Sears associate has to complete both online courses annually, along with exams at the end, and employees must acknowledge they've read the code of conduct in their annual performance reviews.

While that's adequate, he said, sometimes you're in the situation and as much as you know the theory, you really have to practise it. "(This incident is) probably an opportunity for us—certainly in that store, but even across Canada—to re-emphasize with our employees how important behaviour is, especially with customers and fellow associates," said Power. "It gives us pause to make sure that we reinforce this with everybody."

QUESTIONS

1. Given the issues raised in the "incident" between the employee and the customer, how should employees be trained to handle interactions with customers? What are the advantages and disadvantages of using each of the instructional methods listed in Table 5.1?

2. What instructional method(s) do you think is most effective for training salespersons for interacting and communicating with customers? What training method should organizations use to prevent the kind of altercation described in the case? Explain your answer.

Source: Dobson, S. (2014, March 24). Ugly, racist altercation caught on video at Sears. *Canadian HR Reporter*, pp. 1, 12. Reprinted by permission of *Canadian HR Reporter*. © Copyright Thomson Reuters Canada Ltd., (2014), Toronto, Ontario, 1-800-387-5164. Web: www.hrreporter.com

CASE STUDY	THE CUSTOMER-SERVICE TRAINING PROGRAM

Intense competition among retailers has made customer service a top priority. At many stores today, employees welcome customers as they enter the store with cheery greetings and sales staff must have good communication and interpersonal skills to provide customers with excellent service. They also need to be courteous, polite, friendly, and helpful.

A large retail clothing store decided that it needed to improve its customer service to be more competitive, since its customer satisfaction ratings had been declining over the last year and were lower than those of its competitors. It wanted employees to be more active and involved with customers so that they could provide excellent service and improve customer satisfaction ratings.

The company designed a new customer-service training program to train employees to greet customers, offer assistance, help them find what they are looking for, resolve customer complaints and problems, and provide courteous, helpful, and friendly service. An important objective of the program was to provide employees with better interpersonal and communication skills so that they would be able to spend more time interacting with customers and ensure that every customer leaves the store satisfied with his/her shopping experience.

The training program, which was designed in-house and delivered by the company's training staff, began with a lecture in which the trainer described the importance of customer service and the objectives of the training program. Trainees were instructed on the importance of good customer service and how they should behave when they are interacting with customers.

Following the lecture, a video was shown that consisted of different scenarios in which employees were shown interacting with customers. In one scenario, a customer could not find what he was looking for and asked the employee for assistance. The employee was not friendly and told the customer to try looking in another aisle. In another incident, a customer complained to an employee about something she had purchased that was less expensive at another store. She demanded a price reduction or her money back. The customer began raising her voice and the employee yelled at the customer and told her to leave the store. Similar incidents of poor customer service were also shown in the video.

After the video, the trainer asked trainees what was wrong with each scenario and how the employee should have behaved to provide better customer service. At the end of the discussion, the trainer provided a brief lecture outlining the key points shown in the video. This was followed by a video that showed scenarios of employees providing good customer service. A brief discussion and lecture followed in which the trainees were asked to describe what the employee did in each situation to provide good service. The trainer concluded the session by highlighting the key customer-service behaviours.

Trainees then had to take a test on their knowledge of customer service. The test consisted of multiple-choice questions that asked trainees to choose the most appropriate behaviour in different situations with customers. Most of the trainees did very well on the test and received a customer-service qualification certificate upon completion of the training program. Trainees reacted positively to the training program, which was considered to be a success.

However, back on the job some employees had difficulty interacting and communicating with customers. For example, in one incident a customer demanded his money back for a pair of pants that had shrunk after cleaning. He blamed the employee for the store's poor quality and called the employee an idiot. The employee didn't know what to do and just walked away in tears.

In another incident, a customer came into the store to pick up a shirt that he had asked an employee to hold for him. The item had been sold and it was the last one in the store. The employee apologized, saying that it had been sold to somebody else by accident. However, the customer insisted that the employee call the customer who bought the shirt and have him return it. The employee said she could not do that and told the customer how sorry she was. The customer refused to leave the store unless the employee called the person who bought the shirt. The employee threatened to call security if the customer did not leave the store. He finally left but not before causing a big scene in the store in front of many other customers. Later that day the employee quit.

One month after the training program there was no improvement in customer satisfaction ratings, and four of the sales staff who had attended the training program had quit. Management began to wonder whether the training program was effective. They were not sure whether more time was needed to see the effects of the training on customer satisfaction scores or whether the training program was a failure.

QUESTIONS

1. How effective was the customer-service training program? What are its strengths and weaknesses?

2. Describe the instructional methods that were used in the customer-service training program. Do you think these were appropriate methods to use? Explain your answer.

3. What other instructional methods could have been used to make the customer-service training program more effective? Review the methods in Table 5.1 and indicate how effective each method would be using the criteria in the chapter for choosing an instructional methods.

4. If you were to redesign the customer-service training program, what instructional methods would you use, and why?

5. What does this case say about instructional methods and the effectiveness of training programs? What does it say about choosing instructional methods?

FLASHBACK QUESTIONS

1. Refer to the material in Chapter 2 on learning and motivation and consider the following:
   a. What learning outcomes were the focus of the customer-service training program?
   b. What do learning theories tell us about why the customer-service training program was not more effective and how to make it more effective? Be sure to consider conditioning theory, social cognitive theory, and adult learning theory.
   c. What role does training motivation play in understanding the customer-service training program? What should have been done to increase trainees motivation to learn.

2. Refer to the material in Chapter 4 on training design and consider the following:
   a. To what extent was active practice used in the customer-service training program, and was it used appropriately? How else might active practice have been used?
   b. To what extent were the conditions of practice before (pre-training interventions) and during training used in the customer-service training program? What conditions of practice might have been used, and why?
   c. Is adaptive expertise relevant for the customer-service training program? If so, how might the program be designed for adaptive expertise?

FLASH FORWARD QUESTION

1. Do you think the customer-service training program would have been more effective if on-the-job training methods were used? If so, what on-the-job training methods do you think should have been used? Explain your answer. (To answer this question, refer to Table 6.1 in Chapter 6.)

REWRITE THE CASE QUESTION: BEHAVIOUR MODELLING TRAINING AND ROLE PLAYS

Rewrite the case by including a section in which you describe the use of behaviour modelling training or a role play. In other words, the case should have a section that describes how one of these instructional methods was used to train employees on customer service behaviours. Be sure to include all the steps involved in the applicable instructional method.

RUNNING CASE STUDY DIRTY POOLS

QUESTIONS

Refer to the case at the end of Chapter 1 to answer the following:

1. Would off-the-job training be an appropriate and effective way to train pool operators and their employees? Explain your answer.
2. What instructional methods would you recommend to train pool operators and their employees? Review each of the instructional methods in Table 5.1 and explain which ones you would recommend, and why. What instructional method(s) would be most effective?

// REFERENCES

1. Dobson, S. (2013, February 11). Repetitive practice makes close to perfect. *Canadian HR Reporter*, *26*(3), 13.

2. Brown, K. G., & Sitzmann, T. (2011). Training and employee development for improved performance. In S. Zedeck (Ed.), *Handbook of industrial and organizational psychology* (Vol. 2, pp. 469–503). Washington, DC: American Psychological Association.

3. Cotsman, S., & Hall, C. (2018). *Learning cultures lead the way: Learning & development outlook—14th edition*. Ottawa: The Conference Board of Canada; Anonymous (2017, November/December). 2017 Training industry report. *Training Magazine*, *54*(6), 20–33.

4. Silliker, A. (2013, August 12). HR by the numbers (On-site sessions most valued form of training). *Canadian HR Reporter*, *26*(14), 4.

5. Arthur, W., Jr., Bennett, W., Jr., Edens, P. S., & Bell, S. T. (2003). Effectiveness of training in organizations: A meta-analysis of design and evaluation features. *Journal of Applied Psychology*, *88*, 234–245.

6. Milman, N. B. (2012). The flipped classroom strategy: What is it and how can it best be used? *Distance Learning*, *9*(3), 85–87.

7. Renner, P. (1988). *The quick instructional planner*. Vancouver: Training Associates Ltd.

8. Zander, A. (1982). *Making groups effective*. San Francisco: Jossey-Bass.

9. Gabris, G. (1989). Educating elected officials in strategic goal setting. *Public Productivity and Management Review*, *13*(2), 161–175.

10. Conlin, J. (1989). Conflict at meetings: Come out fighting. *Successful Meetings*, *38*(6), 30–36; Renner (1988); Wein, G. (1990). Experts as trainers. *Training and Development Journal*, *44*(7), 29–30.

11. Keller, S., & Chuvala, J. (1992). Training: Tricks of the trade. *Security Management*, *36*(7), 101–105.

12. Yin, R. K. (1985). *Case study research: Design and methods*. Beverly Hills: Sage.

13. Pearce, J. A., Robinson, R. B., Jr., & Zahra, S. A. (1989). *An industry approach to cases in strategic management*. Boston: Irwin Publishing.

14. Wright, P. (1992). The CEO and the business school: Is there potential for increased cooperation? *Association of Management Proceedings: Education*, *10*(1), 41–45.

15. Craig, R. L. (1987). *Training and development handbook: A guide to human resource development* (pp. 414–429). New York: McGraw-Hill Inc.

16. Craig (1987).

17. Craig (1987).

18. Leenders, M. R., & Erskine, J. A. (1973). *Case research: The case writing process*. London, ON: University of Western Ontario Press.

19. Taylor, P. J., Russ-Eft, D. F., & Chan, D. W. L. (2005). A meta-analytic review of behavior modeling training. *Journal of Applied Psychology*, *90*, 692–709.

20. Baldwin, T. T. (1992). Effects of alternative modeling strategies on outcomes of interpersonal-skills training. *Journal of Applied Psychology*, *77*, 147–154; Taylor et al. (2005).

21. Robinson, J. C. (1982). *Developing managers through behaviour modeling*. Austin, TX: Pfeiffer & Co.

22. Taylor et al. (2005).

23. Lauzier, M., & Haccoun, R. R. (2014). The interactive effect of modeling strategies and goal orientations on affective, motivational, and behavioral training outcomes. *Performance Improvement Quarterly*, *27*, 83–102.

24. Baldwin (1992).

25. Lauzier & Haccoun (2014).

26. Buller, M., & McEvoy, G. (1990). Exploring the long-term effects of behaviour modelling training. *Journal of Organizational Change Management*, *3*(1), 32–45.

27. Karve, S. (2011). Setting the stage for effective role plays. *T+D*, *65*(11), 76–77.

28. Klie, S. (2008, October 6). L'Oréal plays games with training. *Canadian HR Reporter*, *21*(17), 26; Klie, S. (2007, October 22). L'Oréal a pretty picture of diversity, training. *Canadian HR Reporter*, *20*(18), 11; www.loreal.ca.

29. Jones, K. P., King, E. B., Nelson, J., Geller, D. S., & Bowes-Sperry, L. (2013). Beyond the business case: An ethical perspective of diversity training. *Human Resource Management*, *52*, 55–74.

30. Karve (2011).

31. Brown & Sitzmann (2011).

32. Salas, E., & Cannon-Bowers, J. A. (2001). The science of training: A decade of progress. *Annual Review of Psychology*, *52*, 471–499.

33. Anonymous. (2014, March 29). Are Ontario hospitals prepared to handle a major urban disaster? *CTV News Toronto*. Retrieved from http://toronto.ctvnews.ca/

34. Musselwhite, C., Kennedy, S., & Probst, N. (2010). Best practices for facilitating simulations. *T+D*, *64*(8), 26–28.

35. Atkins, E. (1999, March). Winning through prevention. *Workplace News*, p. 9.

36. Greenlaw, B., Herron, M., & Ramdon, L. (1962). *Business simulation in industrial and university education*. Englewood Cliffs, NJ: Prentice-Hall.

37. Tannenbaum, S. I., & Yukl, G. (1992). Training and development in work organizations. *Annual Review of Psychology*, *43*, 399–441.

38. Brown & Sitzmann (2011).

39. Revans, R. W. (1982). *The origins and growth of action learning*. Gock, Sweden: Bratt–Institute for Neues Lernen.

40. Revans, R. W. (1984). Action learning: Are we getting there? *Management Decision Journal*, *22*(1), 45–52.

41. Vu, U. (2005, April 25). Action learning popular in Europe, not yet caught on in Canada. *Canadian HR Reporter*, *18*(8), 1, 17.

42. Anonymous. (2011). Best practices & outstanding initiatives. *Training Magazine*, *48*(1), www.adp.com.

43. Brown & Sitzmann (2011).

44. Anonymous. (2008, May 19). CEOs talk: Training & development. *Canadian HR Reporter*, *21*(10), 11–13.

45. Newstrom, J. W. (1980). Evaluating the effectiveness of training methods. *Personnel Administrator*, *25*(1), 55–60; Carrol, S. J., Paine, F. T., & Ivancevich, J. J. (1972). The relative effectiveness of training methods—Expert opinion and research. *Personnel Psychology*, *25*, 495–510.

46. Tannenbaum & Yukl (1992).

47. Callahan, J. S., Kiker, D. S., & Cross, T. (2003). Does method matter? A meta-analysis of the effects of training method on older learner training performance. *Journal of Management*, *29*, 663–680.

48. Landers, A. (2017, January/February). Creating blended learning for small to medium-sized businesses. *Training*, *54*(1), 14–16.

ON-THE-JOB TRAINING METHODS

CHAPTER LEARNING OUTCOMES

AFTER READING THIS CHAPTER YOU SHOULD BE ABLE TO:

- compare and contrast on-the-job training methods
- explain how to train somebody using job instruction training
- explain how and when to use performance aids, job rotation, and apprenticeships for training
- compare and contrast coaching and mentoring, and explain when and how to use them for training
- explain when to use on-the-job versus off-the-job training methods

The youth unemployment rate in Canada is nearly double that of the general population. This makes it difficult for youth to get work experience and learn new skills and without work experience and skills it is difficult to get a job. This has become known as the "no job, no experience" cycle.

To help break this cycle, several years ago RBC started the Career Launch program to provide recent university and college graduates across Canada with work experience so that they can develop the workplace skills that will help them gain a competitive edge in the job market. The program provides youth with a one-year paid internship so that they can acquire real work experience that will help them get into the workforce.

According to program director Rehana Ciriani, "This is a unique opportunity for us to help young grads gain practical, hands-on business experience combined with mentorship, networking, learning, and community engagement."

The one-year program offers 100 recent graduates from across the country the chance to move through multiple job rotations and gain experience in different business areas. The program consists of three separate rotations. The first one is at one of RBC's branches, where associates get hands-on sales and service experience serving retail banking clients, solving problems, and spotting sales opportunities. They learn foundational business, customer service, and workplace skills.

The second rotation is a community/charity rotation that allows associates to use some of the skills they learned to benefit local communities. According to Ciriani, "Associates will gain exposure to the operations of a not-for-profit organization and apply practical business skills contributing value to the organization and the communities and causes it serves. . . . This rotation is also an opportunity for associates to build their networks" and foster "relationships for professional and personal development."

In the third rotation, associates move into a specialized area to gain more specific experience and skills. This gives them further exposure to the variety of roles in organizations today and the opportunity to work in one of RBC's broad-based business areas, such as marketing, technology, human resources, finance, risk, or operations. "During this time, associates will provide project-based support in team-oriented environments to help these departments meet short- and long-term objectives," says Ciriani.

RBC's Career Launch program provides recent university and college graduates with work experience so they can develop workplace skills that will help them gain a competitive edge in the job market.

The program involves more than just the three rotations. It also includes mentoring and networking opportunities. For example, associates are paired with mentors from within RBC who help them get the most out of the program and prepare them for their careers beyond their year at RBC. Networking opportunities encourage associates to build relationships they can take with them when they have finished the RBC program. According to Zabeen Hirji, chief human resources officer at RBC in Toronto, "Relationships matter. So what we'll be doing is giving them that opportunity to meet with people from different sectors, as well as from within RBC, to develop those networks."

The first 100 Career Launch associates began the program in January 2014. In the last three years, the program has run in 17 cities and 8 provinces and involved 300 participants. RBC has been recognized as one of the best workplaces in Canada and one of Canada's Top Employers for Young People.[1]

Sources: Bernier, L. (2014, February 24). Breaking the "no job, no experience" cycle. *Canadian HR Reporter*, pp. 3, 10. Reprinted by permission of *Canadian HR Reporter*. © Thomson Reuters Canada Ltd., (2014), Toronto, Ontario, 1-800-387-5164. Web: www.hrreporter.com; Da Silva-Powell, E. (2014). Inside the RBC Career Launch Program. TalentEgg, http://talentegg.ca/incubator/2014/10/06/rbc-career-launch-program/; Da Silva-Powell, E.(2014). RBC Career Launch Program: An opportunity for recent grads. TalentEgg, http://talentegg.ca/incubator/2014/10/08/rbc-career-launch-program-opportunity-grads/; RBC Career Launch Program. (2017). RBC 2017 impact report, http://www.rbc.com/careers/careerlaunch/_assets-custom/pdf/RBC-Career-Launch-Program-2017-Report.pdf.

// INTRODUCTION

RBC's Career Launch program involves learning on the job, or what is known as on-the-job training. In this chapter, we focus on some of the most common methods of on-the-job training, such as job rotation and mentoring, which are both used in the Career Launch program.

According to the Conference Board of Canada, most Canadian organizations use on-the-job training to train employees.[2] In the United States, 65 percent of organizations place a strong emphasis on on-the-job training to a high or very high extent.[3]

Table 6.1 lists the six types of on-the-job training methods described in this chapter. We begin with the most basic form of on-the-job training—when one person trains another person on how to do something—and conclude with some of the more expensive and time-consuming methods, such as coaching and mentoring.

// ON-THE-JOB TRAINING (OJT) METHODS

On-the-job training
A training method in which a trainee receives instruction and training at his or her workstation from a supervisor or an experienced co-worker

The most common method of training is **on-the-job training**, in which a trainee receives instruction at his/her workstation from a supervisor or an experienced co-worker. Most of us can probably remember a time when a co-worker was assigned the job of training us to perform a task such as operating a cash register or learning how to make a request for supplies. Although on-the-job training has been practised since at least the Middle Ages, the United States army formalized the concept during World War II.

There are a number of approaches for on-the-job training. Table 6.2 provides a description of the various ways in which on-the-job training can be accomplished, such as training a group of employees on the spot, observing performance and providing feedback, and so on.

On-the-job training (OJT) is an important part of training at McDonald's Canada. As one of Canada's largest employers of youth, the company trains thousands of new crew members every year. Although the company once used videos and classroom training, it now uses a buddy system combined with hands-on training and visual aids.

TABLE 6.1

ON-THE-JOB TRAINING METHODS

1. *Job instruction training.* A formalized, structured, and systematic approach that consists of four steps: preparation, instruction, performance, and follow-up.

2. *Performance aid.* A device at the job site that helps an employee perform his/her job.

3. *Job rotation.* Trainees are exposed to many functions and areas within an organization.

4. *Apprenticeship.* Training for skilled trades workers that combines on-the-job training with classroom instruction.

5. *Coaching.* A more experienced and knowledgeable person is formally called upon to help another person develop insights and techniques pertinent to the accomplishment of their job and improvement of their job performance.

6. *Mentoring.* A senior member of an organization takes a personal interest in the career of a junior employee.

TABLE 6.2	
APPROACHES TO ON-THE-JOB TRAINING	

On-the-spot lecture. Gather trainees into groups and tell them how to do the job.
Viewed performance/feedback. Watch the person at work and give constructive feedback, such as when the sales manager makes a call with a new salesperson.
Following Nellie. The supervisor trains a senior employee, who in turn trains new employees (showing the ropes).
Job-aid approach. A job aid (step-by-step instructions or video) is followed while the trainer monitors performance.
The training step. The trainer systematically introduces the task.
Sequence. Follows a planned sequence. For example: Provide an on-the-spot lecture, gather trainees into groups, and tell them how to do the job.

A more experienced employee or "buddy" works with a new member individually on the job. In addition, laminated visual aids are used to show the steps in a task at each station and as a form of visual reinforcement. New crew members can refer to it during training and on the job. The combination of hands-on training and visual reinforcement is believed to result in higher levels of trainee self-efficacy and performance.[4]

OJT is especially useful for small businesses because of the limited investment needed to conduct the training. In fact, a survey found that 43 percent of small- and medium-sized enterprises use training methods such as on-the-job training, tutoring, and mentoring, while just 2 percent use only formal training such as the classroom, seminars, and workshops. Forty-three percent said that they use both on-the-job and formal training methods.[5]

On-the-job training in which a trainee receives instruction at his/her workstation is the most common method of training.

THE PROBLEM WITH ON-THE-JOB TRAINING

Although OJT is the most common approach to training, it has also been described as the most misused.[6] This is because OJT is often not well planned or structured. Another problem is that most people assigned the task of training others on the job have not received training on how to be a trainer. As a result, managers and employees do not have the knowledge and skills required to be effective trainers, nor are they familiar with learning principles such as active practice, feedback, and reinforcement.

Another problem is that poor employees teach undesirable work habits and attitudes to new employees. Also, the traditional ways of doing things get passed on to new employees, which means that existing problems as well as poor attitudes and behaviours will persist.

Other problems occur when those doing the training are worried that newly trained employees will one day take over their jobs. Some trainers might abuse their position by making the trainee do all the dirty work and the trainee might not learn important skills. In addition, OJT can be time consuming, and some employees feel penalized when they can't earn as much money or meet their goals because of the time they have to spend training others. For all these reasons, OJT is not always effective and has been referred to as the most used and misused training method.[7]

The main problem with the traditional unstructured approach to on-the-job training is that it results in training that is inconsistent, inefficient, and ineffective. However, when the process is carefully planned and structured, it can be a highly effective and efficient method of training.[8]

In fact, in one of the few studies to test the effectiveness of on-the-job training, structure was shown to be very important. In the study, a group of newly hired workers received training on how to perform a manufacturing process. One group received traditional on-the-job training in which one worker was trained by the supervisor, and then each person trained another one (similar to the Following Nellie approach described in Table 6.2). A second group was trained by a supervisor who used a structured approach to on-the-job training.

The results showed that the structured approach was considerably more effective. Trainees who received structured on-the-job training reached a predetermined level of skill and productivity in one-quarter of the time it took to train the other group. They also produced 76 percent fewer rejects, and their troubleshooting ability increased by 130 percent. This study highlights the importance of building structure into on-the-job training and the positive effect it can have on trainee learning and performance.[9]

In the next section, we describe a structured approach to on-the-job training called job instruction training.

For more information see Chapter 5, pp. 156–158

> **Job instruction training**
> A formalized, structured, and systematic approach to on-the-job training that consists of four steps: preparation, instruction, performance, and follow-up

// JOB INSTRUCTION TRAINING

While the traditional unstructured approach to on-the-job training has many problems, structured approaches to on-the-job training can be highly effective. The best-known structured approach to on-the-job training is called job instruction training.

Job instruction training is a formalized, structured, and systematic approach to on-the-job training that consists of four steps: preparation, instruction, performance, and follow-up. To some extent, job instruction training incorporates the principles of behaviour modelling training. You might recall from Chapter 5 that behaviour modelling training is a training method in which trainees observe a model performing a task and then attempt to imitate the observed behaviour.

With job instruction training, the trainer demonstrates task performance on the job and then provides the trainee with opportunities to practise while the trainer provides feedback and reinforcement. The trainer then monitors the trainees' performance on the job. Thus, like behaviour modelling training, job instruction training involves observation, rehearsal, reinforcement, and transfer. Let's now consider each of the four steps of job instruction training.

STEP 1: PREPARATION

During the preparation step, the trainer breaks down the job into small tasks, prepares all the equipment and supplies necessary to do the task, and allocates a time frame for learning each task. Key activities during the preparation step are developing a communication strategy that fits the trainee and finding out what the trainee already knows. The trainer needs to understand the background, capabilities, and attitudes of trainees as well as the nature of the tasks to be performed before choosing a technique or combination of techniques. If the training is too easy or difficult for a trainee, the trainer can make adjustments to suit the trainee's needs.

The second part of preparation concerns the trainee. There are three components: putting the trainee at ease, guaranteeing the learning, and building interest and showing personal advantage.[10]

PUTTING THE TRAINEE AT EASE

The trainer must remember that the trainee might be apprehensive. It is unwise to begin too abruptly. Some small talk might be appropriate to relax the trainee and to set the tone for the training session. Most individuals learn more readily when they are relaxed. A short conversation concerning any matter of interest—the weather, sports, a work-related item—should be effective. Obviously, the topic chosen must be suitable for the situation and the trainee.

GUARANTEEING THE LEARNING

When the conversation turns to the training, the trainer needs to assure the trainee that learning is possible. Again, use a simple statement: "Don't worry about this machine, Nadine. In about three hours you will be operating it almost as well as everyone else. I've trained at least 10 people in this procedure." The trainee now knows that it is possible to learn (i.e., learning will take place) and that the trainer has the ability to teach the process, adding to his or her self-efficacy. Recall from Chapter 2 that self-efficacy refers to judgments people have about their ability to successfully perform a specific task, and that it is a key factor in the success of a training program.

For more information see Chapter 2, p. 55

BUILDING INTEREST AND SHOWING PERSONAL ADVANTAGE

Trainees might be apprehensive or might not understand the effect that training will have on the quality of their work. Developing trainee enthusiasm is sometimes difficult, but pointing out some personal gain helps to create interest. The idea that the training will lead to something positive creates the opportunity to design rewards: more self-esteem, easier work, higher-level work, less routine, more control over work, and greater opportunity or security. Once the appropriate reward is found (provided it can be obtained), most employees respond positively.

Some trainees will resist, since training is change and individuals accept change at different rates. The trainee preparation step will identify those who are not responding. Since the trainer is responsible for meeting measurable objectives, it is important to evaluate the likelihood of cooperation among trainees so that individual remedial action can be taken. One way to defuse resistance is to train employees in order of their perceived enthusiasm. When the resisters see others reaping the rewards of training, they usually agree to be trained.

STEP 2: INSTRUCTION

The instruction step involves telling, showing, explaining, and demonstrating the task to the trainee. If the trainee is to perform a task or an operation, he or she should be positioned slightly behind or beside the trainer so that the job is viewed from a realistic angle. The trainer can then proceed in the following manner.

SHOW THE TRAINEE HOW TO PERFORM THE JOB

- Break the job into manageable tasks and present only as much as can be absorbed at one time. Remember that individuals learn at different speeds, so while some trainees might be able to learn six or seven sequences at once, others can absorb only four or five.
- Explain why as well as how.
- Point out possible difficulties and safety procedures.
- Encourage questions.

REPEAT AND EXPLAIN KEY POINTS IN MORE DETAIL

- Stress that safety is especially important.
- Take the time to show how the job fits into any larger systems.
- Show why the job is important.
- Show why key points are more important than others.
- Encourage questions.

ALLOW THE TRAINEE TO SEE THE WHOLE JOB AGAIN

- Ask questions to determine the level of comprehension.
- Encourage questions.

STEP 3: PERFORMANCE

During the performance step, the trainee performs the task under the trainer's guidance and the trainer provides feedback and reinforcement. Each task is learned in a similar way until the whole job can be completed without error. This can be done in the following manner.

ASK THE TRAINEE TO PERFORM LESS DIFFICULT PARTS OF THE JOB

- Try to ensure initial success.
- Don't tell how. If possible, ask questions, but try to keep the trainee's frustration level low.
- Ask the trainee to explain the steps.

ALLOW THE TRAINEE TO PERFORM THE ENTIRE JOB

- Gently suggest improvements where necessary.
- Provide feedback on performance.
- Reinforce correct behaviour.

STEP 4: FOLLOW-UP

Once the performance step is complete, the trainee will be left on his/her own to perform the task. This does not, however, mean that the training is over. In the follow-up step, the trainer monitors the trainee's performance. It is important that the trainer keep track of the trainee's performance and provide support and feedback. The trainer should leave the trainee to work alone, indicate when and where to find help if necessary, supervise closely and check performance periodically, and then gradually taper off instruction as the trainee gains confidence and skill.

TIPS FOR TRAINERS

Sloman developed a set of rules for effective on-the-job training based on a study of three British National Training Award winners.[11] First, job instruction training should not be managed differently from other types of training. Second, it should be integrated with other training methods. Third, ownership must be maintained even when consultants are used. And fourth, trainers must be chosen with care and trained properly. In addition to being experts in the skill area, they must want to be trainers and have good communication skills. Patience and respect for differences in the ability to learn are also important as the trainer sets the initial mood or climate of the learning experience.[12]

Once suitable individuals are found, they should be trained (train-the-trainer) and then recognized and rewarded for training others. It is of little use to give training responsibilities to an already busy employee without restructuring his or her job to include a training element. Nor is increased pay always the most sought-after reward (although it doesn't hurt). Recognition, the chance to add variety to the work day, respect from new employees, training certificates, and the prospect of either promotion or cross-training help to make the experience worthwhile for the individual.

While the steps of job instruction training might seem elaborate, they must be applied with the complexity and possible safety hazards of the job in mind. Very simple tasks might require only one demonstration. As well, employees bring different skills and backgrounds to the workplace, so it is important to make adjustments to suit the needs of each trainee.

// PERFORMANCE AIDS

A **performance aid**, also known as a job aid, is a device at the job site that helps an employee perform his/her job. Performance aids can be signs or prompts ("Have you turned off the computer?"); troubleshooting aids ("If the red light goes on, the machine needs oil"); instructions in sequence ("To empty the machine, follow the next five steps"); a special tool or gauge (a long stick to measure how much gas is in an inaccessible tank); flash cards to help counsel clients; a picture (of a perfectly set table); or posters and checklists.[13]

For example, employees learning about hazardous-waste management might be provided with a checklist that summarizes the major steps for handling radioactive material. This checklist, if prepared as a colourful poster, will increase the chances of employee application. As indicated earlier, McDonald's uses laminated visual aids to remind trainees of the steps in a task and as a form of visual reinforcement that they can

> **Performance aid**
> A device at the job site that helps an employee perform his/her job

refer to during training and on the job. At the Beer Store, "We ID 25" flashes on idle screens between sales to remind employees to ask customers who look 25 or younger for identification.[14]

The reasoning behind the use of performance aids is that requiring the memorization of sequences and tasks can take too much training time, especially if the task is not repeated daily. They are also useful when performance is difficult, is executed infrequently, can be done slowly, and when the consequences of poor performance are serious.[15] As well, new employees can be on the job more quickly if armed with a series of temporary performance aids. Finally, routine (and not-so-routine) troubleshooting and repair responses can be performed much more quickly and with less frustration.

Employees who are placed in positions where they must react very quickly might not be able to rely on memory. A panel operator in a nuclear power plant, for example, may have 15 seconds (or less) to perform a series of safety sequences. In the less hectic world of insurance sales, one manager found that a potentially sound sales trainee constantly neglected to complete the entire sales sequence and paperwork. Both these employees, despite their vastly different work environments, were helped by performance aids.

In the first instance, an indexed manual containing various operating sequences was developed and placed on a wheeled trolley within easy reach of all the operators' positions. The sales problem was solved by creating a checklist containing all the steps or tasks to be completed each time the salesperson visited a prospective client. The employee completed and checked off each step and the sheet was signed and dated. The manager then reviewed each call with the trainee. In this case, the checklist was discarded after about three weeks, by which time the sales trainee was performing to the standards set by management.[16]

For an example of a performance aid that can save lives, see Figure 6.1 and Training Today 6.1, "Operating Room Checklist Saves Lives."

TRAINING TODAY   6.1

OPERATING ROOM CHECKLIST SAVES LIVES

Surgical complications are a common yet often preventable problem that causes the death and disability of patients all around the world. In an effort to reduce the rate of major surgical complications, the World Health Organization (WHO) developed a surgical safety checklist to be used during major operations. The Surgical Safety Checklist (see Figure 6.1) requires surgeons to perform safety checks at three times during surgical procedures: before induction of anaesthesia (Sign In); before skin incision (Time Out); and before the patient leaves the operating room (Sign Out).

The checklist includes a total of 19 checks and is designed to ensure that the correct surgery site is marked, that prophylactic antibiotics are given, that blood loss is closely monitored, that sponge and needle counts are correct,

and that there is effective teamwork by the operating room staff. A check in which members of the surgical team introduce themselves to each other by name is crucial because it increases the chance that a member of the team will speak up when something is going wrong. A checklist coordinator is required to confirm that the team has completed each task on the checklist before proceeding with the operation.

Eight hospitals in eight cities (Toronto, New Delhi, Amman, Auckland, Manila, Ifakara, London, and Seattle) participated in the World Health Organization's Safe Surgery Saves Lives program. Data were collected from 3733 patients who underwent surgery without the use of the Surgical Safety Checklist and from 3955 patients who had surgery after the introduction of the checklist.

(continued)

A comparison of the two groups of patients indicated that the use of the checklist resulted in one-third fewer surgery-related deaths and complications. The rate of major complications following surgery fell from 11 percent to 7 percent after introduction of the checklist. In-patient deaths following major operations fell by more than 40 percent (from 1.5 percent to 0.8 percent).

The Toronto General Hospital was the only Canadian hospital that took part in the study. The results were so impressive that the checklist has also been adopted by the Toronto Western Hospital and the Princess Margaret Hospital.

The chief executive officer of the Canadian Patient Safety Institute is requesting that health ministers in every province and territory have the checklist implemented in all acute-care hospitals. Countries such as England, Ireland, Jordan, and the Philippines have already established nationwide programs to implement the checklist in operating rooms.

The checklist is considered to be a no-cost innovation and one of the most significant safeguards in the past three decades. The use of the checklist in Canada could prevent an estimated 40 000 complications a year and result in enormous savings to the healthcare system.

Sources: Haynes, A. B. et al. (2009). A surgical safety checklist to reduce morbidity and mortality in a global population. *The New England Journal of Medicine, 360*(5), 491–499; Priest, L. (2009, January 15). Simple checklist saves lives in the operating room, study finds. *The Globe and Mail*, p. A4; Checklist helps reduce surgical complications, deaths. World Health Organization, *WHO News Release*, www.who.int/en/

FIGURE 6.1

WORLD HEALTH ORGANIZATION'S SURGICAL SAFETY CHECKLIST

Source: *WHO surgical safety checklist*, http://whqlibdoc.who.int/publications/2009/9789241598590_eng_Checklist.pdf?ua=1. © World Health Organization, 2009. All rights reserved.

TIPS FOR TRAINERS

When designing visual performance aids to help employees remember key information, all the skills of the graphic artist's craft should be used. Ease of reading, space between letters, colour, boldness, symbols, and graphic language ("Pull Here!") are all used to communicate more effectively.[17] Audio aids also must clearly communicate intent. A taped warning ("Connect your safety harness!") may be useless, but a buzzer alarm is hard to ignore.

When designing a training program, it is important to consider how performance aids might save time and money. With ingenuity, not only can the trainee's work life be made easier, but significant improvements in performance, downtime, and safety can result. Performance aids work even better with the use of technology. Performance aids that use technology are called electronic performance-support systems and are described in Chapter 7.

// JOB ROTATION

As indicated at the beginning of the chapter, RBC's Career Launch program provides recent graduates with three job rotations to gain experience in different business areas. **Job rotation** is a training method in which trainees are exposed to different jobs, functions, and areas in an organization. It broadens an individual's knowledge and skills by providing him/her with multiple perspectives and areas of expertise.

For example, at online restaurant and food-ordering company Just Eat, interns work in four different departments (finance, marketing, operations, and sales). Once they have developed a niche or skill set, they are assigned to a specific department. One of the goals of the program is to provide interns with a multi-faceted experience so that by the end of the internship they are highly employable.[18]

Job rotation is often used as part of an ongoing career-development program, especially for employees who are destined to management positions. The objective is for an employee to learn a variety of skills from doing a variety of tasks and by observing the performance of others. Typically, the individual is supervised by a supervisor who is responsible for the individual's training.

Job rotation is an effective method of training employees who need to learn a variety of skills. By providing employees with a series of on-the-job experiences in which they work on a variety of tasks, jobs, and assignments, they acquire the skills needed to perform their current job as well as future job responsibilities.

Job rotation is also an effective way of cross-training employees. **Cross-training** involves training employees to perform each other's jobs so that anyone can step in and perform any member's job if necessary. Cross-training is particularly popular with cross-functional teams. By rotating team members to the various positions on a team, each team member learns the skills required to perform all of the team's tasks and jobs. Cross-training not only provides greater flexibility for organizations, but also enables employees to learn and use more skills. Toronto Hydro uses cross-training for its supervisors so that they can work across specializations.[19]

Research on job rotation has generally been supportive. It not only results in an improvement in knowledge and skills but also has a number of career benefits. These include higher job satisfaction, more opportunities for career advancement, and a higher salary.[20] According to the Conference Board of Canada, job rotation/cross-training is one of the most effective types of training programs, although it is used infrequently compared to other methods.[21]

Job rotation
A training method in which trainees are exposed to different jobs, functions, and areas in an organization

Cross-training
Training employees to perform each other's jobs

Furthermore, despite the benefits of job rotations, a recent survey found that job rotation programs are not promoted by more than half of Canadian organizations surveyed.[22] This might be due to the difficultly of designing effective job rotation programs. An alternative is to provide employees with developmental job experiences or what is generally known as stretch assignments.

Stretch assignments are job assignments that aim to "stretch" employees by having them work on challenging tasks and projects that involve learning new knowledge and skills. Typically they require employees to take on a variety of new tasks that are larger in scope than their current job and involve more responsibility. Many organizations offer their employees stretch assignments as a retention strategy as well as for career development and advancement.

For example, BMO has an organization-wide program that encourages stretching as part of its talent review process and career development and planning. Special projects have been found to be one of the most useful and effective learning programs.[23]

TIPS FOR TRAINERS

Although job rotation has many benefits, a disadvantage is that if an employee does not spend enough time in a department or working on an assignment, he or she might not have sufficient time to get up to speed and complete an assignment. Thus, a trainee might acquire only a superficial understanding of a job or a department, which might result in some frustration. Therefore, it is important that job rotation be carefully planned and structured so that trainees receive sufficient exposure and experience on each assignment to make it a worthwhile learning experience. In addition, the assignments should be tailored to each individual's training needs.

It is also important that job rotation be part of a larger training program and integrated with other training methods. That is, job rotation should be one component of a training program and learning process and supplemented with classroom instruction and coaching or mentoring. Coaching and mentoring are important because trainees need some guidance and supervision throughout the job rotation process.

// APPRENTICESHIPS

Apprenticeships are training methods that combine on-the-job training and classroom instruction. It is the primary method of training for skilled trades workers in Canada. The practical on-the-job training component makes up 80 percent of the training and is used to teach the requisite skills of a particular trade or occupation. Classroom instruction, which usually takes place in community colleges, focuses on technical training and comprises a relatively minor portion of apprenticeship programs (20 percent, or 180 hours).[24]

White Spot, one of British Columbia's most popular restaurants, has an apprenticeship program for chefs that allows them to complete their on-the-job training and classroom instruction in-house.[25] Toronto Hydro developed its own trade school for overhead power-line and underground apprentices.[26] Cameco, which is one of the world's largest producers of uranium, has a trade apprenticeship program that includes a mentorship with an experienced journeyperson. The company also provides apprentices with financial support for tuition and living and travel expenses.[27]

Monkey Business Images/Shutterstock.com

Apprenticeships are the primary method of training for skilled trades workers in Canada.

In Canada, the apprenticeship system covers more than 65 regulated occupations in four occupational sectors: construction (e.g., stonemason, electrician, carpenter, plumber), motive power (motor-vehicle mechanic, machinist), industrial (industrial mechanic, millwright), and service (baker, cook, hairstylist).

The regulation and administration of apprenticeship programs as well as the certification of tradespersons is the responsibility of the provinces and territories. The federal government works with the provinces and territories through the Canadian Council of Directors of Apprenticeship (CCDA) to support the development of a skilled workforce and to facilitate interprovincial mobility of the skilled trades.[28]

In the 1950s, the federal, provincial, and territorial governments established the Interprovincial Standards Red Seal Program (also known simply as the Red Seal Program) to facilitate the interprovincial mobility of skilled workers throughout Canada. The CCDA is responsible for the management of the program, which ensures the standardization of training requirements and certification of 49 skilled trades that are covered under the Red Seal program.[29] White Spot's in-house apprenticeship program provides Red Seal certification for its chefs.

Apprentices must be trained and supervised by at least one qualified tradesperson, known as a journeyperson, and pass a provincial government examination to earn a certificate of qualification. Apprentices who pass an interprovincial examination with a minimum grade of 70 percent are awarded a Red Seal certification and achieve the status of journeyperson.

Apprenticeship training differs from other training methods in that it is regulated through a partnership among government, labour, and industry. In Canada, the federal government pays for in-school training and income support. Provincial governments administer the programs and pay for classroom facilities and instructors. Employers absorb the costs of workplace training and apprentices initiate the process by finding employers to sponsor them.

Unlike corporate-sponsored training programs that address the specific needs of an organization, apprenticeships are focused on the collective training needs of specific occupations in broad industrial categories.[30] As a result, the skills learned through apprenticeship training are transferable within an occupation across Canada. This flexibility provides advantages to the worker and the industry when regional fluctuations occur in the supply and demand of skilled labour.

However, the system is highly dependent on employers, since they must be willing to sponsor apprentices and provide the on-the-job training component, something that many Canadian organizations are not willing to do.[31]

Many employers are reluctant to provide apprentice training because they do not see the benefits. In fact, only 21 percent of employers offer apprenticeships.[32] However, there is evidence that the returns on apprenticeship training investments are realized much sooner than many employers believe. A study by the Canadian Apprenticeship Forum (CAF) found that employers receive a return of $1.47 for every dollar invested in an apprentice, and that an apprentice's productive value exceeds the training costs by the end of the second year or earlier. They also found that "homegrown" journeypersons are more productive than externally trained journeypersons.[33]

TIPS FOR TRAINERS

There has been an increasing demand for skilled tradespersons in Canada, and the registration in apprenticeship programs has increased in recent years to record levels. Tradespeople in Canada represent one in five employed Canadians.[34] However, the number of people completing apprenticeship programs each year has changed very little over the last several decades.[35]

In addition, Canada's aging population means that many workers in the skilled trades are approaching retirement. As a result, there is a growing skills shortage facing many industrial sectors, and it has been predicted that the shortage of skilled workers in Canada could reach one million by the year 2020.[36]

An increased emphasis on apprenticeship training remains the most effective and practical method of teaching skilled trades occupations and dealing with the skills shortage. However, youth interest and entry in apprenticeships has been on the decline, and many employers are reluctant to take on apprentices.

Over the years, the federal government has organized a series of round table meetings with government, business, and labour to find ways to address the skills shortage problem and improve apprenticeship training.[37] A number of programs have been implemented to encourage students to enter and remain in the skilled trades and for organizations to sponsor apprentices.

For example, the Apprenticeship Incentive Grant (AIG) is a taxable cash grant of $1,000 per year up to a maximum of $2,000 that is available to registered apprentices once they have successfully completed their first or second year of an apprenticeship program in one of the Red Seal trades. The Apprenticeship Completion Grant (ACG) is a $2,000 taxable cash grant for apprentices who complete their apprenticeship training and obtain their journeyperson certification in a designated Red Seal trade. The Canada Apprentice Loan is an interest-free student loan for apprenticeship training in designated Red Seal trades. Apprentices registered in a Red Seal trade apprenticeship can receive interest-free loans up to $4,000 for each period of their technical training and do not have to pay back the loan until they have completed their training.[38] Apprenticeship tax credits are also provided by the federal and provincial governments to employers that train apprentices.[39]

Another concern is that not all Canadians participate in apprenticeship programs. Thus, efforts need to be made to encourage Aboriginal people, women, members of visible minorities, and foreign-trained skilled workers to pursue apprenticeship programs and employment in the skilled trades. Several provinces have implemented programs that introduce women to skilled trades and provide them with hands-on experience.[40]

In 2017, the federal government introduced the Union Training and Innovation Program (UTIP) to support union-based apprenticeship training. In addition to providing funding for unions to purchase up-to-date training equipment and materials, the $85 million grant is also aimed at breaking down barriers that deter women and Indigenous people from entering the skill trades. The program provides funding for innovative approaches that target women and Indigenous people. The program's objective is to improve the quality of training and to address barriers that prevent key groups from succeeding in the trades.[41]

Finally, human resource and training professionals have a key role to play in promoting and championing apprenticeship training in their organizations and educating their employers on the benefits of apprenticeships. Apprenticeship training can be an effective recruitment and retention strategy that provides organizations with many benefits and can improve their bottom line.[42]

TABLE 6.3

BENEFITS OF APPRENTICESHIP TRAINING

Effective recruitment strategy. Leads to higher retention rates and lower turnover, and provides a competitive advantage over non-participating organizations.

Two-way skills development. Mentoring apprentices renews and revitalizes journeypersons' skills, leading to greater productivity.

Higher-quality work. Helps maintain high standards and quality on the job, and develops skills and competencies that meet industry standards and build quality products.

Increased productivity. Productivity is increased because apprentices are trained in the company's systems and work processes.

Improved safety. Makes journeypersons more aware of safe work practices as they teach apprentices; makes employees more familiar with the organization's safety practices, leading to fewer accidents and thus reduced compensation costs; and leads to reduced insurance costs for some employers, because insurance companies recognize the lower risk of a skilled workforce.

Improved company reputation. Demonstrates an organization's professionalism, because it shows it is dedicated to delivering high-quality products through employing highly trained and skilled workers.

Source: Canadian Apprenticeship Forum. (2008, July). Strategies to increase employer participation in apprenticeship training in Canada, p. 1. www.caf-fca.org

Table 6.3 provides an overview of the benefits of apprenticeship training for organizations. To learn how to increase employer participation in apprenticeship training, see The Trainer's Notebook 6.1, "Increasing Employer Participation in Apprenticeship Training."

THE TRAINER'S NOTEBOOK 6.1

INCREASING EMPLOYER PARTICIPATION IN APPRENTICESHIP TRAINING

A forum held by the Canadian Apprenticeship Forum made the following recommendations to increase employer participation in apprenticeship training:

- *Educate employers about mentoring.* The process of taking on an apprentice needs to be demystified. Employers may not understand what is involved in mentoring and therefore may be reluctant to take on an apprentice.

- *Inform employers that apprenticeship training is industry driven.* Industry designs the method of delivery in apprenticeship training, and a variety of training delivery options are available.

- *Provide incentives to employers.* Incentives are an important way to maintain and enhance participation in apprenticeship training, and some employers might need clarification on the federal/provincial/territorial incentives available.

- *Ensure apprentices understand their value.* Apprentices need to understand their value to an organization and be informed about wage subsidies and tax credits so they can show what they have to offer to an employer when trying to find a sponsor.

- *Encourage employers to participate in talking to their peers.* Participating employers should inform their

(continued)

colleagues of the benefits of apprenticeship training and encourage non-participating employers to go to schools to discuss with youth a career in the trades; bring non-participating employers to networking events; and give presentations to non-participating employers on the business case for apprenticeship.

- *Build appreciation for skilled labour.* Employers will participate in apprenticeship training if customers and consumers start demanding that they have a skilled labour force and that their employees have trade certification.

Source: Canadian Apprenticeship Forum. (2008, July). Strategies to increase employer participation in apprenticeship training in Canada, p. 15. www.caf-fca.org

// COACHING

Coaching is an on-the-job training and development method in which an experienced and knowledgeable person (the coach) is formally called upon to help another person (the coachee) develop insights and techniques pertinent to the accomplishment of their job and improvement of their job performance.[43]

Coaching is a one-to-one learning and development intervention that consists of four core elements[44]:

1. The formation and maintenance of a helping relationship between the coach and the coachee

2. A formally defined coaching agreement or contract that includes personal development goals and objectives

3. Providing the coachee with tools, skills, and opportunities for growth and development

4. The fulfillment of the agreement and achievement of the objectives

The coaching process begins with a dialogue between coach and coachee, during which a set of goals and objectives is defined. An agreed-upon plan is developed mutually by the coach and the coachee. Coaching opportunities are then identified by a mutual examination of the work environment. A long-term plan is struck, along with an evaluation or measurement procedure. As well, the process is fitted into the employee's career-development goals and made part of the organization's long-term strategies.

The coachee performs the agreed-upon tasks and then reports to the coach both informally and formally during the annual or semi-annual evaluation. They discuss the results of the current program and then plan the next round of activity.[45] With practice, this approach develops into a continual transfer of skills and an ongoing process.[46]

The coaching process involves planned opportunities and activities in the work environment. Development does not occur haphazardly or by chance. The process proceeds in a logical, agreed-upon fashion. The work environment is the training laboratory (sometimes expanded to include the community). Transfers, special assignments, vacation replacements, and conference speaking engagements are all potential coaching opportunities. The necessary formal infrastructure, perhaps attached to the firm's appraisal or evaluation system, must be in place for the system to work.[47]

> **Coaching**
> An experienced and knowledgeable person is formally called upon to help another person develop insights and techniques pertinent to the accomplishment of their job and improvement of their job performance

Coaching has become popular in many organizations today. For example, Sask-Energy has a coaching program to develop successful leadership behaviours. The program includes assessments, workshops, long-term peer-to-peer coaching triangles involving groups of three people with varying levels of experience, and follow-up evaluations.[48]

Joey Restaurants created a coaching culture that involved training 12 successful senior leaders to be internal coaches so that they can develop the coaching skills of the organization's leaders. The company's focus on the "leader as coach" has resulted in more than 30 percent revenue growth and a dramatic reduction in turnover. Joey Restaurant Group has been recognized as one of Canada's most engaged workplaces and one of Canada's best workplaces. In 2011, the company was awarded the International Coaching Federation's (ICF) top prize for organizations that have profited through their commitment to coaching as a leadership strategy.[49]

Coaching programs have been effective in enhancing skills and improving performance in a wide range of areas, including interpersonal skills, communication skills, leadership skills, cognitive skills, and self-management skills. It is especially effective for helping people apply on the job what they have learned in the classroom.[50]

Research has found coaching to be highly effective for both individuals and organizations. A review of coaching research found that coaching has a positive effect on affective outcomes (e.g., attitudes), skill-based outcomes (e.g., competency skills), and results (e.g., productivity).[51] In addition, a recent study on managerial coaching found that the coaching skill of managers was directly and positively related to the annual sales goal attainment of sales representatives that they supervised. Thus, sales representatives whose managers have strong coaching skills are better performers.[52]

In general, the results of coaching studies indicate that individuals who participated in coaching showed improvements in specific skills and overall performance. Coaching has also been found to improve working relationships and job attitudes, and to increase the rate of advancement and salary increases. Benefits to organizations have been found in productivity, quality, customer service, reduced customer complaints, retention, and cost reductions. Thus, coaching is not only popular but also effective.[53]

TIPS FOR TRAINERS

To be most effective, a coach should provide coachees with continuous constructive and developmental feedback, and act as a behavioural model for good performance to demonstrate to employees the behaviour that they should exhibit. The coach should also work with employees to set challenging goals that will motivate performance.[54] In addition, the coachee and the coach must trust each other; otherwise, the coachee will see development as extra work. Indeed, perhaps the most important aspect of the coaching process is ongoing dialogue and feedback. It is only under these conditions that employees participate willingly in a two-way process that often requires extra effort and risk taking.[55]

Thus, it is important that the coach build trust and understanding so that coachees will want to work with him/her. It is also important that a coach be able to relate to the person he/she is coaching. To be most effective, coaching should be used as part of a broader process of learning rather than a stand-alone program.[56]

Finally, like any training program, the effectiveness of coaching should be evaluated. Coaching programs are expensive and time consuming, so it is important to determine whether they are accomplishing what they are supposed to accomplish.

// MENTORING

As indicated in the chapter-opening vignette, participants in RBC's Career Launch program are paired with mentors from within RBC who help them get the most out of the program and prepare them for their careers. But what exactly is mentoring?

Mentoring is an on-the-job training method in which a senior member of an organization takes a personal interest in the career of a junior employee. A mentor is an experienced individual, usually a senior manager, who provides coaching and counselling to a junior employee.

In addition to being a stand-alone method of on-the-job training, mentoring can also be used as part of a larger training program. For example, consulting firm Booz Allen Hamilton included mentoring as part of a 9- to 12- month skills enhancement program. Trainees were matched with mentors to aid in learning and growing functional skills that can be directly applied on the job.[57]

Mentors play two major roles: career support and psychosocial support. **Career support** activities include coaching, sponsorship, exposure, visibility, protection, and the provision of challenging assignments. **Psychosocial support** includes being a friend who listens and counsels, who accepts and provides feedback, and who offers a role model for success.[58]

The mentor–protégé relationship was once an informal one, with a senior person recognizing the talent of a junior employee and wishing to help. However, organizations now recognize mentoring as a valuable employee development tool and have begun to formalize mentor relationships by implementing formal mentoring programs. About half of organizations in Canada that regularly use mentoring programs do so as part of a formal learning program.[59] For example, at Knight Piesold all employees are assigned a mentor and a teammate to provide assistance with assignments. The mentor also has a say in the projects that the protégé is assigned and the project teams with which he/she works.[60]

Like coaching, mentoring is popular in organizations today and is an expensive investment.[61] However, mentoring has a more narrow focus than coaching in that its focus is on the career development of junior employees and it serves a number of purposes for organizations. It can help accelerate the career progress of underrepresented groups; transmit the culture and values to newer managers; and pass on the accumulated wisdom of seasoned leaders.[62] Mentoring involves exposure to senior management activities that are valuable and beneficial for one's growth and development.

Research has found that mentoring is highly effective for those who are mentored and their organizations. Both professional and academic research has found that mentored individuals have greater career prospects and higher incomes than those who have not been mentored. A review of mentoring research found that compared to non-mentored individuals, mentored individuals had more promotions, higher compensation, greater career commitment, and higher career and job satisfaction. Furthermore, career mentoring was more strongly related to objective indicators of career success, such as compensation and promotion, while psychosocial mentoring was more strongly related to satisfaction with the mentor.[63]

The use of technology has opened many new possibilities for mentoring. For example, some organizations have implemented **e-mentoring** programs that allow mentors and protégés to communicate using online technology such as social networks, video conferencing, and teleconferencing.

The main advantage of e-mentoring is that it allows mentors to connect with protégés anywhere in the world and reach a larger number of protégés. It also allows

Mentoring
A senior member of an organization takes a personal interest in the career of a junior employee

Career support
Mentoring activities that include coaching, sponsorship, exposure, visibility, protection, and the provision of challenging assignments

Psychosocial support
Mentoring activities that include being a friend who listens and counsels, who accepts and provides feedback, and who is a role model for success

E-mentoring
Mentoring programs in which the mentor and protégé communicate online

for just-in-time mentoring such that mentees can have their questions answered instantaneously by mentors through texts and emails.[64] To learn how to develop an effective e-mentoring program, see The Trainer's Notebook 6.2, "Developing an Effective E-Mentoring Program."

THE TRAINER'S NOTEBOOK   6.2

DEVELOPING AN EFFECTIVE E-MENTORING PROGRAM

Technology has provided many new ways to develop and implement e-mentoring programs. Here are some guidelines for making e-mentoring programs effective.

- Keep in mind that though there may be less face-to-face interaction in digitally facilitated mentoring, the premise of providing learning and development through a relationship of mutual trust remains the same.

- Enable just-in-time mentoring in which mentor and mentee can connect at the moment a question arises.

- Use video-conferencing technology on computers and mobile devices to allow for virtual "face-to-face" interaction.

- Create internal social networks for training groups, such as for leadership development participants.

- Set goals to track the success of mentoring programs, such as helping employees become ingrained in the culture or getting them up to speed faster so they can hit the ground running.

- Use technology to enable employees to seek, or get matched with, internal career coaches—mentors—who can help them achieve their development goals.

Source: Weinstein, M. (2016, September/October). Mentoring in the digital age. *Training Magazine, 53*(5), 28–31. See https://trainingmag.com/trgmag-article/mentoring-digital-age

TIPS FOR TRAINERS

Mentoring can be an effective method of training that benefits both the mentor and protégés. However, to be effective it is important that the roles and expectations of the mentor and protégés be clear and well understood. It is also important that they agree on how often they will meet, what types of topics they will discuss, and what career activities will be part of the protégé's development.

The mentor and the protégé should have some guidelines on how the process will work. Researchers have highlighted several areas of concern for implementing formal mentoring programs[65]:

- *Choice of mentors.* Mentors must be motivated to participate in the program and to make sufficient time available to their protégé. They also need to be knowledgeable about how the organization really works. Participation should be voluntary. Inevitably, some assigned relationships will not work out. A procedure needs to be in place to allow either party to cancel the arrangement without too much loss of face, and employees should feel free to end the relationship without fear of retaliation.

- *Matching mentors and protégé(s)* Matching is an important process that needs to be handled with care. Should males be matched with males and females with females? There may not be enough senior women to mentor all the junior women.[66] Mentors who are close to retirement perform better in both the career and psychosocial functions.[67] It is important that the relationship remain confidential and for the protégé to know that it will be confidential. The protégé is unlikely to feel comfortable, for example, if the mentor is his or her boss. Research has also found that having input into the matching process is important. Input into the matching process from both mentor and protégé has been found to be related to perceived program effectiveness.[68]

- *Training.* Mentors and protégés need training. This process should entail more than giving mentors a book to read about mentoring. It should, for example, involve the opportunity to share experiences about mentoring. The training of protégés, usually as part of the induction process, should demonstrate the organization's commitment to mentoring and set appropriate expectations for the mentoring relationship. Mentors could be chosen for this training based on their previous track record in developing employees. Research has found that the receipt of training and the quality of training are related to perceived program effectiveness for mentors and protégés.[69]

- *Structuring the mentoring relationship.* Some programs set time limits on the relationship and specify minimum levels of contact. Goals, projects, activities, and resources are spelled out. The program is evaluated and those areas in which either mentors or protégés report dissatisfaction are redesigned. While commitment must be made at all levels, it is at the individual level that the process can most easily break down. Signals sent by derailed mentoring schemes include delay between assignment and first meeting with protégé, poor meeting locations (e.g., the cafeteria), and infrequent contacts.

Finally, to be effective, mentoring programs must receive continued support from management. And because most mentors are volunteers, there should be some benefits and incentives to those who participate as mentors in mentoring programs.

// OFF-THE-JOB VERSUS ON-THE-JOB TRAINING METHODS

In Chapter 5, we discussed some of the factors to consider when choosing off-the-job instructional methods. A related issue is whether to use on-the-job or off-the-job training methods. In the final section of this chapter, we review some of the advantages and disadvantages of on-the-job and off-the-job training methods.

OFF-THE-JOB TRAINING METHODS

ADVANTAGES

A trainer can use a wide variety of instructional training methods when training is off the job. For example, a trainer can combine a lecture with discussion, a case study or case incident, games and simulations, and/or instructional media such as a video and slides. Thus, a trainer has many options when training is off the job and can tailor a training program to the needs and preferences of trainees. The trainer can also choose a combination of methods that will be most effective given the objectives and content of a training program.

Another advantage of off-the-job training is that the trainer is able to control the training environment. In other words, the trainer can choose a training site that is comfortable, free of distractions, and conducive to learning. A trainer does not have as much control of the learning environment when training is on the job.

A third advantage is that a large number of trainees can be trained at one time. This is especially the case when the lecture method is used. Thus, off-the-job training is generally more efficient given that many more trainees can be trained at one time and in one place. This is, of course, a huge advantage when many employees need to be trained as soon and as fast as possible.

DISADVANTAGES

There are also a number of disadvantages of off-the-job training methods. First, off-the-job training can be much more costly than on-the-job training. This is because of the costs associated with the use of training facilities, travel, accommodation, food, and so on. However, as you will see in Chapter 7, these costs can be almost completely eliminated with the use of technology.

A second disadvantage of off-the-job training is that because the training takes place in a training environment that is different from the work environment, trainees might have difficulty applying the training material on the job. For example, while a trainee might be able to perform a training task in a role play during training, he or she might have difficulty performing the same task on the job. Thus, the application of training on the job, or what is known as the transfer of training (see Chapter 9), can be more difficult with off-the-job training.

ON-THE-JOB TRAINING METHODS

ADVANTAGES

A major advantage of on-the-job training methods is that the cost is much lower given that the need for training facilities, travel, accommodation, and so on is eliminated. Thus, on-the-job training tends to be much less costly than off-the-job training.

A second advantage is the greater likelihood of trainees applying the training on the job. That is, because training takes place in the trainees' actual work area, the application is much more direct and in some cases immediate. Thus, there is less difficulty in the transfer of training, since the training environment and work environment are the same.

DISADVANTAGES

There are a number of disadvantages of on-the-job training. First, the work environment is full of distractions that can interfere with learning and interrupt training. Noise might make it difficult for trainees to hear and understand the trainer, and at times the trainer might be interrupted and called away from the training to solve a problem or work on something else.

Second, when trainees are being trained on an actual machine or equipment on the job, there is always the potential for damage to expensive equipment. This could shut down production for a period of time, adding to the cost of repairing or replacing damaged equipment.

A third disadvantage is the disruption of service or slowdown in production that occurs during training. You have probably had the experience of being served by an employee who is being trained. The result is usually slower service and the potential for errors. Thus, on-the-job training can result in a reduction in productivity, quality, and service.

Finally, when safety issues are associated with the use of equipment or dangerous chemicals, on-the-job training can compromise safety. A trainee learning on the job can make a mistake and harm him/herself, other employees, or customers. Therefore, extra precaution and care need to be taken whenever on-the-job training involves working with equipment or dangerous chemicals.

COMBINING ON-THE-JOB AND OFF-THE-JOB TRAINING METHODS

As you can see, there are advantages and disadvantages associated with on-the-job and off-the-job training methods. Being aware of and understanding them can be helpful when choosing a training method. For example, when there is a need to train a large number of employees, off-the-job training is more practical. When the cost of training is an issue, on-the-job training might be more feasible. Thus, issues of practicality and feasibility are important considerations when choosing training methods.

It should be apparent to you that the choice of a training method is not really a matter of whether training should be on the job or off the job. In fact, as noted in Chapter 5, effective training programs often combine on-the-job and off-the-job training methods.

Ultimately, what is most important is mixing and combining training methods to best suit a particular training need and objective. In fact, one study found that a combination of on-the-job and off-the-job training methods is the best approach for getting employees up to speed.[70] Thus, once again the best approach appears to be a blended one that combines different methods of training. This is the case not only with respect to on-the-job and off-the-job training methods, but also for technology-based training methods, which are discussed in Chapter 7.

// SUMMARY

This chapter described some of the most common methods of on-the-job training and complements the off-the-job instructional training methods described in Chapter 5. We noted that on-the-job training is the most common method of training as well as the most misused. However, job instruction training that is carefully planned and structured can have a positive effect on employee learning and performance. On-the-job training can also involve the use of performance aids and job rotation. Apprenticeship programs combine on-the-job training and classroom instruction and are the primary method of training skilled trades workers. Coaching and mentoring are also popular methods of on-the-job training that can be used alone or in combination with other methods. The chapter concluded with a discussion of the advantages and disadvantages of on-the-job and off-the-job training methods. It was noted that effective training programs mix and combine on-the-job and off-the-job training methods as well technology-based training methods, the focus of Chapter 7.

KEY TERMS

apprenticeships p. 189
career support p. 195
coaching p. 193
cross-training p. 188
e-mentoring p. 195
job instruction training p. 182
job rotation p. 188
mentoring p. 195
on-the-job training p. 180
performance aid p. 185
psychosocial support p. 195
stretch assignments p. 189

DISCUSSION QUESTIONS

1. Describe the similarities and differences between coaching and mentoring. When would you use coaching and when would you use mentoring as an on-the-job training method?

2. What are the main issues to consider when developing a mentoring program?

3. How should an organization decide whether it should use on-the-job training? What are the advantages and disadvantages?

4. Why do you think on-the-job training is the most common method of training? Why is it also the most misused method? What can organizations do to avoid the problems of on-the-job training?

5. Describe the objectives of apprenticeships and how they are different from other methods of on-the-job training. What should be done to increase the number of people who pursue apprenticeship training in Canada, and why is this important? What should be done to increase the number of employers that are willing to provide apprenticeship training?

6. Describe the four steps of job instruction training and what you would do in each step if you were training someone on the job. Explain how you would train somebody to drive a car or fix a flat tire if you were using job instruction training.

7. Discuss the advantages and disadvantages of on-the-job and off-the-job training methods.

8. What is job rotation and what are its advantages and disadvantages? What are some ways to make job rotation effective for learning and career development?

9. What is a stretch assignment and what makes it a method of on-the-job training? What is the difference between a stretch assignment and job rotation?

THE GREAT TRAINING DEBATE

1. Debate the following: On-the-job training can result in employees who are poorly trained, and it should be avoided whenever possible.

2. Debate the following: The apprenticeship system in Canada is no longer effective, and organizations would be better off if they implemented their own in-house apprenticeship programs.

3. Debate the following: If an employee can perform a job, then he/she should be able to train others to do the job.

EXERCISES

IN-CLASS

1. Recall the most recent job you had and how you were trained. Were you trained on the job? If so, describe your experience. What exactly did the trainer do and how did it influence your learning? Was your on-the-job training experience effective? Why or why not? What could have been done differently to make it more effective? If you were not trained on the job, describe how on-the-job training might be used to train employees to do your job.

2. As a student, you have probably experienced some problems studying, writing assignments, or perhaps writing exams. If you were to act as a tutor to train another student with some of these problems, what method of training would you use and why? Consider each of the on-the-job training methods in Table 6.1 and indicate how you would use them and how effective they would be for training a student to become a "better" student.

3. Assume that you have just been hired as a trainer in an organization that hires recent college and university graduates every year. The company does not have a formal mentoring program and your job is to try to get one started. Prepare a proposal to convince management of the importance of and need for a formal mentoring program. Include a description of how the program will work and what will be required to get it started. Then have another member of the class review your proposal and provide feedback or present your proposal to the class.

4. Using the job instruction training method, design a training program to perform a task you are familiar with. It could be a task you have had to perform in a current or previous job, or it could be something that is not work related, such as how to fix a flat tire, how to drive a car, or how to ride a bike. Design your training program following the steps outlined in the chapter. Then have another member of the class review your training program and provide feedback. Alternatively, do a demonstration in front of the class and have the class critique your training program and provide feedback.

5. Very often, experienced employees are called on to train a new employee on the job. In most cases, the employee has not received training in how to train others. Chances are that someday you will be asked to train a new employee, or perhaps you have already had to. To prepare yourself for this task, consider how well prepared and qualified you are. What are your strengths and weaknesses? Prepare an action plan to develop areas that you need to improve. If you have already had to train somebody on the job, how effective were you and what do you need to do to improve?

6. On-the-job training can be very effective if the trainer is knowledgeable about learning principles and theories. Make a list of all the principles, concepts, and

CHAPTER 6 On-the-Job Training Methods

theories described in previous chapters of the text that can be used to make on-the-job training more effective. Explain the relevance of each principle, concept, and theory on your list.

IN-THE-FIELD

1. Ask your friends if they would accept a paid training experience that consisted of the following benefits:
   - They would be given structured classroom training and on-the-job assignments.
   - They would be coached and supervised throughout the learning experience.
   - They would be paid to learn.
   - They would be certified at the end of learning the job.
   - They would be guaranteed employment at high wages.

   If they answer "yes," then tell them about becoming an apprentice electrician, carpenter, plumber, or chef. What is their reaction? Do students resist the certification programs in the traditional vocations and embrace certification in human resources or accounting? Why? What can be done to increase the likelihood that students will choose a skilled trade and enter an apprenticeship program?

2. Contact the human resource department of an organization to find out about their use of on-the-job training. In particular, you should inquire about the following:
   - Do they use on-the-job training? If so, what do they use it for (what employees, what kinds of job)? Why do they use it? How effective is it?
   - How formal and systematic is their on-the-job training? Is it carefully planned? Do trainers receive training and instruction? Are the trainers carefully selected? Are they rewarded for their efforts? Are they evaluated?
   - Do they follow the steps of the job instruction training method? How well is each step performed?
   - Based on what you have learned in this chapter, is the organization doing a good job in providing on-the-job training? What is it doing right and wrong?
   - What advice would you give the organization to improve its on-the-job training?

3. Do you have what it takes to be a good mentor? To find out, go to www.mentors.ca, select "All about Peer Mentoring" and then "Take" to take the Mentor Survey. What is your score and what does it say about your potential to be a mentor? What do you have to do to improve your potential to be a mentor?

4. To learn about apprenticeships in Canada, visit the Canadian Apprenticeship Forum (CAF) at www.caf-fca.org. Click on "Apprenticeship 101" and briefly discuss the following:
   a. What is the CAF and what does it do?
   b. What is apprenticeship?
   c. What is involved in becoming an apprentice?
   d. What is involved in hiring an apprentice?
   e. What are apprenticeship regulatory systems?

CASE INCIDENT

DAVCO MACHINE LTD.

Davco Machine Ltd. is located in Grande Prairie in northern Alberta, where it designs and builds equipment for the forestry, construction, and oil and gas industries. The company has 70 employees, most of whom are machinists, welders, mechanics, or millwrights. Davco formed a partnership with technical schools in Edmonton and was able to generate interest among students to apprentice at the company. However, the facility didn't have enough journeypersons to meet the requirement of one journeyperson for every apprentice.

The company representatives travelled to Germany to take part in a job fair hosted by the provincial government. When a worker in Germany is unemployed, the government requires him/her to go back to school. As a result, Germany has a low unemployment rate and a highly educated labour pool. Once in Germany, Davco had no problem recruiting four journeyperson machinists.

QUESTIONS

1. What does this case tell you about the importance and need for apprenticeship training in Canada, and its future as a method of on-the-job training?

2. What should governments and companies like Davco do to increase the number of apprentices and journeypersons in Canada?

Source: Franceschini, T. (2005, December). CloseUp: CEOs talk workforce development. *Canadian HR Reporter*, p. 7. Reprinted by permission of *Canadian HR Reporter*. © Copyright Thomson Reuters Canada Ltd., (2005), Toronto, Ontario, 1-800-387-5164. Web: www.hrreporter.com

CASE STUDY   TPK APPLIANCES

When TPK, a manufacturer of small appliances—electric kettles, toasters, and irons—automated its warehouse, the warehouse crew was reduced from 14 to 4. Every one of the displaced employees was assigned to another department, as TPK had a history of providing stable employment.

Jacob Peters, an employee with more than 15 years of service, was transferred to the toaster assembly line to be retrained as a small-parts assembler. When he arrived to begin his new job, the supervisor said, "This may be only temporary, Jacob. I have a full staff right now, so I have nothing for you to do, but come on, I'll find you a locker."

As there really was no job for him, Jacob did nothing for the first week but odd jobs, such as filling bins. At the beginning of week two, Jacob was informed that a vacancy would be opening the next day, so he reported for work eager to learn his new job.

The operation was very simple. All Jacob had to do was pick up two pieces of metal, one in each hand, place them into a jig so that they were held together in a cross position, and press a button. The riveting machine then put a rivet through both pieces and an air jet automatically ejected the joined pieces into a bin.

"This job is so simple a monkey could do it," the supervisor told Jacob. "Let me show you how it's done," and he quickly demonstrated the three steps involved. "Now you do it," the supervisor said. Of course, Jacob did it right the first time. After watching him rivet two or three, the supervisor left Jacob to his work.

About three hours later, the riveter started to put the rivets in a little crooked, but Jacob kept on working. Finally, a fellow worker stopped by and said, "You're new here, aren't you?" Jacob nodded. "Listen, I'll give you a word of advice. If the supervisor sees you letting the rivets go in crooked like that, he's going to be really mad at you. So hide these in the scrap over there." The co-worker then showed Jacob how to adjust the machine.

Jacob's next problem began when the air ejection system started jamming. Four times he managed to clear it, but on the fifth try, he slipped and his elbow hit the rivet button. The machine put a rivet through the fleshy part of his hand, just below the thumb.

It was in the first-aid station that the supervisor finally had the opportunity to see Jacob once again.

QUESTIONS

1. Comment on the strengths and weaknesses of the on-the-job training that Jacob received. What did the supervisor do that was consistent with job instruction training? What did he fail to do?

2. What does this case tell you about the traditional approach to on-the-job training? What does it tell you about job instruction training?

3. If you were the supervisor, how would you have trained Jacob? What would you do differently, and why?

4. If the job instruction training method was used, how would Jacob's training have been conducted? Explain how each step would proceed.

5. Describe any other on-the-job training methods that might be used to train Jacob. Consider each method listed in Table 6.1. What methods do you think would be most effective? What methods would you use, and why?

FLASHBACK QUESTIONS

1. Describe any off-the-job training methods that might have been used to train Jacob. Consider each method listed in Table 5.1. What methods do you think would be most effective? What methods would you use, and why?

2. Describe how some of the principles, concepts, and theories of learning from Chapter 2 might be relevant for training Jacob. Be sure to consider learning styles, adult learning theory, conditioning theory, and social cognitive theory.

3. Consider the role that active practice played in training Jacob. Did the supervisor provide Jacob with sufficient opportunities for active

practice? If you trained Jacob, what would you have done differently in terms of active practice? Consider the conditions of practice before training (pre-training interventions) and during training (see Table 4.4 in Chapter 4). Which ones would you include in the training, and why?

4. Consider the use of error-management training (EMT) (Chapter 4) for training Jacob. Do you think EMT might have been effective for training Jacob? Would it have prevented his accident? Explain your answers.

FLASH FORWARD QUESTION

1. Do you think the training program would have been more effective if technology-based training methods were used (e.g., computer-based training)? Explain your answer. How might technology have been used to train Jacob?

REWRITE THE CASE QUESTION: JOB INSTRUCTION TRAINING

Rewrite the case so that Jacob's supervisor uses job instruction training. In other words, add a paragraph in which you describe how the supervisor trains Jacob using each of the four steps of job instruction training.

RUNNING CASE DIRTY POOLS

QUESTIONS

Refer to the case at the end of Chapter 1 to answer the following questions.

1. Would on-the-job training be an appropriate and effective way to train pool operators and their employees? Explain your answer.

2. What on-the-job training methods would you recommend to train pool operators and their employees? Review each method in Table 6.1 and explain which ones you would recommend, and why. What on-the-job method(s) would be most effective?

3. Would job instruction training be an effective way to train pool operators and their employees? Review the steps of job instruction training and explain how it can be used to train pool operators and employees. If you prefer, you can describe how to train for a specific pool operator task (e.g., cleaning and sanitizing equipment, or maintaining proper chemical balance, such as pH levels). Be sure to describe what would happen and how you would proceed at each step of job instruction training.

// REFERENCES

1. Bernier, L. (2014, February 24). Breaking the "no job, no experience" cycle. *Canadian HR Reporter, 27*(4), 3, 10; Da Silva-Powell, E. (2014, October 6). Inside the RBC Career Launch Program. *TalentEgg*. Retrieved from http://talentegg.ca/incubator/2014/10/06/rbc-career-launch-program/; Da Silva-Powell, E. (2014, October 8). RBC Career Launch Program: An opportunity for recent grads. *TalentEgg*. Retrieved from http://talentegg.ca/incubator/2014/10/08/rbc-career-launch-program-opportunity-grads/; RBC Career Launch Program, "RBC 2017 Impact report", http://www.rbc.com/careers/careerlaunch/_assets-custom/pdf/RBC-Career-Launch-Program-2017-Report.pdf.

2. Hughes, P. D., & Grant, M. (2007). *Learning & development outlook 2007.* Ottawa: The Conference Board of Canada.

3. Ho, M. (2017, December). Learning investment & hours are on the rise. *TD: Talent Development, 71*(12), 38–43.

4. Anonymous (1999, May/June). McDonald's stresses hands-on training. *The Training Report*, p. 10.

5. Dulipovici, A. (2003, May). Skilled in training: Results of CFIB surveys on training. *CFIB Research*. Retrieved from http://www.cfib.ca/research/reports/training_2003_e.pdf

6. Sisson, G. R. (2001). *Hands-on training.* San Francisco, CA: Berrett-Koehler.

7. Sisson (2001).

8. Sisson (2001).

9. Sisson (2001).

10. Broadwell, M. (1969). *The supervisor and on-the-job training.* Reading, MA: Addison-Wesley.

11. Sloman, M. (1989). On-the-job training: A costly poor relation. *Personnel Management, 21*(2), 38–42.

12. Renner, P. F. (1989). *The instructor's survival kit.* Vancouver: Training Associates Ltd; Tench, A. (1992). Following Joe around: Should this be our approach to on-the-job training? *Plant Engineering, 46*(17), 88–92.

13. Meyers, D. (1991). Restaurant service: Making memorable presentations. *Cornell Hotel and Restaurant Administration Quarterly, 32*(1), 69–73; Ukens, C. (1993). Cards help pharmacists counsel patients in a flash. *Drug Topics, 137*(1), 24–27.

14. Gordon, A. (2014, February 13). Rising to a minor challenge. *Toronto Star*, pp. L1, L4.

15. Ruyle, K. (1991, February/March). Developing intelligent job aids. *Technical and Skills Training*, 9–14.

16. Arajis, B. (1991). Getting your sales staff in shape. *Graphic Arts Monthly, 63*(5), 125–127.

17. Arajis (1991); Cowen, W. (1992). Visual control boards are a key management tool. *Office Systems, 9*(10), 70–72; King, W. (1994). Training by design. *Training and Development, 48*(1), 52–54.

18. Dobson, S. (2013, June 17). Employers recognized for campus recruitment, internship programs. *Canadian HR Reporter, 26*(12), 3, 10.

19. Young, L. (2008, March 24). All in the family at Toronto Hydro. *Canadian HR Reporter, 21*(6), 16.

20. Campion, M. A., Cheraskin, L., & Stevens, M. J. (1994). Career-related antecedents and outcomes of job rotation. *Academy of Management Journal, 37*, 1518–1542.

21. Cotsman, S., & Hall, C. (2018). *Learning cultures lead the way: Learning & development outlook–14th edition*. Ottawa: The Conference Board of Canada.

22. Dobson, S. (2016, May 30). Despite benefits, many employers not offering job rotations: Survey. *Canadian HR Reporter, 29*(10), 3, 12.

23. Ray, R. (2006, April 19). New assignments a stretch but not a yawn. *The Globe and Mail*, pp. C1, C6; Horoszowski, M. (2015, November 13). How to use stretch assignments to support social good. *Harvard Business Review*, https://hbr.org/2015/11/how-to-use-stretch-assignments-to-support-social-good.

24. Ménard, M., Menezes, F., Chan, C. K. Y., & Walker, M. (2007). *National apprenticeship survey: Canada overview report 2007*. Ottawa: Statistics Canada.

25. Klie, S. (2008, June 2). Restaurant's training a recipe for success. *Canadian HR Reporter, 21*(11), 8, 9.

26. Young (2008).

27. Dobson, S. (2013, October 21). Mentorships, events give boost to young workers. *Canadian HR Reporter, 26*(18), 1, 16.

28. Ménard et al. (2007).

29. Ménard et al. (2007).

30. Moskal, B. (1991). Apprenticeship: Old cure for new labor shortage? *Industry Week, 240*(9), 30–35.

31. Galt, V. (2006, March 22). Few employers taking on apprentices: New survey. *The Globe and Mail*, p. C2.

32. Flavelle, D. (2013, March 15). Invest in skilled trades, Stronach urges. *Toronto Star*, p. B3.

33. Dobson, S. (2010, June 14). Disconnect between employers, apprentices with hiring: Report. *Canadian HR Reporter, 23*(12), 6; *It pays to hire an apprentice: Calculating the return on training investment for skilled trades employers in Canada.* (2009, June). Ottawa: Canadian Apprenticeship Forum; *Strategies to increase employer participation in apprenticeship training in Canada.* (2008, July). Ottawa: Canadian Apprenticeship Forum; http://www.caf-fca.org

34. Vander Wier, M. (2017, July 10). Federal government turns focus to trades. *Canadian HR Reporter, 30*(12), 3, 8.

35. Ménard et al. (2007).

36. McCarthy, S. (2001, February 27). Skilled-worker shortage could reach one million. *The Globe and Mail*, p. A1.

37. McCarthy (2001).

38. Bernier, L. (2014, March 10). Ottawa targets skills training. *Canadian HR Reporter, 27*(5), 2.

39. *Apprenticeship training in Canada.* (2006, July 25). Canadian Council on Learning. Retrieved from www.ccl-cca.ca/CCL/Reports/LessonsInLearning/apprenticeship-LinL.htm

40. *Apprenticeship training in Canada.* (2006).

41. Vander Wier (2017).

42. Starrett, T. (2004, February/March). The eager apprentice: Has HR forgotten about a valuable resource? *HR Professional, 21*(2), 32.

43. Jones, R. J., Woods, S. A., & Guillaume, Y. R. F. (2016). The effectiveness of workplace coaching: A meta-analysis of learning and performance outcomes from coaching. *Journal of Occupational and Organizational Psychology, 89*, 249–277.

44. Jones, Woods, & Guillaume (2016).

45. Kroeger, L. (1991). Your team can't win the game without solid coaching. *Corporate Controller, 3*(5), 62–64.

46. Azar, B. (1993). Striking a balance. *Sales and Marketing Management, 145*(2), 34–35; Whittaker, B. (1993). Shaping the competitive organization. *CMA Magazine, 67*(3), 5.

47. Blakesley, S. (1992). Your agency . . . leave it better than you found it. *Managers Magazine, 67*(4), 20–22.

48. Finkelstein, L. (2008, December 1). Coaching SaskEnergy to higher performance. *Canadian HR Reporter, 21*(21), 23.

49. Busse, D., & Hemmingsen, J. (2010, December 13). A pinch of coaching, a dash of training. *Canadian HR Reporter, 23*(22), 25–26; International Coach Federation. (2011, September 26). *Joey Restaurant Group and BC Housing named 2011 ICF International Prism Award winners* [Press release]. Retrieved from http://coachfederation.org/prdetail.cfm?ItemNumber=1934

50. Peterson, D. B. (2002). Management development: Coaching and mentoring programs. In K. Kraiger (Ed.), *Creating, implementing, and managing effective training and development: State-of-the-art lessons for practice* (pp. 160–191). San Francisco, CA: Jossey-Bass.

51. Jones, Woods, & Guillaume (2016).

52. Dahling, J. J., Taylor, S. R., Chau, S. L., & Dwight, S. A. (2016). Does coaching matter? A multilevel model linking managerial coaching skill and frequency to sales goal attainment. *Personnel Psychology, 69*, 863–894.

53. Peterson (2002).

54. Dahling, Taylor, Chau, & Dwight (2016).

55. Kruse, A. (1993). Getting top value for your payroll dollar. *Low Practice Management, 19*(3), 52–57.

56. Peterson (2002).

57. Anonymous (2016). Outstanding training initiatives – Booz Allen Hamilton: Tech Tank. *Training Magazine, 53*(5), 54–55.

58. Noe, R. A. (1999). *Employee training and development.* Boston: Irwin McGraw-Hill.

59. Cotsman & Hall (2018).

60. Dobson (2013).

61. Peterson (2002).

62. Peterson (2002).

63. Allen, T. D., Eby, L. T., Poteet, M. L., Lentz, E., & Lima, L. (2004). Career benefits associated with mentoring for protégés: A meta-analysis. *Journal of Applied Psychology*, *89*, 127–136.

64. Dobson, S. (2011, February 14). Taking mentorship online. *Canadian HR Reporter*, *24*(3), 15; Weinstein, M. (2016, September/October). Mentoring in the digital age. *Training Magazine*, *53*(5), 28–31.

65. Jackson, C. (1993). Mentoring: Choices for individuals and organizations. *The International Journal of Career Management*, *5*(1), 10–16; Noe (1999).

66. Gallege, L. (1993). Do women make poor mentors? *Across the Board*, *30*(6), 23–26.

67. Mullen, E. J. (1998). Vocational and psychosocial mentoring functions: Identifying mentors who serve both. *Human Resource Development Quarterly*, *9*(4), 319–331.

68. Allen, T. D., Eby, L. T., & Lentz, E. (2006). The relationship between formal mentoring program characteristics and perceived program effectiveness. *Personnel Psychology*, *59*, 125–153.

69. Allen et al. (2006).

70. Harding, K. (2003, May 9). Combined training works best, study says. *The Globe and Mail*, p. C1.

CHAPTER
7

TECHNOLOGY-BASED TRAINING METHODS

CHAPTER LEARNING OUTCOMES

AFTER READING THIS CHAPTER, YOU SHOULD BE ABLE TO:

- explain the differences between technology-based training, traditional training, computer-based training, and e-learning
- compare and contrast instructor-led training and self-directed learning as well as asynchronous and synchronous training
- explain how online education and electronic performance support systems are used for training
- explain how a virtual classroom works and how video conferencing, web conferencing, webinars, and webcasts are used
- explain how social media, Web 2.0 technologies, mobile learning, and synthetic learning environments can be used for training
- explain how to design effective computer-based training programs and their advantages and disadvantages for individuals and organizations
- know when to use computer-based training and how to make it effective for learning

Calfrac Well Services designed a blended approach to training that combines online modules and hands-on field training.

Calfrac Well Services of Calgary, Alberta, operates in four countries and is one of the largest hydraulic fracturing companies in the world. Several years ago, Calfrac could not find a classroom large enough for its Employee Responsibility Training (CERT) program so it created one. The result is a blended approach to training that combines online modules and hands-on field training.

CERT provides standardized training across the company's districts, both in content and in delivery. The program includes online training modules relating to each individual piece of equipment used by field operators in conjunction with on-the-job training through peer-to-peer coaching.

As part of the CERT program, Calfrac provides each of its field operators a tablet. This allows greater flexibility and mobility in the organization's on-the-job training by putting a mobile classroom in the hands of every one of its field operators.

The CERT program was originally conceived as a set of manuals. Calfrac uses 30 separate pieces of equipment in its operations and many of these machines are retrofitted to suit specific needs.

In an effort to create standardized training processes, Calfrac worked with several of its field operators and a technical writer to create a manual for each piece of equipment that ranged from 20 to 40 pages. However, according to Human Resource Director Jon Koop, "What we realized really quickly was that probably wasn't the best training method. Sitting these guys in front of stacks of manuals wasn't going to be very effective at keeping them awake, let alone having them learn anything."

So the company decided that a blended approach would be more successful, as the hands-on component would be more in keeping with its tradition of on-the-job training. Field operators were consulted in the creation of best practices, including how to use the equipment as well as safety procedures and environmental factors.

Employees work through the best practices via e-learning courses with their tablets. Once they pass a knowledge exam, they are able to download the necessary on-the-job training forms. Along with a peer trainer, employees complete the forms as they train with the equipment in the field. Following an assessment by a site supervisor, the employee is declared competent and becomes a peer coach for fellow employees undergoing training.

"We don't have a classroom big enough or a teacher smart enough to teach everyone everything they need to know in this business," Koop says, "so we need to rely on each other and be able to teach each other." To facilitate this, an online coaching module was developed for CERT. The module incorporates Calfrac's culture and core values.

The coaching module is indicative of Calfrac's goals moving forward, Koop said. The company sees its CERT program as an opportunity for the organization to become a learning organization and cultivate peer-to-peer training and the sharing of information on an ongoing basis.

By blending online and on-the-job training, Calfrac was able to create a training and development program that is both meaningful and economical. Modules were created for each separate piece of machinery at an average cost of less than $20,000 per module. Calfrac spent about $280,000 to furnish each employee with his/

her own tablet and employees are paid two hours' wages to complete each module, since their learning is done on their own time.

In addition to a positive response from employees, Calfrac has won several awards for the program including the 2015 National HR Award for Best Corporate Training and Development Program and an honourable mention for Blended Learning from the International e-Learning Association. The company is working on translating the program to ensure employees in the United States, Russia, and Argentina are also trained using the same strategy, and plans to expand the program to create modules for its maintenance staff, front-line supervisors, and engineers.[1]

Sources: Based on Foster, L. (2015). Calfrac finds flexibility, mobility – and cost savings – in taking blended approach to training. *Canadian HR Reporter, 28* (15), 18, 20. Reprinted by permission of *Canadian HR Reporter.* © Copyright Thomson Reuters Canada Ltd., (2015), Toronto, Ontario, 1-800-387-5164. Web: www.hrreporter.com; Calfrac, About Us at www. Calfrac.com and Careers at www.calfrac.com/careers.

// INTRODUCTION

Like many organizations today, Calfrac Well Services uses technology to deliver training. Besides being able to offer a wide assortment of training programs, technology-based training can be provided to large numbers of employees at any time, with many benefits to employees and organizations.

In Chapters 5 and 6, we described off-the-job and on-the-job training methods. In this chapter, we focus on technology-based training methods. You will learn about how technology is being used for training, how to design technology-based training programs, and the advantages, disadvantages, and effectiveness of technology-based training. But first, let's be clear about what technology-based training is and how it differs from traditional training methods.

// WHAT IS TECHNOLOGY-BASED TRAINING?

Technology-based training
Training that involves the use of technology to deliver training

Traditional training
Training that does not involve using technology to deliver training

Technology-based training is training that involves the use of technology to deliver training programs, such as Web-based training, computerized self-study, satellite or broadcast TV, and video-, audio-, or tele-conferencing. Calfrac uses technology to deliver training to its field operators who take e-learning courses with their tablets. Any technology that delivers education or training, or supports the delivery of these subjects, would be included in the definition.[2]

By contrast, **traditional training** is training that does not involve the use of technology to deliver training, such as classroom training with a live instructor (regardless of the instructor's or learners' use of technology during the class); non-computerized self-study, such as textbooks or workbooks; non-computerized games; seminars; lectures; or outdoor programs.[3]

Industry, government, and educational organizations are increasingly using technology to deliver training.[4] In Canada, while instructor-led classroom training remains the most widely used training method (used in 94 percent of organizations), more than three-quarters of organizations offer some form of self-paced online learning or e-learning, which represents 20 percent of overall learning time. Furthermore, 69 percent of organizations report that e-learning is strategically important to their organization's learning strategy.[5]

In the United States, 28.6 percent of training hours are delivered via online or computer-based technologies and 88 percent of organizations use e-learning. However, 42 percent of training hours are delivered by an instructor in a classroom. Thirteen percent of organizations use instructor-led classroom training mostly or exclusively, and over 40 percent of small- and mid-sized organizations rely on instructor-led training.[6]

Thus, although the use of technology for training is becoming more common, it is doing so at a relatively slow pace. Furthermore, it has not supplanted instructor-led classroom instruction; rather, it has become an alternative method of training that is not likely to replace learning in the classroom.[7]

That being said, the use of technology for training in Canada has increased over the last decade, and some companies have made major advances.[8] For example, Calfrac now uses technology to deliver standardized training to all of its field operators and is expanding the program for its maintenance staff, front-line supervisors, and engineers. At Cisco Systems Canada Co., most sales training is now done online, compared to just a few years ago when 90 percent was done in the classroom. Employees now access the company's website to find out about new Cisco networking products and how to install products. Because the courses are up and running much faster than traditional classroom programs, employees can learn about new products in one week compared to three months.[9]

As part of an initiative to better meet changing customer requirements that involved replacing existing business processes as well as 200 different business systems, Hydro-Québec now delivers training online for close to 3000 employees.[10]

In the United States, accounting firm EY recently transformed an instructor-led classroom course to a blended learning program for first-year tax professionals. The new blended program consists of e-learning, virtual classroom courses, classroom-based simulations, and just-in-time resources.[11] Vehicle maintenance company Jiffy Lube International, Inc. introduced a training program for a new Point-of-Sale system for more than 1900 service centres. The training program includes e-learning courses to provide training on how to use the new system, two virtual instructor-led training courses, and just-in-time video to refresh training.[12] Thus, technology is increasingly being used to deliver training in many organizations today.

// COMPUTER-BASED TRAINING AND E-LEARNING

In general, using computers to deliver training generally has been referred to as computer-based training or e-learning. Although these terms are often used synonymously, there are some differences. **Computer-based training** is training that is delivered via the computer for the purpose of teaching job-relevant skills. It can include text, graphics, and/or animation, and can be delivered via CD-ROMs, intranets, or the Internet.[13]

> **Computer-based training**
> Training that is delivered via the computer for the purpose of teaching job-relevant knowledge and skills

TABLE 7.1

TRAINING METHODS AS A PERCENTAGE OF OVERALL LEARNING TIME AND USE BY ORGANIZATIONS

	LEARNING TIME	ORGANIZATION USE
Instructor-led (classroom)	48%	94%
Instructor-led (online)	8%	52%
Self-paced (computer-aided, offline)	2%	15%
Self-paced (online)	20%	77%
Collaborative (face-to-face)	8%	64%
Self-paced (non-computer-based)	3%	25%
Instructor-led (blended)	5%	40%
Collaborative (online)	2%	21%

Source: Cotsman, S., & Hall, C. (2018). Learning cultures lead the way: Learning & development outlook—14th edition. Ottawa: The Conference Board of Canada.

E-learning
The use of computer network technology such as the intranet or Internet to deliver information or instruction to individuals

A related and increasingly popular term for technology-based training is e-learning. **E-learning** (also known as Web-based instruction or WBI and online learning) is the use of computer network technology such as the intranet or Internet to deliver information or instruction to individuals.[14] Thus, e-learning is a specific type of computer-based learning in which learners can access training material from a personal computer, a smartphone, or a tablet. Recall that field operators at Calfrac access e-learning courses with their tablets.

Table 7.1 indicates the extent to which different training methods are used for training and by organizations in Canada. Note that although instructor-led classroom training remains the most used for training and by organizations, self-paced online delivery or e-learning are the most used technology-based training methods.

As described in the next section, one of the ways that technology-based training methods differ from traditional training methods is in terms of whether the training is instructor-led or self-directed.

// INSTRUCTOR-LED TRAINING AND SELF-DIRECTED LEARNING

Instructor-led training (ILT)
Training methods that involve an instructor or facilitator who leads, facilitates, or trains online

Like traditional training methods, technology-based training can involve an instructor or facilitator who leads, facilitates, or trains online. Technology-based training that is instructor-led is known as **instructor-led training (ILT)**. Examples of ILT include online discussions and video conferencing.

In some cases, the instructor is very involved in the training and leads the process. In other cases, a course or program involves self-study and the instructor is available for answering questions and providing assistance.[15] However, one of the main advantages of technology-based training is that it can be initiated and controlled by the trainee. This is known as self-directed learning.

Self-directed learning (SDL) occurs when individuals or groups take the initiative and responsibility for learning and manage their own learning experiences. In other words, the responsibility for learning (e.g., what, when, and how to learn) shifts from the trainer to the trainee.[16]

Trainees must seek out the necessary resources to engage in learning that will enhance their careers and personal growth. Employees assess their own needs, use a variety of organizational resources to meet those needs, and are helped with evaluating the effectiveness of meeting their needs.

Self-directed learning has become increasingly popular because traditional methods of training lack the flexibility to respond quickly to dramatic and constant organizational change and trainees' needs. SDL allows trainees to access training materials and programs when they want to, at their own pace, and sometimes in the sequence they prefer. Recall that the field operators at Calfrac take the e-learning courses when they want to on their own time.

Table 7.2 lists some of the benefits and limitations of self-directed learning.

Technology-based training is training that is delivered via the computer for the purpose of teaching job-relevant skills.

> **Self-directed learning (SDL)**
> A process in which individuals or groups take the initiative and responsibility for learning and manage their own learning experiences

---

TABLE 7.2

THE BENEFITS AND LIMITATIONS OF SELF-DIRECTED LEARNING

BENEFITS

- Trainees can learn at their own pace and determine their desired level of expertise.
- Trainees build on their knowledge bases and training time may be reduced; trainees learn what is relevant to their needs.
- Trainees become independent and acquire skills enabling them to learn more efficiently and effectively, reducing dependence on formal training.
- People can learn according to their own styles of learning.

LIMITATIONS

- Trainees may learn the wrong things or may not learn all there is to know; one suggestion to remedy this problem is to negotiate a learning contract with specific learning objectives and performance measures.
- Trainees may waste time accessing resources and finding helpful material; the trainer could become a facilitator, directing employees toward useful resources.
- SDL takes time—employees have to learn active knowledge-seeking skills, acquire knowledge-gathering skills, and learn to tolerate inefficiencies and mistakes; the trainer must learn to give up a power base and move from expert to helper.

// ASYNCHRONOUS AND SYNCHRONOUS TRAINING

Asynchronous
Training that is pre-recorded and available to employees at any time and from any location

Multimedia training
Computer-based training programs that include text, graphics, animation, audio, and video

Synchronous
Training that is live and requires trainees to be at their computer at a specific time

Technology-based training can be asynchronous or synchronous. When training is **asynchronous**, it is available to employees at any time and from any location. For example, an asynchronous program might simply involve the posting of text, information, or instructions on a website.

More sophisticated programs can include text, graphics, animation, audio, and video, thereby providing a **multimedia training** program. This, combined with simulations, interactive exercises, tests, and feedback, can result in a much more engaging and active learning experience. While the use of multimedia results in greater involvement on the part of the trainee, it is much more expensive to design and develop. The e-learning courses that the field operators at Calfrac take with their tablets is an example of asynchronous training.

When training is **synchronous**, it is live and in real time, so trainees must be at their computer at a specific time. A basic synchronous program might simply involve "chat" sessions in which trainees log on at the same time and participate in a discussion of some topic. More sophisticated programs might have trainees from various locations log in to the training at a set time and receive instruction from a trainer who facilitates a discussion, shows slides, answers trainees' questions, and provides feedback.[17]

In the following sections, we describe some of the most common types of asynchronous and synchronous training. Two common methods of asynchronous training are online and distance education and electronic performance support systems.

// ONLINE AND DISTANCE EDUCATION

Online and distance education
The use of computer technology and the Internet to deliver educational content and courses

Online and distance education involves the use of computer technology and the Internet to deliver educational content and courses. Before computers this was known as correspondence programs. Students would receive course materials, which in addition to reading material might include audio- or video-taped lectures and learn the material on their own without actually being in a classroom with an instructor and other students.

With computer technology, students can now take a variety of college and university courses—and earn a degree—through online education. Online courses can include text, graphics, and videos as well as quizzes and downloadable materials. In addition to modules that present the course content, many online courses also include discussion boards for students to post questions, comment on course material, answer questions, and instructor input. Class interactions can also be included by having designated discussion times that involve the entire class.[18]

Colleges and universities have been offering an increasing number of courses and degrees online, and e-learning is a fast-growing trend in post-secondary education.[19] This means that students—in many cases employees—can take courses and earn a degree without having to enter an actual classroom. Rather, they take the course online at their convenience, which allows them to study and work full time. This also benefits employers because it means that employees can take courses and earn a degree without missing work.

Some companies, such as Maple Leaf Foods, encourage their employees to take online courses, allow them to do some of the work during office hours, and offer tuition reimbursements. Maple Leaf Foods helps employees choose courses that are relevant and provides them with mentors to help with course work.[20]

A recent development in online education is **massive open online courses (MOOCs)**. MOOCs are courses that are available on the Internet and are usually free and have open enrolments. Thus, it is possible to have an unlimited number of students from all over the world taking a course. In addition to using traditional teaching methods such as readings and lectures, students and instructors can ask and answer questions and participate in discussions. Thus, MOOCs integrate social and online learning. With thousands of MOOCs now available, an increasing number of organizations have begun to use them as part of their learning programs.[21]

Some organizations have also begun to use **small private online courses (SPOCs)**, which focus on more specific topics and are offered to smaller and more targeted audiences. Thus, the enrolment is limited and the content can be customized and directed to a specific group of employees. As a result, with SPOCs the instructor can be more involved and engaged with the participants.[22]

> **Massive open online courses (MOOCs)**
> Online courses with open enrolments that make it possible to have an unlimited number of students from all over the world
>
> **Small private online courses (SPOCs)**
> Online courses that focus on specific topics and are offered to smaller targeted audiences

// ELECTRONIC PERFORMANCE SUPPORT SYSTEMS

An **electronic performance support system (EPSS)** is a computer-based system that provides access to integrated information, advice, and learning experiences.[23] Thus, it is like a modern-day version of a performance or job aid that uses technology. An EPSS provides several types of support, including assisting, warning, advising, teaching, and evaluating. Employees can obtain information to help solve work-related problems.

The goal of an EPSS is to provide whatever is necessary to aid performance and learning at the time it is needed. When the accounting firm KPMG needed to train all its employees on a new tax planning service, it chose EPSS over classroom training. The EPSS saved in delivery time (consultants did not need to spend three weeks in classrooms) and reduced the costs of updates.[24]

With an EPSS, information is accessed only when it is needed. Only the information that is needed is given; there is no information overload. EPSS is particularly useful for training in high-turnover jobs, like hotel staff, and in tasks that are difficult, performed infrequently, and must be performed perfectly.[25]

Another example of the use of EPSSs is online reference tools that are available to employees to refresh their memories about work-related tasks or provide them with instant help on how to perform a task. Employees access an intranet page where they can download content to a mobile device or a computer. The site might include a short video on topics such as the main features of a product that a retailer sells or the steps involved in performing a task. Thus, not only can employees go online to get what they need when they need it, but they can also get it from wherever they are using a mobile device, which means they don't have to be at their computer.[26]

Home Depot Canada implemented a mobile performance support (mPS) system in its stores to improve sales associate learning and customers' shopping experience. Store associates have been provided with pre-provisioned iPad Minis that function as performance support tools. They can use the iPads to provide customers with product and project information and answer questions on the spot.[27]

> **Electronic performance support system (EPSS)**
> A computer-based system that provides information, advice, and learning experiences to improve performance

// THE VIRTUAL CLASSROOM

Virtual classroom
A Web-based platform to deliver live, instructor-led training to geographically dispersed learners

A common method of synchronous training is the virtual classroom. A **virtual classroom** uses a Web-based platform to deliver live, instructor-led training to geographically dispersed learners. This allows trainees to participate in live discussions with facilitators and co-workers from any location. It also means that shorter training sessions can be held over a period of weeks rather than having to schedule large blocks of time in which trainees have to be away from their jobs to attend a training program in a classroom.[28]

For example, several years ago Economical Insurance decided to use a virtual classroom for its Accident Benefits Claims Regulations training program, which is divided into modules of five short sessions over a period of three days.[29] The main advantage of a virtual classroom is the cost savings and convenience. An increasing number of organizations are using virtual classrooms to provide training.

Virtual classrooms are made possible through the use of video- and web-conferencing technology. **Video conferencing** involves linking a subject-matter expert or trainer to employees by means of two-way television and satellite technology. This can involve the transmission of television signals via cable or through satellite technology. Whatever the means of transmission, the basic idea is that people at two or more locations are able to see, hear, and speak with one another, thus permitting simultaneous meetings in different locations.

Video conferencing
Linking an expert or trainer to employees via two-way television and satellite technology

Scotiabank has used interactive training sessions broadcast to employees across the country by satellite television. This makes it possible to train employees in branches across Canada. For example, a program on RRSPs trained 2000 employees at 25 locations across the country. Trainees had to use the Internet to review course materials online prior to attending the training. To keep employees engaged, they completed quizzes and participated in opinion polls throughout the session by pushing buttons on their phone sets, and asked questions by telephone. During breaks, group discussions and case study analyses were led by previously trained managers at each meeting site.

With employees spread all over the country, Scotiabank was able to train thousands of employees at one time without having to bring them together in one location or send

An increasing number of organizations are using virtual classrooms to provide training.

trainers all over the country. It also ensures that a consistent message is sent to all employees and everyone "hits the ground running" at the same time. In fact, employees return to their branches the day after training and begin to apply their new product knowledge.

An added benefit to employees is the opportunity to learn about what their fellow employees around the country are doing and to share ideas and best practices. This also helps to create a sense of cohesion, which is difficult in such a large and geographically diverse organization.[30]

The disadvantage of video conferencing is that less personal attention is given to trainees. However, this problem can be remedied by having a facilitator on site or by allowing for interactive questioning while training takes place.

Virtual classrooms are also made possible through the use of Web conferencing and webinars. Web conferencing is similar to a video conference except that the trainees are connected to the trainer and each other via the Internet and participate from their own computer. Thus, **web conferencing** is a live meeting or conference that takes place on the Internet.

Similar to Web conferencing is a **webinar**, which is a seminar or workshop that takes place live over the Web (a Web-based seminar). It can be a presentation, lecture, or workshop, and can be interactive by allowing participants to ask and answer questions. Many organizations prefer a webinar over a seminar because it reduces the costs associated with renting a room, travel, and catering.[31]

A **webcast** is a live or recorded video or audio broadcast over the Internet. Webcasts are used primarily for presentations, while Web conferencing and webinars are used for live meetings and seminars, respectively. Webcasts are usually one-way communications that do not have an interactive component.[32]

To be most effective, virtual classrooms should be designed from scratch and treated as a unique type of learning experience rather than just converting a traditional classroom training program into a virtual training program.[33] To learn more about how to design an effective virtual training program, see The Trainer's Notebook 7.1, "Designing Effective Virtual Training Programs."

> **Web conferencing**
> A live meeting or conference that takes place on the Internet
>
> **Webinar**
> A seminar that takes place live over the Web
>
> **Webcast**
> A live or recorded video or audio broadcast over the Internet

THE TRAINER'S NOTEBOOK 7.1

DESIGNING EFFECTIVE VIRTUAL TRAINING PROGRAMS

To be effective, live virtual training has to be designed from the ground up as a unique type of learning experience, as follows.

- Design a series of short modules—about 60 to 90 minutes—each followed by a work assignment that immediately applies the learning to the job.
- Move from monologue to dialogue for the delivery.
- Ensure that the delivery is interactive: ask questions, facilitate conversation, conduct brainstorming sessions, and use breakout rooms.

- Include multimedia content to illustrate complex concepts, such as short pre-recorded audio and video segments.
- Keep the classroom size to a maximum of 20 to 25 learners.
- Attempt to model programs on the structure and style of a phone-in radio show, including guests and compelling narrative.

Source: Lewis, M. (2011, July). Moving into the live virtual classroom. *T+D*, p. 76.

// SOCIAL MEDIA AND WEB 2.0 TECHNOLOGY

Social media
The use of technology for sharing and exchanging information

Knowledge sharing
Providing task information and know-how to help and collaborate with others to solve problems, develop new ideas, or implement policies or procedures

Communities of practice
Groups of employees who share similar concerns and problems and meet regularly to share their experiences and knowledge, learn from each other, and identify new approaches for working and solving problems

Web 2.0
Internet tools that enable the communication and sharing of information and knowledge

Generative learning
A self-initiated and learner-controlled form of collaborative learning in which individuals in a social network share ideas and information, and in the process solve problems and create new knowledge

Blog
A website that contains commentary and information on a subject

Wiki
A webpage or collection of webpages in which users share, contribute, and modify information on a topic

In the last two decades we have seen the emergence of social media and new learning technologies for training and development. **Social media** refers to the use of technology for sharing and exchanging information. According to the Conference Board of Canada, the use of social and collaborative approaches to learning is on the rise in Canadian organizations, with an increasing number of organizations offering online social networking and online peer information sharing.[34] Thus, social media is increasingly being used for knowledge sharing and learning.

Knowledge sharing involves providing task information and know-how to help and collaborate with others to solve problems, develop new ideas, or implement policies or procedures.[35] Research has found that knowledge sharing is positively related to team performance and organizational financial performance, and contributes to an organization's competitive advantage.[36]

One of the ways that employees share knowledge is through the use of communities of practice. **Communities of practice** are groups of employees who share similar concerns and problems and meet regularly to share their experiences and knowledge, learn from one another, and identify new approaches for working and solving problems.[37] In effect, a community of practice is a social system in which individuals interact to share and develop knowledge.[38]

The core principles of communities of practice are that learning is social and people learn from each other while working together on the job.[39] Thus, people in communities of practice share information and knowledge and in the process learn with and from each other. Members ask each other for help, exchange best practices, and share information.[40]

Communities of practice can exist within a department in an organization as well as across departments and regions and even include members from different organizations. Some communities of practice meet regularly face-to-face, while others use technology to communicate.[41] The technology used for knowledge sharing and communities of practices is typically known as Web 2.0 technology.

Web 2.0 refers to Internet tools that enable communicating and sharing information and knowledge. With Web 2.0 technology, anybody can create and distribute knowledge and collaborate with others in the process.[42]

One of the benefits of Web 2.0 technologies is that they facilitate generative learning. **Generative learning** is a self-initiated and learner-controlled form of collaborative learning in which individuals in a social network share ideas and information, and in the process solve problems and create new knowledge. This involves much more than the traditional approach to learning, in which trainees learn the training material provided to them in instructor-led training programs. With generative learning, individuals initiate and control what they learn, when they learn, and how they learn. Web 2.0 technologies make generative learning possible.[43]

You are probably familiar with Web 2.0 technologies such as social media networks and interest groups like Facebook, Twitter, wikis, and chat rooms. Some of the most popular Web 2.0 technologies for training are blogs, wikis, and podcasts.

A **blog** is a website that contains commentary and information on a subject. It is like a journal in which an individual posts information about a topic or subject. Blogs can include text, video, audio, and links to other individuals' blogs. Thus, they provide a network of conversations and the exchange of information on a particular topic, subject, or issue.[44]

A **wiki** is a webpage or collection of webpages in which users share, contribute, and modify information on a topic. Although there are many public wikis (Wikipedia is the best known), some companies have internal wikis that focus on particular topics, such as company products. The content can be created and shared among the users of the website on an ongoing basis. Wikis enable relevant information to be obtained on demand and training material to be constantly revised and updated. Many large organizations now use wikis for team projects.[45]

A **podcast** is a short audio or video recording that can be downloaded and played on a mobile device such as an iPod or smartphone. Employees can access information on demand from any location at their convenience. For example, a sales team can learn about new products directly from the designers, and truck drivers can learn how to drive in a storm while they're actually driving.[46]

Although Web 2.0 technologies are still relatively new and many organizations have not yet adopted them, the next evolution, or Web 3.0, is already on the horizon. **Web 3.0** represents an evolutionary and fundamental shift in how people interact with the Web and consists of three components: the semantic Web, the mobile Web, and the immersive Internet.[47]

The semantic Web involves technology that can understand the meaning of data and create customized experiences in which information is tailored to a user's needs, location, and identity. The mobile Web allows one to use the Web seamlessly across devices and locations. The immersive Internet involves the use of immersive technologies such as virtual worlds, augmented reality, and 3-D environments, which are described later in the chapter.[48]

Web 3.0 technologies are expected to improve learning and performance and represent the future of learning. Let's now take a closer look at one of the components of Web 3.0, mobile or m-learning.

// MOBILE LEARNING (M-LEARNING)

Technology has made it possible for employees to learn whenever they need to and from any location. This is known as **mobile learning** or **m-learning** and involves the use of mobile or portable technologies such as iPods, MP3 players, and smartphones. Like the field operators at Calfrac who take courses on their tablets, employees can obtain information and training at any time and from any location with the use of mobile technologies. Thus, mobile technology makes learning accessible across time, location, and device.[49]

Mobile devices can be used to deliver short videos or small amounts of bite-sized chunks of focused information to meet a specific learning outcome or what is known as **microlearning**. Microlearning is often used to reinforce and supplement training programs and to provide just-in-time or on-demand learning content.[50] For example, if an employee is away from the workplace and needs to learn a specific procedure, he/she can access a short video or information on the company's intranet using a mobile device. As a result, employees can stay current and up to date with the latest knowledge and information.[51]

Several years ago, Black & Decker replaced paper-based training materials with m-learning content to train its 300 field reps. The field reps are responsible for setting up store displays for retailers. In the past, they were provided with manuals, photographs, and other paper materials. Now they receive short two- to three-minute learning modules directly to their PDA (personal digital assistant). In addition to learning about the products and displays, the modules include task lists, images, quizzes, and short videos about the products. The use of mobile learning costs less, takes less time, and provides better quality control over training.[52]

A number of hotels have begun to use mobile learning for security training. Hotel staff are encouraged to take their mobile phones with them on breaks and have small "snacks" of training throughout the day. In this way, they can learn about security

Podcast
A short audio or video recording that can be downloaded and played on a mobile device such as an iPod or smartphone

Web 3.0
A fundamental shift in how people interact with the Web that consists of the semantic Web, the mobile Web, and the immersive Internet

Mobile learning (m-learning)
The use of mobile or portable technologies across locations for obtaining information and training

Microlearning
Small amounts of bite-sized chunks of focused information to meet a specific learning outcome

Mobile learning or m-learning involves the use of mobile or portable technologies such as iPods, MP3 players, and smartphones.

protocols such as emergency evacuation procedures without having to take time away from work.[53]

Mobile learning is especially effective for short sessions (two to six minutes) that address a single learning point or summarize previously learned material. It is also ideal for providing information and support for employees when they are away from the office.[54]

However, a downside of mobile learning is the potential for distractions that stem from the environment in which a trainee is using the device for training and from the device itself (e.g., texts, notifications). Distractions can reduce a trainee's ability to attend to the training content and interfere with learning and retention. Therefore, it is important that some guidelines be in place for mobile learning to avoid distractions and facilitate learning.[55]

// SYNTHETIC LEARNING ENVIRONMENTS (SLEs)

Technology is increasingly being used to create ever-more realistic environments for learning and training or what we referred to earlier as immersive technologies. These new technologies are known as synthetic learning environments (SLEs).

Synthetic learning environments refer to technology-based training media that augment, replace, create, and/or manage a learner's experience with the world by providing realistic content with instructional features. The essence of SLEs is that they provide trainees with realistic synthetic experiences to enhance learning and performance.[56] Two examples of SLEs are virtual reality and augmented reality.

Virtual reality (VR) uses computers to create an artificial 3-D experience that simulates and recreates an actual environment. It uses computer graphics, sounds, and images to create an electronic version of a real-life situation.[57]

VR can be used to simulate various conditions in which trainees can immerse themselves in highly realistic situations to solve real work-related problems, such as police officers learning how to deal with a shooter or manufacturing workers practising emergency response procedures during a fire. Walmart uses VR to train employees for difficult customer interactions and UPS is using VR technology for driver training.[58] For another example of an organization that uses VR for training, see Training Today 7.1, "Virtual Reality Training at BNSF Railway."

> **Synthetic learning environments (SLEs)**
> Technology-based training media that augment, replace, create, and/or manage a learner's experience with the world
>
> **Virtual reality (VR)**
> The use of computers to create an artificial 3-D experience that simulates and recreates an actual environment

---

TRAINING TODAY   7.1

VIRTUAL REALITY TRAINING AT BNSF RAILWAY

BNSF Railway is one of the oldest and largest railroads in North America. The railroad's 42 000 employees serve the western two-thirds of the United States. For BNSF, safety is at the foundation of everything the company does and is based on having well-trained employees.

When it comes to safety, BNSF is a leader in the rail industry.

In response to a federal regulation on Brake System Safety Standards, BNSF Railway developed a 3-D e-learning training program called Virtual Power Brake Law (VPBL).

(continued)

The virtual reality learning program serves as the proficiency-based training program for brake inspection. The course places employees as avatars in a realistic, three-dimensional, virtual simulation, where they perform comprehensive brake inspections on a "consist" of rail cars.

The program enhances decision making by testing employees' ability to not only identify but also correct malfunctions—many of which prove difficult to demonstrate even in live training environments. With this training solution (including nine individual 3-D virtual scenarios), BNSF incorporates all defects and functionality, reducing the safety risk that comes from inspections in live training environments. In addition, BNSF can efficiently cover all inspection requirements.

BNSF developed four different modules for instructors to choose from for each class. Participants must complete, with 100 percent accuracy, one full module per class. When students complete the performance verification at 100 percent (individually and as a team), they can "move" the train out of the virtual inspection cycle. This creates a "team challenge."

The 30-minute program features high-end graphics, user-friendly functions, and realistic functionality, including car components, hand brakes, angle cocks, and air hoses—all key components to proper inspection. Students also have the ability to work through the program under nighttime conditions. In addition, hand controls and critical "hot spots" allow the program to flow in a user-friendly way.

At the end of the program, participants must pass a knowledge-based assessment for final completion. Throughout the class, instructors provide coaching and feedback so that learning is dynamic and targeted directly to the concept taught. All training is conducted in BNSF field locations by certified instructors. There is an eight-student maximum per session.

In 2015, BNSF trained more than 6200 employees with this program. The results have been very positive. One hundred percent of learners passed the knowledge and performance assessments. This program and other safety-focused training contributed to record safety performance in 2015 and injuries have been reduced by 17 percent since 2012. BNSF has been approached by other railroads interested in purchasing the training and plans to seek a patent for it.

Source: Based on Best practices & outstanding training initiatives (BNSF Railway: Virtual Power Brake Law (VPBL)). (2017, January/February). *Training Magazine, 54*(1), 102; Who We Are, BNSF, https://jobs.bnsf.com/content/who/

Augmented reality (AR) is a technology in which computer-generated virtual imagery (e.g., graphics, text, and other visual elements) information is overlaid or superimposed onto a real-world environment in real time. It integrates physical reality with digital information to augment or enhance certain aspects of the environment.[59]

Unlike virtual reality, AR contains some aspect of reality and is designed to augment the real environment with information integrated into the individual's real world. Thus, while virtual reality creates an artificial environment that replaces the real world, AR supplements and augments the real world. The environment is real with AR but it is augmented with additional information and imagery.[60]

Augmented reality is increasingly being used in medical settings where surgeons can practise surgical procedures prior to actually performing them and even during the actual procedures. Several studies have shown that the use of AR for training has positive effects on learning outcomes and improving performance in medical settings.[61]

Now that we have described how technology is being used for training, let's consider how to design effective technology-based training programs.

> **Augmented reality (AR)** Computer-generated virtual imagery (e.g., graphics, text, and other visual elements) information is overlaid onto a real-world environment in real time

// DESIGNING EFFECTIVE TECHNOLOGY-BASED TRAINING PROGRAMS

How do you design an effective training program using technology? For starters, it is important to keep in mind that when designing technology-based training programs, the technology is just the medium for delivering the training content. Technology

For more information
see Chapter 4, p. 126 and
Chapter 5, p. 152

itself has no direct influence on learning.[62] Whether a training program is effective for learning and other training outcomes depends on how it is designed rather than the sophistication of the technology used to deliver it.

As described in Chapter 4, to maximize trainee learning and retention, training programs should include active practice and conditions of practice (e.g., feedback). In addition, many of the instructional methods described in Chapter 5 can be used, such as games, simulations, and role plays. Other design factors that can be used include stories, customizing and personalizing the training, human interaction, and feedback.

COMPUTER SIMULATIONS Computer simulations provide trainees with hands-on training for a particular task. They are reality based in that they are designed to replicate on-the-job experiences by providing trainees with opportunities to practise and master knowledge and skills in an interactive environment. Computer simulations can provide trainees with a realistic experience on tasks that might be too dangerous to learn in the work environment. Research has found that simulations can improve learning outcomes in a variety of contexts, such as training pilots and military personnel.[63]

Mr. Lube uses an online simulation for new technicians to learn how to perform an oil change. The simulation takes trainees through all the checks and assessments and times them on the tasks. The simulation provides new technicians with a safe learning environment to learn and master their job before they actually work on a vehicle. As a result, on-the-job training time and errors are reduced. The program also ensures that the same process is used by all technicians across the country. Computer simulations are also being used for soft-skills training for various skills, such as leadership, sales, customer service, and financial services.[64]

Advances in technology have provided more realistic types of simulations. For example, **virtual worlds** use computers to provide elaborate simulations that involve interactions among and between multiple trainees and objects.[65]

Virtual worlds
Elaborate simulations that involve interactions among and between multiple trainees and objects

GAMES Computer-based games are designed to engage trainees with realistic and entertaining experiences. It is important to note that games are often simulations in that they simulate work-related tasks and experiences. What distinguishes them from simulations is that they are meant to be both entertaining and competitive, and they include common game features, such as competition, rules, and a scoring system.

Computer-based simulation games have been defined as "instruction delivered via personal computer that immerses trainees in a decision-making exercise in an artificial environment in order to learn the consequences of their decisions."[66]

Learning games such as crossword puzzle games have been used in the presentation and practice of training material. Games can improve trainee learning and performance by increasing the appeal of e-learning, encourage trainees to practise, and facilitate the discovery of patterns and relationships in the training material.[67]

Canon Inc. uses a game simulation to train employees to repair copy machines. Trainees have to drag and drop parts into the right spot in a copy machine. Like the board game Operation, a light flashes and a buzzer sounds when trainees make a mistake.[68]

The use of games in the workplace has been receiving increasing attention as a way to improve employee engagement and motivation and has led to the development of **gamification**, which refers to the use of game mechanics and elements from video games to engage and motivate employees in the workplace.[69] Gamification is also being used for training and development to make learning more interactive, engaging, and fun. For example, Sun Life Financial used gamification to design a training program to encourage

Computer-based simulation games
Instruction delivered via personal computer that immerses trainees in a decision-making exercise in an artificial environment in order to learn the consequences of their decisions

Gamification
The use of game mechanics and elements from video games to engage and motivate employees in the workplace

the employees of its clients to learn about workplace retirement and savings plans and to increase their financial literacy. The online game, called "money UP," breaks the program into a series of levels called missions that are progressively more challenging. As employees progress through the levels, they have a series of goals, receive feedback, complete short quizzes, and compete against colleagues. Employees can also share their mission scores with friends on Facebook and Twitter.[70]

To be most effective, gamification should involve three key elements: a story that provides the context and includes characters and settings that are relevant to trainees; parameters that indicate the basic framework and rules for how the game is played; and rewards that highlight and recognize player achievement.[71]

How effective are computer-based games? A study that reviewed the research on computer-based games found that trainees who received instruction via a simulation game had higher self-efficacy, declarative knowledge, procedural knowledge, and retention than trainees in a comparison group. The study also found that simulation games resulted in more learning when they actively engaged trainees in learning the course material rather than passively conveying the material; when trainees have unlimited access to the simulation game rather than limited access; and when the simulation game was used as a supplement to other instructional methods rather than as a stand-alone instructional method. However, it is worth noting that other instructional methods were just as effective as simulation games when they actively engaged trainees in the learning material.

Thus, to be most effective, simulation games must actively engage trainees in learning the training material and they should be used in conjunction with or as a supplement to other instructional methods (e.g., lecture, discussions). Furthermore, learning principles must be incorporated into the design of simulation games.[72]

ROLE PLAYS Role plays can also be used with technology-based training programs. For example, Rogers Wireless Communications Inc. has an interactive customer-service training program for sales representatives that includes online role playing. Trainees interact with animated characters who present different customer-service challenges and learn different approaches for interacting with them. An animated coach provides guidance and feedback.

Rogers noticed improvements in service and employee satisfaction not long after the program was implemented. The role playing makes the program engaging and the lessons—which are based on real-life scenarios—are improving employees' performance.[73]

STORIES Stories and narratives have also been used in e-learning in order to engage trainees. Abstract concepts and dry material can be livened up with stories that involve dialogue and characters. The characters can be created to be similar to the trainees and learning can occur as the characters solve problems in the story.

Sprint and Volvo have used stories to train employees on how to deliver the company's brand image when interacting with customers. Trainees also practise communicating the brand image in simulated customer interactions.[74]

CUSTOMIZATION **Customization** involves tailoring instructional elements to meet trainee preferences and needs. This can increase trainee satisfaction with the training and improve learning. Hewlett-Packard is an example of one company that has been very successful at customization. The company has found that preferences for e-learning and other training media differ around the world. For example, it found that employees in Asia prefer instructor-presented or blended learning, while in the United States and Europe employees prefer self-paced and instructor-presented learning approaches, respectively. Differences in e-learning preferences indicate that one type of e-learning program is not likely to meet the needs and preferences of all employees.[75]

Training content can also be customized specially to the needs of each trainee with the use of adaptive learning technology. **Adaptive learning** tailors and adjusts training content and material to the specific needs of trainees. That is, based on trainee knowledge and level of performance the technology can change and adapt the training content and material so that the training is tailored to each trainee's specific needs. As a result, trainees learn only what they need to learn and do not waste time on material they have already learned and mastered.[76]

PERSONALIZATION **Personalization** refers to structuring the program so that trainees feel they are engaged in a conversation with the program. This can be achieved by using conversational rather than formal language in the on-screen text and audio recordings.[77]

HUMAN INTERACTION A potential problem of computer-based training for some trainees is the lack of face-to-face interaction with an instructor and other trainees. This can result in trainees feeling isolated and less motivated to learn. One way to overcome this is to include human interaction in the design of computer-based training programs.

Human interaction refers to the extent to which trainees are able to interact with the instructor and one another during a training program. This can be built into computer-based programs using a number of formats, including email exchanges, chat rooms, discussion boards, and group projects. There is some evidence that more interaction with the instructor and among trainees is associated with higher motivation, more positive attitudes toward learning, and improved learning outcomes.[78]

FEEDBACK Regardless of the nature of the training experience, it is important that feedback be provided to trainees. In fact, students who received feedback in computer-based training have been found to learn more than students who were not given feedback.[79]

Feedback can be incorporated into computer-based training in many ways. It can range from a simple prompt indicating that an answer to a question or a quiz is right or wrong to the execution of another program segment in which trainees are routed through a complex maze of reviews and reinforcements based on their responses and answers.

Feedback can also be incorporated into simulations and role plays. For example, in a role play in which trainees must choose from a number of options regarding how to respond to different customers, immediate feedback can be provided following each response chosen by a trainee. In addition, an on-screen virtual coach can be used to provide trainees with feedback about the correctness of their choices, what they did wrong, and hints on how to proceed and improve. Trainees can then take the program again until their performance improves.

At Verizon, retail store representatives practise and record mock responses to virtual role plays with customers. The responses are then sent to a manager or coach who provides the employee with specific and tailored feedback.[80]

To learn about some additional design principles for computer-based training, see The Trainer's Notebook 7.2, "Design Principles for Computer-Based Training."

For more information see Chapter 4, p. 133

THE TRAINER'S NOTEBOOK   7.2

DESIGN PRINCIPLES FOR COMPUTER-BASED TRAINING

The following principles cover many aspects of computer-based training design and are well grounded in both theory and research.

- *The multimedia principle.* Graphics and text should be used rather than simply text alone. Trainees will engage in a deeper and more active processing of the learning material.

- *The contiguity principle.* When text is used to explain a graphic or vice versa, the text and graphics should be placed near each other on the screen. This permits trainees to focus on the instructional material rather than on trying to match a miscellaneous set of pictures to text.

- *The modality principle.* Audio technology, rather than on-screen text, should be used to present information. Trainees are likely to become overwhelmed with visual information when presented with only text, graphics, illustrations, and figures during learning.

- *The personalization principle.* Text should be written in first and second person, and trainees should have access to on-screen virtual coaches that provide guidance and direction. This will help trainees to see the computer as a conversational partner rather than as an information delivery agent.

Sources: DeRouin, R. E., Fritzsche, B. A., & Salas, E. (2005). E-Learning in organizations. *Journal of Management, 31*, 920; Clark, R. C., & Mayer, R. E. (2003). *E-learning and the science of instruction: Proven guidelines for consumers and designers of multimedia learning.* San Francisco: Jossey-Bass.

// BENEFITS OF TECHNOLOGY-BASED TRAINING

Many see technology as the future for all training programs. However, just like on-the-job and off-the-job training methods, technology-based training has advantages and disadvantages for trainees and organizations.

ADVANTAGES

TRAINEES

A major advantage for trainees is flexibility. Recall that the field operators at Calfrac can take the e-learning courses on their own time when they want to. Thus, trainees do not have to coordinate and arrange their schedule and workload to accommodate training schedules. Trainees do not have to take courses when they are scheduled or wait until a group of trainees is ready to take a course. They can learn when they want to or "just in time." Trainees also do not have to leave work to attend training and can even learn while they are at home or away from work. Thus, geographic flexibility is a major advantage.

Another advantage for trainees is greater control over their learning, or what is known as learner control. **Learner control** refers to the degree to which the trainee has control over various instructional features during a lesson or training program, such as the content, sequence, and/or the pace of training.[81] In other words, trainees can choose the content they want to view, the order in which they will view the content, enter and leave training as they choose, and progress at their own pace. Thus, with greater learner control trainees must manage the learning process themselves and make decisions about what and how much to study and practise.[82]

Self-pacing means that trainees can work on training tasks as quickly or as slowly as they want. In some cases, trainees even have control over various instructional elements of a program, such as the sequence of instructional material, the content of instruction, the amount of instruction during training, and even the level of practice difficulty or what is known as **learner-controlled practice difficulty**.

A recent study on learner-controlled practice difficulty found that some trainees who were learning a complex video game were more likely to choose higher levels of difficulty for practice. In particular, trainees who were encouraged to make errors (recall the discussion of error-management training in Chapter 4), had more prior experience playing video games, and had higher general mental ability and pre-training self-efficacy chose more difficult levels of practice. Furthermore, practice difficulty was positively related to task knowledge and post-training performance. It was also indirectly related to adaptive performance (performance on a novel game that was more difficult and complex than the training game) through its effect on task knowledge and post-training performance.[83]

Although learner control can have a positive effect on trainee motivation and satisfaction with training, there is some evidence that too much learner control can detract from the learning experience and have a negative effect on learning.[84] This is because trainees do not always accurately assess their level of knowledge and make bad decisions, such as skipping over important sections of the training and terminating study and practice sessions before they have completed the training and learned the required material.[85] Thus, a number of strategies are necessary for learner control to be effective and for trainees to realize its benefits.

For example, trainees should be provided with some structure and guidance so that they know what content to learn and the best way to learn it. They also need to know what they should be studying and practising to improve their learning and performance. This type of guidance is known as **adaptive guidance**, which is an instructional strategy to assist trainees in making effective learning decisions. Adaptive guidance has been found to have a positive effect on the way trainees study and practise, as well as their self-efficacy, knowledge, and performance. Thus, learner control is more effective when it is supplemented with adaptive guidance.[86]

Research has also found that trainees are more likely to learn the training material and less likely to drop out of training when they begin training with a plan for when, where, and how much time they will devote to training and when they follow through with their plans.[87] In addition, self-regulation prompts (as discussed in Chapter 2) can help trainees make better use of learner control because they encourage them to regulate their learning, which has been shown to improve learning and performance.[88] Thus, learner control will be most effective when trainees are provided support and guidance.

For more information see Chapter 2, p. 57

ORGANIZATIONS

A major advantage for organizations is that they can ensure that all trainees receive the same training regardless of where they are located. Thus, organizations can deliver standardized and consistent training to large numbers of employees across the organization and even worldwide. This is especially important when employees in many locations require training. Leaving the training to each location could result in differences in content, delivery, and effectiveness. Recall that by using online e-learning courses for its CERT program, Calfrac was able to standardize the training across the company's districts—both in content and in delivery—and plans to do the same in other countries where it operates.

Another advantage is that large numbers of employees can be trained in a short period of time. There is no limit to the number of employees who can be trained, as one is not constrained by the number of instructors available or the need for classroom space.

Computer-based training also makes it possible to track employees' enrolment, attendance, and completion of training programs as well as their performance on learning exercises and tests with the use of a learning management system (LMS).

A **learning management system (LMS)** is software that is used for the administration, delivery, and management of an organization's training and development programs. An LMS allows organizations to manage all of their learning activities and to deliver online courses. It also tracks and records course enrolments as well as employees' progress and completion of training and development programs.[89] At Calfrac, supervisors are able to track employees' training progress in real time.

A record of employees' completion and performance is especially important for training programs that are mandatory and completion, certification, and attaining a certain level of performance is legally mandated. An LMS can generate test results that can provide legal documentation of proof of competency levels. When an accident or safety incident results in a lawsuit, the employer can prove that a training program was completed and that a desired level of competence was achieved. Such training statistics can reduce corporate liability. The software also allows trainees to track their progress and receive feedback about their performance. Ideally, to be most effective an organization's LMS should be integrated with other systems, such as talent and performance management systems.[90]

Perhaps the greatest advantage for organizations is the reduction in the cost of training by eliminating the cost of travel, training facilities, hotel rooms, meals, trainers, and employee time off work to travel to and attend training.[91] In addition, the high overhead costs of traditional training make computer-based training especially advantageous to companies with national or international employees.

> **Learning management system (LMS)**
> Software that is used for the administration, delivery, and management of an organization's training and development programs

DISADVANTAGES

TRAINEES

A disadvantage of technology-based training for trainees is that there is less interpersonal contact and interaction with other trainees. Furthermore, individuals have learning preferences and styles, and if a trainee prefers to receive training in a classroom with a trainer and other trainees, then technology-based training disadvantages that employee. One solution to this problem is a face-to-face pre-training socialization session in which trainees are given the opportunity to get to know one another and to establish relationships prior to training. One study found that trainees who participated in a face-to-face pre-training socialization session performed better than trainees who received online socialization and no socialization prior to training.[92]

Trainees who are not computer literate might also resist and fear computer-based training. A low-threat opportunity to allow trainees to test the technology is to place the learning stations in the classroom.[93] However, industry analysts perceive these barriers as temporary problems. Technology-based training will become a standard way of providing training, particularly for the current generation, which is comfortable with computers and technology.

ORGANIZATIONS

For organizations, the major disadvantage of technology-based training is the up-front cost of development, especially for sophisticated multimedia programs. Estimates are that it takes 200 to 300 hours of design and development time to produce one hour of instruction.[94] Full-motion colour and sound courseware would likely cost $200,000 for 30 hours of instruction. This requires a considerable up-front investment in information technology and staff. At Motorola, where about 30 percent of employee training is computer based, it was estimated that $20 million to $27 million will be spent in one year on e-learning.[95]

Another disadvantage is that some employees are uncomfortable with computers and might refuse technology-based training. For example, individuals with greater computer literacy and higher computer self-efficacy tend to be more willing and able to learn from computer-based training programs. Thus, some trainees might require assistance and guidance to improve their computer literacy and self-efficacy. The good news is that after taking a computer-based training program, trainees report satisfaction with their learning experience, more positive attitudes toward technology-based training, and a willingness to try it again.[96]

// EFFECTIVENESS OF TECHNOLOGY-BASED TRAINING

Many have claimed that technology-based training is more effective than classroom instruction. One of the main reasons for this is that it provides a greater variety of instructional methods that are tailored to individual needs and preferences for learning. Other explanations include greater learner ease, control, flexibility, and immediate feedback. Some argue that it is a more cost-effective method of training than face-to-face instruction.[97] But is technology-based training more effective than traditional classroom training?

A review of 96 studies that compared computer-based training to classroom instruction found that, on average, computer-based training was 6 percent more effective than classroom instruction for declarative knowledge. However, both methods were equally effective for procedural knowledge. In addition, trainees were equally satisfied with both methods.

However, the effectiveness of computer-based training for declarative knowledge was found to depend on several factors. For example, computer-based training was more effective than classroom instruction for older trainees, while classroom instruction was more effective for younger trainees. Computer-based training was not more effective for employees than it was for college/university students.

Computer-based training was also more effective than classroom instruction when the instructional methods (i.e., the techniques used to deliver the training content, such as lecture, video, textbooks) were different. However, computer-based training and classroom instruction were equally effective when the instructional methods were the same.

This is an important finding because it suggests that one of the reasons some studies have found computer-based training to be more effective than classroom instruction is because the instructional methods differ, such as when classroom instruction involves a lecture and computer-based training involves a variety of instructional methods. In fact, the authors found that computer-based training was 11 percent more effective than classroom instruction for teaching declarative knowledge when different instructional methods were used. This suggests that instructional methods are more important for learning than the media used to deliver the training (computer versus face-to-face).

Another important factor was trainee choice of training method. Computer-based training was more effective than classroom instruction when trainees were able to choose the training method. When trainees were not able to choose a training method (i.e., they were randomly assigned to computer-based training or classroom instruction), classroom instruction was 10 percent more effective. This suggests that there might be pre-existing differences between trainees who choose a computer-based program compared to those who choose classroom instruction (e.g., motivation, cognitive ability, computer experience, skills, and self-efficacy), and these differences might be the reason why some studies have found computer-based training to be more effective than classroom instruction. For example, the authors found that trainees with more computer experience learned more from computer-based training.

Computer-based training was also more effective than classroom instruction when trainees had greater learner control and the training included practice and feedback, especially when classroom instruction did not include practice and feedback. However, it should be noted that both training methods were effective when they included opportunities for practice and feedback.

Finally, computer-based training was more effective than classroom instruction when the length of the training program (i.e., number of days) was greater.[98]

There is also some evidence that computer-based training can result in a reduction in the time to completion. However, this appears to be most likely when trainees have some prior experience using technology. In some cases, such as when trainees do not have experience or when trainees experience technology problems and interruptions, the time to completion might actually be greater for computer-based training compared to classroom training.[99]

In addition, there is some evidence that employees are not likely to take or complete computer-based training courses that are optional or have little impact on them. That is, unless a course is required or there is a strong reason for employees to complete it, they are not likely to do so. Employees have been found to be more likely to complete a computer-based training program when there is an incentive for doing so, some form of accountability, or when the program content is job relevant and useful.[100]

It is also important to keep in mind that classroom instruction is more effective for certain types of learning outcomes. For example, a study on the training of sailors in the use of a sophisticated sonar system in the U.S. Navy found that computer-based training increased the costs of parts for maintenance, corrective maintenance actions, and maintenance labour hours. The additional cost of maintenance is estimated to be in the millions of dollars.

Thus, although the replacement of traditional instructor-led training with computer-based training was meant to reduce training time and costs, it turned out to be very costly. The results of this study support anecdotal evidence that computer-based training did not prepare new sailors to operate and maintain sophisticated equipment and that they are not as well prepared as classroom-trained sailors of the past. Thus, computer-based training does not appear to be as effective as traditional classroom instruction for highly skilled Navy operations, and this might also be the case for other complex skills.[101]

Finally, it is worth noting that blended training, in which computer-based training is used to supplement classroom instruction, has been found to be 13 percent more effective than classroom instruction for teaching declarative knowledge, and 20 percent more effective for teaching procedural knowledge.[102] Recall that the Calfrac used a blended approach to training that combined online training with on-the-job training.

Thus, once again a blended approach that combines different instructional methods and includes classroom instruction, on-the-job training, and the use of computers and technology is most effective.

// SUMMARY

This chapter described technology-based training methods and serves as a complement to Chapters 5 and 6, which described on-the-job and off-the-job training methods. First, we described the meaning of technology-based training, computer-based training, and e-learning. Then the differences between instructor-led training and self-directed learning, and between asynchronous and synchronous training, were noted. This was followed by a discussion of different types of technology-based training, including online and distance education and electronic performance support systems, the virtual classroom, video and Web conferencing, webinars and webcasts, and the use of social media, Web 2.0 technologies, mobile learning, and synthetic learning environments. We then described how to design technology-based training programs and their advantages and disadvantages for individuals and organizations. The chapter concluded with a discussion of the effectiveness of technology-based training methods.

KEY TERMS

adaptive guidance p. 228
adaptive learning p. 226
asynchronous p. 216
augmented reality (AR) p. 223
blog p. 220
communities of practice p. 220
computer-based simulation games p. 224
computer-based training p. 213
customization p. 226
e-learning p. 214
electronic performance support system (EPSS) p. 217
gamification p. 224
generative learning p. 220
human interaction p. 226

DISCUSSION QUESTIONS

1. In Canada and the United States, the use of technology for training has fallen below projections; in fact, the adoption of training technologies has been relatively slow and most training still takes place in the classroom. What are some of the reasons for this, and what are the potential barriers to the adoption of training technologies?

2. Compare and contrast technology-based training methods to traditional training methods. Why would an organization choose to use technology-based training methods rather than traditional training methods? Are there some types of industries, organizations, or jobs in which technology-based training or traditional training would be more appropriate and effective?

3. What are the advantages and disadvantages of technology-based training for trainees, trainers, and organizations?

4. If you had the choice, would you choose a computer-based training program or a traditional classroom program? Which would you prefer, and why? Do you think your satisfaction, learning, and performance would differ in a computer-based program versus a traditional classroom program? Explain your reasoning.

5. Discuss how technology-based training programs can be designed to engage trainees and improve their motivation and learning.

6. Discuss how games, simulations, and role plays can be used in technology-based training programs. If you were designing a technology-based training program, when and why would you use each method?

7. Some have argued that there is nothing uniquely advantageous about technology-based training methods, and that any effect they have on learning is not due to the use of any particular technological device. Do you agree or disagree with this position? Explain your reasoning, and why you think this view might be true or false.

8. Research on the effects of computer-based training has found that it is more effective than classroom instruction when trainees can choose the program (computer-based or classroom) and when the instructional methods used to deliver the programs are different. What are the implications of these two findings for understanding the effects of computer-based training and for the design and delivery of computer-based training programs?

9. What is Web 2.0 technology and how can it be used for training? Do you think organizations should use Web 2.0 technologies for training? Explain your answer.

10. What does learner control refer to and what role does it play in technology-based training? Why is learner control not always effective? What can be done to make it more effective?

11. What is a synthetic learning environment (SLE) and how can it make technology-based training programs more effective? What are its advantages and disadvantages?

THE GREAT TRAINING DEBATE

1. Debate the following: Given the many benefits of technology-based training, organizations should convert all of their classroom training programs to technology-based programs and eliminate formal classroom training.

2. Debate the following: There is nothing inherently superior about technology-based training. The effectiveness of a training method depends on how it is designed rather than how it is delivered.

3. Debate the following: The use of technology for training is just the latest fad and it will never be as effective as classroom instruction.

EXERCISES

IN-CLASS

1. Describe the objectives, content, methods, and conditions of practice of the most recent classroom training program you attended. Now think about how the program might be converted to a technology-based training program. Describe what the program would be like and how you would design it. Do you think it would be more or less effective than the classroom training program?

2. Choose a class from a course you are currently taking and describe it in terms of the following design factors from Chapter 4:

   - What are the objectives?
   - What is the content?
   - What training methods are used?
   - What kinds of active practice are provided?

   Now consider how the class might be designed and delivered as an online course. Use your answers for each of the above design factors to redesign the class as an online course. What would be the objectives, content, methods, and type of active practice? How effective do you think the course would be as an online course? Compare and contrast it to the classroom course. What are the advantages and disadvantages for students, instructors, and the university or college? Which approach would you prefer and why?

3. One of the concerns about technology-based training is the tendency to focus too much on the technology and not enough on learning and the conditions of practice. Refer to Chapter 4 and the conditions of practice in Table 4.4. Describe how each of the conditions of practice can be included in the design of a computer-based training program.

4. After learning about technology-based training, you realize that your organization can benefit by converting some of its traditional classroom training programs to computer-based programs. Describe how you would proceed if you were to convert a particular training program (e.g., customer service, sales, negotiations) to a computer-based program. What would you have to do to convert the program? How would you proceed?

5. You have just been hired by an organization to help convert some of its classroom training programs to computer-based programs. However, the company does not have a tradition of using computers in the workplace and there is likely to be a great deal of resistance from managers and employees. You have to meet with employees and managers to help them understand why computer-based training will be better for them and the organization than classroom training. Prepare a brief presentation of what you will tell the employees and managers, and then present it to another student or the class.

IN-THE-FIELD

1. Contact the human resource department of an organization and ask them if you can conduct a brief interview with the training staff about their use of technology-based training methods. Some of the things you might consider include the following:

   a. Do they use computers or other electronic devices for training? If so, what forms of computer-based training or electronic devices are they using, and what are they using them for?

   b. Why did they decide to use technology for training?

   c. How effective has the use of technology been for training? How have they evaluated its effectiveness? What has the impact been on employees and the organization?

   d. Do they plan to use technology-based training in the future? If so, in what way, for what purposes, and for what reasons?

2. Contact the human resource department of an organization to find out if they have technology-based training programs. Once you have found an organization that has developed a technology-based program, find out how they designed the program and how effective it is. Some of the things to consider include the following:

   a. What are the training objectives?

   b. What is the training content?

   c. Who are the trainees?

   d. How has the program been designed, and does it include interactive elements?

   e. Does the program include active practice and conditions of practice? If so, how have they been incorporated into the program?

   f. How effective has the program been and how does it compare to traditional classroom training? How have trainees reacted to it?

3. Contact the human resource department of an organization to find out if they use social media for training and if they are using any Web 2.0 tools for learning. Once you have found an organization that uses social media for training and is using Web 2.0 tools, find out the following:

   a. What Web 2.0 tools are being used?

   b. What are the tools being used for and who is using them?

   c. How have employees reacted to the use of Web 2.0?

   d. How effective has Web 2.0 been for learning?

   e. What are some of the benefits and limitations of using Web 2.0 for learning?

4. To find out about technology-based training in Canada, visit Industry Canada at www.collectionscanada.gc.ca/webarchives/20060201093632/http://strategis.ic.gc.ca/epic/internet/incts-scf.nsf/en/h_sl00009e.html Summarize the main findings by answering these questions:

   a. What is the impact of learning technologies?

   b. Does e-learning help companies save money and improve productivity?

   c. How can you find out which learning technology is right for you?

   d. How can you assess the quality of e-learning products and services?

   e. Briefly summarize how each case-study organization has used technology-based learning and the benefits and outcomes that resulted from it.

CASE INCIDENT

PLAYING VIDEO GAMES TO LEARN

Davis Controls Ltd., based in Oakville, Ontario, is an instrument and control company that was founded in 1933. Several years ago, the company introduced a training program to its sales force that involves playing a video game. The game consists of real-world, simulated sales call scenarios. The goal of the game is to secure a meeting with an avatar who represents a virtual client.

Davis Controls introduced the game to its sales staff with a one-day class, but the training takes place online on their own time. Sales reps are expected to complete three missions every two weeks. They can take time out during their day or play online from home after hours.

The game is structured around six basic principles: business skills, influencing, negotiation, change technology, assertiveness, and presentation. Sales reps also learn about different customer styles, such as the "finisher" or "adapter." The scenarios change with every mission but the core strategies are the same.

Players are presented with a series of choices as they move along, with each one eliciting a different reaction from the avatar. The player's performance depends on how well he/she learned strategies earlier in the game. The scenarios become increasingly difficult and more complex at each level. Trainees receive feedback at the end of every round. With 120 story-based missions, each taking from 20 to 30 minutes to play, it could take up to one year to finish all of the levels.

QUESTIONS

1. Describe the design factors that are used in the video game training program. How do these design factors contribute to trainee learning?

2. What are the advantages of the video game training program for employees and the organization? What are the disadvantages?

3. How effective do you think the video game training program will be for trainees? Be specific about what you think the game might or might not be effective for in terms of various outcomes (e.g., learning, sales performance).

Source: Based on Harder, D. (2012, February 13). Gaming on the job. *Canadian HR Reporter*, pp. 16, 17. Reprinted by permission of *Canadian HR Reporter*. © Copyright Thomson Reuters Canada Ltd., (2012), Toronto, Ontario, 1-800-387-5164. Web: www.hrreporter.com

---

CASE STUDY E-LEARNING AT FLOTATION LTD.

Jenny Stoppard was excited about her new position as vice president of human resources at Flotation Ltd., a manufacturer of life jackets and other flotation devices. However, she knew she had her work cut out for her.

The president of the company had clearly stated that one of her first tasks was to take a close look at the training function. Although Flotation Ltd. had a reputation as a company with a well-trained workforce, the president now wanted to see some hard evidence to back up the company's training investment. The president wanted to increase productivity per person by 50 percent over the next three years, and Jenny was expected to spearhead the effort.

Sam was the company's veteran trainer and was liked by everybody in the organization. For 25 years he had been training employees at Flotation Ltd. He was only two years away from retirement and was not likely to respond favourably to Jenny and her new mandate.

The president introduced Jenny to Sam as his new boss and the key player in the drive to increase the company's competitiveness. He also asked Sam to do everything in his power to cooperate with her.

Jenny had to revamp the training function and she had to deal with Sam, who was pretty much set in his ways. How was she going to achieve the president's goals and at the same time get Sam on board?

After thinking about her situation for several days, Jenny came across an article on e-learning and how it has saved some companies millions of dollars a year in training costs. Suddenly, she had an idea.

"Why not convert some of Sam's training courses to e-learning programs on the company's website?" she thought to herself. "This would certainly be a whole new approach and I could save the company money and get Sam involved, since he would be responsible for preparing his course material for the program. Surely Sam would be excited to know that his training courses would continue even after he has retired."

Both the president and Sam were very excited about the potential of e-learning at Flotation Ltd. Jenny was given the go-ahead to begin designing the first course. Jenny and Sam decided that the first course would be Sam's sales training program, which was one of his best. It would be especially useful for the company's sales staff who would be able to take the program while they were on the road selling.

The first thing Jenny did was arrange for Sam to be videotaped delivering the course. Then she had Sam prepare some text material and additional information about some of the key learning points. With the help of the IT people, the video and text were placed on the company's website. The program was designed so that employees could watch the video of Sam, and at certain points during the video they could click on an icon for more information. The video would then stop, and the additional information would appear on the screen. After reading the material they could return to the video.

When the program was set up and ready to go, the sales staff received a memo telling them about the company's first e-learning program and how to access it on the company's website. The memo was titled "Learn how to improve your sales skills on the road" and "Attend Sam's best training program anytime and anywhere." Everybody was very excited about this new approach to training, and Sam was thrilled to know that he was the main attraction.

However, although the program was launched with much fanfare, the results were less than glowing. In fact, after the first six months very few of the sales staff had taken the course. Many said that they did not have time to take it. Of those who did, fewer than half actually completed it.

When asked about the program, some of the sales staff said that it was not very interesting. Some said they would rather attend a live version of the course in the classroom, and others said they didn't see the advantage of taking an e-learning course. Some thought it was just a big waste of the company's time and money.

The president asked to see Jenny to find out how things were going and if they were on track for achieving the company's productivity goals. Jenny did not know what she would tell him. Sam tried to console her by telling her that it had only been six months and the sales staff just needed a little more time to get used to e-learning. Jenny wasn't so sure. She began to wonder if the e-learning strategy was really a good idea or just a big mistake.

QUESTIONS

1. Do you think e-learning was a good idea for Flotation Ltd.? Could e-learning help the company realize the president's productivity goals?

2. Comment on the e-learning program that Jenny and Sam designed. What are the indicators that suggest it has not been a success? Is it possible there are other indicators that might indicate that it is more effective than it appears?

3. If you were Jenny, what would you tell the president and what would you do about e-learning at Flotation Ltd.? Should Jenny give up on e-learning, or wait another six months before making a decision?

4. What do you think are the main reasons for the negative reaction to the e-learning program? What are the most important things that need to be changed to improve the program? What changes would you make if you had to redesign it?

5. Consider the use of social media and Web 2.0 technologies for the sales training program. What Web 2.0 technologies would you recommend and how should they be used as part of the sales training program? Would social media and Web 2.0 technologies be effective for employee learning? Explain your answer.

FLASHBACK QUESTIONS

1. Comment on the design of this e-learning program in terms of the material described in Chapter 4, such as active practice and the conditions of practice. Do you think the program could be redesigned and more effective? Refer to Table 4.4 and discuss the use of the conditions of practice in the redesign of the e-learning program.

2. Consider the use of active learning and adaptive expertise for the e-learning program. Do you think the program should be designed for adaptive expertise and active learning? Explain your answer. If you were to redesign the program for active learning, explain what you would do, and why.

3. Consider the material in Chapter 2 on learning theories. How can learning theories help us understand why the e-learning program was not more effective? What are the implications of the learning theories for the design of the e-learning program? What would you do to make it more effective?

FLASH FORWARD QUESTION

1. Two important considerations for training delivery involve the choice of a trainer and the trainees. For example, good trainers have expertise on the training content and are able to motivate trainees. Trainees should be ready to learn and to benefit from a training program. Is it possible that the negative reaction to the e-learning training program was due in part to the trainer and/or the trainees? Explain your answer and indicate any changes in the trainees and/or trainer that might make the program more effective.

REWRITE THE CASE QUESTION: TRAINING DESIGN

Rewrite the case to include design elements that will make the e-learning program more effective and maximize trainee motivation, learning, and retention. In other words, rewrite the section on the design of the program so that it includes various design elements that might make it a more effective training program.

PART 1

The Korea Ginseng Corporation (KGC) is one of the leading companies in the world health food market. It specializes in red ginseng – an herbal supplement often used to strengthen the immune system and ward off stress and disease. During the past decade, the company has grown rapidly due to increasing global interest in health and also owes its success to the company's dedicated local employees.

As KGC's business has thrived, the amount of information that the employees need to know has grown. The dissemination rate, however, has not kept pace with the growth of the company. This lack of understanding about the company caused communication problems between business units and made each unit a silo.

When a Korean current affairs TV program raised a question about the high price of KGC's product compared with its competitors, many KGC employees found themselves subject to questions from their acquaintances about the issue and red ginseng more broadly. The company's leadership immediately realized it needed to address this lack of understanding on the part of employees.

KGC felt strongly about the necessity to train its people, so its human resource development (HRD) department created a taskforce to collect core organizational knowledge and business information and then disseminate it to employees. To identify the issues and core knowledge that was necessary to impart, HRD managers thoroughly reviewed the company's yearly and long-term business plans, performance evaluation index of each department, and other internal documents. From reviewing these documents, the HRD managers listed keywords from seven business units covering product/brand information, the food sanitation act, the manufacturing process, and other business-related issues. They then sent the keywords to each business unit to ask consent to share their business issues and knowledge with every company employee.

After getting each department head's approval, HRD finalized a core knowledge list of 101 keywords. Next the HRD managers selected internal subject-matter experts (SMEs) on each issue and worked with them to write scripts around each keyword. The manuscripts were uploaded to the knowledge management system and then disseminated to employees.

Short video clips based on the manuscripts were developed by HRD in coordination with the SMEs, and then made available to employees. Printed manuscripts also were distributed to each team so that people could refer to the information in that format. But despite all these efforts, employees weren't taking advantage of the learning resources and materials.

Before reading Part 2 of the case, answer the following questions:

1. Why did KGC decide to design a training program, and what were its objectives? Do you think a training program was necessary? Explain your answer.

2. Describe how KGC designed the training program and the program itself. What are some of the strengths and weaknesses of the process and the program?

3. Why do you think that employees at KGC were not taking advantage of the learning resources and materials?

4. What else could KGC do so that employees will take advantage of and refer to the learning resources and materials? What would make the training program more effective?

PART 2

To entice employees to update their knowledge through the available learning resources on the knowledge management system, and to stimulate employees' interest in doing so, the HRD department decided to introduce a game and contest. To allow for greater flexibility in time and place for the employees' learning, HRD made sure the game application could be used on mobile devices.

The idea for mobile gamification was first proposed by the chief learning officer, but it faced opposition from HRD managers for many reasons. First and foremost, nobody had experience in developing mobile game content, and HRD practitioners did not want to take the risk of trying a new solution. They also worried about employees' low participation and indifference, because the cost of developing the mobile game application was expensive.

Persuaded by the CLO, the HRD managers took the challenge as an opportunity to improve their competencies. The CLO secured an extra budget allocation for this project from top management, and the HRD managers converted the learning resources into a mobile gamification format. Collaborating with an IT company that provided tech support, the HRD managers worked to develop a mobile quiz application. Finally, the KGC mobile game application was complete and mobile quiz contests were held three times from July to August.

To promote the content, HRD regularly posted notifications to the company's intranet that encouraged employees to download the game from the Google app store. To further promote the quiz contest, HRD team members spread the word to their colleagues and demonstrated the game by visiting other offices.

Before reading Part 3 of the case, answer the following questions:

5. Do you think it was a good idea to covert the learning resources into a mobile gamification format? What are the advantages and disadvantages of doing so?

6. How do you think employees will react to the new format? Will it be more effective than the previous format? Explain your answer.

PART 3

Although playing the mobile game and taking part in the competition was voluntary for employees, the participation rate was high. Server data reveal that 90 percent of possible users used the game app, and employees even played the game on weekends.Feedback from management and employees also was encouraging. Many employees testified that the game was very helpful to learn about the company and it was fun. One executive recounted that he did not know a name of a new employee until the employee sent him a playing request.

Before reading Part 4 of the case, answer the following questions:

7. Why do you think the new format was more effective than the previous format?

8. What does this case say about the design of training programs and the use of technology for training? What does it say about the use of games and gamification?

9. What lessons does this case provide to organizations that are considering adapting mobile gamification to their workplaces?

PART 4

KGC's successful initiative yields several lessons to organizations that are considering adapting mobile gamification to their workplaces. First, the game's rules and the app's interface design were purposely very simple so people could easily master how to use the app and play. Each round consisted of five quizzes, with employees needing to answer questions quickly and correctly.

The faster they answered the questions, the more points the employees received. The quiz consisted of multiple-choice and true-false questions. This was by design to keep the items short and clear. Because the game was simple to learn and easy to play, more employees could enjoy it regardless of age group.

Second, the game was designed to have players compete against each other, with top players listed on a leaderboard with their full names and pictures. Employees could check the rankings of teams and business departments on the leaderboard, which were updated in real time.

Individuals were strongly motivated because it brought social capital to high-scoring employees. Team leaders and heads of business departments also encouraged employees to play because they wanted their teams to be listed among the high rankings.

The game was only available for one month, with the time limitation making employees more focused. The top 20 players won prizes of KGC products (about $200 worth), which also was a strong enticement.

Third, in addition to the overall competition and leaderboard, the game was designed to be played against another employee. Individuals could either send a play request to someone specific against who they wanted to play or choose a random opponent.

Many employees said that once they received a play request from a stranger, they searched for that person's HRD profile on the intranet. Employees came to know more people in the organization, as well as learned about the organization itself. Many employees said that they began by playing only with people they knew, but continuously broadened their networks.

Fourth, the game was designed to provide instant feedback as to whether an answer was right or wrong. If a player answered incorrectly, the app provided a detailed explanation. An identification number of the feedback page matched with the knowledge management database content; players who wanted to learn more could refer to the database.

The uptick in employee hits on the knowledge management pages suggests that the mobile gamification encouraged important connections between mobile learning and rich database-provided company content. Furthermore, this relationship facilitated self-directed, in-depth study on the part of employees.

Mobile gamification appealed to employees, but many said they were too busy to download the application and play the game. Moreover, employees who struggled with technology needed extra support. HRD managers posted a manual on the intranet summarizing how to download the game application, but the manual didn't provide enough guidance for many employees.

Whenever HRD managers visited employee offices, they asked whether employees had downloaded the app; if an employee had not yet done so, the manager helped with the download and demonstrated how to play. Also, the HRD team randomly picked young employees to provide assistance. These younger employees agreed to help their peers download and play the game.

Employees were intrigued with the HRD department's new approach to promote learning, but it seemed the interest did not last long. Some employees suggested that more game factors—unexpected events, extra points, or graphical components—be included to hold users' interests. Others complained that they got bored after a few weeks.

HRD managers also found that many quiz items needed to be included in the app. About 800 total questions were used; however, this proved too small for the one-month competition. Some employees said that they learned something when the same quiz items repetitively showed up. But once they were familiar with the items, solving the quiz questions was like a knee-jerk reaction with no new learning.

Integrating feedback from both employees and the HRD department, recommendations for the next generation of mobile gamification include the following:

1. Novelty wears off quickly, so there should be some changes in the game factors.
2. Fun is as important as learning for the players. Not all games are fun, so when designing learning, make sure the game is interesting.
3. A high amount of content is needed to keep learning happening.
4. Design is not enough; introducing and promoting the game are vital to the success of mobile gamification.

QUESTIONS

10. What does this case teach us about the use of technology and gamification for training?
11. Do you think it was a good idea for KGC to use gamification as part of the training program? What are some of the advantages and disadvantages?
12. What other information might be useful for determining how effective the gamification program was? What do we not know about its effectiveness?
13. What advice would you give organizations about using gamification as part of a training program?

Source: Republished with permission of the Association for Talent Development (ATD), from Yang, G. H., & Lee, J. Y. (2016, May). Learning while playing. *TD Magazine*, *70*(5), 48–52. Permission conveyed through Copyright Clearance Center, Inc.

RUNNING CASE STUDY DIRTY POOLS

Refer to the case at the end of Chapter 1 to answer the following questions.

1. Would technology-based training be an appropriate and effective way to train pool operators and their employees? Explain your answer.
2. Describe how technology-based training methods might be used to train pool operators and employees. What are the advantages and disadvantages of using technology-based methods? Would it be more or less effective than off-the-job and on-the-job training methods?

3. If you were to design a computer-based training program to train pool operators and employees, what instructional methods and design factors would you use? To answer this question, refer to the "Designing Effective Technology-Based Training Programs" section and discuss the usefulness of each of the design factors.

// REFERENCES

1. Foster, L. (2015). Calfrac finds flexibility, mobility – and cost savings – in taking blended approach to training. *Canadian HR Reporter*, *28*(15), 18, 20; Calfrac, About Us at www. Calfrac.com and Careers at www.calfrac.com/careers.

2. Dolezalek, H. (2005). 2005 industry report. *Training Magazine*, *42*(12), 14–28.

3. Dolezalek (2005).

4. Tomlinson, A. (2002, March 25). T & D spending up in U.S. as Canada lags behind. *Canadian HR Reporter*, *15*(6), 1; Sitzmann, T., Kraiger, K., Stewart, D., & Wisher, R. (2006). The comparative effectiveness of web-based and classroom instruction: A meta-analysis. *Personnel Psychology*, *59*, 623–664.

5. Cotsman, S., & Hall, C. (2018). *Learning cultures lead the way: Learning & development outlook—14th edition*. Ottawa: The Conference Board of Canada.

6. Anonymous (2017, November/December). 2017 Training industry report. *Training Magazine*, *54*(6), 20–33; Ho, M. (2017, December). Learning investment & hours are on the rise. *TD: Talent Development*, *71*(12), 38–43.

7. Hall, C. (2014). *Learning & development outlook—12th edition: Strong learning organizations, strong leadership*. Ottawa: The Conference Board of Canada; Cotsman & Hall (2018).

8. Harris-Lalonde, S. (2001). *Training and development outlook*. Ottawa: The Conference Board of Canada.

9. Ray, R. (2001, May 25). Employers, employees embrace e-learning. *The Globe and Mail*, p. E2.

10. Anonymous (2007, December 3). Hydro-Quebec takes training online. *Canadian HR Reporter*, *20*(21), 28.

11. Anonymous (2016, January/February). Outstanding training initiatives (EY: Tax 1 Blended Program). *Training Magazine*, *53*(1), 56–60.

12. Freifeld, L. (2016, January/February). Jiffy Lube is leader of the pack. *Training Magazine*, *53*(1), 26–32.

13. Brown, K. G., & Ford, J. K. (2002). Using computer technology in training: Building an infrastructure for active learning. In K. Kraiger (Ed.), *Creating, implementing, and managing effective training and development: State-of-the-art lessons for practice* (pp. 160–191). San Francisco, CA: Jossey-Bass.

14. Welsh, L. T., Wanberg, C. R., Brown, K. G., & Simmering, M. J. (2003). E-learning: Emerging uses, empirical results and future directions. *International Journal of Training and Development*, *7*, 245–258.

15. Welsh et al. (2003).

16. Salas, E., Tannenbaum, S. I., Kraiger, K., & Smith-Jentsch, K. A. (2012). The science of training and development in organizations: What matters in practice. *Psychological Science in the Public Interest, 13*, 74–101.

17. Welsh et al. (2003).

18. Weidman, E. (2014, November 3). Distant but within reach. *Canadian HR Reporter, 27*(19), 20.

19. Ellis, F. (2013, March 21). Have a question? Hit the raise-hand key. *Toronto Star*, p. M4.

20. Grant, C. (2013, September 23). Online education appealing to busy employees. *Canadian HR Reporter, 26*(16), 16.

21. Ubell, R. (2017). Making the most of MOOCs. *TD: Talent Development, 71*(10), 22–23; Noe, R. A., Clarke, A. D. M., & Klein, H. J. (2014). Learning in the twenty-first century workplace. *Annual Review of Organizational Psychology and Organizational Behavior, 1*, 245–275.

22. Freifeld, L. (2016, September/October). Do's & don't for MOOCs & SPOCs. *Training Magazine, 53*(5), 20–26; Saunderson, R. (2016, September/October). Live, learn, and prosper with SPOC. *Training Magazine, 53*(5), 62–63.

23. Raybould, B. (1990). Solving human performance problems with computers—A case study: Building an electronic performance support system. *Performance and Instruction, 29*(10), 4–14.

24. Smith, K. (1996, April). EPSS helps accounting firm reduce training time, improve productivity during transition to new service emphasis. *Lakewood Report on Technology for Learning*, p. 8.

25. Gebber, B. (1991). Help! The rise of performance support systems. *Training Magazine, 28*(12), 23–29; Ruyle, K. (1991, February/March). Developing intelligent job aids. *Technical and Skills Training*, 9–14.

26. Weinstein, M. (2006, October). On demand is in demand. *Training Magazine, 43*(10), 31–35.

27. Bernier, L. (2014, December 15). Training goes high-tech. *Canadian HR Reporter, 27*(22), 3, 20.

28. Lewis, M. (2011, July). Moving into the live virtual classroom. *T+D, 65*(7), 76–77.

29. Freifeld, L. (2011, January/February). TEIG locks in on leadership. *Training Magazine, 48*(1), 34–39.

30. Galt, V. (2003, January 22). Bank tunes in to TV training. *The Globe and Mail*, pp. C1, C5.

31. Shankar, C. (2006, September 25). Rise in webinars among e-learning trends. *Canadian HR Reporter, 19*(16), 19, 21.

32. Anonymous (2008, September). What does it cost to host web conferences and webcasts? *T+D, 62*(9), 88.

33. Lewis (2011).

34. Hall (2014).

35. Wang, S., & Noe, R. A. (2010). Knowledge sharing: A review and directions for future research. *Human Resource Management Review, 20*, 115–131.

36. Mesmer-Magnus, J. R., & DeChurch, L. A. (2009). Information sharing and team performance: A meta-analysis. *Journal of Applied Psychology, 94*, 535–546;

Milia, L. D., & Birdi, K. (2010). The relationship between multiple levels of learning practices and objective and subjective organizational financial performance. *Journal of Organizational Behavior, 31*, 481–498; Noe, Clarke, & Klein (2014).

37. Wenger, E. C., & Snyder, W. M. (2000). Communities of practice: The organizational frontier. *Harvard Business Review, 78*(1), 139–145.

38. Chang, J., & Jacobs, R. L. (2012). Determinants and outcomes of employee participation in a strategic community of practice: A mixed-method approach. *Human Resource Development Quarterly, 23*, 341–362.

39. Stamps, D. (1997). Communities of practice. *Training Magazine, 34*(2), 34–42.

40. Stamps (1997); Salopek, J. (2008). Knowledge in numbers. *T+D, 62*(7), 24–26.

41. Wenger & Snyder (2000).

42. Jarche, H. (2008, April). Skills 2.0. *T+D, 62*(4), 22–24.

43. London, M., & Hall, M. J. (2011). Unlocking the value of Web 2.0 technologies for training and development: The shift from instructor-controlled, adaptive learning to learner-driven, generative learning. *Human Resource Management, 50*, 757–775.

44. Jarche (2008).

45. Shankar (2006).

46. Shankar (2006); Anonymous (2006). Podcast popularity grows. *Training Magazine, 43*(4), 14.

47. Green, M. (2011). Better, smarter, faster: Web 3.0 and the future of learning. *T+D, 65*(4), 70–72.

48. Green (2011).

49. Wasserman, M. E., & Fisher, S. L. (2018). One (lesson) for the road? What we know (and don't know) about mobile learning. In K. G. Brown (Ed.), *The Cambridge handbook of workplace training and employee development* (pp. 293–317). New York: Cambridge University Press.

50. Moore, A. (2017, November). 2017 trends. *TD: Talent Development, 71*(9), 28–32.

51. Ally, M. (2008, February 11). Learn anywhere, anytime. *Canadian HR Reporter, 21*(3), 18.

52. Fister Gale, S. (2008, May 29). Dial M for mobile learning. *Workforce Management Online*. Retrieved from www.workforce.com

53. Weinstein, M. (2010). Be our guest—safely. *Training Magazine, 47*(1), 32–33.

54. Garff, M. (2012). Implementing M-learning: Make the dream a reality. *T+D, 66*(1), 16.

55. Wasserman & Fisher (2018).

56. Cannon-Bowers, J. A., & Bowers, C. A. (2010). Synthetic learning environments: On developing a science of simulation, games and virtual worlds for training. In S. W. J. Kozlowski and E. Salas (Eds.), *Learning, training, and development in organizations* (pp. 229–261). Mahwah, NJ: Erlbaum.

57. Moore (2017); Franchi, J. (1994). Virtual reality: An overview. *TechTrends, 39*, 23–26; Gronstedt, A. (2016, June). From immersion to presence. *TD: Talent Development, 70*(6), 54–59.

58. Gronstedt, A. (2016); Moore (2017); Ellis, R. (2018, February 21). Get in the driver's seat: UPS explores VR training. *Association for Talent Development*, https://www.td.org/insights/get-in-the-drivers-seat-ups-explores-vr-training

59. Green, J., Green, T., & Brown, A. (2017). Augmented reality in the K-12 classroom. *TechTrends, 61*, 603–605; Keebler, J. R., Patzer, B. S., Wiltshire, T. J., & Fiore, S. M. (2018). Augmented reality systems in training. In K. G. Brown (Ed.), *The Cambridge handbook of workplace training and employee development* (pp. 278–292). New York: Cambridge University Press; Lee, K. (2012). Augmented reality in education and training. *TechTrends, 56*, 13–21; Moore (2017).

60. Keebler, Patzer, Wiltshire, & Fiore (2018).

61. Keebler, Patzer, Wiltshire, & Fiore (2018).

62. Bell, B. S., Kanar, A. M., & Kozlowski, S. W. J. (2008). Current issues and future directions in simulation-based training in North America. *The International Journal of Human Resource Management, 19*, 1416–1434.

63. Bell, Kanar, & Kozlowski (2008); Cannon-Bowers & Bowers (2010).

64. Bowness, A. (2004, September 27). Hands-on learning through computer simulations. *Canadian HR Reporter, 17*(16), 15.

65. Bell, Kanar, & Kozlowski (2008).

66. Sitzmann, T. (2011). A meta-analytic examination of the instructional effectiveness of computer-based simulation games. *Personnel Psychology, 64*, 489–528.

67. DeRouin, R. E., Fritzsche, B. A., & Salas, E. (2005). E-learning in organizations. *Journal of Management, 31*, 920–940.

68. Sitzmann (2011).

69. Green, S. (2013, August 12). Get in the game. *Canadian HR Reporter, 26*(14), 11; Smolkin, S. (2014, August 11). Turning work into a game. *Canadian HR Reporter, 27*(14), 12.

70. Smolkin (2014); www.sunlife.ca

71. Ortiz, C. C. (2016, December). Game on a dime. *TD: Talent Development, 70*(12), 76–77.

72. Sitzmann (2011).

73. Galt, V. (2004, June 12). Employers jumping on e-learning bandwagon. *The Globe and Mail*, p. B10.

74. DeRouin et al. (2005).

75. DeRouin et al. (2005).

76. Posner, Z. (2017, May). Data-driven personalization comes to learning. *Talent Development, 71*(5), 32–36; Posner, Z. (2018, January). Personalizing adaptive learning. *Talent Development, 71*(1), 24–28.

77. DeRouin et al. (2005).

78. Sitzmann et al. (2006).

79. Sitzmann et al. (2006).

80. Leone, P., & Pinkston, R. (2017, May). Practice makes perfect. *Talent Development, 71*(5), 62–63.

81. Sitzmann et al. (2006); Orvis, K., Fisher, S. L., & Wasserman, M. E. (2009). Power to the people: Using learner control to improve trainee reactions

and learning in Web-based instructional environments. *Journal of Applied Psychology, 94*, 960–971.

82. Bell, Kanar, & Kozlowski (2008).

83. Hughes, M. G., Day, E. A., Wang, X., Schuelke, M. J., Arsenault, M. L., Harkrider, L. N., & Cooper, O. D. (2013). Learner-controlled practice difficulty in the training of a complex task: Cognitive and motivational mechanisms. *Journal of Applied Psychology, 98*, 80–98.

84. Orvis et al. (2009).

85. Bell, Kanar, & Kozlowski (2008).

86. Bell, B. S., & Kozlowski, S. W. J. (2002). Adaptive guidance: Enhancing self-regulation, knowledge, and performance in technology-based training. *Personnel Psychology, 55*, 267–306.

87. Sitzmann, T., & Johnson, S. K. (2012). The best laid plans: Examining the conditions under which a planning intervention improves learning and reduces attrition. *Journal of Applied Psychology, 97*, 967–981.

88. Sitzmann, T., Bell, B. S., Kraiger, K., & Kanar, A. M. (2009). A multilevel analysis of the effect of prompting self-regulation in technology-delivered instruction. *Personnel Psychology, 62*, 697–734; Sitzmann, T., & Ely, K. (2010). Sometimes you need a reminder: The effects of prompting self-regulation on regulatory processes, learning, and attrition. *Journal of Applied Psychology, 95*, 132–144.

89. Weinstein, M. (2017, September/October). LMS data deep dive. *Training Magazine, 54*(5), 30–33.

90. Anonymous (2015, September/October). LMS surveys say. . . . *Training Magazine, 52*(5), 6.

91. Brown & Ford (2002).

92. Yanson, R., & Johnson, R. D. (2016). An empirical examination of e-learning design: The role of trainee socialization and complexity in short term training. *Computers & Education, 101*, 43–54.

93. O'Keefe, B. (1991). Adopting multimedia on a global scale. *Instruction Delivery Systems, 5*(5), 6–11.

94. Miles, K. W., & Griffith, E. R. (1993, April/May). Developing an hour of CBT: The quick and dirty method. *CBT Directions*, 28–33.

95. Eure, R. (2001, March 21). Companies embrace e-training. *The Globe and Mail*, p. B16.

96. Welsh et al. (2003).

97. Sitzmann et al. (2006).

98. Sitzmann et al. (2006).

99. Welsh et al. (2003).

100. Welsh et al. (2003).

101. McNab, R. M., & Angelis, D. I. (2014). Does computer-based training impact maintenance costs and actions? An empirical analysis of the US Navy's AN/SQQ-89(v) sonar system. *Applied Economics, 46*(34), 4256–4266.

102. Sitzmann et al. (2006).

CHAPTER 8

TRAINING DELIVERY

CHAPTER LEARNING OUTCOMES

AFTER READING THIS CHAPTER, YOU SHOULD BE ABLE TO:

- develop a detailed lesson plan
- describe the characteristics of an effective trainer
- determine who should attend a training program
- explain the role of ethics in training and development
- explain how to create a positive learning climate
- explain how to use Gagné's nine events of instruction
- develop solutions to training delivery problems

The Canadian Broadcasting Corporation (CBC) is Canada's national public broadcaster providing news and entertainment from coast to coast. The Crown corporation employs over 6000 permanent, full-time-equivalent employees and operates 27 television stations, 88 radio stations, and one digital station. The CBC has two main television networks, one English and one French, as well as five specialty television channels and four Canada-wide radio networks, two in each official language.

Several years ago, CBC launched a project to equip all its televisions stations in Canada with high-definition cameras and equipment. This meant that staff across the country had to be trained to use the new technology. But how could they train so many staff across the country? The answer was staff instructors, who make up 70 percent of the 30 or so instructors at the CBC.

To support their development, staff instructors received four days of training—two focused on e-learning and two focused on higher-level "train the trainer." Senior staff trainers were partnered with newer members of the training group and they worked collaboratively on developing material.

Staff instructors primarily provide technical and infrastructure training, such as new equipment training, as well as journalism and programming training, including journalism skills, writing, and producing. A handful of staff instructors also provide soft-skills and business skills

Staff instructors make up 70 percent of the 30 or so instructors at the CBC.

training, including facilitation, internal negotiation, dealing with complex work environments, and providing feedback.

Senior staff members also play a key role in training at the CBC. For example, several years ago the CBC launched a "conversation series" in which younger staff got to talk to veteran journalists, producers, and editors. In addition, the employee intranet features a variety of videos of more senior employees offering their expertise.[1]

Sources: Silliker, A. (2013, April 22). Staff instructors offer training at CBC. *Canadian HR Reporter, 26*(8), 10; CBC Annual Report 2015–2016. About us, Our operations.; www.cbc.radio-canada.ca/site/annual-reports/2015-2016/about-us/our-operations-en.html

// INTRODUCTION

In the previous four chapters, we described how to design training programs and the different methods of training. However, as you can tell from the description of training and development at the CBC, there are other important aspects of training and development, such as deciding who should attend training, who should be the trainer, and how to train the trainers. These issues have to do with the delivery of training programs, the focus of this chapter.

Table 8.1 lists the main activities associated with training delivery that are described in this chapter. The starting point is the development of a lesson plan.

// THE LESSON PLAN

Lesson plan
The blueprint that outlines the sequence of activities that will take place in the training program

Once a training program has been designed, the trainer needs to develop a lesson plan. The **lesson plan** is the blueprint that outlines the sequence of activities that will take place in the training program. As such, it is a guide for the trainer that provides a step-by-step breakdown for conducting a training program. A lesson plan should be

TABLE 8.1

TRAINING DELIVERY ACTIVITIES

1. Develop a lesson plan.
2. Choose the trainer.
3. Decide on the trainees who should attend a training program.
4. Determine the training materials and equipment required.
5. Prepare the training site.
6. Schedule the training program.
7. Administer the training.
8. Implement the training program.

developed for each lesson in a program. A **lesson** is a cohesive unit of instruction with a specific learning objective.[2]

A good lesson plan should be developed in advance of a training program and be detailed enough that any trainer could use it to guide him/herself through the program. Most of what is required to deliver a training program is indicated in the lesson plan. Although there is no one best format for lesson plans, a good rule of thumb is to focus on what the trainee will be doing.[3] A lesson plan should reflect the interaction of content, sequence, trainer, trainee, and the norms of the organization.[4]

Some of the things that should be listed on the first page or cover of a lesson plan are the training objectives, the trainees, the trainer, time allocation, location, classroom requirements, seating, training materials and equipment, and supplies and handouts.[5]

The detailed lesson plan for each lesson should indicate the activities that will occur during the lesson as well as what the trainer and trainees will be doing and when they will be doing it.

An important consideration in the development of a lesson plan is the sequencing or ordering of the content for the training program. There is no one best way to order the training content, since it will depend on the nature of the content and the trainees. However, there are a number of general approaches for content sequencing that are based on ease of learning, such as general to specific, easy to difficult, concrete to abstract, old to new, simple to complex, familiar to unknown, practical to theoretical, and present to future.[6]

Beginning with the simple and familiar is generally recommended because it builds trainee self-efficacy and allows trainees to see how their current levels of knowledge and experience are relevant for the training. This also provides some comfort to trainees and lowers their anxiety about learning.

Table 8.2 presents the cover page of a lesson plan for a one-day training program on structured employment interviews. As shown in Table 8.3, a detailed lesson plan should indicate what will happen and when, as well as what the trainees and the trainer will be doing. Note that if this training program lasted for more than one day there would be a detailed lesson plan for each day of the program.[7]

The development of a lesson plan is a critical phase in the design of a training program. It allows for the approval and the smooth operation of training activities; enables expenditures to be budgeted for and monitored; and sets the stage for the implementation of the training program. A lesson plan is also a signal to other members of the organization that training is to be conducted in a professional manner.

In the following pages, we describe the main elements in the lesson plan in more detail. For some guidance on what to include in a lesson plan, see The Trainer's Notebook 8.1, "Guidelines for Developing a Lesson Plan."

Lesson
A cohesive unit of instruction with a specific learning objective

TABLE 8.2

LESSON PLAN COVER PAGE FOR STRUCTURED EMPLOYMENT INTERVIEWS

Organization:	Vandalais Department Stores
Department:	Human Resources
Program Title:	Structured Employment Interviews
Instructor(s):	Interview Training Consultant
Time Allocation:	1 day
Trainees:	All employees in the Human Resources Department
Where:	Vandalais Learning Centre

TRAINING OBJECTIVES

Employees will be able to conduct a structured behaviour description interview and correctly perform the seven key behaviours.

CLASSROOM REQUIREMENTS

Seating for 50 people that allows for high involvement.

TRAINING MATERIALS AND EQUIPMENT

DVD player and TV monitor; DVD: *How to Conduct a Structured Employment Interview*; computer and projector with screen; flipchart; paper; markers.

TRAINEE SUPPLIES

Pen and paper.

TRAINEE HANDOUTS

1. Course objectives and outline.
2. Article on structured employment interviews.
3. Article on behaviour description interviews.
4. List of the seven key behaviours for conducting a structured employment interview.
5. Copy of the behaviour description interview for the sales associate position, with interview questions and scoring guide and instructions.
6. Role-play exercise.

THE TRAINER'S NOTEBOOK   8.1

GUIDELINES FOR DEVELOPING A LESSON PLAN

Use the following guidelines to develop a lesson plan.

1. Write the lesson objective (what the trainee will be able to do at the end of the lesson).

2. Determine the knowledge and skills the trainee must learn to accomplish the objective. This enables the developer to determine the subtopics of the lesson.

3. Put the subtopics in a preliminary sequence in a way that is most meaningful to the trainee and enables the trainee to master the knowledge and skills.

4. Identify the content of the various subtopics of the lesson. Answer the question: "What must the trainee know or be able to do for satisfactory performance of each lesson subtopic?"

(continued)

5. Select the instructional procedures appropriate to the learning of each lesson subtopic. Identify materials and equipment needed.

6. Review the instructional sequence. Adjust as necessary to provide variety and movement for the trainees.

7. Provide a means of monitoring and trainee feedback.

8. Prepare a test to evaluate the degree to which trainees have achieved the learning objective of the lesson.

Source: Republished with permission of Jossey-Bass Publishers, from A.P. Carnevale, L. J. Gainer & A. S. Meltzer, *Workplace basics training manual*, (1990) p.139; permission conveyed through Copyright Clearance Center, Inc.

TABLE 8.3

DETAILED LESSON PLAN FOR STRUCTURED EMPLOYMENT INTERVIEWS

OBJECTIVE

Employees will be able to conduct structured behaviour description employment interviews and correctly perform the seven key behaviours.

Trainees:	Members of the Human Resources Department
Time:	9 a.m.–5 p.m.

COURSE OUTLINE

9:00–10:00	Introduction lecture on the problem of poor employee performance and high turnover, and the use of structured and unstructured employment interviews for selection.
10:00–10:30	Show DVD of an unstructured employment interview followed by a discussion.
10:30–10:45	Break
10:45–11:15	Show DVD of a structured employment interview followed by a discussion.
11:15–12:00	Review the seven key behaviours of conducting a structured employment interview.
12:00–1:00	Lunch
1:00–2:00	Lecture on behaviour description interview questions and review of the interview questions and guide developed for sales associates.
2:00–2:30	Review of the seven key behaviours in conducting a structured employment interview.
2:30–2:45	Break
2:45–3:30	Role-play practice exercise: In groups of three, assign participants the roles of interviewer, interviewee, and observer. Review script for roles and instruct trainees to demonstrate the seven key behaviours of a structured interview using the sales associate behaviour description interview questions. Have observer provide feedback using guidelines contained in the role-play exercise booklet and evaluate the interviewer's performance on the seven key behaviours using the evaluation form provided. Switch roles until each group member has played the role of the interviewer.
3:30–4:30	Regroup for discussion of role-play exercise. Discuss how it felt to be the interviewer and the interviewee, and get the observer's feedback and evaluation.
4:30–4:45	Review the seven key behaviours of the structured employment interview, the importance of using structured interviews, and the behaviour description interview for hiring sales associates.
4:45–5:00	Closing. Review objectives and give pep talk about conducting structured employment interviews and using the behaviour description interview. Thank participants and hand out training certificates.

// THE TRAINER

The lesson plan cover sheet in Table 8.2 indicates that the trainer will be a consultant. But how do you decide who the trainer will be? At first, this might seem like a trivial question. After all, isn't this the job of the human resources department or the training and development staff? In some cases the answer is yes, but in many training situations the answer to this question depends on a number of factors.

First, it is important to realize the role of a good trainer. Regardless of how well a training program is designed, the success of a program rests in large part on the trainer. In other words, no matter how good the training program, if the trainer is ineffective the program will suffer.

What are the qualities of a good trainer? This question should be easy for students to answer if they consider the courses they have enjoyed and those that they found less memorable. One of the first things that might come to mind is the extent to which the instructor was knowledgeable about the course material. Is the trainer a subject-matter expert?

A **subject-matter expert (SME)** is someone who is familiar with the knowledge, skills, and abilities required to perform a task or a job and has subject-matter expertise. In Chapter 4, we noted the importance of subject-matter experts in determining the content of a training program.

A trainer should also be an expert on the topic or content area being taught. Not only will trainees learn more, but the trainer will be perceived as more credible. As indicated in the chapter-opening vignette, staff instructors make up 70 percent of the instructors at the CBC, and senior staff members also play a key role in training.

An effective trainer must also have the ability to make the material interesting. Students probably have had instructors who knew the material and were able to deliver it, but they did not make it very interesting. A good trainer should be enthusiastic and excited about the training material and capable of motivating and arousing the interest of trainees.

One way for trainers to generate interest and increase trainee motivation is by being expressive during the delivery of a training program. **Trainer expressiveness** refers to the degree to which a trainer uses linguistic devices and is physically animated. Expressive trainers are physically animated (e.g., posture, gesturing, and eye contact) and use linguistic devices such as an animated and enthusiastic voice rather than a monotone voice, and vocal fluency rather than speaking with hesitancies (e.g., "ums").

Research has found that trainees recall a greater amount of the training content when a trainer is more expressive. There is also evidence that a trainer's expressiveness enhances trainees' training motivation and self-efficacy.[8]

In Chapter 4 the importance of active practice for learner engagement was described. Learner engagement is also influenced by the trainer. Thus, in addition to being expressive, a good trainer should also be engaging. In other words, a good trainer is able to draw trainees into the training program and keep them interested, focused, and engaged in learning. No doubt you can think of course instructors you have had who either put you to sleep or kept you on the edge of your seat as you were absorbed in what was being taught. When a trainer is engaging, trainees are more likely to be motivated to learn, and they are attentive and absorbed in the learning process.

Subject-matter expert (SME)
A person who is familiar with the knowledge, skills, and abilities required to perform a task or a job

Trainer expressiveness
The degree to which a trainer uses linguistic devices and is physically animate

For more information see Chapter 4, p. 125

Expressive trainers are physically animated and use linguistic devices such as an animated and enthusiastic voice.

One way a trainer can do this is by using seductive details while delivering the training program. **Seductive details** consist of entertaining and interesting information (such as cartoons, stories, and jokes) that is irrelevant or only tangentially related to the training material and not necessary for achieving the training objective.[9]

Although seductive details might be interesting and entertaining for trainees, it might impair their learning and retention, something known as the **seductive details effect**.[10] Research has found some evidence for the seductive details effect. However, the presence of the effect depends on a number of factors, such as the kind of seductive detail. The seductive details effect is also more likely when trainees have a time limit for completing training. In addition, while seductive details have been found to have a positive effect on the attention of trainees with high pre-training knowledge of the training content, they have a negative effect on those with low pre-training knowledge. There is also some evidence that when seductive details are combined with an expressive trainer it has a positive effect on problem solving.

Thus, trainers can make their instructional material entertaining and engaging by using seductive details and by being expressive. However, given that seductive details can impair learning and retention for some trainees, trainers should limit the use of seductive details and use them sparingly.[11]

To learn more about how a trainer can engage trainees, see The Trainer's Notebook 8.2, "Getting Trainees Engaged."

For more information see Chapter 4, p. 152

> **Seductive details**
> Entertaining and interesting information that is irrelevant or only tangentially related to the training material and not necessary for achieving the training objective
>
> **Seductive details effect**
> Seductive details impair learning and retention

THE TRAINER'S NOTEBOOK   8.2

GETTING TRAINEES ENGAGED

Trainers play an important role in getting trainees engaged in a training program. Here are some things that a trainer can do to engage trainees:

- Encourage trainees to answer questions instead of being the first to comment.
- Ask clear and specific questions one at a time.
- Probe with questions that elicit deeper thought and responses from trainees.

- Demonstrate an empathetic level of listening rather than listening to respond.
- Go beyond covering the prescribed content and make the content relevant to trainees so that they see the application to work situations.
- Encourage interaction, discussion, and collaboration, and provide clear directions for activities.
- Manage time and adhere to course objectives and flow, but adapt to trainee needs and expectations.

Source: Republished with permission of the Association for Talent Development (ATD), from Laborie, K., & Stone, T. (2016, January). Interact + engage. *TD, 70*(1), 36–39. Permission conveyed through Copyright Clearance Center, Inc.

TRAIN-THE-TRAINER

One of the difficulties of finding a good trainer is that individuals who are skilled trainers often do not have the subject-matter expertise to deliver a training program in their organization. On the other hand, individuals who have subject-matter expertise often are not experienced trainers.

Students know, perhaps all too well, that no matter how well informed or knowledgeable an instructor might be, a course can still be poor if the instructor is not effective in delivering the material. In addition to subject-matter expertise, good trainers must also have good verbal and communication skills, interpersonal skills, and organizing and planning skills. The trainer must be able to deliver the training material in a manner that is understandable to trainees. Trainees are more likely to learn and recall training content when the trainer is well organized and presents the material in a structured manner that is easy to follow and understand.[12]

One solution to this problem is to teach subject-matter experts how to be effective trainers. This is what the CBC does to develop staff instructors. These programs are known as train-the-trainer and focus on the skills that are required to be an effective trainer.

Train-the-trainer refers to training programs that teach subject-matter experts how to design and deliver training programs. With the increasing use of technology in the workplace, more SMEs are being asked to become trainers and attend train-the-trainer programs. To learn more about train-the-trainer programs, see The Trainer's Notebook 8.3, "Train-the-Trainer Fundamentals."

> **Train-the-trainer**
> Training programs that teach subject-matter experts how to design and deliver training programs

---

THE TRAINER'S NOTEBOOK   8.3

TRAIN-THE-TRAINER FUNDAMENTALS

Subject-matter experts (SMEs) are often asked to design and/or deliver a training program because of their unique knowledge, the needs of a particular group of training participants, or the requirements of a specific project. However, they may not have experience as a trainer and will require some training on how to be an effective trainer. Here are some things to consider when you need to train-the-trainer:

1. Explain the specific reasons that the SME was selected for the role.

2. Review the training materials with the SME and make sure they are well scripted and marked up with plenty of visual cues for the trainer.

3. Coach the SME on facilitation skills and provide detailed information about the participants.

4. Give the SME permission to delegate tasks during the training (e.g., a volunteer for clicking through the slides).

5. Prepare the SME by providing a checklist of the basics of engaging facilitation, including setting up the room to meet the participants' needs and establishing rapport with the participants by presenting a friendly demeanour and sharing stories. Incorporate tips such as using interactive activities. Review the checklist with the SME and explain the reasons behind each tip.

6. Discuss adult learners' needs and learning styles so that the SME understands how and why to vary the training activities to maximize learning. Help the SME think about charts, illustrations, and other visuals that would help participants understand the content. Make sure the SME understands the need to design interactive activities that appeal to visual, kinesthetic, and auditory learning styles.

7. Teach the SME how to facilitate a workshop accurately without reading from the leader's guide. Offer tips for remembering content such as creating note cards with key points.

8. Watch the SME conduct a practice session and provide feedback beginning with all the positive behaviours demonstrated and include one or two constructive comments that the SME can work on before the actual training program.

9. Offer assistance during the training with flipcharts or distributing materials.

10. Provide SMEs who must design their programs with PowerPoint templates, sample training materials, and examples they can build on.

11. Provide access to experienced instructional designers who can assist the SME when he/she has questions.

12. Provide the SME with access to a content reviewer to make sure everything is covered clearly and effectively for participants who are not experts.

Source: Adams, T., Kennedy, A., & Marquart, M. (2008, March). The reluctant trainer, *T+D*, *62*(3), 24. Reprinted by permission of Association for Talent Development (ATD).

// THE TRAINEES

The lesson plan cover page indicates that the trainees will be members of the human resources department. This raises another question. Who should attend a training program? This is an important question because money and time can be wasted, and performance problems are likely to continue, if the wrong people attend training and those who require training do not attend.

According to Donald Kirkpatrick, the following four questions need to be asked when selecting participants for a training program[13]:

1. Who can benefit from the training?
2. What programs are required by law or by government edict?
3. Should the training be voluntary or compulsory?
4. Should the participants be segregated by level in the organization, or should two or more levels be included in the same class?

Some employees stand to benefit from a training program given the tasks they perform and the extent to which the training will provide them with knowledge and skills that will help them improve their performance. This was the case at the CBC, where employees at all of its television stations had to learn to use high-definition cameras and equipment. Some training programs are required by law, such as health and safety programs for employees who work with hazardous materials. Other training programs are compulsory for all employees in a particular job category or role. According to Kirkpatrick, some training programs should be compulsory, otherwise some employees who will benefit from the training might not attend.[14]

As for segregating participants by organizational level or including them in the same training session, this really depends on the culture of the organization and the rapport that exists between different levels. The main issue is whether employees will feel comfortable enough to speak and participate if their supervisors are present. If they will, it is often a good idea for different levels to attend a training program together.

Another issue that requires some consideration is the extent to which the trainees belong to different generations and if they should be placed together in a training program. As described in Training Today 8.1, "Training a Multi-Generational Workforce," generations differ in their learning preferences and how a training program should be delivered.

TRAINING TODAY 8.1

TRAINING A MULTI-GENERATIONAL WORKFORCE

In Canada today, we have four distinct generations in the workforce. This is the first time in history that a generational mix of this proportion has existed in this country—and a significant shift is happening, which will reach its peak by 2020.

The workforce includes Traditionalists, born between 1945 and 1949; Baby Boomers (born 1946–1964); Generation X (1965–1981); and Millennials (1982–1990).

Forty percent of senior positions are held by Baby Boomers. But by 2020, Millennials will be the dominant group, one full generation removed from Boomers.

As we are largely a product of our times, the era in which we were born shapes our tastes, beliefs, and work ethic. Because each generation shares a place in history its members tend to develop personalities based on that common experience. While not everyone fits their

(continued)

generational type perfectly, Traditionalists value hard work and order and respect authority. Baby Boomers tend to be competitive and think workers should pay their dues. Gen Xers are more likely to be skeptical and independent-minded. Millennials like teamwork, feedback, and technology.

Being aware of the working styles, preferences, and how each generation believes they should be treated as employees can help organizations deliver effective employee training. By keeping their characteristics in mind, you can cater your training to this multi-generational workforce.

One solution is to ensure you have a mix of learning methods. For example, Millennials tend not to like to read long, detailed case studies, so they need to be replaced with short, timely examples. Boomers like relevancy in their learning, so those examples should be relevant to the workplace and result in actions or knowledge that can be applied to their jobs. Generation Xers and Millennials appreciate feedback, so be sure to provide opportunities to give and receive feedback during the training session. Gen Xers tend to prefer working independently, while Millennials like to work in teams. This is possibly a reflection of how the current education system puts emphasis on group projects, while the education model for Boomers and Gen Xers was for students to sit in rows and work independently. This insight can help you to plan a training session that includes a balance of both.

The key to effective training for a multi-generational workforce is to know your audience. Have a variety of learning methods and be prepared to adapt as you work through the training. And remember, generation is just one dimension of a person. A trainer also needs to keep in mind other facets, including culture, personality, life experiences, and education. This will ensure you deliver the most valuable training that will help all of your employees develop and succeed.

Source: McCarthy, A. (2016, May/June). Train a multi-generational workforce. *Training Magazine*, 53(3), 14. Trainingmag.com

TRAINABILITY TEST

Trainability test
A test that measures an individual's ability to learn and perform training tasks

One way to know whether an employee is ready to attend a training program is to have him/her take a trainability test. A **trainability test** is a test that measures an individual's ability to learn and perform training tasks in order to predict whether an individual will successfully complete a training program.[15]

This is typically done by having individuals take a mini-course or learn a sample of the training that is representative of the content of a training program. They then take a test that measures their learning and performance of the tasks. For example, consulting firm Booz Allen Hamilton used a technical pre-test as part of the criteria to select employees for a skills enhancement training program that was designed to build a pool of technical talent. The selection process involved a highly competitive five-step process.[16]

Trainability tests have been shown to be effective in predicting training success and job performance in many jobs, such as carpentry, welding, dentistry, and forklift operating. Although they have most often been used for psychomotor skills, they are just as applicable for other types of skills and knowledge tests. Training pre-tests can also be used to determine what kind of remedial training an individual might require to prepare them for a training program or to tailor a training program to one's needs. Thus, managers can maximize trainee learning by assessing employees' readiness to learn and trainability prior to training.[17]

Training plan
Indicates who in an organization needs training, the type of training that is needed, and how the training will be delivered

Information on who requires training can be incorporated into a training plan. A **training plan** indicates who in an organization needs training (e.g., human resources staff), the type of training needed (e.g., structured employment interviewing), and how the training will be delivered (e.g., in a formal classroom).[18]

// TRAINING MATERIALS AND EQUIPMENT

All training programs require the use of training materials, supplies, and equipment, and this should be indicated on the lesson plan cover page. The content of a training program as well as the methods and exercises determine the materials, supplies, and equipment that will be required.

Training materials refer to expendable items such as note pads, pens, markers, tape, and so on. Common supplies include computer equipment, a projector, and workbooks or manuals. Handouts such as course outlines that indicate the course objectives, the material to be covered, a schedule of training activities, articles, and copies of the trainer's slides are often required and have to be prepared in advance. Equipment refers to things that have a life beyond a single use, such as projectors, computers, and DVD players. The trainer must identify the materials and equipment that will be required for a training program.[19]

As shown in Table 8.2, the materials and equipment needed for the structured employment interview training program include a TV monitor and DVD player, a DVD on how to conduct a structured employment interview, a computer and projector with screen, a flipchart, pen, paper, and markers. Handouts for trainees include a course outline, readings, a list of the key learning behaviours, and a role-play exercise.

With the determination of the materials and equipment necessary, the cost of training is more easily determined, and the actual training session is more likely to run smoothly.

> **Training materials**
> Expendable items such as note pads, pens, markers, and tape

// TRAINING SITE

The **training site** is the facility or room where the training will take place. Off-the-job training can take place at the organization if rooms are available, at an organization's headquarters, or at a rented facility such as a hotel or conference centre. As indicated in Table 8.2, the structured employment interview training program takes place at the company's learning centre.

Some organizations have their own learning centre for training and development. For example, the Bank of Montreal has a corporate facility called the Institute for Learning. Organizations that do not have a learning centre or training rooms must find suitable facilities to conduct the training. In this case, important concerns are the travel time required for trainees to get to the training site and ensuring that trainees have transportation. If trainees have to stay overnight, plans for transportation, accommodation, and meals will have to be made and included in the training budget. This of course can be expensive and can result in employees being away from work for several days.

Regardless of where a training program takes place, a number of factors need to be considered to ensure the training program runs smoothly. First, the training site should be conducive to learning. This means that the training environment should be comfortable in terms of things like space, lighting, and temperature. This might seem like a trivial point, but have you ever attended a class and the room temperature was on the cold side? Or a classroom that was too crowded and you had to stand or sit on the floor because there was not enough seating? Chances are it caused you some discomfort and interfered with your learning.

Second, the training site should be free of noise and distractions that might interfere with or disrupt learning. How often have you been in a class where you had to strain

> **Training site**
> Facility or room where the training will take place

Moriyama & Teshima Architects

The Bank of Montreal has a corporate learning facility called the Institute for Learning.

to hear the instructor over the chatter coming from outside the classroom? Obviously, noise can interfere with learning. Distractions can also be a problem. This is one reason why it is sometimes preferable to conduct a training program away from the organization. Otherwise, trainees might be tempted to step out of the training session to take care of business. This, of course, is not likely if they are far from their desk and the workplace.

Third, the training site should be set up in a manner that is appropriate for the training program. For example, if trainees will be viewing a DVD, will they be able to see the screen and hear the sound? If trainees will be working in groups, will there be sufficient room for them to move around the room and interact with group members? Are break-out rooms necessary for group work? Are the seats arranged in a way that will allow trainees to interact and work with one another, and will the trainer be able to interact with trainees? Are the chairs movable or fixed? These are important considerations that the trainer needs to determine before the training.

Given the importance of the training room for trainee motivation and learning, trainers should inspect and prepare the room in advance of a training program to ensure that it will be conducive to learning. The trainer should arrive early on the day of the training to make sure that the room is properly set up and that the required equipment has arrived and is functioning. As discussed in the next section, one of the most important things that the trainer needs to prepare is the seating arrangement.

// SEATING ARRANGEMENT

It is easy to understand how important seating is when you consider that many students choose a seat in the first class and then continue to sit in the same seat all term. The seating arrangement is also important because it can facilitate or limit trainee involvement and participation. It can also energize or inhibit trainees, and it communicates the trainer's style.[20]

Figure 8.1 shows examples of different seating arrangements for low, moderate, and high levels of trainee involvement. The low-involvement seating represents a traditional classroom arrangement, in which the instructor is in control and stands or sits at the front of the room behind a desk or a table. With this seating arrangement, communication is one-way and flows from the instructor to trainees. Communication among the trainees is not possible. This arrangement is most common for the lecture method.

When a moderate amount of involvement is desired, the instructor is still at the front of the room. However, trainees are seated around a table, thereby allowing them to interact and exchange ideas with one another. Although the instructor remains in control and one-way communication still dominates, participants can also communicate with and learn from one another.

Finally, with a high-involvement seating arrangement, small groups of trainees are seated together around small tables. As a result, group members can interact and work together on projects. The instructor's role is more of a resource person or a facilitator.

260   Managing Performance through Training and Development   NEL

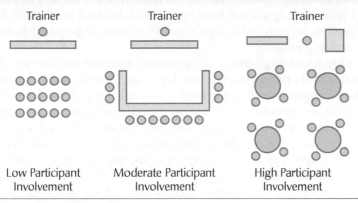

FIGURE 8.1

SEATING ARRANGEMENTS

Trainer	Trainer	Trainer
Low Participant Involvement	Moderate Participant Involvement	High Participant Involvement

Source: Eitington, J. E. (1989). The winning trainer: Winning ways to involve people in learning. Houston, TX: Gulf Publishing Company. Reprinted with permission from Elsevier.

This allows the instructor to present material to the class (the work table and flipchart are at the front of the room), engage the class in discussions, move around the room and listen in on groups, provide help, and spend time with each group while they work on projects and solve problems.[21]

The seating arrangement has important implications for the trainer and trainees and should be determined by the objectives of a training program and the desired level of trainee involvement and interaction. Thus, the trainer needs to carefully choose a seating arrangement that is appropriate for a particular training program and the methods, activities, and exercises that will be used.

// SCHEDULING THE TRAINING PROGRAM

As indicated in Table 8.2, the structured employment interview training program is scheduled as a one-day program. Scheduling a training program must take into consideration a number of factors. In effect, one has to arrange the training schedule to accommodate all of the participants.

For example, when is the best day of the week, time of day, and time of year for employees to attend a training program? When will the participants be available to attend training? This will probably depend on the organization and the nature of its business. Most businesses have periods or seasons when they are especially busy; scheduling a training program during these times is likely to result in some resistance and low attendance.

It is also important to be sensitive to the needs and desires of employees and their supervisors. Would it be preferable to hold the training during office hours or after hours, such as in the evenings or on the weekend? Employees and their supervisors should be consulted to determine the best time for them to attend a training program.[22]

Another factor to consider is the availability of the trainer. Whether the trainers are from the human resources department or elsewhere in the organization, they will likely have responsibilities that will restrict their availability. Trainers from within the organization will have to receive release time from their other duties to prepare and deliver the training program. If the trainers are from outside the organization, they will also have some restrictions regarding their availability and will have to be contracted for a particular date.

A third consideration in scheduling a training program is the availability of the training site, equipment, materials, and so on. If the training site and facilities are used frequently, a training program will have to be scheduled well in advance. In addition, if materials need to be designed or purchased, they must be prepared and available in time for the training program.

Finally, when scheduling a training program one must also consider whether it would be best to offer it all at one time, such as one day versus four two-hour sessions in the case of an eight-hour program, or all in one week versus one day each week for five weeks (or once a month for five months) in the case of a five-day program. Recall from Chapter 4 that this distinction refers to massed versus distributed practice. Massed practice is practice with no rest periods, while distributed practice includes rest intervals. There are also issues of resources and logistics. Sometimes it is just not feasible to conduct a training program over a longer period of time. Kirkpatrick recommends that it is best to spread the training out as an ongoing program, such as a three-hour session once a month.[23]

For more information see Chapter 4, pp. 132–133

// TRAINING ADMINISTRATION

Once the lesson plan has been completed, a number of activities must be undertaken to manage and administer a training program. **Training administration** involves the coordination of all the people and materials involved in a training program. The maintenance of trainee records, training histories, customized learning opportunities, schedules, and course and material inventories is a routine, but necessary, activity.

In addition to tracking registrations for programs, it is also useful to track individual career development and learning plans. As was noted in Chapter 7, learning management systems (LMSs) are often used to do all these things.

Employees and their supervisors have to be informed of the objectives and content of training programs as well as where and when the training will take place. In addition, employees who are required to attend a training program must be notified and enrolled in the program. Trainers must also be informed, since they need to know how many trainees will be attending a training program.

If trainees are to receive training materials prior to a program, arrangements have to be made for this. In addition, all of the materials and equipment must be ordered and prepared in time for the training program. The training site must be booked, and equipment must be made available. In some cases, this might involve renting equipment. As well, supplies such as pens and paper must be ordered.

Finally, the training administrator has to prepare a budget that includes the costs of all of the expenses incurred in the design and delivery of a training program. The calculation of the costs and benefits of training programs is discussed in Chapter 11.

Training administration
The coordination of all the people and materials involved in the training program

// THE ROLE OF ETHICS IN TRAINING AND DEVELOPMENT

Before implementing a training program, it is important to be aware of and understand the role of ethics in training and development. **Ethics** involves the use of systematic thinking about the moral consequences of one's actions and decisions for various

Ethics
The use of systematic thinking about the moral consequences of one's actions and decisions on various stakeholders

TABLE 8.4

ETHICAL GUIDELINES FOR TRAINING AND DEVELOPMENT PROFESSIONALS

Trainers must conduct themselves according to a set of ethical guidelines and standards as follows:

- Voluntary consent: Trainers should not implicitly coerce unwilling or skeptical participants into self-revealing or physical activities.

- Discrimination: Age, sex, race, or handicaps should not be used as barriers to determine who receives training.

- Cost-effectiveness: Training activities should be based on demonstrated utility, should show a demonstrated benefit vis-à-vis costs, and should not be undertaken simply to spend a training budget.

- Accurate portrayal: Claims for the benefits of training need to be accurate; training should be consistent across time and trainers; training materials should be appropriately depicted.

- Competency in training: Teaching methods that do not work, such as talking down to audiences, should be avoided.

- Values: Trainers should believe in the value of what they teach.

Source: Lowman, R. L. (1991). Ethical human resource practice in organizational settings. In D. W. Bray (Ed.), *Working with organizations.* New York: Guilford.

stakeholders. **Stakeholders** are people inside or outside the organization who might be affected by the organization's actions and decisions.

With respect to training and development, ethics involves following a set of standards and principles in the design, delivery, and evaluation of training and development programs. Training professionals must adhere to a set of ethical principles that guide their behaviour and they must serve as role models of proper ethical conduct to the rest of the organization.

One ethical issue of particular concern is refusing to allow some employees to attend a training program, which can result in workplace discrimination and human rights complaints. In fact, there have been a number of cases in which an employee who was denied training filed a complaint of discrimination. The federal *Canadian Human Rights Act* and the provincial human rights codes govern human rights issues such as an employee being denied training.[24]

Table 8.4 describes the kinds of ethical issues and guidelines that are important for training and development professionals.

> **Stakeholders**
> People inside or outside the organization who might be affected by the organization's actions and decisions

// IMPLEMENTING THE TRAINING PROGRAM

Once the lesson plan has been prepared and the administrative activities have been completed, the training program is ready to be implemented. For many trainers and especially novices, this is the most difficult part of the training process. There are, however, a number of important steps to follow when implementing a training program. In this section, we describe how to create a climate for learning and Gagné's nine events of instruction.

LEARNING CLIMATE

When implementing a training program, the trainer has to ensure that the **learning climate** is conducive to learning. This means that trainees should feel relaxed, comfortable, and safe in the training environment. Creating a climate that is conducive to learning involves four elements: pre-arrival factors, greeting participants, the learning facility/environment, and the trainer's style and behaviour.[25]

PRE-ARRIVAL FACTORS

A trainer can begin to create positive perceptions of the learning climate before trainees arrive for training. For example, contacting trainees before the training begins can help set a positive tone. This might just be a welcome message that describes the program and its objectives. However, it can also include information about the location, when the program starts and ends, meals, clothes to wear, what to bring, and so on.

Pre-arrival activities might include pre-work readings or assignments, a pre-session get-together (to hand out materials or perhaps a cocktail party or dinner), or an attempt to find out about trainees' needs, ideas, and input for the program.

GREETING PARTICIPANTS

Trainees might be anxious about the training and some will be skeptical about its value. Others will be upset that they are spending time away from work. Therefore, the trainer should meet and greet participants and make them feel welcome when they arrive for training. A nice touch is to have a welcome message posted on the board or a flipchart in the room. Some trainers like to have trainees write their name on a name card to get them doing something simple when they arrive rather than sitting alone and waiting for the program to start. An early-morning welcome session with coffee and other refreshments can facilitate interactions among trainees and create a relaxed and comfortable atmosphere.

LEARNING FACILITY/ENVIRONMENT

An important factor in trainees' climate perceptions is the training site itself. In this regard, the trainer should ensure that the physical set-up of the training room is attractive, comfortable, bright, relaxing, and clean.

Some of the things that the trainer needs to pay attention to include lighting, noise, space, and room temperature, as discussed earlier. Making sure that drinks, refreshments, and lunch arrive on time is also important for creating a positive training climate.

TRAINER'S STYLE AND BEHAVIOUR

Trainees' perceptions of the learning climate are also based on how the trainer interacts with trainees and conducts the training. If the trainees do not know the trainer, then one of the first things trainers should do is to provide a brief personal introduction about themselves and their involvement in the training program.

The trainer should let trainees know how they can address him/her (e.g., first name is fine) and should address trainees by their first name. He/she should circulate throughout the room during training and at times be seated rather than standing at the front of the room throughout the session. It is also a good idea to take advantage of opportunities to interact with trainees. This can be achieved by mingling with trainees during breaks and joining them at lunch and other meals.

Finally, key to creating a positive learning climate is the style of the trainer. A trainer can create a positive climate by listening with empathy, accepting different ideas, showing sensitivity to the communication process, supporting people who take risks, providing a fun-type atmosphere, stressing opportunities for discovery, making learning gradual, asking for feedback, and making him/herself accessible for questioning.[26]

In summary, creating a positive climate that is conducive to learning is a critical factor in the successful implementation of a training program. Also important is how the trainer actually delivers the training, our next topic.

Robert Gagné is responsible for the development of the nine events of instruction

GAGNÉ'S NINE EVENTS OF INSTRUCTION

How should a trainer deliver a training program? According to Robert Gagné, a training program should have nine events of instruction. **Events of instruction** are external events that are designed to help learning occur. Their purpose is to stimulate and activate trainees' internal learning processes, which will then lead to learning.[27] You might notice that some of the design principles discussed in previous chapters are incorporated into the events of instruction.

Table 8.5 lists Gagné's nine events of instruction along with the relevant training design principles.[28] Let's now take a closer look at the nine events of instruction.

> **Events of instruction** External events that are designed to help learning occur

TABLE 8.5

GAGNÉ'S NINE EVENTS OF INSTRUCTION AND TRAINING DESIGN PRINCIPLES

Gagné's nine events of instruction reflect important principles of training design discussed in previous chapters.

1. *Gain attention.* Reflects adult learners' need to know why they are learning something and their training motivation.

2. *Describe the objectives.* This follows from the purpose of training objectives for trainees. It also reflects adult learners' need to know how the learning relates to their job, and the importance of goals as indicated in goal-setting theory.

3. *Stimulate recall of prior knowledge.* Reflects adult learners' existing knowledge and experience and how that can be linked to the training material. Providing a framework for learning is similar to an advance organizer.

4. *Present the material to be learned.* Reflects task sequencing and incorporating adult learners' job-relevant experiences into the training content.

TABLE 8.5 *(Continued)*
GAGNÉ'S NINE EVENTS OF INSTRUCTION AND TRAINING DESIGN PRINCIPLES
5. *Provide guidance for learning.* Reflects the use of metacognitive strategies, attentional advice, and advance organizers.
6. *Elicit performance practice.* Reflects the importance of active practice and experiential training methods (e.g., role plays, games, simulations).
7. *Provide informative feedback.* Reflects the importance of feedback and knowledge of results during practice.
8. *Assess performance.* Reflects the importance of linking training objectives to trainee learning and ensuring that the objectives are being met as well as the stages of learning.
9. *Enhance retention and transfer.* Reflects generalization from conditioning theory and self-regulation and self-efficacy from social cognitive theory.

1. GAIN ATTENTION

The first thing a trainer needs to do is draw trainees into the learning process. In other words, get the attention of trainees (recall the earlier discussion of learner engagement). This can be achieved in a number of ways. For example, the trainer might present a thought-provoking problem.

For the structured employment interview training program, the trainer might ask trainees, "What should we do to ensure that we hire great employees?" Other questions might focus trainees on the problem at hand and the need for training, such as "How do you conduct a valid employment interview?" Or the trainer might point out that bad hiring is costing the organization thousands of dollars.

Having the CEO make an impassioned plea on the importance of the training program can also get the attention of trainees. Getting trainees interested, engaged, and motivated is an important way to begin a training program. Trainees should know why the training program is important for them and the organization.

2. DESCRIBE THE OBJECTIVES

For more information see Chapter 4, p. 118

In Chapter 4, we discussed the purpose of training objectives for trainees, trainers, and managers (refer to Table 4.2). Therefore, the trainer must communicate to trainees what they will learn in a training program, what to expect, and what they will be able to accomplish at the end of the program. Trainees should understand what they will learn and how they will be able to use it on the job.

The trainer might even provide a demonstration of the desired performance to help trainees form a mental picture of the skill to be performed. This will help trainees begin to focus on what they will need to learn and do after training and think about goals for learning.

3. STIMULATE RECALL OF PRIOR KNOWLEDGE

It is important to show trainees that they already know some things that are related to what they will learn in training. This enables trainees to think about what they know and can do that is related to what they will learn in the training program.

You might recall from the discussion of andragogy and adult learning theory in Chapter 2 that adults have a great deal of knowledge and work-related experience that the trainer should ask about and incorporate into the training. One way to stimulate recall of prior knowledge is for the trainer to discuss what trainees already know that is relevant to the training material (facts, rules, procedures, or skills).

The trainer might also provide a framework to help trainees learn and retain the training material. By providing a solid grounding, trainees will feel more confident about their ability to learn. For example, trainees in the structured employment interview training program might begin to think about what they have already learned about hiring and interviewing and how they currently conduct employment interviews.

For more information see Chapter 2, p. 59

4. PRESENT THE MATERIAL TO BE LEARNED

The organization and presentation of the training material should be done in a logical and consistent manner. As discussed in Chapter 4, this involves teaching the material in a meaningful sequence or one sub-task at a time (i.e., task sequencing). The trainer can ensure learning and understanding by asking questions at various points during the training and by asking trainees to provide examples from their own work experience.

For the structured employment interview training, the trainer might present each of the seven key behaviours in a logical order and ask trainees how they perform the behaviours when conducting employment interviews (e.g., How do you decide what questions to ask job candidates?).

For more information see Chapter 4, p. 133

5. PROVIDE GUIDANCE FOR LEARNING

The trainer should provide trainees with guidance and direction on how best to learn the material. This can be done by providing trainees with relevant examples that demonstrate what they need to learn and asking questions to help them generate ideas and solutions. The combination of examples, questions, and discussion should help guide trainees toward the main learning points.

6. ELICIT PERFORMANCE PRACTICE

Trainees should be given the opportunity to practise and apply the training material. You might recall from Chapter 4 that providing trainees with opportunities to practise performing a task or using knowledge during training is called active practice. Trainers should provide sufficient time for trainees to do something with the information they have received during training.

In a training program on the employment interview, trainees have the opportunity to practise conducting an interview. If they have been taught seven key learning points, they practise them in a mock interview during training.

For more information see Chapter 4, p. 126

7. PROVIDE INFORMATIVE FEEDBACK

Trainees should receive feedback on their performance during training. Recall the discussion of feedback and knowledge of results in Chapter 4, where we described the importance of feedback as a condition of practice during training. It is essential that

For more information see Chapter 4, p. 134

trainees know and understand what they did correctly, what they did wrong, and how to correct what they did wrong to improve their performance. Trainees should leave training with an understanding of what they can do well and what they need to improve.

8. ASSESS PERFORMANCE

For more information see Chapter 2, pp. 46–50

It is important to test trainees on their learning during and after a training program. Ideally, learning should be assessed after each topic is completed. The assessment of learning can be declarative (recall the discussion of learning outcomes and the stages of learning in Chapter 2), in which case trainees are simply asked to recall information. Or, the assessment of learning can involve knowledge compilation or procedural knowledge, in which case trainees have to explain how they would do something or display the learned behaviour in a role play or behavioural demonstration. The assessment of performance can involve a formal test, or it might simply involve an informal question-and-answer session. The main issue is to ensure that trainees have learned the material before moving on to new topics.

9. ENHANCE RETENTION AND TRANSFER

Trainees need to know how their learning can be used and applied on the job. Therefore, it is important that trainers discuss how the training material can be applied on the job and in actual work situations.

The trainer might show trainees how the material they are learning applies to actual situations that they will encounter at work. Asking trainees to describe situations in which they will be able to use the training content in their job can also enhance retention and transfer. More detail about transfer of training and what a trainer can do to facilitate it is described in Chapter 9.

CLOSING A TRAINING PROGRAM

Once a training program has ended, the trainer must close the program. Like the rest of the program, the closing should be well planned and include a closing activity that signals the successful completion of the program. Some kind of event or form of recognition is common, such as a ceremony in which certificates are awarded to trainees who have completed the program. The lasting impression following the closing should be that the next step is a change in behaviour and performance.[29]

// TRAINING DELIVERY PROBLEMS

In this last section of the chapter, we consider some of the problems that trainers might experience during the delivery of a training program. One of the most common problems is an uncooperative and difficult trainee. While most trainees are cooperative, some can make it difficult for a trainer to deliver a training program by talking too much, putting others down, complaining, displaying negative or hostile behaviour, or just being plain irritating.

TABLE 8.6

TYPES OF PROBLEM PARTICIPANTS

Some of the most common types of problem participants in training include the following:

1. *The hesitant one.* Shy, reluctant, and silent most of the time.
2. *The monopolizer.* The "big talker" who will use up all of the available air time if permitted.
3. *The voice of experience.* Has a strong need to be heard and to bring in incidents and anecdotes that are tedious and unnecessary.
4. *The arguer.* Constantly looks for opportunities to disagree, to show up the other participants and the trainer.
5. *The non-listener.* Tends to interrupt, cuts others off, leaps in before others have had their say, and does not listen to others.
6. *The idea zapper.* Puts down other participants' ideas and anything new or different.
7. *The complainer.* A problem magnifier who finds the world unfair and is a specialist in blaming and fault-finding.
8. *The rigid one.* Staunchly takes a position on an issue and will rarely, if ever, move from it.
9. *The hostile one.* Presents highly hostile questions that are designed to embarrass or inflame the trainer.
10. *The angry one.* Will find loopholes in your ideas and present impossible "what-if" scenarios.
11. *The negative one.* Finds the gloomy side of things and will dredge up gripes, past grievances, and cantankerous complaints.
12. *The clown.* Has an abundance of ill-fitting and sometimes irritating and annoying humour.
13. *The show-off.* Likes to parade his/her knowledge before everyone.
14. *The tangent-taker.* Has interesting inputs but they do not relate to the topic.

Source: Eitington, J. E. (1989). *The winning trainer: Winning ways to involve people in learning.* Houston, TX: Gulf Publishing Company. Reprinted with permission from Elsevier.

Table 8.6 lists different types of problem participants. Dealing with problem participants requires patience and avoiding arguments and put-downs. In most cases, it is best to deal with them politely and, if possible, let the group decide how to manage them.[30]

To learn about the types of problems that a trainer might encounter, Richard Swanson and Sandra Falkman conducted a study in which they asked novice trainers about the problems they have had when delivering a training program. After analyzing the responses, the authors identified the following 12 common training delivery problems[31]:

1. *Fear.* Fear that is due to a lack of confidence and a feeling of anxiety while delivering the training program.
2. *Credibility.* The perception that they lack credibility in the eyes of the trainees as subject-matter experts.
3. *Personal experiences.* A lack of stories about personal experiences that can be used to relate to the training content.
4. *Difficult learners.* Don't know how to handle problem trainees who may be angry, passive, or dominating.
5. *Participation.* Difficulty getting trainees to participate.

6. *Timing.* Trouble with the timing and pacing of the training material and worries about having too much or too little material.

7. *Adjusting instruction.* Difficulty adjusting the training material to the needs of trainees or being able to redesign the presentation of material during delivery.

8. *Questions.* Difficulty using questions effectively and responding to difficult questions.

9. *Feedback.* Unable to read trainees and to use feedback and evaluations effectively.

10. *Media, materials, facilities.* Concerns about how to use media and training materials.

11. *Opening, closing techniques.* The need for techniques to use as ice-breakers, introductions, and effective summaries and closings.

12. *Dependence on notes.* Feeling too dependent on notes and having trouble presenting the material without them.

These 12 common delivery problems of novice trainers have three basic themes:

1. Problems pertaining to the trainer
2. Problems pertaining to how the trainer relates to the trainees
3. Problems pertaining to presentation techniques

The authors also asked expert trainers for strategies and solutions for dealing with the 12 delivery problems. For example, to deal with the problem of fear, a trainer should be well prepared, use ice-breakers, begin with an activity that relaxes the trainees and gets them talking and involved, and acknowledge his/her own fear, understanding that it is normal.[32]

See The Trainer's Notebook 8.4, "Solutions to Training Delivery Problems," for solutions to all 12 delivery problems.

THE TRAINER'S NOTEBOOK   8.4

SOLUTIONS TO TRAINING DELIVERY PROBLEMS

1. **Fear.**
   A. Be well prepared and have a detailed lesson plan.
   B. Use ice-breakers and begin with an activity that relaxes trainees.
   C. Acknowledge the fear and use self-talk and relaxation exercises prior to the training.

2. **Credibility.**
   A. Don't apologize. Be honest about your knowledge of the subject.
   B. Have the attitude of an expert and be well prepared and organized.
   C. Share personal background and talk about your area of expertise and experiences.

3. **Personal experiences.**
   A. Relate personal experiences.
   B. Report experiences of others and have trainees share their experiences.
   C. Use analogies, refer to movies or famous people who relate to the subject.

4. **Difficult learners.**
   A. Confront the problem learner and talk to them to determine the problem.
   B. Circumvent dominating behaviour by using non-verbal behaviour such as breaking eye contact or standing with your back to the person.
   C. Use small groups to overcome timid behaviour and structure exercises where a wide range of participation is encouraged.

5. **Participation.**

   A. Ask open-ended questions and provide positive feedback when trainees participate.

   B. Plan small-group activities such as dyads, case studies, and role plays to increase participation.

   C. Invite participation by structuring activities to allow trainees to share early in the program.

6. **Timing.**

   A. Plan for too much material and prioritize activities so that some can be omitted if necessary.

   B. Practise presenting the material many times so that you know where you should be at 15-minute intervals.

7. **Adjusting instruction.**

   A. Determine the needs of the group early in the training and structure activities based on them.

   B. Request feedback by asking trainees how they feel about the training during breaks or periodically during the training.

   C. Redesign the program during breaks and have a contingency plan in place.

8. **Questions.**

   Answering questions

   A. Anticipate questions by writing out key questions that trainees might have.

   B. Paraphrase and repeat a question so everyone hears the question and understands it.

   C. Redirect questions you can't answer back to the trainees and try to find answers during the break.

   Asking questions

   A. Ask concise and simple questions and provide enough time for trainees to answer.

9. **Feedback.**

   A. Solicit informal feedback during training or breaks on whether the training is meeting their needs and expectations; watch for non-verbal cues.

   B. Do summative evaluations at the conclusion of the training to determine whether the objectives and needs of trainees have been met.

10. **Media, materials, facilities.**

    Media

    A. Know how to operate every piece of equipment you will use.

    B. Have back-ups such as extra bulbs, extension cords, markers, tape, and so on, as well as bringing the material in another medium in case one has problems.

    C. Enlist assistance from trainees if you have a problem and need help.

    Materials

    A. Be prepared and have all the material placed at trainees' workplace [in the training room] or ready for distribution.

    Facilities

    A. Visit facility beforehand to see the layout of the room and where things are located and how to set up.

    B. Arrive at least one hour early to set up and handle any problems.

11. **Opening, closing techniques.**

    Openings

    A. Develop a file of ideas based on experimentation and observation.

    B. Develop and memorize a great opening.

    C. Relax trainees by greeting them when they enter, taking time for introductions, and creating a relaxed atmosphere.

    Closings

    A. Provide a simple and concise summary of the course contents using objectives or the initial model.

    B. Thank participants for their time and contribution to the course.

12. **Dependence on notes.**

    A. Notes are necessary.

    B. Use cards with an outline or key words as prompts.

    C. Use visuals such as notes on the frames of transparencies or your copy of the handouts.

    D. Practise and learn the script so you can deliver it from the key words on your note cards.

Source: Republished with permission of Jossey-Bass Inc., from Swanson, R. A., & Falkman, S. K. (1997). Training delivery problems and solutions: Identification of novice trainer problems and expert trainer solutions. *Human Resource Development Quarterly, 8*(4), 305–314. Permission conveyed through Copyright Clearance Center, Inc.

// SUMMARY

This chapter described the steps involved in training delivery. We began the chapter with the development of the lesson plan, which describes how a training program will proceed and how it will be implemented. This was followed by a description of the characteristics of effective trainers and how to determine which trainees should attend a training program. We also described the training materials and equipment, the training site and seating arrangement, scheduling a program, training administration, and the role of ethics in training and development. We then described how to create a positive climate for learning and Gagné's nine events of instruction. The chapter concluded with a discussion of common training delivery problems and solutions.

KEY TERMS

ethics, p. 262
events of instruction p. 265
learning climate p. 264
lesson p. 251
lesson plan p. 250
seductive details p. 255
seductive details effect p. 255
stakeholders p. 263
subject-matter expert (SME) p. 254
train-the-trainer p. 256
trainability test p. 258
trainer expressiveness p. 254
training administration p. 262
training materials p. 259
training plan p. 258
training site p. 259

DISCUSSION QUESTIONS

1. Discuss Gagné's nine events of instruction and how they relate to training design principles and adult learning theory.

2. What are some of the common problems and solutions encountered in training delivery?

3. What are the characteristics of a good trainer, and what effect do these characteristics have on learning? Do you think you can learn to be a good trainer, or is it something you are born with?

4. How can you decide whether an employee should attend a training program?

5. Describe the different types of problem trainees and how a trainer might manage them during training.

6. What factors need to be considered when deciding on a training site?

7. Why is it important for subject-matter experts to design and/or deliver training programs? What can organizations do to prepare SMEs for delivering training programs?

8. What is a train-the-trainer program, and how would you proceed if you had to develop and deliver one?

9. What are seductive details? Should they be included in the delivery of a training program? If yes, explain how to do this and provide some examples. What is the seductive details effect and what are its implications?

10. What is the meaning of "ethics" and what are some of the ethical issues that training professionals are likely to face?

THE GREAT TRAINING DEBATE

1. Debate the following: Great trainers are born, not made.
2. Debate the following: All training programs should be compulsory.

EXERCISES

IN-CLASS

1. Think about the last time you attended a course or training program. How effective was the instructor/trainer and what effect did this effectiveness have on your training motivation and learning? What was it about the instructor/trainer that had a positive or negative effect on your motivation and learning? What could the instructor/trainer have done differently to improve your motivation and learning?

2. How expressive are you as a trainer? To find out and improve your expressiveness, prepare a short lecture (5 to 10 minutes) on a topic of interest to you or perhaps something on training from the text. Then give your lecture to the class. The class can then evaluate your verbal and non-verbal expressiveness. Make a list of the things you can do to improve your expressiveness. Be sure to refer to your verbal and non-verbal behaviour.

3. Choose a class you are taking and evaluate your instructor's use of Gagné's nine events of instruction. Evaluate the instructor on each of the following events of instruction using a 5-point scale where 1 = strongly disagree, 2 = disagree, 3 = neither agree nor disagree, 4 = agree, and 5 = strongly agree.

   The instructor does this event during most classes:
   - gain attention
   - describe the objectives
   - stimulate recall of prior knowledge
   - present the material to be learned
   - provide guidance for learning
   - elicit performance practice
   - provide informative feedback
   - assess performance
   - enhance retention and transfer

   Based on your evaluation, how effective was your instructor? How can he/she improve?

4. Recall a training program that you attended in a previous or in a current job. Describe the extent to which the trainer used Gagné's nine events of instruction. Provide specific examples of how each event was applied. How effective was the training program, and what might the trainer have done differently to make it more effective?

5. Consider some of the factors that make a training site conducive to learning. Now consider the room of one of your courses. Is the room adequate for learning? What factors, if any, affect your ability to learn? What needs to be improved?

6. Think about the last time you attended a training program, or about one of the courses you are currently taking. Describe the climate for learning and its effect on your motivation, engagement, learning, and satisfaction with the program or course. What could the trainer or instructor have done to improve the climate?

7. Think about the last time you attended a training program, or one of the courses you are currently taking. Describe the seating arrangement and its effect on your motivation, engagement, learning, and satisfaction with the program or course. Do you think the seating arrangement was/is appropriate? If you could change the seating arrangement, how would you change it? Why?

8. Consider the ethics of the most recent training experience you have had in a current job or in a previous job. Review the six ethical guidelines listed in Table 8.4 and use them to determine the extent to which the training program was conducted in an ethical manner. Based on your analysis, were the trainer and the training program ethical? What should have been done differently to make the program more ethical? Be prepared to explain and defend your answer.

IN-THE-FIELD

1. Contact the human resources department of an organization and request a meeting with somebody in the department who you can interview about the organization's training programs. Develop some questions to learn about each of the following issues with respect to a particular training program that the organization has implemented.

   - Was a detailed lesson plan prepared for the program? If not, why? If so, what things were included in it?
   - Who is the trainer of the program and how was he or she chosen?
   - Who were the trainees and how and why were they chosen to attend the program?
   - What training materials and equipment were used?
   - Describe the training site and why it was chosen.
   - Describe the seating arrangement and why it was chosen.
   - Describe the scheduling of the training program and how it was determined.
   - Who administered and coordinated the training program? What did this involve?
   - How was the training program implemented (refer to Gagné's nine events of instruction)?
   - What are some problems that have occurred in the delivery of the training program? What strategies are used to deal with them?

   Based on the information you have acquired, how effectively do you think each of the training delivery activities was performed? List some recommendations for improvement.

2. To find out what it means to be a Certified Training Practitioner (CTP) and a Certified Training and Development Professional (CTDP) in Canada, visit the Institute for Performance and Learning at http://performanceandlearning.ca/ and click on "Certification" and then "Get certified."

Answer the following questions:

a. What does it mean to be a CTP and a CTDP?

b. What are the objectives and requirements of a CTP and a CTDP?

c. Describe the CTP and CTDP process.

CASE INCIDENT

TRAINING THE TRAINER AT THE RUNNING ROOM

The Running Room is a family-owned business and North America's largest specialty retailer of sporting goods, apparel and footwear for runners and walkers. The company currently operates 110 corporately owned stores in Canada and the United States and has plans for expansion. The Running Room does not have an HR department and relies heavily on a train-the-trainer approach to training. The store managers are in effect the human resource managers and training takes place at the store level.

Each year, all store managers are brought together to talk about training issues, initiatives, and challenges. The focus is usually floor sales training because customer service on the floor is the essence of the business. Training is dynamic and interactive and does not rely on lectures. Role playing is used to teach such things as how to greet customers, how to do merchandising, how to handle security, and how to sell. The goal is to make it fun and enjoyable.

QUESTIONS

1. What do you think about the train-the-trainer approach to training used at the Running Room? What are the advantages and disadvantages?

2. As the company grows and expands, do you think it will have to change its approach to training and development? If so, how should it change and why?

Source: Rabinovitch, R. (2004, May 17). Close up: Training and development. *Canadian HR Reporter*, p. 7. Reprinted by permission of Canadian HR Reporter. © Copyright Thomson Reuters Canada Ltd., (2004), Toronto, Ontario, 1-800-387-5164. Web: www.hrreporter.com; www.runningroom.com

CASE STUDY   THE HOUGHTON REFRIGERATION COMPANY

Houghton Refrigeration Company builds refrigerators for large appliance companies. It employs about 300 people, mostly assembly line workers, and is located in a small town in Ohio. The company typically builds, on a contract basis, chest-type freezers and small bar-type refrigerators. On occasion, however, it also builds standard-size refrigerators. The president of the company is a former engineer, as are most of the other executives. These individuals are very knowledgeable about engineering, but have received little training in the basic principles of management.

During the summer months, volume at the factory increases significantly, and the company needs to hire about 40 new employees to handle the heavy workload. Most of these new employees are college students who attend a small private college located about 15 minutes from the plant. Some high school students are hired as well.

When a new employee is hired, the company asks him or her to complete an application blank and then to show up at the plant gate ready for work. Employees receive no orientation. The worker is shown to a work station and, after a minimum amount of on-the-job training, the new employee is expected to start performing a job. Most of the jobs are quite simple and the training is typically completed within 10 minutes. The first-line supervisor usually shows the employee how to do a job once, then watches while the employee does the job once, leaves, and comes back about 20 minutes later to see how the employee is progressing. Typical jobs at the plant include screwing 14 screws into the sides of a freezer, placing a piece of insulation into the freezer lid, and handing out supplies from the tool room.

The company has had excellent experience with college students over the years. Much of the success can be attributed to the older workers coming to the aid of the new employees when difficulties arise. Most new employees are able to perform their jobs reasonably well after their on-the-job training is completed. However, when unexpected difficulties arise, they are usually not prepared for them and therefore need assistance from others.

The older workers have been especially helpful to students working in the "press room." However, Joe Gleason, the first-line supervisor there, finds it amusing to belittle the college students whenever they make any mistakes. He relishes showing a student once how to use a press to bend a small piece of metal, then exclaims, "You're a hot-shot college student; now let's see you do it." He then watches impatiently while the student invariably makes a mistake and then jokingly announces for all to hear, "That's wrong! How did you ever get into college anyway? Try it again, dummy."

One summer, the company experienced a rash of injuries to its employees. Although most of the injuries were minor, the company felt it imperative to conduct a series of short training programs on safe material-handling techniques. The company president was at a loss as to who should conduct the training. The human resource director was a 64-year-old former engineer who was about to retire and was a poor speaker. The only other employee in the human resource department was a new 19-year-old secretary who knew nothing about proper handling techniques. Out of desperation, the president finally decided to ask Bill Young, the first-line supervisor of the "lid-line," to conduct the training.

Bill had recently attended a training program himself on safety and was active in the Red Cross. Bill reluctantly agreed to conduct the training. It was to be done on a departmental basis with small groups of 10 to 15 employees attending each session.

At the first of these training sessions Bill Young nervously stood up in front of 14 employees, many of whom were college students, and read his presentation in a monotone voice. His entire speech lasted about one minute and consisted of the following text:

> Statistics show that an average of 30 persons injure their backs on the job each day in this state. None of us wants to become a "statistic."
>
> The first thing that should be done before lifting an object is to look it over and decide whether you can handle it alone or if help is needed. Get help if there's any doubt as to whether the load is safely within your capacity.

Next, look over the area where you're going to be carrying the object. Make sure it's clear of obstacles. You may have to do a little housekeeping before moving your load. After you have checked out the load and route you're going to travel, the following steps should be taken for your safety in lifting:

1. Get a good footing close to the load.
2. Place your feet 8 to 12 inches apart.
3. Bend your knees to grasp the load.
4. Bend your knees outward, straddling the load.
5. Get a firm grip.
6. Keep the load close to your body.
7. Lift gradually.

Once you've lifted the load, you'll eventually have to set it down. So bend your legs again and follow the lifting procedures in reverse. Make sure that your fingers clear the pinch points. And, finally, it's a good idea to set one corner down first.

After Bill's speech ended, the employees immediately returned to work. By the end of the day, however, everyone in the plant had heard about the training fiasco and all except the president were laughing about it.

Source: From Nkomo/Fottler/Mcafee. *Applications in Human Resource Management*, 5E. © 2005 South-Western, a part of Cengage, Inc. Reproduced by permission. www.cengage.com/permissions

QUESTIONS

1. Comment on the president's choice to have Bill Young conduct the training. Was it a good idea for Bill to be the trainer? How else might the president have chosen a trainer?

2. How effective was Bill Young as a trainer? What characteristics of an effective trainer did he display and which did he not display? What could he have done to make the training more effective?

3. Discuss how the company determined who should attend the training program. Was this a good way to decide who should attend training? How else might they have decided who the trainees should be?

4. Describe the climate for learning. How positive was it? What might Bill Young have done to create a more positive learning climate?

5. Evaluate Bill Young's delivery of the training program in terms of Gagné's nine events of instruction. What events did he use and which ones were absent? Describe what he might have done differently if he had used all nine of Gagné's events of instruction.

6. What were the most serious problems in Bill's delivery of the training program? What advice would you give Bill next time he delivers the training program?

FLASHBACK QUESTIONS

1. Comment on the on-job-training that new employees receive. What is the approach used (see Table 6.2 in Chapter 6)? Is it effective?

2. To what extent is Houghton's on-the-job training consistent with job instruction training? What changes are necessary to better reflect the steps of job instruction training?

3. Comment on Joe Gleason's approach to on-the-job training. What effect might his approach have on the student workers? If you were the company president, what would you say to him?

4. Comment on Bill Young's training method. What training method did he use (refer to Table 5.1 in Chapter 5)? How effective was it?

5. What other instructional methods might have made Bill Young's training program more effective? Refer to Table 5.1 in Chapter 5.

6. If you were to redesign the training program that was delivered by Bill Young, what changes would you make? Refer to the training design activities in Table 4.1 in Chapter 4 to answer this question.

FLASH FORWARD QUESTION

1. How likely is it that employees who attended the training program will apply what they learned on the job? What are some of the reasons that they might not apply the training on the job? What can be done to increase the likelihood that employees will apply the training on the job?

REWRITE THE CASE QUESTION: EVENTS OF INSTRUCTION

Rewrite the case so that Bill Young uses Gagné's nine events of instruction. In other words, describe what he does and how he delivers the training for each of the nine events of instruction.

RUNNING CASE DIRTY POOLS

QUESTIONS

Refer to the case at the end of Chapter 1 to answer the following questions.

1. Develop a lesson plan for a training program for pool operators and employees. Be sure to indicate the training objective, classroom requirements, training materials and equipment, supplies, and handouts. Also include the sequence of activities and events that will occur during the training program and the timing of them.

2. Who should be the trainer for a training program to train pool operators and employees? Explain your answer.

3. Explain how you would use Gagné's nine events of instruction to train pool operators and employees. Be sure to give specific examples for each event of instruction.

// REFERENCES

1. Based on Silliker, A. (2013, April 22). Staff instructors offer training at CBC. *Canadian HR Reporter*, *26*(8), 10; CBC Annual Report 2015–2016. About us, Our operations. Retrieved from http:/www.cbc.radio-canada.ca/site/annual-reports/2015-2016/about-us/our-operations-en.html

2. Carnevale, A. P., Gainer, L. J., & Meltzer, A. S. (1990). *Workplace basics training manual*. San Francisco, CA: Jossey-Bass.

3. Carnevale et al. (1990).

4. Nadler, L. (1982). *Designing training programs: The critical events model*. Reading, MA: Addison-Wesley.

5. Donaldson, L., & Scannell, E. E. (1986). *Human resource development: The new trainer's guide* (2nd ed.). Reading, MA: Addison-Wesley.

6. Nadler (1982).

7. Nadler (1982).

8. Towler, A. J., & Dipboye, R. L. (2001). Effects of trainer expressiveness, organization, and trainee goal orientation on training outcomes. *Journal of Applied Psychology*, *86*, 664–673.

9. Towler, A. (2009). Effects of trainer expressiveness, seductive details, and trainee goal orientation on training outcomes. *Human Resource Development Quarterly*, *20*, 65–84.

10. Rey, G. D. (2012). A review of research and a meta-analysis of the seductive detail effect. *Educational Research Review*, *7*, 216–237; Sitzmann, T., & Johnson, S. (2014). The paradox of seduction by irrelevant details: How irrelevant information helps and hinders self-regulated learning. *Learning and Individual Differences*, *34*, 1–11.

11. Towler (2009); Rey (2012); Sitzmann & Johnson (2014).

12. Towler & Dipboye (2001).

13. Kirkpatrick, D. L. (1994). *Evaluating training programs: The four levels.* San Francisco, CA: Berrett-Koehler.

14. Kirkpatrick (1994).

15. Tannenbaum, S. I., & Yukl, G. (1992). Training and development in work organizations. *Annual Review of Psychology*, *43*, 399–441.

16. Anonymous (2016). Outstanding training initiatives—Booz Allen Hamilton: Tech Tank. *Training Magazine*, *53*(5), 54–55.

17. Goldstein, I. L., & Ford, J. K. (2002). *Training in organizations*. Belmont, CA: Wadsworth.

18. Ford, J. K., Major, D. A., Seaton, F. W., & Felber, H. K. (1993). Effects of organizational, training system, and individual characteristics on training director scanning practices. *Human Resource Development Quarterly*, *4*, 333–351.

19. Nadler, L., & Nadler, Z. (1994). *Designing training programs*. Houston, TX: Gulf Publishing.

20. Eitington, J. E. (1989). *The winning trainer*. Houston, TX: Gulf Publishing.

21. Eitington (1989).

22. Kirkpatrick (1994).

23. Kirkpatrick (1994).

24. Macdonald, N. C. (2004, November 22). Workplace discrimination prohibited—and that includes training. *Canadian HR Reporter*, *17*(2), G3, G11.

25. Eitington (1989).

26. Eitington (1989).

27. Gagné, R. M., Wager, W. W., Golas, K. C., & Keller, J. M. (2005). *Principles of instructional design* (5th ed.). Belmont, CA: Wadsworth.

28. Gagné et al. (2005); Zemke, R. (1999). Toward a science of training. *Training Magazine*, *36*(7), 32–36.

29. Nadler & Nadler (1994).

30. Eitington (1989).

31. Republished with permission of Jossey-Bass Inc., from Swanson, R. A. & Falkman, S. K. (1997). Training delivery problems and solutions: Identification of novice trainer problems and expert trainer solutions. *Human Resource Development Quarterly*, *8*(4), 305–314. Permission conveyed through Copyright Clearance Center, Inc.

32. Swanson & Falkman (1997).

CHAPTER 9

TRANSFER OF TRAINING

CHAPTER LEARNING OUTCOMES

AFTER READING THIS CHAPTER, YOU SHOULD BE ABLE TO:

- compare and contrast positive, negative, zero, far, near, horizontal, and vertical transfer
- explain the major barriers to transfer of training, when they occur, and who is responsible for them
- describe the factors that influence the transfer of training using Baldwin and Ford's model
- explain what managers, trainers, and trainees can do before, during, and after training to improve the transfer of training
- explain how to use transfer of training interventions and post-training supplements to improve the transfer of training
- analyze the transfer system and its implications for improving the transfer of training

Courtesy of Nutrien Ltd

Nutrien embarked on a total renewal of its company training process with the goal of becoming one of the safest resource companies in the world.

In January of 2018, Potash Corporation of Saskatchewan (PotashCorp) and Agrium Inc. completed a merger creating Nutrien Ltd., the world's largest provider of crop nutrients, inputs, and services. Nutrien has approximately 20 000 employees with operations and investments in 14 countries.

Several years ago, Nutrien (PotashCorp before the merger) wanted a training program that would stay with participants long after the training ended. According to Candace Laing, Nutrien senior director of sustainability and stakeholder relations, "Lots of companies know what good looks like, but actually making it stick—the transfer of learning—is difficult. You can give people a good dip into a one-day course but then how do you sustain it?"

In 2014, Nutrien embarked on a total renewal of its company training process with the goal of becoming one of the safest resource companies in the world. The company combined the power of the HR department and the safety and health team and came up with a coaching-for-safety engagement training program, developed in-house.

The company's new way of training incorporates continuous learning, which includes education (an eight-hour classroom session), experience (on-site coaching), exposure (time with other leaders), and environment (improvement via feedback and action plans). The training begins with a one-day classroom session for team leaders and is designed to promote continuous safety learning through a focus on coaching techniques.

In the training session, participants work on creating coaching strategies that reinforce the company's hazard identification, mitigating, and coaching process, which is Nutrien's company-wide safety standard. "All leaders need the ability to facilitate effective and engaging dialogue about safety every day with their team members," says Laing.

The training promotes a set of 15 behaviours, including visibility on job sites, discussion of safety before shifts, getting to know employees, addressing safety problems by collaboration, and creating an atmosphere where workers feel comfortable.

In 2015, 489 leaders of the company's Canadian operations attended the classroom training course. Of those, 363 received in-field coaching afterward. Company-wide, 90 percent of supervisors have so far received the training. Nutrien also employs follow-up coaching in the field to ensure continuous learning.

Nutrien now has eight safety leadership coaches who visit all sites and provide follow-up instruction to the managers who have taken the coach-for-safety engagement program. Coaches also provide weekly updates to management.

Leaders also receive feedback from crew members through a survey. From there, they are expected to create individual action plans. These plans and their implementation are regularly tracked by the company.

"Sites are held accountable for ensuring supervisors receive the training, coaching, and crew feedback, and the results of the site assessments are used to help calculate the site's resulting amount for the annual short-term incentive plan," says Laing.

The company has also started a half-day program for workers. This was initiated after hearing positive feedback from the supervisors who attended the coaching course, so Nutrien reworked the course for front-line workers. The company knew the employee training had to stick, so it worked through a number of pilots to get it just right.

Nutrien (PotashCorp) has won awards for its training program as well as for safety. In 2017, it received the Green Cross Safety Excellence Award from the National Safety Council in the United States.

Sources: Based on Dujay, J. (2016). Coaching at the heart of PotashCorp's training program. *Canadian HR Reporter, 29*(15), 18. Reprinted by permission of *Canadian HR Reporter.* © Copyright Thomson Reuters Canada Ltd., (2016), Toronto, Ontario, 1-800-387-5164. Web:www. hrreporter.com; Agrium and PotashCorp merger completed forming Nutrien, a leader in global agriculture, https://www.nutrien.com/investors/news-releases/2018-agrium-and-potashcorp-merger-completed-forming-nutrien-leader-global ; Nutrien Fact Sheet, https://www.nutrien.com/sites/default/files/uploads/2017-12/NutrienFactSheetDecember2017.pdf

// INTRODUCTION

When it comes to training, many companies like Nutrien are concerned about making it "stick." This is because trainees do not always apply and make use of what they learn in training on the job. As a result, organizations like Nutrien design training programs with strategies to facilitate trainees' application of training on the job so that training will "stick." This is known as the transfer of training, and it is the focus of this chapter.

// WHAT IS TRANSFER OF TRAINING?

Organizations are increasingly concerned about the value added of human resource programs and its impact on employee and organization performance. When it comes to training, they are concerned about the transfer of training.

Transfer of training is the application of the knowledge and skills acquired in a training program on the job and the maintenance of acquired knowledge and skills over time.[1] There are two conditions of transfer of training. **Generalization** refers to the use or application of learned material to the job, and **maintenance** refers to the use or application of learned material on the job over a period of time.

While generalization involves the application of knowledge and skills learned in training to different settings, people, and situations, maintenance reflects the fact that some trainees will increase their use of trained skills over time while other trainees will decrease their use of trained skills over time.[2] In general, transfer of training occurs when knowledge and skills learned in training are generalized to the job and maintained over a period of time on the job.

There are several types of transfer of training (see Table 9.1). For example, the extent to which a training program transfers to the job can be positive, zero, or negative. When transfer is **positive**, trainees apply new knowledge, skills, and attitudes acquired in training on the job. If transfer is **zero**, trainees are not using new knowledge and skills on the job. When transfer is **negative**, training has had a negative effect and trainees are performing worse as a result of a training program. The purpose of this chapter is to find out why transfer is sometimes zero or negative and what can be done to make it positive.

Transfer of training
The generalization of knowledge and skills learned in training on the job and the maintenance of acquired knowledge and skills over time

Generalization
The use or application of learned material to the job

Maintenance
The use or application of learned material on the job over a period of time

Positive
Trainees apply new knowledge, skills, and attitudes acquired in training on the job

Zero
Trainees do not use new knowledge, skills, and attitudes acquired in training on the job

Negative
Training has had a negative effect and trainees are performing worse as a result of a training program

TABLE 9.1

TYPES OF TRANSFER OF TRAINING

- *Positive transfer.* Trainees apply new knowledge, skills, and attitudes acquired in training on the job.
- *Zero transfer.* Trainees do not use new knowledge, skills, and attitudes acquired in training on the job.
- *Negative transfer.* Training has had a negative effect and trainees are performing worse as a result of a training program.
- *Near transfer.* The extent to which trainees can apply what was learned in training to situations that are very similar to those in which they were trained.
- *Far transfer.* The extent to which trainees can apply what was learned in training to novel or different situations from those in which they were trained.
- *Horizontal transfer.* The transfer of knowledge and skills across different settings or contexts at the same level.
- *Vertical transfer.* Transfer from the individual or trainee level to the organizational level, or the extent to which changes in trainee behaviour or performance transfer to organizational-level outcomes.

Near transfer
The extent to which trainees can apply what was learned in training to situations that are very similar to those in which they were trained

Far transfer
The extent to which trainees can apply what was learned in training to novel or different situations from those in which they were trained

Horizontal transfer
The transfer of knowledge and skills across different settings or contexts at the same level

Vertical transfer
Transfer from the individual or trainee level to the organizational level, or the extent to which changes in trainee behaviour or performance transfer to organizational-level outcomes

Transfer of training can also be defined in terms of the type of situations in which trainees apply what was learned in training the job. For example, **near transfer** refers to the extent to which trainees apply what was learned in training to situations that are very similar to those in which they were trained. On the other hand, **far transfer** refers to the extent to which trainees apply what was learned in training to novel or different situations from those in which they were trained.[3]

A final distinction is whether transfer is horizontal or vertical. **Horizontal transfer** involves the transfer of knowledge and skills across different settings or contexts at the same level. This is the focus of this chapter and is consistent with how we have defined "transfer of training." That is, we are concerned about the extent to which trainees transfer what they learn in training from the training environment to the work environment.

Vertical transfer refers to transfer from the individual or trainee level upward to the organizational level. In other words, it is concerned with the extent to which changes in trainee behaviour and performance transfer to organizational-level outcomes. For example, will a change in trainees' customer service behaviour and performance result in an improvement in the organization's service and customer satisfaction? Vertical transfer represents the link between employee behaviour and organization results.

This is an important distinction because transfer to the job (i.e., horizontal transfer) might not lead to changes in organization outcomes (i.e., vertical transfer). Furthermore, there are differences in how to improve each type of transfer. The focus of this chapter is on horizontal transfer, which is a necessary condition for vertical transfer.[4]

// THE TRANSFER OF TRAINING PROBLEM

For decades, it has been reported that there exists a transfer of training problem in organizations. Although the estimates of transfer have varied over the years, they have generally been low, with studies reporting that between 60 and 90 percent of what is learned in training is not applied on the job.[5]

According to a study by the Conference Board of Canada, only 46 percent of organizations indicated that employees apply learning immediately after a training program to a large extent or completely. This number drops to 18 percent six months after training and to 16 percent one year after training (see Table 9.2).[6]

There are many reasons why training does not always transfer. Table 9.3 provides a list of some of the major barriers to the transfer of training. One of the things you will

TRANSFER OF TRAINING IN CANADIAN ORGANIZATIONS

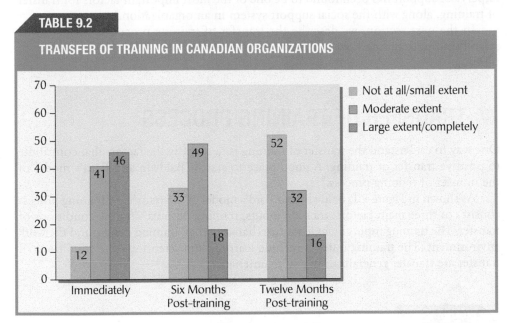

Source: Hall, C., & Cotsman, S. (2015). *Learning & development outlook—13th edition: Learning as a lever for performance.* Ottawa: The Conference Board of Canada, p. 76.

TABLE 9.3

BARRIERS TO THE TRANSFER OF TRAINING

- Immediate manager does not support the training.
- The culture in the work group does not support the training.
- No opportunity exists to use the skills.
- No time is provided to use the skills.
- Skills could not be applied to the job.
- The systems and processes did not support the skills.
- The resources are not available to use the skills.
- Skills no longer apply because of changed job responsibilities.
- Skills are not appropriate in our work unit.
- Did not see a need to apply what was learned.
- Old habits could not be changed.
- Reward systems don't support new skills.

Source: Phillips, J. J., & Phillips, P. P. (2002). 11 reasons why training and development fail . . . and what you can do about it. *Training Magazine, 39*(9), 78. Trainingmag.com

notice is that many of the barriers have to do with factors in the work environment, such as the culture in the work group. Furthermore, many of the barriers have to do with a lack of support from supervisors and the organization.

As you can see in Table 9.3, the number one barrier to transfer of training is the immediate manager's lack of support for training. **Supervisor support** has to do with the extent to which supervisors reinforce and encourage the use of learning on the job.[7] Supervisor support has been found to be one of the most important factors for transfer of training, along with the social support system in an organization.[8]

In the next section, we describe the transfer of training process, which sets the stage for understanding how to remove transfer barriers and facilitate the transfer of training.

> **Supervisor support**
> The extent to which supervisors reinforce and encourage the use of learning on the job

// TRANSFER OF TRAINING PROCESS

One way to understand the transfer of training is to identify the factors that contribute to positive transfer of training. A good place to start is Baldwin and Ford's model of the transfer of training process.[9]

As shown in Figure 9.1, Baldwin and Ford's model of the transfer of training process consists of three main factors: training inputs, training outputs, and the conditions of transfer. The training inputs include trainee characteristics, training design, and the work environment. The training outputs include learning and retention. The conditions of transfer are transfer generalization and maintenance.

FIGURE 9.1

BALDWIN AND FORD'S MODEL OF THE TRANSFER OF TRAINING PROCESS

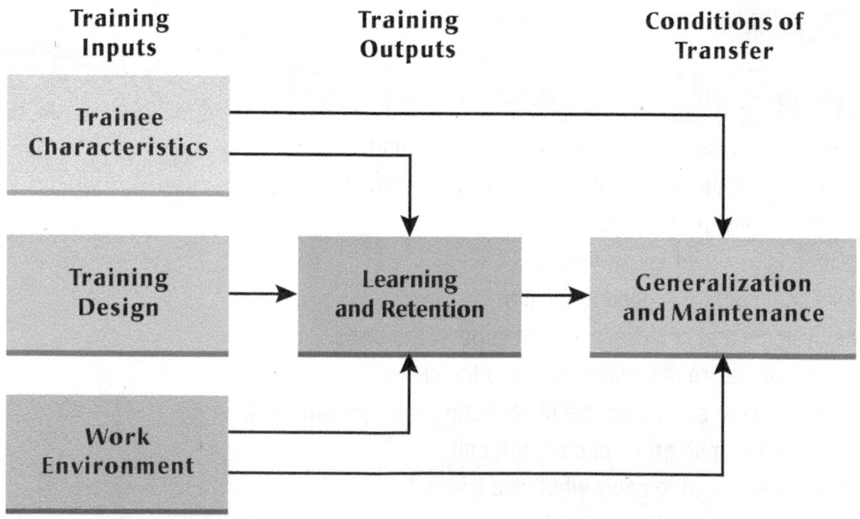

Source: Republished with permission of Blackwell Publishing, Inc., from Baldwin, T. T., & Ford, J. K. (1988). Transfer of training: A review and directions for future research, *Personnel Psychology*, *41*(1), 63–105. Permission conveyed through Copyright Clearance Center, Inc.

According to the model, trainee characteristics, training design, and the work environment have a direct effect on learning and retention. Trainee characteristics, the work environment, and learning and retention have a direct effect on transfer generalization and maintenance.

An important implication of the model is that learning and retention are a necessary but not sufficient condition for transfer. This is because trainee characteristics and the work environment also have an effect on whether trainees apply on the job what they learn in training. To better understand the role of training inputs, let's take a closer look at each of them.

TRAINEE CHARACTERISTICS

Trainee characteristics are trainees' capabilities (e.g., cognitive ability), personality traits (e.g., locus of control), motivational factors (e.g., self-efficacy), values and interests (e.g., occupational interests), attitudes and emotions (e.g., motivation to learn), and perceptions (e.g., climate for learning).[10]

In Chapter 2, you learned that trainee characteristics are important predictors of trainee learning and retention. Thus, it should not surprise you that trainee characteristics are also important for the transfer of training. In fact, the same trainee characteristics that influence learning and retention are also important for transfer. Trainee differences in these characteristics can help us understand why some trainees are more likely to transfer their learning than others.

In Chapter 2, cognitive ability, training motivation, self-efficacy, goal orientation, job attitudes, and personality traits were discussed in relation to learning and retention. Each of these trainee characteristics also has a direct effect on transfer. In other words, trainees with higher cognitive ability, higher training motivation, higher self-efficacy, and a learning goal orientation are more likely to transfer. In addition, trainees with an internal locus of control and a high need for achievement are more likely to apply on the job what they learn in training, and employees with higher job involvement, job satisfaction, and organizational commitment are more likely to learn and transfer. Among the trainee characteristics, cognitive ability has been found to be the most strongly related to transfer.[11]

Another trainee characteristic that is important for transfer is motivation to transfer. Recall from Chapter 2 that training motivation refers to the direction, intensity, and persistence of learning-directed behaviour in training contexts.

Motivation to transfer is a trainee's intended efforts to use on the job skills and knowledge learned in training. Motivation to transfer has been found to be a significant positive predictor of transfer generalization and transfer maintenance. In other words, trainees who are more motivated to transfer are not only more likely to transfer, but they are also more likely to increase their use and application of what they learn in training over time.[12]

TRAINING DESIGN

A number of design elements that are known as learning principles also affect the transfer of training. These learning principles include identical elements, general principles, and stimulus variability.

> **Trainee characteristics**
> Trainee capabilities, personality traits, motivational factors, values and interests, attitudes and emotions, and perceptions

For more information see Chapter 2, pp. 65–66

> **Motivation to transfer**
> A trainee's intended effort to use on the job skills and knowledge learned in training

IDENTICAL ELEMENTS

Identical elements
Training experiences and conditions that closely resemble those in the actual work environment

For more information see Chapter 5, p. 162

Identical elements involve providing trainees with training experiences and conditions that closely resemble those in the actual work environment. Identical Elements theory states that transfer will occur only if identical elements are present in both the old (training course) and new situations.[13] Identical elements are especially important for near transfer, and they have been shown to increase trainees' retention of motor and verbal behaviours.[14]

But what exactly is identical? In Chapter 5 it was noted that to be most effective, simulations should have physical and psychological fidelity. Physical fidelity involves making the conditions of a training program, such as the surroundings, tasks, and equipment, similar to those in the work environment. Psychological fidelity has to do with the extent to which trainees attach similar meanings to the training experience and the job context.

GENERAL PRINCIPLES

General principles
The general rules and theoretical principles that underlie the application of trained knowledge and skills

Teaching trainees the general rules and theoretical principles that underlie the application of trained knowledge and skills is called **general principles**. In other words, the training program provides trainees with an explanation of the theory and principles behind a skill or a task that they are learning to perform. On-the-job application is more likely when trainees are taught the general rules and theoretical principles that underlie training content.[15]

STIMULUS VARIABILITY

Stimulus variability
A variety of training stimuli and experiences, such as multiple examples of a concept and practice experiences in a variety of situations

Incorporating **stimulus variability** into a training program involves providing trainees with a variety of training stimuli and experiences, such as multiple examples of a concept or practice experience in a variety of situations. The idea is that trainees' understanding of training material can be strengthened by providing several examples of a concept because they will see how the concept can be applied in a variety of situations. This enables greater generalization of the new skills and prevents the potential problem of learning being limited to a narrow range of situations.[16]

Stimulus variability can be incorporated into a training program by using different models that vary in their characteristics (e.g., gender or age), by modelling different situations (e.g., different types of negotiation scenarios for a training program on negotiation skills), and by using models with different levels of competence in performing the training task (successful and unsuccessful).

Trainers can also increase stimulus variability by describing a variety of examples and experiences related to the training content, and by asking trainees to discuss their own work experiences in relation to the training material. Using several examples has been found to be more effective than simply repeating the same example.[17]

WORK ENVIRONMENT

Characteristics of the work environment before training (the pre-training environment) and after training (the post-training environment) also influence transfer of training.

PRE-TRAINING ENVIRONMENT

Management actions prior to a training program send signals and messages to employees about the importance of training and the extent to which the organization supports training. These messages can influence employees' training motivation.

For example, if management actions convey messages that training is not important, employees will not be motivated to attend training and will be less likely to learn. In addition, if employees face constraints in their job, such as a lack of time, equipment, and/or resources, they will not be highly motivated to learn—the work environment prevents them from using new skills.[18]

POST-TRAINING ENVIRONMENT

Events that occur after a training program in the post-training environment can also influence transfer. Factors in the post-training environment can encourage, discourage, or prevent employees from applying new knowledge and skills on the job.

As indicated earlier, one of the most important characteristics of the post-training environment is the amount of support provided by trainees' supervisors and co-workers. In fact, both supervisor support and peer support have been found to be strong predictors of transfer. Trainees who have supervisors and colleagues who are supportive of training are more likely to be motivated to attend training, to learn and retain training content, and to transfer what they learn in training on the job.[19]

Another key factor in the post-training environment is the opportunity to perform trained tasks on the job. **Opportunity to perform** refers to the extent to which a trainee is provided with the opportunity to perform trained tasks on the job. Training programs that include opportunities to practise newly learned skills have been shown to have higher rates of transfer.[20]

In Chapter 3 we described the importance of the organizational context as part of an organizational analysis. At that time, two important aspects of the work environment were described: the training transfer climate and a continuous learning culture.

TRAINING TRANSFER CLIMATE

As described in Chapter 3, a **training transfer climate** refers to characteristics in the work environment that can either facilitate or inhibit the application of training on the job. A positive transfer climate is one in which there exist cues that remind employees to apply training material on the job, positive consequences such as feedback and rewards for applying training on the job, and supervisor and peer support for the use of newly acquired skills and abilities.[21]

A positive and supportive transfer climate has been shown to result in greater learning, retention, and transfer of training. Further, a review of transfer research found that among the work environment factors, a positive transfer climate was the strongest predictor of transfer.[22]

CONTINUOUS LEARNING CULTURE

A **continuous learning culture** is a culture in which members of an organization believe that knowledge and skill acquisition are part of their job responsibilities and that learning is an important part of work life in the organization.

Opportunity to perform
The extent to which a trainee is provided with the opportunity to perform trained tasks on the job

For more information see Chapter 3, pp. 88–89

Training transfer climate
Characteristics in the work environment that can either facilitate or inhibit the application of training on the job

Continuous learning culture
A culture in which members of an organization believe that knowledge and skill acquisition are part of their job responsibilities and that learning is an important part of work life in the organization

Recall the description of the training program at Nutrien and how it was designed to promote continuous safety learning. Research has shown that the transfer of training is greater in organizations that have a continuous learning culture.[23]

// TRANSFER OF TRAINING STRATEGIES

Barriers to the transfer of training can occur before, during, and after training. Therefore, transfer of training strategies need to consider the barriers at all time periods throughout the training and development process.

In this section, we describe transfer of training strategies that can be implemented before, during, and after training to improve the transfer of training. We also show that positive transfer of training requires the involvement of three key role players (management, trainers, and trainees) and describe transfer strategies for each role player at each of the three time periods.

Table 9.4 summarizes the transfer of training strategies at each time period.

TABLE 9.4

TRANSFER OF TRAINING STRATEGIES

TRANSFER OF TRAINING STRATEGIES BEFORE TRAINING

MANAGEMENT

- Decide who should attend training.
- Meet with employees prior to training to discuss training programs (e.g., WIIFM).
- Get employee input and involvement in the training process.
- Provide employees with support for learning and training (e.g., release time to prepare for training).

TRAINER

- Ensure application of the ISD model.
- Find out supervisor and trainee needs and expectations.
- Make sure that trainees and supervisors meet and discuss the training.
- Make sure that trainees are prepared for the training.

TRAINEES

- Find out about training programs prior to attendance.
- Meet with supervisor to discuss the training program and develop an action plan.
- Prepare for the training program.

TRANSFER OF TRAINING STRATEGIES DURING TRAINING

MANAGEMENT

- Participate in training programs.
- Attend training programs before trainees.
- Reassign employees' work while they are attending training.

TABLE 9.4 (*Continued*)

TRANSFER OF TRAINING STRATEGIES

TRANSFER OF TRAINING STRATEGIES DURING TRAINING

TRAINER

- Incorporate conditions of practice, adult learning principles, and other learning principles (e.g., identical elements) in the design of training programs.
- Include content and examples that are relevant and meaningful to trainees.
- Provide transfer of training interventions at the end of the content portion of a training program (e.g., relapse prevention, self-management, goal-setting).
- Have trainees prepare and commit to a performance contract for the transfer of trained skills on the job.

TRAINEES

- Enter a training program with a positive attitude and the motivation to learn.
- Engage in the training program by getting involved and actively participating.
- Develop an action plan for the application of training on the job.

TRANSFER OF TRAINING STRATEGIES AFTER TRAINING

MANAGEMENT

- Ensure that trainees have immediate and frequent opportunities to practise and apply on the job what they learn in training.
- Encourage and reinforce trainees' application of new skills on the job.
- Provide positive feedback for the use of new skills on the job.
- Develop an action plan with trainees for transfer and show support by reducing job pressures and workload, arrange practice sessions, publicize transfer successes, give promotional preference to employees who have received training and transfer, and evaluate employees' use of trained skills on the job.

TRAINER

- Stay involved in the training and transfer process by conducting field visits to observe trainees' use of trained skills, provide and solicit feedback, and continue to provide support and assistance to trainees.

TRAINEES

- Begin using new knowledge and skills on the job as soon and as often as possible.
- Meet with supervisor to discuss opportunities for transfer.
- Form a "buddy system" or a network of peers who also attended the training program.
- Consider high-risk situations that might cause a relapse and develop strategies for overcoming them and avoiding a relapse.
- Set goals for transfer and use self-management.

// TRANSFER OF TRAINING STRATEGIES BEFORE TRAINING

Strategies for positive transfer of training should begin before a training program. A number of factors in the pre-training work environment have a direct effect on trainees' motivation to learn, learning, and transfer. The pre-training work environment sends messages to employees about the importance of training and should therefore be constructed and managed carefully. This means that management has an especially important role to play.

MANAGEMENT

One of the first things that a manager should do before a training program is decide who should attend training. This involves more than just the identification of employees' needs for training. Recall from our earlier discussion that trainee characteristics are an important determinant of learning and retention as well as transfer. Therefore, it is important that trainees selected to attend training programs will learn the training material and apply what they learn on the job. As indicated in Chapter 3, a person analysis can help to identify important trainee characteristics associated with training success as well as the extent to which a trainee is ready for training.

The extent to which a trainee is likely to learn and benefit from a training program is known as readiness to learn or trainability. **Readiness to learn/trainability** refers to the extent to which an individual has the knowledge, skills, abilities, and the motivation to learn the training content. An equation for readiness to learn and trainability combines ability, motivation, and perceptions of the work environment as follows[24]:

Readiness to Learn and Trainability = (Ability × Motivation × Perceptions of the Work Environment)

According to this equation, trainees are more likely to learn and are more trainable when they have the ability to learn the training content, are motivated to learn, and perceive the work environment as supportive of their learning and their use of new knowledge and skills on the job. All three of these components are important and they are not additive. In other words, being high on one factor will not make up for or compensate for a low rating on another factor.

For example, a trainee might have the ability to learn and be motivated to learn, but if he/she does not believe that the work environment will support learning, then he/she will score low on readiness to learn and trainability. Therefore, it is important that all three components are high before trainees attend a training program.

One way to determine whether an employee has the ability to learn the training content is to have him/her take a trainability test, as described in Chapter 8. A trainability test measures an individual's ability to learn and perform training tasks.

If employees lack the motivation to attend training, there are several ways for managers to increase training motivation. First, they can meet with employees to discuss their training needs and decide on a training plan to meet those needs. Prior to actually attending a training program, managers should discuss the program and its benefits with employees and set goals for learning and applying what they learn on the job. They should also discuss the objectives of a training program so that employees know what is expected and what they will be accountable for in terms of learning and using new knowledge and

Readiness to learn/ trainability
The extent to which an individual has the knowledge, skills, abilities, and motivation to learn the training content

For more information see Chapter 8, p. 274

skills on the job. Trainees who know that they will be required to participate in follow-up activities or will be evaluated have stronger intentions to transfer.[25]

Employees also need to know why they are attending a training program and the potential benefits. It is up to management to inform trainees about the importance and relevance of a training program and the benefits of learning and transfer. Trainees need to know what's in it for them, or what is sometimes called **WIIFM** (What's in it for me?). This is best represented by what is known as **valence**, which refers to trainee beliefs about the desirability of outcomes obtained from training. Valence has been found to be strongly related to motivation to learn and transfer. Thus, managers should emphasize the benefits that trainees will receive from training (e.g., improved performance, promotions, career mobility) in an effort to strengthen trainees' valence.[26]

Some evidence exists that trainees are more motivated and more likely to learn when they are given the choice of attending a training program than when attendance is mandatory. In one study, managers who could choose whether to attend a performance-appraisal workshop achieved more from attending the workshop than those who were forced to attend. Providing detailed information about the workshop that was designed to facilitate the managers' attendance decision—rather than just providing the typical positive overview—also resulted in greater achievement.[27]

Some, however, argue that it is better to make attendance mandatory. The idea behind this argument is that by making attendance mandatory, managers communicate the importance of training and ensure that all employees are using the same skills.[28] One study found that a mandatory training course resulted in higher intentions to transfer.[29] However, this appears to be the case when training is highly valued in an organization. When training is not so highly valued, providing employees with some choice is beneficial. The main point is that trainee involvement and input in the training process, whether discussing training needs, allowing trainees to decide what training programs to attend, and/or providing input regarding training content and methods can enhance training motivation, learning, and transfer.

Finally, managers also need to show their support for training before an employee attends a training program. One way to do this is to have them complete a survey and respond to questions about the need for and potential application of training material. For example, managers who have requested training might be required to answer questions such as: "What is the training need? What are the employees doing now and what should they be doing? Why do you believe that training will solve the problem? What do you want employees to be able to do after the training?"

Having managers complete a contract can also commit them to a training program and ensure their support for it (an example of a contract is shown in Table 9.5). Supervisors can also demonstrate their support for training by providing employees release time to prepare for training and by providing encouragement.[30]

TRAINER

One of the first things a trainer should do before training is ensure that the training system is operating according to the instructional systems design (ISD) model. That is, a trainer should ensure that a needs analysis has been conducted, that appropriate training objectives have been developed, and that important learning and design principles have been incorporated into the design of the training program.

Second, the trainer should ensure that supervisors and trainees are prepared for the training program. For example, the trainer should make sure that supervisors have taken

TABLE 9.5

TRAINING SUPPORT CONTRACT: SUPERVISOR

I, _____, agree to

- provide time for the employee to complete pre-course assignments
- provide release time for attendance, and ensure that the employee's workload is undertaken by others to eliminate interruptions
- review the course outline with the employee, and discuss situations in which the newly acquired knowledge and skills can be used
- provide timely opportunities to implement the skills and reinforce new behaviours when the trainee returns

Signature _____

Title _____

appropriate actions with respect to trainees' readiness to learn/trainability. The trainer should also make sure that supervisors and trainees have met to discuss the training objectives and content and the benefits of the training program, and that trainees know what they are expected to learn and do after training.

Third, the trainer should know what supervisors and trainees expect from the trainer and the training program. Thus, to some extent a trainer might have to tailor a training program to the particular needs and expectations of supervisors and trainees. The trainer should also be aware of the needs of trainees in terms of relevant content, examples, and methods. In other words, the trainer must ensure that the training program is relevant and meaningful for trainees.

Finally, the trainer should ensure that trainees have taken any required prerequisite courses and have the necessary readings, assignments, and/or pre-training exercises. Preparation might also include asking trainees to think about work-related problems and issues they are currently dealing with and how the training program might help solve them. Thus, when trainees show up for a training program they should be ready and motivated to learn.

TRAINEES

Trainees often attend training programs with little knowledge of what they are going to learn or what is expected of them. This is obviously not going to lead to a high level of motivation, learning, or transfer. Trainees must be involved in their training and the training process. But what can trainees do before a training program to increase their involvement and the likelihood that they will learn and transfer?

First, trainees should find out why they are being asked to attend a training program, what the training objectives are, and what is expected of them in terms of learning and on-the-job behaviour and performance. Second, trainees should meet with their supervisor to discuss the training program and develop a plan of action for learning and transfer. Trainees should also ask their supervisor about the support they can expect while they are away from work and attending a training program, and the support they will receive when they return to work.

Finally, trainees should prepare for the training program to ensure that they are ready to learn and that they will benefit from the training. This might involve preparatory reading, pre-training exercises or assignments, or simply thinking about work-related problems that they can bring with them to discuss during the training program. These activities will help ensure that trainees are knowledgeable about the training program and its objectives, and that they are prepared and motivated to learn.

// TRANSFER OF TRAINING STRATEGIES DURING TRAINING

There are also strategies that managers, trainers, and trainees can perform during training to improve learning and transfer.

MANAGEMENT

During training, managers can facilitate transfer by showing their support for training. One way of doing this is to attend a training program. If managers cannot attend a training program, they should consider speaking about the importance and relevance of the training at the start of a program or, if possible, participate as a trainer. At the very least, they should visit the training session at some time to show their support.[31]

It also helps if managers have already taken a training program. Managers are more likely to support training if they have been trained or have participated as trainers in a training program. In this way, managers can model the behaviour and observe

Managers can facilitate the transfer of training by speaking about the importance and relevance of the training and participating as a trainer.

its occurrence. Senior executives at Vancouver-based Finning Ltd., the world's largest Caterpillar dealer, are the first to attend training and help deliver the training.[32] This cascading effect tells employees that management is serious about learning and the application of new skills on the job. In addition, when managers are required to teach the new skills, they learn them very well. They are also aware that their employees are watching them to see if they practise what they preach.[33]

Management can also do a number of things to assist employees while they are away from work and attending a training program. For example, they can reassign some of their workload so that they don't worry about falling behind while they are being trained. They can also ensure that trainees are not interrupted during training. This not only puts trainees at ease while they are being trained, but also signals to employees that management supports training and considers it a high priority.

TRAINER

For more information see Chapter 4, pp. 126–133 and Chapter 2, p. 58

There are several things a trainer can do during training to facilitate the transfer of training. For starters, as described in Chapter 4, training programs should include active practice and the conditions of practice (e.g., task sequencing, feedback, and knowledge of results) to maximize learning and transfer. In addition, as discussed earlier in this chapter, the principles of learning (identical elements, general principles, and stimulus variability) are especially important design factors for transfer of training. Adult learning theory should also be considered (Chapter 2).

Trainers can also increase trainees' training motivation during training. This can be achieved by explaining the value of a skill and by using training content and examples that are familiar and meaningful to trainees.[34] As noted in Chapter 4, trainees learn and remember meaningful content more easily than material unrelated to their work.[35] Trainers can use information, problems, and anecdotes collected from the needs analysis to demonstrate the link between the training material and work situations. New material should be introduced using terms and examples familiar to trainees.

Trainers can also have trainees prepare a performance contract. A **performance contract** is a statement that is drafted by the trainee and the trainer jointly near the end of a training program. It outlines which of the newly acquired skills are beneficial and how they will be applied to the job. A copy can then be given to the trainer, a peer, or the supervisor, who will monitor progress toward these goals. Trainees submit progress reports to human resources and their supervisor. A variation on the timing (i.e., signing the contract jointly before a training program) alerts the trainee to the critical elements of the program and commits the supervisor to monitoring progress.[36]

Performance contract
An agreement outlining how the newly learned skills will be applied to the job

TRAINEES

Trainees should begin a training program with a positive attitude and be motivated to learn. During the training, trainees should engage themselves by taking notes, participating in discussions and exercises, asking and answering questions, and interacting with the trainer and the other trainees.

Before leaving a training program, trainees should set goals for transfer, develop an action plan for applying the training on the job, and be prepared to discuss their goals and action plan with their supervisor and co-workers. You might recall from the chapter-opening vignette that leaders are expected to create individual action plans, which are then tracked by the company.

// TRANSFER OF TRAINING STRATEGIES AFTER TRAINING

After a training program has ended and trainees return to work, they may be motivated to use their new skills on the job. However, only some trainees are able to do so successfully. Some will stop trying after a few attempts because they receive no support or reinforcement for the use of their new knowledge and skills on the job. Others will give up because they encounter barriers and obstacles that make it difficult if not impossible for them to apply their new knowledge and skills. Still others will give up just because the old ways of doing things are easier and faster. Therefore, it is important that managers, trainers, and trainees implement strategies after training that facilitate the transfer of training.

MANAGEMENT

One of the most important things that managers can do after a training program is ensure that employees have immediate and frequent opportunities to practise what they learned in training on the job. As indicated earlier, opportunities to perform newly learned skills are related to higher rates of transfer.[37] Thus, assignments and opportunities to try new skills should be given as soon as trainees return from a training program. Managers can also help by allowing trainees time to experiment using new behaviours without adverse consequences.

Managers should also encourage and reinforce the application of new skills on the job. In fact, one of the major reasons for a lack of transfer is that reinforcement is usually infrequent or nonexistent. Behaviour that is not reinforced is not repeated. If the sales representative dutifully submits the reports as learned in training but no one even notices they are filed, then the representative will waste no further energy doing this task. Thus, trainees who use new skills on the job should be provided with praise, recognition, more challenging assignments, additional opportunities for training, and other extrinsic rewards.

It is also important that managers provide trainees with positive feedback about their use of new knowledge and skills on the job. The use of feedback is an important component of the Nutrien coaching-for-safety training program. Feedback has been found to be a significant predictor of transfer of training.[38]

Recognition and positive feedback not only directly reinforce employees for their transfer behaviour, but also send a signal to other employees that training is important and learning and transfer will be rewarded. In effect, they help to demonstrate management support and to create a positive transfer climate.

Managers can do many other things to facilitate transfer, such as developing an action plan for transfer, reducing job pressures and workload, arranging for co-workers to be briefed by trainees about a training program, arranging practice sessions, publicizing

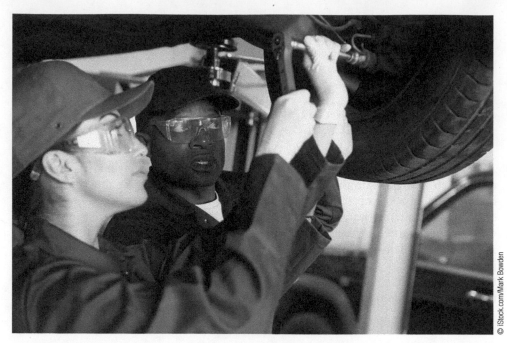

After a training program, managers should give employees immediate and frequent opportunities to practise on the job what they learned in training.

successes, giving promotional preference to employees who have received training, and evaluating employees' use of trained skills on the job.[39]

Calgary-based Western Gas Marketing Ltd., a subsidiary of TransCanada PipeLines Ltd., rates its managers on the application of new skills on their performance-appraisal forms.[40] At the Bank of Montreal, managers conduct performance assessments to gauge the transfer of learning to the job.[41]

TRAINER

Some trainers might believe that their job is finished after a training program has been delivered. However, it is important for trainers to remain involved in trainees' learning and transfer after a training program has been delivered. Trainers should maintain their involvement in the training and transfer process by conducting field visits to observe trainees' use of trained skills, provide and solicit feedback, and provide continued support and assistance to trainees.[42]

Sometimes a trainer might meet with trainees for a follow-up session to review the training program and discuss transfer problems and solutions (see the section on booster sessions later in the chapter). As described at the beginning of the chapter, Nutrien has leadership coaches who visit all sites and provide follow-up instruction to the managers who have taken the coach-for-safety engagement program, and the coaches provide weekly updates to management.

To find out more about the effects of follow-up sessions on transfer, see Training Today 9.1, "The Effects of Follow-Up Sessions on the Transfer of Training."

THE EFFECTS OF FOLLOW-UP SESSIONS ON THE TRANSFER OF TRAINING

It has long been believed that follow-up sessions are an effective way to improve the transfer of training. To find out, the Institute for Work & Health (IWH) conducted a study on the effectiveness of ergonomics training for office workers.

The study compared the effectiveness of four different methods of delivering ergonomics training: online, classroom, online with follow-up, and classroom with follow-up. More than 400 office workers from five organizations across southern Ontario in the municipal, education, and utility sectors participated in the study.

The classroom and online training offered the same evidence-based, standard-compliant, nine-module content. Both took about 90 minutes to complete, though online learners had the flexibility to leave and pick up the nine 10-minute modules anytime they wanted during a two-week window.

Study participants were broken into five groups: One group received only the classroom training and another only the online training. The third group was given the classroom training plus follow-up, and the fourth group was given the online learning plus follow-up. The fifth group was a control group that did not receive the training—they were provided with links to ergonomics information on the website of the Ontario Ministry of Labour.

The follow-up consisted of three half-hour group sessions that took place once per month for three months after the initial training. In the follow-up sessions, trainees worked in pairs doing ergonomics assessments on each other, and then supported each other to do assessments on colleagues who didn't take part in the training. The focus was on building their self-efficacy.

Supervisors and managers of the two follow-up groups took part in a 60-minute group session on ways to support workers. The focus was on supporting a healthy computing culture, helping them understand the importance of role modelling, and helping them build their own self-efficacy.

To test the effects of the training, several variables were measured before the training and at three, six, and nine months after the training, including trainee self-efficacy to solve workstation problems and help co-workers, and knowledge about ergonomics, trainee postures, workstation configurations, workstation adjustments, and pain symptoms.

The results indicated more positive outcomes for trainees who received training regardless of whether it was online or classroom training. Both methods of training were equally effective. However, in the groups that did not receive the follow-up sessions, the improvements started to level off after three months. In contrast, the two groups that received the follow-up sessions continued to make improvements. They had higher self-efficacy, lower postural risk, and greater likelihood of having properly configured and adjusted workstations. The only variable where differences were not found was for pain symptoms.

The results of this study highlight the beneficial effects of follow-up sessions for the transfer of training and the importance of focusing on trainees' self-efficacy.

Sources: Based on King, T. (2014, April 21). The secret to making training stick. *Canadian HR Reporter, 27*(8), 8. Reprinted by permission of *Canadian HR Reporter.* © CopyrightThomson Reuters Canada Ltd., (2014), Toronto, Ontario, 1-800-387-5164. Web: www.hrreporter.com; Anonymous (2014, Winter). Study finds supporting learner confidence to apply new skills key to effective training. *At Work, 75*, Institute for Work & Health, Toronto; Anonymous (2014, January 28). Study shows way to make health and safety training for office workers more effective. Institute for Work & Health, www.iwh.on.ca/media/2014-jan28.

TRAINEES

After attending a training program, trainees should begin to use their new knowledge and skills on the job as soon as possible. Failure to use the training material when a trainee returns to work is likely to result in a low likelihood of transfer. To

Michael Jung/Shutterstock.com

A buddy or a network of peers who have attended a training program can provide assistance and support for using trained skills on the job.

ensure adequate opportunities for skill application and support, trainees should meet with their supervisor and discuss opportunities for transfer.

Trainees might also benefit by establishing a "buddy system," or a network of peers who have attended a training program and can provide assistance and support and reinforce each other for using their trained skills on the job.[43]

Now that we have described transfer of training strategies, you might be wondering which ones are most effective. To find out, see The Trainer's Notebook 9.1, "Best Practice Strategies for Transfer of Training." You might also be wondering about how technology can be used to facilitate the transfer of training. To learn more, see Training Today 9.2, "Using Technology to Facilitate Transfer of Training."

THE TRAINER'S NOTEBOOK 9.1

BEST PRACTICE STRATEGIES FOR TRANSFER OF TRAINING

According to a sample of training professionals, the best practice strategies for transfer of training are the following:

1. *Supervisory support and reinforcement.* Recognize and reinforce the use of new knowledge and skills on the job.

2. *Coaching and opportunities to practise.* Provide time to practise skills immediately when returning from training.

3. *Use of interactive activities to encourage participation.* Collaborative activities, role plays, and small group exercises.

4. *Post-training evaluation of skills.* Tracking and measuring transfer of training.

5. *Making the content relevant to actual job duties.* Activities that resemble work behaviours, challenges, and scenarios.

Source: Republished with permission of Jossey-Bass, Inc., from Burke, L. A., & Hutchins, H. M. (2008). A study of best practices in training transfer and proposed model of transfer. *Human Resource Development Quarterly, 19,* 107–128. Permission conveyed through Copyright Clearance Center, Inc.

TRAINING TODAY 9.2

USING TECHNOLOGY TO FACILITATE TRANSFER OF TRAINING

Given that many organizations now use social media and technology for training, is it possible to also use technology to facilitate the transfer of training?

A recent study by Andrea Hester, Holly Hutchins, and Lisa Burke-Smalley suggests that the use of Web 2.0 technologies (e.g., blogs, wikis, podcasts) might be a

less intrusive, more efficient and integrated approach for supporting transfer of training. The authors argue that "Web 2.0 tools have the potential to accelerate employee application of acquired skills in their work through electronic performance cuing and tracking of acquired skills, sharing new learning through social

(continued)

media, and engaging expertise through live chats and wikis."[44]

To learn about the use of Web 2.0 technologies for transfer of training, the authors conducted a study in which they asked training professionals about the use of technology to support transfer of training in their organization. The authors wanted to know what Web 2.0 tools are being used and what factors predict their usage.

With respect to the use of Web 2.0 tools, the training professionals reported that their organizations use Web video-conferencing tools, social or professional networking applications, screencast or capture tools, instant messaging, file-sharing, and course management or e-learning systems most frequently to support transfer of training.

There was a preference for using highly visual modes such as Web or video-conferencing as well as technologies to obtain virtual feedback from networks such as instant messaging, file-sharing, and screencasts.

In terms of using Web 2.0 tools, the authors found that both individual and situational factors were important. With respect to individual factors, perceived usefulness of a Web 2.0 tool predicted its usage, and perceived usefulness was predicted by perceived ease of use. As for situational factors, a supportive learning climate also predicted Web 2.0 usage.

The results of this study indicate that Web 2.0 technologies are being used by training professionals as an organizational learning tool to support and facilitate the transfer of training.

Source: Based on Hester, A. J., Hutchins, H. M., & Burke-Smalley, L. A. (2016). Web 2.0 and transfer: Trainers' use of technology to support employees' learning transfer on the job. *Performance Improvement Quarterly, 29*(3), 231–255.

// TRANSFER OF TRAINING INTERVENTIONS

In addition to transfer of training strategies at each time period, transfer of training can also be facilitated through the use of **transfer of training interventions**, which are provided at the end of a training program after all of the training content has been delivered. In this section, we discuss three types of transfer of training interventions: relapse prevention, self-management, and goal-setting.

RELAPSE PREVENTION

Relapse prevention (RP) is an intervention that instructs trainees to anticipate transfer obstacles and high-risk situations in the work environment and to develop coping skills and strategies to overcome them.

A **relapse** occurs when trainees revert back to using the old skills or their pre-training behaviour. Relapse prevention sensitizes trainees to the possibilities of a relapse and "immunizes" them against obstacles in the environment that might cause one.[45] RP sensitizes trainees to barriers in the workplace that might inhibit or prevent successful transfer of training.

Relapse prevention interventions make trainees aware that relapses can occur and that temporary slips are normal. Trainees are asked to identify obstacles and barriers to transfer and high-risk situations in which a relapse is likely to occur. Some high-risk situations that might lead to a relapse are time pressure and deadlines; work overload; lack of necessary tools, equipment, and resources; and the lack of opportunities to apply trained skills on the job.[46]

For each barrier or high-risk situation, trainees develop a coping strategy. For example, if workers think they will abandon their new skills when there is too much work, time-management techniques could be discussed and used to prevent a relapse. Thus, RP prepares trainees to anticipate, prevent, and recover from temporary lapses. Table 9.6 provides an outline of a relapse prevention intervention.

Transfer of training interventions
Interventions provided at the end of a training program to facilitate the transfer of training

Relapse prevention (RP)
An intervention that instructs trainees to anticipate transfer obstacles and high-risk situations in the work environment and to develop coping skills and strategies to overcome them

Relapse
When trainees revert back to using old skills or their pre-training behaviour

TABLE 9.6

RELAPSE PREVENTION INTERVENTION

Step 1. State the trained skill you wish to apply and maintain from this training.

Step 2. Set your skill maintenance goal, based on this training. Set a specific, measurable, short-range goal. Then, specifically define a slip and a relapse.

Skill Maintenance Goal _____

Slip: _____

Relapse: _____

Step 3. Understand positive and negative consequences of using the skill at work.

Positive consequences of using your new skills: _____

Negative consequences of *not* using your new skills: _____

Positive consequences of *not* using your new skills: _____

Negative consequences of using your new skills: _____

Step 4. Apply the relapse prevention strategies to maintain trained skills.

1. Understand the relapse process (i.e., slip, then relapse).

2. Understand the difference between the training environment and job contexts.

3. Create a support network.

4. Be aware of subordinate skepticism of new skills.

5. Identify high-risk situations.

6. Apply skills in the appropriate setting.

7. Understand seemingly unimportant behaviours that may lead to a relapse.

8. Reduce interfering and unproductive emotions.

9. Retain your self-confidence, despite slips.

10. Diagnose support skills needed to maintain training.

11. Review disruptive lifestyle patterns.

12. Mix enjoyable and tedious work tasks.

13. Diagnose support back at work for skill application.

14. Create meaningful self-rewards for skill retention.

Step 5. Describe the nature of circumstances that will likely surround a first slip.

Step 6. Generate ideas for how you will deal with such difficult situations.

Step 7. Monitor your behaviour at work using a self-monitoring record.

Sources: Burke, L. A. (2001). Training transfer: Ensuring training gets used on the job. In L.A. Burke (Ed.), *High-impact training solutions: Top issues troubling trainers.* Westport, CT: Quorum Books; Republished with permission of SAGE Publications, from Hutchins, H. M., & Burke, L. (2006). Has relapse prevention received a fair shake? A review and implications for future transfer research. *Human Resource Development Review, 5*(1), 8–24. Permission conveyed through Copyright Clearance Center, Inc.

Relapse prevention programs have been found to be effective. Trainees who receive RP interventions have higher levels of course knowledge and use the knowledge on the job more than trainees who do not receive it. RP has also been found to improve trainees' ability and desire to transfer. There is also evidence that relapse prevention interventions are especially effective when the transfer climate is not very supportive of training.[47]

For more information see Chapter 2, pp. 56–58

SELF-MANAGEMENT

In Chapter 2, we discussed self-regulation as one of the components of social cognitive theory. We also noted that employees can be trained to learn how to regulate their behaviour and the use of self-regulation prompts.

Self-management interventions focus on behavioural change and have their basis in self-regulation and social cognitive theory. Self-management interventions teach trainees to perform a series of steps to manage their transfer behaviour.

The steps of self-management interventions include anticipating performance obstacles, planning to overcome obstacles, setting goals to overcome obstacles, monitoring one's progress, and rewarding oneself for goal attainment.

Research has found that self-management interventions result in greater skill generalization and higher performance of a transfer task.[48]

> **Self-management**
> A post-training transfer intervention that teaches trainees to manage their transfer behaviour

GOAL-SETTING

In Chapter 2, we described goal-setting theory and its implications for training, and in Chapter 4 we described how learning goals can be set as a pre-training intervention to improve learning during practice sessions. Many studies have shown that individuals who set specific, difficult, and challenging goals achieve higher levels of performance.[49]

The importance of goal-setting for training has been the focus of many studies. From these studies, we know that learning and transfer is more likely when trainees set specific and challenging goals. Therefore, it makes sense to use goal-setting as a transfer intervention.

Goal-setting interventions teach trainees about the goal-setting process and how to set specific goals for using trained skills on the job. This usually involves a discussion of why goal-setting is important and a definition of goals; a description of the goal-setting process; characteristics of effective goals (specific and challenging); an explanation for the effectiveness of goals; examples of how goal-setting has been used in organizations; and a discussion of how goal-setting can be effective in one's own organization.

Following a discussion of how to set specific and challenging goals, trainees develop their own goal-setting plan that indicates the steps they will take to achieve their goals and the date by which each step will be achieved.[50]

Goal-setting interventions have been shown to improve learning and the extent to which trainees apply their newly learned skills on the job. In addition, one study found that goal-setting was particularly effective for enhancing transfer for trainees who work in a supportive work environment.[51]

For more information see Chapter 2, pp. 61–63 and Chapter 4, pp. 130–131

> **Goal-setting interventions**
> An intervention that instructs trainees about the goal-setting process and how to set specific goals for using trained skills on the job

// POST-TRAINING SUPPLEMENTS

A final approach for improving the transfer of training is to provide trainees with support and guidance after they return to work. These approaches are known as post-training supplements.

Post-training supplements are transfer interventions that take place on the job following a training program and include booster sessions, self-coaching, and upward feedback.

BOOSTER SESSIONS

A common post-training supplement is a booster session or refresher course that is provided sometime after a training program. **Booster sessions** are extensions of training programs that involve a review of the training material.

A booster session can also involve **debriefs**, which are discussions about trainees' transfer experiences as well as transfer obstacles and problems they are having using trained knowledge and skills on the job. Debriefs can then lead to plans for overcoming transfer obstacles and the establishment of transfer goals.[52]

SELF-COACHING

Self-coaching involves reflecting on one's performance and setting transfer goals for several weeks following completion of a training program. Trainees complete an assessment in which they examine the extent to which they have engaged in trained behaviours and then establish performance maintenance and improvement goals.

UPWARD FEEDBACK

An **upward feedback** supplement involves providing trainees with data on the frequency with which they engaged in the trained behaviours along with written comments from subordinates on their performance. Trainees then establish performance maintenance and improvement goals.[53] The leaders who attend the Nutrien coaching-for-safety training program received feedback from crew members through a survey that they used to create individual action plans.

A study of newly hired managers at a large restaurant chain found that both self-coaching and the upward feedback supplements resulted in greater post-training performance following a training program on interpersonal skills development. Thus, both post-training supplements proved to be effective extensions of formal classroom training for improving transfer of training.[54]

// TRANSFER SYSTEM

In this chapter, we have described strategies and interventions that can facilitate and improve the transfer of training. These strategies can occur throughout the training process and involve the training program itself as well as trainees, trainers, management, and the organization. One way of thinking about all the factors that can influence and facilitate the transfer of training is in terms of a transfer system.

According to Elwood Holton and colleagues, the **transfer system** is all factors in the person, training, and organization that influence transfer of learning to job performance.[55] The 16 factors that make up the transfer system are important predictors of transfer of training that we have already discussed in the chapter, such as trainee ability, motivation, and the work environment. Learning and the transfer system factors influence transfer performance, which in turn influences organizational performance.[56]

Holton and his colleagues have developed a diagnostic instrument called the Learning Transfer System Inventory (LTSI) to assess the transfer system in organizations. The instrument consists of 16 factors that have been found to be the most important in transfer research.

Some of the factors are used to assess a specific training program, such as motivation to transfer and opportunities to use, while others are general factors, such as performance-outcomes expectations that are important for all training programs.

The LTSI can be used by organizations to diagnose their transfer system. It is usually administered to trainees after a training program to identify potential barriers in an organization's transfer system and to determine the type of intervention needed to overcome barriers and facilitate transfer. Those factors with the lowest scores (e.g., supervisor support) can be the focus of transfer interventions.[57]

One of the benefits of the LTSI is that it recognizes the importance of a systematic approach to the transfer of training. Organizations are able to diagnose their transfer system, identify barriers, and implement programs to eliminate the barriers. This is important because transfer systems differ across organizations, which means that the barriers and the most effective interventions to eliminate them also differ across organizations.[58]

It should also be evident that there is no one best strategy for improving the transfer of training, and that multiple transfer strategies should be used in combination as the best approach for improving the likelihood that training will transfer.[59]

// MODEL OF TRAINING EFFECTIVENESS—TRANSFER OF TRAINING

Let's now return to the model of training effectiveness that was presented in Chapters 2 and 4. Recall that the model shows that: (1) training and development has a direct effect on learning and retention; (2) trainee characteristics (cognitive ability, training motivation, personality, goal orientation, self-efficacy, and attitudes) and training design (training methods, active practice, conditions of practice, active learning, and error-management training) have a direct effect on trainee learning and retention; (3) learning and retention have a direct effect on individual behaviour and performance; and (4) individual behaviour and performance have a direct effect on organizational effectiveness.

As shown in Figure 9.2, we can now add a number of other factors to the model based on the material presented in this chapter. First, we can add the work environment, which includes the training transfer climate and a continuous learning culture. Second, we can add the learning principles (i.e., identical elements, stimulus variability, and general principles) and transfer of training interventions to the training design factors.

In terms of the linkages, we can add a direct link from trainee characteristics and the work environment to individual behaviour and performance. This follows from Baldwin and Ford's model of the transfer process. We can also add a direct link from training design to individual behaviour and performance given that the learning principles and transfer of training interventions are important for transfer.

The model now shows that individual behaviour and performance (i.e., transfer) is influenced by trainee characteristics, training design, the work environment, and learning and retention.

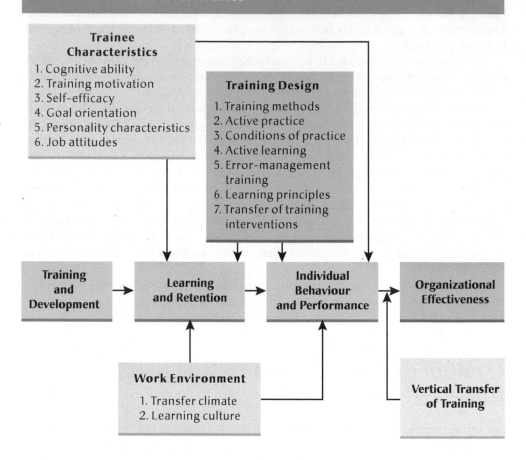

FIGURE 9.2

MODEL OF TRAINING EFFECTIVENESS

Trainee Characteristics
1. Cognitive ability
2. Training motivation
3. Self-efficacy
4. Goal orientation
5. Personality characteristics
6. Job attitudes

Training Design
1. Training methods
2. Active practice
3. Conditions of practice
4. Active learning
5. Error-management training
6. Learning principles
7. Transfer of training interventions

Training and Development → Learning and Retention → Individual Behaviour and Performance → Organizational Effectiveness

Work Environment
1. Transfer climate
2. Learning culture

Vertical Transfer of Training

The final linkage in the model is from transfer behaviour and performance to organizational effectiveness. Recall that this linkage is called "vertical transfer." Vertical transfer refers to the link between individual-level training outcomes and organizational outcomes.

While a change and improvement in employees' behaviour and performance (i.e., horizontal transfer) is necessary for vertical transfer, it is important to realize that the relationship is not one-to-one. In other words, positive horizontal transfer does not guarantee vertical transfer, because many other factors also contribute to organizational effectiveness.

// SUMMARY

This chapter described the transfer of training process and the transfer problem in organizations. Baldwin and Ford's model was presented as a framework for understanding the transfer process, and strategies for facilitating the transfer of training were described in terms of when they can be used (before, during, and after training) by managers, trainers, and trainees. The use of transfer of training interventions and post-training supplements for improving transfer were also described. The chapter concluded with a discussion of the transfer system and the importance of a systematic approach to transfer of training that involves all of the key stakeholders throughout the training process, and the need to use multiple transfer strategies to improve the transfer of training in organizations.

KEY TERMS

booster sessions p. 304
continuous learning culture p. 289
debriefs p. 304
far transfer p. 284
general principles p. 288
generalization p. 283
goal-setting intervention p. 303
horizontal transfer p. 284
identical elements p. 288
maintenance p. 283
motivation to transfer p. 287
near transfer p. 284
negative p. 283
opportunity to perform p. 289
performance contract p. 296
positive p. 283
post-training supplements p. 304
readiness to learn/trainability p. 292
relapse p. 301
relapse prevention (RP) p. 301
self-coaching p. 304
self-management p. 303
stimulus variability p. 288
supervisor support p. 286
trainee characteristics p. 287
training transfer climate p. 289
transfer of training p. 283
transfer of training interventions p. 301
transfer system p. 304
upward feedback p. 304
valence p. 293
vertical transfer p. 284
WIIFM p. 293
zero p. 283

DISCUSSION QUESTIONS

1. Refer to Table 9.3, "Barriers to the Transfer of Training." For each of the barriers, indicate who is responsible for the barrier (trainer, trainee, management) and when the barrier is most likely to occur (before, during, and/or after).

2. Refer to Table 9.3, "Barriers to the Transfer of Training." For each of the barriers, describe what can be done to remove the barrier and facilitate the transfer of training. Be sure to indicate at what stage in the training process you would do something to remove the barrier (before, during, and/or after), and who would be involved (manager, trainer, and/or trainee).

3. Refer to the Nutrien vignette at the beginning of the chapter and describe the strategies that were used to facilitate the transfer of training. At what point during the training process were these strategies implemented?

4. What is the difference between horizontal and vertical transfer? How are they related? What is the difference between near transfer and far transfer, and what should a trainer do to maximize each of them?

5. Describe the main factors in Baldwin and Ford's model of the transfer of training process and how they are related. What are the practical implications of the model for improving transfer of training?

6. What is the transfer system and how can it be used by organizations to improve the transfer of training?

7. Discuss how technology can be used to facilitate the transfer of training in organizations. Be specific in describing the technology and how it can be used.

8. Who is responsible for the transfer of training? Explain your answer and indicate why you believe that someone is or is not responsible. For those who you believe are responsible, explain what you think they should do as part of their responsibility to faciliate the transfer of training.

THE GREAT TRAINING DEBATE

1. Debate the following: Low rates of transfer of training are inevitable and will always be a problem for trainers and organizations; there is nothing you can do about it.

2. Debate the following: Trainers should be responsible only for trainee learning and retention because what happens when trainees return to work and the transfer of training is beyond their control.

3. Debate the following: Trainees and only trainees are responsible for the transfer of training and they should be held accountable for applying on the job what they learn in training.

EXERCISES

IN-CLASS

1. After the final exam, many students claim to forget most of what they learn in their courses. How could you design a course for students so they will remember and use what they learned in the classroom after the course has ended?

2. Think about the most recent training experience you had in a current or previous job. What did you learn and to what extent did you apply what you learned on the job? Did you transfer immediately after training? Six months after training? One year after training? What factors explain why you did or did not transfer on the job what you learned in training? Is there anything that the trainer or your

supervisor could have done to increase your transfer? Is there anything you could have done yourself to improve your transfer? (Note: This exercise can also be done by interviewing somebody—such as a classmate, friend, or family member—about their training experiences.)

3. Students acquire a great deal of knowledge and information from their courses, but does it transfer to their work experiences? Describe any courses you have taken that resulted in transfer to a job. What factors do you think contributed to your transfer? Could they be used in the design of other courses?

4. Describe how your university or college instructor could use identical elements, general principles, and stimulus variability to improve your learning and transfer. In other words, how can an instructor incorporate these learning principles into his/her classes?

5. Assume the role of a training consultant who has been hired by an organization that has a problem with transfer of training. Your task is to conduct a diagnosis of the transfer system to find out why there is a transfer problem. To do this, you need to develop a diagnostic tool to find out what barriers exist. Using the material in this chapter, develop some questions that take into account the different time periods of the training process (i.e., before, during, and after) and the main role players (management, trainer, and trainees) to assess the transfer problem in the organization. What questions will you ask and who will you interview and/or survey?

6. Review the transfer of training interventions (relapse prevention, self-management, and goal-setting) described in the chapter and think about how they might be used to help students learn their course material and apply it on the job. You could consider your course on training and development or perhaps a course on managerial skills. Your task is to design one of the following interventions: relapse prevention, self-management, or goal-setting. You can then have another member of the class review your intervention and provide feedback or, if time permits, present your intervention to the class.

IN-THE-FIELD

1. To find out about transfer of training in an organization, contact the human resources department of an organization and ask the following questions:
   - To what extent do trainees apply on the job what they learn in training immediately after training, six months after training, and one year after training?
   - What are the main barriers or obstacles to transfer of training in your organization, and who is responsible for them?
   - What strategies do you use to facilitate the transfer of training?
   - Are there things you do before, during, and after training to facilitate the transfer of training?
   - What are the responsibilities of managers, trainers, and trainees for the transfer of training?
   - What have you found to be most effective for ensuring that trainees apply on the job what they learn in training?

   Based on your interview, how well do you think the organization is managing the transfer of training process? What recommendations do you suggest for the organization to improve its transfer system and the transfer of training?

2. Conduct a transfer of training audit of an organization to find out if they are using the transfer of training strategies before, during, and after training. Using Table 9.4, conduct an audit of the transfer strategies used in an organization you currently work in or have worked in; or, if possible, interview a person or persons currently employed in an organization. If possible, interview an employee, a manager, and somebody in HR involved in training and development. Based on your audit, answer the following questions:

   a. To what extent are transfer strategies before, during, and after training being used by the organization? What strategies are used the most and least often?

   b. To what extent are transfer strategies being used by management, trainers, and trainees? What strategies are used the most and least often?

   c. Based on your audit, do you think the organization is using a sufficient number of strategies before, during, and after training?

   d. Based on your audit, do you think the organization is using a sufficient number of strategies by each role player (management, trainer, trainees)?

   e. What recommendations would you make to the organization to improve its use of transfer strategies? What strategies should they begin using before, during, and after training, and what role players need to become more involved?

CASE INCIDENT

BC ASSESSMENT

BC Assessment is a provincial Crown organization whose 350 to 400 professional appraisers determine the market value of land and improvements for taxation purposes. Each year, about 2 percent of property owners file a formal complaint or appeal with the agency.

Complex appeals that are not resolved might proceed to an appeal board, which could lead to a formal hearing. The appeal process represents a significant cost, mainly in staff time. To help cut back, the agency decided to train appraisers to develop the skills needed to resolve appeals earlier.

Thirty-six appraisers took part in a two-day, face-to-face workshop that included group discussions, team summaries, case studies, and mock role-playing exercises. Before training, 20 percent of the trainees rated their knowledge and skill levels as high. After training, that number rose to 56 percent. In addition, 69 percent of the trainees said they had a high level of confidence in applying the learning to their jobs effectively.

However, six months after the training the value of the course was significantly diminished at the transfer of learning stage. More than one-half of respondents saw little or no improvement in tasks associated with appeals management.

QUESTIONS

1. What effect did the training have on trainees? What should the trainees be able to do on the job after attending the training program?

2. Use Baldwin and Ford's model of the transfer of training process (Figure 9.1) to explain why so many of the trainees reported little or no improvement in tasks associated with appeals management.

3. Discuss some of the strategies you would recommend before, during, and after training to improve trainees' performance of tasks associated with appeals management. Be sure to indicate strategies for the trainer, trainees, and managers.

Source: Dobson, S. (2010, March 22). Logitech, BC Assessment fine-tuning training. *Canadian HR Reporter*, p. 8. Reprinted by permission of *Canadian HR Reporter*. © Copyright Thomson Reuters Canada Ltd., (2010), Toronto, Ontario, 1-800-387-5164. Web: www.hrreporter.com

CASE STUDY THE SCHOOL BOARD

For years, parents, students, and teachers complained that nobody listened, that decisions were made without participation, and that good ideas went unacknowledged. A needs analysis that involved a survey of teachers and students confirmed that these problems were widespread.

Carlos DaSilva, who was recently appointed trainer at the school board and had a strong background in teaching, had to address the communications problem as his first assignment. He designed what he considered to be an excellent three-day communications program. He spent months on the design: finding videos, exercises, and games that taught active listening, upward communication, brainstorming, and other areas identified in the survey.

Carlos was excited to deliver his new training program and was sure that the participants would like it. On the first day, Carlos began with a brief introduction on the importance of communication, followed by a lecture on communication channels. Afterwards, he showed a video about manager–employee communication problems and how to improve communication. This was followed by a discussion of the key points in the video and what the trainees might do to improve their communication skills.

On day two of the training program, Carlos began with a lecture on brainstorming. He then had trainees participate in a group brainstorming exercise. Each group had to brainstorm as many ideas as possible for improving communication in the school board. Afterward, the groups presented their ideas followed by a discussion of the most creative ways to improve communication with teachers, students, and parents.

On the third day of the training program, Carlos began with a lecture on active listening. Trainees then participated in an exercise in which they had to develop a message and then communicate it to the other trainees. At the end of the exercise, each trainee had to recall the message sent by the other trainees. This was followed by a discussion of how to be a more effective listener and tips on active listening.

Carlos ended the training program by having trainees participate in a communication game. First, he had trainees complete a self-assessment of how they send messages and the channels they use for communication. Then groups of trainees had to develop a message that they would communicate to the other groups. Each group had to determine the best way for their message to reach the other groups as accurately and quickly as possible. At the end of the game, each group read out the message they received from the other groups. Carlos then scored each group in terms of the accuracy of the message received by the other groups and how long it took for each group to receive the message.

The game was a lot of fun for the participants, who left the training program on a high. Carlos thanked them for attending the program and encouraged them to apply what they learned in training when they returned to work. The trainees applauded Carlos and thanked him for providing such an enjoyable training experience.

Two months after the training program, Carlos was sitting at his desk, thinking about his meeting scheduled for 2 p.m. with the school board superintendent. He was looking forward to the meeting, knowing that he would be praised for the successful interactive communications program he had designed and delivered.

However, the meeting with the superintendent went poorly. Although some participants had loved the exercises and games in the communications course, most had not changed their work behaviour. Furthermore, a review of the situation showed that the old problems persisted and communication remained a serious problem at the school board. Carlos did not know what to say or what he should do.

Several days later, Carlos approached some of the participants who had attended the training program and asked them how things were going. One participant laughed and said, "Well that was a lot of fun, but training is training and work is work. Besides, nothing ever changes around here." Carlos asked her what she meant and she explained to him that supervisors don't get it and continued to call the shots. "The only thing they know about communication is downward," she said. "Maybe they should have attended your training program!"

QUESTIONS

1. What are some reasons that Carlos's training program did not transfer?

2. Discuss some of the barriers to transfer that might be operating at the school board. Who is responsible for these barriers and when do they occur during the training process?

3. Describe some of the things that Carlos might have done before, during, and after the training program to improve the transfer of training. What could the trainees and supervisors have been asked to do before, during, and after training to improve transfer?

4. Discuss the training transfer climate and the transfer system at the school board. How might they have contributed to the transfer problem?

5. What should Carlos do about the transfer problem at the school board? What changes should he make next time he delivers a training program? What should he do differently and why?

FLASHBACK QUESTIONS

1. Describe the training methods that were used in Carlos's communications training program. Do you agree with the use of these methods? Do you think they were appropriate given the content and objectives of the training program?

2. What other training methods would you recommend for the communications training program? Refer to Table 5.1 in Chapter 5 and consider each of the instructional methods. Explain why you would recommend some methods, and why they might be more effective than the methods Carlos used.

3. Describe how some of the principles, concepts, and theories of learning from Chapter 2 might be relevant for understanding why the communications

training program was not more effective. What can Carlos learn from the material in Chapter 2 that would make the training program more effective if he were to redesign it?

4. If you were to redesign the communications training program, what changes would you make? Refer to the training design activities in Table 4.1 in Chapter 4 to answer this question.

FLASH FORWARD QUESTION

1. How was the communications training program evaluated? Describe the information provided in the case that pertains to the evaluation of the training program. What does this information tell you about the effectiveness of the program? What other information might be obtained to evaluate the training program? What do you think the additional evaluation information will tell Carlos about the effectiveness of the training program?

REWRITE THE CASE QUESTION: TRANSFER OF TRAINING STRATEGIES AND INTERVENTIONS

Rewrite the case so that it includes transfer of training strategies and/or interventions. In other words, describe some transfer of training strategies and interventions that Carlos might include in the design of the training program. Be sure to consider and describe transfer of training strategies before, during, and after training, as well as transfer of training interventions.

RUNNING CASE DIRTY POOLS

QUESTIONS

Refer to the case at the end of Chapter 1 to answer the following questions.

1. Do you think there would be any transfer problems of a training program for pool operators and employees? Refer to the barriers to transfer of training in Table 9.3 and discuss some of the barriers that might inhibit the transfer of the pool operators training program. Who is responsible for these barriers? When will they occur?

2. What can be done when designing the training program for pool operators and employees to increase the likelihood that the program will transfer? Be sure to discuss how each of the learning principles (identical elements, general principles, and stimulus variability) can be used in the design of the training program.

3. What strategies can be used before and after the training program to increase the probability that the training will transfer? Be sure to indicate strategies that can be used by the trainer, trainees, and management. What do you think will be most important for ensuring that the training program will transfer?

// REFERENCES

1. Baldwin, T. T., & Ford, J. K. (1988). Transfer of training: A review and directions for future research. *Personnel Psychology*, *41*, 63–105.

2. Huang, J. L., Ford, J. K., Ryan, A. M. (2017). Ignored no more: Within-person variability enables better understanding of training transfer. *Personnel Psychology*, *70*, 557–596.

3. Broad, M. L., & Newstrom, J. W. (1992). *Transfer of training*. Reading, MA: Addison-Wesley.

4. Kozlowski, S. W. J., Brown, K. G., Weissbein, D. A., Cannon-Bowers, J. A., & Salas, E. (2000). A multilevel approach to training effectiveness: Enhancing horizontal and vertical transfer. In K. J. Klein & S. W. J. Kozlowski (Eds.), *Multilevel theory, research, and methods in organizations* (pp. 157–210). San Francisco: Jossey-Bass.

5. Phillips. J. J., & Phillips, P. P. (2002). 11 reasons why training and development fails . . . and what you can do about it. *Training Magazine*, *39*(9), 78–85.

6. Hall, C. & Cotsman, S. (2015). *Learning as a lever for performance: Learning & development outlook—13th edition*. Ottawa: The Conference Board of Canada.

7. Cromwell, S. E., & Kolb, J. A. (2004). An examination of work-environment support factors affecting transfer of supervisory skills training to the workplace. *Human Resource Development Quarterly*, *15*, 449–471.

8. Tracey, J. B., Tannenbaum, S. I., Kavanagh, M. J. (1995). Applying trained skills on the job: The importance of the work environment. *Journal of Applied Psychology*, *80*, 239–252.

9. Baldwin & Ford (1988).

10. Bell, B. S., Tannenbaum, S. I., Ford, J. K., & Noe, R. A. (2017). 100 years of training and development research: What we know and where we should go. *Journal of Applied Psychology*, *102*, 305–323.

11. Colquitt, J. A., Lepine, A., & Noe, R. A. (2000). Toward an integrative theory of training motivation: A meta-analytic path analysis of 20 years of research. *Journal of Applied Psychology*, *85*, 678–707; Blum, B. D., Ford, J. K., Baldwin, T. T., & Huang, J. L. (2010). Transfer of training: A meta-analytic review. *Journal of Management*, *36*, 1065–1105.

12. Burke, L. A., & Hutchins, H. M. (2007). Training transfer: An integrative literature review. *Human Resource Development Review*, *6*, 263–296; Huang, Ford, & Ryan, (2017).

13. Bass, B. M., & Vaughn, J. A. (1969). *Training in industry: The management of learning*. Belmont, CA: Wadsworth.

14. Baldwin & Ford (1988).

15. Baldwin & Ford (1988).

16. Baldwin & Ford (1988).

17. Baldwin & Ford (1988).

18. Tannenbaum, S. I., & Yukl, G. (1992). Training and development in work organizations. *Annual Review of Psychology*, *43*, 399–441.

19. Baldwin & Ford (1988); Tannenbaum & Yukl (1992); Blum et al. (2010); Martin, H. J. (2010). Workplace climate and peer support as determinants of training transfer. *Human Resource Development Quarterly*, *21*, 87–104.

20. Ford, J. K., Quinones, M. A., Sego, D. J., & Sorra, J. S. (1992). Factors affecting the opportunity to perform trained tasks on the job. *Personnel Psychology*, *45*, 511–527.

21. Rouiller, J. Z., & Goldstein, I. L. (1993). The relationship between organizational transfer climate and positive transfer of training. *Human Resource Development Quarterly*, *4*, 377–390.

22. Blum et al. (2010).

23. Tracey et al. (1995).

24. DeSimone, R. L., Werner, J. M., & Harris, D. M. (2002). *Human resource development*. Orlando, FL: Harcourt.

25. Baldwin, T. T., & Magjuka, R. J. (1991). Organizational training and signals of importance: Linking pretraining perceptions to intentions to transfer. *Human Resource Development Quarterly*, *2*, 25–36.

26. Colquitt, Lepine, & Noe (2000).

27. Hicks, W. D., & Klimoski, R. J. (1987). Entry into training programs and its effects on training outcomes: A field experiment. *Academy of Management Journal*, *30*, 542–552.

28. Broad & Newstrom (1992).

29. Baldwin & Magjuka (1991).

30. Tannenbaum & Yukl (1992).

31. Burke, L. A. (2001). Training transfer: Ensuring training gets used on the job. In L. A. Burke (Ed.), *High-impact training solutions: Top issues troubling trainers*. Westport, CT: Quorum Books.

32. Clemmer, J. (1992, September 15). Why most training fails. *The Globe and Mail*, p. B26.

33. Clemmer (1992).

34. Bass & Vaughn (1969).

35. McGehee, W., & Thayer, P. W. (1961). *Training in business and industry*. New York: Wiley.

36. Leifer, M. S., & Newstrom, J. W. (1980, August). Solving the transfer of training problems. *Training and Development Journal*, *34*(8), 42–46.

37. Taylor, P. J., Russ-Eft, D. F., & Taylor, H. (2009). Transfer of management training from alternative perspectives. *Journal of Applied Psychology, 94*, 104–121.

38. Velada, R., Caetano, A., Michel, J. W., Lyons, B. D., & Kavanagh, M. J. (2007). The effects of training design, individual characteristics and work environment on transfer of training. *International Journal of Training and Development, 11*, 282–294.

39. Broad & Newstrom (1992).

40. Clemmer (1992).

41. Waxer, C. (2005). Bank of Montreal opens its checkbook in the name of employee development. *Workforce Management, 84*(11), 46–48

42. Burke (2001).

43. Baldwin & Ford (1988); Burke (2001).

44. Hester, A. J., Hutchins, H. M., & Burke-Smalley, L. A. (2016). Web 2.0 and transfer: Trainers' use of technology to support employees' learning transfer on the job. *Performance Improvement Quarterly, 29*(3), p. 232.

45. Tziner, A., Haccoun, R. R., & Kadish, A. (1991). Personal and situational characteristics influencing the effectiveness of transfer of training improvement strategies. *Journal of Occupational Psychology, 64*(2), 167–177.

46. Burke (2001).

47. Burke (2001).

48. Gist, M., Bavetta, A., & Stevens, C. (1990). Transfer training method: Its influence on skill generalization, skill repetition, and performance level. *Personnel Psychology, 43*, 501–523; Gist, M., Stevens, C., & Bavetta, A. (1991). Effects of self-efficacy and post-training intervention on the acquisition and maintenance of complex interpersonal skills. *Personnel Psychology, 44*, 837–861.

49. Locke, E. A., & Latham, G. P. (1990). *A theory of goal setting and task performance*. Englewood Cliffs, NJ: Prentice-Hall.

50. Richman-Hirsch, W. L. (2001). Posttraining interventions to enhance transfer: The moderating effects of work environments. *Human Resource Development Quarterly, 12*, 105–120; Wexley, K. N., & Nemeroff, W. F. (1975). Effectiveness of positive reinforcement and goal setting as methods of management development. *Journal of Applied Psychology, 60*, 446–450.

51. Richman-Hirsch (2001).

52. Salas, E., Tannenbaum, S. I., Kraiger, K., & Smith-Jentsch, K. A. (2012). The science of training and development in organizations: What matters in practice. *Psychological Science in the Public Interest, 13*, 74–101.

53. Tews, M. J., & Tracey, J. B. (2008). An empirical examination of posttraining on-the-job supplements for enhancing the effectiveness of interpersonal skills training. *Personnel Psychology, 61*, 375–401.

54. Tews & Tracey (2008).

55. Holton, E. F., III. (2003). What's really wrong: Diagnosis for learning transfer system change. In E. F. Holton III & T. T. Baldwin (Eds.), *Improving learning transfer in organizations*. San Francisco, CA: John Wiley & Sons.

56. Holton (2003).

57. Holton (2003).

58. Holton, E. F., III., Chen, H., & Naquin, S. S. (2003). An examination of learning transfer system characteristics across organizational settings. *Human Resource Development Quarterly, 14*, 459–482.

59. Blum et al. (2010).

CHAPTER 10

TRAINING EVALUATION

CHAPTER LEARNING OUTCOMES

AFTER READING THIS CHAPTER, YOU SHOULD BE ABLE TO:

- define "training evaluation" and the main reasons for conducting evaluations
- discuss the barriers to evaluation and the factors that affect whether it is conducted
- describe the different types of evaluations
- discuss the models of training evaluation and their interrelationships
- describe the main variables to measure in a training evaluation and how they are measured
- discuss the types of designs for training evaluation, their requirements, their limits, and when they should be used

Bloomberg/Getty Images

The training evaluations launched by Bell led to modifying the training strategy.

Years ago, when Bell Canada installed a new telephone system for its business clients, it also sent out service advisers whose task it was to train the employees to use the new system. These training sessions consisted of "show-and-tell" activities in which the instructors demonstrated the use of the telephone. Simple as the training was, it was expensive, costing millions of dollars annually. With the introduction of electronic equipment, the functionality of the telephone systems—and complexity for the users—increased exponentially.

Initially, the company tried to use its traditional training approach with purchasers of the electronic systems. However, a training evaluation was conducted and it showed that following the training experience, customer knowledge of the operation of the electronic telephones was quite low. The training was not effective.

A number of attempts were then made to improve the situation. Different types of training, presented by either Bell Canada or user personnel, were tried and evaluated. None made any significant difference in terms of training effectiveness.

However, these training evaluation studies did detect an important fact. No matter how training was conducted, the users' knowledge of a limited number of functions—those they used a lot—increased after training, indicating that practice seemed to have a significant effect on learning.

This suggested that providing end users with an instructional aid might help them gain greater benefit from the electronic system. To that end, a special instruction booklet was carefully prepared and trainees were provided with a brief instructional session teaching the users how to use the instruction booklet. The evaluation of this approach showed, empirically, that the use of the instruction booklet resulted in greater user mastery than the formal training course.

Thus, the training evaluations conducted throughout this process demonstrated that (1) the traditional training method was ineffective, (2) changing the instructors had no effect, but (3) the use of a well-developed instruction booklet had greater effect.

This demonstrates the two main objectives of training evaluation: to assess the effectiveness of training and, equally important, to identify ways of enhancing that effectiveness. At Bell, the traditional program was discontinued and replaced with an inexpensive booklet that was both more effective and considerably cheaper.

// INTRODUCTION

Training programs are designed to affect learning and behaviour. However, as the Bell Canada story demonstrates, they do not always achieve these goals. Fortunately, in that case, the organization launched an evaluation program that involved several studies. These studies contributed to the development of a novel and successful training strategy.

// WHAT IS TRAINING EVALUATION?

Organizational training and development is intended to improve technical competencies (e.g., learning new software), to modify attitudes (e.g., preparing a manager for an international assignment), and/or to modify behaviours (e.g., better communication skills). Organizations invest in this organizational function because it is expected that training makes a positive contribution to them and to their employees.

Training evaluation is concerned with whether these expected outcomes materialize as a result of training. They are designed to assist decision making: Should the organization cancel or continue a training program? Should it be modified? How?

Training evaluation is a process designed to assess the value–the worthiness–of training programs to employees and to organizations. Using a variety of techniques, objective and subjective information is gathered before, during, and/or after training to establish that worthiness. Trainees, supervisors, or others familiar with the trainees and the job are important information sources, as are objective performance records.

Training evaluation is not a single procedure. Rather, it is a continuum of techniques, methods, and measures. At one end of the continuum are simple evaluations that mainly focus on the reactions of the trainees to the program. Are the trainees satisfied with the training sessions? Do they think they are helpful? Easily conducted, these evaluations entail few if any costs. However, the information they provide is limited, leading at times to misleading conclusions about the worthiness of a training program.

At the other end of the training evaluation continuum lie procedures that are more elaborate. They rely on more complete and more solid information-extensive questionnaires, interviews, and objective data. They use detailed information of a richer quality about the value of a training program. Hence, their conclusions can be stated with greater confidence and precision. They answer key questions such as: Have the trainees learned the skills? Are they motivated to apply them? Are they confident they can? Will the work environment support or discourage the display of the new skill on the job?

However, these sophisticated evaluation procedures are more costly, complex, and difficult to implement. They may entail disruptions to the training program and/or to the job; in some cases they may require the services of specialized (and expensive) consultants. Such sophistication is often unnecessary and a simple and cheap procedure will do.[1]

In the end, training evaluation choices involve the usual trade-off: quality/completeness versus complexity/costs. One needs to balance the informational needs of decision makers with the difficulty and costs of obtaining that information.

> **Training evaluation**
> A process to assess the value—the worthiness—of training programs to employees and to organizations

// WHY CONDUCT TRAINING EVALUATIONS?

Organizations invest in the training of employees and managers because it is necessary for competitiveness in the current global environment. With chronic understaffing (organizations do not always fully replace employees who retire or leave), the amount of time available for training has become smaller and must be used more wisely. In this context, management has a stake in ensuring that the resources invested in training bear fruit. Training evaluation is therefore of value to

- help fulfill the managerial responsibility to improve training
- assist managers in identifying the training programs most useful to employees and in determining who should be trained
- determine the cost benefits of a program and help ascertain which program or training technique is most cost-effective (see Chapter 11)
- determine whether the training program has achieved the expected results or solved the problem it was meant to solve
- diagnose the strengths and weaknesses of a program and pinpoint needed improvements
- use the evaluation information to justify and reinforce, if merited, the value and credibility of the training function to the organization

DO ORGANIZATIONS CONDUCT TRAINING EVALUATIONS?

By the year 2000, most organizations in North America were conducting some evaluation of most of the training programs offered to their employees. [2] This was the case in Canada, as reported by the Conference Board of Canada in its bi-annual survey of training practices. Figure 10.1 shows these results from 2000 to 2016/17. The chart

FIGURE 10.1

THE PERCENTAGE OF ORGANIZATIONS THAT EVALUATE THEIR TRAINING AND DEVELOPMENT EFFORTS

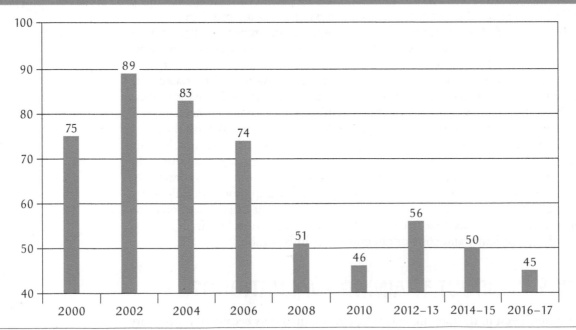

Source: Adapted from Cotsman, S. and Hall, C. (2018). *Learning cultures lead the way: Learning and development outlook—14th edition:* Ottawa: The Conference Board of Canada.

confirms that training evaluation activity has changed over time in Canada. Prior to 2008, the majority (three-quarters or more) of organizations conducted evaluations. Starting in 2008 and thereafter, that proportion dropped to half or less.

As stated in the opening paragraphs, evaluations range from simple to complex. Complexity is largely a function of the information—the data—required. Evaluations that rely on trainee reactions are the simplest to plan and conduct. It is not surprising that, as the Conference Board data report, most organizations that do evaluate training rely principally on a simpler evaluation strategy.

Evaluations that assess trainee learning are only marginally more complex and costlier to implement. Hence, learning is the second most frequent measure used to evaluate training effectiveness. Assessing job performance improvement, organizational impact, and the cost–benefit of training, however, can be a major challenge. Consequently, rare are the organizations that conduct such high-level evaluations. The more complex the evaluation outcome assessed, the fewer the organizations that conduct them. Figure 10.2 summarizes the Canadian situation in 2016/17.

These data confirm the trend: organizations with stronger learning cultures conduct more evaluations at all levels, including the more sophisticated ones.

To summarize: Do organizations conduct evaluations? Roughly 50 percent do, but most focus on easily measured reactions and, to a substantial though lesser degree, on learning. Organizations with stronger learning cultures conduct more evaluations and sophisticated ones are more frequently used. Yet it remains—organizations rarely assess behaviour, impact, or the cost and benefits of training programs.

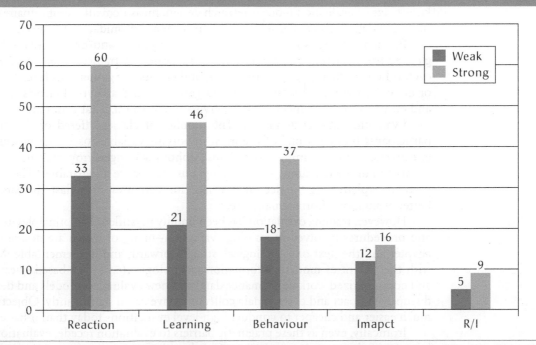

FIGURE 10.2

TRAINING OUTCOMES EVALUATED IN ORGANIZATIONS WITH WEAK OR STRONG LEARNING CULTURES

Source: Adapted from Cotsman, S. and Hall, C. (2018). *Learning cultures lead the way: Learning and development outlook—14th edition:* Ottawa: The Conference Board of Canada.

This is a paradoxical result. The latest Conference Board of Canada study reports that improving individual (behaviour) and organizational performance are both the central objectives of training for organizations and the least frequently evaluated. It is to this apparent paradox that we now turn: the barriers to training evaluation.

// BARRIERS TO TRAINING EVALUATION

Studies conducted with training professionals show that more sophisticated training evaluations are rarely used because they are perceived as being too complicated to implement, too time consuming, and/or too expensive.[3] Measuring higher-level variables (such as behaviour change) is indeed more difficult. Collecting job performance data requires supervisors to devote time and resources to systematic performance monitoring and observation. It is not easy for trainers to obtain such collaboration.[4]

In some cases, training managers resist evaluation because of the difficulty of isolating from other variables the unique impact that training has on employee effectiveness. In other cases, they do not evaluate the value of training efforts because top management does not ask for it, while still others may not because they do not wish to know. Thus, barriers to training evaluation fall into two categories: pragmatic and political.

PRAGMATIC BARRIERS TO TRAINING EVALUATION

Presumably, as with all other departments, training departments need to demonstrate their usefulness, their contribution to job performance improvements, and ultimately to the company's bottom line. Yet evaluation remains a relatively marginal activity.

As you will learn in this chapter, taking on the training evaluation task requires knowledge of evaluation models, research design, measurement, questionnaire construction, and data analysis. For some, that can seem an intimidating prospect.

Fundamentally, evaluation requires that perceptual and/or objective information gleaned from performance records and/or furnished by trainees, their supervisors, and even others—such as peers, subordinates, and clients—be gathered before, during, and/ or after the training session. These data gathering and analytical efforts require time and effort from the trainees, their supervisors, and so on. That is not always available.

Evaluation also costs money. The number of classes offered or the number of participants trained is one of the most important variables used as a measure of the effectiveness of the training departments. Siphoning budgets from this main task to the evaluation of the remaining training programs may prove unpalatable.[5] These concerns partially explain both the decline in evaluation activities in the last 10 years and why better evaluation efforts remain rare.

However, training evaluation has been unduly mystified. The principles, techniques, and procedures involved in training evaluation—many of which are described in this chapter and the next one—are logical, straightforward, and implementable. Moreover, with the advent of modern information technologies (e.g., Web-based questionnaires and computerized work-performance data) and new evaluation models and designs, the disruptive impact and costs of data collection have eased significantly. Objectively, it is much easier and cheaper to conduct high-level evaluations today than it has ever been.

Ironically, even as these pragmatic barriers to evaluation recede, evaluation activity is becoming less prevalent, not more. Clearly technical issues are not the only inhibitors of evaluation. We label these other issues the political barriers to training evaluation.

POLITICAL BARRIERS TO TRAINING EVALUATION

Some trainers do not evaluate training programs on ethical grounds. How can the person (or department) responsible for training also be the one responsible for evaluating its effectiveness? To avoid a perceived or actual conflict of interest they believe that external professionals—not trainers—should conduct evaluations. Conflict of interest, although always a possibility, is unlikely when training managers make use of the established methods of evaluation, many of which are described in this chapter.

Evaluation can be threatening as it may reveal that part of a training program—or even an entire training approach—is ineffective. While this can be a valuable finding (as in the chapter-opening vignette), some trainers fear that this will reflect poorly on them, the training function, and/or the service they offer.

Training is an investment. As with all investments, it is of importance to ascertain if it is a "good" or "poor" one. In the absence of evaluation, the training function's ability to defend the value of training is handicapped. But even more importantly, without evaluation it becomes impossible to know if and how to improve the organization's ability to develop the competencies of its employees. Good programs might be dropped and poor one perpetuated. In either case, this may be a disservice to the training function as well as to the organization.

This resolves to an issue of accountability. Burke and Saks have strongly argued that training will serve organizational success more clearly when trainees, their managers, and those who develop and administer training programs are more accountable for results.[6] Empirically that is not happening. As the latest Conference Board (2016/17) survey reports, it is neither the trainer nor the employee's manager who is considered responsible for applying learning to the job. That is the responsibility of employees. But employees operate under the instructions of the manager. When the manager does not support and encourage learning applications on the job, employees are less likely to do so.

This last result throws into focus the role of management. Evaluations are conducted when there is pressure to do so. In the absence of such demands, many training managers would rather forgo the exercise. (See Training Today 10.1, "Upper Management's Role in Training Evaluation.") Upper management needs to demand of the training function that it evaluate its own effectiveness.

TRAINING TODAY 10.1

UPPER MANAGEMENT'S ROLE IN TRAINING EVALUATION

A few years ago, there was a rash of serious work accidents in a large transportation company. Some of these accidents were the direct or indirect result of operator errors due to the consumption of drugs and alcohol. As a result, the firm declared a zero-tolerance policy concerning the use of such substances. The policy required that no employee use substances that may impair effective and safe job performance, whether or not these substances are legal. The key element of the policy was that all supervisors were directly and personally responsible for enforcing the policy. Supervisors who failed to enforce the policy would themselves be subject to sanctions that could include dismissal.

The training department was directed to develop and administer a training program to all supervisory and managerial personnel in the company that was aimed at teaching the policy and its implementation. However, the CEO of the company also insisted that the training program be evaluated to ensure that it was effective. As a result,

(continued)

the training department, which normally only administered "smile sheets" to evaluate their training programs, launched a much more sophisticated training evaluation program that included three measurement times and the collection of information on dozens of variables. Clearly, this effort was launched because the training program had attained high visibility and because top management demanded it. The training evaluation did uncover some problems with the training program and suggested a number of changes.

However, none of these changes was ever implemented. This was because top management showed no interest in the results of the evaluation study, since these became available only several months after the training program was administered.

The moral of the story is that high-level visibility can stimulate evaluation actions. However, maintaining that visibility is important to ensure that the evaluation results will prove of practical use.

// TYPES OF TRAINING EVALUATION

Evaluations can be distinguished from one another with respect to the data gathered and analyzed and the fundamental purpose for which the evaluation is being conducted. Most training evaluations focus on trainee perceptions, which are typically assessed through questionnaires administered immediately after training. The more complete evaluations also assess behavioural data that may be collected in various ways, including self-reports, observation, and performance data.

1. **The data collected.** Evaluations differ with respect to the type of information that is gathered and how that is accomplished.

   a. The most common training evaluations rely on *trainee perceptions at the conclusion of training* (Did the participants like it?), while more sophisticated evaluations go further to analyze the extent of trainee learning and the post-training behaviour of trainees.

   b. More recently, there has been a growing emphasis on evaluation studies that also assess the *psychological states* with which trainees leave training and that affect outcome measures such as learning and behaviour change. Research in this area has helped to identify several of these states[7] (affective, cognitive, and skills-based) that are important training outcomes because of the influence they have on learning and on improvements in job behaviours.

   c. Finally, information about the *work environment*–transfer climate and learning cultures–is useful in evaluation.[8] Understanding the organization's culture, climate, and policies can strongly affect training choices and effectiveness.[9] The degree to which opportunities exist for on-the-job practice of new skills and the level of support provided by others to new learners have, among other things, been found to influence training success.[10] Training courses that are strongly aligned with the firm's strategic vision tend to be more effective. It has also been shown that training programs are more likely to improve job performance when using the new skill improves the performance of participants whose remuneration depends on performance.[11]

2. **The purpose of the evaluation.** Evaluations also differ with respect to their purposes. Worthen and Sanders distinguished between *formative evaluation* and *summative evaluation*.[12]

   a. **Formative evaluations** are designed to help evaluators assess the value of the training materials and processes with the key goal of identifying

Formative evaluations
Provide data about various aspects of a training program

improvements to the instructional experience (the clarity, complexity, and relevance of the training contents, how they are presented, and the training context). Hence, formative evaluation provides data that are of special interest to training designers and instructors.

b. **Summative evaluations** are designed to provide data about a training program's worthiness or effectiveness: Has the training program resulted in payoffs for the organization? Cost–benefit analyses (see Chapter 11) are usually summative. Economic indices are often an integral and important part of these types of evaluations, and for this reason summative evaluations are of greatest interest to senior management. Ironically, these are rarely conducted by training departments!

A further distinction can be made between *descriptive* and *causal evaluations*. **Descriptive evaluations** provide information describing trainees once they have completed the program. Have the trainees learned the skill? Are they confident about and motivated to use the skill? Are they using the new skill on the job? Most evaluation designs have some descriptive components. **Causal evaluations** are used to determine whether the training *caused* the post-training learning and/or behaviours. Causal evaluations require more complex data gathering and statistical procedures. They are infrequently used (see Figure 10.2).

// MODELS OF TRAINING EVALUATION

Models of training evaluation specify the information (the variables) to be measured and their interrelationships. The dominant training evaluation model is Donald Kirkpatrick's hierarchical model.[13] However, research and practical experience have indicated that Kirkpatrick's model can be improved. The COMA model and the Decision-Based Evaluation model are two recent efforts in that direction and are discussed below.[14]

KIRKPATRICK'S HIERARCHICAL MODEL: THE FOUR LEVELS OF TRAINING EVALUATION

Kirkpatrick's hierarchical model of training evaluation is the oldest, best known, and most frequently used training evaluation model. For example, the Conference Board of Canada data summarized in Figure 10.2 is organized using his model. It identifies four fundamental measures, called levels, to assess training. According to this model, a training program is "effective" when

L1. Trainees report positive reactions to a training program (Level 1 = reactions).
L2. Trainees learn the training material (Level 2 = learning).
L3. Trainees apply on the job what they learn in training (Level 3 = behaviours).
L4. Training has a positive effect on organizational outcomes (Level 4 = impact or results).

In a more recent articulation, an additional level has been added to the Kirkpatrick model. Level 5 refers to return on investment (ROI). It attempts to assess the organizational benefits provided by training relative to its costs. In this chapter we concentrate on the original four levels of the Kirkpatrick evaluation model. Chapter 11 is fully devoted to the fifth level, the issue of cost–benefit analysis of training programs.

Summative evaluations
Provide data about the worthiness or effectiveness of a training program

Descriptive evaluations
Provide information that describes the trainee once he/she has completed a training program

Causal evaluations
Provide information to determine whether training caused the post-training behaviours

The Kirkpatrick model states that the four levels are arranged in a hierarchy such that each succeeding level provides more important (though more difficult to obtain) information than the previous one. Importantly, the model suggests *that each level has a causal link* to the next level. Thus, success at a particular level causes success at the next one. For example, training has strong organizational impact (L4) because individual behaviours have changed (L3), behaviours changed because trainees have learned the training material (L2), and they have learned it because the course was positively experienced (L1).

Originally proposed in 1959, Kirkpatrick's model provides managers and trainers with a systematic training evaluation framework that makes sense. It is simple and logical. It has clearly demystified training evaluation and most organizations that evaluate training programs rely on it and, to its credit, Kirkpatrick's model has stimulated much training evaluation research. We now know a great deal about the model, a topic to which we now turn.[15]

RESEARCH ON KIRKPATRICK'S MODEL

The hierarchy of cascading effects is essential for the practical use of Kirkpatrick's model. Programs that receive positive reaction scores are deemed "successful" because—according to the hierarchy—those positive reactions trigger positive results at the learning, behavioural, and results levels. That has real-life implications. Measuring trainee reactions is very easy, which is why most organizations do it. And if it were the case that reactions cause learning and behaviour change, organizations would then be perfectly justified to base their evaluations on the measurement of reactions.

However, that is not the case. Alliger et al's meta-analysis reports little correlation between the four levels of the model. Evaluations based on level 1 reactions, for example, indicate little about learning (L2), or behaviour change on the job (L3), or impact on the organization (L4). This invalidates the hierarchical characteristic of the model.

Not being hierarchical seriously limits the model's usefulness for organizations interested in formative evaluations. Recall that formative evaluations identify the aspects of training that need improvements. As the relationship between reactions, learning, and behaviour is very small (as shown in the Alliger meta-analysis), improving L1 (reactions) or L2 (learning) is unlikely to improve the impact of training at the behaviour (transfer) level.

Even as it is not useful for formative evaluations, Kirkpatrick's model remains useful for summative evaluations as long as one measures the appropriate level. If, for example, one is interested in determining if participants liked the training experience or learned from it, respectively measuring reactions (Level 1) or learning (Level 2) is appropriate. If the criterion of training success is job improvement, then measuring Kirkpatrick's Level 3 (behaviours) is mandatory. But the model cannot infer success at (say Level 3) by measuring Levels 1 and/or 2.

It has also been observed that the Kirkpatrick model lacks precision. The same label—reactions, learning, behaviour, impact—can be defined in a great many ways. As you will learn by consulting Table 10.2, some reaction measures are affect based (they assess how much training was enjoyed) while others are utility based (how useful it is perceived to be). These are quite different variables, though both are "reactions." Similar ambiguity exists for the other levels: L2 "learning" (declarative? procedural? see Chapter 2); L3 "behaviours" (reproduction of a specific learned task? generalization of the new skill to several job aspects? improvement in job performance?).

In recognition of Kirkpatrick's ambiguities and limitations, alternative evaluation models have been developed. Three of these are COMA, DBE, and the Learning Transfer System Inventory (see Training Today 10.2).

COMA MODEL

The **COMA** model is inspired by the Kirkpatrick model. It is intended principally for conducting formative evaluation. COMA enhances the usefulness of training evaluation questionnaires by identifying and measuring those variables that research has shown to be important for the transfer of training.[16] Instead of relying exclusively on reaction and declarative learning measures, COMA suggests the measurement of variables that fall into four categories: cognitive, organizational environment, motivational, and attitudinal variables (spelling the acronym COMA). These are measured by questionnaires that are administered to trainees immediately after the training session (and sometimes before).

> **COMA**
> A training evaluation model designed for formative evaluation that involves the measurement of cognitive, organizational, motivational, and attitudinal variables

- *Cognitive* variables refer to the level of learning that the trainee has gained from a training program. Both declarative and procedural learning might be measured, but the latter is more important because it is more strongly related to transfer than the former.

- *Organizational* environment refers to a cluster of variables that are generated by the work environment and that impact transfer of training. These include the learning culture, the opportunity to practise, the degree of support that is expected, and the level of support actually provided to trainees once they return to the job.

- *Motivation* refers to the desire to learn and to apply the learned skill on the job. Motivation is a powerful and persistent influence on transfer of training. COMA suggests that training motivation (measured at the onset of the program) and motivation to transfer (measured immediately after) both be measured.

- *Attitudes* refers to individuals' feelings and thinking processes. Chief among these beliefs are self-efficacy, perceptions of control, and expectations about self and the environment.

According to the COMA model, training evaluation should assess the degree to which trainees have mastered the skills (C) accurately perceive the degree to which the organizational environment (including peers and supervisors) will support and help them apply the skills (O) are motivated to learn and to apply the skills on the job (M) have developed attitudes and beliefs that allow them to feel capable of applying their newly acquired skills on the job (A).

At the conclusion of training, the trainees answer questionnaires that assess the COMA components. The questionnaires list each skill for which training is provided. The participants indicate, for each, whether they know the learned skills (C), are motivated to display them (M), are confident they can display the skills (A), and have realistic expectations of support (the degree to which the job environment will provide help and encourage them to use the skill on the job (O). When scores on the COMA variables are positive, the chances of transfer are greater. However, the reverse is also true: when scores are negative on one or more COMA dimensions, transfer is likely to be weaker. An analysis of each of the COMA dimensions helps identify the specific element (C, O, M, or A) that is problematic, pinpointing where to improve the training experience.

COMA improves upon the Kirkpatrick model in four ways:

- It transforms and improves the typical reaction questionnaires by incorporating a greater number of measures (the COMA variables).
- It is especially useful for formative evaluations.
- The variables it measures *are* causally related to transfer of training (see Chapter 9).
- It defines these new variables with greater precision.

However, the COMA model does have limits. As it is relatively new, it is too early to draw conclusions as to its value. Further, COMA is focused exclusively on an analysis of the factors that affect transfer. Moreover, because it does not specifically require measurement of on-the-job behaviours, is not well suited for summative evaluation purposes. Finally, COMA has one very large practical drawback: the questionnaires are required to list the trained skills. Therefore, different questionnaires must be constructed for different training programs.

Kirkpatrick's approach may be more suited to summative evaluations, while COMA is better for formative ones. Decision-Based Evaluation, the third evaluation model to be discussed, is an attempt at more versatility. It provides a template to guide the evaluator through a number of choices.

Decision-Based Evaluation (DBE)
A training evaluation model that specifies the target, focus, and methods of evaluation

DECISION-BASED EVALUATION MODEL

Decision-Based Evaluation (DBE) is a model developed by Kurt Kraiger. It requires evaluators to select their evaluation techniques and variables as a function of the uses to which the results of the evaluation will be put. That is, evaluation choices depend on the decisions needed. As with the COMA model, DBE specifies the categories of variables to be measured, but DBE goes further. It invites evaluators to custom fit their evaluations to the requirements of the situation. Hence, assessors need to identify the *target* of the evaluation (What do we want to find out from the evaluation?), identify its *focus* (What are the variables we will measure?), and suggest the *methods* that may be appropriate for conducting the evaluation.

The model specifies three potential "targets" for the evaluation: (1) trainee change; (2) organizational payoff; and (3) program improvement. Once those are decided, the evaluator specifies the "focus" of the change, as there are many changes that can be measured. Are we interested in assessing the level of trainee changes with respect to learning behaviours, or to the psychological states (such as motivation and self-efficacy)? Each evaluation study may include one or more foci. Once the focus or foci are selected, the model suggests the appropriate data collection method (e.g., surveys, job sample information, objective data, questionnaires, interviews).

DBE may well be a marked improvement, for different reasons, over both Kirkpatrick's model and the COMA model. Unlike Kirkpatrick's model and COMA, it allows for different variables (focus) to be measured depending on the goals (target) of the evaluation. DBE is the only training evaluation model that clearly specifies that evaluations must always be guided by key questions, chief among which are: What do we choose to evaluate? and How can we do so?

Kurt Kraiger: "Evaluation choices depend on the decisions needed."

In contrast to COMA and Kirkpatrick, DBE is more flexible, being useful for both formative and summative evaluations. However, as with COMA, this model is recent and still needs to be tested.

The Kirkpatrick, COMA, and DBE models of training evaluation all require that for each training program people with somewhat specialized skills develop the evaluation measures and questionnaires, and analyze and interpret the data. In some organizations, such resources are not always available. To help alleviate this constraint on training evaluation, Elwood Holton and his colleagues have proposed a more generic approach, described in Training Today 10.2, "The Learning Transfer System Inventory (LTSI)."[17]

TRAINING TODAY   10.2

THE LEARNING TRANSFER SYSTEM INVENTORY (LTSI)

The Holton–Bates approach is the Learning Transfer System Inventory (LTSI), which was described in Chapter 9. It is a questionnaire containing 89 questions that assess 16 variables that are important for the transfer of training. These variables include all of the COMA dimensions plus additional ones such as learner readiness (e.g., "I knew what to expect from the training before it began"), resistance/openness to change (e.g., "People in my group are open to changing the way they do things"), and opportunity to use learning (e.g., "The resources I need to use what I learned will be available to me after training"). Trainees answer the 89 questions using a five-point scale (strongly agree to strongly disagree). The LTSI is available in both English and French (advantageous for use in organizations that operate in different cultural milieux). Importantly, the LTSI is also a research instrument that is being constantly refined, with questions added or withdrawn depending on research results.

There are, however, some limitations with LTSI. It is a proprietary instrument, and organizations that wish to use it must obtain the authors' permission, must administer all 89 questions, and are required to provide the data collected to the authors. Organizations that do not wish to release their training evaluation data (e.g., for confidentiality or legal reasons), that believe the questionnaire taps dimensions of no relevance to their assessment, and/or that are unable to administer a lengthy questionnaire may judge this approach less applicable.

Source: Devos, C., Dumay, X., Bonami, M., Bates, R., & Holton, E., III. (2007). The Learning Transfer System Inventory (LTSI) translated into French: Internal structure and predictive validity. *International Journal of Training and Development, 11*, 181–199.

// TRAINING EVALUATION VARIABLES

Training evaluation requires the measurement of variables–those specified in the evaluation models. Table 10.1 provides a list of the main variables measured in training evaluation, while Table 10.2 shows sample questions and formats for measuring each type of variable.

REACTIONS

Trainee opinions and attitudes about a training program–so-called *reaction measures*–are the most common variables measured in evaluation studies. Reaction measures are easy to administer, collect, and analyze, and the questions may focus on the trainees' overall reactions to a training program (e.g., Overall, how satisfied were you with the training

TABLE 10.1

THE MAIN VARIABLES MEASURED IN TRAINING EVALUATION

VARIABLE	DEFINITION	HOW MEASURED
Reactions	trainee perceptions of the program and/or specific aspects of the course	questionnaires, focus groups, interviews
Learning	trainee acquisition of the program material – Declarative learning is knowing the information – Procedural knowledge is being able to translate that knowledge into a behavioural sequence.	– declarative: multiple choice or true–false tests – procedural: situational and mastery tests
Behaviour	on-the-job behaviour display, objective performance measures	self-reports, supervisory reports, direct and indirect observations, production records
Motivation	trainee desire to learn and/or transfer skills	questionnaires
Self-efficacy	trainee confidence in learning and/or behaviour display on the job	questionnaires
Perceived and/or anticipated support	the assistance trainees obtain and/or expect	questionnaires
Organizational perceptions	how trainees perceive the organization's culture and climate for learning and transfer	standardized questionnaires
Organizational results	the impact of training on organizational outcomes	organizational records

TABLE 10.2

EXAMPLES OF QUESTIONS AND FORMATS USED IN TRAINING EVALUATIONS

VARIABLE	EXAMPLE OF QUESTION	EXAMPLE OF ANSWER FORMAT
Reactions	How much of the course content can be applied in your job? (utility reaction measure) How satisfied were you with the content of the program? (affective reaction measure)	1 = None, 2 = Little, 3 = Some, 4 = Much, 5 = All 1 = Not at all satisfied, 2 = Not satisfied, 3 = Somewhat satisfied, 4 = Satisfied, 5 = Very satisfied
Declarative learning	Declarative: True or False: Earth is square. Multiple choice: What statement best describes Earth?	Declarative: True ___ False ___ Multiple choice: round, square, triangular, flat

TABLE 10.2 (*Continued*)

EXAMPLES OF QUESTIONS AND FORMATS USED IN TRAINING EVALUATIONS

VARIABLE	EXAMPLE OF QUESTION	EXAMPLE OF ANSWER FORMAT
Procedural learning	Procedural Mastery: You need to write a letter using a computer. From the list below pick the four steps required to do so and list them in the order with which they should be performed.	

Step	Required?	Order
Turn computer on	Yes	1
Set the margins	Yes	4
Select "new document"	Yes	3
Open the word processor	Yes	2
Test the hard drive	No	—

VARIABLE	EXAMPLE OF QUESTION	EXAMPLE OF ANSWER FORMAT
Behaviour	Self-report: How many "cold calls" have you made in the last week? Observation: By others including the supervisor and the analyst. May also include subordinates or customers.	Open-ended frequency scale (number of times) or rating scale: 1 = Many, 2 = Some, 3 = A few, 4 = None
Motivation	How important is it to reduce accidents at work?	1 = Very important, 2 = Important, 3 = Neither important nor unimportant, 4 = Somewhat unimportant, 5 = Very unimportant
	What are the consequences to you if you apply at work that which you learned in training?	Will make my job: 1 = much harder, 2 = somewhat harder, 3 = no effect, 4 = somewhat easier, 5 = much easier
	How likely is it that if you do apply the trained behaviours there will be fewer accidents?	1 = Extremely likely, 2 = Somewhat likely, 3 = Neither likely nor unlikely, 4 = Unlikely, 5 = Extremely unlikely
	The product of the three sets of questions produces the motivator scores.	
Self-efficacy	How confident are you that you can explain the new policy to your subordinates?	1 = Not at all confident, 2, 3, 4, to 5 = Very confident
Perceived and/or anticipated support	My supervisor helps me (perceived support); I expect that my supervisor will help me apply (anticipated support) my new skills on the job.	1 = Completely disagree, 2, 3, 4, to 5 = Completely agree
Organizational perceptions	Supervisors give recognition and credit to those who apply new knowledge and skills to their work.	Standardized questionnaires
Organizational results	How much has quality improved as a result of the training program?	Number of units rejected per day; number of items returned per month; number of customer complaints per week

Participants answer a questionnaire that assesses their perceptions of the training program.

Nicholas Monu/Getty Images

program?) and/or on specific elements of a program (e.g., To what extent were you satisfied with the instructor?).

Trainee reactions are typically and most frequently measured by questionnaires immediately following training. The same questionnaires can be used for many different courses, which reduces costs and allows easy comparisons between courses. Table 10.3 lists a variety of ways in which reaction questions may be formatted. Most rating scales have between four and seven response choices, though more or fewer points can be used.

In other cases, trainees answer in their own words so-called open-ended questions, such as "What improvements should be made to the course?" Personal or group interviews (focus groups) are sometimes used to gather reactions. Such qualitative approaches can provide richer, more nuanced data. However, they depend in part on the openness and verbal abilities of participants, as well as on the skills and objectivity of the analysts (for written comments) and on the interviewer (for focus groups). If analyst/interviewer biases slant or taint the discussion, the results may be quite worthless. Hence someone other than the course designer or instructor should conduct these tasks.

In a major study involving thousands of responses to reaction questionnaires, Morgan and Casper identified six dimensions that underlie reaction measures: satisfaction with the instructor, the training process, the materials, the course structure, the assessment process, and the perceived usefulness (utility) of the training.[18]

Reaction measures can be quite different, but two types have received the most attention: affective and utility reaction measures. **Affective reactions** assess trainees' *likes and dislikes* of a training program. **Utility reactions** assess the degree to which trainees perceive the training program to be *useful*.

Affective reaction measures appear to bear little relationship to other important training outcomes such as learning and behaviour. By contrast, utility reaction measures are generally preferable, since they demonstrate some relationship to these higher-level outcomes.[19] However, the data gathered in a 2008 study nuance the previously thought advantage of utility measures over affective ones.[20] Whereas this study confirms that affective reactions bear little relationship to higher-level outcomes, it reports significant correlations between affective reactions and outcomes *for courses that use a high level of technology, such as Internet courses*: People who dislike an Internet course are less likely to derive benefits from it than those who like it. This suggests the importance for Internet-delivered courses to include design elements that can maintain the trainee's attention. They need to be interesting and engaging to the learner. Trainees who dislike or are bored by a training course (low affective reactions) can, and often do, simply shut off their computers!

Trainee reaction measures for training evaluation are extremely popular because: (1) they provide trainers with immediate feedback on their course; (2) they are easy to collect and analyze, and are easily understood by managers and employees; (3) trainees who have had a chance to comment on a program and make suggestions for improvements might be more motivated to transfer their learning than others who leave a program without providing input.

However, it remains the case that reaction questionnaires are unable to estimate transfer levels. Hence, in practice they are more often than not used to evaluate the performance of the trainers rather than to assess the value of a course. In universities, for example, student ratings of courses partially determine promotion and/or retention decisions, especially for lecturers and part-time faculty.

Affective reactions Reaction measures that assess trainees' *likes and dislikes* of a training program

Utility reactions Reaction measures that assess the perceived *usefulness* of a training program

For more information see Chapter 2, pp. 48-50

TABLE 10.3

REACTIONS RATING FORM

Course or Session: _____

Instructor: _____

CONTENT:

Please answer the following questions using the scale below:
1. Strongly disagree 2. Disagree 3. Neither disagree nor agree 4. Agree 5. Strongly agree

____ The material presented will be useful to me on the job.
____ The level of information was too advanced for my work.
____ The level of information presented was too elementary for me.
____ The information was presented in manageable chunks.
____ Theories and concepts were linked to work activities.
____ The course material was up to date and reliable.

INSTRUCTOR:

Please rate the instructor's performance along the following dimensions:

____ Needs improvement.
____ Just right, or competent, effective.
____ Superior or very effective performance.

THE INSTRUCTOR:

____ Described the objectives of the session.
____ Had a plan for the session.
____ Followed the plan.
____ Determined trainees' current knowledge.
____ Explained new terms.
____ Used work and applied examples.
____ Provided opportunities for questions.
____ Was enthusiastic about the topic.
____ Presented material clearly.
____ Effectively summarized the material.
____ Varied the learning activities.
____ Showed a personal interest in class progress.
____ Demonstrated a desire for trainees to learn.

PERCEIVED IMPACT:

____ I gained significant new knowledge.
____ I developed skills in the area.
____ I was given tools for attacking problems.
____ My on-the-job performance will improve.

Please indicate what you will do differently on the job as a result of this course.

OVERALL RATING:

Taking into account all aspects of the course, how would you rate it?
____ Excellent ____ Very Good ____ Good ____ Fair ____ Poor
Would you take another course from this instructor? ____ Yes ____ No
Would you recommend this course to your colleagues? ____ Yes ____ No

LEARNING

It is important to assess learning. Research has shown that participants anticipating a post-training test are more attentive and more motivated to learn the training material.[21] They also attach more importance to the training.

The measurement of learning is also very important in other cases. Electricians, lawyers, and doctors, to name but three professions, all require certification to earn the right to practise. Certification requires passing the professional exams. In cases of accidents and litigation, the employer can prove that the employee was trained to the necessary levels. For trainees at General Dynamics, this was important because they were not allowed access to the manufacturing resource planning software until they had passed a competency tests.

Learning tests are very useful in formative evaluations because they provide diagnostic information. If trainees consistently score low on some aspect, the trainer is alerted to the fact that this component may need revision. More information may be required, or exercises might have to be added to ensure that learning does occur.

Although many types of learning outcomes can be measured (Jonassen and Tessmer identify more than 10), most training evaluations measure declarative learning.[22] In rare cases, some evaluators also assess procedural learning. The distinction between declarative and procedural learning is important in training evaluation. Declarative learning is relatively easy to measure, but research has shown that it has slight if any relationship to behaviours. Procedural learning is much more difficult to measure. However, it is related significantly to behaviours and to transfer of training.

Declarative learning is by far the most frequently assessed learning measure. It refers to the acquisition of facts and information. Students familiar with college or university exams know about tests of declarative learning. The most popular (and easiest to construct) declarative learning tests are formatted as multiple choice or true–false questions. However, other techniques are available; Table 10.4 presents several of these.

Part A of Table 10.4 lists declarative learning tests that are objectively scored. With objective testing, there is only one correct answer and the test corrector has no leeway in defining a correct or incorrect response to a test item.

Part B exemplifies subjectively scored learning measures. These can take various forms, including essay questions, oral interviews, journals, and diaries. Several different answers might be equally correct, and markers have some latitude in their interpretation of the correctness of the answer. Of course, that flexibility comes with a price—the risk of scorer biases.

Procedural learning involves the organization of facts and information into a smooth behavioural sequence. Many techniques are available to measure it, but all are more complex to develop and use than declarative learning measures. As a result, rare are the organizations that measure procedural learning in their evaluations of training.

Desjardins developed a procedural learning measure for a course training police officers in the do's and don'ts of how to protect a crime scene.[23] She interviewed task experts who demonstrated the proper actions and proper sequence of behaviours required and then summarized these steps, added some unnecessary and incorrect steps, and shuffled the order of the steps. Trainees had to distinguish between the required and erroneous steps and reposition them into the correct order. Completing this task successfully requires procedural understanding of the training content.

Cheri Ostroff measured procedural learning with a different approach. Education managers were trained to interact effectively with parents in tense conflict situations.[24] At the completion of the training program, trainees were presented with a number of

Declarative learning Acquiring facts and information; is by far the most frequently assessed learning measure

Procedural learning Organizing facts and information into a smooth behavioural sequence

TABLE 10.4

DECLARATIVE LEARNING TEST FORMATS

PART A: OBJECTIVELY SCORED TESTS

TRUE OR FALSE

1. A test is valid if a person receives approximately the same result or score at two different testing times. True ___ False ___

MULTIPLE CHOICE

2. The affective domain of learning refers to
   a) ___ skills
   b) ___ attitudes
   c) ___ knowledge
   d) ___ all of the above
   e) ___ (b) and (c)

MATCHING

3. For each of the governments listed on the left, select the appropriate responsibility for training and place its letter next to the term.

   ___ 1. federal   a. displaced workers

   ___ 2. provincial   b. language training

   ___ 3. municipal   c. student summer work

SHORT ANSWER

4. Kirkpatrick identified four levels of measurement. These are:

   ___

   ___

   ___

   ___

PART B: SUBJECTIVELY SCORED TESTS

ESSAY

5. Describe the similarities among Kirkpatrick, COMA, and DBE.

ORAL

6. The measurement of training has many potential benefits. Identify these benefits. Discuss why, given these benefits of measurement, most trainers do not evaluate training.

OBSERVATION CHECKLIST

7. The customer-service representative:

   ___ greeted the customer

   ___ approached the customer

   ___ offered to help

TABLE 10.4 (*Continued*)				
DECLARATIVE LEARNING TEST FORMATS				
RATING SCALE				
8.	Indicate the degree to which you agree or disagree with the statements below: Scale: 1 = Strongly disagree, 2 = Disagree, 3 = Agree, 4 = Strongly agree During a selection interview, the interviewer: – used behavioural-based questions 1 2 3 4 – looked for contrary evidence 1 2 3 4 – used probing questions 1 2 3 4				
DIARIES, ANECDOTAL RECORDS, JOURNALS				
9.	In your journal, write about your experiences working with someone from a different culture. Record the date, time, and reason for the interaction. Describe how you felt and what you learned.				

conflict situations. Four different ways of handling the conflict were listed for each. The conflict cases were drawn from real situations and the four response options were carefully constructed. Trainees who had acquired a limited comprehension of the principles of conflict management (low procedural knowledge) would tend to select one option, while those with sophisticated comprehension levels (high procedural knowledge) would select another. The intermediate choices reflected comprehension (and procedural learning) levels between these extremes.

Procedural learning measures can also involve simulations conducted in realistic situations. For example, a pilot could be tested in a virtual-reality airplane. The skills of a drug counsellor could be tested using actors as drug addicts. A test could be conducted as a role play (for negotiation skills) or a practice session (for tennis certification). These tests are usually called performance tests or work sample tests.

Clearly, it is very important and useful for training evaluations to include the measurement of knowledge acquisition. However, scoring well on tests does not necessarily result in performance changes on the job. It is on the measurement of behaviour at work and its impact on job performance that the real assessments of the worthwhileness of training is revealed.

For more information see Chapter 9, p. 283 and Chapter 4, p. 129

BEHAVIOUR

"Behaviour" refers to the display of the newly learned skills or competencies on the job. This is also what we called "transfer of training" in Chapter 9, and is arguably the most important of all training effectiveness criteria.[25] The behaviours assessed should be those identified by the training objectives (see Chapter 4).

Behaviours can be measured using three basic approaches:

a. *Self-reports*: The trainee indicates if and/or how often the newly trained behaviours are used on the job. Use of self-reports is dominant in the field because they are the easiest and most practical measure to collect.

b. *Observations*: Others observe and record whether and/or how often the trainee has used the newly trained behaviours on the job. Typically, it is supervisors who provide these observations, but depending on the opportunity to observe, the trained person, trainers, subordinates, or even clients can provide it.

c. *Production indicators*: The trainee's objective output is assessed through productivity records, such as sales or absenteeism.

Self-reports remain the most frequently used measures of behaviour.[26] However, the accuracy of self-report measures can be problematic. How do we know that people are accurately remembering and reporting their own behaviours? It is generally agreed that self-reports tend to be *inaccurate*, although they might yet be *valid*. The distinction between accuracy and validity is important. Studies comparing self-reports of absenteeism with company records of absence show that, in general, people tend to report fewer absences than were actually taken (low accuracy). However, people who are more absent tend to self-report more absences than those who have fewer absences (validity). Hence, although self-reports are unable to measure transfer in absolute terms, they are able to reveal trends.

On-the-job behaviour is sometimes assessed through observations by others (mainly supervisors). Typically, the observer rates whether the person has used the behaviour and/or how often that has occurred. As with self-reports, the issues of accuracy and validity are of significance. For both self-report and observational data, it is important that the measure zero-in on specific behaviours (How many times in the last month has the trainee used the new machine?) as opposed to general ones (Has the trainee applied the skill on the job?). Measures of specific behaviours are more likely to be valid and accurate. Moreover, the validity and accuracy of observational data are enhanced when the observer has a clear understanding of the behaviours the employee is expected to display or avoid and when he/she has extensive contact with the trainee.[27] To help focus the observations on the relevant behaviours, checklists are frequently provided.

Performance indices (sometimes called "objective" measures) are a third type of behaviour data that might be gathered in an evaluation of training effectiveness. Performance indicators, such as sales performance drawn directly from company records, are the measures needed in summative evaluations, where measuring the cost–benefits of training are key (see Chapter 11). They are the desired data when the evaluation is a time series (see Data Collection Designs in Training Evaluation later in this chapter).

In some cases, performance records can provide highly precise data on specific behaviours. For example, "number of times a trainee has accessed a database" can be automatically recorded by the computer, providing highly accurate behaviour data for evaluating a training program designed to train people in the use and application of a database. In the Bell Canada chapter-opening vignette, computerized records were used to accurately measure, for each trainee, his/her extent of use of each feature of the electronic telephone.

However, performance indices are not always available (how would one measure the objective performance of a doctor?). Further, even when available they may not be the best measure, since they sometimes contaminate individual performance with other events that impact performance. For example, one "objective" measure of a call centre operator might be the number of calls he/she has taken in an hour. But that is not necessarily a good indicator of performance, since the number of calls that can be answered is limited by the number of incoming calls. This may engender inaccurate conclusions.

Xerox uses many methods to ascertain behaviour, including post-course observations of trainees performing their jobs, interviews with their managers, and a review of performance-appraisal forms.[28] TD Bank uses a very simple approach. Participants in training programs are asked to describe three or four examples of when they used the new knowledge or skill on the job.[29]

Whatever the approach used, behaviour data collection should take place only after the trainee has become comfortable with the newly acquired skills and has had opportunities to demonstrate them on the job. The time lag for the assessment of behaviour can range from a few weeks to two years or more in the case of managerial skills. It is recommended that the measurement of behaviour take place at several points following a training program in order to determine the long-term effects of a training program.

For more information see
Chapter 2, p. 45 and
Chapter 9, p. 281

MOTIVATION

Training evaluators consider the measurement of two types of motivation in the training context: training motivation and the motivation to transfer the skill on the job.

As described in Chapter 2, training motivation refers to the direction, intensity, and persistence of learning-directed behaviour in training contexts. This is usually administered before the start of the training program. Motivation to transfer, on the other hand, is typically assessed after training is completed. It is especially important to measure motivation to transfer. As discussed in Chapter 9, transfer is arguably the single most important reason for conducting training in organizations, and motivation levels have a decided impact on transfer.

A number of scales have been designed to measure training motivation and motivation to transfer.[30] One important technique for measuring transfer motivation relies on expectancy theory. Three sets of items are used to measure the valence (the attractiveness of transfer outcomes), instrumentalities (the positive or negative consequences of transfer), and expectancies (the probability that transfer will result in successful performance). The principle is that trainees will be motivated to apply the training when they attach importance to the end result of training (valence), that the attainment of that end result leads to positive consequences or avoids negative ones (instrumentalities), and that applying the training is likely to lead to the desired end result (expectancies).

A study by Haccoun and Savard exemplifies the measurement of motivation to transfer.[31] Trainees (supervisors) were trained to apply a new organizational policy designed to reduce employee absenteeism (among other things). Motivation was measured through three sets of questions: (1)Valence: How important is it that absence be reduced in your work group? (2)Instrumentality: If you reduce absence, what would be the consequences (positive or negative) for you? and (3)Expectancy: If you did apply the behaviours taught in training, how likely is it that absence levels would drop? Each question was rated on a five-point rating scale. The product of the three sets of answers (Valence × Instrumentality × Expectancy) produces the transfer motivation score.

For more information see
Chapter 2, p. 60

SELF-EFFICACY

As described in Chapter 2, self-efficacy refers to the beliefs that trainees hold about their ability to successfully perform the behaviours that were taught in a training program. That is, self-efficacy assesses a person's confidence in engaging in specific behaviours or achieving specific goals. Changing one's work behaviour is often a difficult process, as many obstacles and ambient forces in the work environment may not be supportive of it. Thus, self-efficacy is important because people who do not feel capable of applying a new skill at work are unlikely to exert much effort to do so, especially when they are faced with obstacles. This is crucial especially in the many cases in which the work environment (e.g., co-workers, supervisors) is less than supportive of behaviour changes.

Measures of self-efficacy vary, but most tend to focus on assessing trainees' level of confidence for learning the material and/or for displaying specific behaviours or performing specific tasks. Self-efficacy is measured relative to a specific behavioural target.

In one option trainees rate the likelihood of obtaining a certain result followed by ratings of the confidence they have in obtaining that result. For example, a measure of self-efficacy for an exam on this chapter might read as follows: "Are you likely to obtain 50%, 60%, 70%, 80%, 90%, 100% on an exam on training evaluation?" (Yes/No response to each option). Next, the person rates how confident they are about obtaining the grade for each "Yes" response. The question might read, "How confident are you that you can obtain that grade?" (0 = Not confident at all, 10 = Total confident).

Another simple method lists the key behaviours demonstrating transfer and asks trainees to rate each on a confidence scale, such as: "How confident are you that you will obtain at least 70 percent on the training evaluation exam?" The response scales range from totally confident to not at all confident. Although 10-point rating scales are common, scales using a smaller number of points are also frequently used.

For more information see Chapter 9, p. 288

PERCEIVED AND/OR ANTICIPATED SUPPORT

As indicated in Chapter 9, the support provided to trainees as they return to work is a very important component of transfer and training effectiveness. Two important measures of support are perceived support and anticipated support. **Perceived support** refers to the degree to which the trainee reports receiving support in his/her attempts to transfer the learned skills. **Anticipated support** refers to the degree to which the trainee *expects* to be supported in his/her attempts to transfer the learned skills.

Specific questions can be designed to include the source of the support (e.g., supervisor, co-workers, or the organization) and the support (perceived or anticipated) in applying the training content in general and/or in transferring specific aspects of the training program.

For example, in a study on the effects of a training program that trained nurses on a model of nursing, questions about anticipated support included "If I am having difficulty writing a nursing care plan, I know I can obtain (very little–very much) help from my supervisor." An alternative phrasing could be "Based on my previous experiences, I think I can count on (very little–very much) support from my co-workers in applying the training content to my job."

Notice that in the nursing study, the first formulation of the question refers to a specific component of the training program (i.e., nursing care plan), while the latter refers to the training program content in general. These two items also differ in terms of the source of support, with the former being one's supervisor and the latter being co-workers.

Anticipated support measures are collected before and/or immediately following training. Actual support, on the other hand, is measured weeks or months after the trainees have returned to work. In their study, Haccoun and Savard measured anticipated support in the last minutes of the training day (as part of the immediate post-training reaction questionnaire). Two years later, they returned to the organization and measured

Perceived support
The degree to which the trainee reports receiving support in his/her attempts to transfer the learned skills

Anticipated support
The degree to which the trainee expects to be supported in his/her attempts to transfer the learned skills

both the transfer levels the trainees reported as well as their perceptions of the level of support they had actually received in applying the new skill on the job.

Two of their results are particularly important: (1) expected support was best able to predict transfer, but more importantly (2) the relationship between expected support and transfer was *negative*! Trainees who *expected more support* than they actually received *transferred significantly less*! Further statistical analyses showed that trainees who expected much support but who actually received little transferred the least. On the other hand, those whose support expectations matched the support levels they got transferred more. This highlights the importance for trainees of leaving the training session with realistic expectations of support. In the world of training, overselling is not a good idea.

For more information see Chapter 3, p. 90 and Chapter 9, pp. 288-290

ORGANIZATIONAL PERCEPTIONS

Several researchers have designed scales to measure perceptions of the transfer climate and a learning culture, as discussed in Chapter 3 and Chapter 9. Transfer climate can be measured via a questionnaire developed by Janice Rouiller and Irwin Goldstein.[32] The measure consists of a number of questions that identify eight sets of "cues" that can trigger trainee reactions that encourage or discourage the trainee to transfer the skill. The eight scales include goal cues, social cues, task and structural cues, positive feedback, negative feedback, punishment, no feedback, and self-control. Trainees are asked questions about training-specific characteristics of the work environment, such as "In your organization, supervisors set goals for trainees to encourage them to apply their training on the job" (1 = Strongly disagree, 5 = Strongly agree). Rouiller and Goldstein have shown that transfer is stronger when the organizational transfer climate is more favourable.

In addition, J. Bruce Tracey, Scott Tannenbaum, and Michael Kavanagh proposed a scale to measure whether an organization has a continuous learning culture. The questions measure trainees' perceptions, beliefs, expectations, and values with regard to individual, task, and organizational factors that support the acquisition and application of knowledge, skill, and behaviour. The Trainer's Notebook 3.1 in Chapter 3 presents some of the items from this scale. Once again, research indicates that transfer levels are higher in organizations that have a stronger learning culture.

Finally, the LTSI approach (described in Training Today 10.2) is an example of yet another approach to assessing the role of the organization in fostering training transfer.

ORGANIZATIONAL RESULTS

An evaluation may also focus on "results criteria." These criteria relate to the effects of training on the organization rather than on the trainee. How has the organization benefited from the training program? Have profits increased? Results criteria may include such measures as turnover, productivity, quality, profitability, customer satisfaction, and accidents. However, some of these may be difficult to measure. More importantly, it is very difficult to clearly determine if it is training or something else that has caused improvements in these organizational level variables. Testing causality requires experimental designs that are generally difficult to implement in organizations (see the section on Data Collection Designs in Training Evaluation later in this chapter). In some instances, the objective is to cost the program and determine the net benefit. Chapter 11 is devoted to procedures for doing cost–benefit analysis.

Phillips has produced a useful taxonomy of hard data and soft data that may be measured in training evaluations.[33] **Hard data** are objective measures that fall in one of four categories:

- quantity (the number of items sold or produced)
- quality (scrap rates and product returns)
- time (downtime or time to complete assignments)
- costs (sales expenses, benchmarks)

Hard data are of particular and direct relevance to upper management partly because of their objectivity, but mainly because they assess the bottom line.

ACCO Brands Corporation, a manufacturer of school supplies ranging from paper clips to binders, uses hard data (quantity) to track the effect of training on new production hires. After training, new hires were able to produce vinyl binders at a 5 to 10 percent higher rate than tenured operators, a clear payoff to the organization.[34]

Few organizations collect hard outcome measures in the training evaluations. This is the case for two reasons:

- Such data are not always available, and/or collecting it may be too expensive or difficult.
- It is not necessarily the case that training caused the hard data changes.

Many things unrelated to training may have caused any improved productivity. To illustrate, consider the ACCO Brands case showing that the new hires, trained with a new program, were more effective. But was that improvement because of the new training or did it really occur because the participants were more motivated, as new hires tend to be?

Even when available, hard data are not always essential to the purpose of the evaluation. For formative evaluations, where the goal is to improve training, the use of soft data is prevalent.

Soft data are measures of beliefs, attitudes, and perceptions and usually involve judgments, observations, or perceptions of an outcome. These include measures of self-efficacy, motivation, post-training support, and the elements covered by the LTSI questionnaire. Self-reports are frequently measured when it is difficult to measure some skills, such as decision making.

Unlike hard data, soft data are not direct indicators of organizational outcomes (providing dollar values). Rather, soft data are important because the feelings, beliefs, and attitudes they measure are linked to concrete results. For example, communication skills are not bottom-line measures, but they may ultimately affect the organization's bottom line. Self-efficacy is another type of soft data that might indirectly affect the bottom line because of its influence on the display of communication skills.

In some cases, it is difficult or impossible to adequately assess the impact of training directly either with hard or soft data. An alternative is to calculate **return on expectations**. Those who are involved in training decide exactly what they expect from the training. These expectations form the goals for training, and sometime later the course managers decide whether the performance results are in line with their expectations.

For example, an organization restructured into product-performance teams (where collaboration between members of teams was critical) was unable to place a dollar value on the cross-functional training employees had received. However, managers noticed that 95 percent of deadlines were now being met by teams that received training. This was taken as a sign of improved collaboration among team members, which of course was the goal of training. They could not measure collaboration directly but they could surmise from the results that the training had met the expectations held of it.

Hard data
Results that are assessed objectively

Soft data
Results that are assessed through perceptions and judgments

Return on expectations
The measurement of a training program's ability to meet managerial expectations

Thus far in this chapter, we have discussed the nature, purpose, uses, and constraints of training evaluation as well as its models and variables. In all cases, training evaluation requires the collection of data. We now turn to this important issue. How are we to organize—design—the collection of evaluation data? As with everything else about training evaluation, the design we choose depends on the information needed.

// DATA COLLECTION DESIGNS IN TRAINING EVALUATION

There are a number of data collection alternatives available to the evaluator. Some of them require just a single data gathering effort, while others may require two or more. The data may be perceptual (subjective) or objective, and they may be gathered from one or more sources: the trainees, their supervisors, or performance records. But all training evaluations involve one or more of these three comparisons:

- Trainee states relative to a predetermined criterion (e.g., After having studied this chapter, can you pass a knowledge test?)
- Trainee changes (e.g., After studying this chapter, is your knowledge of training evaluation greater than it was before?)
- Trainees compared to non-trained people (e.g., Compared to students who have not read this chapter, do you know more about training evaluation than they do?)

As with all other aspects discussed in this chapter, the approach selected depends on the information we require and on the practical constraints to getting it—as the information need increases, so does the complexity of the data collection design. All designs rely on measurements, and these may be of attitudes, knowledge, and/or behaviours of participants following training. We begin with three descriptive models: the post-only, the pre-post, and the time series designs.

DESCRIPTIVE TRAINING EVALUATION MODELS

Descriptive data collection schemes indicate the post-training states of trainees in terms of attitudes, knowledge, and/or behaviours. However, they *cannot* prove that training caused those outcomes. Three descriptive models are relatively popular.

THE POST-ONLY DATA COLLECTION DESIGN: HAVE TRAINEES ATTAINED A PREDETERMINED LEVEL?

Often, especially for certification purposes, the organization is required to demonstrate that its employees have attained, after training, a predetermined level of proficiency. In that case, the post-only design is required. As the name implies, trainees are measured on the relevant variable only once the course is completed. Training effectiveness is inferred when on average (or when most of) the trainees attain that specified level. Driving tests and university exams are common examples of the post-only data collection design, as are the certification exams for many professions, including law and medicine.

In practice, most organizations use the post-only design and measure trainee reactions as it is the simplest and easiest method to use. Of course, as we have seen, reactions are very limited measures of training effectiveness. However, even with better outcome measures—learning, behaviours, and even job performance—valid interpretation of the results of a post-only design is difficult. As students know all too well, performance on exams may be excellent (or poor) because we learned a lot from the course but—and equally important—it may also be because the exam was especially easy (or hard), because we felt comfortable (or not) during it, because we had slept well (or poorly), and so on. Moreover, as the post-only design only measures the trainees after training, it cannot indicate if the trainees improved.

To help solve some of these problems, evaluators can turn to a somewhat more sophisticated evaluation design: the pre-post.

THE PRE-POST DESIGN: HAVE TRAINEES CHANGED?

The pre-post design is indicated when the goal of the training evaluation is to assess trainee improvement in knowledge, skills, and/or performance. With this design, trainee attitudes, knowledge, skills, and/or job performance are measured twice, once before (pre) and once after (post) the program is completed. Training effectiveness is inferred when the post-training scores are significantly higher than the pre-training ones.

The pre-post assesses if change has occurred, which is a measure of effectiveness, and it can assess the size or extent of that change, which is a measure of efficiency. When two training programs produce equivalent trainee change, the less expensive one is more efficient.

As with the post-only, the pre-post design is not a causal model. Hence, it cannot prove that training is responsible for the changes. There are many reasons that might explain a pre-post change and training is but one of them (see The Trainer's Notebook 10.1, "Understanding Pre-Post Differences"). And since only one post-training measure is taken, it is impossible to know whether the change is long lasting or ephemeral. To help alleviate these problems—at least to some degree—evaluators sometimes turn to a third data collection approach, the time series design.

THE TRAINER'S NOTEBOOK   10.1

UNDERSTANDING PRE-POST DIFFERENCES

Suppose we wish to evaluate this chapter's effectiveness in teaching training evaluation. We select a pre-post design in which knowledge is measured with a multiple-choice test administered on the first day of class (pre-test) and again on the last day (post-test). The results show the average score of the students on the post-test is significantly higher than the pre-test scores. Can it be concluded that reading this chapter *caused* this gain in knowledge? Before jumping to conclusions, you should consider four alternative explanations:

- *History or Time.* Events that coincide with this course and that have nothing to do with it may have caused pre-to-post changes. For example, the class may have done better because many students saw a PBS program on training evaluation that was aired the week before the final exam.

- *Maturation.* People mature and change over time. As the students are taking this course they are also taking other courses. Even if none of the other courses deals explicitly with training evaluation, they may have helped the students develop higher levels of reasoning and critical thinking skills. This growing general competence may translate into better performance on the post-test.

- *Testing.* Taking the pre-test may have made it easier for students to perform better on the post-test. Some students may have remembered

(*continued*)

---

some of the questions asked on the pre-test, while others may have gained a better "feel" for the kinds of questions that are asked. Hence, the post-test performance may be due, at least in part, to the mere experience of being pre-tested.

- *Mortality.* Whereas most students who enroll in a course stay until the end, it is almost always the case that some students drop the course. Those who remain in the course may obtain higher scores on the final exam because they are systematically different from those who dropped out—they may be more interested in the subject matter, be more motivated, be better prepared, and/or have more time to meet the course demands. It is not the training per se, but rather the other elements that may have caused the pre-post differences.

Source: Adapted from Cook, T. D., & Campbell, D. T. (1979). *Quasi-experimentation: Design and analysis issues for field settings.* Skokie, IL: Rand McNally.

THE TIME SERIES DESIGN: DO THE POST-TRAINING RESULTS PERSIST?

The time series design extends the pre-post by collecting the same outcome measures several times before and several times after training. Most time series–based evaluations rely on objective performance records, since this information is repeatedly collected without disturbing the employees. As with the pre-post design, training effectiveness is indicated when a significant improvement is noted immediately following training. The time series is an improvement over the pre-post as it assesses the degree to which that improvement persists.

Organizations will choose this evaluation design when objective performance data are easily available. For example, an organization that trains its sales people on closing techniques would record monthly sales obtained by each trainee for the six months preceding and the six months following training. The course is considered a success if sales volumes increase immediately after training and remain at the higher level thereafter.

THE LIMIT OF THE THREE DESCRIPTIVE EVALUATION MODELS

These three designs are practical to implement and they can provide some useful information. They can certainly assess if employees possess the required skills after training. However, as training can be expensive and disruptive in an organization, it matters to ascertain that it is the training experience that "created" those skills. The demonstration of causality requires the use of an evaluation design in which the effects of training are isolated from the effects of the other potential causes. These are known as *experimental designs*.

Wise organizations choose these causal evaluation designs when they are considering implementing an expensive and/or strategically important training program, and/or when they must select one from several course offerings.

// CAUSAL EVALUATION DESIGNS

Typical causal evaluation designs collect data from two "identical" groups of employees: one is trained and the other is not. The same training-relevant outcome data, collected from both the trained and the untrained group, is compared statistically. Training is judged to be effective when the trained group outperforms the untrained group on the relevant post-training measures. In practice, a causal evaluation is produced when the performance data of an untrained group are added to the descriptive designs—the post-only, the pre-post, and the time series.

The development of a causal training evaluation requires five steps.

1. Select the basic designs (post only, pre-post, time series) as a function of the constraints and of the informational needs of the organization.
2. Identify a group of "identical" employees for whom the need for the specific training is pertinent.
3. Randomly divide these employees into two groups. One group is to attend training, the other, called the *control* group, is not.
4. Measure both groups on the same outcome variables at the same time.
5. Statistically compare the outcomes achieved by both groups.

Evaluation designs that follow these five steps are called "experimental."

Many organizations find it very difficult to fulfill the random assignment required of experimental designs. In those cases, they can turn to quasi-experimental designs, in which the trained group is compared to a group of employees who do a similar job in similar circumstances. For example, the same training program might be delivered to the tellers of one branch but not to those from a different branch of the same bank. The untrained tellers, in that case, would be part of the *comparison* group in that *quasi-experimental* training evaluation design.

Random assignment ensures that the trained and untrained groups are statistically identical (if the number of participants is adequate). However, with quasi-experimental designs we do not have random assignment to the trained and untrained group. Consequently, it is less certain that the two groups are identical before training. If they differ after training, we are less certain that the training caused that difference . . . we are quasi-certain!

Confidence in the results is greater with experimental than with quasi-experimental designs and both are clearly superior to the nonexperimental data collection designs. However, descriptive models are the easiest and most practical data collection models and hence the most popular in organizations.

This creates a dilemma: Evaluation models that can prove effectiveness (i.e., experimental and quasi-experimental designs) are impractical, while practical designs (such as the pre-post or time series) cannot prove effectiveness. A hybrid quasi-experimental design has been proposed to help solve the problem. It is called the *Internal Referencing Strategy* or *IRS*.[35] This design allows causal inference without the need to include a control/comparison group.

// THE INTERNAL REFERENCING STRATEGY (IRS): A COMPROMISE EVALUATION MODEL

With the IRS design, data are collected exclusively from the trained group using a pre-post design. However, on both the pre and post measures, two types of outcomes are measured. One of these outcomes is the one for which training is provided. It is called the *relevant* outcome. The other outcome is one for which training could have been provided but was not. It is called the *irrelevant but germane* outcome. If training is effective, there should be greater pre-post change on the relevant outcomes (for which training is given) than change on the irrelevant but germane outcome (for which training is not provided).

Suppose that we evaluate the extent to which the six data collection schemes discussed in this chapter have been learned using a (non-causal) pre-post design. Analysis shows significant improvement. Did training cause that improvement?

With the classic pre-post scheme, improvement in the trainees' understanding of the six evaluation designs is tested. The IRS design additionally tests knowledge improvements of evaluation designs that *are not discussed* in this chapter. For example, knowledge of the Solomon Four Group and the Cross-Panel Evaluation Designs would also be tested in addition to knowledge of the six designs discussed in the chapter. The Solomon Four Group design or the Cross-Panel Evaluation are two legitimate training evaluation designs. These designs are germane because they are legitimate training evaluation schemes. However, they are *irrelevant* because they are not covered in the chapter.

Causality is proved when the pre-post change is statistically larger for the relevant outcomes than is the case for the irrelevant but germane outcomes. If, however, the pre-post change is equivalent on both the relevant and the irrelevant contents, we cannot claim that this was "caused" by this chapter and we would need to conclude that training was not effective!

Research has shown that the IRS provides inferences equivalent to those that can be drawn from the more complex pre-post experimental (or quasi-experimental) models.[36] As such, it is an important addition to the evaluator's tool box, since it provides a relatively simple procedure to improve the very common pre-post design.

Figure 10.3 shows the data collection schemes currently used for training evaluation.

FIGURE 10.3

TRAINING EVALUATION DATA COLLECTION DESIGNS

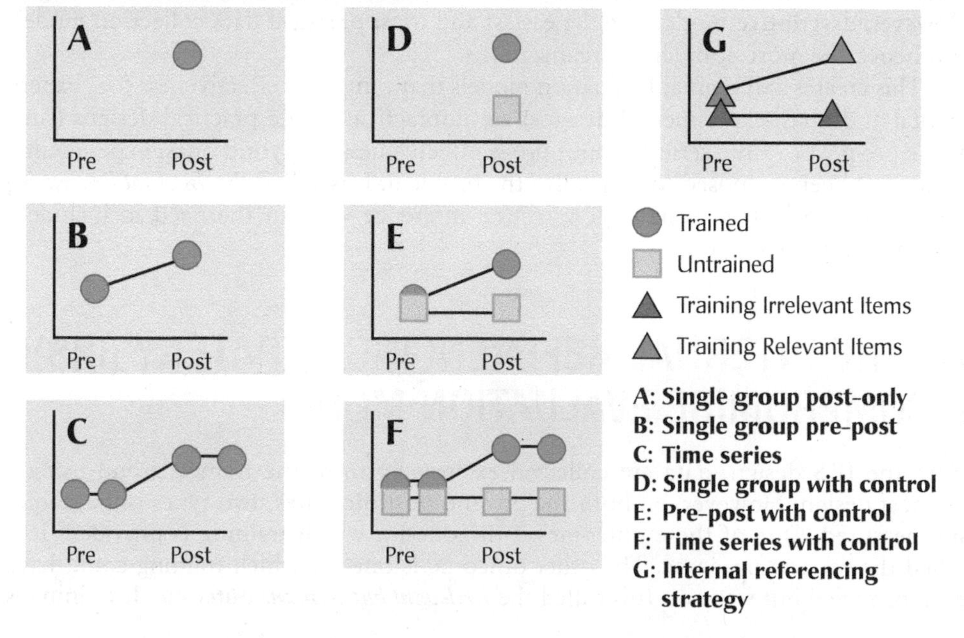
A
Pre
Post
D
Pre
Post
G
Pre
Post
B
Pre
Post
E
Pre
Post
C
Pre
Post
F
Pre
Post
Trained
Untrained
Training Irrelevant Items
Training Relevant Items
A: Single group post-only
B: Single group pre-post
C: Time series
D: Single group with control
E: Pre-post with control
F: Time series with control
G: Internal referencing strategy

// SUMMARY OF DATA COLLECTION DESIGNS

As stated at the onset of this chapter, the choice of evaluation strategies always involves trade-offs (between the quality and scope of the information gathered and its costs and practicality). The same is true of data collection approaches. More complex designs yield much better data and more convincing conclusions, but using them is more complicated, difficult, and costly. The evaluator will need to choose the design that provides management the information it needs. But when evaluators are compelled to make use of lower-quality designs, it is of importance to advise management that by doing so the quality of the information—specifically the conclusions that are possible—may be compromised.

// A FINAL INTEGRATIVE COMMENT: MODELS, OUTCOMES, AND DATA COLLECTION DESIGNS

When tasked with an evaluation problem, trainers might profitably begin by using Decision-Based Evaluation. Hence, they would first need to consider the target: Do they wish to assess whether the trainee has attained a specified level on particular outcomes, or trainee changes? The answer to that question will dictate if a post-only or pre-post design is required. Next, is it critical to establish whether the training experience has caused the outcome? That determines whether a causal or non-causal data collection design is required. Trainers then need to focus on the variables to be measured, which depend on whether the evaluation is summative (Has the program met its objectives?) or formative (Is program improvement the goal?). Kirkpatrick's model is indicated if the purpose of the evaluation is summative. If the purpose is more formative, COMA or LTSI might be better choices.

One then needs to consider the type and the source of the data; a number of questions require consideration. Are performance indicators available, and are they objective or perceptual? If perceptual, will ratings be collected from supervisors, customers, direct observations, and/or the trainees themselves? Will the indicators be collected individually (questionnaires? interviews?) or collectively (focus groups?).

And these decisions will be driven by the information needs and by practical considerations. Both evaluators and management should keep in mind that the evaluation choices they make will have a decided impact on the legitimacy of the conclusions reached.

// SUMMARY

This chapter reviewed the main purposes for evaluating training and development programs and the barriers that prevent training evaluation. Models of training evaluation were presented, contrasted, and critiqued. Although Kirkpatrick's evaluation model is the most common and most frequently used model, for formative evaluations at least, the COMA or LTSI models may be more appropriate, while the DBE model is useful for both formative and summative evaluation. Also described are the variables required for an evaluation and some of the methods and techniques required to measure them. Whereas many of these are measured with questionnaires administered to trainees, their supervisors, or others, objective data can also be used. Advantages and disadvantages of each option were discussed. Descriptive and causal data-collection designs were described, along with the limits to the interpretation they permit. The choice of data collection design, as with most aspects of training, is a trade-off between costs, practicalities, and the information needs of management.

KEY TERMS

affective reactions p. 332
anticipated support p. 339
causal evaluations p. 325
COMA p. 327
Decision-Based Evaluation (DBE) p. 328
declarative learning p. 334
descriptive evaluations p. 325
formative evaluations p. 324
hard data p. 341
perceived support p. 339
procedural learning p. 334
return on expectations p. 341
soft data p. 341
summative evaluations p. 325
training evaluation p. 319
utility reactions p. 332

DISCUSSION QUESTIONS

1. Discuss the similarities and the differences among the evaluation models discussed in the chapter. Be sure to address the practical implications of preferring one model over another.

2. You have two training programs: (a) a course designed to teach the use of a PC, and (b) a course to improve supervisory feedback to employees. Which evaluation design would you use in each case? Which design would you use to determine whether training caused the outcome?

3. Many organizations conduct some sort of training evaluation, but Company A does not. Convince the senior managers of Company A to evaluate their training programs. What would you tell them?

4. Consider the section on Barriers to Training Evaluation and the Conference Board data (Figures 10.1 and 10.2) that summarize training evaluation. Can you suggest ways that would improve the situation in organizations?

5. Distinguish from each other the different types of training evaluations. What is the difference between formative and summative evaluation? between descriptive and causal evaluation?

6. Discuss the assumptions of Kirkpatrick's hierarchical model of training evaluation. What are the implications for training evaluation if the assumptions are valid? What are the implications if the assumptions are not valid?

7. Explain each of the following and give an example of it: hard data, soft data, return on expectations. What are the advantages and disadvantages of each type of measure?

8. Under what circumstances would you recommend the implementation of each of the data collection designs described by Figure 10.3?

THE GREAT TRAINING DEBATE

Conducting evaluation studies using full experimental designs and sophisticated data collection is almost impossible in real organizations. Some managers argue that training evaluations can provide meaningful conclusions only when conducted using these techniques. They therefore conclude that, in most cases, training evaluations are a waste of time and money.

Debate the following: Training evaluations should be conducted only when it is possible to use the more sophisticated procedures. (In preparation for this debate, you should review the chapter's sections on barriers to training evaluation, models of training evaluation, and data collection designs.)

EXERCISES

IN-CLASS

1. Training evaluation principles and variables can be used to make important individual decisions.

   Following her graduation, your best friend Sally felt she lacked "work-life skills." To remedy her perceived problem, she enrolled in a private school that specializes in "enhancing the skills needed for a successful work life." You are graduating at the end of the year and, for the same reasons, are considering enrolment in that program. The school fees are very high, but you'll accept that burden provided you believe that graduates of this program are indeed better prepared for the world of work.

   Six months into her program, you meet Sally for lunch. Assume that Sally is your only source of information about the school and remember that she has yet to enter the world of work.

   What are the changes in Sally that you will be looking for to help you decide whether the school program is worthwhile? Are there specific questions you would ask Sally? Refer to the models and variables of training evaluations to guide your thinking. Remember that Sally has not yet completed her course, so we cannot know at this point whether she is indeed better prepared for work.

2. In most universities and colleges, students fill out an end-of-course questionnaire in which they evaluate the course. Describe how these evaluations are typically conducted in your university or college. What variables are measured, how is that done, and what type of data collection design is used? Keeping in mind each model and the variables in Table 10.1, what other variables do you think should be included as part of the evaluation process? Design an evaluation form that you would like to see used to evaluate your university's or college's courses. For each variable you include, develop one sample question and/or a procedure for measuring it.

3. Suppose your university or college has decided to switch all computers from PC to Mac (or, if your university's current system uses Mac, to PC). Although some staff members already know both systems, the majority will need to learn and master the new system. The university administration has therefore authorized human resources and the IT group to work together to develop and deliver a compulsory training program to all staff members. The top university administration has hired you to conduct an evaluation of the effectiveness of this program, since it needs to know if the training program was worthwhile. Design the required evaluation.

IN-THE-FIELD

1. Identify the training manager of a local company, set up an appointment, and meet with him/her. During that interview, obtain the following information:
   - What types of training programs are given in that company, and what types of training evaluations (if any) are conducted?
   - Is the same type of evaluation used across different programs, or are different evaluation designs adopted for different ones?
   - How are the evaluation data used, and by whom?

   Using the information you gather, assess the quality of the company's evaluation efforts. What can the company conclude about training effectiveness given the types of evaluations it conducts, and what can it not conclude?

2. Identify a family member or friend who is currently working and who has recently taken a training course. Interview that person and estimate the likelihood that the training program was "effective." Establish the interview guide (the questions you will ask) in advance of the interview. Your questions should focus on the dimensions to be measured using both the Kirkpatrick and the COMA models.

CASE INCIDENT

THE SOCIAL AGENCY

A large governmental social agency, employing thousands of social workers and other specialized workers, trained all of its front-line professionals on a new service-delivery system. Simultaneously, it taught managers how to actively support and encourage their employees to implement the new system—that is, to transfer their new skills. A consultant was asked to evaluate the effectiveness of the program directed to the managers and to offer suggestions for improvements.

QUESTIONS

1. What information should be collected and from whom should it be collected?
2. Discuss when and how the information should be collected.
3. What should the criteria for "effectiveness" be?

THE ALCOHOL/DRUG ABUSE PREVENTION PROGRAM (ADAPP)

The North American Transportation Company (NATC) is a very large organization that provides continent-wide facilities for the shipping of goods, from tonnes of wheat and iron ore to individual parcels. Headquartered in Canada, the company uses all forms of heavy equipment to load, transport, and deliver goods and materials for its clients.

In recent years, a number of accidents and near-accidents have occurred. In some cases the accidents caused injuries to people (mainly employees, though some injuries were sustained by bystanders). In three cases in the last five years, people were killed. They also caused substantial material damage to property and/or the environment.

Investigation of these accidents indicated that drug and/or alcohol abuse by company personnel was relatively common and that these may have been contributing factors to the accidents. This analysis also uncovered that absenteeism and job performance problems were also the result of drug/alcohol use by employees.

The CEO of the company asked the HR department to solve the problem. In response, the department formulated a zero-tolerance policy toward workplace alcohol and drug abuse. The policy outlawed alcohol/drug use on the job and made the implementation and enforcement of the policy the direct responsibility of all supervisory personnel in the company. They further developed and implemented a training program to instruct all supervisors on the policy, the means to implement it, and the specific behaviours expected of them. This training program became known as the Alcohol/Drug Abuse Prevention Program (ADAPP).

The day-long training program explained that it was the responsibility of supervisors to be vigilant with respect to drug/alcohol use on the job and to act immediately when there was a problem.

The training program focused on three main aspects of the ADAPP policy that supervisors were to learn and to transfer to the job: (1) explain the policy to their employees as a group; (2) watch for employees who show signs of being under the influence; and (3) choose the specific supervisory action required correctly.

Supervisor were instructed to (a) assess the situation with the employee; (b) immediately relieve the employee from his/her post should the impairment prevent safe and effective job performance; and (c) direct the person to the Employee Aid Program for further investigation and treatment. Supervisors who failed to implement the procedure would face disciplinary actions including, in some cases, immediate dismissal.

The training program consisted of lectures and video presentations, followed by various role-playing exercises and discussions designed to help supervisors learn the policy, motivate them to implement it, and enhance their confidence in their ability to do so.

QUESTIONS

1. Design a training evaluation for the ADAPP. The training evaluation must be both summative (Has ADAPP led to an increase in the desired supervisory behaviours and to a decrease in employee absence and workplace accidents and injuries?) and formative (What aspects of the training program, if any, should be improved?).

2. What model or models of training evaluation would seem appropriate in this case? Explain your answer.

3. What variables should be measured and how should this be done?

   a. Determine the main variables to measure.

   b. Determine the information to be collected to address potential improvements to the program, if necessary.

4. What data collection design or designs would you consider most appropriate for the evaluation? Explain your reasoning.

FLASHBACK QUESTIONS

1. Suppose that the ADAPP evaluation results showed little transfer. Refer back to the sections on trainee characteristics and the other conditions of transfer described in Chapter 9. What would you suggest be done to improve the situation? Should the company change the training? If so, how?

2. The ADAPP mobilized the entire company, costing it thousands of work hours. One of the main advantages of e-learning (Chapter 7) is that it can considerably reduce those costs. Do you think this a viable alternative in this case? What e-learning approach would you think appropriate in the situation? In thinking about your answer, consider, among other things, the issue of active practice discussed in Chapter 4.

3. Trainee motivation to learn and transfer are important elements that should be assessed in a training evaluation because of their known impact on the adoption of new job behaviours. Chapter 2 deals extensively with motivation. What kinds of interventions to the ADAPP program during training would enhance the managers' motivation? What can be done on the job to maintain and enhance motivation?

FLASH FORWARD QUESTION

1. One of the main thrusts of the ADAPP program was to create new work behaviours that would yield cost reductions. But the training program itself involves important costs to the organization including direct costs (such as program development costs and trainer salaries) as well as indirect costs (trainee salaries, travel costs, loss of productivity during training, etc.). Are these costs acceptable given the benefits that the course yielded? What are the benefits likely to be in monetary terms, and are they be worth it given the costs? This is the issue of cost–benefit analysis, which is sometimes referred to as "Level 5" of the Kirkpatrick model.

REWRITE THE CASE QUESTION: EVALUATION VARIABLES

Rewrite the case so that it includes a description at the end of how the training program will be evaluated using both formative and summative evaluations. Be sure to indicate what variables will be measured, when they will be measured, and whether the evaluation will be descriptive or causal.

QUESTIONS

Refer to the case at the end of Chapter 1 to answer the following questions. A consulting firm contracted by the health department has developed a formal training course aimed at solving the problem of the dirty pools in Toronto. You are to develop a plan to evaluate that training program.

1. Suppose the health department wants to know if the training course has achieved its purpose.

   • Would you recommend a summative or a formative evaluation in this case?

   • Based on your choice, what evaluation model would you choose, what variables would you measure, and when would you measure them?

2. Now suppose the health department is principally interested in determining how the training course should be improved.

   • Would you recommend a summative or a formative evaluation?

   • Based on your choice, what evaluation model would you choose, what variables would you measure, and when would you measure them?

3. Suppose that after the training Toronto pools have become significantly cleaner. Now, an audit of pools in Vancouver discovers that they suffer the same deficiencies noted in Toronto. Consequently, some Vancouver officials wish to hire the consulting firm to implement Toronto's training program in Vancouver. However, other officials are unconvinced—they think that the improvement in Toronto pools was not caused by the training program but by other things (such as the pool cleaners being shamed by the press reports). Consequently, a pilot study is launched in Vancouver in which the training program will be delivered to the employees of only a few pools in the city.

   • Develop a training evaluation study for Vancouver that would demonstrate if the training program causes improvements in the pools.

   • What are some of the constraints you are likely to encounter in conducting your study, and how do you intend to deal with them?

// REFERENCES

1. Sackett, P. R., & Mullen, E. J. (1993). Beyond formal experimental design: Towards an expanded view of the training evaluation process. *Personnel Psychology, 46*, 613–627.

2. Twitchell, S., Holton, E. F., III, & Trott, J. R., Jr. (2001). Technical training evaluation practices in the United States. *Performance Improvement Quarterly, 13*(3), 84–109.

3. Grider, D.T. (1990). *Training evaluation. Business Magazine, 17*(1), 20–24.

4. Haccoun, R. R., & Lauzier, M. (2014, April/May) Le superviseur: Au cœur d'une approche intégrée en matière de formation (The supervisor: At the heart of the training). *Revue Effectif*, pp. 48–51.

5. Laroche, R., & Haccoun, R. R. (2003). Buts complémentaires et contradictoires de la formation du personnel: Une typologie intégratrice [Complementary and contradictory goals of employee training: An integrative typology]. *Psychologie du travail et des organisations*, *9*, 3–4, 147–166; Kennedy, P. E., Chyung, S. Y., Winiecki, D. J., & Brinkerhoff, R. O. (2013). Training professionals' usage and understanding of Kirkpatrick's Level 3and Level 4 evaluations. *International Journal of Training and Development*, *18*(1), 1–21.

6. Saks, A. M., & Burke, L. A. (2012). An investigation into the relationship between training evaluation and the transfer of training. *International Journal of Training and Development*, *16*(2), 118–127.

7. Kraiger, K., Ford, J. K., & Salas, E. (1993). Application of cognitive, skill based and affective theories of learning outcomes to new methods of training evaluation. *Journal of Applied Psychology*, *78*(2), 311–328; Colquitt, J. A., Lepine, J. A., & Noe, R. A. (2000). Toward an integrative theory of training motivation: A meta-analytic path analysis of 20 years of research. *Journal of Applied Psychology*, *85*(5), 678–707.

8. Roullier, J. Z., & Goldstein, I. L. (1993). The relationship between organizational transfer climate and positive transfer of training. *Human Resource Development Quarterly*, *4*(4), 377–390; Tracey, J. B., Tannenbaum, S. I., & Kavanagh, M. J. (1995). Applying trained skills on the job: The importance of the work environment. *Journal of Applied Psychology*, *80*(2), 239–252.

9. Tracey, J. B., Hinkin, T. R., Tannenbaum, S., & Mathieu, J. E. (2001). The influence of individual characteristics and the work environment on varying levels of training outcomes. *Human Resource Development Quarterly*, *12*(1), 5–23.

10. Quinones, M. A. (1995). Pretraining context effects: Training assignment as feedback. *Journal of Applied Psychology*, *80*, 226–238.

11. Montesino, M. U. (2002). Strategic alignment of training, transfer-enhancing behaviors and training usage: A posttraining study. *Human Resource Development Quarterly*, *13*(1), 89–108; Saks, A. M., Tagger, S., & Haccoun, R. R. (2002). Is training related to firm performance? *The HRM Research Quarterly*, *6*(2).

12. Worthen, B. R., & Sanders, J. R. (1987). *Educational evaluations: Alternative approaches and practical guidelines*. White Plains, NY: Longman.

13. Kirkpatrick, D. L. (1976). Evaluation of training. In R. L. Craig (Ed.), *Training and development handbook: A guide to human resource development* (2nd ed.). New York: McGraw-Hill.

14. Kraiger, K. (2002). Decision-based evaluation. In K. Kraiger (Ed.), *Creating, implementing, and managing effective training and developmen: State-of-the-art lessons for practice* (pp. 331–375). San Francisco: Jossey-Bass.

15. Holton, E. F., III. (1996). The flawed four-level evaluation model. *Human Resource Development Quarterly*, *7*, 5–21; Alliger, G. M., Tannenbaum, S. L., Bennett, W., Traver, H., & Shortland, A. (1997). A meta-analysis on the relations among training criteria. *Personnel Psychology*, *50*, 341–342.

16. Haccoun, R. R., Jeanrie, C., & Saks, A. M. (1999). Concepts et pratiques contemporaines en évaluation de la formation: Vers un modèle diagnostic

des impacts [Contemporary concepts and practices in training evaluation: Towards a diagnostic model of impacts]. In D. Bouthilier (Ed.), *Gérer pour la performance*. Montréal: Presses de HEC.

17. Holton, E. F., Bates, R. A., & Ruona, W. E. A. (2000). Development of a generalized learning transfer system inventory. *Human Resource Development Quarterly*, *11*(4), 333–360.

18. Morgan, R. B., & Casper, W. (2000). Examining the factor structure of participant reactions to training: A multidimensional approach. *Human Resource Development Quarterly*, *11*, 301–317.

19. Alliger, G. M., Tannenbaum, S. L., Bennett, W., Traver, H., & Shortland, A. (1997). Meta analysis of the relationship among training criteria. *Personnel Psychology*, *50*, 341–357.

20. Sitzmann, T., Brown, K. G., Casper, W. J., Ely, K., & Zimmerman, R. D. (2008). A review and meta-analysis of the nomological network of trainee reactions. *Journal of Applied Psychology*, *93*(2), 280–295.

21. Smith, J. E., & Merchant, S. (1990). Using competency exams for evaluating training. *Training and Development Journal*, *44*(8), 65–71.

22. Jonassen, D., & Tessmer, M. (1996/97). An outcomes-based taxonomy for instructional systems design, evaluation and research. *Training Research Journal*, *2*, 11–46.

23. Desjardins, D. (1995). *Impact de la présentation d'un organisateur avancé sur l'apprentissage et le transfert en formation du personnel* [The impact of advanced organizers on trainee learning and transfer]. Unpublished master's thesis. Université de Montréal, Département de Psychologie.

24. Ostroff, C. (1991). Training effectiveness measures and scoring schemes: A comparison. *Personnel Psychology*, *44*, 353–374.

25. Flynn, G. (1998). The nuts and bolts of valuing training. *Workforce Management*, *17*(11), 80–85; Kozlowski, S. W. J., & Salas, E. (1997). A multilevel organizational systems approach for the implementation and transfer of training. In J. K. Ford (Ed.), *Improving training effectiveness in work organizations* (pp. 247–287). Hillsdale, NJ: Erlbaum.

26. Salas, E., & Cannon-Bowers, J. A. (2001). The science of training: A decade of progress. *Annual Review of Psychology*, *52*, 471–499.

27. Barrette, J., & Haccoun, R.R. (1995) La précision de l'évaluation du rendement: Une vérification de la théorie de Wherry [The accuracy of performance evaluation: Testing Wherry's theory]. *Canadian Journal of Administrative Sciences 12*(4), 324–338.

28. Olian, J. D., & Durham, C. C. (1998). Designing management training and development for competitive advantage: Lessons from the best. *Human Resource Planning*, *21*(1), 20–31.

29. Larin, N. (1998, April). Who understands return on investment better than a bank? *Canadian HR Reporter*, pp. 2–8.

30. Noe, R. A., & Schmitt, N. (1986). The influence of trainee attitudes on training effectiveness: Test of a model. *Personnel Psychology*, *39*, 497–523.

31. Haccoun, R. R., & Savard, P. (2003). Prédire le transfert des apprentissages à long terme rôle du soutien anticipé et perçu, de la motivation et de

l'efficacité personnelle [Predicting long term transfer of learning: The role of anticipated and actual support, motivation, and self efficacy]. In G. Delobbe, C. Karnas, & C. Vandenberghe (Eds.), *Evaluation et développement des compétences au travail* (pp. 507–516). Presses Universitaire de Louvain.

32. Roullier, J. Z., & Goldstein, I. L. (1993). The relationship between organizational transfer climate and positive transfer of training. *Human Resource Development Quarterly, 4*(4), 377–390; Tracey, J. B., Tannenbaum, S. I., & Kavanagh, M. J. (1995). Applying trained skills on the job: The importance of the work environment. *Journal of Applied Psychology, 80*(2), 239–252.

33. Phillips, J. (1996). How much is the training worth? *Training & Development, 50*(4), 20–24.

34. Flynn, G. (1998). The nuts and bolts of valuing training. *Workforce, 17*(11), 80–85.

35. Haccoun, R. R., & Hamtiaux, T. (1994). Optimizing knowledge tests for inferring learning acquisition levels in single group training evaluation designs: The internal referencing strategy. *Personnel Psychology, 47*, 593–604.

36. Frese, M., Beimel, S., & Schoenborn, S. (2003). Action training for charismatic leadership: Two evaluation studies of a commercial training module on inspirational communication of vision. *Personnel Psychology, 56*, 671–697; Neuhengen, M. J., Cigularov, K., & Scott, S. B. (2010). *Effectiveness of the internal referencing strategy design for training evaluation.* Paper made available to participants at the Society for Industrial and Organizational Psychology (SIOP) conference; Taylor, P. J., Russ-Eft, D. F., & Taylor, H. (2009). Transfer of management training from alternative perspectives. *Journal of Applied Psychology, 94*(1), 104–121.

TRAINING COSTS AND BENEFITS

CHAPTER LEARNING OUTCOMES

AFTER READING THIS CHAPTER, YOU SHOULD BE ABLE TO:

- explain why training and human resource professionals should calculate the costs and benefits of training programs in their organization
- calculate the various costs of training programs
- compare and contrast cost-effectiveness evaluation and cost–benefit evaluation
- conduct a net benefit analysis, benefit–cost ratio, return on investment, and utility analysis
- explain what credibility means when estimating the benefits of training programs

MW Canada is an innovative and leading manufacturer of textile window covering textiles and speciality materials located in Cambridge, Ontario. The company's 65 employees manufacture window coverings, filtration composite, and energy-related fabrics that are sold to manufacturers and wholesalers. The company uses advanced technologies for specialty materials; thus, ongoing training is critical.

In an effort to adapt to increasingly competitive markets, MW Canada implemented a new learning initiative in 2013 called the Technical Skills Certificate Program (TSCP). The program was designed to improve communication and discussion of technical issues and improve problem solving of its production staff. The two main business objectives were to improve product quality and reduce equipment downtime.

The 90 hours of training was delivered in two-hour sessions twice a week over six months. The program consisted of a blended delivery method that included online modules, in-plant instructor-led methods for hands-on training, and on-the-job coaching with MW Canada production managers.

Following the training, production managers observed an increased level of independent thinking in the workplace as a result of the skills training program. For example, loom mechanics now start jobs "without requiring supervisors to coax or push them." In the morning, upon reviewing the tasks of the day, "employees pick their jobs and independently start them." And addressing complex problems has become a great deal easier "since staff feel they have more knowledge and more confidence."

In addition, approximately three-quarters of those who were trained applied their learning on the job, improved their performance, and perceived the training as a worthwhile investment for MW Canada. And just more than half of the participants reported that the training

MW Canada's Technical Skills Certificate Program resulted in an annual savings of $20,400 and a return on investment of 17 percent.

improved organizational outcomes such as quality and productivity.

In terms of the two main business objectives, improving product quality and a reduction in downtime, the total annual savings from improvement in these two areas was $20,400. With a total cost of $17,500, the return on investment of the TSCP program was .17, or 17 percent. In other words, every dollar spent on training was returned plus an additional $0.17 as a result of reducing equipment downtime. However, the return to the organization will be much higher, since the benefits will continue to accrue in subsequent years.[1]

Sources: Gillis, L., & Bailey, A. (2014, January). *Workplace literacy and essential skills research: MW Canada Ltd. Technical Skills Certificate Program Impact Analysis.* Canadian Manufacturing Network, Div. of Excellence in Manufacturing Consortium; Giroux, J. P. (2014, October 3). MW Canada—Essential Technical and Manufacturing Skills Certificate. Canadian Manufacturing Network, www.emccanada.org; *Executive summary*, MW Canada: Technical Skills Certificate Program. Canadian Manufacturing Network, Workplace Literacy and Essential Skills Research Project (WLESR), www.emccanada.org

// INTRODUCTION

Organizations have become increasingly concerned about the costs and benefits of their training and development programs, and the value added to the bottom line. As you can see from MW Canada's Technical Skills Certificate Program (TSCP), it is possible to calculate the benefits of training programs in monetary terms and the return on training investments. For MW Canada, the return on investment of the TSCP was 17 percent.

Several years ago, Accenture, a global management consulting firm, demonstrated that the net benefit of its training and development programs was $1.27 billion, and that for every dollar invested in training there was a return of $3.53, or an ROI of 353 percent.[2] Thus, training can have a substantial financial impact on an organization's bottom line by maximizing the return on training.

Information on the costs and benefits of training programs is an important part of training evaluation. In fact, some experts consider the calculation of return on investment (ROI) to be Level 5 in Kirkpatrick's model of training evaluation (see Chapter 10).[3]

In this chapter, you will learn how to calculate the costs, benefits, net benefit, benefit–cost ratio, return on investment (ROI), and utility of training and development programs. But first, let's discuss training and the bottom line.

For more information see Chapter 10, pp. 324–325

// TRAINING AND THE BOTTOM LINE

In Chapter 10, we described the process of training evaluation. This usually involves measuring trainees' reactions, learning, and behaviour, and organization results. The intent is to show some improvement in employees' knowledge, on-the-job behaviour, and organizational outcomes. Typically, one hopes to see an improvement in employees' learning and on-the-job behaviour and a positive effect on organizational outcomes such as sales or customer satisfaction.

But what about the cost of a training program? What if a training program is very expensive? That is, what if the cost of training is greater than the benefits? Would improvements in employee behaviour and organizational outcomes be worthwhile? Would the training program be worth the cost?

Without information on the cost of training and the monetary value of training benefits, one cannot adequately answer these questions. Clearly, the effectiveness of a training program also depends on its costs and benefits. Managers might be pleased to know that a training program has improved customer satisfaction, but they will be even more impressed by the financial value of an improvement in customer satisfaction.

Costing is a complex and time-consuming process that many training specialists prefer to avoid. Some managers are skeptical about the theoretical underpinnings of costing, while others suggest, rightly, that in business not everything is quantifiable. Indeed, many managers suggest that some attitudes and behaviours—such as job satisfaction and communication techniques—make people feel good about themselves and the company they work for, and you just cannot put a dollar value on them.

However, there is increasing pressure for human resource and training professionals to demonstrate the financial value of their programs. Organizations increasingly want to know the return on their training investments, and in a time of declining budgets, the training function faces increased pressure to justify the costs of training programs.[4] In fact, a survey of CEOs found that 96 percent of them want to see learning and development connected to business impact data. And while 74 percent want to see ROI data, it happens in only 4 percent of cases.[5]

Therefore, trainers and HR professionals must learn how to calculate and indeed demonstrate the financial benefits of training and development investments. This shows the value of training programs to management and the organization and it also justifies the training function's share of the budget. It also improves its status and influence within the organization.[6]

In addition, other members of an organization are more likely to see training and development as an investment rather than a cost, and training budgets are less likely to be slashed during economic downturns when the financial benefits of training and development programs can be clearly demonstrated.

You might recall from Chapter 1 that many organizations in Canada view training and development as an operating expense or cost that should be minimized rather than as an investment. In fact, most executives view training and development as a cost rather than as an investment.[7]

Calculating the costs and benefits of training programs is necessary for viewing training as an investment. Financial information about the benefits of training programs places human resource and training professionals on an equal footing with other functional areas in an organization.

The starting point for demonstrating the financial benefits of training and development programs is to identify the desired end result of training. To learn more, see The Trainer's Notebook 11.1, "Business Impact-Driven Learning."

THE TRAINER'S NOTEBOOK 11.1

BUSINESS IMPACT-DRIVEN LEARNING

Effectively managing learning programs involves a bottom-line approach that starts with clearly identifying the end goal of training—specifically, how well employees are applying their knowledge to the job and achieving target job outcomes as a result. This is called business impact-driven learning. Business impact-driven learning involves four steps:

- Identify the job performance outcomes or results you expect from your employees. Start with the end result you want to achieve: business outcomes and performance objectives.

- Define how they will achieve those results—key behaviours employees must exhibit continually to affect the business. Define behaviours associated with performance objectives.

- Design a learning program to teach employees the knowledge they need to perform the desired behaviours.

- Collect the right data to actively track behaviours and measure outcomes; identify deficits that are affecting performance; and design and adjust training in real time to ensure that employees consistently have the knowledge needed to perform to their potential.

Source: Republished with permission of the Association for Talent Development (ATD), from Leaman, C. (2016, March). Measuring what matters most in your training. *TD, 70*(3), 76–77. Permission conveyed through Copyright Clearance Center, Inc.

// TRAINING AND THE BOTTOM LINE IN CANADIAN ORGANIZATIONS

Although most training programs in Canada are evaluated at Level 1 (trainee reactions), only 20 percent of organizations conduct Level 5 (cost–benefit analysis) evaluations and only 19 percent of courses are evaluated at this level.[8] However, more organizations, such as MW Canada, are beginning to conduct financial evaluations of their training and development programs.

For example, several years ago supervisors at Firestone Canada attended a problem-solving workshop after a lack of skills was identified as the source of an internal problem. After the training the supervisors used their new skills to solve the problem. An assessment of the program's impact on the supervisors indicated that supervisors acquired new problem-solving skills, strengthened their analytical thinking, participated in more dynamic teamwork, and had better quality control. As for the bottom line, the company realized a cost savings of $10,000 per month.[9]

In order to calculate the effect of training and development on the bottom line, you must calculate the costs and benefits of training and development. In the next section, we describe how to calculate training and development costs; in subsequent sections we describe how to calculate the benefits of training and development.

// COSTING TRAINING PROGRAMS

Costing is the process used to identify all the expenditures used in training. This is an important procedure in both the design and evaluation of a training program. In Chapter 8, we noted that the trainer must prepare a budget that includes the costs of all of the expenses incurred in the delivery of a training program.

The cost of MW Canada's TSCP was $17,500. But where exactly do the costs come from? The calculation of the cost of a training program usually involves the assignment of various costs to a number of meaningful cost categories. Over the years, a number of approaches have been developed. One approach categorizes the costs of training according to the stages of the training process. For example, one might calculate the cost of needs analysis, training design, delivery, and evaluation. These costs are usually listed on a costing worksheet. One can then calculate and compare the cost of each stage as well as the total cost of a training program.

Another approach to costing training programs is to categorize the costs according to the nature or kind of cost. An example of this approach uses the following five cost categories: direct costs, indirect costs, development costs, overhead costs, and trainee compensation costs.[10]

Costing
The process of identifying all the expenditures used in training

DIRECT COSTS

Direct costs are costs that are linked directly to a particular training program. This includes the trainers' salary and benefits, equipment rental, course materials, instructional aids, food and refreshments, and the cost of travel to and from the training site. These costs are so directly linked to a particular training program that they would not be incurred if the training program were cancelled.

Direct costs
Costs that are linked directly to a particular training program

INDIRECT COSTS

Indirect costs are costs that are not part of a particular training program per se but are expenses required to support training activities. Indirect costs include clerical and administrative support, trainer preparation and planning, training materials that have already been sent to trainees, and the cost of marketing training programs. These costs would still be incurred even if a training program were cancelled. In other words, unlike the direct costs, these costs cannot be recovered.

Indirect costs
Costs that support training activities and are not directly linked to a particular training program

DEVELOPMENTAL COSTS

Developmental costs Costs that are incurred in the development of a training program

Developmental costs are incurred in the development of a training program. This would include the cost of doing a needs analysis, the cost of developing instructional media such as video, the design of training materials, and the cost of evaluating a training program.

OVERHEAD COSTS

Overhead costs Costs incurred by the training department but not associated with any particular training program

Overhead costs are incurred by the training department but not associated with any particular training program. Such costs are required for the general operation of the training function, such as the cost of maintaining training facilities (e.g., heat and lighting) and equipment and the salaries of clerical and administrative support staff. A portion of these costs must be allocated to each training program.

TRAINEE COMPENSATION COSTS

Trainee compensation The cost of the salaries and benefits paid to trainees while they are attending a training program

Trainee compensation refers to the cost of the salaries and benefits paid to trainees while they are attending a training program. This might also include the cost of replacing employees while they are in training. The logic behind this cost is simply that employees must be paid while they are not working and this is a cost of the training program.

// TRAINING COSTS AT THE WOOD PANEL PLANT

Table 11.1 presents a training cost analysis using the five cost categories described above. The example is from a company that produces wood panels. The company had three problems that it wanted solved. First, it wanted to improve the quality of wood panels because they were experiencing a 2 percent rejection rate each day due to poor quality. Second, they wanted to lower the number of preventable accidents, which was higher than the industry average. Third, they wanted to improve the housekeeping of the production area, which was considered poor and a cause of some of the preventable accidents. Visual inspections that used a 20-item checklist indicated an average of 10 problems in housekeeping each week.[11]

The solution was to train supervisors in performance-management and interpersonal skills. Forty-eight supervisors, seven shift superintendents, and a plant manager attended a three-day behaviour-modelling skill-building training program. The objectives of the program were to teach the supervisors how to discuss quality problems and poor work habits with employees, to recognize improvements in employee performance, to teach employees on the job, and to recognize employees for above-average performance.

The cost of the training program was calculated for each of the five cost categories. As shown in Table 11.1, the total cost of the training program was $32,564, or $582 per trainee. This was based on total direct costs of $6,507; indirect costs of $1,161; development costs of $6,756; overhead costs of $1,444; and compensation costs of $16,696.

It is important to recognize that the costing process presented in Table 11.1 is only an example. It represents one approach for categorizing training costs and might need to be modified to suit an organization's unique circumstances. The idea is to identify the main costs of a training program and not to worry too much about the labels assigned

TABLE 11.1

TRAINING COST ANALYSIS FOR WOOD PANEL PLANT

Direct costs. The travel and per diem cost was zero, because training took place adjacent to the plant. Classroom space and audio-visual equipment were rented from a local hotel; refreshments were purchased at the same hotel. Because different supervisors attended the morning and afternoon sessions, lunch was not provided.

DIRECT COSTS	
Outside instructor	0
In-house instructor—12 days × $125 a day	$ 1,500
Fringe benefits—25 percent of salary	375
Travel and per-diem expenses	0
Materials—$60 × 56 participants	3,360
Classroom space and audio-visual equipment—12 days × $50 a day	600
Refreshments—$4 a day × 3 days × 56 participants	672
Total direct costs	**$ 6,507**

Indirect costs. Clerical and administrative costs reflect the amount of clerical time spent on making arrangements for the workshop facilities, sending out notices to all participants, and preparing class rosters and other miscellaneous materials.

INDIRECT COSTS	
Training management	0
Clerical and administrative salaries	750
Fringe benefits—25 percent of clerical and administrative salaries	187
Postage, shipping, and telephone	0
Pre- and post-learning materials —$4 × 56 participants	224
Total indirect costs	**$ 1,161**

Development costs. These costs represent the purchase of the training program from a vendor. Included are instructional aids, an instructor manual, videotapes, and a licensing fee. The instructor-training costs are for a one-week workshop the instructor attended to prepare for facilitating the training. Front-end assessment costs were covered by the corporate training budget.

DEVELOPMENT COSTS	
Fee to purchase program	3,600
Instructor training	
Registration fee	1,400
Travel and lodging	975
Salary	625
Benefits (25 percent of salary)	156
Total development costs	**$ 6,756**

Overhead costs. These represent the services that the general organization provides to the training unit. Because figures were not available, we used 10 percent of the direct, indirect, and program-development costs.

OVERHEAD COSTS	
General organization support, 10 percent of direct, indirect, top management's time and development costs	....
Total overhead costs	**$ 1,444**

Compensation for participants. This figure represents the salaries and benefits paid to all participants while they attended the workshop.

COMPENSATION FOR PARTICIPANTS	
Participants' salaries and benefits (time away from the job)	
Total compensation	**$ 16,696**
Total training costs	**$ 32,564**
Cost per participant	**$ 582**

Source: Republished with permission of the Association for Talent Development (ATD), from Robinson, D. G., & Robinson, J. (1989, August). Training for impact. *T+D, 43*(8), 34–42. Permission conveyed through Copyright Clearance Center, Inc.

Supervisors of a wood panel plant attended a three-day behaviour-modelling training program on performance-management and interpersonal skills.

to them. The trainer should be most concerned about how to design a costing approach that has credibility within the organization and that will be accepted by management.

Once the costs of a training program have been calculated, they can be used for at least two purposes. First, they can be used to prepare a budget for a training program and to compare and contrast the costs of different programs. This is important when making decisions about whether to adopt a particular training program. Second, they can be used along with benefit information to calculate a training program's net benefit, benefit–cost ratio (BCR), and ROI. In the next section, we describe how to determine the benefits of training programs.

// THE BENEFITS OF TRAINING PROGRAMS

Cost-effectiveness evaluation
A comparison of the monetary cost of training to the benefit of training in monetary terms

Cost–benefit evaluation
A comparison of the cost of training in monetary terms to the benefits of training in non-monetary terms

The benefits of a training program can be calculated in monetary or non-monetary terms. For example, recall that the benefits of MW Canada's TSCP included an improvement in product quality and a reduction in downtime (non-monetary benefits) and a total annual savings from these improvements of $20,400 (monetary benefit). When the benefit is calculated in monetary terms, it is referred to as a cost-effectiveness evaluation. A **cost-effectiveness evaluation** involves comparing the monetary cost of training to the benefit of training in monetary terms.

Sometimes, however, it is not possible to determine the monetary value of training benefits or to express them in financial terms. Further, in some cases there might be important benefits of a training program that are not monetary benefits. This kind of evaluation is called a cost–benefit evaluation.

A **cost–benefit evaluation** compares the cost of training in monetary terms to the benefits of training in non-monetary terms. Non-monetary benefits are similar to what was described as results or Level 4 evaluation criteria in Chapter 10. These benefits involve organization outcomes such as the rate of turnover, absenteeism, customer satisfaction, and so on. It is worth noting that such benefits might have a financial effect on the performance of an organization even though they might not be described in monetary terms.

For example, if a training program is expected to reduce the amount of scrap in the production of a product, then a cost–benefit evaluation would indicate how much the training program cost and the amount or percentage reduction in scrap. On the other hand, a cost-effectiveness evaluation would calculate the monetary value of the reduction in scrap.

Once we know the cost of a training program as well as the benefit in monetary terms, it is possible to determine the net benefit of the program. The **net benefit** of a training program refers to the benefit minus the cost of the training program. Thus, to conduct a net benefit analysis one simply subtracts the cost of a training program from its financial benefit. The net benefit of MW's TSCP is therefore $2,900 ($20,400 − $17,500). A related calculation is the **benefit–cost ratio (BCR)**, which is derived by dividing the benefit by the cost. Thus, the BCR for MW's TSCP is 1.17 ($20,400/$17,500).

Another way to determine the financial benefit of a training program is the calculation of the ROI, which is described in the next section.

Net benefit
The estimated value of the benefit minus the cost of the training program

Benefit–cost ratio (BCR)
The benefit divided by the cost of the training program

// RETURN ON INVESTMENT (ROI)

The most popular approach for determining the financial benefits of a training program is return on investment. As indicated in the chapter-opening vignette, MW Canada realized a return on investment of 0.17 or 17 percent.

Return on investment (ROI) involves comparing the cost of a training program to its benefits by dividing the net benefit by the cost of the training program. For example, Cisco Systems calculates the ROI of e-learning by having employees complete a Web-based survey shortly after they have attended a training program. Employees are asked to select a percentage range that indicates the time savings or quality improvement in their performance since taking the course. The results are used to calculate the ROI of e-learning, which has been found to be 900 percent per course. In other words, every dollar the company spends on training results in a gain of $9 in productivity.[12]

Return on investment (ROI)
A comparison of the cost of a training program to its benefits by dividing the net benefit by the cost of the training program

However, many companies in Canada do not calculate the ROI of their training programs. As indicated earlier, only 20 percent of organizations in Canada conduct a Level 5 evaluation. This is due in large part to the difficulty and complexity involved in the process. To help companies learn how to calculate the ROI of their training programs, a program called Investing in People was launched several years ago to provide Canadian organizations with methods and tools to assess the impact of their training investments. To learn more about this program, see Training Today 11.1, "The Investing in People Project."

The calculation of ROI involves dividing the net benefit (benefits – cost of the program) by the cost of a training program:

$$\text{Return on Investment} = \frac{\text{Benefits} - \text{Cost of the program}}{\text{Cost of the program}}$$

Return on investment involves comparing the cost of a training program to its benefits by dividing the net benefit by the cost of the training program.

As an example, if a training program costs $100,000 and the financial benefit is $300,000, then the calculation of ROI is $300,000 − $100,000/$100,000 = 2 . In other words, there is a return of $2 for every $1 spent on training (1:2). The percentage return can also be calculated simply by multiplying the ratio by 100; thus, in this case, the return is 200 percent. This can also be described as a 200 percent ROI (the gain of $200,000 is 200 percent of the $100,000 investment).

Returning to MW's TSCP, the ROI is calculated as follows: $20,400 − $17,500/$17,500 = 0.17 , or a return of 17 percent (17 × 100).

TRAINING TODAY   11.1

THE INVESTING IN PEOPLE PROJECT

A project called Investing in People was launched in 2007 to help Canadian organizations evaluate the return on investment (ROI) of training programs and to provide evidence that training results in positive business outcomes. The main objective of the project was to provide evidence that training results in a positive ROI and is crucial to business success and economic growth. The program also aims to encourage Canadian organizations to invest more in training and to identify best training practices based on the most successful training programs.

Investing in People was a three-year project sponsored by Human Resources and Social Development Canada (HRSDC) as part of the Workplace Skills Initiative (WSI). The $1.3-million project was awarded to the Canadian Society of Training and Development (now known as The Institute for Performance and Learning) and was implemented by Learning Designs Online.

ROI case studies were carried out in 12 organizations where a chosen training program was evaluated. The project involved organizations from all geographic regions and includes a wide variety of training programs across the country.

The aim of the program was to develop practical and innovative methods, tools, and instruments for Canadian organizations to use for assessing the impact of their training investments. The program focused on small and medium-sized companies in the manufacturing, services, and retail sectors. The results of the project along with the best practices and evaluation tools have been made available to other Canadian organizations.

To calculate ROI, Learning Designs uses a methodology called the Learning Value Chain, which evaluates a training program at each of four "links" (capability, transfer, business results, and ROI). At each link, data are gathered to assess the extent to which the training has achieved key outcomes, added value, and enabled the next critical event in the chain to occur.

Business Development Bank of Canada (BDC) is one of the 12 workplaces that participated in the program. The Crown corporation has 1700 employees and invests on average about 4.5 percent of its payroll in training. BDC evaluated a coaching program for banking branch managers that achieved an ROI of 74 percent. A training program at WestJet on running efficient meetings achieved an ROI of 558 percent.

Sources: Dobson, S. (2009, October 19). Rallying for ROI around training. *Canadian HR Reporter*, p. 15; Dobson, S. (2008, April 21). Project connects dots between T&D, profit. *Canadian HR Reporter*, p. 3; Bailey, A. (2008, Fall). Meeting Canada's productivity challenge. *The Canadian Learning Journal*, p. 25; Gillis, L., & Bailey, A. (2010). *Meta study of evaluation findings.* Toronto: Canadian Society for Training and Development.

Let's now return to the wood panel plant. Recall that a supervisor training program that cost $32,564 was designed to improve the quality of wood panels by lowering the daily rejection rate, to improve the housekeeping of the production area, and to reduce the number of preventable accidents.[13]

Table 11.2 shows how the benefits were measured in each of the three areas. The results in each area before and one year after training are shown, as well as the differences. First, before training, the rejection rate of wood panels was 2 percent per day,

TABLE 11.2

BENEFITS CALCULATION WORKSHEET FOR WOOD PANEL PLANT

OPERATIONAL RESULTS AREA	HOW MEASURED	RESULTS BEFORE TRAINING	RESULTS AFTER TRAINING	DIFFERENCES (+ OR −)	EXPRESSED IN $
Quality of panels	Percent rejected	2 percent rejected: 1440 panels per day	1.5 percent rejected: 1080 panels per day	5 percent 360 panels	$720 per day $172,800 per year
Housekeeping	Visual inspection using 20-item checklist	10 defects (average)	2 defects (average)	8 defects	Not measurable in $
Preventable accidents	Number of accidents	24 per year	16 per year	8 per year	$48,000 per year
	Direct cost of each accident	$144,000 per year	$96,000 per year	$48,000	

Total savings: $220,800

Net Benefit = $220,800 − $32,564 = $188,236

Benefit–cost ratio = $220,800/$32,564 = 66.8

$$\text{ROI} = \frac{\text{Benefits} - \text{Training Costs}}{\text{Training Costs}} = \frac{\$220,880 - \$32,564}{\$32,564} = 5.78 \times 100\% = 578\%$$

Source: Republished with permission of the Association for Talent Development (ATD), from Robinson, D. G., & Robinson, J. (1989, August). Training for impact. *T+D, 43*(8), 34–42. Permission conveyed through Copyright Clearance Center, Inc.

or 1,440 panels. After training, this was reduced to 1.5 percent or 1,080 panels. The difference of 0.5 percent per day—360 wood panels—was calculated to be a saving of $720 per day or $172,800 per year.

Second, housekeeping was measured in terms of a visual inspection using a 20-item checklist. Before the training there was an average of 10 defects per week; after training it was reduced to two defects. Thus, the training program resulted in a reduction of eight defects per week (this could not be calculated in monetary terms).

Third, the number of preventable accidents before training was 24 per year at a cost of $144,000. After training this was reduced to 16 per year or 8 fewer accidents at a cost of $96,000 and a savings of $48,000.

By comparing this information to the cost information in Table 11.1, we can calculate the net benefit, BCR, and ROI of the training program. Recall that the total cost of the training program was $32,564. The net benefit of the training program in monetary terms can be determined by adding the savings from the reduction in rejected wood panels ($172,800) to the savings from the reduction in preventable accidents ($48,000), and then subtracting the cost of the training program ($32,564). Thus, the net benefit of the training program is $220,800 − $32,564 = $188,236. The BCR is $220,800/$32,564 = 6.78 .

To calculate the ROI, we divide the net benefit of the program ($188,236) by the cost of the training program ($32,564): $188,236/$32,564 = 5.78 . Therefore, the ROI for one year after training is equal to 5.78 or 578 percent.

TABLE 11.3

METHODS TO CALCULATE THE FINANCIAL BENEFITS OF TRAINING AND DEVELOPMENT PROGRAMS

MW's TSCP Training Program:
Program cost: $17,500
Total annual savings: $20,400
Net Benefit: The benefit minus the cost of the training program: Benefit − Cost
MW's TSCP Training Program: $20,400 − $17,500 = $2,900
Benefit–cost ratio (BCR): The benefit divided by the cost: Benefit/Cost
MW's TSCP Training Program: $20,400/$17,500 = 1.17
Return on investment (ROI): The net benefit divided by the cost of training:
Net benefit/Cost
Return: ROI × 100
MW's TSCP Training Program: $2,900/$17,500 = 0.17
Return: 0.17 × 100 = 17 percent

It is worth noting that while this analysis is an example of cost-effectiveness evaluation, the results for housekeeping (i.e., a reduction of eight defects per week) is an example of cost–benefit evaluation.

In summary, this example provides a good illustration of how the benefits of training programs can be measured in a way that is consistent with the objectives of a training program (e.g., reduction in preventable accidents), and can then be translated into monetary terms and used to calculate a training program's net benefit, BCR, and ROI.

Table 11.3 provides a summary of the different methods to calculate the financial benefits of training and development programs using the cost and benefit data from MW's TSCP Training Program. To learn more about how to convert benefits into monetary values, see The Trainer's Notebook 11.2, "Converting Benefits to Monetary Values."

THE TRAINER'S NOTEBOOK   11.2

CONVERTING BENEFITS TO MONETARY VALUES

One of the most difficult aspects of calculating the ROI of training and development programs is determining the monetary value of the benefits of training. Jack Phillips, one of the leading experts on the calculation of ROI, suggests the following five steps for converting benefits to monetary values.

Step 1: Focus on a single unit. Identify a particular unit of improvement in output (e.g., products, sales), quality (e.g., errors, product defects), time (to respond to a customer order or complete a project), or employee behaviour (e.g., one case of employee turnover).

Step 2: Determine a value for each unit. Place a value identified on the single unit identified in step 1. This will be easier for hard measures such as production, quality, and time because most organizations record the value of one unit of production or the cost of a product defect. It will be more difficult to do for softer measures such as the cost of one employee absence.

Step 3: Calculate the change in performance. Determine the change in performance following training after factoring out other potential influences. This change in units of performance should be directly attributable to the training.

Step 4: Obtain an annual amount. The industry standard for an annual performance change is equal to the total change in the performance data during one year.

Step 5: Determine the annual value. The annual value of improvement equals the annual performance change, multiplied by the unit value.

Source: Phillips, J. J. (1996, April). How much is the training worth? *T+D*, pp. 20–24. Reprinted by permission of Association for Talent Development (ATD).

// UTILITY ANALYSIS

As described in Chapter 10, in a typical training evaluation study a training group is compared to an untrained or control group that did not receive training in order to determine how effective a training program is for learning, change in behaviour, and/or job performance.

For more information see Chapter 10, pp. 342–346

While the results of this comparison might indicate a significant difference between the two groups, they do not indicate the dollar value associated with the change or improvement in learning, behaviour, or job performance. Utility analysis, however, can do this; it is another approach for determining the financial benefits of training and development programs.

Utility analysis is a method used to forecast the financial benefits that result from human resource programs such as training and development. Utility analysis involves procedures in which the effectiveness of a training program is translated into dollars and cents.[14]

Utility analysis
A method to forecast the financial benefits that result from human resource programs such as training and development

To calculate the utility of a training program, several factors must be considered. One of the most important is the effectiveness of the training program. In other words, what is the difference in job performance between employees who are trained and those who do not receive training? This difference is called the *effect size*. The larger the effect size, the more effective a training program is and the greater its utility.

A second factor is the *standard deviation of job performance* in dollars of untrained employees. This has to do with how much of a difference there is in the job performance of untrained employees and the monetary value of this difference.

The standard deviation of job performance in dollar terms is an important factor because in jobs in which the performance of individual employees is widely different, an effective training program will improve the performance of a greater number of employees and will, therefore, result in larger dollar gains. When the job performance of employees is relatively similar, an effective training program is less likely to result in large dollar gains. Therefore, it is necessary to estimate the standard deviation of job performance of untrained employees to make estimates of utility.

There are several approaches for doing this, such as asking supervisors to provide an estimate of the dollar value of performance. The larger the standard deviation of job performance of the untrained group the greater the utility of a training program.

A third factor is the *number of employees trained*. The more employees trained, the greater the utility. A fourth factor is the expected length of *time that the training benefits will last*. The longer the effects of training will last, the higher the utility of a training program.

Utility is equal to the multiplication of all of these factors minus the *cost of the training program* (cost per employee × number of employees trained). The following formula is used to estimate the utility of a training program[15]:

$$\Delta U = (T)(N)(d_t)(SDy) - (N)(C)$$

where

ΔU	=	utility, or the dollar value of the program
T	=	the number of years the training has a continued effect on performance
N	=	the number of people trained
d_t	=	the true difference in job performance between the average trained and untrained employee in standard deviation units (effect size)
SDy	=	the standard deviation of job performance in dollars of the untrained group
C	=	cost of training each employee

Consider the following example. To increase the number of toys produced in a toy factory, a training program is implemented and 50 of the plant employees attend. Compared to a group of workers who do not attend the training program, the performance of the 50 trained employees is found to be twice as high (e.g., they produce 100 toys per day compared to 50 produced by untrained workers). We will assume that this equals an effect size of 2. We also assume that the standard deviation of job performance of the untrained employees is $100. The expected length of time that the training will last is estimated to be five years. The cost of the training program is $300 per employee.

Using the utility equation above, we can calculate the utility of the training program as follows:

$$\Delta U = 5(50)(2)(\$100) - 50(\$300)$$
$$\Delta U = \$50,000 - \$15,000$$
$$\Delta U = \$35,000$$

Thus, the expected utility of the training program for the 50 employees trained is $35,000. This amount might be even greater if the training program lasts longer than five years or if the untrained employees learn how to improve their performance by working with and observing the trained employees. The BCR can also be calculated by dividing the utility by the total cost of the program ($35,000/$15,000 = 2.33) and the ROI can be calculated by dividing the net benefit of the program by the total cost of the program ($35,000 − $15,000/$15,000 = 1.33).

BREAK-EVEN ANALYSIS

An extension of the use of the utility formula is to conduct a **break-even analysis** or to find the value at which benefits equal costs and utility is equal to zero.[16] This can be calculated for any of the terms in the utility equation. However, it is most meaningful to conduct a break-even analysis for the effect size or the standard deviation.

Break-even analysis Finding the value at which benefits equal costs and utility is equal to zero

Managing Performance through Training and Development

For example, what is the break-even effect size for the scenario presented above? This can be calculated by dividing the cost of the training program ($15,000) by the multiplicative function of the other factors: (N)(T)(SDy) or (50)(5)(100). The calculations are as follows:

$$d_t = 15,000/25,000$$
$$d_t = 0.6$$

Thus, a training program with an effect size of 0.6 will result in a utility of zero, and an effect size greater than 0.6 will result in a utility that is greater than zero. Therefore, a training program that is considerably less effective than the one in the example would still be likely to result in a financial gain as long as the effect size is greater than 0.6.

Break-even analysis can be very useful because it helps reduce the uncertainty associated with the estimates of the various parameters used to calculate utility. For example, to the extent that the break-even effect size is far below the actual effect size used to calculate utility, the greater the confidence one can have in the results.[17]

// THE CREDIBILITY OF BENEFIT ESTIMATES

We have been discussing the costs and benefits of training programs and how to calculate ROI and utility. However, it is important to realize that this is not an exact science. Assumptions and judgments are made when estimating the monetary benefits of a training program. As a result, the process works only if managers and clients accept the assumptions. The estimation of benefits is an inexact procedure and trainers should be concerned about professional credibility.

Credibility is a major issue in cost-effectiveness evaluation, and the data must be accurate and the process believable.[18] Consider the example of a large bank that was experiencing a high rate of turnover.

A training program was designed to counter the turnover problem. The cost of employee turnover needed to be estimated to calculate the ROI. However, the actual cost calculation was difficult because of the many interacting variables–administrative costs, interviewing, testing, relocation, orientation, increase in supervisory time, initial less-than-optimal performance, on-the-job training–that make up the cost of replacing one person. As the bank did not want to devote the considerable resources necessary to develop a precise calculation, turnover was classified as a soft cost and a combination of approaches was used to derive an acceptable figure.

Initially, a literature search was used to determine that another institution in the same industry had calculated a cost of $25,000 per turnover. This figure, derived by an internal-audit unit and verified by a consulting specialist in turnover reduction, was used as a starting point. The application of this statistic to another (even though quite similar) organization, however, was in question. The training staff then met with senior executives "to agree on a turnover cost value to use in gauging the success of the program. Management agreed on an estimate that was half the amount from the study, $12,500. This was considered very conservative because other turnover studies typically yield statistics of greater value. Management felt comfortable with the estimate, however, and it was used on the benefits side of program evaluation. Although not precise, this exercise yielded a figure that was never challenged."[19]

The term "never challenged" is significant. Trainers must perform cost-effectiveness evaluations from a position of strength. In this example, senior managers were brought on-side when they were used as experts. It mattered little that the turnover cost was set at $12,500 rather than $25,000, because the benefit estimation produced from these data was credible and accepted by those with the power to make investment decisions.

Thus, despite the appearance of quantitative rigour, virtually all but the simplest cost-effectiveness evaluations are dependent to a greater or lesser extent on some assumptions and expert opinion.[20]

Trainers must ensure that their clients and management agree on the cost factors and the measurement and estimation of benefits. Management and clients must perceive benefit estimates as credible, believable, and acceptable. It is therefore critical that trainers find out what management deems to be most important in terms of the benefits and expected results and, whenever possible, obtain cost estimates (e.g., the cost of turnover) from management.

It also helps to use internal and external experts to assist in making benefit estimates. Because they are experts who are familiar with the situation, they are likely to be seen as credible by management. For example, if one wanted to estimate the cost of employee grievances, a good expert would be a manager of labour relations. Estimates might also be obtained from other sources that are close to the situation, such as trainees and their supervisors.[21]

For some guidelines on how to increase the credibility of the estimates of training benefits, see The Trainer's Notebook 11.3, "Increasing the Credibility of Benefit Estimates."

THE TRAINER'S NOTEBOOK 11.3

INCREASING THE CREDIBILITY OF BENEFIT ESTIMATES

Following these guidelines can increase the credibility of estimates of the benefits of a training program.

1. Take a conservative approach when making estimates and assumptions.

2. Use the most credible and reliable sources for estimates.

3. Explain the approaches and assumptions used in the conversion.

4. When results appear overstated, consider adjusting the numbers to achieve more realistic values.

5. Use hard data whenever possible.

Source: Phillips, J. J. (1996, April). How much is the training worth? *T+D*, p. 20. Reprinted by permission of Association for Talent Development (ATD).

// SUMMARY

This chapter described the methods and approaches for calculating the costs and benefits of training and development programs. Cost and benefit information is important not only for budgeting purposes and for comparing training programs, but also for training evaluation. Five cost categories for costing training programs were described, as well as the differences between cost-effectiveness evaluation and cost–benefit evaluation. Descriptions and examples were then provided for the calculation of the net benefit, benefit–cost ratio (BCR), and return on investment (ROI) of training programs. Utility analysis was also described as an alternative approach for calculating the financial benefits of training programs. The chapter concluded with a discussion of the importance of credibility when estimating the financial benefits of training and development programs.

KEY TERMS

benefit–cost ratio (BCR) p. 365
break-even analysis p. 370
cost–benefit evaluation p. 364
cost-effectiveness evaluation p. 364
costing p. 361
developmental costs p. 362
direct costs p. 361
indirect costs p. 361
net benefit p. 365
overhead costs p. 362
return on investment (ROI) p. 365
trainee compensation p. 362
utility analysis p. 369

DISCUSSION QUESTIONS

1. Discuss the pros and cons of calculating the ROI of training programs. Should trainers always do this as part of a training evaluation? Explain your answer.

2. What can trainers do to increase the credibility of monetary estimates of the benefits of a training program?

3. What is the difference between cost–benefit evaluation and cost-effectiveness evaluation? Provide an example of each. What are some situations in which a trainer might want to calculate a cost–benefit evaluation and a cost-effectiveness evaluation?

4. What is a utility analysis and how is it used to determine the cost and benefits of a training program? What is a break-even analysis and how is it useful in determining the value of a training program?

5. Why should trainers be concerned about calculating the costs and benefits of training programs? What are the advantages and disadvantages of doing so?

6. What are the different costs associated with training programs? What information is required to calculate each type of cost?

7. Why do so few Canadian organizations evaluate the financial benefits of training programs? Do you think more organizations should do so? What needs to be done to increase the number of organizations that evaluate the financial benefits of training programs?

8. Explain how to calculate each of the following: net benefit, benefit–cost ratio (BCR), return on investment (ROI), and utility. What are the differences among these calculations?

THE GREAT TRAINING DEBATE

1. Debate the following: Calculating the monetary benefits and ROI of training and development is the most important way to evaluate training and development programs.

2. Debate the following: The calculation of a training program's ROI is more art than science and should not be part of the training evaluation process.

EXERCISES

IN-CLASS

1. In order to calculate the benefits of training programs, measures have to be developed that are consistent with the training program and its objectives. As well, some of these measures will need to be converted into monetary terms. For each of the following training programs, identify some of the benefits and how they can be measured for the purpose of cost–benefit evaluation and cost-effectiveness evaluation:
   a. Sales training
   b. Ethics training
   c. Customer-service training
   d. Health and safety training
   e. Total quality management training
   f. Sexual and racial harassment training
   g. Diversity training

   To learn more about these training programs, refer to Chapter 12.

2. Consider a situation in which you are a trainer for an organization that manufactures sportswear. You must present information on the costs and benefits of a training program to management, which is about to decide whether the program will be implemented organization-wide. You have already designed the training program and delivered it to one group of employees, and you want to begin offering it to the rest of the organization. How will you present the information to management? Will you present information on the net benefit, BCR, ROI, and/or utility analysis? Will you present cost–benefit information or cost-effectiveness information? What are the advantages and disadvantages of presenting information on each of these? Do you think trainers should present financial information about the benefits of training to management? What are the advantages and disadvantages of doing so?

3. Consider the costs and benefits of a university or college course such as the training and development course you are now taking. Using the five cost categories discussed in the chapter, identify the major costs of the course and try to estimate the costs of each category. Now consider the benefits. What benefits would you include if you were to conduct a cost-effectiveness analysis and a cost–benefit analysis? How would you determine the ROI and utility of your course? Consider the costs and benefits from the institution's perspective and the student's perspective.

4. Think about the last time you attended a training program. Based on what you know about the program, make a list of the costs in each of the following cost categories: direct costs, indirect costs, development costs, overhead costs, and compensation

for participants. In addition, make a list of the potential benefits of the program. What information would you need to determine the monetary value of these benefits? What additional information do you require to calculate the utility of the program?

IN-THE-FIELD

1. To find out about the costs and benefits of training in an organization, contact the HR department of an organization and ask the following questions:
   - To what extent do you determine the cost of training programs? How do you do it, and who does it? What cost categories are used?
   - Do you determine the benefits of training programs? If so, how do you do it? Who is involved in calculating the monetary value of training?
   - Do you conduct a cost-effectiveness evaluation and a cost–benefit evaluation? If so, who does it?
   - Do you determine the net benefit, benefit–cost ratio (BCR), and return on investment (ROI) of training programs? If so, who is responsible for it?
2. To find out about organizations that have calculated the costs and benefits of their training programs, visit the Canadian Manufacturing Network at https://www.emccanada.org/search?usterms=roi. Choose one of the case studies about an organization that participated in the Workplace Literacy and Essential Skills Research (WLESR) and prepare a brief report (written or a class presentation) of the organization in which you discuss the following:
   a. What is the WLESR and what is its purpose?
   b. Provide an overview of the organization.
   c. Describe the training program (e.g., objectives, methods, participants, etc.).
   d. Describe the costs and benefits of the training program.
   e. Discuss how the program was evaluated and the evaluation results obtained.

CASE INCIDENT 1

THE HARMONY REMOTE

The Harmony remote is a universal remote control that can replace up to 15 remote controls. While it sounds simple, many consumers have questions and they keep Harmony's call centre very busy. Maintaining this centre can be expensive and poorly trained support agents can affect customer satisfaction and, subsequently, the success of the product.

So Logitech, makers of the remote, decided to redesign the training program used to educate new support agents about the Harmony technology. Harmony's redesigned training program blended e-learning technology with a traditional classroom setting while reducing the training from 12 to eight days.

The goal for Logitech was to improve the support experience for customers in terms of quality and call-handle time, and reduce the overall cost of the training. For the purpose of evaluation, they looked at the average handle time of a call, customer satisfaction ratings, and first-call resolution (dealing with the customer's concerns during the first call without any follow-up required).

Immediately after the training, the 162 participants completed a survey about the training program. The results revealed considerable success in enhancing capability—78 percent said they had acquired a high level of knowledge and skills and 74 percent had a high level of confidence in their ability to apply their learning in their new jobs. When it came to the transfer of learning to the job, 73 percent of respondents reported a high level of learning application and proficiency one month after training.

Sources: Based on Dobson, S. (2010, March 22). Logitech, BC Assessment fine-tuning training. *Canadian HR Reporter*, p. 8. Reprinted by permission of *Canadian HR Reporter*. © Copyright Thomson Reuters Canada Ltd., (2010), Toronto, Ontario, 1-800-387-5164. Web: www.hrreporter.com; Weisser, L. (2009, Spring). Is training the answer? Project partners discover what's really important in measuring training initiatives. *The Canadian Learning Journal*, p. 14.

QUESTIONS

1. Describe how you would do a cost-effectiveness evaluation and a cost–benefit evaluation of the Harmony remote training program. What additional information do you require?

2. Describe how you would calculate the net benefit, BCR, and ROI of the Harmony remote training program. What additional information is required?

3. How would you conduct a utility analysis of the Harmony remote training program? What information do you have? What additional information do you require to conduct a utility analysis?

CASE INCIDENT 2

RENSWARTZ REALTY COMPANY

As the housing market began to heat up, the Renswartz Realty Company set high goals for increasing the number of listings and sales. In order to accomplish these goals, the company president believed they would have to do two things. First, they would have to market the company's superior customer service. Second, they would have to train their agents to improve their sales and customer-service skills.

Choosing an advertising company turned out to be much easier than choosing a training program. Two consulting firms were contacted to provide a proposal to design and implement a training program that would be attended by all 200 of the company's sales agents.

The first consulting firm proposed a five-day program that would consist of lectures on "how to get more listings," "how to improve your service," and "making the sale," and would involve videos and behaviour-modelling training. According to the consulting firm, research has shown that the sales performance of those who have attended the training is significantly better than those who have not; the effect size of the program is 0.35. The training is expected to last for two years and will cost $1,500 per employee.

The second consulting firm proposed a similar program for only two days and would consist of sessions on "how to improve your sales," and "providing excellent service." Research on the training program has found it to be highly effective, with an effect size of 0.25. The effects have been found to last for one year at which time follow-up sessions are required. The cost of the training program is $450 per employee.

Based on the current sales performance of all 200 sales agents at Renswartz Realty, the standard deviation of sales is $15,000.

QUESTIONS

1. Calculate the utility of the training programs proposed by each of the consulting firms.
2. Calculate the break-even effect size for both training programs.
3. Calculate the BCR and ROI of each training program.
4. What are the advantages and disadvantages of each training program?
5. Which training program should the company purchase? Explain your answer.
6. What are the advantages and limitations of this approach for calculating the benefits of a training program?

CASE STUDY   DATAIN

DATAIN is a company that was started by two students who saw an opportunity to make some money and help pay for their education. As an increasing number of organizations today survey their customers and employees, the two students saw a need for data input and analyses.

With a loan from their parents, they rented space, purchased 20 used computers, and set up shop. They hired other students to do data input and analyses and began advertising their services.

Within a relatively short period of time they were having trouble keeping up with demand. In fact, business was so good they had to hire more students and purchase more computers.

After about six months, however, they began to notice some problems. The data files were often full of mistakes, and the data analysis was often incomplete and incorrect. As a result, almost 40 percent (20 jobs per month) of all jobs had to be completely redone. This turned out to be a rather costly problem. Each job took approximately 10 hours and cost the company $150 (students were paid $15 per hour).

To make matters worse, they began to notice that their new hires were quitting after only a few months on the job. In the last six months, they had lost an average of four employees a month. Every time an employee quit, they had to replace him/her and the cost of this was beginning to get very expensive. The cost of advertising, interviewing, and hiring a new employee was estimated to be about $5,000.

In order to cut down on these unanticipated costs, DATAIN decided to invest in a training program to reduce the mistakes and errors in data input and analyses and to improve employee retention. They contacted a training consultant to conduct a needs analysis, design and deliver a training program, and conduct the training evaluation.

Based on the figures provided by the consultant, DATAIN thought it would be a good idea to determine whether the training program would be a worthwhile investment. The consultant estimated that the needs analysis and training evaluation would each take about 20 hours at a cost of $100 per hour. The fee to purchase the actual training program would be $5,000. The training program itself would be for one day (8 hours) at a cost of $200 per hour to the consultant.

In addition to the consultant fees, DATAIN would also have to give its 25 employees one full day (8 hours) of pay ($15 per hour); lunch that would cost $10 per employee; and coffee and snacks at a cost of $50 for the day. The training would take place at DATAIN so the only cost for classroom space would be a portion of the cost associated with room heating, lighting, and maintenance, which was estimated to be $100 for the day. As well, some administrative support work would be required to plan and prepare for the training, which would involve about two days (8 hours per day) of work on the part of DATAIN's administrative assistant, who is paid $15 an hour.

According to the training consultant, DATAIN could anticipate an 80 percent drop in mistakes and errors and a 90 percent reduction in turnover. In other words, instead of 20 jobs a month only four would have to be redone, and instead of four quits a month there would be on average fewer than one.

This sounded like a great investment; however, DATAIN was concerned about the loss of a full day of work while employees attended the program. So they decided to get an estimate from a vendor that specialized in e-learning training programs.

The e-learning vendor told DATAIN that she could design an e-learning program for $25,000. The program would take four hours to complete and would include interactive exercises and opportunities for practice. Employees would be able to take the course on their own time and at their own pace. The anticipated benefits are a 90 percent reduction in mistakes and errors and a 60 percent reduction in turnover.

DATAIN does not know how to calculate the potential benefits of the two training programs. As a result, they do not know which training program to purchase.

QUESTIONS

1. Calculate the costs of the consultant's proposed training program in terms of the different categories for determining training costs. What is the cost of each category and the total cost of the training program?

2. Calculate the benefit, net benefit, benefit–cost ratio, and return on investment of the consultant's program and the vendor's e-learning program. Based on your calculations, are the training programs a good investment? Which one would you recommend, and why?

3. What other factors should the company consider in deciding whether to purchase one of the proposed training programs?

4. If the company wants to conduct a utility analysis, what additional information does it require? How can it obtain this information? In other words, what would DATAIN or the consultant and vendor have to do to obtain the necessary information?

FLASHBACK QUESTIONS

1. Do you think training is the best solution to DATAIN's problems? Explain your answer using Mager and Pipe's performance analysis flowchart for determining solutions to performance problems (see Chapter 3, Figure 3.2). What are some other possible solutions to the problems described in the case?

2. What do you think the objectives should be for the proposed training programs? Refer to Chapter 4 and write several training objectives for the training programs that DATAIN is considering. Be sure to include the five key elements of training objectives and the three key components of training objectives (i.e., performance, condition, and criterion).

3. DATAIN has not prepared a request for proposal (RFP). What are some possible consequences of this? If they were to create an RFP, what should it include and what should they consider when creating it? (Refer to the section in Chapter 4 on Request for Proposal and The Trainer's Notebook 4.1.)

4. Describe how the proposed training programs should be evaluated according to: (a) Kirkpatrick's model, (b) the COMA model, and (c) the decision-based evaluation (DBE) model. Be specific about what should be measured.

5. If you were to evaluate the proposed training programs, how would you design your evaluation study? Refer to Figure 10.3 in Chapter 10 and describe how you would evaluate the proposed training programs using each of the designs. What design would you recommend, and why?

FLASH FORWARD QUESTION

1. What kind of training program do you think DATAIN needs to solve its problems? Refer to Table 12.2 in Chapter 12 (Types of Training Programs) and consider the potential of each type of program for DATAIN. What types of training programs would you recommend, and why?

REWRITE THE CASE QUESTION: FINANCIAL BENEFITS OF THE TRAINING PROGRAMS

Rewrite the case by adding a section at the end that compares the two training programs in terms of costs and benefits. Be sure to describe the costs of each program as well as the benefits, including the net benefit, the benefit–cost ratio, and the ROI.

RUNNING CASE DIRTY POOLS

QUESTIONS

Refer to the case at the end of Chapter 1 to answer the following questions.

1. What will be the main costs for a facility that provides training to its pool operators and employees? Refer to the main types of costs described in the chapter and estimate how costly the training program will be.

2. What are some of the benefits that will result from a training program for pool operators and employees? If you were to conduct a cost-effectiveness evaluation and a cost–benefit evaluation, what information would you need? What would you include in your calculations?

3. Describe how you would determine the net benefit, BCR, and ROI of a training program for pool operators/employees.

4. Do you think the benefits of a training program for pool operators/employees would be greater than the costs? Explain your answer.

// REFERENCES

1. Gillis, L., & Bailey, A. (2014, January). *Workplace literacy and essential skills research: MW Canada Ltd. Technical Skills Certificate Program Impact Analysis.* Canadian Manufacturing Network, Div. of Excellence in Manufacturing Consortium; Giroux, J. P. (2014, October 3). MW Canada–Essential Technical and Manufacturing Skills Certificate [Web log post]. Retrieved from http://www.emccanada.org/group_spaces/canadian_manufacturing_network/news_blogs/blogs/making_essential_skills_training_profitable_early_findings_show_busi; *Executive summary*, MW Canada: Technical Skills Certificate Program. Canadian Manufacturing Network, Workplace Literacy and Essential Skills Research Project (WLESR), https://www.emccanada.org/gallery/canadian_mfg_network_june_2014/manufacturing_essentials/wlesrfinalprojectsummarycomplete20150420pdf

2. Vanthournout, D., Olson, K., Ceisel, J., White, A., Waddington, T., Barfield, T., Desai, S., & Mindrum, C. (2008). *Return on learning: Training for high performance at Accenture.* Evanston, IL: Agate.

3. Phillips. J. J. (1996). ROI: The search for best practices. *Training and Development, 50*(2), 42–47.

4. Salas, E., & Cannon-Bowers, J. A. (2001). The science of training: A decade of progress. *Annual Review of Psychology, 52*, 471–499; Lavis, C. (2011). *Learning & development outlook 2011: Are organizations ready for Learning 2.0?* Ottawa: The Conference Board of Canada.

5. Phillips, J. J., & Phillips, P. P. (2010). Confronting CEO expectations about the value of learning. *T+D, 64*(1), 52–57.

6. Phillips, J. J., & Phillips, P. P. (2009). Measuring what matters: How CEOs view learning success. *T+D, 63*(8), 44–49.

7. Phillips & Phillips (2017).

8. Hall, C., & Cotsman, S. (2015). *Learning as a lever for performance: Learning and development outlook—13th edition*. Ottawa: The Conference Board of Canada.

9. Everson, B. (2007, November 5). Canadian companies lag foreign firms in training. *Canadian HR Reporter, 20*(19), 23.

10. Robinson, D. G., & Robinson, J. (1989). *Training for impact. Training & Development Journal, 43*(8), 34–42.

11. Robinson & Robinson (1989).

12. Gale, S. F. (2002). Measuring the ROI of e-learning. *Workforce, 81*(8), 74–77.

13. Robinson & Robinson (1989).

14. Cascio, W. F. (1991). *Costing human resources: The financial impact of behavior in organizations*. Boston, MA: Kent.

15. Schmidt, F. L., Hunter, J. E., & Pearlman, K. (1982). Assessing the economic impact of personnel programs on workforce productivity. *Personnel Psychology, 35*, 333–347.

16. Cascio (1991).

17. Mathieu, J. E., & Leonard, R. L., Jr. (1987). Applying utility concepts to a training program in supervisory skills: A time-based approach. *Academy of Management Journal, 30*, 316–335.

18. Bedinham, K. (1998). Proving the effectiveness of training. *Education & Training 40*(4), 166–167; Phillips. J. J. (1996). How much is the training worth? *Training & Development, 50*(4), 20–24.

19. Phillips, J. J. (1991). Measuring the return on HRD. *Employment Relations Today, 18*(3), p. 337.

20. Geroy, G. D., & Wright, P. C. (1988). Evaluation research: A pragmatic program-focused research strategy for decision makers. *Performance Improvement Quarterly, 1*(3), 17–26; Wright, P. C. (1990). Validating hospitality curricula within associated-sponsored certification programs: A qualitative methodology and a case study. *Hospitality Research Journal, 14*(1), 117–132.

21. Phillips (1996).

CHAPTER 2

TRAINING PROGRAMS

CHAPTER LEARNING OUTCOMES

AFTER READING THIS CHAPTER, YOU SHOULD BE ABLE TO:

- compare and contrast the different types of training programs
- explain why an organization would provide the various types of training programs
- identify situations in which the various types of training described in the chapter are required by an organization
- explain the potential benefits that an organization can realize by implementing each type of training

North York General Hospital (NYGH) is a community and academic hospital that primarily serves north-central Toronto and southern York Region. It is one of the largest Family and Community Medicine programs in Canada, and its emergency department is one of the most visited in the country.

Several years ago, the manager of the emergency psychiatric consultation team recognized that newly hired nurses with English as a second language (ESL) had problems writing their assessments, which were often sparse or incomplete. They missed key points, lacked attention to significant details, reflected difficulty using and understanding common vernacular or idioms, and showed limited awareness of behavioural norms common in diverse cultures. The assessments lacked sufficient depth for the emergency department's on-call psychiatrist, who relies on the assessments to determine a patient's follow-up treatment.

To address the problem, a specialized, innovative orientation component for nurses with ESL was added to the requisite one-month orientation for all new nurses hired by the psychiatric unit. During this orientation, the nurses work directly with an experienced mental health nurse at the hospital who specializes in crisis assessment. Using a variety of teaching techniques, the nurse identifies and addresses gaps in the new nurses' communication skills, and provides one-on-one role modelling and mentorship.

The role-modelling and mentorship are essential because mental health nurses in the emergency department work autonomously and have to make on-the-spot recommendations, referrals, and decisions in collaboration with the on-call psychiatrist. They work under extreme pressure and require strong crisis resolution skills. Therefore, in addition to improving communication skills, the training with the crisis nurse was designed to help the new nurses become more comfortable working independently. Role plays were also

North York General Hospital developed a specialized, innovative orientation program for new nurses with ESL.

used, in which the experienced nurse demonstrated how to gently probe patients to elicit detailed responses.

Because some of the nurses come from cultures where all decision making is left up to the doctor, this training is essential to develop the nurses' ability to make rapid, well-founded, and confident decisions independently. During their orientation, new hires with ESL also shadow staff in related mental health programs at the hospital, enabling them to make better recommendations for follow-up treatments.

Upon completion of their enhanced orientation, the nurses have reported increased confidence in their ability to prepare comprehensive assessments. Colleagues have reported increased satisfaction with the new nurses' assessments as well as improved confidence resulting in a more cohesive working team and optimal patient care.[1]

Source: O'Hare, M. A., Quint, F., & Rosenbaum, L. (2013, October 7). Nothing lost in translation at Toronto hospital. *Canadian HR Reporter*, p. 27. Reprinted by permission of *Canadian HR Reporter*. © Copyright Thomson Reuters Canada Ltd., (2013), Toronto, Ontario, 1-800-387-5164. Web: www.hrreporter.com; www.nygh.on.ca.

// INTRODUCTION

By now you should be familiar with the training and development process. We have covered the major steps of the instructional systems design (ISD) model of training and development: needs analysis, training objectives, training design, training methods, training delivery, transfer of training, and the evaluation and costing of training and

TABLE 12.1

TRAINING CONTENT IN CANADIAN ORGANIZATIONS

TRAINING CONTENT	% OF OVERALL CONTENT	% OF ORGANIZATIONS OFFERING
Management and supervisory skills	17	95
Interpersonal skills	11	83
New employee orientation	8	82
Occupational health and safety/compliance	12	74
Executive development	7	78
Customer relations and/or service	7	73
Information technology skills training	6	58
Professional and technical training	13	64
Quality, competition, and business practices	4	51
Product knowledge	7	48
Sales (excluding product knowledge)	4	44
Basic skills (e.g., literacy, numeracy)	1	12
Other	2	7

Source: Cotsman, S., & Hall, C. (2018). *Learning cultures lead the way: Learning and development outlook—14th edition.* Ottawa: The Conference Board of Canada.

development programs. At this point, you might be asking yourself, "What types of training programs do organizations provide their employees?"

Organizations offer many types of training, one example of which is the orientation training for nurses with English as a second language at North York General Hospital. The purpose of this chapter is to describe the major types of training programs that are designed and delivered by organizations.

Table 12.1 shows the percentage of overall content for different types of training programs and the percentage of organizations in Canada that offer each type. Notice that most organizations offer all of the training content listed except for basic skills training, which is offered by only 12 percent of organizations. Management and supervisory skills is the most-provided training content, followed by interpersonal skills, new employee orientation, executive development, and occupational health and safety.

Table 12.2 lists 17 common types of training programs that are described in this chapter. As you read about each type of training, you might think about how some of the material described in earlier chapters (e.g., needs analysis, training methods, transfer of training, and training evaluation) is important for making each type of training program effective. Let's now take a closer look at the different types of training programs.

TABLE 12.2

TYPES OF TRAINING PROGRAMS

1. *Orientation training.* Programs that introduce new employees to their job, the people they will be working with, and the organization.

2. *Essential skills training.* Training programs that are designed to provide employees with the essential skills required to perform their job and adapt to workplace change.

3. *Technical skills training.* Training in specific job-related skills that all employees need to perform their jobs.

4. *Non-technical skills training.* Training in a variety of skills that employees require for working and interacting with others.

5. *Information technology training.* Training programs that focus on the use of computers and computer systems.

6. *Computer software training.* Training programs that focus on how to use a specific computer software application.

7. *Health and safety training.* Training programs that educate employees in safe work methods and practices and how to recognize the chemical and physical hazards in the workplace so that they are prepared and capable of taking corrective action in the event of an accident.

8. *Total quality management (TQM) training.* Training programs that involve team training and training in the use of statistical tools that are used for problem-solving and decision-making processes.

9. *Team training.* Training programs that are designed to improve the functioning and effectiveness of teams in areas such as communication and coordination.

10. *Sales training.* Training programs that are designed to upgrade sales professionals' skills and help them deal with new competitive challenges.

11. *Customer-service training.* Training programs that are designed to provide employees with interpersonal and service skills that are required for interacting with customers and for providing quality service.

12. *Sexual and racial harassment training.* Training programs that are designed to educate employees about sexual and racial harassment and the organization's policies and procedures regarding sexual and racial harassment.

13. *Ethics training.* Training programs that educate employees about the organization's values and ethical policies and on making ethical decisions.

14. *Diversity training.* Training programs that focus on differences in values, attitudes, and behaviours of individuals with different backgrounds.

15. *Cross-cultural training.* Training programs that prepare employees for working and living in different cultures and for interactions with persons from different backgrounds.

16. *Health and wellness training.* Training programs that educate employees on how to improve their health and lifestyle.

17. *Mental health training.* Training programs on how to recognize mental health problems and how to provide assistance and support to those experiencing a mental health problem.

// ORIENTATION TRAINING

The chapter began with a description of a specialized and innovative orientation training program provided to newly hired nurses with English as a second language (ESL) at North York General Hospital. But what exactly is orientation training?

Orientation training refers to training programs that introduce new employees to their job, the people they will be working with, and the organization.[2] Formal orientation and training programs are one of the main methods used by organizations to socialize new employees.[3]

Most organizations provide some type of orientation for new employees. For example, a study of 100 major British organizations found that an overwhelming majority provided new hires with formalized, off-the-job induction training within four weeks of entry. Most of the organizations provided standardized programs that were designed and conducted by in-house human resource practitioners. The content of induction training was general in nature and pertained mostly to health and safety, terms and conditions of employment, organizational history and structure, and human resource management policies and procedures.[4]

Employees who attend orientation training programs have been found to be more socialized in terms of their knowledge and understanding of the organization's goals, values, history, and involvement with people, and to have higher organizational commitment.[5]

Effective orientation programs can also shape corporate culture, increase new employees' speed to proficiency, and lower turnover.[6] Furthermore, a study on the training of new hires in a large fast-food organization found that those units that used the new-hire training program to a greater extent had higher customer-service performance, greater retention, and higher financial performance.[7]

// ESSENTIAL SKILLS TRAINING

Many working adults today have difficulty reading, writing, and understanding mathematics. They lack what are known as essential skills.

Essential skills are the skills required for work, learning, and life. They are necessary and a foundation for learning other skills and being able to adapt to workplace change. The Government of Canada and other agencies have identified nine types of essential skills: reading text, document use, numeracy, writing, oral communication, working with others, continuous learning, thinking skills, and computer use. Essential skills are required for most occupations and in one's daily life.[8]

Many of the essential skills (e.g., reading text, document use, and numeracy) are known as literacy skills. **Literacy** refers to the ability to understand and use printed information in daily activities, at home, at work, and in the community—to achieve one's goals, and to develop one's knowledge and potential.[9]

A report by the Conference Board of Canada found that 42 percent of all Canadians aged 16 to 65 score at the lowest literacy levels and are only semi-literate. About 4.7 million Canadians score in the upper Level 2 and low Level 3 range, and their limited literacy skills pose a significant challenge to their workplace performance and success. Further, only 58 percent of Canadian adults can read well enough to meet most day-to-day requirements, and half of Canadian adults do not have the required level of literacy to succeed in a modern knowledge-based economy.

It has been reported that low literacy levels cost Canadian businesses $2.5 billion each year in lost productivity and the Canadian economy $80 billion in lost economic opportunities.[10]

It is becoming increasingly clear that organizations must provide their workforces with essential skills training if they are to compete and survive in a global and high-tech workplace. Evidence suggests that without first providing trainees with essential skills training, other programs and initiatives will not succeed.

Essential skills training provides employees with the essential skills that are required to perform their job and adapt to workplace change. Organizations that have implemented essential skills training not only have experienced improvements in productivity, efficiency, and quality, but some also report a decrease in absenteeism and the number of workers' compensation claims made, and an improvement in cross-cultural communication and morale.[11]

A study on firms in the accommodation and food services sector found that literacy and essential skills training resulted in a net benefit of $577 per participant and an average return on investment of 23 percent. The training resulted in improvements in job performance, higher rates of job retention, and increased customer satisfaction.[12]

A survey of the skilled trades found that 45 percent of employers provide essential skills training. The median investment of $1,125 per employee was found to result in a total benefit of $4,071 and a return of $3.08 for every dollar invested.[13]

Unfortunately, Canadian organizations spend very little on essential skills training. As shown in Table 12.1, only 1 percent of overall training content is devoted to basic skills and only 12 percent of organizations indicated that they provide basic skills training.

The Conference Board of Canada has described this underinvestment as "troubling," given that employees who improve their essential skills are more likely to learn new job-related skills more quickly and accurately, make fewer mistakes, work more efficiently, and be less resistant to change. Literacy is critical to productivity, which in turn is essential to Canadian competitiveness and prosperity.[14]

Essential skills training
Training programs that are designed to provide employees with the essential skills required to perform their job and adapt to workplace change

// TECHNICAL AND NON-TECHNICAL SKILLS TRAINING

Technical skills training is training in specific job-related skills that all employees need to perform their jobs. Among manufacturing firms, training for specific job skills is the most frequent type of training provided. This is not surprising given the changes in the workplace that have occurred over the last several decades.

With increasing global competition, organizations have had to find new ways to stay competitive and to survive, often by adopting new technologies and the redesign of work arrangements and systems. As a result, employees have had to undergo a considerable amount of technical skills upgrading and training. Nowhere is this more apparent than in the manufacturing sector, where low-skilled employees have had to become highly skilled to keep their jobs and for their organizations to survive.[15]

In addition to technical skills, non-technical or "soft" skills have also become increasingly important today. **Non-technical skills training** refers to training in a variety of skills that employees require to work and interact with others, such as communication skills, interpersonal skills, and negotiation skills. Many of the changes taking place in

Technical skills training
Training in specific job-related skills that all employees need to perform their jobs

Non-technical skills training
Training in a variety of skills that employees require for working and interacting with others

organizations such as flatter organization structures and the use of work teams have led to the increased importance of non-technical skills.

Today even entry-level employees need to have soft skills in addition to technical skills.[16] Some of the most common types of non-technical skills training programs such as team training are described later in the chapter.

// INFORMATION TECHNOLOGY TRAINING

Information technology training refers to training in computers and computer systems. Information systems training is a key factor in the successful implementation of information systems technology.[17] Research has shown that technological failures in the workplace are most often the result of training issues rather than the technology.[18]

Information technology training usually involves either introductory computer training programs, in which trainees learn about computer hardware and software, or applications training, in which trainees are instructed on specific software applications to be used in the organization.[19] Applications training is required whenever an organization upgrades its computer systems.

One of the most common types of information technology training is computer software training. **Computer software training** focuses on how to use a specific computer software application.[20] Computer software training has been shown to increase trainees' ability to use the system and their motivation to use the software.

// HEALTH AND SAFETY TRAINING

Workplace health and safety has become an increasing concern in Canadian organizations. The costs of work-related injuries and illnesses are on the rise and present a serious threat to employees and their organizations.

Approximately 1000 workers die each year in Canada as a result of workplace accidents, and some 340 000 workers suffer an injury serious enough to warrant missing time from work, which is known as a lost-time injury. The cost of workplace injuries is estimated to exceed $12 billion a year.[21]

One of the most important ways to prevent accidents before they occur is education. **Health and safety training** programs educate employees in safe work methods and practices and how to recognize the chemical and physical hazards in the workplace so that they are prepared and capable of taking corrective action in the event of an accident. Unfortunately, many workers in Canada do not receive adequate safety training. It has been reported that only one in five Canadians receive safety training in the first year of a new job.[22]

However, safety training is so important that one of the recommendations of a report by the Ministry of Labour in Ontario was to provide mandatory health and safety awareness training for all workers and supervisors. The report was the result of a construction accident in Toronto in 2009, in which four construction workers fell to their death.[23]

In July of 2014, a new regulation under the *Ontario Occupational Health and Safety Act* (OHSA) came into effect that requires all workers and supervisors in Ontario to complete a mandatory health and safety awareness training program. The occupational health and safety awareness training provides a basic understanding of the OHSA; the rights and responsibilities of workers, supervisors, and employers; and how the act is enforced.

Health and safety training programs educate employees in safe work methods and practices and how to recognize the chemical and physical hazards in the workplace.

An important component of health and safety training involves the handling of hazardous materials and chemicals. The **Workplace Hazardous Materials Information System (WHMIS)** legislation is designed to ensure that workers across Canada are aware of the potential hazards of chemicals in the workplace and are familiar with emergency procedures for the clean-up and disposal of a spill.

An important component of WHMIS legislation is employee training. Training in WHMIS is designed so that employees can identify WHMIS hazard symbols, read WHMIS supplier and workplace labels, and read and apply the information on material safety data sheets (MSDS), which outline the hazardous ingredient(s) in a product and the procedures for the safe handling of that product.[24]

Research on safety training has found that it can have a significant positive effect on employee learning (i.e., safety knowledge) and safety performance. However, the effectiveness of safety training depends on the training method and the severity of exposure to workplace hazards.

Safety training that involves the use of highly engaging instructional methods (e.g., behaviour modelling, simulations, and hands-on training) is more effective for both learning and safety performance than less engaging instructional methods (e.g., lectures, films, reading materials, and video-based training). This is especially the case when the training is for work situations that involve high exposure to hazardous conditions that could result in severe illness, injury, or death.[25]

> **Workplace Hazardous Materials Information System (WHMIS)** Legislation to ensure that workers across Canada are aware of the potential hazards of chemicals in the workplace and are familiar with emergency procedures for the clean-up and disposal of a spill

// TOTAL QUALITY MANAGEMENT TRAINING

To remain competitive, many organizations have implemented quality programs. One of the most popular examples is total quality management.

Total quality management (TQM) is a systematic process of continual improvement of the quality of products and services. In addition to an emphasis on quality and continual improvement, TQM also involves teamwork and a customer focus.[26]

TQM places the training function in a pivotal position, as the process often requires significant changes in employees' skills and the way employees work.

TQM training involves team training as well as training in the use of statistical tools that are used for problem-solving and decision-making processes. Most TQM advocates emphasize the importance of training and development.[27] Training and development is the primary method of reinforcing employee commitment to the consistent delivery of high-quality products and services.[28]

// TEAM TRAINING

Many organizations now rely on teams as the primary work arrangement. Although teams have the potential to be effective, teams face many challenges and often require training.[29]

Team training is designed to improve the functioning and effectiveness of teams in areas such as communication, coordination, mutual performance monitoring, exchange of feedback, and adaptation to varying situational demands.[30]

Team training is an "attempt to improve a group's process through the use of interventions targeted at specific aspects of the process such as effective communication."[31]

Group processes are usually the focus of team training; however, because team members are often expected to perform a variety of the group's tasks, they often must also receive technical training to become multi-skilled.

Thus, team training focuses on two general types of skills: *task-work skills*, which are skills that are required to perform the team's tasks, and *teamwork skills*, which are skills that team members need in order to interact, communicate, and coordinate tasks effectively with other team members.

Both types of skills need to be included in team training programs, and it is recommended that team members first master task-work and technical skills before they are trained on teamwork skills.[32]

A good example of a specific type of team training is crew resource management (CRM) training, which is a specialized type of team training for flight crew teams that focuses on communication and decision making.

Crew resource management training teaches team members to use all available resources—people, information, and equipment—to ensure safe and efficient flight operations. CRM training focuses on critical cognitive and interpersonal skills such as communication, problem solving, and decision making to improve crew coordination and performance. Research on CRM training has found that it has a positive effect on attitudes, learning, and behavioural changes on the job.[33]

Another area where team training is especially important is in healthcare, where team training can reduce preventable errors and patient harm. A large-scale study that reviewed the findings of research on healthcare team training found that it improves trainee reactions, learning, task and teamwork performance, and results. In terms of results, healthcare team training improves organizational outcomes, including safety climate, and patient outcomes, such as patient mortality.[34]

In general, research has found that team training improves team functioning and has a positive effect on cognitive outcomes (e.g., declarative knowledge), affective outcomes (e.g., trust), teamwork processes (e.g., communication), and performance

Crew resource management training focuses on cognitive and interpersonal skills to improve flight crew communication and coordination.

outcomes (efficiency and effectiveness). Team training has also been found to result in fewer medical errors and safer air travel, and to improve organizations' bottom line.[35]

// SALES TRAINING

Sales professionals need to be knowledgeable about their products, their business, and their customers' businesses. As a result, sales training has become more than simply sending the sales troops off to a motivational pep rally.[36]

Sales training programs upgrade sales professionals' skills and help them deal with new competitive challenges. At the centre of these training initiatives is an emphasis on "relationship-based" sales training.

Sales professionals are trained to develop strategic and complex relationships with clients, and to create relationships across client functions. They are also trained to become knowledgeable about their customers' business needs, and to develop customized sales strategies. Rather than just selling a commodity, integrated teams of people from sales, support, and service are learning to sell solutions that combine support and service agreements.

// CUSTOMER-SERVICE TRAINING

Organizations with a strong commitment to customer service invest heavily in training their employees. **Customer-service training** programs are designed to provide employees with interpersonal and customer-service skills that are required for interacting with customers and for providing quality service.

Sales training
Training programs that are designed to upgrade sales professionals' skills and help them deal with new competitive challenges

Customer-service training
Training programs that are designed to provide employees with interpersonal and service skills that are required for interacting with customers and for providing quality service

Employees at the Canadian National Exhibition receive customer-service training that is tailored to the needs of each department.

Aaron Lynett/Toronto Star/Getty Images

The training can be informal or formal. Informal training might involve pairing new hires with the organization's best employees in terms of customer-service behaviour and philosophy. The kind of formal training required depends on the type of service business that an organization is in and its service strategy. In other words, the training program must be tailored to an organization's strategy, characteristics, and customers.[37]

The Canadian National Exhibition hires 1200 employees every year and provides them with customer-service training that is tailored to the needs of each department. All front-line employees are trained on how to interact with guests and how to handle situations that they are likely to encounter on the job.[38]

Service employees must have both the *ability* and *motivation* to perform effectively. Because you cannot always hire people with the required abilities or motivation, you must be able to train them. Many organizations that have reputations for superb customer service are successful because of their commitment to training. Organizations that provide the best service also provide the most training.

// SEXUAL AND RACIAL HARASSMENT TRAINING

Sexual harassment continues to be a serious problem for many organizations; this has become very evident following the many accusations of sexual harassment and abuse in the United States and Canada recently.

Consultations conducted by the federal government found that many incidents of sexual harassment are unreported and those that are reported are often not handled appropriately. As a result, the Canadian government has updated its sexual harassment legislation, and the Ontario government amended the *Occupational Health and Safety Act* (OHSA) (Bill 132: *The Sexual Violence and Harassment Action Plan Act*), which expands organizations' responsibilities to investigate and address incidents of workplace sexual harassment.[39] In addition, all new judges in Ontario are now required to undergo mandatory training on sexual assault issues.[40]

Sexual harassment is defined as "unwelcome sexual advances, requests for sexual favours, and other verbal or physical conduct of a sexual nature ... when submission to requests for sexual favours is made explicitly or implicitly a term or condition of employment; submission to or rejection of such requests is used as a basis for employment decisions; or such conduct unreasonably interferes with work performance or creates an intimidating, hostile, or offensive work environment."[41]

Racial harassment and discrimination is also a concern for organizations with increasing reports of racist incidents at public establishments such as hotels, restaurants, and banks.[42] As a result, organizations have to become proactive and prepared to handle racist and discriminatory incidents.

The most effective way for organizations to deal with and prevent sexual and racial harassment is to develop sexual and racial harassment policies, develop procedures for filing complaints, and provide **sexual and racial harassment training** to educate employees about sexual and racial harassment and the organization's policies and procedures regarding sexual and racial harassment.[43]

Sexual harassment
Unwelcome sexual advances, requests for sexual favours, and verbal or physical conduct of a sexual nature that is a condition of employment, interferes with work performance, or creates a hostile work environment

Sexual and racial harassment training
Training programs that are designed to educate employees about sexual and racial harassment and the organization's policies and procedures regarding sexual and racial harassment

Training is especially important because the definition of what constitutes sexual harassment is not always clear or understood, and problems have occurred in situations in which employees and managers were unaware of an organization's sexual harassment policy or did not know how to report it and proceed with a complaint.

In addition, many organizations do not have anti-discrimination policies and procedures in place and employees are not prepared to handle racist incidents. Canadian human rights legislation requires organizations to respond to racist incidents, so organizations need to develop anti-discriminatory policies and procedures and train employees on their policies and on how to respond to racist and discriminatory incidents.

In 2018, Starbucks closed its stores in Canada and the United States for an afternoon to provide racial bias education training to all of its employees following an incident in a Starbucks store in which two black men were arrested while waiting for a friend. Organizations have a responsibility to create a work environment that is free of sexual and racial harassment and a key part of doing this effectively involves training.[44]

// ETHICS TRAINING

Several years ago, six current and former employees of the Toronto Transit Commission (TTC) were charged with theft, fraud, and conspiracy. As a result, then TTC CEO Andy Byford announced that all TTC managers and supervisors will attend mandatory ethics training.[44]

While many companies provide ethics training to comply with legal mandates and to gain liability protection, ethics training is also important for creating an ethical culture and workplace, and for attracting and retaining the right type of employee.

Ethics training programs educate employees about the organization's values and ethical policies and on making ethical decisions. This usually involves opportunities for employees to practise applying company values and its code of ethics to hypothetical situations. It is important that ethics training programs go beyond ethical guidelines and focus on how to effectively recognize and respond to common ethical problems in the workplace. As a result, employees learn to recognize ethical dilemmas and how to respond to them.[45]

To be most effective, ethical training programs should be mandatory for all employees and include a copy of the organization's code of ethics, a discussion of relevant compliance laws, an ethical decision-making model, resources for help, and role-playing scenarios. Organizations should first set standards for ethical behaviour and determine what the training should accomplish. Key elements of strong ethical programs are responsibility, respect, fairness, honesty, and compassion.

Employees should also be trained on the laws that apply to their jobs as well as decision-making models with questions they can ask themselves to help them make ethical decisions. Employees should also be taught how to report ethics violations and where they can go for assistance.

Practical scenarios should be included in the training so employees can test their ethical knowledge. Ethical topics

> **Ethics training**
> Training programs that educate employees about the organization's values and ethical policies and on making ethical decisions

TTC managers and supervisors attend mandatory ethics training.

CHAPTER 12 Training Programs

can include workplace romance, email appropriateness, Internet use, confidentiality, security, and harassment (physical, verbal, and emotional).[46]

Molson Coors Brewing Company has one of the most comprehensive ethics programs in North America. Its training program includes interactive online courses, ethics leadership training, a decision map, a detailed set of policies, and a help line that complements and supports a user-friendly and accessible code of conduct.[47]

// DIVERSITY TRAINING

Diversity training
Training programs that focus on differences in values, attitudes, and behaviours of individuals with different backgrounds

Diversity training programs are designed to address the differences in values, attitudes, and behaviours of individuals with different backgrounds. They are one of the most common and effective ways for organizations to manage diversity.

The objectives are to increase awareness and understanding of cultural diversity, and to improve interaction and communication among employees with different backgrounds and between employees and the organization's customers and clients.

Diversity training is one of the most widely used strategies for managing diversity in the workplace, and there has been a dramatic rise in the use of diversity training programs.[48] According to the Conference Board of Canada, 37 percent of organizations provide diversity learning and development programs to help employees understand and work with non-traditional groups.[49]

Diversity training has three main objectives: (1) increase awareness about diversity issues, (2) reduce biases and stereotypes, and (3) change behaviours to those required to work effectively in a diverse workforce.[50]

Some diversity training programs are designed to change people's attitudes by creating an awareness of diversity and an understanding of differences in values and behaviours. The expectation is that by creating awareness and understanding of these differences, people will change their behaviour and overcome any stereotypes they might hold. Another approach to diversity training is to change behaviour. This approach emphasizes learning new behaviours that might then lead to changes in attitudes.[51]

Diversity training, however, has been controversial. Some organizations believe that it is well worth the investment while others believe it is a waste of time and does not work.[52]

However, a study on diversity in the workplace found that diversity experts rated training and education programs as one of the best strategies for managing diversity. The study also suggested that diversity training should focus on increasing *awareness* of what diversity is and why it is important; providing *skills* required to work effectively in a diverse workforce; and providing *application* strategies to facilitate the use of diversity awareness and skills to improve work performance, interactions, and communication.[53]

In Canada, many organizations have implemented diversity programs. For example, L'Oréal Canada has an intergenerational training program that was designed to help different age groups communicate with each other. The program has become one of the company's most popular training programs.[54]

The Winnipeg Division of Boeing Canada Technology provides diversity training that includes formal classes on respecting and honouring the origins, leanings, and affiliations in four target groups of co-workers (women, Aboriginal people, members of visible minorities, and people with disabilities).[55]

// CROSS-CULTURAL TRAINING

Many companies send their managers and employees on assignments in foreign countries. While these foreign assignments can be good for an employee's career, they can be difficult if an individual is not familiar with the foreign culture.

Foreign assignments often result in failure, with the employee returning home early. According to one survey, 42 percent of managers fail in overseas assignments and only 58 percent are considered to be successful.[56]

One way to improve the success rate of overseas assignments is to provide managers and employees with cross-cultural training. The purpose of **cross-cultural training** is to prepare employees for overseas assignments by developing the skills and attitudes they need to interact successfully with persons from different backgrounds.[57]

A critical factor in the success of cross-cultural training is training rigour. **Training rigour** refers to "the degree of mental involvement and effort that must be expended by the trainer and the trainee in order for the trainee to learn the required concepts."[58] Training rigour also refers to the length of time spent on training.

Table 12.3 lists some of the most common methods of cross-cultural training. Cross-cultural training programs that are considered to have a high degree of rigour include interactive language training, cross-cultural simulations, and field trips. Programs with a moderate degree of training rigour include role plays, cases, and survival-level language. Cross-cultural training programs that are considered to be the lowest in terms of training rigour include lectures, films, books, and area briefings. More rigorous cross-cultural training programs require trainees to be much more active and involved in practising cross-cultural skills.[59]

The degree of cross-cultural training rigour required by an expatriate for a particular foreign assignment depends on three dimensions: cultural toughness, communication toughness, and job toughness.

Cultural toughness refers to how difficult it is to adjust to a new culture. Generally speaking, cultural toughness increases as the difference or distance between one's own culture and the foreign culture increases.

> **Cross-cultural training**
> Training programs that prepare employees for working and living in different cultures and for interactions with persons from different backgrounds
>
> **Training rigour**
> The degree of mental involvement and effort that must be expended by the trainer and the trainee in order for the trainee to learn the required concepts

---

TABLE 12.3

CROSS-CULTURAL TRAINING METHODS

- Environmental briefings about a country's geography, climate, housing, and schools.
- Cultural orientation to familiarize expatriates with cultural institutions and the value systems of the host country.
- Cultural assimilators that use programmed learning approaches to expose persons of one culture to the concepts, attitudes, role perceptions, and customs of another culture.
- Language training.
- Sensitivity training to develop attitudinal flexibility.
- Field experience such as visiting the country where one will be assigned to see what it is like to work and live with people in a different culture.

Source: Tung, R. L. (1982). Selection and training procedures of U.S., European, and Japanese multinationals. *California Management Review, 25*(1), 57.

Communication toughness is a function of the extent to which the expatriate will have to interact with the locals of the host country. When an expatriate will be required to have frequent interactions with host nationals that will involve face-to-face informal communication, the level of communication toughness will be high and more rigorous communication training will be required.

Job toughness refers to how difficult the tasks will be for the expatriate compared to what he/she is used to doing. If the expatriate will be working in a new area and the demands of the job will be different and require new responsibilities and challenges, then the degree of job toughness will be greater. As a result, the expatriate will require more rigorous job-specific training.[60]

As the levels of these three dimensions increase, the type of cross-cultural training required will need to be more rigorous. In addition to pre-departure training, it is also important that the expatriates and their families receive follow-up or in-country cross-cultural training in the host country.[61]

Research on cross-cultural training has found that it is effective for enhancing an expatriate's success on overseas assignments and is related to expatriate adjustment and performance. However, the effectiveness of cross-cultural training depends on a number of factors, such as the timing of the training and the cultural differences between one's own country and the assignment country.[62]

For guidelines on how to design a cross-cultural training program, see The Trainer's Notebook 12.1, "How to Design an Effective Cross-Cultural Training Program."

THE TRAINER'S NOTEBOOK 12.1

HOW TO DESIGN AN EFFECTIVE CROSS-CULTURAL TRAINING PROGRAM

Here are some recommendations for the successful design and implementation of a cross-cultural training program:

1. Cross-cultural training should be considered a mandatory process.

2. The location of training should be established in accordance with the needs of the family as part of the preparation process, and corporations need to accept that training can be done at home or in the host country.

3. The depth of training is of utmost importance. If corporations are going to provide cross-cultural training, it needs to be done properly with depth and with care.

4. Families must be incorporated into the training process. Training for expatriates alone is only sufficient if the expatriate is on an individualized assignment.

5. Language training should be incorporated into cross-cultural training wherever possible and should be encouraged as an ongoing aspect of the assignment.

6. Education and expectations of training must be laid out by training companies for international human resource professionals and in turn be easily translated for the preparation of each individual expatriate. This can be through appropriate written information being prepared for the expatriate and reinforced by the service provider reiterating the goals and expectations prior to the training.

Source: Bross, A. Churchill, A., & Zifkin, J. (2000, June 5). Cross-cultural training: Issues to consider during implementation. *Canadian HR Reporter*, p. 10.

// HEALTH AND WELLNESS TRAINING

There has been increasing concern about people's health and well-being. This stems in part from reports concerning the increasing number of Canadians who live unhealthy lifestyles. For example, nearly two-thirds of Canadian adults are overweight or obese, and obesity is one of the main risk factors for heart disease, hypertension, and Type 2 diabetes. These illnesses can have a negative effect on productivity and increase absenteeism.[63]

In response, many organizations have implemented **health and wellness training** programs that educate employees on how to improve their health and lifestyle. Health and wellness programs are on- or off-site services that promote and sustain good employee health, identify health-related risks in the employee population, and attempt to correct potential health-related problems.[64] In addition to providing healthy food choices in the cafeteria and during meetings, health and wellness programs often include education and training on nutrition and making healthy food choices.

For example, TOTAL E&P Canada of Calgary has a nutrition program that educates employees on how to make healthy food choices. As well, employees can receive weekly one-on-one sessions with a nutritionist.[65] TELUS offers employees a variety of wellness programs that focus on nutrition, active living, and cold and flu readiness, and provides screenings for osteoporosis, blood pressures, cholesterol, and cancer. The company also implemented a program that provides health coaching on risk factors. For example, it provided coaching on heart disease to 500 middle managers that resulted in a return on investment of $3.80 for every dollar spent.[66]

According to the Conference Board of Canada, the majority of Canadian organizations offer at least one workplace wellness initiative. However, only about one-quarter have an integrated and comprehensive strategy, which is essential for realizing the benefits of a healthy workplace.[67]

In addition to physical health and wellness, there has also been an increased concern and awareness of mental health in the workplace. According to the Mental Health Commission of Canada, more than 70 percent of Canadian employees are concerned about the psychological health and safety of their workplace.[68]

It has been estimated that mental illness costs Canadian organizations billions of dollars a year in lost productivity and absenteeism, and mental health problems and illnesses are a major cause of short-term and long-term disability claims in Canada.[69]

In 2013, a Canadian national standard called Psychological Health and Safety in the Workplace was introduced for workplace mental health and safety. The standard provides organizations with guidelines, tools, and resources on how to promote mental health in the workplace. A key part of improving mental health in the workplace is training.

Mental health training provides information on how to recognize mental health problems and how to provide assistance and support to those experiencing a mental health problem.

To learn more about mental health training, see Training Today 12.1, "Mental Health Training at the Government of the Northwest Territories."

Health and wellness training
Training programs that educate employees on how to improve their health and lifestyle

Mental health training
Training programs on how to recognize mental health problems and how to provide assistance and support to those experiencing a mental health problem

MENTAL HEALTH TRAINING AT THE GOVERNMENT OF THE NORTHWEST TERRITORIES

Canadian organizations have come to realize that supporting and promoting workplace mental health offers real advantages in terms of reduced absenteeism, increased productivity, and better overall employee well-being. However, only 39 percent of organizations have implemented a mental health strategy.

One of the reasons for this is a lack of corporate knowledge on how to do so. An effective mental health strategy focuses on specific workplace needs. Although there is no single approach that is applicable to all organizations, most organizations agree that one essential component for a mental health strategy is training, although when and how training should be provided, and who should receive it, varies.

Before developing a mental health training program, it is important to develop a comprehensive strategy so the organization has a clear idea of how training fits into the big picture and complements other wellness initiatives. This involves understanding what issues exist in the workplace, what needs to change, and how training can help effect the transformation.

For many organizations, flexibility in how the program is delivered is essential. The Government of the Northwest Territories (GNWT) implemented mental health training in January 2016. To address the high cost of travelling to and from Northern Canada, the government chose a provider that offered online training.

"Organizations facing similar challenges should find a provider that can deliver training in different ways, such as online training or in a classroom," says Glorianna Shearme, health and wellness consultant at the GNWT in Yellowknife. "Webinars provide an opportunity to train staff who work in remote regions and allow them equal access to training."

Flexibility is especially important if an organization decides to offer different training for various roles. For example, the GNWT offers one-hour mental health webinars to employees while managers and supervisors can sign up for half-day workshops that teach them how to recognize signs an employee may be dealing with an issue, and provide them with a framework for supporting the employee.

Metrics to evaluate the effectiveness of mental health initiatives are under review at the GNWT, says Shearme. "Employees, however, want additional in-person training to allow for more in-depth discussion, and managers want support, such as hands-on tools, to assist them in having conversations with employees with mental health issues."

The GNWT is acting on these requests through updates to its employee and family assistance site, and additions to its learning and development calendar.

Mental health training is one initiative in a larger strategy to address workplace mental health. But to maximize effectiveness, it is important to ensure the organization has not only laid the groundwork for training, but has chosen the most appropriate program.

Source: Based on Delfosse, J., & Richardson, D. (2017). The importance of training for mental health: Choosing the right program critical to ensuring maximum effectiveness. *Canadian HR Reporter*, *30*(11), 24. Reprinted by permission of *Canadian HR Reporter*. © Copyright Thomson Reuters Canada Ltd., (2017), Toronto, Ontario, 1-800-387-5164. Web: www.hrreporter.com

// SUMMARY

This chapter has provided an overview of the different types of training programs provided by organizations. You should now be familiar with orientation training, essential skills training, technical and non-technical skills training, information technology training, computer software training, health and safety training, total quality management training, team training, sales training, customer-service training, sexual and racial harassment training, ethics training, diversity training, cross-cultural training, health and wellness training, and mental health training. Many of these training programs have become key components of organizations' business strategies and are major factors in their efforts to remain competitive.

KEY TERMS

computer software training p. 388
crew resource management training, p. 390
cross-cultural training p. 395
customer-service training p. 391
diversity training p. 394
essential skills p. 386
essential skills training p. 387
ethics training p. 393
health and safety training p. 388
health and wellness training p. 397
information technology training p. 388
literacy p. 386
mental health training p. 397
non-technical skills training p. 387
orientation training p. 386
sales training p. 391
sexual and racial harassment training p. 392
sexual harassment p. 392
team training p. 390
technical skills training p. 387
total quality management (TQM) p. 390
total quality management (TQM) training p. 390
training rigour p. 395
Workplace Hazardous Materials Information System (WHMIS) p. 389

DISCUSSION QUESTIONS

1. Diversity training programs have been criticized for doing more harm than good. In fact, there is some evidence that they may be ineffective at best and harmful at worst. Why do you think this is the case? Do you think this is true, and should organizations abandon diversity training or embrace it?

2. Why do you think Canadian organizations invest so little in essential skills training (see Table 12.1, basic skills)? What are the implications of this for employees, organizations, and society? Should Canadian organizations spend more on essential skills training? What would be the advantages and disadvantages?

3. What would be your reaction if your employer wanted to send you on an overseas assignment? What would be your reaction if the assignment was in (a) England, (b) France, (c) China, or (d) Egypt? Would you accept the assignment? If so, what training would you require? Describe the content and methods of the training you would need.

4. What aspects of a cross-cultural training program affect its degree of training rigour? Discuss the factors that need to be considered to determine the degree of

cross-cultural training rigour required by an expatriate for a foreign assignment. If you were sent on a foreign assignment to France to manage a restaurant chain, what degree of cross-cultural training rigour would you require?

5. What is the Workplace Hazardous Materials Information System (WHMIS) and what are its implications for safety training? What content should be included in a health and safety training program?

6. Why is team training important for organizations that want to implement teams? What skills should be the focus of team training programs?

7. Why should an organization provide orientation training? If you were going to design an orientation program, what content would you include and how would your program be delivered?

8. Who is responsible for literacy in the workplace and what is the effect of low literacy levels on individuals, organizations, and the economy?

9. Research has found that the effectiveness of safety training depends on the instructional method and the severity of workplace hazards. Explain the nature of this relationship and its implications for organizations and employees.

10. What is mental health training and why is it important for organizations to have a mental health strategy and to provide mental health training?

11. What is sexual and racial harassment and what should organizations do to prevent it in the workplace? What should be included in training programs on sexual and racial harassment?

THE GREAT TRAINING DEBATE

1. Debate the following: Diversity training programs result in more harm than good and organizations should abandon them.

2. Debate the following: Essential skills and literacy training are the responsibility of government, not organizations.

EXERCISES

IN-CLASS

1. The extent to which organizations provide certain types of training programs is often driven by external and internal factors. In other words, social, political, and economic changes in the external environment, as well as internal changes to organizational systems and work arrangements, have a substantial influence on training activities (see the section on the context of training and development in Chapter 1 and Figure 1.2). Choose one of the types of training programs in Table 12.2 and discuss the role of external and internal factors and how these factors might influence the need for that type of training.

2. Assume you are a training director for a large retail organization. To increase your training budget for next year, you have to make a persuasive argument to convince other members of the organization of your need for an increase in resources. An important part of your argument will involve proving the need for and importance of several training programs. For one of the training programs listed in Table 12.2, describe how you will argue that it is important, the impact it will

have on employee attitudes and behaviour, the benefits it will have for employees and the organization, and how it can help the organization gain a competitive advantage.

3. Design a training program for one of the types of training discussed in this chapter. In designing your program, specify each of the following:

   a. The training objectives
   b. The training content
   c. The trainer
   d. The trainees who should attend the program
   e. The training methods to be used
   f. The required training materials and equipment
   g. The training site
   h. The schedule for the training program
   i. The lesson plan
   j. The criteria you will use to evaluate the program

4. Describe the orientation training you received in the most recent job you have held. Some of the things to consider are as follows:

   a. How long was the orientation training?
   b. What content was included?
   c. What methods were used?
   d. What did you learn from it?
   e. Were you satisfied with the program, and did it help you perform your job?
   f. What did you like about it, and what did you not like?
   g. How would you change the orientation training you received to make it more effective?

5. Choose one of the types of training programs described in this chapter that you have attended in a current or previous job. Describe the content and methods used and how effective the training was for your learning, on-the-job behaviour, job performance, and career. Based on the material in the chapter, how effective was the training program? How would you change it, improve it, and make it more effective?

6. Imagine your employer has just informed you that you are going on a foreign assignment for three years to a country that you have never been to and know nothing about. Furthermore, the culture is very different from your own. Your employer has said you will be receiving some written information about the country and its culture, as well as a DVD to help you prepare for your assignment. Prepare a memo to your employer in which you evaluate this training and describe the type of cross-cultural training that you require if you are going to accept the assignment.

7. Students often have to work in groups on course projects without any knowledge of how groups function and what it takes for them to be effective. Some students experience difficulties when working in groups and some groups fall apart and the work is not completed. Therefore, it might be helpful for students to receive team training. Your task is to design a training program for students to prepare them for group work. Describe the nature of your training program, including the objectives, content, and methods.

8. Prepare a brief presentation to convince management to invest in essential skills and literacy training. Be sure to explain why investing in this training is important, the consequences of investing in it, and the consequences of not investing in it.

IN-THE-FIELD

1. To learn more about the training programs discussed in this chapter, contact a training professional or an HR professional to arrange an interview about the types of training programs provided in their organization. Choose one or two of the types of training programs described in this chapter and ask them the following questions:
   - Does your organization provide this type of training?
   - What are some of the reasons you do or do not provide this type of training?
   - What are the objectives of this type of training program?
   - What is the content of this type of training?
   - How is this training program designed (e.g., methods, techniques, etc.) and who is the trainer?
   - What effect does this type of training have on employees' attitudes and behaviours?
   - What effect does this type of training have on the organization?

   Based on your interview, what is your evaluation of the training program(s) provided by the organization? Do you think it or they could be improved? If so, what would you recommend, and why?

2. Contact several people you know who work in different organizations, and ask them the following questions about one or two of the types of training programs discussed in the chapter:
   - Have you ever attended this type of training program?
   - If yes, why did you attend the training program?
   - What were the objectives of the training program?
   - What was the content of the training program?
   - How was the training program designed (e.g., methods, techniques, etc.), and who was the trainer?
   - What was your reaction to the training program, and what did you learn?
   - What effect did the training have on your behaviour and job performance?
   - What effect did the training have on the organization?

   Based on your interview, do you think the training program(s) was or were effective? What changes would you recommend to make it more effective?

3. To learn more about workplace literacy and essential skills in Canada, visit ABC Life Literacy Canada at http://abclifeliteracy.ca.

   Click on the workplace literacy link and answer the following questions:

   a. What are the nine essential skills needed for success in the workplace?

   b. What are the benefits of basic/essential skills training?

   c. What are some of the tools and resources provided by the website?

4. To learn more about the types of safety training programs available, visit the Canadian Centre for Occupational Health and Safety at www.ccohs.ca/education/.

   Answer the following questions:

   a. What kinds of training programs are available?

   b. Choose one of the programs and find out what the program is about, the topics covered, the program objectives, the target audience, and the delivery options.

5. To find out about WHMIS education and training go to the Canadian Centre for Occupational Health and Safety at https://www.ccohs.ca/oshanswers/chemicals/whmis_ghs/general.html

   Answer the following questions:

   a. What is WHMIS?

   b. Is WHMIS law?

   c. What is the status of the new WHMIS regulations?

   d. What products does WHMIS cover? What products are not covered by WHMIS?

   e. What are the suppliers' duties under WHMIS?

   f. What are the employers' duties under WHMIS?

   g. What are the workers' duties under WHMIS?

CASE INCIDENT

SAVING THEATRE CALGARY

Theatre Calgary is one of the largest professional theatres in western Canada. However, lagging ticket sales and competing claims on the philanthropy dollar brought Theatre Calgary to near bankruptcy in 1996.

A decision was made to overhaul the company's marketing approach that would raise the standard of performance expected from employees, especially those in the areas of sales and customer service.

To support the new approach, the company invested in training for aggressive marketing and up-selling. Employees attended seminars on a range of techniques from how to cross-sell to how to analyze demographics for marketing opportunities and how to create a customer profile from the client database. Employees also had to improve their customer contact skills, from telephone manner to up-selling to meet-and-greet. They spent time developing scripts and rehearsing how to deal with people and how to deal with people with problems.

QUESTIONS

1. How important is training for saving Theatre Calgary from bankruptcy? What type of training is required?

2. What do you think about the training programs provided to employees at Theatre Calgary? What would you recommend for improving them?

Source: Rabinovitch, R. (2004, May 17). Close up: Training and development. *Canadian HR Reporter*, p. 7. Reprinted by permission of *Canadian HR Reporter*. © Copyright Thomson Reuters Canada Ltd., (2004), Toronto, Ontario, 1-800-387-5164. Web: www.hrreporter.com

| CASE STUDY | THE FOREIGN ASSIGNMENT |

Fred Bailey gazed out the window of his 24th-floor office at the tranquil beauty of the Imperial Palace amid the hustle and bustle of downtown Tokyo. It had been only six months since Fred had arrived with his wife and two children for this three-year assignment as the director of Kline & Associates' Tokyo office.

Kline & Associates is a large multinational consulting firm with offices in 19 countries worldwide. Fred was now trying to decide whether he should simply pack up and tell headquarters that he was coming home or whether he should try to convince his wife, and himself, that they should stay and finish the assignment. Given how excited they all were about the assignment to begin with, it was a mystery to Fred how things had gotten to this point. As Fred watched the swans glide across the water in the moat that surrounds the Imperial Palace, he reflected on the past seven months.

Seven months ago, Dave Steiner, the managing partner of the main office in Boston, asked Fred to lunch to discuss business. To Fred's surprise, the business they discussed was not about the major project that he and his team had just finished; instead, it was about a very big promotion and career move. Fred was offered the position of managing director of the firm's relatively new Tokyo office, which had a staff of 40, including seven Americans. Most of the Americans in the Tokyo office were either associate consultants or research analysts. Fred would be in charge of the whole office and would report to a senior partner. Steiner implied to Fred that if this assignment went as well as his past projects, it would be the last step before becoming a partner in the firm.

When Fred told his wife about the unbelievable opportunity, he was shocked at her less-than-enthusiastic response. His wife, Jennifer (or Jenny as Fred called her), thought that it would be rather difficult to have the children live and go to school in a foreign country for three years, especially when Christine, their older daughter, would be starting middle school next year. Besides, now that the kids were in school, Jenny was thinking about going back to work, at least part-time. Jenny had a degree in fashion merchandising from a well-known university and had worked as an assistant buyer for a large women's clothing store before having the two girls.

Fred explained that the career opportunity was just too good to pass up and that the company's overseas package would make living overseas terrific. The company would pay all the expenses to move whatever the Baileys wanted to take with them. The company had a very nice house in an expensive district of Tokyo that would be provided rent free, and the company would rent their house in Boston during their absence. Moreover, the firm would provide a car and driver, education expenses for the children to attend private schools, and a cost-of-living adjustment and overseas compensation that would nearly triple Fred's gross annual salary. After two days of consideration and discussion, Fred told Steiner he would accept the assignment.

The current Tokyo office managing director was a partner in the firm but had been in the new Tokyo office for less than a year when he was transferred to head a long-established office in England. Because the transfer to England was taking place right away, Fred and his family had about three weeks to prepare for the move. Between transferring responsibilities at the office to Bob Newcome, who was being promoted to Fred's position, and getting furniture and the like ready to be moved, neither Fred nor his family had much time to find out about Japan, other than what was in the online encyclopedia.

When the Baileys arrived in Japan, they were greeted at the airport by one of the young Japanese associate consultants and the senior American expatriate. Fred and his family were quite tired from the long trip, and the two-hour ride to Tokyo was a rather quiet one. After a few days of just settling in, Fred spent his first full day at the office.

Fred's first order of business was to have a general meeting with all the employees of associate consultant rank and higher. Although Fred didn't notice it at the time, all the Japanese staff sat together and all the Americans sat together. After Fred introduced himself and his general idea about the potential and future directions of the Tokyo office, he called on a few individuals to get their ideas about how the things for which they were responsible would likely fit into his overall plan.

From the Americans, Fred got a mixture of opinions with specific reasons about why certain things might or might not fit well. From the Japanese, he got very vague answers. When Fred pushed to get more specific information, he was surprised to find that a couple of the Japanese simply made a whistling sound as they breathed and said that it was "difficult to say." Fred sensed the meeting was not achieving his objectives, so he thanked everyone for coming and said he looked forward to them all working together to make the Tokyo office the fastest-growing office in the company.

After they had been in Japan about a month, Jenny complained to him about the difficulty she had getting certain everyday products like maple syrup, peanut butter, and good-quality beef. She said that when she could get the items at one of the specialty stores, they cost three or four times what they would cost at home. She also complained that since the washer and dryer were much too small, she had to spend extra money by sending things out to be dry-cleaned. On top of all that, unless she went to the American Club in downtown Tokyo, she never had anyone to talk to. After all, Fred was gone 10 to 16 hours a day. Unfortunately, while Jenny talked, Fred was preoccupied, thinking about a big upcoming meeting between his firm and a significant prospective client, a top-100 Japanese multinational company.

The next day, Fred, along with the lead U.S. consultant for the potential contract, Ralph Webster, and one of the Japanese associate consultants, Kenichi Kurokawa, who spoke perfect English, met with a team from the Japanese firm. The Japanese team consisted of four members: the vice-president of administration, the director of international personnel, and two staff specialists.

After shaking hands and a few awkward bows, Fred said that he knew the Japanese gentlemen were busy and he didn't want to waste their time, so he would get right to the point. Fred then had the other American lay out their firm's proposal for the project and what the project would cost. After the presentation, Fred asked the Japanese what their reaction to the proposal was. The Japanese did not respond immediately, so Fred launched into his summary version of the proposal, thinking that the translation might have been insufficient. Again, the Japanese had only the vaguest of responses to his direct questions.

The recollection of the frustration of that meeting was enough to shake Fred back to reality. In the five months since that first meeting, little progress had been made and the contract between the firms was yet to be signed. "I can never seem to get a direct response from Japanese," he thought to himself. This feeling of frustration led him to remember a related incident that happened about a month after this first meeting with this client.

Fred had decided that the reason not much progress was being made with the client was that he and his group just didn't know enough about the client to package the proposal in a way that was appealing to the client. Consequently, he called in Ralph Webster, the senior American associated with the proposal, and asked him to develop a report on the client so that the proposal could be re-evaluated and changed where necessary.

Jointly, they decided that one of the more promising Japanese research associates, Tashiro Watanabe, would be the best person to take the lead on this report. To impress upon Tashiro the importance of this task and the great potential they saw in him, they decided to have the young Japanese associate meet with both Fred and Ralph. In the meeting, Fred and Ralph laid out the nature and importance of the task, at which point Fred leaned forward in his chair and said to Tashiro, "You can see that this is an important assignment and that we are placing a lot of confidence in you by giving it to you. We need the report by this time next week so we can revise and represent our proposal. Can you do it?"

After a long pause, Tashiro responded hesitantly, "I'm not sure what to say." At that point, Fred smiled, got up from his chair, walked over to the young Japanese associate, extended his hand, and said, "Hey, there's nothing to say. We're just giving you the opportunity you deserve."

The day before the report was due, Fred asked Ralph how the report was coming. Ralph said that, since he had heard nothing from Tashiro, he assumed everything was under control but that he would double-check. Ralph later ran into one of the U.S. research associates, John Maynard. Ralph knew that John was hired for Japan because of his Japanese language ability and that, unlike any of the other Americans, John often went out after work with some of the Japanese research associates, including Tashiro. So Ralph asked John if he knew how Tashiro was coming on the report.

John then recounted that at the office the previous night Tashiro had asked if Americans sometimes fired employees for being late with reports. John had sensed that this was more than a hypothetical question and asked Tashiro why he wanted to know. Tashiro did not respond immediately, and since it was 8:30 in the evening, John suggested they go out for a drink. At first Tashiro resisted, but then John assured him that they would grab a drink at a nearby bar and come right back. At the bar, John got Tashiro to open up.

Tashiro explained the nature of the report that he had been requested to produce. He continued to explain that, even though he had worked long into the night every night to complete the report, it was just impossible and that he had doubted from the beginning whether he could complete the report in a week. At this point, Ralph asked John, "Why didn't he say something in the first place?" Ralph didn't wait to hear whether John had an answer to this question. He headed straight to Tashiro's desk.

Ralph chewed out Tashiro and then went to Fred, explaining that the report would not be ready and that Tashiro, from the start, didn't think it could be. "Then why didn't he say something?" Fred asked. No one had any answers, and the whole episode left everyone more suspect and uncomfortable with each other.

Other incidents, big and small, had made the last two months especially frustrating, but Fred was too tired to remember them all. To Fred, it seemed that working with Japanese both inside and outside the firm was like working with people from another planet. Fred felt he couldn't communicate with them, and he never could figure out what they were thinking. It drove him crazy. On top of all this, Jenny laid a bombshell on him.

She wanted to go home, and yesterday was not soon enough. Even though the kids seemed to be doing all right, Jennifer was tired of Japan—tired of being stared at, of not understanding anybody or being understood, of not being able to find what she wanted at the store, of not being able to drive and read the road signs, of not having anything to watch on television, of not being involved in anything. She wanted to go home and could not think of any reason why they shouldn't. After all, she reasoned, they owed nothing to the company because the company had led them to believe this was just another assignment, like the two years they spent in San Francisco, and it was anything but that!

Fred looked out the window once more, wishing that somehow everything could be fixed, or turned back, or something. The traffic below was backed up. Though the traffic lights changed, the cars and trucks didn't seem to be moving. Fortunately, beneath the ground, one of the world's most advanced, efficient, and clean subway systems moved hundreds of thousands of people about the city and to their homes.

QUESTIONS

1. Why is Fred thinking about leaving his three-year assignment as director of Kline & Associates' Tokyo office after only six months?

2. Do you think it was a good idea for Fred to accept the assignment to the Tokyo office? What are the pros and cons for doing so? What might he have done differently before accepting the assignment?

3. Comment on the preparation that Fred and his family had prior to moving to Tokyo. What was wrong with it, and how might it have been better?

4. What are some of the difficulties and frustrations that Fred and Jennifer experience in Tokyo? Refer to some specific incidents in the case that have led to their difficulties and frustrations. Why are they having these difficulties and frustrations? What might have lessened or even prevented them?

5. Consider Fred's assignment to Tokyo in terms of cultural toughness, communication toughness, and job toughness. Given the toughness of the assignment, what degree of cross-cultural training rigour does Fred require?

6. Refer to Table 12.3 on cross-cultural training methods and consider the effectiveness of each type of training for Fred and his family. How effective do you think each method would be? Which method(s) do you recommend, and why?

7. Describe how you would design a cross-cultural training program for Fred and his family. Refer to The Trainer's Notebook 12.1 to answer this question.

8. Do you think Fred should pack up and go home, or should he try to convince his wife and himself that they should stay and finish the assignment? Explain your answer.

FLASHBACK QUESTIONS

1. Do you think a needs analysis should have been performed before Fred accepted the assignment in Tokyo? If a needs analysis had been conducted, what would some of the outcomes of organizational, task, and person analyses have been?

2. If a training program had been designed for Fred and his family before they left for Tokyo, what would have been the objectives and content of the program?

3. What training methods should have been used for a cross-cultural training program for Fred and his family? How effective would off-the-job, on-the-job, and technology-based methods have been, and would you recommend them? If you had to choose instructional methods, what instructional methods in Table 5.1 would you choose, and why?

4. What does *transfer of training* mean for Fred and his family? If they had received cross-cultural training, what strategies would you suggest to ensure that the transfer of training is positive?

FLASH FORWARD QUESTION

1. *Management* is the process of getting things done, efficiently and effectively, through and with other people. *Management development* refers to the complex processes by which individuals learn to perform effectively in managerial roles. Do you think Fred is an effective manager? Refer to specific examples from the case to support your answer. Do you think Fred should have received management development before he left for Tokyo? Explain your answer.

REWRITE THE CASE QUESTION: CROSS-CULTURAL TRAINING

Rewrite the case by including a section at the end of the case in which you describe how Fred and his family decide to attend a cross-cultural training program. Be sure to describe the nature and design of the program, such as the content and the methods used. Use the material in Table 12.3 on cross-cultural training methods and The Trainer's Notebook 12.1 on the design of cross-cultural training programs for your description of the training that Fred and his family receive.

RUNNING CASE STUDY DIRTY POOLS

QUESTIONS

Refer to the case at the end of Chapter 1 to answer the following question.

1. What type of training do you think pool operators and their employees should receive? Review each of the types of training in Table 12.2 and discuss the relevance and importance of it for the training of pool operators and their employees. What types of training would you recommend, and why?

// REFERENCES

1. O'Hare, M. A., Quint, F., & Rosenbaum, L. (2013, October 7). Nothing lost in translation at Toronto hospital. *Canadian HR Reporter, 26*(17), 27; www.nygh.on.ca.

2. Klein, H. J., & Weaver, N. A. (2000). The effectiveness of an organizational-level orientation training program in the socialization of new hires. *Personnel Psychology, 53*, 47–66.

3. Feldman, D. C. (1989). Socialization, resocialization, and training: Reframing the research agenda. In I. L. Goldstein (Ed.), *Training and development in organizations* (pp. 376–416). San Francisco: Jossey-Bass.

4. Anderson, N. R., Cunningham-Snell, N. A., & Haigh, J. (1996). Induction training as socialization: Current practice and attitudes to evaluation in British organizations. *International Journal of Selection and Assessment, 4*, 169–183.

5. Klein & Weaver (2000).

6. Ostroff, C., & Kozlowski, S. W. J. (1992). Organizational socialization as a learning process: The role of information acquisition. *Personnel Psychology, 45*, 849–874; Schettler, J. (2002). Welcome to ACME Inc. *Training, 39*(8), 36–43.

7. Van Iddekinge, C. H., Ferris, G. R., Perrewé, P. L., Perryman, A. A., Blass, F. R., & Heetderks, T. D. (2009). Effects of selection and training on unit-level performance over time: A latent growth modeling approach. *Journal of Applied Psychology, 94*, 829–843.

8. Employment and Social Development Canada. (2014). Guide to essential skills profiles. Retrieved from http://www.esdc.gc.ca/eng/jobs/les/profiles/guide.shtml

9. Campbell, A. (2005, December). *Profiting from literacy: Creating a sustainable workplace literacy program.* Ottawa: The Conference Board of Canada.

10. Campbell (2005); Anonymous (2012, March 26). Literacy skills a foundation of national productivity and prosperity. *The Globe and Mail*, p. B4.

11. Kuri, F. (1996). Basic-skills training boosts productivity. *HR Magazine 41*(9), 73–79; www.abclifeliteracy.ca/workplace_literacy_facts.

12. Gyarmati, D., Leckie, N., Dowie, M., Palameta, B., Shek-wai Hui, T., Dunn, E., & Hébert, S. (2014, August). *UPSKILL: A credible test of workplace literacy and essential skills training.* Ottawa: Social Research and Demonstration Corporation. Retrieved from http://www.srdc.org/media/199774/upskill-technical-report-en.pdf

13. Anonymous (2014, October 20). HR by the numbers: Supporting skills training. *Canadian HR Reporter, 27*(18), 4.

14. Harris-Lalonde, S. (2001). *Training and development outlook.* Ottawa: The Conference Board of Canada; Campbell (2005).

15. Baker, S., & Armstrong, L. (1996, September 30). The new factory worker. *BusinessWeek*, 59–68.

16. Bernier, L. (2016, April 4). Skill requirements evolving rapidly. *Canadian HR Reporter, 29*(6), 10.

17. Harp, C. G., Taylor, S. C., & Satzinger, J. W. (1998). Computer training and individual differences: When method matters. *Human Resource Development Quarterly*, *9*, 271–283.

18. Martocchio, J. J. (1992). Microcomputer usage as an opportunity: The influence of context in employee training. *Personnel Psychology*, *45*, 529–552.

19. DeSimone, R. L., & Harris, D. M. (1998). *Human resource development* (2nd ed.). Fort Worth, TX: Dryden Press.

20. Harp et al. (1998).

21. Kelloway, E. K., & Francis, L. (2008). *Management of occupational health and safety* (4th ed.). Toronto: Nelson Canada.

22. Kelloway & Francis (2008); Cooper, A. (2014, February). Safety training: The small investment with big benefits. *Toronto Star*, Workplace Safety Supplement, p. 4.

23. Silliker, A. (2011, January 17). Ontario report calls for overhaul of OHS. *Canadian HR Reporter*, *24*(1), 1, 23.

24. Kelloway & Francis (2008).

25. Burke, M. J., Salvador, R. O., Smith-Crowe, K., Chan-Serafin, S., Smith, A., & Sonesh, S. (2011). The dread factor: How hazards and safety training influence learning and performance. *Journal of Applied Psychology*, *96*, 46–70.

26. Dean, J. W., Jr., & Bowen, D. E. (1994). Management theory and total quality: Improving research and practice through theory development. *Academy of Management Review*, *19*, 392–418.

27. Oakland, J. S. (1989). *Total quality management*. Oxford: Butterworth-Heinemann Ltd; Schonberger, R. J. (1992). Total quality management cuts a broad swath—through manufacturing and beyond. *Organizational Dynamics*, *20*(4), 16–28; Tenner, A. R., & DeToro, I. J. (1992). *Total quality management, three steps to continuous improvement*. Reading, MA: Addison-Wesley.

28. Harper, L. F., & Rifkind, L. J. (1994). A training program for TQM in the diverse workplace. *Human Resource Development Quarterly*, *5*, 277–279.

29. Salas, E., DiazGranados, D., Klein, C., Burke, C. S., Stagl, K. C., Goodwin, G. F., & Halpin, S. M. (2008). Does team training improve team performance? A meta-analysis. *Human Factors*, *50*, 903–933.

30. Tannenbaum, S. I., & Yukl, G. (1992). Training and development in work organizations. *Annual Review of Psychology*, *43*, 399–441.

31. Bottom, W. P., & Baloff, N. (1994). A diagnostic model for team building with an illustrative application. *Human Resource Development Quarterly*, *5*, 317–336.

32. Salas, E., Burke, C. S., & Cannon-Bowers, J. A. (2002). What we know about designing and delivering team training: Tips and guidelines. In K. Kraiger (Ed.), *Creating, implementing, and managing effective training and development: State-of-the-art lessons for practice* (pp. 234–259). San Francisco, CA: Jossey-Bass.

33. O'Connor, P. O., Campbell, J., Newon, J., Melton, J., Salas, E., & Wilson, K. A. (2008). Crew resource management training effectiveness: A meta-analysis and some critical needs. *The International Journal of Aviation Psychology*, *18*, 353–368; Salas, E., Wilson, K. A., Burke, C. S., & Wightman, D. C. (2006).

Does crew resource management training work? An update, an extension, and some critical needs. *Human Factors, 48*, 392–412.

34. Hughes, A. M., Gregory, M. E., Joseph, D. L., Sonesh, S. C., Marlow, S. L., Lacerenza, C. N., . . . , & Salas, E. (2016). Saving lives: A meta-analysis of team training in healthcare. *Journal of Applied Psychology, 101*, 1266–1304.

35. Salas et al. (2008).

36. Stamps, D. (1997). Training for a new sales game. *Training, 34*(7), 46–52.

37. Schneider, B., & Bowen, D. E. (1995). *Winning the service game.* Boston, MA: Harvard Business School Press.

38. Akkerman, E. (2014, September 8). 'Let's go to the Ex.' *Canadian HR Reporter, 27*(15), 14.

39. Vander Wier, M. (2017, November 27). Why is sexual harassment not going away? *Canadian HR Reporter, 30*(20), 1, 8; Gergin, M. (2016, October 5). Understanding and employing Bill 132 in the workplace. *The Globe and Mail, https://www.theglobeandmail.com/report-on-business/careers/leadership-lab/ understanding-and-employing-bill-132-in-the-workplace/article32231651/.*

40. Rushowy, K. (2017, May 18). New judges to undergo mandatory training. *Toronto Star*, pp. A1, A18; Hasham, A. (2017, July 2). As courts adapt to societal change, judges go back to school. *Toronto Star*, pp. A1, A4.

41. Schneider, K. T., Swan, S., & Fitzgerald, L. F. (1997). Job-related and psychological effects of sexual harassment in the workplace: Empirical evidence from two organizations. *Journal of Applied Psychology, 82*, 401–415.

42. Vander Wier, M. (2017, March 20). Rise of racial incidents challenging employers. *Canadian HR Reporter, 30*(5), 1, 12.

43. Ganzel, R. (1998). What sexual harassment training really prevents. *Training, 35*(10), 86–94; Peirce, E., Smolinski, C. A., & Rosen, B. (1998). Why sexual harassment complaints fall on deaf ears. *Academy of Management Executives, 12*, 41–54.

44. Siegel, R., & Horton, A. (2018, April 18). Starbucks to close 8,000 stores for racial sensitivity training. *Toronto Star*, pp. A1, A9; Kalinowski, T. (2014, June 12). Current, ex-TTC staff face theft, fraud charges. *Toronto Star*, p. GT2.

45. Tyler, K. (2005). Do the right thing: Ethics training programs help employees deal with ethical dilemmas. *HR Magazine, 50*(2), 99–102; Sekerka, L. E. (2009). Organizational ethics education and training: A review of best practices and their application. *International Journal of Training and Development, 13*, 77–95.

46. Tyler (2005).

47. Greengard, S. (2005). Golden values. *Workforce Management, 84*(3), 52–53.

48. Chrobot-Mason, D., & Quinones, M. A. (2002). Training for a diverse workplace. In K. Kraiger (Ed.), *Creating, implementing, and managing effective training and development: State-of-the-art lessons for practice* (pp. 117–159). San Francisco, CA: Jossey-Bass; Wentling, R. M., & Palma-Rivas, N. (1998). Current status and future trends of diversity initiatives in the workplace: Diversity experts' perspective. *Human Resource Development Quarterly, 9*, 235–253.

49. Hughes, P. D., & Campbell, A. (2009). *Learning & development outlook 2009: Learning in tough times*. Ottawa: The Conference Board of Canada.

50. Hanover, J. M. B., & Cellar, D. F. (1998). Environmental factors and the effectiveness of workforce diversity training. *Human Resource Development Quarterly*, *9*, 105–124.

51. Noe, R. A., & Ford, J. K. (1992). Emerging issues and new directions for training research. *Research in Personnel and Human Resources Management*, *10*, 345–384.

52. Cocchiara, F. K., Connerley, M. L., & Bell, M. P. (2010). "A GEM" for increasing the effectiveness of diversity training. *Human Resource Management*, *49*, 1089–1106.

53. Wentling & Palma-Rivas (1998).

54. Klie, S. (2007, October 22). L'Oréal a pretty picture of diversity, training. *Canadian HR Reporter*, *20*(18), 11.

55. Shaw, A. (2008, May 5). Boeing puts diversity to work—silently. *Canadian HR Reporter*, *21*(9), 18.

56. Silliker, A. (2013, July 15). HR by the numbers (2 in 5 managers fail in overseas assignments). *Canadian HR Reporter*, *26*(13), 4.

57. Noe & Ford (1992).

58. Black, J. S., Gregersen, H. B., & Mendenhall, M. E. (1992). *Global assignments*. San Francisco, CA: Jossey-Bass, p. 97.

59. Black et al. (1992).

60. Black et al. (1992).

61. Black et al. (1992).

62. Aguinis, H., & Kraiger, K. (2009). Benefits of training and development for individuals and teams, organizations, and society. *Annual Review of Psychology*, *60*, 451–474.

63. Silliker, A. (2013, September 9). Nutrition programs popular with employers. *Canadian HR Reporter*, *26*(15), 3, 8.

64. Chenier, L., Hoganson, C., & Thorpe, K. (2012). Making the business case for investments in workplace health and wellness. Ottawa: The Conference Board of Canada.

65. Silliker (2013, September 9).

66. Silliker, A. (2012, September 10). Employers not evaluating effectiveness of wellness programs: Conference Board. *Canadian HR Reporter*, *25*(15), 8, 10.

67. Chenier et al. (2012).

68. Gergin (2016).

69. Delfosse, J., & Richardson, D. (2017, June 12). The importance of training for mental health: Choosing right program critical to ensuring maximum effectiveness. *Canadian HR Reporter*, *30*(11), 24; Bradley, L. (2015, May). Workplace safety and wellness: The ripple effect of creating psychologically safe and healthy workplaces. *Media Planet*, 3.

MANAGEMENT AND LEADERSHIP DEVELOPMENT

CHAPTER LEARNING OUTCOMES

AFTER READING THIS CHAPTER, YOU SHOULD BE ABLE TO:

- define "management" and "management development" and explain how these differ from employee training

- describe the main roles, functions, and critical skills of managers

- discuss the issue of leadership development

- understand the differences between transactional, transformational, and authentic leadership

- explain emotional intelligence and its relevance for management and leadership

- describe the models of management skill development

- discuss how error-management training can be used for management development

- describe the content of programs used to develop conceptual, technical, and interpersonal managerial skills

- discuss the different types of management development programs, including management education, management training, and on-the-job management development

- explain the relationship between After-Event Reviews (AERs) and experiential training

- discuss the effectiveness of management and leadership development programs and how that can be improved

The Société des Transports de Montréal (STM) is Montreal's public transit organization that runs buses and subways throughout the city. As with most such organizations in Canada, it is financed by the public purse and by the fares paid by users. For environmental and financial reasons, increasing ridership is a top priority. Senior management believed it could be achieved through service and performance improvements.

Consequently, the STM's top leadership decided on a strategic plan designed to meet that challenge. The strategy focuses on improved technology (modernization of subways and user-friendly information technology applications) and on the employee–customer relationship. Whereas the employee–customer relationship has been a priority for many years, the STM thought it was important to emphasize this element further. Achieving that goal is contingent on the employee's engagement with the strategy—their buy-in.

This brings into focus management and leadership. Based on the general premise that employees are more likely to engage in and adopt particular values when they are active participants in them, senior management believed it was critically important that supervisors adopt leadership behaviours that are more collaborative, with open communication that encourages joint problem solving.

As part of an overall multi-facetted organizational development strategy that includes the development of future managers, performance management, and continuous support, a major management development project was launched. Top management, the HR specialists, and university academics collaborated to create and implement a training program compulsory for all supervisors at all levels of the organization. This integrated program was designed to help managers adopt the communicational and participative attitudes and behaviours needed to ensure employee engagement in the required customer service and performance orientations.

Cohorts of 12 to 15 managers at similar organizational levels but drawn from different functions were assembled. Each cohort stayed together for the entire year-long program that involved five specific steps. The first step was conducted at the STM, but the groups met at the university for the other four steps. The trainers were academics who, through preliminary work including site visits and orientations, had become very familiar with the STM.

Step 1: In a preparatory two-hour meeting, the HR personnel and senior executives discussed the overall

The management development program conceived and launched by the Société des Transports de Montréal (STM) specifically supports an organizational strategy.

strategy and explained the specific aims of the development program. At that time supervisors self-rated themselves on the required behaviours and developed their own specific development goals.

Step 2: Some time later, each cohort met with an external trainer in a day-long session designed to help managers develop a personal understanding of the plan. Following preliminary presentations by the trainer who proposed techniques and tools, the bulk of the training session was devoted to discussions that helped managers define the implementation strategies and goals applicable to their specific work environments. Managers then returned to their jobs to put into practice the elements developed that day.

Step 3: Several weeks after completing and practising Step 2 on the job, the cohorts returned to the university for a two-day session that focused on the development of cooperation and teamwork. It followed the usual format. Trainers explained the relevant principles and specific useful tools. This was followed by extensive discussions aimed at enhancing comprehension and helping participants develop strategies for implementing these skills in their own work groups. The trainees then returned to the job and practised them.

Step 4: A similar process was pursued at this stage in a two-day session dealing with leadership and effective communication. Lectures that introduced the concepts and explained relevant tools were followed by extensive discussions. Finally, trainees returned to the job and practised the skills.

Step 5: The final step of the program was the follow-up, which included the evaluation of participants' reactions to the training program and self-reports on the degree to which the training participants used the new skills at work.

Throughout all training sessions participant practice was prevalent and both participants and instructors worked hard to provide constructive feedback to each other. Each trainee was encouraged to plan and implement the training objectives in a manner with which he or she was comfortable and that was adapted to their specific work context.

To foster on-the-job application of the trained skills, a coordinated support structure was implemented. Organizational development (OD) specialists attached to the HR department were assigned to the project full-time. They acted as liaison officials to inform, support, and encourage all—from top management to first-level supervisors—to engage in the project, and to help all actors play their expected supportive role at the right time and in an appropriate manner. Beyond this, on-the-job coaching provided by HR personnel was a further integral supportive aspect of the entire program. This service was made available to managers who requested advice on solving any application issues and difficulties they encountered. Hence, the training participants and their own bosses received on-the-job support. Equally important, the display of the trained behaviours (or lack thereof) was considered as part of the performance appraisal process. In turn, that job performance rating affected salary reviews.

The reactions to the training program and the degree of usefulness formed the basis of the self-reported evaluation of the program. Here the results were extremely positive (with well over 90 percent approval and enthusiasm for the program). Structured interviews conducted with training participants indicated that they held the attitudes and behaviours consistent with the goals of the development program.

Source: Chantal Lamoureux, Division Head, Diversity and Organizational Development, Department of Human Resources, STM (personal communication, January 2015).

// INTRODUCTION

The management of our global economy is no simple matter, challenging companies, even smaller ones, to excellence.[1] Evidence indicates that the single characteristic that best distinguishes a successful organization, large or small, from others is the calibre of the management team.[2] As exemplified in the chapter-opening vignette, leadership and management skills can be critical to the successful implementation of organizational strategies and goals. Like many companies, the STM understands the critical impact that managers can have on the company's performance.

This is particularly important as major shifts in the business environment can and often do impact the management of organizations. For example, at the time of this writing, the North American Free Trade Agreement (NAFTA) is being reviewed. This in turn might create massive change to some organizations' client base and/or performance standards. Those changes, of course, will prove a major challenge for management.

This chapter is near the end of the book, but not because the training of managers is unimportant or an afterthought. On the contrary, developing managers is among the most important, complex, and difficult of the challenges that trainers face today. In 2016 and again in 2017, the Conference Board of Canada launched major surveys of Canadian organizations with the express purpose of assessing the development of leadership within its managerial ranks.[3] The report concludes, without surprise, that strong and effective leadership is a fundamentally important driver of organizational effectiveness. Indeed the majority of Canadian organizations (55 percent, according to a Conference Board report) consider the development of their leadership a top development priority.[4]

The development of managers and of leadership is a particularly critical issue right now because of a very important demographic change: the baby boom generation is retiring.

Organizations must recruit and/or develop high-potential men and women—referred to as "bench strength"—to take over the leadership of organizations (see Training Today 13.1, "Bench Strength").[5] To meet this challenge, management development experts need to rely on the full slate of principles and techniques described in the earlier chapters.

TRAINING TODAY 13.1

BENCH STRENGTH

Surveys of managerial and leadership development practices and priorities conducted in North America indicate that organizations are concerned with managerial development, but more pointedly with the development of future managers (known as the development of "bench strength"). Clearly, as the baby boom generation retires the replenishment of the leadership pipeline is an increasingly urgent priority. Interestingly, although companies still make use of the full gamut of development activities, including formal courses and informal learning, they are increasingly turning to three mechanisms for creating that bench strength: leader-led development, action learning, and executive coaching.

Leader-led development refers to having top executives share their experiences and insights with future leaders. Action learning refers to job rotations and special assignments specifically designed to enhance certain specific competencies. Executive coaching remains a very important development activity, the use of which is increasing.

Of the many mechanisms used for development purposes, mentoring and coaching are increasingly favoured. This trend is also evident in Quebec. Daoud and Gosselin,

researchers from the École des Hautes Études Commerciales in Montreal, report a qualitative study conducted with Quebec-based pharmaceutical and insurance companies. In-depth interviews held with managers from these companies reveal that whereas both are assigning increasing importance to managerial development, insurance companies are motivated to do so, as with the USA study, because of the demographic concerns (i.e., retirement of the baby boomers). Pharmaceutical companies in Quebec are smaller and more recently created than are insurance companies, and as such are likely to have a younger work force. Yet both emphasize the same techniques for growing their future managers.

The broader North American studies, as well as the narrower Quebec study, report the same fundamental issue: All see the development of managers as a critical priority and, within this, the development of soft skills—such as human interaction skills—as much more important than the development of hard skills—such as technical ones. Clearly, these results are telling us that new managers should be better at handling people.

Sources: Bolt, J. F. (2007). Mapping the future of leadership development. *The 2007 Pfeiffer Annual: Leadership development*. San Francisco, CA: John Wiley & Sons; Daoud, M., & Gosselin, A. (2007). *Évolution récente du développement des gestionnaires dans les secteurs pharmaceutique et de l'assurance au Québec*. Paper presented at the annual meeting of Administrative Sciences Association of Canada, Ottawa; Hall, C. (2014) *Learning and development outlook—12th edition: Strong learning organizations, strong leadership*. Ottawa: The Conference Board of Canada.

As you have learned, successful training and development involves four key aspects:

- the identification of training needs, which requires an understanding of the jobs and an identification of the skills people need to do them (see Chapter 3)
- the choice of training design and delivery techniques (see Chapters 4 through 8)
- an integration, within the training experience, of elements that contribute not only to learning, but also to other psychological forces, such as motivation and self-efficacy (see Chapter 2)
- on-the-job practice and support

As discussed in Chapter 9, these enhance the odds of successful transfer, as demonstrated in training evaluation studies (see Chapter 10).

To grasp management training, it is important to explore, as this chapter does, what managers do (their roles and functions) and the critical skills they need. We describe the techniques and guiding principles that create the training experience (management training design and delivery). The chapter also describes several types of management development programs and their content, and it explores the issue of leadership development, a topic related though distinct from managerial development. Finally, the chapter closes with a research-based analysis of the effectiveness of management and leadership development. We begin by explaining what management is.

// WHAT IS MANAGEMENT?

The work of managers is to orchestrate the work of others: "**Management** refers to the process of getting things done, efficiently and effectively, through and with other people."[6] Figure 13.1 describes what managers do—their roles (interpersonal, informational, and decisional) and the functions these roles serve (controlling, organizing, and planning). Most managers need to engage in these fundamental functions, but their relative saliency differs depending on the specific environment in which they work, the responsibilities they hold, and the organizational level they occupy. For example, controlling budgets or organizing a task may have very different meanings for the National Ballet of Canada or

> **Management**
> The process of getting things done, efficiently and effectively, through and with other people

FIGURE 13.1

MANAGERIAL ROLES, FUNCTIONS, SKILLS, AND DEVELOPMENT APPROACHES

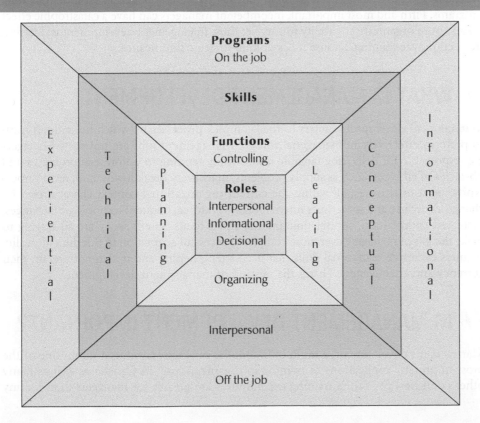

Petro-Canada managers. Yet in both these organizations managers perform tasks requiring them to have conceptual, technical, and interpersonal skills, as grouped in Figure 13.1. Whereas purely technical skills may be critical for some lower-level managers, as one climbs the corporate ladder, conceptual skills may become increasingly important.

It is axiomatic to management development that managerial skills and competencies are learnable and that they can and should be nurtured and developed through training and related experiences. These development experiences (indicated in Figure 13.1) occur on and/or off the job with instructional systems that are informational and experiential.

// MANAGEMENT DEVELOPMENT VERSUS EMPLOYEE TRAINING

In this book we discuss management and employee development separately and in different chapters because they differ in several ways. First, although some management development programs are strictly technical (e.g., project planning or budget preparation), it is the case that managers work mainly through other people—they are effective when those they manage (the subordinates) are effective. Hence, most management training programs are focused on the development of "people skills," a training task of considerable difficulty.

Second, managerial development relies more heavily on experiential techniques. Third, managerial behaviours are highly influenced by the manager's personality and preferences, so training needs to take into account these important individual differences. Fourth, management development is a *longitudinal and gradual process*. Developing the complex skills needed by effective managers requires on-the-job experiences as well as traditional training programs. Fifth and most important, incompetent managers can have a catastrophic effect on an entire organization's ability to survive; thus, management development is different from employee training because it has unique strategic significance.

// WHAT IS MANAGEMENT DEVELOPMENT?

Management development refers to the "complex processes by which individuals learn to perform effectively in managerial roles."[7] Management jobs are not easy. Managers are responsible for delivering tangible results while tending to unforeseen problems and obstacles of all types, such as supply problems, machinery breakdowns, and, most importantly, personnel issues, all within the current organizational context characterized by change. A diverse and sometimes international workforce, frequent technological changes, increased competition, shorter time frames, and a focus on efficiency are all serving to make the job of managing ever more complex. Successful adaptation to this difficult reality requires extensive managerial skills that need strengthening and updating to retain their currency and effectiveness. That is the mission of management development.

Management development
The complex process by which individuals learn to perform effectively in managerial roles

// IS MANAGEMENT DEVELOPMENT IMPORTANT?

Management development, a multi-billion-dollar business, is without doubt one of the most important applications of training in organizations.[8] In Canada as well as many other countries, per capita training expenditures are greater for managers than for any other category of employees; more managers are trained and more is spent on each of them. North American corporations pour billions of dollars into management development as they fund courses, seminars, executive education, and university business schools. This high level of commitment to managerial development is true in countries as diverse as the United Kingdom, Lithuania, Spain, and Iran.[9] This is because the development of managers is a prudent business investment.

To a very large degree, managers are responsible for ensuring that the organization functions effectively and efficiently. They define the organization and are most responsible for its financial and psychological health. Organizations are systems composed of people, technologies, procedures, and communications designed to achieve specific, valued objectives. It is management's purpose to define these objectives (products and services) and to ensure that they are completed on time and with acceptable levels of quality. In effect, organizations invest more heavily in managers and in their development because theirs is *the* pivotal role in organizations.

// MANAGEMENT DEVELOPMENT

As you will see, the fundamental roles that managers play in organizations are interpersonal, informational, and decisional ones. These three roles are core for the main functions of managers: controlling, organizing, and planning (which makes the convenient acronym COP). However, especially in recent years, some but not all organizations require of managers one other skill: leadership.

Leadership refers to the individual qualities and behaviours that define and shape the direction of the organization and that inspire others to pursue that direction in the face of obstacles and constraints. Leadership is commonly required of managers in the highest sphere of the organization. But, it is the case today that many organizations believe that middle or even first-line managers need to exercise leadership.

Indeed, a 2017 report from the Conference Board of Canada specifically targets the behaviour of Canadian companies in the development of the leadership of middle managers.[10]

The starting point for a discussion of management development is the identification of training needs. To define these needs (as discussed in Chapter 3) a thorough understanding of the managerial job is required. We therefore begin by reviewing research that describes what managers do in order to identify the skills they require. This is particularly important, as research shows that the effectiveness of training programs is highly influenced by the quality and accuracy of job information. After all, programs that teach skills that are—or are perceived to be—irrelevant can hardly be expected to improve performance or be used on the job.

> **Leadership**
> The qualities and behaviours that shape the direction of the organization and that inspire others to pursue that direction in the face of obstacles and constraints

// CORE MANAGERIAL ROLES

Henry Mintzberg analyzed management from the perspective of the manager's day-to-day activities.[11] Derived from the formal authority and status that a manager has, Mintzberg broke these activities into three roles: interpersonal, informational, and decisional. This research is important because it helps define, with greater precision, the skills required of managers and hence the focus of training and development efforts.

INTERPERSONAL ROLES

Interpersonal roles are the relationships that managers develop with other people because these people can provide significant help (or obstacles) to the attainment of group goals. As such, the manager is the organizational person who provides *leadership* (motivates others), and who *liaises* with others within and outside the unit with the goal of securing information that is of use to the attainment of goals. The manager also plays a *figurehead* or representational role, wherein he/she stands in for the managed group in routine (e.g., administrative meetings), social (e.g., local school board), and legal contexts (e.g., municipal zoning hearings).

INFORMATIONAL ROLE

Managers must *monitor* the environment (both internal and external) to accumulate information pertinent to the attainment of organizational goals. He/she reciprocates by assuming the role of *disseminator* of information by informing others about the unit and informing the unit about relevant developments occurring outside the unit. The manager also acts as a *spokesperson*, informing others and "selling" them on the plans, values, or goals of the unit (such as explaining to others the environmental impact of a new plant). Hence, managers require communication skills.

DECISIONAL ROLE

Managers must make decisions about people, goals, and the means to attain those goals. As an initiator of change, the manager is an *entrepreneur*, moving the unit in directions that take advantage of opportunities or shifting the activities of the group to reduce threats. The manager *allocates resources*, choosing from competing proposals and projects those that are encouraged and funded and those that are not. Downsizing or staff expansions are such resource-allocation decisions.

The manager is also called upon to act as a *negotiator*, interacting and bargaining with others in the external (e.g., regulatory agencies, suppliers) and internal (e.g., budget allocation, policy choices) environments. Mintzberg's data note that the manager is also a *troubleshooter* reacting to unanticipated and unplanned environmental events that can severely disrupt the unit (e.g., a sudden job action or a delivery problem).

// MANAGERIAL FUNCTIONS

Functions of management
Controlling, Organizing, Planning, and Leading

Traditionally, the **functions of management** have been summarized as controlling, organizing, and planning (COP). That is, managers are responsible for ensuring that things get done. They monitor the work processes and progress toward goal attainment (controlling), they allocate resources and tasks (organizing), and they establish what should be done and how (planning). As is discussed below (see "Leadership: A Critical Function of Management?"), they are also tasked to maintain the motivation and zeal of those who do the work. That is, they are to lead. In completing these functions, they rely on their interpersonal, informational, and decisional skills in a way that inspires and builds the commitment and engagement of their subordinates.

CONTROLLING

Controlling, as its name suggests, refers to the process by which the activities of the organization and its members are monitored to ensure that they contribute positively to the attainment of organizational goals and objectives. It involves establishing mechanisms to monitor and resolve performance gaps and to address constraints and problems that hinder the attainment of performance goals.

ORGANIZING

The accomplishment of most contemporary organizational goals requires the efforts of a diversity of units, each composed of many individuals. Major activities are identified and components of these major tasks are assigned to units and individuals. The manager's job is to establish systems that ensure these efforts are coordinated and organized efficiently and effectively.

PLANNING

In the context of management, planning refers to where the efforts of individuals are to be directed. It involves defining objectives and developing goals for the organization and the departments or units for which the manager is responsible. The scope of the goals and objectives depends on the level of management, and the specifics of the planning tasks depend on the nature of the managerial responsibility. As one moves from the lowest to the highest levels of the organization, the objectives and goals become broader and more strategic.

LEADING

Leading is a critical people-oriented function of management. It entails influencing the actions of others such that these actions are coordinated to produce the desired outcomes. Since managers mainly operate through others, they require people skills.

LEADERSHIP: A CRITICAL FUNCTION OF MANAGEMENT?

In the past, the "leadership" function was thought to belong exclusively to the apex of the organizational pyramid: the senior managers.[12] Although that remains true, many organizations today have come to believe that the exercise of leadership is a function of *all* management (e.g., Kotter, Whetten and Cameron, and the Conference Board of Canada).[13] It is important to understand that leadership does not replace good management; good leaders are also good managers. Hence, in many organizations the functions of managers are now thought to be controlling, organizing, planning, and leading (which makes COPL, though some prefer the less literal but more colourful acronym CLOP).

The 2014 Conference Board of Canada survey shows that for the majority (59 percent) of the organizations sampled, the development of leaders is the top learning and development priority, a result statistically higher than was the case in their 2010 report. The 2017 Conference Board of Canada survey specifically focuses on the development of leadership of middle managers. Although the development of the leadership at the top level of organizations is improving, that report indicates that the development of leadership at middle levels is considerably weaker.

Managers need to demonstrate leadership because they are responsible for attaining goals and keeping employees committed to their goals. Such commitment is more likely when employees believe that the attainment of the goal is important, when they believe that attaining the goal will result in positive outcomes, and when they believe that their individual efforts make a difference in goal attainment. A leader, according to Kouzes and Posner, is successful by being a role model (i.e., leading by example), by inspiring a shared vision, by challenging the status quo and encouraging others to do the same (asking why), and by recognizing the contributions of others (through verbal feedback and tangible outcomes).[14]

Adapting to the global economy and its competitive pressures requires ever-increasing levels of resiliency and flexibility in organizations. This flexibility requires that people at all levels of the organization, from the top to the bottom, adapt their job behaviours in response to the changing requirements of their jobs and the contexts in which they are to be performed. As Kotter explains, leaders propel this process of adaptation to change. From first-line supervisors to CEOs, from production to R&D, managers need to have the knowledge, skills, attitudes, and behaviours that enable them to foster in the people they manage the attitudes and behaviours that are conducive to the attainment of the individual and organizational goals. This chapter's opening vignette exemplifies the STM's efforts to encourage and develop that important leadership function. And the STM is far from unique in this regard.

LEADERSHIP AND ITS DEVELOPMENT: A WORK IN PROGRESS

The Conference Board of Canada's research shows that leadership development is among the very top priority for organizations. However, the development of leaders is very difficult and not always successful. The Conference Board of Canada reports that most Canadian organizations (two-thirds) believe that their leadership development efforts have not been satisfactory, and the Canadian experience is far from being unique (see Leadership Training: What's Wrong and What Is Needed?).

"Leadership" is defined as an influence process in which one person (the leader) influences others (the subordinates) to pursue valued organizational goals effectively. Effective leadership means getting results from the subordinates, and that requires an understanding of what makes a leader.

In the first half of the 20th century, it was believed that leaders were born and not made, which made training irrelevant. Only those few who possessed the required personal characteristics (called "traits") could be leaders. Despite thousands of studies, no clear list of those traits emerged, leading to the gradual abandonment of that view of leadership.

Following World War II, solid research (generally known as the Ohio State University and the University of Michigan Leadership Studies) developed the view that it was specific behaviours (and not traits) that distinguished good from poor leaders and, most importantly, that these behaviours could be learned. Hence developing leaders meant training people to display specific behaviours and attitudes.

By about the 1970s, however, it was becoming apparent that this approach to leadership was problematic. The same leadership behaviours could be effective in one context and much less so in another.

This led to the so-called situational approach to leadership, in which effective leadership had to be analyzed as a function of the context in which it was displayed. The skills required would therefore be simultaneously identified through an analysis of the individual leaders as well as the situation in which they exercised their role. However, the specification of situations proved highly complex. For example, the same leader may or may not be successful depending on the cultures of the countries in which the organization functions, differences between the types of subordinates and the tasks they perform, and differences between organizational cultures within the same countries and/ or jobs.

By the beginning of the 21st century, it has become increasingly clear that in the development of leadership one needs to consider leader traits, leader behaviours, and the organizational environment. From this, two basic notions of leadership have emerged: transactional and transformational leadership.

Transactional leadership refers to the styles adopted by some, in which leaders make clear to the followers the behaviours and attitudes that are associated with rewards and punishment. Subordinates follow transactional leaders because they clarify the path employees need to follow in order to obtain rewards and avoid unpleasant consequences. In these cases, the main task of leaders is providing clarity: specifying individual goals and monitoring individual work behaviours relevant to those goals. The leader of the sales team who specifies the size of bonuses merited as a function of the volume of sales is transactional. From a development viewpoint, leaders would then need to learn how to set specific goals, how to evaluate attainment of those goals, and how to reward the attainment.

By contrast, **transformational leaders** influence their followers by inspiring them into engaging wilfully in the attainment of goals. That is they inspire subordinates to forgo self-interest to pursue the common good, to understand that their individual tasks are meaningful and relevant for the attainment of a valued greater purpose. These leaders when they successfully engage the feelings and emotions of the followers are often called *charismatic leaders*.

Charismatic leaders display two fundamental characteristics. They (1) present an idealized vision, an overarching goal that promises a better future that matters to the followers, and (2) they convince the followers that the vision can be achieved. They motivate others by enhancing their self-efficacy, they use their own behaviours to exemplify (model) their personal commitment to the vision, and they communicate that vision through words and actions that engage the emotions of the followers. They are perceived to be authentic (see Training 13.2, "Authentic Leadership") and appear to have high levels of emotional intelligence. Subordinates follow charismatic leaders because they want to, because they feel that the path to be followed is right and good.

Transformational leadership theory combines trait, behaviours, and situations. Charismatic leaders have—or at least project—certain personal traits, chief among which are self-confidence and unconventionality. They engage in specific behaviours, principally supported by exceptional communication skills. And, contextually, charisma tends to emerge when the followers feel concern and anxiety about the current situation, and when they feel a strong need for change.

> **Transactional leadership**
> Leaders make clear to the followers the behaviours and attitudes that are associated with rewards and punishment
>
> **Transformational leaders**
> Leaders influence their followers by inspiring them into engaging wilfully in the attainment of goals.

Martin Luther King was a charismatic leader; he inspired others by projecting an achievable vision for a better world.

AUTHENTIC LEADERSHIP

In the last decade, the concept of authentic leadership, the roots of which can be traced to ancient Greek philosophy, has inspired interest. Authentic leaders think and behave in ways that truly reflect what they believe to be true and morally right, especially in their relationships with other members of the organization.

Although there are many nuanced definitions of "authentic leadership," all describe a pattern of leader behaviours that is essentially positive. Such leaders are self-aware, ethical, and transparent with regards to others. They seek improvements in themselves and in their subordinates, and are truly devoted to building organizational success. They are trusted by others, since their actions are perceived to be guided by a genuine concern for them and for the mission of the organization. Self-interest is not, and is not perceived to be, the dominant motive for their actions.

Authentic leadership results in many positive consequences for the organization and for its members. Among these, research has shown that the subordinates of authentic leaders enjoy greater job satisfaction, are less likely to burn out, are more likely to engage in organizational citizenship behaviour, and are more likely to produce better individual job performance. Research also shows that authentic leadership yields greater employee commitment to the organization, more positive organizational climate, and better firm performance on financial indicators.

The programs that strive to develop this authenticity focus on helping managers, through questionnaires, discussions, and role-play exercises, to develop more confidence in their values and beliefs, more self-awareness, and more transparency in dealing with others by, for example, admitting their errors.

Source: Gardner, W. L., Cogliser, C. C., Davis, K. M., & Dickens, M. (2011). Authentic leadership: A review of the literature and research agenda. *The Leadership Quarterly, 22*, 1120–1145.

But this raises a question: Can charismatic leadership be developed? The answer to that question, as strange as this sounds, may well be partially "yes." It may not be possible to train leaders into the development of the overarching vision. However, if a leader does hold one, it is possible to develop in them the skills to project it charismatically. This involves the development of presentational skills, such as communicating emotions through body language, using voice modulations and hand motions to emphasize points, and illustrating the vision through examples familiar to the followers. Research has shown that these critical skills can be learned.[15]

However, one needs to be cautious. Whereas some charismatic leaders, such as Martin Luther King, have motivated others into pursuing a vision that has affected the world in a positive way, this is not always the case. History is rife with charismatic leaders who inspired their followers to follow a vision that led to ruin.

Although managers are still viewed as those responsible for "getting things done" through the functions of controlling, organizing, planning, and leading, increasingly managers must provide support to their employees, assist them in the development of new skills, and act as coaches and facilitators for employee task accomplishment.[16]

Some leading organizations have formalized these functions by integrating them into the performance appraisal system for managers. To learn more about this, see Training Today 13.3, "Taking Management Development Seriously: The PricewaterhouseCoopers Story."

Finally, an additional component of transformational leadership has been gaining some currency. Labelled "servant leadership," it describes a leadership style that focuses

TAKING MANAGEMENT DEVELOPMENT SERIOUSLY: THE PRICEWATERHOUSECOOPERS STORY

PricewaterhouseCoopers (PwC) is one of the largest professional services organizations in the world. PwC takes the development of its people seriously. It has instituted widespread coaching and mentoring programs for managers, and has gone one step further.

As part of the performance management program, all managers must indicate the steps they have taken to develop their own subordinates. The performance assessment—and the rewards and bonuses paid out to managers based on it—is determined, in part, by the degree to which they have helped their employees achieve higher levels of competencies, both managerial and technical.

Moreover, all partners in the firm are offered a series of workshops delivered by leading professionals to help them gain a deeper understanding of the help they can provide to their employees and the importance of that function for the organization.

Why would a prestigious organization like PwC attach importance to this policy? Because it is good for their employees and good for business! Such policies help the company retain its valued employees and help them service their clients even better. Developing and growing the competencies of employees also increases their employability, both on client projects with PwC and even if they should leave the organization.

In the end, the value of these practices is that they seamlessly and simultaneously provide benefits to both the organization and its employees. It's a win-win scenario.

---

on the needs of employees.[17] They empower subordinates and serve their need for growth, autonomy, and competence. Some empirical research shows that this particular style of leadership has a positive effect on both the employees and the organization.[18]

// MANAGEMENT SKILLS

Skills are defined as sets of actions that individuals perform and that lead to valued outcomes.[19] The literature is replete with descriptions of the types of skills needed to accomplish the managerial roles and functions. Two types of approaches have been used to identify the skills required of managers. Some authors rely on their extensive experience with management to infer the skills needed for effective management (or leadership). They then propose mechanisms by which these skills can be developed.

> **Skills**
> Sets of actions that individuals perform and that lead to valued outcomes

Others have used empirical surveys of managers, sometimes within a single firm and sometimes across several, to guide their prescriptions. Managers rate the importance of many potential skills, and statistical analyses are used to identify the skills and competencies that distinguish successful managers from their less successful counterparts.

One such comparative study involved observations of 52 successful managers and less successful ones in three organizations. Successful managers were better equipped with technical skills (such as paperwork, planning, and goal-setting) as well as in working with people (building power and influence, communicating, managing conflict, decision making, and developing others).[20] Unsuccessful managers tend to be poorer in both technical and people skills, such as providing feedback, clarifying expectations, delegating, and encouraging teamwork.

Some further research has helped identify the relative importance of the various managerial skills. Cameron and Tschirhart asked a large sample of managers working in

150 organizations to identify the most important skills and competencies required of managers.[21] The results showed that the managerial skills fall into four basic clusters. One cluster focuses on human relations skills and includes skills such as providing support, communication, and team building. Another focused on competitiveness and control. A third cluster focused on behaviours that foster individual entrepreneurship and innovativeness, and the fourth focused on order and rationality. Hence, effective managers support and encourage the work of their employees (cluster 1) while staying focused on achievement and results (cluster 2). They encourage employees to display innovation and creativity (cluster 3) while maintaining control and rationality (cluster 4).

Reread the previous paragraph. You might note, as Cameron and Tschirhart do, that the skills required of successful managers seem paradoxical and contradictory; for example, fostering individual entrepreneurship (cluster 3) is the opposite of maintaining control (cluster 4). Yet Whetten and Cameron showed that successful managers resolve this paradox. Even as they are controlled, stable, and rational, they are still able to foster employee creativity and flexibility.

These research studies identified a number of critical managerial skills. Table 13.1 presents a summary of the most frequently mentioned skills of effective managers. As you will see, many of these involve "people skills" (communicating, motivating others, delegating, self-awareness, team building, and conflict management). This emphasizes that the "people" side of management and its subsequent salience for management development cannot be underestimated. As an example, the Stanford Graduate School of Business produces a large number of briefing videos to support the development of managers. Delivered by corporate and academic stars, the videos cover a wide range of topics. However, the single most frequent topic, about a third of all videos, focuses on dealing with people (such as coaching and providing feedback).

One of the most important aspects of management involves interacting, communicating, and dealing with other people both within and outside the organization; some people are better at this than others. Those who are better tend to have higher levels of a specific type of intelligence called "emotional intelligence," a topic to which we now turn.

TABLE 13.1
THE MOST FREQUENTLY CITED SKILLS OF EFFECTIVE MANAGERS
Verbal communication (including listening)
Managing time and stress
Managing individual decisions
Recognizing, defining, and solving problems
Motivating and influencing others
Delegating
Setting goals and articulating a vision
Self-awareness
Team building
Managing conflict

Source: *WHETTEN, DAVID A.; CAMERON, KIM S., DEVELOPING MANAGEMENT SKILLS*, 5th Ed., ©2002. Reprinted by permission of Pearson Education, Inc., New York, New York.

// EMOTIONAL INTELLIGENCE

Most human interactions have an emotional component, and the success of these interactions often depends on how well emotions—one's own and other people's—are managed. These skills have been labelled *emotional intelligence* (EI).[22]

Search the Internet using the key words "emotional intelligence" or "emotional quotient (EQ)" to obtain an appreciation for the prominence of this concept. You will find thousands of entries!

Emotional intelligence is the ability to manage and cope with emotions—one's own emotions as well as those of others. This involves five sets of skills.

1. *Self-awareness:* Being aware of, and understanding, oneself and one's emotions when interacting with others.

2. *Self-control:* Managing and regulating one's emotions (both positive and negative) that arise from encounters and events.

3. *Motivation or drive:* Channelling emotions and energies in support of one's goals.

4. *Empathy:* "Reading" and recognizing the emotions of others and responding to them appropriately.

5. *Interpersonal skills:* The ability to manage interactions with others effectively through an understanding, integration, and management of emotions.

> **Emotional intelligence**
> The ability to manage your own and others' emotions and your relationships with others

Notice that the components of EI (self-awareness, interpersonal skills, etc.) are listed as skills. Unlike intellectual intelligence (IQ), which is a relatively stable and enduring characteristic of people's cognitive abilities, EI is believed to be a learnable and changeable factor (see the following section, "Project Management and Emotional Intelligence"). However, unlike technical skills associated with management, people-oriented skills and EI are labelled as "soft skills" (see Chapter 10 for a discussion of hard and soft skills).

It is believed that EI, like other soft skills, can be developed indirectly, through exposure and feedback about their conduct with others.[23] As people learn, for example, to receive and deliver feedback, to manage stress, or to defuse conflicts, they simultaneously enhance their own levels of emotional intelligence. Training in EI involves group and individual activities that include role plays, assessments, and practical exercises, all of which serve to enhance self-management and empathy.

This is extremely important because empirical research has shown that managers with higher levels of EI are more effective and successful than managers with lower levels of EI. They are more likely to rise, through promotions, to the highest levels of management in their organizations. Furthermore, while cognitive intelligence level (IQ) is important, in some cases EI is even more important than IQ in predicting a managerial success. Not surprisingly, research indicates that some organizations prefer to fill management positions with people who have higher levels of the skills associated with emotional intelligence.[24]

In summary, emotional intelligence involves the ability to manage one's own and others' emotions and relationships with others. Given that managers spend most of their time interacting and communicating with others and that the main functions and roles of management involve people, EI is a critical factor in management development and effectiveness. Therefore, in addition to training experiences that are directly focused on its development, programs that include activities and experiences that encourage self-awareness, self-control, motivation, empathy, and interpersonal skills serve to enhance emotional intelligence.

PROJECT MANAGEMENT AND EMOTIONAL INTELLIGENCE

Whereas some managers are involved with project *planning*, most if not all are tasked with the *management* of projects. Planning involves determining the resources (human, technical, and financial) required to achieve an objective and organizing these resources such that they will converge to achieve the final product within the projected time frames and budgets. Managing a project, on the other hand, requires managers to control, organize, plan, and lead (COPL) the workforce to achieve the desired end result. Project management, therefore, refers to the day-to-day functioning of the manager in the accomplishment of the plan.

While poorly planned projects are unlikely to be successful, research has shown that well-planned projects can and sometimes do fail. That unfortunate result often stems from weak project management. Planning is one thing—getting it done is another.

All plans, once initiated, are subject to unexpected and disruptive events: poor weather, wildcat strikes, supply problems, and influenza outbreaks are but four examples. Anyone who has undergone a kitchen renovation knows that even under the best of circumstances, changes to the plan are practically certain.

Managing a project invariably means managing feelings. These may include the frustrations of workers who must sometimes redo work, the concerns of clients who fear delays and cost overruns, the anxieties that accompany the heavy responsibility for achieving specific results within tight time frames, and the anger and conflicts that occur when people are under pressure.

This raises two interrelated questions. First, is it the case that managers with higher levels of emotional intelligence—that is, those who cope better with emotions—manage projects better? Second, can EI be developed through structured training in the context of project management? The answer to both questions appears to be "yes."

Research conducted by Muller and Turner analyzed leader cognitive and emotional intelligence across different types of projects run in different countries.[25] Their results show that EI dimensions and success in project management are closely related. Leaders with high levels of both critical thinking skills (a traditional IQ dimension) and emotional intelligence are more likely to be successful. Intelligence is important for successful project management—especially when it is emotional.

Clarke provided EI training to a sample of project managers.[26] The two-day training program focused on three elements. First, trainee motivation and readiness was enhanced by presenting information that demonstrated the importance of EI for successful completion of projects. Second, participants received specific feedback on their own emotional intelligence. This was designed to provide baseline data to the managers and allow them to eventually gauge their own progress. Thirdly, the managers waded through a number of structured exercises designed specifically to help managers develop an understanding of their own behaviours with others.

A pre-post evaluation (see Chapter 10) showed that following this two-day program, participants showed a significant growth in their EI. However, the difference did not emerge immediately after training. It showed up six months later! Clearly, EI can be learned and modified by training and it can have an impact at the job level. However, this result also shows that, as with all other training programs, the conditions of the work environment remain important determinants of training success.

Clearly, managers require myriad skills. Whereas some fortunate managers excel in all, most managers have strengths and weaknesses, some of which require development. What are the principles that underlie how we are to go about developing managerial skills? Models of management skill development provide an answer to this question.

// MODELS OF MANAGEMENT SKILLS DEVELOPMENT

A model of management skills development is a basic blueprint that identifies the components or steps to be included in the development of training programs. Many skills development models exist in the management literature, some specifying a greater number of steps than others (e.g., Whetten and Cameron list five steps, while Hunsaker lists 10—see The Trainer's Notebook 13.1, "The TIMS (Training in Management Skills) Procedure").[27]

THE TRAINER'S NOTEBOOK   13.1

THE TIMS (TRAINING IN MANAGEMENT SKILLS) PROCEDURE

Phillip Hunsaker provides the following 10-step process to management development that he refers to as TIMS, or Training in Management Skills.

1. self-assessment
2. learn skill concepts
3. check concept learning
4. identify behaviours that define the skill
5. model the skill (i.e., observe others performing the skill)
6. practise the skill during training (to build self-efficacy and contribute to procedural learning)
7. re-assess skills (to test for progress and intervene when skill changes are insufficient)
8. questions to assist in skill application (questioning trainees to ensure that they have a clear understanding of the situations in which the application of the trained skill is warranted and to identify constraints and coping strategies for overcoming these constraints)
9. exercises to reinforce skill application (as well as self-efficacy and procedural learning)
10. planning for future development (as a specific preparation for transfer)

The TIMS model (and most other models) helps training developers and management trainers focus their efforts by providing a template of the activities required to increase the odds that managerial skill levels do improve as a result of training. Although somewhat more detailed than others, this model reflects the key dimensions common to all: skill-assessment (steps 1 and 7), learning (steps 2 through 5), and practice and preparation for application on the job (steps 6, and 8 through 10).

Source: HUNSAKER, PHILLIP L., Training in Management Skills, 1st Ed., ©2001. Reprinted by permission of Pearson Education, Inc., New York, New York.

However, most models of management skill development share four basic commonalities. That is, management development programs that minimally include the following sequenced steps are more likely to be successful:

1. initial skills assessment (identifying where people are)
2. skill acquisition (learning and understanding the basic principles associated with the specific skill of interest)
3. skill practice (developing procedural learning by integrating the principles into smooth behavioural actions)
4. skill application on the job (applying the learned principles in job situations that require the skills)

TABLE 13.2

THE BASIC COMPONENTS OF MANAGEMENT DEVELOPMENT AND THEIR EXPECTED IMPACT ON TRAINEES

	MOTIVATION	SELF-EFFICACY	LEARNING	BEHAVIOUR CHANGE (TRANSFER)
Initial skills assessment	X			
Skill acquisition			X	
Skill practice	X	X	X	
Skill application on the job	X	X	X	X

Table 13.2 summarizes these four basic components of management development programs and identifies the outcome each influences. Following is a brief discussion of each component.

a. *Skill assessment.* Beyond the mere determination of skill levels, this initial step serves the critical purpose of helping managers become *self-aware* of their own strengths and weaknesses relative to the skill in question. This is essential because people must recognize a need for development before development can take hold. That is, skill assessment affects and contributes to training motivation.

Initial skill assessment also identifies the learning and behavioural styles of managers that need to be taken into account when developing and implementing training programs. Remember that the purpose of management development is *not* to change individual personalities, but rather to help managers translate these personal preferences into practices and behaviours that are appropriate to their work context and that are effective in meeting the goals of the organization. Skill assessment developed in close symmetry with the learning objectives (see Chapter 4) is a key component of successful training and development programs.

Initial skill assessment is usually (though not necessarily) established through self-administered (and often self-scored), standardized, validated questionnaires. These are relatively short, easily administered, and scored under themes that reflect the training content directly. For example, the initial (PRE-TRAINING) questionnaire for a stress-coping program would ask trainees to describe the degree to which they engage in behaviours that are known to be associated with stress reactions. Typically, trainees keep their answers so they can compare them to their answers after training. Following training, participants answer the same questionnaire (POST-TRAINING) again. Comparing the pre- and post-answers allows managers to see their own progress, if any.

The before-after approach to skill assessment is immediately useful to the trainer (to know how things are going), but it also contributes to the motivation of the learner. Management development is a gradual process, where *improvement* in skills is the main objective. Observing one's own progress is self-reinforcing, and reinforcement contributes to motivation. It encourages managers to practise the skill and, as we will soon see, it is through practice that skill mastery and the development objectives are achieved.

b. *Skill learning.* Learning is the core focus of training programs. However, in contrast to most technical training, in which the trainee is taught specific procedures and steps for accomplishing a task, the managerial role is more diffuse, requiring that managers recognize the need for the skill in a diverse number of circumstances and the importance of using the skill in different ways for different cases. This requires that they learn managerial principles and processes that are applicable in different ways, depending on the manager's personal style in the conditions they are likely to meet on the job. These programs include substantial lectures or presentations that outline the reasons for and the principles behind the training. But most importantly they generally include group discussions and role plays that help participants discover the opportunities for application that may exist on the job, the obstacles that may inhibit skill use, and the strategies and tactics that may be used to circumvent these obstacles.

The ultimate objective of these development programs is to help managers attain procedural learning (see Chapter 2). Attaining that goal generally requires *practice*, the third major component of management development programs.

c. *Skill practice.* As described in Chapter 4, practice is the key to learning how to do most things well. The practice of learned skills serves three fundamental purposes. First and most obvious, practice reinforces learning and, more formally, helps shift the learning from the declarative to the procedural learning stage (see Chapters 2 and 10). This is essential if the manager is to integrate the learned skill with his/her own style. Second, practice enhances the manager's belief in his/her ability to perform the skill: it builds self-efficacy, a key ingredient of successful training (see Chapters 2 and 10). Managers who feel more confident in their capacity to learn and display the skill on the job are more likely to learn and transfer that skill. Third, skill practice can take a variety of forms, including role plays, simulations, and videotaped behaviour with feedback. These activities are inherently more active, maintaining trainee interest, attention, and motivation on the learning task. However, as training time is invariably limited in the North American context, it is not realistic to expect that the amount of time devoted to practice during training will be sufficient to automatically produce high levels of transfer on the job. Since rehearsal and practice on the job are essential, all development models include as a final component "skill application on the job."

For more information see Chapter 4, p. 126 and Chapter 10, p. 334 Chapter 2, p. 55

d. *Skill application on the job (transfer).* This final step in management development deals with the transfer of training process (see Chapter 9). Managers establish, during the training session, specific plans for the application of the learning on the job. Once on the job, however, organizational support in the form of follow-ups, additional coaching, and reinforcement is required to ensure that managers transfer their newly learned skills. The reason for this is that in light of the many tasks that managers perform, usually under pressure, it is very easy and tempting for them to relapse into their traditional, well-honed pre-training behaviours. Specific, immediate post-training interventions such as relapse prevention (see Chapter 9) integrated into the training can augment the odds of successful transfer, especially when the job environment contains barriers to transfer.

For more information see Chapter 9, pp. 286–290 and p. 300

In summary, models of management skill development focus on a number of important steps or stages in the development process. This usually begins with self-assessment and then proceeds to skill learning, practice, and application. These steps favour the development of the motivational, self-efficacy, learning, and transfer outcomes that define successful training.

// ERROR TRAINING FOR MANAGEMENT DEVELOPMENT

For more information see Chapter 4, pp. 135–136

Traditional models such as TIMS regard errors as undesirable and detrimental to learning. Trainees are taught skills that are sequentially practised and then applied. This approach focuses the training content and processes on error reductions with the goal of eliminating errors at the application stage. However, errors are inevitable when mastering new content or a new task, and that can be very discouraging (see Chapter 4). As most students know, it is very difficult to exercise continued effort in the face of failure.

In Chapter 4 we discussed error-management training (EMT), which involves allowing and encouraging trainees to make errors. Let us consider how EMT is useful for management development.

Recall that EMT is more effective when the trainee has to generalize learning to new tasks. Thus, if the training transfer task is to simply reproduce—more or less mechanically—a learned skill, EMT programs do not offer much advantage over traditional ones designed using TIMS approaches. However, for jobs that require problem-solving skills, where reproduction of learned behaviours is not sufficient, EMT may prove superior.

This latter result is of special relevance for management jobs, where constant adaptation to an ever-changing environment is the norm. Trained managers must be able to use new skills flexibly in a variety of contexts. In Chapter 4 this was called adaptive expertise. As EMT appears pointedly more effective in producing adaptive expertise, and since that type of transfer is required for management jobs, organizations might consider EMT when developing managers.

// THE CONTENT OF MANAGEMENT DEVELOPMENT PROGRAMS

Based on our earlier discussion, management skills fall into three general categories: conceptual, technical, and interpersonal skills. These three clusters of skills are rarely independent. For example, the mastery of conceptual skills (planning a project) often requires technical skills (such as linear programming). Similarly, interpersonal skills (e.g., convincing R&D scientists of the importance of respecting deadlines) often require specific technical skills (understanding the complexities of research). Nevertheless, this categorization provides a useful way to organize management development programs.

We now describe the content of programs used to develop some of these managerial skills. More complete descriptions of management development programs are available in texts specialized in management development (e.g., Whetten and Cameron, or Hunsaker).

CONCEPTUAL SKILLS

To accomplish the control, organizing, and planning functions of management, managers require various conceptual skills. We will limit the discussion to three especially important conceptual skills—problem solving and decision making, planning, and performance management.

a. *Problem-solving and decision-making skills.* Because managers are required to make myriad decisions—small and large—it is essential that they have the skills to do so.

Many years ago, James March and Herbert Simon, in one of the most influential studies of managerial decision making, showed that most people are uncomfortable making decisions. Moreover, as Mintzberg showed, managers are invariably under time pressure. They need to make very quick decisions.[28] Because of these pressures, they typically tend to select the first solution that minimally solves the problem. That is, they choose "adequate" rather than "optimal" solutions. That is not always a good idea.

Contemporary decision-making training programs train managers to avoid this tendency. As a result, most programs are organized into four basic steps:

1. definition of the problem

2. generation of alternative solutions

3. evaluation and selection of a solution

4. implementation of the solution and follow-up

The actual training programs include introductory lectures that explain and defend the four basic elements of effective decision making. Videotapes, role plays, and structured individual exercises reinforce each learning point and provide some of the all-important skills practice.

b. *Planning skills.* Planning, that essential requirement of management, involves first the clarification and specification of the goals the manager wishes to achieve. Next, the manager learns how to scan the environment to ensure that the plans are relevant and likely to succeed. This second step is called a "SWOT" analysis. That is, the manager is taught how to identify the strengths (S) and weaknesses (W) of the unit managed (i.e., its capabilities and weaknesses) relative to the opportunities (O) and threats (T) that exist in the environment. The manager learns how to translate these strengths and weaknesses, opportunities, and possible threats into action plans that include strategies, tactics, and specific actions. Finally, managers learn how to evaluate the success (or lack thereof) of the plan.

c. *Performance management and goal-setting skills.* Almost all organizations in North America require managers to review, assess, and manage the performance of their units and the people in them. Performance appraisal involves two distinct steps: assessing the performance of people (to provide feedback on past performance and to ensure that rewards and sanctions are applied fairly) and establishing goals and directions to encourage improved future performance. Although these formal performance reviews are traditionally conducted in a yearly session, it is increasingly the case that managers are encouraged to review the performance of their subordinates on an ongoing basis.[29] Motivating employees to improve performance is one of the key skills that successful managers possess.

Goal-setting is an integral part of this process. As discussed in Chapter 2, goals have strong motivational effects. They are one of the most important mechanisms for managing one's own performance and the performance of others.[30] Goals focus and direct one's efforts and can be self-reinforcing by providing specific feedback information that allows people to evaluate their progress.

However, in order for goals to be motivational, they must be SMART. As described in Chapter 1, they must be Specific, Measurable, Achievable, Relevant, and specified in Time. Managers who attend these programs learn how to structure such SMART goals. Moreover, challenging and achievable goals are motivating only when there is commitment to goal attainment. Therefore, most goal-setting training programs also teach managers how to obtain employees' commitment to the set goals.

For more information see
Chapter 1, p. 5–7

Goal-setting is now an integral part of performance management, and many Canadian organizations, including PricewaterhouseCoopers, the National Research Council of Canada, and Bell Canada, provide performance management and assessment training courses that include goal-setting as one of the key dimensions of the program.

These training programs emphasize, through lectures and discussions, the key advantages of performance reviews and the fundamental difficulties of the process. (Performance assessment is a stressful process for both the employee and the manager). The training techniques include many experiential components, such as role plays and simulations.

TECHNICAL SKILLS

Managers of marketing departments know something about marketing, and research directors know something about research. Such knowledge and skills are generally acquired through university programs that may be general (such as a general MBA) or more specialized (such as a university program in human resource management, marketing, statistics, or accounting). Additionally, specific courses instruct managers on very specific skills. For example, controlling budgets requires expertise in computer spreadsheet programs such as Excel, and the informational role requires presentation skills, which in turn often requires knowledge of how to use presentation programs such as PowerPoint.

As additional examples, university professors tend to build technical skills by reading scientific journals and attending conferences, and medical doctors and pharmacists in Canada are required to attend a certain number of conferences and workshops that instruct them on new research, treatments, or diagnostic procedures in their areas of practice. Accountants and lawyers are also required to attend periodic specialized information sessions (to ensure they are up to date with changes to auditing standards, tax regulations, or laws). These are essentially informational interventions.

INTERPERSONAL SKILLS

Interpersonal skills refer to the manager's ability to interact with others in a constructive manner. This includes skills in communication, in coaching (see "Coaching" further on in this chapter), and in managing conflict and stress. Although we limit our discussion in this chapter to these skills, it is important to note that other skills are also important. For example, there is a growing recognition of the importance for managers to develop "political" skills designed to help them gain power and influence. Moreover, as organizations move toward knowledge-based systems, they require that their members increasingly self-manage their behaviour and show initiative in their own development, including innovative ways of integrating Web-based learning.[31] Although that particular approach is somewhat controversial, it remains that managers need to learn how to function in this new environment by learning how to empower and motivate their employees and to build effective teams.[32]

For more information see
Chapter 7, p. 220

a. *Communication.* Communication skills are central to most management positions because much of a manager's time involves gathering information from the environment and disseminating it to the people in the unit and from the unit to higher management and/or to the external environment. Often, managers must communicate expectations to employees and provide feedback—not all of which is positive—to employees. In communicating effectively, managers must recognize their own *biases and styles* in hearing and in speaking with others. Hence, managers need to understand their *frame of reference* (knowing "where they are coming from"), how their interpretations are affected by their *values*, and their *trusts* or distrusts of others. These in turn affect *selective listening* (hearing what we want to hear) and *filtering* (telling only what others want to hear). In addition to alerting managers to these tendencies that obscure communication, most training programs teach managers the principles and practice of effective communication. This involves *congruency* (ensuring that the message sent is in line with their own actions), *clarity* (using language that is appropriate for the listener), and—most importantly— ensuring *comprehension* by actively soliciting feedback from the listener. Effective communication training programs place a large emphasis on practice. The training content includes role plays and analyzing cases, and the main role of the instructor is to provide constructive feedback.

b. *Managing conflict.* Managing conflict is an essential skill for managers because they are invariably competing for resources with other managers and because they may be involved in managing competition and conflict between employees.

Conflict can be described as being one of two types—conflict that is *interpersonal* (co-workers who may dislike one another) or *issue-based* (people who may have conflicting views on a problem or its solution).[33] Conflict is not an inherently "bad" thing, because issue-based disagreements often enhance the quality of the final decision.[34] However, improperly managed conflict can quickly create organizational problems.

There are five ways of managing conflict: *avoidance* (ignoring it), *accommodation* (giving in), *forcing* (getting your way), *compromise* (providing each party with some of the things they want), and *collaboration* (finding a solution together that gives the parties what they both want).

Collaboration is the ultimate conflict resolution outcome but it is not always possible. Forcing, for example, may be appropriate when the resolution requires an unpopular decision and when gaining the commitment of people to that decision is not important. Managers learn to recognize and choose the conflict management response that is appropriate to the circumstances they face. This, above all, requires managers to pay attention to the emotional aspects of the conflict. To do so requires that the manager

- treats the parties with respect
- listens to the other party and ensures that they know they have been heard and understood
- shares his/her needs and feelings

c. *Managing stress.* Considering the scope, time pressures (managers spend about nine minutes on each problem!), difficulties, responsibilities, and ambiguities of managerial life, it is no surprise that managerial jobs tend to be very stressful. A stress reaction is a person's emotional and physical response to a perceived threat. Stress reactions, like pain, are useful warning mechanisms that inform people that "something is wrong" and that they should do something about it. However, how a person deals with stress may or may not be particularly functional. Reacting to the stress of being cut off on the highway with a heavy foot on the accelerator and vengeance on your mind is unlikely to lead to an enjoyable or safe driving experience.

Stress reactions are responses to events that emanate from the work itself and/ or from the organization. For example, two well-known work-related stressors are role conflict and role ambiguity. *Role conflict* is associated with having contradictory task demands (e.g., jobs that require experimentation and innovation in organizations that do not tolerate errors); *role ambiguity* refers to not knowing what is expected. Stressors that affect work behaviours might also find their source in non-work events (a family or health problem, for example). Managers need to recognize stress reactions both in themselves and in those they manage, because some stress reactions can be quite dysfunctional, damaging one's health and/or work performance.

The *Canadian HR Reporter* published several articles that describe what it calls "problem managers"; that is, managers who "abuse" or make inappropriate comments to employees.[35] Indeed, harassment and abuse at work are now illegal at both the provincial and federal levels in Canada. Although abusive or even cruel managers do exist, these dysfunctional behaviours are often a result of the stresses the manager is experiencing.[36]

There are two basic ways to deal with stress. First, one can change the environment by removing the stressors. Second, one can learn to cope with and manage stressors more effectively. As individuals are generally better able to learn how to react to stressful situations than they are able to change organizational environments, the second approach is more likely to be successful.

Most people experience stress and are unaware of it. In learning how to cope with stress, the first and most important step, then, is to recognize when one is experiencing it. As a result, the initial skills assessment phase of stress training is critical, and these programs spend considerable time helping managers become aware of their own stresses and their reactions to them. The manager can then learn proactive behavioural and cognitive responses (learning how to perceive these situations differently) that will reduce the harmful effects of a stress reaction.

Stress-related training programs rely on the typical informational (reviewing basic principles related to stress and its management) and experiential (principally simulations and role plays) techniques. Usually, these programs offer concrete stress-reduction techniques that can be beneficial to managers not only in the context of work but also in their non-work lives.

In summary, management development programs are designed to focus on the development of conceptual, technical, and interpersonal skills. There are, of course, many different approaches and methods for developing these managerial skills, which occur on or off the job. We now turn to this topic.

// METHODS OF MANAGEMENT DEVELOPMENT

Management development programs can and often do make use of all of the on-the-job and off-the-job training methods described in Chapters 5 and 6. However, the balance between informational and experiential programs differs. Many short-term programs (such as the Stanford Graduate School of Business DVDs) are essentially informational: they focus on learning principles. At the other extreme, some are more fully experiential, providing few if any formal informational components.

At the informational level, management-training programs focus on the principles and the applications of the skill or technique. That is, they teach principles relevant to specifics in the core roles and functions of management. Most if not all management training programs have a strong informational component. This is of great importance.

You may have noticed that in the sections describing management training programs (conflict management, decision making, emotional intelligence, etc.), we emphasized their principles as opposed to specific behaviours. Management development cannot consist of memorizing and applying a set of behaviours. Managers operate in fluid and varied environments and individuals need to develop their own idiosyncratic ways of comfortably applying the principles learned in training. It is only by understanding and integrating the principles taught that different managers can correctly apply them in a manner that is appropriate to them and to the work group situation. To anchor that comprehension, direct experience is important.

Indeed, direct experience is the main crucible for managerial and leadership development.[37] This has placed a great emphasis on experiential learning as a development tool for managers. **Experiential learning** is learning by experience.

People mainly learn through experience. Organizations help provide that experience in many ways. These include direct job experiences such as job rotation and special assignments. They also learn through formal instructor-led courses that include role-playing and off-the-job experiences such as outdoor wilderness training (see Training Today 13.4, "The Origins of Outdoor Wilderness Training"). Active exercises designed to engage the learner are the key component of these development efforts. Direct experience allows managers to derive personal lessons and understandings that shape future behaviours.

> **Experiential learning**
> Skill practices exercises that actively engage and involve the learner

TRAINING TODAY 13.4

THE ORIGINS OF OUTDOOR WILDERNESS TRAINING

During World War II, the allied navies played a major role, conveying and protecting ships supplying England. German U-boats attacked these convoys, taking a heavy toll on men and ships. Hundreds of ships were torpedoed, forcing thousands to confront the rigours of survival in rafts and lifeboats. Many successfully escaped their burning ships only to perish awaiting a rescue that did not come.

Paradoxically, casualty reports revealed that older, less physically able shipwrecked men had better survival rates than younger, fit sailors. Discussions held with survivors indicated that younger sailors adopted unsuccessful life strategies such as panic, while the older sailors, those with greater life experience, remained calmer and

hence were better able to meet the demands of their extreme situation.

Years after the war ended, this experience spawned outdoor wilderness training, an experiential team and management development technique. For several days, trainees are tasked with arduous and/or hazardous duties that are intentionally stressful, such as winter wilderness camping or rock climbing.

These stressful situations bring out the best and the worst in ourselves and others, allowing us to gain direct experience with what we and others are capable of doing. With its exposure to extreme conditions, outdoor wilderness training is intended to build "life experience" which, in turn, is supposed to contribute to the development of coping skills.

Experiential approaches build procedural knowledge and motivation to transfer (two important aspects of transfer; see Chapters 9 and 10). However, recent work has suggested that the lessons learned from experiences are not always what should have been learned! To reduce this risk, some training departments use a special technique, called **After-Event Reviews (AERs)**. AERs are formal, structured debriefings held immediately following an experiential learning situation. Led by a facilitator, the participants discuss the task objectives, the outcomes realized, and the specific behaviours—their own and those of others—that facilitated or inhibited that achievement. Recent evaluation research shows that AERs significantly improve the value of experiential training, especially for trainees with certain personality characteristics (those with higher levels of openness to experience, conscientiousness, and emotional stability).[38]

There are three general approaches to and techniques for management development: management education programs, management training programs, and on-the-job management development.

For more information see Chapter 9, p. 288 and Chapter 10, pp. 334–336 and p. 338

> **After-Event Reviews (AERs)**
> Formal, structured debriefings held immediately following an experiential learning situation

MANAGEMENT EDUCATION PROGRAMS

The development of managers has typically involved management education. **Management education** activities conducted by colleges and universities help develop a broad range of knowledge, principles, and general conceptual abilities relevant to the managerial role.[39]

These education programs and classes target the development of the principles and techniques required to control, organize, plan, and lead effectively. They frequently include lectures and discussions focused on those principles. Additionally, management education supplements these lectures with case studies. Case studies are management problems that are solvable by the techniques and principles introduced in the lectures. These case studies serve two purposes. First, they exemplify the principles and techniques discussed during the lectures. Second, and even more importantly, by working through the case studies, trainees test and modify their understandings of the principles. That is, they provide feedback.

The ever-popular MBA that most business schools offer provides the classic example of a management education program. Executive MBA programs are especially desirable for individuals who are already in managerial roles and who want to advance in their organization. These programs provide individuals with a general education in management. Although they tend to be highly informational, they typically include some experiential learning and case studies as well. Students in most MBA programs learn management concepts and theory that underlie the managerial skills listed in Table 13.1.

Management education programs use the full gamut of instructional methods described in Chapter 5 including lectures, group discussions, role plays, games, simulations, and behaviour modelling training. But the study of cases remains central for the development of management skills in MBA programs.

A second, complementary approach to management education has been the development of corporate universities. To learn more, see Training Today 13.5, "Are Corporate Universities Useful?"

For more information see Chapter 5, p. 152

TRAINING TODAY   13.5

ARE CORPORATE UNIVERSITIES USEFUL?

A corporate university (CU) is a function or department, independent of the human resource department that offers an integrated set of learning and development experiences that are strategic for that specific organization or industrial sector. The main objective of a CU is to develop individual competencies that are of relevance to the organization. They do not replace training departments. Rather, they operate in parallel to them, developing in managers and employees competencies and attitudes (including attitudes toward learning itself) that will be beneficial to their actual and future performance in the company.

Although they are owned by the companies, corporate universities are sometimes affiliated with universities that provide some of the teaching. The Eaton School of Retailing, developed with Ryerson University in Toronto, is one such partnership. In some cases, CU participation can contribute credits toward formal degrees and diplomas. Other examples of corporate universities include BMO's Institute for Learning (Canada); the Federal Express Leadership Institute (USA); and the Lufthansa School of Business (Europe).

Organizations accept the large investment required by corporate universities because, in part, it is thought that they will contribute to improved individual job performance. However, this remained an untested hypothesis until Morin and Renaud conducted an evaluation of a Canadian financial institution's corporate university.

Over a two-year period, annual individual job performance data, demographics, and other variables were gathered from more than a thousand employees, some of whom had enrolled in one or more courses provided

(continued)

---

in the CU (the "experimental" group), while others had not enrolled in any (the "comparison" group). The results showed that CU participation had a very small, though statistically significant, effect on job performance. At first glance, the corporate university's impact on individual job performance appears to be marginal at best.

Whereas advocates of corporate universities may be disappointed that participation in it had such a small impact on overall job performance, they may take solace in that the data also showed a statistically significant interaction between pre-training performance and participation in the CU. Those employees who demonstrated the most improvement following participation in the CU were those who had poorer pre-training job performance. This suggests that CU participation may provide its greatest benefit to those organizational members who need it most. The implication of that finding is obvious. Rather than dismissing sub-performing managers and employees, organizations that have CUs may be able to recuperate them through their enhanced job performance.

In addition to providing insight into corporate universities, this study demonstrates the advantage of the pre-post with comparison design over both the post-only and the simple pre-post designs as described in Chapter 10. Had either of these other designs been used, we would have been compelled to conclude that corporate universities have little impact on job performance. However, through the inclusion of "before—after" measurements and the comparison group, it was possible to detect the all-important interaction between CU participation and improvement in job performance. That interaction, more than any other result of the study, may well indicate the true importance and value of corporate universities to organizations.

Source: Morin, L., & Renaud, S. (2004). Participation in corporate university training: Its effect on individual job performance. *Canadian Journal of Administrative Sciences*, *21*(4), 295. Reprinted with the permission of the authors and the *Canadian Journal of Administrative Sciences* (CJAS).

MANAGEMENT TRAINING PROGRAMS

Management training refers to training programs that involve activities and experiences designed to develop specific, immediately applicable managerial skills (e.g., communication, decision making) in a particular organizational setting. Many of the specific training programs described in the technical, conceptual, and interpersonal skills development efforts discussed in this chapter's section on the content of management development programs fall in this category.

> **Management training**
> Programs and activities designed to develop specific managerial skills

Management training programs usually focus on specific topics or particular skills. Some management training programs take place in classrooms and consist of specialized workshops and seminars. Management training programs can also take place outside of the classroom in any number of settings. Outdoor wilderness training is one example of an off-the-job management development activity.

Outdoor wilderness training programs are typically organized as a series of outdoor tasks that expose individuals to physically and psychologically demanding activities with which the trainees have had little or no prior experience, such as rock climbing, whitewater rafting, or winter camping. Generally, the successful and safe accomplishment of these tasks requires self-reliance as well as teamwork, strong communication skills, and the development of trust in others. This in turn is expected to help enhance the individual skills of trainees—such as leadership skills—and to improve the individual's ability to function collaboratively with others (teamwork).

> **Outdoor wilderness training**
> Highly experiential programs designed to help managers develop greater levels of "life experience" by participating in physically and psychologically demanding tasks and activities

Notwithstanding its popularity, one key question remains: How effective is wilderness training? Research on Outward Bound Australia trainees indicates that an overwhelming proportion of participants retain highly positive reactions to their training experience.[40] Moreover, the research indicates that such training appears to have effects on a very wide set of variables from leadership ability and mood to social skills and well-being, and that this effect may be very durable. In addition, these programs appear to have their largest impact in increasing the participants' self-efficacy and their ability to manage time. However, the research also shows considerable variation among programs, some being more successful than others. Beyond some mild indications that shorter programs (one to three days) are less successful than longer ones, we do not know with much clarity what makes one program more successful. Hence, whereas it is possible that such programs do lead to improvements in managerial job performance, the research data—being principally based on self-reports—remain insufficient to draw a firm conclusion.

SOURCES AND LENGTHS OF MANAGEMENT TRAINING SESSIONS

In North America, training courses tend to be of relatively short duration (one-half to three days is typical). The trainers are typically employees of the company's HR department. In some cases, when internal subject-matter expertise is lacking or in smaller organizations, specialized external trainers are hired. Although the perceived credibility of the trainer is important, there is no evidence that internal or external trainers are differentially effective.

The HR departments of some companies develop their own proprietary training packages using their own resources or external consultants. These highly customized training products can be very effective or not, depending on the degree to which they (a) are constructed around solid need analyses, (b) strongly respect adult learning principles, and (c) integrate practice and other active learning experiences.

Other companies rely on training programs supplied by specialized firms (such as Xerox). These commercially available programs are well developed, as they incorporate adult learning principles as well as some practices and/or role plays. They are generally affordable and the training packages include all required materials, including those needed by the trainer (acetates, lecture notes, etc.). However, as they are designed for and used in different organizations, their content may sometimes be inappropriate. For example, a role play simulating a sales context may be less meaningful to trainees in construction jobs. Concerns about "identical elements" (see Chapter 9) are pertinent here.

An increasing number of management development programs are available through electronic media (see Chapter 7). IPM, for example, offers an integrated package of 12 CD-based training modules that covers key management skills including staffing, performance management, team building, and employee relations. (More details are available from www.workplace.ca.)

ON-THE-JOB MANAGEMENT DEVELOPMENT

On-the-job management development programs intend to provide individuals with managerial learning experiences on the job. Two of the most common examples are job rotation and coaching.

JOB ROTATION

Recall from Chapter 6 that **job rotation** is a planned process that involves posting the manager to different jobs, areas, or functions of the organization. In effect, once a manager has mastered one job, he/she moves to a different one. Job rotation develops managers by giving them the opportunity to use existing and new skills in a diversity of ways, with different people, and in different functional contexts. This develops and enhances

On-the-job
management
development
Programs designed to
provide individuals with
managerial learning
experiences on the job

Job rotation
Exposing an individual
to different areas and
experiences throughout
the organization

For more information see
Chapter 6, p. 188

their skills. Job rotation also helps the participant learn about the organization itself. This development technique is particularly beneficial when the match between the skills the managers have and the skills they need in the new job is thought out. Rotating managers to jobs that require the manager's skills and provide opportunity for building others are best. As indicated in the TIMS model, accurate initial skills assessment is important for companies that make use of job rotation to develop managers.

COACHING

In Chapter 6 it was noted that coaching and mentoring are common methods of on-the-job training. Both are very popular tactics for the development of managerial competencies, especially because they focus on the organization to which the manager belongs. That is, they are highly congruent with and relevant to the specific organizational culture. In most cases they involve one-on-one sessions held between the manager and another person who acts as a mentor or coach. Mentoring and coaching share the same distal goal of helping managers be more effective.

Coaching and mentoring have grown into major management development approaches for many companies. The 2007 Conference Board of Canada *Learning and Development Outlook* reports that more than one-third of Canadian organizations maintain coaching and/or mentoring programs, and 55 percent of these consider them effective tools for the development of their people.[41]

For more information see Chapter 6, pp. 193–197

MENTORING **Mentors** contribute to the strategic development of managers by helping less experienced managers understand and gain perspective on the general managerial problems and difficulties they confront. They are usually continuous interventions in which trainees and mentors might work together for years and are most useful as career

> **Mentors**
> Help less experienced managers gain insight and perspective on the general managerial problems and difficulties with which they are confronted

Seniors mentoring juniors: the key to leadership development

© iStock.com/Steve Debenport

development strategies. Although the mentor and the manager may discuss specific problems, the goal of mentoring is broader and more diffuse. The mentor's task is to nurture the manager's growth as a manager.

COACHING On the other hand, **coaching** is more specifically goal-oriented than mentoring. It is a one-on-one structured learning experience to help the manager develop the insights and techniques pertinent to the accomplishment of specific aspects of their job. The key to successful coaching is the qualities of the coach and the manager's openness to the coaching experience.

The coach interacts with and provides feedback to the manager with the intent of developing his or her insight, skills, attitudes, and motivation for dealing with more specific challenges. For example, a coach might help a manager develop presentation skills.

Coaches may be external or internal to the company depending on budgets, coaching goals, and the organizational contexts. For example, the CEO who is struggling with a downsizing decision may well prefer a coach who is not an employee. However, the manager who needs to hone her political skills might benefit more from a trusted internal coach.

Many coaches are specialized in specific sectors, such as pharmaceuticals or manufacturing, or in specialized contents, as the following example illustrates. A marketing manager recently promoted to head the organizational learning group within HR had to develop and present a training plan for the marketing division. Lacking direct experience with training, she hired an external coach with expertise in training and with extensive experience of the pharmaceutical industry. The coach's role was *not* to produce the training plan, but rather to help the manager develop hers. They held weekly two-hour coaching sessions to discuss best practices, the pros and cons of various options, the obstacles likely to be encountered, how best to prepare for them, and how to present the plan, including setting up the actual slides for the presentation. This coaching episode ended six weeks later, when the manager presented (successfully, as it turns out) her training plan.

In this very typical case, the coach was an external consultant hired to help a manager complete one major task within an established time frame. However, many organizations require that managers serve as coaches to subordinate employees and managers on an ongoing basis. In that case the mandate may be much broader (the issues to be coached are not specified in advance) and/or more open-ended (without a specific end date). The coaching system in place in the Canadian branch of PricewaterhouseCoopers (see Training Today 13.3, "Taking Management Development Seriously: The PricewaterhouseCoopers Story") provides one such example.

When coaching is provided to all employees on an ongoing basis, managers are sometimes expected to serve as coaches. However, to be competent in that role, supervisors need to be trained in the science of coaching. David Peterson has uncovered some of the key ingredients of a great coach. Three of these stand out: Great coaches are goal-oriented, challengers, and person-focused.[42]

1. *Goal orientation.* Great coaches are great listeners who empathize with learners and who are honestly interested in helping them achieve their goals. They work diligently to help managers clarify the goals pursued.

2. *Challengers.* Great coaches are able to "feel" the mood state of the learner and know when to listen and when to challenge the beliefs and thinking of the learner. They know when to be supportive and when to be critical.

3. *Person-focused.* Great coaches focus their efforts and attention on the learner. They do not impose their views on the learner, nor do they insist that there is "one best way" to do things. Rather, they focus on helping the learner use

Coaching
One-on-one individualized and structured learning experience in which a more experienced and knowledgeable person helps another person develop the insights and techniques pertinent to the accomplishment of their job

his/her own previous knowledge and experience to develop his/her own perspective, understanding, and styles in dealing with the task.

Coaches are most helpful when they structure their efforts to help managers develop five key elements. Peterson labels these five the "development pipeline."

- *Insight.* Recognizing and understanding their own strengths and weaknesses.
- *Motivation.* Understanding and caring about changing how they operate.
- *Capabilities.* Identifying resources and best practices for dealing with complex decisions/situations and exploring alternative ways of dealing with them.
- *Real-world practices.* Identifying opportunities to implement, on a day-to-day basis, the little changes that should be made and developing the critical perspective needed to assess what works, what does not, and why.
- *Accountability.* Encouraging the manager to demonstrate the new skills and knowledge through commitment to specific actions.

To achieve these objectives, coaches face a number of important challenges. First and foremost, coaches must act to gain the trust of the "coachee." Confidentiality, discretion, and honesty are three of the key behaviours coaches must demonstrate. With this developing trust it becomes easier for the coach to provide feedback that stands a better chance of being perceived as constructive.

Applying new skills is difficult and attempts to do so are often subject to obstacles and hurdles that can discourage their deployment. Coaches have a special responsibility to be attentive to these situations and to help managerial persistence. Building self-efficacy, helping managers construe obstacles as problems rather than failures, and providing emotional support are three techniques successful coaches use. Finally, coaches who are in a position to do so sometimes intervene elsewhere in the organization to remove obstacles. That is, successful coaches are sometimes proactive as opposed to strictly passive in their interventions. Compared to external ones, internal coaches are often in a better position to help in this way.

A number of research studies have shown that coaching does help managers become more successful and more effective in accomplishing their tasks. Coached executives showed progress in a number of dimensions, including the management of people, relationships with others, communication skills, goal-setting, engagement, and productivity.[43] These positive outcomes are greater when the coaches are committed to change and when the organizational environment actively supports them in their attempts to change. Yet another study—this one relying on a very large sample of executives using a quasi-experimental research design—showed similar results, although here the changes were significant but somewhat modest.[44] Finally, other research has shown that managers who received coaching as part of their executive education program in a university also reported higher levels of self-efficacy and improved skills in developing others.

// IS MANAGEMENT DEVELOPMENT EFFECTIVE?

We now conclude this chapter by turning to the key question: *How effective is management development?* It is important to note that most of the research has relied on self-report measures to assess the effectiveness of management development; these are not necessarily accurate substitutes for objective criteria.

Consistently and over several reports, the Conference Board of Canada found that most organizations are not satisfied with the results of their development practices.[45]

The Conference Board results are derived from perceptions rather than from hard facts, and they represent the results of specific surveys conducted at specific moments. More general results have been obtained from meta-analyses.

A meta-analysis is a powerful statistical technique that allows researchers to summarize, in quantitative terms, the results obtained from many evaluation studies that have focused, in this case, on the effectiveness of management training. The results of these meta-analyses tend to be highly congruent with those reported by the Conference Board.

In 1986, Burke and Day analyzed all studies conducted prior to the early 1980s and concluded that management training was, at best, "modestly" effective.[46] However, because few studies actually collected objective data and even fewer measured Level 3 or 4 outcomes (see the discussion of the Kirkpatrick model in Chapter 10), the results of that meta-analysis are tentative.

Twenty years later, Collins and Holton returned to the literature and reported a meta-analysis of all pertinent studies published since Burke and Day.[47] Here, the focus was on investigating the degree to which managerial leadership development efforts produced positive results with regard to learning, expertise, and organizational outcomes. Both perceptual and objective data were included in this study, as were many types of training evaluation studies both with and without control or comparison groups (see Chapter 10).

The results indicate that training programs are highly effective in increasing learning levels. However, they are only moderately effective in building expertise, though that result varies depending on the specific training evaluation design used. As for organizational outcomes—such as impact on company effectiveness or profits—the results are less complete, as few studies actually assessed such outcomes. Fewer still were able to isolate the effect of management training from all other potential impacts on these outcomes. Nevertheless, the data indicate that, on average, leadership development programs do seem to contribute to the organization's effectiveness. Management training has a major impact on learning and a more modest one on expertise and organizational outcomes.

Perhaps more important is the finding that there remains much variation in results across development efforts. Some training programs are effective but others are not. Unfortunately, the data available from the Collins and Holton study are unable to identify the characteristics of training programs that are effective versus those that fail. For example, we do not clearly understand the conditions under which coaching or mentoring programs are effective.

Taylor, Russ-Eft, and Taylor provide data that begin to explain the difference between successful and less successful training programs.[48] Their meta-analysis integrates the results of 107 management training evaluation studies that focus on transfer of training. In those studies, managerial effectiveness—the degree of training transfer—was assessed in some studies by self-reports and/or by the trainee's boss, peers (other managers), or own subordinates. They also related certain characteristics of the training program to the transfer outcome for different types of training programs. In particular, they researched evaluation studies that focused on training programs centred on the development of the manager's interpersonal skills. The data analysis uncovered some significant trends.

Although different studies reported somewhat different results, in general trainees and their supervisors self-report reasonably high levels of transfer. However, the managers' employees and/or their peers do not agree. They rated transfer levels as negligible! In other words, managers and their bosses tended to view managerial training as being quite effective though others were less certain.

A deeper analysis of Taylor et al.'s data suggests that compared to less effective training programs, effective programs are distinguished by two characteristics: (1) the contents are developed following a thorough needs analysis, and (2) during training they provide significantly more time for the practice of the learned skills. This may be taken as an indication that organizations that invest more efforts into—and who are more mindful of—the development of skills are more successful at it. This interpretation of the meta-analysis finds support from all recent (2014–2017) Conference Board of Canada surveys: *Organizations that have stronger learning cultures report greater success and satisfaction with their training and development efforts.*

// LEADERSHIP TRAINING: WHAT'S WRONG AND WHAT IS NEEDED?

According to the Conference Board of Canada reports, the development of leadership is a top development priority for Canadian organizations.[49] Internationally, training expenditures hover around the $400 billion and the development of managers and leadership receives the lion's share of that amount. However, surveys of organizations as well as scientific research indicate that the return on investment for this massive effort is disappointing. Trainees do learn, but for the most part this does not produce noticeable behaviour changes and performance improvements on the job. Transfer of training is insufficient.

For over half a century, we have known (or at least suspected) that organizational support is of critical importance in transfer of training. In the absence of such support, especially for leadership development, training will prove disappointing.

Recently, Michael Beer and his colleagues identified several common organizational situations that prevent transfer of training in organizations.[50] They identify six such situations that they label the "silent killers."

1. unclear organizational priorities and strategies
2. lack of commitment to change by upper management
3. a reluctance to allow honest discussions of problems
4. lack of coordination across different elements of the organization
5. inability to identify and nurture talented individuals
6. managers' reluctance (fear?) to tell the truth about barriers to behaviour change on the job

It is traditional to believe that the cause of individual performance issues lies within the individual. Consequently, it is reasonable and logical for the individual to be the focus and the target for change. That view has dominated the practice of leadership training in organizations. However, perusal of the six silent killers suggests that the target for change should be the organization and not the individual. In effect, Beer and his colleagues suggest that leadership training and development needs to be tied to organizational development efforts. This has strong implications for the organization and its view of training and development.

Top leadership should be clear as to its priorities and strategies, and it needs to champion change and adopt policies that enable and encourage frank and honest discussions of performance problems. In a word, senior management needs to be directly involved with the development of leadership.

But it also suggests major changes for the human resource departments. HR needs to provide more than a list of static classes. It needs to accept some responsibility for the transfer of skills to the job. HR needs to carefully assess training needs but, equally important, it needs to ensure congruency between the behaviours they train and the acceptability of these skills to local management. Training programs that contradict organizational norms of behaviours are unlikely to transfer.

Trainers also need to recognize that the display of newly learned behaviours can be difficult and that providing on-the-job support helps. Help lines, job aides, and mentoring and coaching can all enhance the chance of transfer.

Clearly, both HR and senior management need to better understand the larger role they need to play in the development of leadership. Doing less will not be helpful.

// SUMMARY

This chapter described the roles, functions, and critical skills of managers and how they are developed. Managers engage in a number of interpersonal, informational, and decisional activities in order to accomplish their organizational goals of controlling, organizing, planning, and leading the work of others. This requires them to master and display conceptual, technical, and interpersonal skills, and to have emotional intelligence. Management development programs are designed to develop these skills. Moreover, managers must lead, and the development of leaders is a crucial task in modern organizations. However, understanding how that is to be done remains a work in progress. Models of development involve skill assessment, skill acquisition, skill practice, and skill application. The content of programs was described in terms of conceptual, technical, and interpersonal skills. Management/leadership development programs involve both informational and experiential learning and include management education, management training, and on-the-job management development. Management education programs, such as an MBA, provide individuals with a general management education. A popular example of a highly experiential management training program is outdoor wilderness training. Examples of on-the-job development include job rotation, mentoring, and coaching. The chapter concluded with a review of the research findings on the effectiveness of management and leadership development, and suggested strategies for improvement.

KEY TERMS

After-Event Reviews (AERs) p. 437
coaching p. 442
emotional intelligence p. 427
experiential learning p. 437
functions of management p. 420
job rotation p. 440
leadership p. 419
management p. 417
management development p. 418
management education p. 438
management training p. 439
mentors p. 441
on-the-job management development p. 440
outdoor wilderness training p. 439
skills p. 425
transactional leadership p. 423
transformational leadership p. 423

DISCUSSION QUESTIONS

1. What are some of the differences between management development and employee training?

2. Why is management development important?

3. Imagine the CEO of a company who has read this chapter and the section on coaching. She decides that coaching is a good idea and sends a memo to all managers telling them to personally coach each of their subordinates. Is this a good idea? How likely is it to improve performance? Had the CEO consulted you prior to announcing her decision, what would you have suggested she do?

4. Compare and contrast management education, management training, and on-the-job development. What are the advantages and disadvantages of each of these approaches for management development? How effective do you think each approach is for teaching the skills listed in Table 13.1?

5. What is emotional intelligence (EI) and what does it have to do with management and managerial skills? Can managers be trained to improve their EI? If so, how?

6. What is outdoor wilderness training and how effective is it for developing managers? What would be your advice to an organization that was considering sending its managers to an outdoor wilderness program?

7. What is the difference between informational learning and experiential learning? When should each be used for management development?

8. Describe the four basic commonalities of models of management skill development.

9. What is the difference between the traditional models of skill development and error-management training?

10. Martin Luther King is widely regarded as a charismatic leader. Based on your knowledge of his life, discuss if that is justified. Was he an "authentic" leader? (Viewing the biographical movie *Selma* might prove helpful for this discussion.)

THE GREAT TRAINING DEBATE

1. Debate the following: Some people have argued that management development is a waste of time and money because great managers are born, not made. Is it the case that managers cannot be developed?

EXERCISES

IN-CLASS

1. In an article called "The Smart-Talk Trap," Jeffrey Pfeffer and Robert Sutton described a phenomenon in organizations that they call the knowing–doing gap.[51] According to the authors, many managers are knowledgeable and very good at talking but not very good at doing or acting. In other words, talk substitutes for action. An especially dangerous form of talk is "smart talk," in which the speaker is particularly good at sounding confident, articulate, and eloquent. Unfortunately, smart talk tends to focus on the negative and is often unnecessarily complicated. It tends to result in inaction or what the authors call the "smart-talk trap." Problems are discussed and plans for action might

be formulated, but in the end nothing is done. This can have serious negative consequences for organizations. The authors suggest that one of the main reasons for the knowing–doing gap and the smart-talk trap is that managers have been trained to talk.

    a. What do you think about the knowing–doing gap and the smart-talk trap? Do you think this is a serious problem in organizations?

    b. The authors argue that one of the reasons for the existence of the knowing–doing gap and the smart-talk trap is the training that managers receive. Do you agree with this assertion? How can management training result in so much knowing and talking and so little doing?

    c. Discuss the knowing–doing gap and the smart-talk trap with somebody you know in a managerial position. Find out what they have to say about the prevalence of it in their organization, why it might or might not be a problem, and what can be done to avoid it.

    d. What advice would you give organizations about how to develop managers in order to avoid the knowing–doing gap and the smart-talk trap?

2. This task will help you integrate much of the material in this book. Starting with the TIMS model, construct a table similar to Table 13.2. In it, indicate for each of the 10 steps of the model the probable impact of that step on trainees.

3. Think of your manager from a current or previous job. Keeping in mind his/her behaviours and performance, how effective do you think he/she is? Your response has to be structured around the core functions and roles of management. What skills do you think he/she needs to improve? What would you recommend your manager do to improve his/her performance and managerial skills?

4. Imagine you are hired in a managerial position. The company asks you to design your own plan for development. What would you do? Refer to the section on models of management skill development, and for each step in the process develop a plan for your own management development. Be sure to indicate what you will do in each step.

5. Review the chapter-opening vignette dealing with the management and leadership development program the STM has launched. To what degree do you think the STM's efforts are consistent with the TIMS model?

6. Suppose that your university or college has instituted a new policy whereby more senior students are to coach first year students in being successful in their studies. One such student has been assigned to you to coach him or her on taking effective lecture notes. Keeping in mind Peterson's key elements for successful coaching described on pages 442–443, how would you structure your coaching behaviour in this case?

IN-THE-FIELD

1. To find out more about management development, contact a human resource professional and ask about management development in his/her organization. To guide your discussion, consider the following issues:

    • Describe the main skills that are the focus of management development programs. What are these skills and why are they the focus of management development?

    • Describe the process of management development. What are the main steps involved in the process?

    • Describe the content of management development programs.

- What types of management development programs are used, and why? Does the organization use experiential learning approaches? If so, what are they? Does the organization use management education programs, job rotation, and/or coaching? If so, how effective are they?
- How effective is management development for improving managerial and organizational effectiveness?

2. Contact and interview several people who work full-time for an organization. In each case, focus the interview on their perceptions of their immediate supervisor, manager, or boss. Focus on the skills of managers as described in the chapter. Do they perceive their manager as competent? What are the skills they think the manager should most urgently improve? Summarize your results in a report in which you discuss the extent and nature of management skills that subordinates believe should be improved.

CASE INCIDENT

MIDDLE MANAGER BURNOUT

In their article published in the *Harvard Business Review*, Morison, Erikson, and Dychtwald surveyed more than 7000 mid-career employees between the ages of 35 and 55.[52] The authors report that many middle managers are burned out, dissatisfied, or believe they are in dead-end jobs; most find that their work is no longer stimulating. Feeling neglected, many are actively searching for new jobs. As a result, many organizations face a stark choice: risk losing some of their best people or continue to work with a host of unhappy managers.

Your consulting advice is requested by the company president. She is asking you to provide suggestions for combating this growing managerial apathy in her organization.

QUESTIONS

1. What do you think are some of the causes of this growing problem?
2. In order to improve the situation, what, if anything, should top management do with and/or for the middle managers, the bosses of the middle managers, and the subordinates of the middle managers?

CASE STUDY   MARKET RESEARCH INC.

Market Research Inc. is a Vancouver-based firm that specializes in conducting surveys and interviews with members of the general public. The company has a number of teams that work on different projects for its many corporate clients. It is usually the case that several projects are conducted at the same time.

The company is composed of three departments: production, technical, and marketing. The marketing group is responsible for selling the company's services to corporate clients. The technical department is mainly composed of research personnel who develop and analyze the results of the surveys, focus groups, and interviewing studies for the clients. The production department is composed of several teams of interviewers. It is that department's job to conduct the data collection. They are responsible for identifying the people who are to be interviewed or surveyed, for enlisting their cooperation, and for conducting the interviews by phone or by mail, depending on the project.

Thomas Waterfall (Tom) is the manager of the production department. The department is responsible for ensuring that all of the data-collection projects are conducted in a professional and timely manner. More specifically, Tom must ensure that there is always enough staff on hand to conduct each study (never too many or too few), for hiring (or dismissing) the interviewers, for training them on the specific project requirements, and for ensuring and controlling the quality of the work done by the production department. He must keep himself informed of the activities of the marketing and technical departments to ensure that his department meets the demands of these other groups. Finally, the production department is a high-pressure environment where tensions among interviewers and between interviewers and the technical staff can sometimes flare up, threatening the efficient and effective production of the studies. The production manager must often act as an arbiter of disputes and soothe people when they get upset, a skill for which Tom is famous.

Mary Milend has been working for the last five years in the production department of Market Research Inc., where she is an interviewer. She has been doing a remarkable job, conducting her interviews with professionalism and competence. She always meets her deadlines and has never been the object of a complaint, either by consumers or by her co-workers. She has always shown great cooperation, often volunteering to help other interviewers with their tasks when they were submerged. Finally, in the tense atmosphere of conducting the data collection under tight deadlines, she has maintained extremely good relationships with the technical staff with whom the production department interacts routinely.

Tom, the manager of the production department, has announced that he will be retiring next year. Because of her superb record as an employee and her extensive hands-on knowledge of the production department, the vice president has offered to promote Mary to the job of production manager when Tom retires.

Mary is quite interested in the job, as this would mean a much higher salary, better benefits, longer vacations, and greater influence in the company. However, as Mary is a very honest person, she told the VP that although she was keenly interested in the job, she was not sure that she was the best choice. She explained that she had never acted in a managerial role before and that she felt uncertain that she had the skills to do the job well. Impressed by Mary's honesty, the VP indicated that he would be willing to provide her with all the training she needs to acquire the managerial skills that she will need to perform her new job.

QUESTIONS

1. What are the main skills that Mary will need to develop if she accepts the promotion?

2. What are some of the training experiences that might benefit Mary?

3. Should Tom be invited to play a role in Mary's development? If so, what could that role be?

4. How effective do you think each of the following programs would be for Mary's development: management education programs, management training programs (i.e., outdoor wilderness training), and on-the-job development (i.e., job rotation and coaching). What are the advantages and disadvantages of each? Which one(s) do you recommend for Mary, and why?

FLASHBACK QUESTIONS

1. Clearly, Mary's managerial skills need development. However, this may take quite a long time. Can you identify training methods that could be delivered more quickly? In answering this question, think back to Chapter 7, which discusses technology-based training.

2. Thinking back to Chapter 6 (about on-the-job training programs), can you suggest some of the things that can be done, on the job, to sharpen Mary's skills?

3. Chapter 10 discusses training evaluation and Chapter 11 describes the costs and benefits of training programs. How would you evaluate the effectiveness of the training and development provided to Mary?

FLASH FORWARD QUESTION

1. Organizational learning refers to the process of creating, sharing, diffusing, and applying knowledge. Organizational learning focuses on the systems used to create and distribute new knowledge on an organization-wide basis. It is a dynamic process of creating and sharing knowledge and it is an important determinant of organizational competitiveness and survival. To what extent will Mary's development be influenced by organization learning? In other words, will the development of Mary and her success as the production manager be influenced by organizational learning? What if her organization is not very good when it comes to organizational learning? Explain your answer.

REWRITE THE CASE QUESTION: THE METHODS OF MANAGEMENT DEVELOPMENT

Rewrite the case so that it concludes with a description of the development activities that are provided to Mary. In other words, provide a detailed account of the various development programs Mary attends and the skills that they are meant to develop.

// REFERENCES

1. Schettler, J. (2002, March). Training top 100: IBM. *Training Magazine, 39*(3), 48–49; Schettler, J. (2003, March). Training top 100: Best practices. *Training Magazine, 40*(3), 58–59; Johnson, G., Johnson, H., Dolezalek, H., Galvin, T., & Zemke, R. (2004). Top five profile and ranking. *Training Magazine, 41* (3), 42–58.

2. McCallum, J. (1993). The manager's job is still to manage. *Business Quarterly, 57* (4), 61–67; Brown, T. L. (1995). Leadership is everyone's business. *Apparel Industry Magazine, 56* (9), 14; Tannenbaum, S. I., & Yukl, G. (1992). Training and development in work organizations. *Annual Review of Psychology, 43*, 399–441.

3. Hall, C., & Burnett-Vachon, D. (2017). *The leadership outlook: Leadership perspectives from the middle.* Ottawa: The Conference Board of Canada; Hall, C., Burnett-Vachon, D., & O'Brien, K. (2016). *The leadership outlook: Leadership driving organizational performance.* Ottawa: The Conference Board of Canada.

4. Hall, C., & Cotsman, S., (2015). *Learning as a lever for performance: Learning and development outlook—13th edition.* Ottawa: The Conference Board of Canada.

5. Bolt, J. F. (2007). Mapping the future of leadership development. *The 2007 Pfeiffer annual: Leadership development.* San Francisco, CA: John Wiley & Sons; Hall, C. (2014). *Learning and development outlook—12th edition: Strong learning organizations, strong leadership.* Ottawa: The Conference Board of Canada; O'Leonard, K. (2010). *The corporate learning factbook 2009: Benchmarks, trends and analysis of the U.S. training market.* Oakland, CA: Bersin & Associates.

6. Robbins, S. P., De Cenzo, D. A., Condie, J. L., & Kondo, L. (2001). *Supervision in Canada today.* (3rd ed.). Toronto: Prentice-Hall, p. 7.

7. Whetten, D. A., & Cameron, K. S. (2002). Developing management skill. (5th ed.) Upper Saddle River, NJ: Prentice Hall, p. 270.

8. Baldwin T. T., & Patgett, M. Y. (1994). Management development: A review and commentary. In C. L. Cooper & I. T. Robertson (Eds.), Key reviews in managerial psychology. New York: Wiley.

9. Marquardt, M. J., Nissley, N., Ozag, R., & Taylor, T. L. (2000). International briefing 6: Training and development in the United States. *International Journal of Training and Development, 4*(2), 138–149; Mabey, C., & Thomson, A. (2000). Management development in the UK: A provider and participant perspective. *International Journal of Training and Development, 4*(4), 272–286; Cornuel, E., & Kletz, P. (2001). An empirical analysis of priority sectors for managers' training. *Journal of Management Development, 20*(5), 402–413; Agut, S., & Grau, R. (2002). Managerial competency needs and training requests: The case of the Spanish tourist industry. *Human Resource Development Quarterly, 13*(1), 31–51; Analoui, F., & Hosseini, M. H. (2001). Management education and increased managerial effectiveness. The case of business managers in Iran. *Journal of Management Development, 20*(9), 785–794.

10. Hall, C., & Burnett-Vachon, D. (2017). *The leadership outlook: Leadership perspectives from the middle.* Ottawa: The Conference Board of Canada.

11. Mintzberg, H. (1973). *The nature of managerial work.* New York: Harper & Row; Mintzberg, H. (1975). The manager's job: Folklore and fact. *Harvard Business Review, 53*(4), 49–61.

12. London, M. (2002). *Leadership development.* Mahwah, NJ: Lawrence Erlbaum Associates; Tichy, N. M., & Cardwell, N. (2002). *The cycle of leadership: How great leaders teach their companies to win* (3rd ed.). New York: HarperCollins; Ketz de Vries, M. (2001). *The leadership mystique.* London: Prentice-Hall.

13. Kotter, J. P. (1996). *Leading change.* Boston, MA: Harvard Business School Press; Whetten & Cameron (2002).

14. Kouzes, J. M., & Posner, B. Z. (2002). *Leadership challenge* (3rd ed.). San Francisco, CA: Jossey-Bass.

15. Frese, M., Beimel, S., & Schoenborn, S. (2003). Action training for charismatic leadership: Two evaluation studies of a commercial training module on inspirational communication of vision. *Personnel Psychology, 56,* 671–697.

16. Orth, C. D., Wilkinson, H. E., & Benfari, R. C. (1987, Spring). The manager's role as coach and mentor. *Organizational Dynamics, 15*(4), 67–74.

17. Van Dierendonck, D. (2011). Servant leadership: A review and synthesis. *Journal of Management 37*(4), 1228–1262.

18. Chiniara, M., & Benstein, K. (2016). Linking servant leadership to individual performance: Differentiating the mediating role of autonomy, competence and relatedness need satisfaction. *The Leadership Quarterly*, 27, 124–141.

19. Whetten & Cameron (2002).

20. Luthans, F., Rosenkrantz, S. A., & Hennesy, H. W. (1985). What do successful managers really do? An observation study of managerial activities. *Journal of Applied Behavioral Science*, 21, 255–270.

21. Cameron, K., & Tschirhart, M. (1988). Managerial competencies and organizational effectiveness. Working Paper, School of Business Administration, University of Michigan.

22. Goleman, D. (1998). *Working with emotional intelligence*. New York: Bantam.

23. Ryan, A. M., Brutus, S., Greguras, G. J., & Hakel, M. D. (2000). Receptivity to assessment-based feedback for management development. *Journal of Management Development*, 19(4), 252–276.

24. Pfeffer, J. (1998). *The human equation: Building profits by putting people first.* Boston, MA: Harvard Business School Press.

25. Muller, R., and Turner, R. (2010). Leadership competency profiles of successful project managers. *International Journal of Project Management, 28,* 437–448.

26. Clark, N. (2010). The impact of a training programme designed to target the emotional intelligence abilities of project managers. *International Journal of Project Management, 28,* 461–468.

27. Hunsaker, P. L. (2001). *Training in management skills.* Upper Saddle River, NJ: Prentice Hall.

28. March, J. G., & Simon, H. A. (1958). *Organizations.* New York: Blackwell.

29. Lawler, E. E., III. (2008). *Talent: Making people your competitive advantage.* San Francisco, CA, Jossey-Bass.

30. Locke, E. A., & Latham, G. P. (1990). *A theory of goal setting and task performance.* Englewood Cliffs, NJ: Prentice-Hall.

31. Kraiger, K. (2008). Transforming our models of learning and development: Web-based instruction as enabler of third-generation instruction. *Industrial and Organizational Perspectives: Perspectives on Science and Practice, 1,* 454–467.

32. Saks, A. M., & Haccoun, R. R. (2008). Is the "third-generation model" new and is it the holy grail of adaptive learning? *Industrial and Organizational Perspectives: Perspectives on Science and Practice, 1,* 480–483.

33. Eisenhardt, K. M., Kahwajy, J. L., & Bourgeois, L. J., III. (1997). How management teams can have a good fight. *Harvard Business Review, 75,* 77–85.

34. Haccoun, R. R., & Klimoski, R. J. (1975). Negotiator status and accountability source: A study of negotiator behavior. *Organizational Behavior and Human Performance, 14,* 342–359.

35. Klie, S. (2011, January 17). "Problem" managers a big problem: Survey. *Canadian HR Reporter, 24,* 1.

36. Burton, J.P., Hoobler, J.M., & Scheuer, M.L. (2012). Supervisor workplace stress and abusive supervision: The buffering effect of exercise. *Journal of Business and Psychology*, *27*(3) 271–279.

37. McCall, M. W. (2010). Recasting leadership development. *Industrial and Organizational Psychology*, *3*, 3–19.

38. DeRue, D. S., Nahrgang, J. D., Hollebeck, J. R., & Workman, K. (2012). A quasi-experimental study of after-event reviews and leadership development. *Journal of Applied Psychology*, *97*(5), 997–1015.

39. Wexley, K. N., & Baldwin, T. T. (1986). Management development. *Journal of Management*, *12*, 277–294.

40. Hattie, J., Marsh, H. W., Neill, J. T., & Richards, G. E. (1997). Adventure education and Outward Bound: Out-of-class experiences that have a lasting effect. *Review of Educational Research*, *67*, 43–87.

41. Hughes, P. D., & Grant, M. (2007). *Learning and development outlook 2007*. Ottawa: The Conference Board of Canada.

42. Peterson, D. B. (2002). Management development: Coaching and mentoring programs. In K. Kraiger (Ed.), *Creating, implementing, and managing effective training and development: State-of-the-art lessons for practice* (pp. 160–191). San Francisco, CA: Jossey-Bass.

43. Kombarakaran, F., Yang, J., Baker, M., & Fernandes, P. (2008). Executive coaching: It works! *Consulting Psychology Journal: Practice and Research*, *60*(1), 78–90.

44. Smither, J. W., London, M., Flautt, R., Vargas, Y., & Kucine, I. (2003). Can working with an executive coach improve multisource feedback ratings over time? A quasi-experimental field study, *Personnel Psychology*, *56*, 23–44.

45. Grant, M. P., & Hughes, D. (2007). *Learning and development outlook 2007: Are we learning enough?* Ottawa: The Conference Board of Canada; Hall, C. (2014). *Learning and development outlook–12th edition: Strong learning organizations, strong leadership*. Ottawa: The Conference Board of Canada.

46. Burke, M. J., & Day, R. R. (1986). A cumulative study of the effectiveness of managerial training. *Journal of Applied Psychology*, *71*, 232–246.

47. Collins, D. B., & Holton, F. E., III. (2004). The effectiveness of managerial leadership development programs: A meta analysis of studies from 1982 to 2001. *Human Resource Development Quarterly*, *15*(2), 217–248.

48. Taylor, P. J., Russ-Eft, D. F., & Taylor, H. (2009). Transfer of management training from alternative perspectives. *Journal of Applied Psychology*, *94*(1),104–121.

49. Hall, C., Burnett-Vachon, D., & O'Brien, K. (2016). *The leadership outlook: Leadership driving organizational performance*. Ottawa: The Conference Board of Canada.

50. Beer, M., Finnstrom, M., & Schrader, D. (2016, October). Why leadership training fails—and what to do about it. *Harvard Business Review*, 50–58.

51. Pfeffer, J., & Sutton, R. I. (1998). The smart-talk trap. *Harvard Business Review*, *77*(3), 134–42.

52. Morison, R., Erikson, T. J., & Dychtwald, K. (2006, March). Managing middlescence. *Harvard Business Review*. Retrieved from https://hbr.org/2006/03/managing-middlescence (April 26, 2018).

THE EVOLUTION AND FUTURE OF TRAINING AND DEVELOPMENT

CHAPTER LEARNING OUTCOMES

AFTER READING THIS CHAPTER, YOU SHOULD BE ABLE TO:

- describe the evolution of learning in organizations, and define "Learning 2.0" and "social constructivism"
- evaluate the learning system in an organization using the multilevel systems model of organizational learning
- describe the changing role of learning professionals and the skills and competencies required to be a learning professional
- describe how to make training and development programs effective

TELUS is a national telecommunications company in Canada that provides a wide range of communications products and services, including data, Internet protocol (IP), voice, entertainment, and video. The company has 23 000 employees in Canada and over 40 000 globally with an annual revenue of more than $12.8 billion.

In 2008, TELUS completely restructured all aspects of its existing corporate learning by creating an organization-wide vision called "Learning 2.0." At TELUS, Learning 2.0 represented a fundamental shift from the traditional model of "training as an event" to "learning as a continuous, collaborative, connected, and communicative process." This ideological shift required an approach to learning that encompassed three interconnected facets of learning: formal, informal, and social.

The impetus for the shift at TELUS was a recognition that learning does not occur solely in a classroom and dissatisfaction with the existing delivery methods and distribution of learning expenditures. Prior to the restructuring, TELUS dealt with more than 250 external learning providers, as 95 percent of its learning offerings were provided through outsourced instructor-led training. External providers were typically self-selected by team members in search of learning opportunities. This largely individualized outsourced approach led to frequent inconsistencies in the ways that vendors interpreted TELUS's specific training needs. As a result, the two main goals of the restructuring were to reduce the number of external providers used and to ensure that all learning providers delivered material consistent with the Learning 2.0 vision and philosophy.

After conducting a thorough assessment of external providers and team member learning needs, the move to Learning 2.0 allowed TELUS to reduce the number of external providers from 250 to roughly 70; shift expenditures from 95 percent outsourced formal learning to 60 percent formal and 40 percent informal within only two years; include more opportunities for social, team-member-driven, and developed learning; and maintain spending at previous levels through a "value-for-money" mindset.

Accomplishing such a radical shift in such a short time frame required a two-pronged approach. First, TELUS mobilized its 25-person Learning and Collaboration team to manage the change process. Those new to social learning educated themselves quickly through consultations with the Learning 2.0 experts who were brought on board.

TELUS restructured all aspects of its existing corporate learning by creating an organization-wide vision called "Learning 2.0."

Additionally, a grassroots 2.0 Adoption Council was formed within the organization. This group met biweekly to share their collective intelligence and discuss the ways in which social media could be used to benefit the organization and drive some of their social learning goals.

When the time came to pilot the new approach, TELUS relied on ambassadors and on early adopters to use as case studies for promoting Learning 2.0 within the organization. Once the seeds were sown by these early cases, Learning 2.0 was launched enterprise-wide and has been met with enthusiasm throughout the organization.

TELUS has since developed other tools for social learning and collaboration and has been recognized for its culture of continuous learning and development. An internal social network site called Jam allows employees to create and share knowledge and experiences. Employees can join learning groups to share and exchange knowledge and recommend content to colleagues.

TELUS's training and skills development program has been rated as exceptional, and in 2015 the Association for Talent Development named TELUS the first company to win the Best of the BEST award for employee talent development. In 2017, TELUS was named one of Canada's and British Columbia's Top employers.[1]

Sources: Lavis, C. (2011). *Learning & development outlook 2011: Are organizations ready for learning 2.0?* Ottawa: The Conference Board of Canada; Anonymous (2017, October). Building talent: The very best of 2017—TELUS. *TD: Talent Development, 71*(10), 68; Anonymous (2016, October). Building talent: The very best of 2016—TELUS. *TD: Talent Development, 70*(10), 84; www.about.telus.com.

// INTRODUCTION

The restructuring of the learning function at TELUS and its Learning 2.0 vision is an excellent example of how training and development is changing and evolving in organizations.

In this chapter, we discuss the evolution of training and development, a multilevel systems model of organizational learning, and the changing role of training professionals. We conclude the chapter with a review of how to make training and development programs effective.

// THE EVOLUTION OF LEARNING IN ORGANIZATIONS

As indicated in the chapter-opening vignette, TELUS has completely restructured all aspects of its learning system and created a new organization-wide vision that represents a fundamental shift in learning that includes formal, informal, and social learning. These changes represent how learning in organizations has evolved and is changing.

Throughout this textbook you have learned about a variety of ways in which employees learn, such as informal and formal learning, social learning, on-the-job and off-the-job training methods, and the use of technology and e-learning. When one considers these various approaches, one can begin to see how training, development, and learning in organizations has evolved.

As shown in Figure 14.1, learning has evolved from classroom instructor-led training to e-learning, then blended learning, and most recently to a more employee-driven and collaborative process. This evolution represents a shift from formal learning to social learning and from an individual focus to a group focus. This paradigm shift is known as Learning 2.0, and it involves the use of technology.[2]

Learning 2.0 represents a shift from learning as a product that is created for learners by organizations to a learner-initiated collaborative process. Learning 2.0 can involve informal learning (e.g., during meetings) as well as formal learning (e.g., mentoring programs, apprenticeships), and it can happen either face-to-face or through the use of social media.[3]

> **Learning 2.0**
> A shift from learning as a product that is created by organizations for learners to a learner-initiated collaborative process

FIGURE 14.1

THE EVOLUTION OF LEARNING

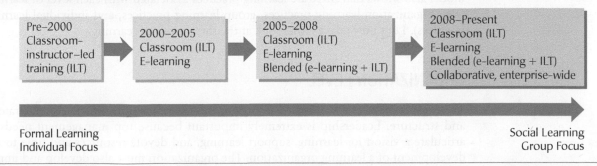

Source: The Conference Board of Canada. (2011). "The evolution of learning," *Conference Board of Canada Learning and Development Outlook 2011*, Exhibit 1, p. 4.

This shift in learning places greater emphasis on the learner and learning through social interaction rather than formal training. Kurt Kraiger has referred to this as **social constructivism** in which "the goal of instruction should be to create interactive learning environments in which training participants learn from instructors, participants learn from each other, and the instructor learns from participants." Technology and Web-based instruction is especially well suited for fostering such interactive learning environments.[4]

As described in the chapter-opening vignette, TELUS restructured its corporate learning based on a Learning 2.0 vision and philosophy that involves a fundamental shift in how it provides training and development. This approach is consistent with the notion of social constructivism, in which employees learn through social interactions and collaboration.

The evolution of learning toward Learning 2.0 and social constructivism is a result of changes in the workplace and the changing nature of work (e.g., knowledge- and team-based), shifting demographics, an increase in employee-initiated learning, and social media.[5]

As a result of these changes, learning can no longer be treated as a static and organization-driven event or product. Rather, learning is becoming a more continuous, fluid, and employee-driven collaborative process. Thus, Learning 2.0 and social constructivism represent an important trend in training and development—an increasing number of organizations like TELUS are likely to embrace Learning 2.0 and social constructivism in the coming years.[6]

// A MULTILEVEL SYSTEMS MODEL OF ORGANIZATIONAL LEARNING

Although the focus of this textbook has been individual learning, it is important to realize that learning occurs at three levels in organizations. At the highest level of the learning system is organizational learning, which sets the stage for learning at the other two levels.

Organizational learning refers to the process of creating, sharing, diffusing, and applying knowledge. Organizational learning focuses on the systems used to create and distribute new knowledge on an organization-wide basis. Thus, organizational learning is a dynamic process of creating and sharing knowledge and it is an important determinant of organizational competitiveness and survival. As discussed below, organizational learning influences and is influenced by individual and group learning.

Figure 14.2 presents a multilevel systems model of organizational learning. The model shows that there are three levels of learning in organizations: the organization level, the group level, and the individual level. Each level is connected to the levels above and below it, which means that learning at each level is influenced by the other levels. The model also shows that there are learning practices associated with each level of learning (e.g., organization learning practices, group learning practices, and individual learning practices). Let's now take a closer look at the three levels of learning.

ORGANIZATION LEVEL

The organization level consists of an organization's leadership, culture, vision, strategy, and structure. Leadership is extremely important because top management needs to articulate a vision for learning, support learning, and devote resources and time to the development of a learning organization. The organization must also develop and implement strategies for individual and group learning.

FIGURE 14.2

A MULTILEVEL SYSTEMS MODEL OF ORGANIZATIONAL LEARNING

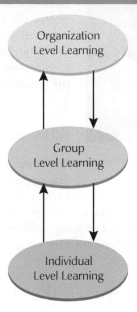

Organization learning practices

An environment for learning and the acquisition and exchange of knowledge and information.

Organization Level Learning

Group learning practices

The opportunity for groups to interact, communicate, and share information.

Group Level Learning

Individual learning practices

Individuals must have formal and informal opportunities for learning. Learning and the transfer of knowledge and information must be rewarded.

Individual Level Learning

Organization practices are necessary for the organization and its members to acquire and share information and to distribute it throughout the organization. Thus, an organization must create processes, practices, policies, and structures that enable the acquisition, exchange, and distribution of information and knowledge throughout the organization. As well, the organization's culture for learning will influence the extent to which teams and individuals seek out new information and learning opportunities, and transfer new knowledge and skills on the job. Thus, there must be a culture that supports and encourages continuous learning.

Organizations that are particularly good at this are known as learning organizations. A **learning organization** is an organization that creates, acquires, organizes, shares, and retains information and knowledge, and uses new information and knowledge to change and modify its behaviour in order to achieve its objectives and improve its effectiveness.

Learning organizations have established systems and structures to acquire, code, store, and distribute important information and knowledge so that it is available to those who need it, when they need it. As a result, a learning organization is able to transform itself by acquiring and disseminating new knowledge and skills throughout the organization. Thus, it has an enhanced capacity to learn, adapt, and change its culture.[7]

> **Learning organization**
> An organization that creates, acquires, organizes, shares, and retains information and knowledge, and uses new information and knowledge to change and modify its behaviour in order to achieve its objectives and improve its effectiveness

GROUP LEVEL

Important factors that influence learning at the group level include group climate, culture, norms, dynamics, and processes, as well as the complexity of the group task and task interdependence.

Organizational learning influences and is influenced by individual and group learning.

For example, the extent to which informal learning occurs is influenced by the group's culture and norms for learning. The nature of the group's tasks will also influence learning. Groups that perform more complex tasks are more likely to realize the benefits of learning. When the tasks that group members perform are interdependent, there is a greater need for the group to interact and share information. Thus, group-level factors influence the extent to which learning occurs at the group level.

INDIVIDUAL LEVEL

At the individual level, employees must have formal and informal opportunities to learn. This means that the organization needs to provide structured and formal training and development programs so that employees can acquire new knowledge and skills, and have opportunities to share and exchange information. In addition, employees must be rewarded for learning and applying what they learn on the job.

LINKAGES BETWEEN THE LEVELS

The multilevel systems model of organizational learning shows that learning is a dynamic process that involves three levels that are interconnected. For example, the systems and processes that exist at the organization level influence the extent to which learning occurs at the group and individual levels, and group-level factors influence learning at the individual level. In addition, individual learning influences group learning, and individual and group learning influence organization learning.[8]

In summary, the multilevel systems model of organizational learning demonstrates the importance of learning practices and systems at each level of the organization and how learning at each level is influenced by and in turn influences learning at the other levels.

Finally, it is important to recognize that learning at each level is influenced by HR practices and the HR system. Research has found that HR practices such as learning and career development opportunities have a positive effect on all three levels of learning, and the three levels of learning have a positive effect on organization performance.[9] The relationships between the HR system, learning, and organization performance are shown in Figure 14.3.

FIGURE 14.3

THE HR SYSTEM, LEARNING, AND ORGANIZATION PERFORMANCE

HR System → Individual Learning / Group Learning / Organization Learning → Organization Performance

// THE CHANGING ROLE OF LEARNING PROFESSIONALS

During the last several decades, the trainer's traditional role as a staff employee of HR has been changing, and there has been a significant transformation of the training and development function.[10] Trainers have begun to move out of the training department to work with management to solve organizational problems and create learning opportunities that support the organization's strategy. This reflects a movement and evolution of the trainer from staff employee to strategic business partner.

While many training professionals spend most of their time designing and delivering training programs, they are increasingly involved in strategic functions such as facilitating organizational change, managing organizational knowledge, career planning, and talent management.[11] Thus, training professionals are increasingly being called on to provide learning solutions that will drive key business outcomes.[12]

According to the Conference Board of Canada, the role of learning and development professionals is shifting from knowledge-keeper to that of learning facilitator. This involves creating environments and activities that enable and facilitate knowledge sharing and transfer between employees.[13] Thus, training and talent development professionals will increasingly be responsible for creating environments for learning and helping organization members find the resources and tools for learning and performance improvement.[14]

The training and development function is transforming into a learning and talent development function. It will focus more on results rather than activities, and it will be integrated into the business of the organization at a strategic level; learning will be embedded into the jobs that individuals perform.[15] In addition, training functions will become performance consulting centres, and training professionals will become performance and learning consultants.

As a **performance consultant**, the role of the trainer is not just to provide training and development. Trainers must now also provide solutions to performance problems and be proactive in identifying emerging learning needs and taking steps to prepare and support the organization by offering solutions and learning programs to address future skills and performance gaps. This also means that training professionals must have a thorough understanding of the organization and its business.[16]

Finally, given the increasing importance of continuous learning in organizations, the role of the trainer is shifting from training to learning. Thus, the role of the trainer is to facilitate and create learning opportunities throughout the organization, and to help organizations manage the transition to a learning organization and the creation of a learning environment.

A **learning environment** is defined as "a deliberately curated collection of materials and activities to support the development of a specific knowledge base or skill."[17] An effective learning environment provides a variety of resources and activities that employees can access to manage their own learning. To learn more, see the Trainer's Notebook 14.1, "Learning Material and Activities in a Learning Environment."

So what does all this mean in terms of the skills and capabilities required by learning professionals today and in the future? In Canada, the Institute for Performance and Learning (I4PL) has developed a set of competencies for performance and learning professionals. As shown in Figure 14.4, the competencies

> **Performance consultant**
> A training professional responsible for providing solutions to performance problems
>
> **Learning environment**
> A deliberately curated collection of materials and activities to support the development of a specific knowledge base or skill

Training professionals are becoming performance consultants who facilitate learning and provide solutions to performance problems.

LEARNING MATERIAL AND ACTIVITIES IN A LEARNING ENVIRONMENT

There are many kinds of learning materials and activities that exist in a learning environment. The key is that a learning environment consists of various materials and resources that offer learners choice and just-in-time learning. Here are some examples of materials and activities found in learning environments.

1. **Resources**: Study and reference materials in a variety of formats, including Web pages, manuals, books, videos, and podcasts.

2. **People**: Active interpersonal connections that support learning, including peers supporting one another.

3. **Training and education**: Formal courses, workshops, and modules that address specific learning objectives.

4. **Development practices**: Company- or manager-defined on-the-job learning activities.

5. **Experiential learning practices**: Learners' own on-the-job action and reflection, and learning-by-doing activities.

Source: Lombardozzi, C. (2016, January). Cultivating valuable learning environments. *TD: Talent Development*, *70*(1), 54–58.

FIGURE 14.4

INSTITUTE FOR PERFORMANCE AND LEARNING COMPETENCIES FOR PERFORMANCE AND LEARNING PROFESSIONALS

Source: Courtesy of The Institute for Performance and Learning.

are organized into seven categories: partnering with clients, assessing performance needs, designing curricula, designing learning experiences, facilitating learning, supporting transfer of learning, and evaluating learning.

Within each competency category there are first-, second-, and third-level competencies. These competencies form the basis of the I4PL certification process, which includes two designations—Certified Training Practitioner, or CTP, and Certified Training and Development Professional, or CTDP.[18] In addition, an increasing number of organizations use these competencies for the hiring and development of learning professionals.

In the United States, the Association for Talent and Development (ATD) has developed a competency model for talent development professionals that indicates the skills and knowledge that training and development professionals require now and in the future.

As shown in Figure 14.5, the model includes six foundational competencies (business skills, interpersonal skills, global mindset, personal skills, industry knowledge, and technology literacy) that are important for all training and development professionals, as well as 10 specific areas of expertise (performance improvement, instructional design, training

FIGURE 14.5

ATD COMPETENCY MODEL

delivery, learning technologies, evaluating learning impact, managing learning programs, integrated talent management, coaching, knowledge management, and change management) that represent areas of expertise and specialized knowledge, skills, and abilities required by persons in specific roles.

The competency model can be used by learning professionals to identify their own skills gaps and guide their development, as well as by those who want to enter the field and become a Certified Professional in Learning and Performance.[19]

// MAKING TRAINING AND DEVELOPMENT PROGRAMS EFFECTIVE

Much of what you have learned in this book has focused on how to make training and development programs effective. This is no small feat, since there is ample evidence that many training and development programs are not effective. According to one recent survey, 46 percent of employees indicated that the formal training they receive is not very effective.[20] Therefore, in this final section of the chapter and textbook, we briefly review some of the key factors that contribute to making training and development programs effective.

A good place to start is with individual differences or trainee characteristics, which—as described in Chapters 2 and 9—influence a number of training outcomes. Although some individual differences such as cognitive ability are stable, others can be changed. Therefore, to make training programs effective, trainers should strengthen trainees' training motivation, self-efficacy, and motivation to transfer, which are strong predictors of learning and transfer of training.

Second, the design of training programs (Chapter 4) should include active practice so that trainees have opportunities to use newly acquired knowledge and skills during training. In addition, careful consideration should be given to the conditions of practice before and during training. Although the use and need for particular conditions of practice will vary across training programs, all training and development programs should include feedback and knowledge of results, which are fundamental for learning.

Third, a variety of instructional methods (Chapters 5, 6, and 7) should be used depending on the training objectives and learning outcomes. As noted earlier in the text, blended training is most effective as it not only appeals to trainees with different learning styles, but is also most likely to achieve a variety of learning outcomes. Thus, trainers should use a combination of off-the-job, on-the-job, and technology-based training methods whenever possible.

Fourth, when delivering a training program (Chapter 8) it is advisable to use Gagné's nine events of instruction: gain attention, describe the objectives, stimulate recall of prior knowledge, present the material to be learned, provide guidance for learning, elicit performance practice, provide informative feedback, assess performance, and enhance retention and transfer. This provides a meaningful structure for the delivery of a training program and ensures that many critical factors (e.g., objectives, practice, and feedback) are included in training and development programs.

Fifth, the pre- and post-training environments (Chapter 9) should be favourable for learning and transfer. For example, supervisors should provide encouragement and support for trainees before and after training. The transfer climate should be positive and consist of cues that remind employees to apply learning on-the-job, supervisor and peer support, and feedback and positive reinforcement. In addition, trainees should be provided with ample opportunities to practise and use newly acquired knowledge and skills on the job.

The Trainer's Notebook 14.2, "Making Training and Development Programs Effective" summarizes the main factors for making training and development programs effective.

It should now be clear to you that training and development is an important part of the management of performance in organizations. Training and development plays a critical role in helping organizations meet the challenges of an increasingly complex and competitive environment.

Unfortunately, training programs often fail to achieve their objectives and, as a result, hinder an organization's ability to remain competitive. The good news is that the science of training, as described in this textbook, contains practical information on how to design, deliver, and evaluate effective training and development programs. By applying the theories, concepts, and principles described in this textbook, it is possible to design and deliver effective training and development programs that will benefit employees, organizations, and society.

You now know the science of training and how to make training and development programs effective; it is up to you to translate training science into training practice!

// SUMMARY

This chapter began with a discussion of the evolution of learning in organizations, and the trend toward Learning 2.0 and social constructivism. The importance of a multilevel systems perspective of organizational learning, the changing role of learning professionals, and the competencies required to be a learning professional today were discussed. The chapter concluded with a discussion and review of how to make training and development programs effective.

KEY TERMS

Learning 2.0 p. 457
learning environment p. 461
learning organization p. 459
organizational learning p. 458
performance consultant p. 461
social constructivism p. 458

DISCUSSION QUESTIONS

1. How has the role of training and development professionals changed? What are the new and emerging competencies and roles of trainers?

2. Describe the evolution of training and development in organizations and the implications for the design and delivery of training programs. What are the main changes taking place? What are the implications of these changes for trainers and employees?

3. Define "Learning 2.0" and "social constructivism," and discuss how they are different from more traditional approaches to learning. What are the implications of Learning 2.0 and social constructivism for employees, trainers, and organizations?

4. Discuss the multilevel systems model of organizational learning. How are the three levels related, and what should organizations do to facilitate learning at each level?

5. What is the meaning of "learning organization" and "organizational learning"? How are they related and how can they influence training and development in organizations?

6. What are some of the most important things that a trainer can do to make training programs effective?

THE GREAT TRAINING DEBATE

1. Debate the following: The training and development function and the role of trainers will become obsolete in the near future.

EXERCISES

IN-CLASS

1. If an organization wants to hire a training professional today, what should it look for? Find several job advertisements for training managers or director positions in your local area. Bring the advertisements to class and summarize the main competencies and responsibilities of the positions. Describe how the jobs match the traditional role of a trainer as well as the more current roles and competencies described in the chapter.

2. Think about your knowledge and skills and the extent to which you are prepared for the new competencies and roles expected of training professionals today. Conduct a self-assessment using the material presented in this chapter, with particular attention to the ATD competency model (Figure 14.5) and the I4PL competencies for learning professionals (Figure 14.4). What competencies do you have, and which ones do you

still need to develop? Prepare an action plan that describes some of the things you can do to develop your competencies.

3. Recall the most recent training program you attended at a current or former employer and evaluate the program in terms of the five factors in The Trainer's Notebook 14.2. How effective was the training program in terms of your learning and transfer of training? To what extent did the trainer do each of the five factors for making training programs effective? What could the trainer have done to make the program more effective?

IN-THE-FIELD

1. Contact a training and development professional in an organization to find out how his/her role has changed and how it will change in the future. What was his/her role five years ago? What is his/her role today? What will be his/her role in five years? What skills and experiences do trainers need in order to perform their current and future roles, and how has this changed over the last 5 to 10 years?

2. Contact a training and development professional in an organization to find out how learning, training, and development have changed in their organization in the last 5 to 10 years. Using Figure 14.1, interview them about the extent to which they provide classroom instructor-led training, e-learning, blended learning, and social and collaborative learning. Based on your interview, where in the evolution of learning would you place the organization? To what extent is Learning 2.0 part of the learning system in the organization? What advice would you give the organization for advancing learning, training, and development?

3. Contact a training and development professional in an organization to find out if they use the five factors in The Trainer's Notebook 14.2. Interview them about the extent to which each of the five factors is performed. Based on your interview, to what extent does the organization perform each of the five factors? What factors do they need to focus on and improve to make their training and development programs more effective?

RUNNING CASE STUDY: DIRTY POOLS

QUESTIONS

Refer to the case at the end of Chapter 1 to answer the following questions.

1. The case points out that some organizations have repeatedly failed to meet health and safety standards and continue to put bathers at risk. Do you think that some organizations are more likely than others to violate public health and safety rules? Is it possible that learning organizations are less likely to violate public health and safety rules? Explain your answer.

2. Explain how a multilevel approach to learning might be necessary for organizations to improve the health and safety of their pools and hot tubs and to lower the number of health infractions. What can we learn about making pools and hot tubs safer from the multilevel systems model of organizational learning?

// REFERENCES

1. Based on Lavis, C. (2011). *Learning & development outlook 2011: Are organizations ready for Learning 2.0?* Ottawa: The Conference Board of Canada; http://about.telus.com/community/english/about_us; Mediacorp Canada Inc. (2015). Canada's top 100 employers.
   Retrieved from http://www.canadastop100.com/national/

2. Lavis (2011).

3. Lavis (2011).

4. Kraiger, K. (2008). Transforming our models of learning and development: Web-based instruction as enabler of third-generation instruction. *Industrial and Organizational Psychology, 1,* 461.

5. Lavis (2011).

6. Lavis (2011).

7. Bennet, J. K., & O'Brien, M. J. (1994, June). The building blocks of the learning organization. *Training Magazine, 31*(6), 41–49.

8. Kozlowski, S. W. J., & Salas, E. (1997). A multilevel organizational systems approach for the implementation and transfer of training. In J. K. Ford, S. W. J. Kozlowski, K. Kraiger, E. Salas, & M. S. Teachout (Eds.), *Improving training effectiveness in work organizations*. Mahwah, NJ: Lawrence Erlbaum Associates.

9. Cho, S. H., Song, J. H., Yun, S. C., & Lee, C. K. (2013). How the organizational learning process mediates the impact of strategic human resource management practices on performance in Korean organizations. *Performance Improvement Quarterly, 25,* 23–42.

10. Giulioni, J. W. (2017, August). L&D for L&D. *TD: Talent Development, 71*(8), 50–54.

11. Vu, U. (2004, July 12). Trainers mature into business partners. *Canadian HR Reporter, 17*(13), 1, 2.

12. Giulioni (2017).

13. Lavis (2011).

14. Lombardozzi, C. (2016, January). Cultivating valuable learning environments. *TD: Talent Development, 70*(1), 54–58.

15. Robinson, D. G., & Robinson, J. C. (2005, Anniversary issue). A heightened focus on learning and performance. *HR Magazine, 50*(13), 65–67.

16. Giulioni (2017).

17. Lombardozzi (2016).

18. *Competencies for performance and learning professionals*. The Institute for Performance and Learning. https://performanceandlearning.ca/competency-wheel/

19. Arneson, J., Rothwell, W., & Naughton, J. (2013). Training and development competencies redefined to create competitive advantage. *T+D, 67*(1), 42–67.

20. Anonymous (2017, March). Effectiveness of formal workplace training uncovered. *TD: Talent Development, 71*(3), 19.

APPENDIX

INTEGRATIVE CASE STUDIES

// INTEGRATIVE CASE STUDY 1

TRAINING SECURITY GUARDS

In 1999, Patrick Shand was wrestled to the ground by security guards at a grocery store in Toronto. He was handcuffed and kept face-down on the ground, where he died of asphyxiation after being accused of shoplifting baby formula.

In February of 2004, a coroner's inquest ruled that Shand's death was accidental, and that he died of restraint asphyxia with complications from chronic and acute cocaine use. One of the findings of the inquest was that Shand might not have died if the guards who apprehended him had been trained in the use of force and life-saving.

The inquiry made 22 recommendations to reform Ontario's security industry. For example, it recommended that all in-house security guards and bouncers in Ontario be licensed and receive mandatory training (in areas such as first aid, CPR, and the use of force) that identifies the hazards of restraint asphyxia and excited delirium, and appropriate training in the use of handcuffs and expandable batons. The inquest concluded that "It is important that the government act quickly, responsibly, and diligently."

The Ontario government responded to the inquest's 22 recommendations with amendments to the *Private Security and Investigative Services Act* in 2005. This was the first time the Act had been updated since it was passed in 1966. The updated Act went into effect in August 2007, and specified August 2008 as the deadline for 22 000 previously unlicensed security guards and bouncers to get licensed.

In addition to mandatory licensing for all security personnel and standards for uniforms, equipment, and vehicles used by security personnel, the Act also includes mandatory training standards. The basic training standard would be developed to include knowledge of relevant legislation (the new *Private Security and Investigative Services Act*, and the *Trespass to Property Act*); power of arrest; use of force; communications and public relations skills; first aid and cardiopulmonary resuscitation (CPR); on-the-job skills (report writing, note taking, and diversity sensitivity); and the use of equipment (batons, handcuffs).

Security guards and bouncers in Ontario now must pay $80 to meet the new requirements. However, the Ministry of Community Safety and Correctional Services did not implement the training program that is part of the licensing. Those in the industry were left questioning the law.

Thus, despite a proposed curriculum and government plans for a 40-hour mandatory training program, the licence requirements only required in-house security guards and bouncers to submit an application to the ministry, pay a fee, and pass a criminal record check. No use-of-force training or first-aid training was required. As a result, security guards continued to work at local stores and nightclubs without the basic training needed to safeguard lives.

In May of 2008, the Ministry announced that it was pushing back plans to implement the training program from November 2008 to an undetermined later date because the curriculum for training had only recently been finalized. However, according to the director and registrar of the Ministry's private security and investigative services branch, which is responsible for the new licensing procedures, "The onus of responsibility is at this state on the employer to make sure that their staff are adequately trained." As for the province's slow pace in implementing the training, he said that it takes time to implement such a wide range of changes in an industry that has never had to be licensed or trained.

However, other provinces already have similar training programs in place. British Columbia has a 40-hour course for security guards that is taught by the same people who train the police.

Unfortunately, the problem has not gone away. In 2008, a 20-year-old man died in Hamilton after being pinned to the ground by a security guard and store employees who suspected him of stealing a $15 radiator hose from a Canadian Tire store.

In June of 2008, bouncers found a woman unconscious and frothing from the mouth in the back of an after-hours club. The bouncers did not have first-aid training and did not know how to help the woman, who later died.

In February of 2009, two security guards at St. Michael's Hospital in Toronto were dismissed following the alleged beating of a man who had broken ribs and a punctured lung. The hospital said that it will assess and review its use-of-force policy and procedures, and that it intends to provide additional diversity training to its security officers.

Finally, on April 15, 2010, the new basic Training and Testing Regulation came into effect. The regulation requires that individuals must take a mandatory basic training course and pass the basic ministry test before they are eligible to apply for a security guard or private investigator licence.

The security guard basic training program must consist of at least 40 in-class hours and must include certification in Emergency Level First Aid. Basic security guard training obtained through Web-based, instructor-led distance learning (e.g., virtual classroom) meets the ministry's requirement for in-class training. However, Web-based courses must include some real-time interaction with an instructor.

Sources: Popplewell, B. (2008, July 14). Training lag angers guards. *Toronto Star*, pp. A1, A9; Security industry cleanup overdue. (2007, August 23). *Toronto Star*, p. A6; Black, D. (2004, April 24). Tough rules on security demanded: "This is Patrick's legacy," Shand's mother says of coroner's jury findings. *Toronto Star*, p. B1; McGuinty government introduces new legislation to make Ontarians safer. (2004, December 9). Ministry of Community Safety and Correctional Services, Government of Ontario. Retrieved from www.ogov.newswire.ca/ontario (March 16, 2009); Henry, M. (2009, February 19). Man says ribs broken by hospital guards. *Toronto Star*, p. A2; Henry, M. (2009, February 27). Hospital CEO apologizes to beaten man. *Toronto Star*, p. GT4.

QUESTIONS

CHAPTER 1

1. Explain how a mandatory training program for security guards is an example of performance management. What effect will it have on security guards and their organizations?

2. Describe the role of the environmental context for mandatory security guard training. How will the organizational context and the HR system in organizations influence the training and the effect it has on organizations and society?

3. Explain how the instructional systems design (ISD) model can be used in the development, delivery, and evaluation of a security guard training program.

CHAPTER 2

4. What are the learning outcomes of security guard training?

5. Explain the relevance of learning styles for a security guard training program. How can Kolb's four learning modes be used to train security guards? How can the VARK model be used to train security guards?

6. What are the implications of conditioning theory and social cognitive theory for the security guard training program? How can principles from each theory be used in the training of security guards?

7. What are the implications of adult learning theory for the security guard training program? Explain how adult learning theory principles might be included in the training.

8. How important is training motivation for the training of security guards? Explain what can be done to ensure that security guards are high in training motivation.

CHAPTER 3

9. Refer to the needs analysis process in Figure 3.1 and explain its use and relevance for the mandatory security guard training program.

10. Explain the relevance and use of an organizational, a task, and a person analysis for the security guard training program. What information can be obtained from each level of needs analysis, and how can it be useful in the design of the training program?

11. What methods and sources would you use to conduct an organizational, a task, and a person needs analysis? Explain your reasoning for each method and source.

12. Run the situation through Mager and Pipe's Performance Analysis Flowchart (Figure 3.2) to determine solutions to the problem described in the case. Is training the best solution? Are there other possible solutions? Explain your answer.

CHAPTER 4

13. Write some training objectives for the security guard training program.

14. Describe the content of the program and some potential training methods that should be considered.

15. Explain how active practice can be used for the security guard training program. How can the conditions of practice before (pre-training interventions) and during training be used? Explain the use and relevance of each condition of practice.

16. Is active learning and adaptive expertise relevant for the security guard training program? Explain how active learning elements might be included in the training.

17. Is error-management training (EMT) relevant for the security guard training program? Explain how you might use EMT in the training and its potential effects.

CHAPTER 5

18. What off-the-job training methods should be used for the security guard training program? Consider each of the instructional methods described in Table 5.1. Which methods would you recommend, and which ones would you not use? Explain your answer.

CHAPTER 6

19. Consider each of the on-the-job training methods described in Table 6.1 for the security guard training program. Which methods would you recommend, and which ones would you not use? Explain your answer.

CHAPTER 7

20. Can technology-based training methods be used for the security guard training program? How might technology-based methods be used? Do you think they would be effective? What would be the advantages and disadvantages of using them? Explain your answer.

21. Review the material on the design of technology-based training programs in Chapter 7. If you were to design a technology-based training program for security guards, what instructional methods and design factors would you use? Be sure to explain your reasoning for using or not using the methods and design factors described in Chapter 7.

CHAPTER 8

22. Develop a lesson plan for the security guard training program. Be sure to indicate the training objective, classroom requirements, training materials and equipment, supplies, and handouts. You should also indicate the sequence of activities and events that will occur during the training program and the timing of them.

23. Who should be the trainer for the security guard training program? Explain your answer.

24. Explain how you would use Gagné's nine events of instruction for the security guard training program. Be sure to give specific examples.

25. What are some training delivery problems that might occur in the security guard training program? What can a trainer do to avoid them or manage them during training?

26. What are some barriers that might inhibit the transfer of the security guard training program? Who is responsible for these barriers?

27. How can the security guard training program be designed to facilitate the transfer of training?

28. What are some strategies that can be used before, during, and after training to facilitate the transfer of training? Be sure to indicate strategies for the trainer, trainees, and management.

CHAPTER 10

29. How should the security guard training program be evaluated? Be sure to indicate the type of data to be collected, the purpose of the evaluation, and whether it should be a descriptive and/or causal evaluation.

30. Explain the application of Kirkpatrick's model, the COMA model, and the decision-based evaluation model for evaluating the security guard training program. What model would you recommend, and why?

31. What variables would you include in the evaluation of the security guard training program? How would you measure them?

32. What data collection design would you use to evaluate the security guard training program? Explain the advantages and disadvantages of nonexperimental, experimental, and quasi-experimental designs. What design would you use, and why?

CHAPTER 11

33. What are the main costs of the security guard training program? Be sure to indicate the main cost categories.

34. What are the main benefits of the security guard training program? Explain how you would conduct a cost-effectiveness evaluation and a cost–benefit evaluation.

35. How would you estimate the net benefit, benefit–cost ratio, return on investment, and utility of the security guard training program? Be sure to indicate what you would include in the estimation of each (e.g., what costs and what benefits).

// INTEGRATIVE CASE STUDY 2

THE LEARNING A CULTURE OF SAFETY PROGRAM

Given the staggering cost of workplace injuries, it is critical that occupational health and safety (OHS) training be as effective as possible to reduce incidents and claims. Unfortunately, most OHS training takes up one full day or more in a classroom, with a presenter and 500 slides, each with reams of legislation that is then read to the audience. Even the best students can barely stay awake, much less learn anything.

Some companies and unions have worked hard to develop more engaging OHS training, but the bulk of it has little effect in keeping workers safe. Even engaging programs do not seem to make much of a difference.

To try to make a difference, Canadian Manufacturers & Exporters (CME) set up a two-year national project titled *Essential Skills through Safety and Health (ESSH)*—funded by the Office of Literacy and Essential Skills at Human Resources and Skills Development Canada (HRSDC)—with the mandate to embed essential skills in OHS training.

The program was housed in CME's provincial offices in five regions—British Columbia, the Prairies and the West, Ontario, Quebec, and the Atlantic provinces—with principal investigators in each of the regions. Each interviewed 25 manufacturing companies, for a total of 125 companies across the country, to gain a snapshot of issues confronting employers in delivering OHS training and data on the types of hazards faced in the specific company.

What came out of the interviews clearly supported labour market data and research around the future labour force. It is estimated that almost all manufacturing new hires (this is less true in the Atlantic provinces) in the next decade will be immigrants. In the Prairies and the West, the First Nations population will also be providing the future labour force.

So, it was obvious that OHS efforts needed to focus on workers who do not have English or French as their first language, as well as those who have literacy issues. And it was critical that trainers and employers be supported in working with immigrant workforces.

Interviews were conducted with recent immigrant workers in their own language about health and safety, both in their home countries and in Canada. The three largest linguistic populations were chosen: Chinese (Mandarin), Punjabi, and Tagalog (Philippines). Researchers who were native speakers of each of the languages conducted and recorded the interviews, then translated and analyzed them for commonalities that might provide more contexts for the training.

The results demonstrated the critical importance of workplace OHS as the first means of acculturation for the new Canadians to the workforce. It is the area in which the differences between the country of origin and Canada are most obvious to the immigrants. How it is taught and supported by management colours all future perceptions of the employers.

There were three stakeholders: industry, workers, and the funders. To satisfy industry employers, the results needed to be visible on the job and the solution had to provide the least disruption to production requirements. For the workers, OHS training had to be innovative so they could learn and practise safety on the job. Ultimately, the success of the program had to be determined by their supervisors and managers. Finally, the program would also serve as a model for other types of workplace training.

The course was constructed through discussions with supervisors, safety officers, and employees at manufacturing companies across Canada. The essential skills embedded in the course had behavioural components that supervisors could see in action back on the job.

The Learning a Culture of Safety program aimed to have the smallest impact on production, running over 10 weeks with one hour per week. Each of the 35 companies that participated in the pilot selected two workers who had some knowledge of English or French to be in the program. The training was delivered both face-to-face as well as over the Internet on a platform called Adobe Connect, which functioned as a live classroom in which participants and a facilitator could see and speak with each other.

The homework assignments were carried out back on the job. For example, participants were required to speak up at a safety meeting, complete a simple job task analysis as well as a job hazard analysis, develop a job aid for their respective jobs, and deliver a presentation to management at the end of the program.

To support the learning, new media products were developed so the class could check their understanding or practise. The learning products were fun but also extremely strong educationally, and each was facilitated as a group activity. One of the products taught participants how to conduct a task analysis and hazard analysis (with a video of a tire being changed). By starting with the familiar in order to understand the more difficult, participants were able to practise the skills of observation and analysis, which they would then apply to their workplaces and specific jobs.

The other products checked for understanding. One asked participants to determine whether a phrase constituted the responsibility of workers or employers under the OHS legislation in the specific province in which the class was being taught. Another was a series of scenarios, both at home and at work, in which participants would decide the best place for a job aid. Another was an animated video that took a humorous look at the four levels of dealing with a hazard.

The most intricate was a simulation of a shop floor called Safety Shift to be played in groups of four. Each player could choose one of three activities to advance around the shop floor: "Speaking Up," in which the player was given a situation and asked to say something required of the specific situation; "It's Your Choice," a series of multiple-choice questions about OHS legislation and training; and "Document Dilemma," in which players were presented with a chart or job aid and asked a question they could ascertain from the material presented.

The program succeeded beyond initial expectations. In many cases, supervisors and senior management asked for help in rolling out the program throughout their companies. One of the unexpected outcomes was the sense of personal agency that developed in each of the participants regarding their safety.

For example, one man worked for a manufacturing company in the Prairies. He was an immigrant who had been living in Canada for two years. After the first session of the course, his assignment was to ask a question of his supervisor about safety. He looked up some potential safety hazards related to the chemicals used for his job and realized wearing a mask would be very important, but the mask wasn't located anywhere near his work station. As a result, he often didn't wear one because it was too inconvenient. So the employee mentioned the issue to his supervisor and within a couple of weeks, there were new hooks next to his machine for a mask and goggles.

Through the program, positive changes were seen, at the companies and with the individuals—changes in morale and efficiencies as well as individuals' practice of their role and responsibilities in maintaining a safe workplace.

Source: Faulk, J. (2012, March 12). Conveying safety messages—in any language. *Canadian HR Reporter, 25*(5), 11, 18. Reprinted by permission of *Canadian HR Reporter.* © Copyright Thomson Reuters Canada Ltd., (2012), Toronto, Ontario, 1-800-387-5164. Web: www.hrreporter.com

QUESTIONS

CHAPTER 1

1. Discuss the potential benefits of the Learning a Culture of Safety program for organizations, employees, and society. What are the implications for each group without the program?

2. Explain how the instructional systems design (ISD) model has been used for the Learning a Culture of Safety program. Be sure to refer to needs analysis, training design and delivery, and evaluation.

CHAPTER 2

3. What are the learning outcomes of the Learning a Culture of Safety program?

4. Which of Kolb's learning modes have been incorporated into the training? Be sure to provide examples of each learning mode. What learning mode or modes have not been considered? What could be done to include it or them? What modalities of the VARK model have been used? Which ones have not been used, and what could be done to include them?

5. What aspects of conditioning theory and social cognitive theory were used in the Learning a Culture of Safety program? What components of each theory should be given more attention? How can the program be changed to incorporate them?

6. Has adult learning theory been used in the design and delivery of the Learning a Culture of Safety program? What principles are lacking? How would you incorporate them into the training?

7. Discuss trainees' motivation to learn. What factors might have contributed to it? What might be done to improve it?

CHAPTER 3

8. Refer to the needs analysis process in Figure 3.1 to explain the needs analysis process for the Learning a Culture of Safety program. Be sure to explain each part of the process.

9. What aspects of an organizational, a task, and a person analysis have been considered with respect to the Learning a Culture of Safety program? What needs analysis information suggested the need for a training program?

10. What methods and sources were used for the needs analysis? Were they effective? Do you think other methods and/or sources should have been used? Explain your answer.

11. Run the problem through Mager and Pipe's Performance Analysis Flowchart (Figure 3.2) to determine solutions to performance problems. Do you think training was the best solution in this case? Are there other solutions that should be considered? Explain your answer.

CHAPTER 4

12. What are the training objectives for the Learning a Culture of Safety program? Write a training objective for the program using the four elements and three key components of training objectives.

13. Describe the content of the Learning a Culture of Safety program. What training methods were used to deliver the content?

14. To what extent is active practice used in the Learning a Culture of Safety program? Provide some examples and explain what they are used for.

15. Are any of the conditions of practice before (pre-training interventions) and during training used in the program? Explain the use and relevance of each condition of practice for the Learning a Culture of Safety program.

16. What is more relevant to the Learning a Culture of Safety program, adaptive expertise or routine expertise? Explain your answer. What are the implications of your answer for the design of the program?

CHAPTER 5

17. What off-the-job training methods are used in the Learning a Culture of Safety program? Consider each of the instructional methods described in Chapter 5 (Table 5.1). Which methods would you recommend, and which ones would you not use? Explain your answer.

CHAPTER 6

18. What on-the-job training methods are used in the Learning a Culture of Safety program? Consider each of the on-the-job methods described in Chapter 6 (Table 6.1). Which methods would you recommend and which ones would you not use? Explain your answer.

CHAPTER 7

19. What technology-based training methods are used in the Learning a Culture of Safety program? Is technology-based training an appropriate and effective approach to use for this program? Explain your answer.

CHAPTER 8

20. Describe the lesson plan for the Learning a Culture of Safety program. Would you change anything? If so, what would you change, and why?

21. To what extent have Gagné's nine events of instruction been used in the Learning a Culture of Safety program? Be sure to provide examples of each event of instruction. What events are missing? How would you include them?

CHAPTER 9

22. What are some barriers that might inhibit the transfer of the Learning a Culture of Safety program? Who is responsible for these barriers?

23. How successful do you think the transfer of training of the Learning a Culture of Safety program has been? What factors do you think have contributed to the transfer of the program?

24. What other strategies might have been used before, during, and after training to facilitate the transfer of the Learning a Culture of Safety program? Be sure to indicate strategies for the trainer, trainees, and management.

25. How was the Learning a Culture of Safety program evaluated? What type of data were collected? What was the purpose of the evaluation? Was the evaluation descriptive or causal?

26. How would you evaluate the Learning a Culture of Safety program using Kirkpatrick's model, the COMA model, and the decision-based evaluation model? What model would you recommend, and why?

27. What data collection design has been used to evaluate the Learning a Culture of Safety program? Explain the advantages and disadvantages of nonexperimental, experimental, and quasi-experimental designs. What design would you recommend, and why?

CHAPTER 11

28. What are the main costs of the Learning a Culture of Safety program? Be sure to refer to each cost category.

29. What are the main benefits of the program? Explain how you would conduct a cost-effectiveness evaluation and a cost–benefit evaluation of the program.

30. How would you estimate the net benefit, benefit–cost ratio, return on investment, and utility of the Learning a Culture of Safety program? What approach would you recommend, and why?

INDEX